THE OXFORD HANDBC

AMERICAN IMMIGRATION AND ETHNICITY

THE OXFORD HANDBOOK OF

AMERICAN IMMIGRATION AND ETHNICITY

Edited by
RONALD H. BAYOR

OXFORD
UNIVERSITY PRESS

OXFORD
UNIVERSITY PRESS

Oxford University Press is a department of the University of Oxford. It furthers
the University's objective of excellence in research, scholarship, and education
by publishing worldwide. Oxford is a registered trade mark of Oxford University
Press in the UK and certain other countries.

Published in the United States of America by Oxford University Press
198 Madison Avenue, New York, NY 10016, United States of America.

© Oxford University Press 2016

First issued as an Oxford University paperback, 2021

Library of Congress Cataloging-in-Publication Data
Names: Bayor, Ronald H., 1944–
Title: The Oxford handbook of American immigration and ethnicity / edited by
Ronald H. Bayor.
Other titles: Handbook of American immigration and ethnicity
Description: New York, NY : Oxford University Press, 2016. | Includes
bibliographical references and index.
Identifiers: LCCN 2015047823 | ISBN 978-0-19-976603-1 (hardback : acid-free paper) |
ISBN 978-0-19-752991-1 (paperback : acid-free paper)
Subjects: LCSH: United States—Emigration and immigration—History. | United
States—Ethnic relations—History. | United States—Race
relations—History. | Immigrants—United States—History. |
Ethnicity—United States—History. | Nationalism—United States—History.
Classification: LCC JV6450 .O94 2016 | DDC 304.8/73—dc23
LC record available at http://lccn.loc.gov/2015047823

Contents

Contributors

Richard Alba is Distinguished Professor of Sociology at The Graduate Center, CUNY. His most recent books are *The Children of Immigrants at School: A Comparative Look at Integration in the United States and Western Europe*, with Jennifer Holdaway (2013); *The Next Generation: Immigrant Youth in a Comparative Perspective*, with Mary Waters (2011); and *Blurring the Color Line: The New Chance for a More Integrated America* (2009).

James R. Barrett is Professor of History and African American Studies at the University of Illinois at Urbana-Champaign. He is author or editor of numerous publications on working-class history and race and ethnicity in American cities, including *The Irish Way: Becoming American in a Multi-Ethnic City* (2012). He is a contributing editor to *Labor: Studies in Working Class History of the Americas* and the *Journal of American Ethnic History*, and co-editor of the series, *The Working Class in American History*, with more than 120 volumes in print.

Ronald H. Bayor is Emeritus Professor of History at Georgia Tech, a former president of the Immigration and Ethnic History Society, and founding editor of the *Journal of American Ethnic History*. His most recent book is *Encountering Ellis Island: How European Immigrants Entered America* (2014). Other publications include *Multicultural America: An Encyclopedia of the Newest Americans* (2011); *The New York Irish*, co-edited with Timothy Meagher (1996); *Race and the Shaping of Twentieth-Century Atlanta* (1996); and *Neighbors in Conflict: the Irish, Germans, Jews, and Italians of New York City, 1929–1941*(1978).

David Brundage is a Professor of History at the University of California, Santa Cruz. He has published widely in the areas of U.S. immigration and labor history and is the author of *Irish Nationalists in America: The Politics of Exile, 1798–1998* (2016).

John J. Bukowczyk is Professor of History at Wayne State University in Detroit, editor of the *Journal of American Ethnic History*, and author of numerous publications on various immigration and ethnic topics. He received the American Historical Association's inaugural William Gilbert Award for Best Article on Teaching History for his article, "The American Family and the Little Red Schoolhouse: Historians, Class, and the Problem of Curricular Diversity" and the Albert B. Corey Prize of the American Historical Association and the Canadian Historical Association for his coauthored book, *Permeable Border: The Great Lakes Basin as Transnational Region, 1650–1890* (2005). He is past recipient of Wayne State University's President's Award for Excellence in Teaching.

Steven Alan Carr is Graduate Program Director and Associate Professor of Communication at Indiana University-Purdue University Fort Wayne, a 2002–2003 Center for Advanced Holocaust Studies Postdoctoral Fellow at the U.S. Holocaust Memorial Museum in Washington, DC, a 2010–2011 Loewenstein-Wiener Marcus Research Fellow at the American Jewish Archives, and co-director of the IPEW Institute for Holocaust and Genocide Studies. He is the author of *Hollywood and Anti-Semitism: A Cultural History up to World War II* (2001) as well as numerous essays on the evolving response of the American Film industry to Nazi anti-Semitism and the Holocaust.

Gregory T. Carter is Associate Professor of History at the University of Wisconsin-Milwaukee. Focusing on racial mixing, civil rights, intellectual history, and popular culture, his writing has appeared in *Ethnic Studies Review, Journal of American Ethnic History*, and *Mixed Race Hollywood*, edited by Mary Beltran and Camilla Fojas. He is the author of *The United States of the United Races: A Utopian History of Racial Mixing* (2013).

Steven Conn is Professor of History at Miami University of Ohio. He is the author of five books including, most recently, *Nothing Succeeds Like Failure: The Sad History of American Business Schools* (2019), *Americans Against the City: Anti-Urbanism in the Twentieth Century* (2014), and *Do Museums Still Need Objects?* (2010).

Will Cooley is Associate Professor of American History at Walsh University. He has published articles in the *Journal of Urban History, Labor History*, and the *Journal of Sport and Social Issues*, and a chapter in the book, *Building the Black Metropolis: African American Entrepreneurship in Chicago*. Cooley studies race and social mobility in urban America.

Steven P. Erie is Professor of Political Science and Adjunct Professor of History at the University of California, San Diego. He is the author of *Rainbow's End: Irish Americans and the Dilemmas of Urban Machine Politics, 1840–1995* (1988) and other books and articles on urban politics. His research interests include ethnic and racial politics, urban politics, public policy, and governance.

Yen Le Espiritu, originally from Vietnam, is Professor and former Chair of the Department of Ethnic Studies at the University of California, San Diego. She has published widely on Asian American panethnicity, gender and migration, and U.S. colonialism and wars in Asia. Her most recent book is *Body Counts: The Vietnam War and Militarized Refuge(es)* (2014).

Joshua A. Fishman is the late emeritus professor of Social Sciences at Yeshiva University, Albert Einstein College of Medicine and founding editor of *International Journal of the Sociology of Language*. He was a leading scholar on multilingualism, bilingual education, the Yiddish language, language and ethnicity and religion, and language movements. His publications include numerous books and articles dealing with various aspects of language, including *Language Loyalty in the United States: The Maintenance and Perpetuation of Non-English Mother Tongues by*

American Ethnic and Religious Groups (1966); *Yiddish in America: Socio-Linguistic Description and Analysis* (1965); *The Rise and Fall of the Ethnic Revival: Perspectives on Language and Ethnicity* (1985); *Bilingual Education* (1991); *Language and Ethnicity* (1991); and *Can Threatened Languages Be Saved?* (2000).

Donna R. Gabaccia is Professor of History at the University of Toronto Scarborough where she teaches courses on international migration, world history, and gender and women's studies. She has written many books and articles on immigration to the United States, on Italian migration worldwide, and on international, interdisciplinary, and gender perspectives on human migrations, including a book she coauthored with sociologist Katherine Donato, *Gender and International Migration: From the Slavery Era to the Global Age* (2015).

María Cristina García is the Howard A. Newman Professor of American Studies in the Department of History at Cornell University. She is author of *Havana USA: Cuban Exiles and Cuban Americans in South Florida* (1997); *Seeking Refuge: Central American Migration to Mexico, the United States, and Canada* (2006); and several articles and book chapters on immigration history. Her forthcoming book focuses on U.S. refugee and asylum policy in the post-Cold War period.

Gary Gerstle is the Paul Mellon Professor of American History at Cambridge University. His publications include his book, *American Crucible: Race and Nation in the Twentieth Century* (2001); *E Pluribus Unum?: Contemporary and Historical Perspectives on Immigrant Political Incorporation*, co-edited with John Mollenkopf (2001); and "Acquiescence or Transformation: Divergent Paths of Political Incorporation in America," in *Outsiders No More? Models of Immigrant Political Incorporation*, edited by Jennifer Hochschild, Jacqueline Chattopadhyay, Claudine Gay, and Michael Jones-Correa (2013).

David G. Gutiérrez is Professor and Chair of the Department of History at the University of California, San Diego, where he specializes in the history of Mexican America, immigration history, and the history of citizenship and civil rights. He is the author of *Walls and Mirrors: Mexican Americans, Mexican Immigrants, and the Politics of Ethnicity* (1995); editor of the *Columbia History of Latinos in the United States since 1860* (2004); and co-editor with Pierette Hondagneu-Sotelo of *Nation and Migration: Past and Future* (2009). He is currently working on a monograph on the historical evolution of the immigrants' rights movement and with co-editor Luis Alvarez, *The Routledge Handbook of the History of Mexican America* (forthcoming 2016).

Dirk Hoerder Emeritus Professor at Arizona State University and the University of Bremen, taught North American social history, global migrations, borderland issues, and sociology of migrant acculturation. His publications include *Cultures in Contact: World Migrations in the Second Millennium* (2002), *The Historical Practice of Diversity: Transcultural Interactions from the Early Modern Mediterranean to the Postcolonial World* (2003), on which he was co-editor; and *Migrants and Migration in Modern North America* (2011).

Madeline Y. Hsu is Associate Professor of History and past director of the Center for Asian American Studies at the University of Texas at Austin. She is the author of *Dreaming of Gold, Dreaming of Home: Transnationalism and Migration Between the United States and South China, 1883–1943* (2000), which received the 2002 Association of Asian American Studies History Book Award; and *The Good Immigrants: How the Yellow Peril Became a Model Minority* (2015), which explores intersections between American foreign policy goals, immigration laws and practices, and shifting racial ideologies through the migration of Chinese intellectuals.

Peter Kivisto is the Richard A. Swanson Professor of Social Thought at Augustana College and Visiting Research Fellow at the University of Helsinki. His research focuses on immigration, social integration, and civil society. His most recent books include *Solidarity, Justice, and Incorporation: Thinking Through The Civil Sphere*, which he co-edited with Giuseppe Sciortino (2015), and *Religion and Immigration: Migrant Faiths in North America and Western Europe* (2014).

Wendy Kline is the Dema G. Seelye Chair in the History of Medicine in the Department of History at Purdue University. She is the author of several articles and two books: *Bodies of Knowledge: Sexuality, Reproduction, and Women's Health in the Second Wave* (2010) and *Building a Better Race: Gender, Sexuality, and Eugenics from the Turn of the Century to the Baby Boom* (2011). Her current book project, under contract to Oxford University Press, is entitled *Coming Home: Medicine, Midwives, and the Transformation of Birth in Late Twentieth-Century America*.

Vladimir Kogan is Assistant Professor in the Department of Political Science at Ohio State University. He is coauthor of *Paradise Plundered: Fiscal Crisis and Governance Failures in San Diego* (2011), which won the best book award from the Urban Political Section of the American Political Science Association. His research has been published in *American Politics Research, Political Communication, State Politics and Policy Quarterly, Urban Affairs Review*, and the *Rutgers Law Journal*.

Mary E. Odem is Associate Professor in the Department of History and the Latin American and Caribbean Studies Program at Emory University. A U.S. historian, her research interests include immigration, race and ethnicity in the modern United States, and gender and women's history. Her current research examines Latin American immigration to the U.S. South. She has published numerous articles on this topic and co-edited *Latino Immigration and the Transformation of the U.S. South* (2009).

David M. Reimers is Emeritus Professor of History at New York University. He has written extensively about immigration. Among his books are *Still the Golden Door: The Third World Comes to America* (2d ed. 1992) and, with coauthor Leonard Dinnerstein, *The World Comes to America: Immigration to the United States Since 1945* (2014).

David R. Roediger is the Foundation Professor of American Studies at the University of Kansas where he teaches and writes on race and class in the United States. His recent books include *Seizing Freedom: Slave-Emancipation and Liberty for All* (2014) and, with coauthor Elizabeth Esch, *The Production of Difference* (2014). His writings on race and immigrant history include *The Wages of Whiteness* (1991) and *Working Toward Whiteness* (2006).

Amanda I. Seligman is Associate Professor of History and Urban Studies at the University of Wisconsin-Milwaukee. She is the author of *Block by Block: Neighborhoods and Public Policy on Chicago's West Side* (2005) and *Is Graduate School Really for You?: The Whos, Whats, Hows, and Whys of Pursuing a Master's or Ph.D.* (2012) and co-author of the *Bibliography of Metropolitan Milwaukee* (2014). Her current projects include a monograph on the history of block clubs in Chicago, and the *Encyclopedia of Milwaukee*.

Suzanne M. Sinke is Director of Graduate Studies and Associate Professor in the Department of History at Florida State University. She is the author of numerous articles and book chapters on migration and gender; co-editor of three books on migration, including *Letters Across Borders: The Epistolary Practices of International Migrants* (2006); and author of *Dutch Immigrant Women in the United States, 1880–1920* (2002). Her research often draws on and examines the letters of international migrants.

Stephen Steinberg is Distinguished Professor of Urban Studies at Queens College and the PhD Program in Sociology at the CUNY Graduate Center. He is the author of *The Ethnic Myth: Race, Ethnicity, and Class in America* (1981, 1989, 2001); *Turning Back: The Retreat from Racial Justice in American Thought and Policy* (1995, 2001); and *Race Relations: A Critique* (2007).

Joe W. Trotter is Giant Eagle Professor of History and Social Justice at Carnegie Mellon University in Pittsburgh. He is a member of the American Academy of Arts and Sciences, and also directs Carnegie Mellon's Center for Africanamerican Urban Studies & the Economy (CAUSE). His publications include *Race and Renaissance: African Americans in Pittsburgh Since World War II*, with Jared Day (2010); *Coal, Class, and Color: Blacks in Southern West Virginia, 1915–1932* (1990); and *Black Milwaukee: The Making of an Industrial Proletariat, 1915–1945* (1985, 2007).

Allison Varzally is an Associate Professor at California State University, Fullerton. Her first book, *Making a Non-White America: Coloring Outside Ethnic Lines, 1925–1955*, won the Theodore Saloutos Prize from the Immigration and Ethnic History Society for best book on any aspect of Immigration History in the United States. She is currently completing a book about the immigration of adopted Vietnamese and Amerasians and their families since 1965.

R. Stephen Warner is Emeritus Professor in the Sociology Department at the University of Illinois at Chicago, where generations of students made him aware of the variety and vitality of the religious institutions of post-1965 immigrants. Under funding from the Lilly Endowment and the Pew Charitable Trusts, he directed, with Judith Wittner, the New Immigrant and Ethnic Congregations Project, which produced *Gatherings in Diaspora: Religious Communities and the New Immigration* (1998). He is also the author of *A Church of Our Own: Disestablishment and Diversity in American Religion* (2005) and co-editor with Ho-Youn Kwon and Kwang Chung Kim of *Korean Americans and Their Religions: Pilgrims and Missionaries from a Different Shore* (2001).

INTRODUCTION

The Making of America

RONALD H. BAYOR

THE immigration and ethnic history field has expanded not only in volume since the early years of study in the 1930s and 1940s but also in terms of topics and interpretations. Initial historians who studied immigration mostly focused on one group or on western and northern Europeans, sometimes in a way designed to illustrate the important place that a particular group held in American life. The concentration for these historians, who were often of the same background as the group they studied, consisted of placing value on the immigrant's historical contribution to America. Theodore Blegen's work on Norwegians and Carl Wittke's work on Germans as well as on the Irish and on northwestern Europeans in general, illustrate this methodology.[1] Oscar Handlin, in his book on the Boston Irish, introduced a social history approach that set the tone for later works and in his *The Uprooted* (1951) placed the immigration topic before the reading public.[2]

Studies therefore tended to focus on single groups, on white Europeans, on men, and on assimilation, often as a straight-line process. Non-white immigrant groups faced a decidedly different history and traditionally have received less scholarly attention from immigration historians. Their American experience entailed a denial of citizenship status and discrimination beyond what the white ethnics had to endure. African Americans came to America before the founding of the nation yet had few or no rights; Latinos could be found in early America on the land before the English arrived, and were an important element in U.S. history but were often disregarded as legitimate parts of American history. The treatment of America's non-white people reveals the role of race in regard to assimilation, politics, intermarriage, transnationalism, gender, acceptance, panethnicity, and other facets of immigration history. Neither Plymouth Rock nor Ellis Island tells the complete story of American immigration; the non-white groups complicate and enhance the telling of the American saga. As Paul Spickard relates: "The immigrant assimilation model . . . has no explanation for the stubborn fact that today American-born U.S. citizens of Asian and Mexican descent are regarded as foreigners in their native land by Whites, even those whose ancestry in the United States may be of substantially shorter duration."[3] The immigrant story is a multifaceted one, far more complex than early immigration historians envisioned. Furthermore, it is a story of world migration patterns that include regions containing nontraditional sending countries. Atlantic and Pacific migrations taking people across the world along numerous transportation routes is a clearer view of what occurred.

Race, traditionally considered a biological term—although now seen as a culturally constructed category—often became confused and conflated with ethnicity, a cultural description, and with nationality, indicating national background. Chinese immigrants could be defined as a racial group, an ethnic one, or one based on their nationality. Germans, however, would signify ethnicity and nationality, but not race; however, for much of the eighteenth to twentieth centuries, they found themselves described in racial terms. Ethnicity as a classification replaced nationality and race in the 1940s for white groups.

Before the 1965 Immigration Act, therefore, the field was a bifurcated one. Students of race—particularly sociologists and historians researching African Americans— and students of immigration and ethnicity took up complementary but different lines of inquiry. A rich publication variety developed in these areas. The immigration and ethnicity scholars looked at an increasingly more complicated history with important research done on assimilation and incorporation, ethnic succession, comparative analysis of two or more groups and in more than one receiving country, migration patterns that revealed the chain migration that occurred, religious mores, cooperation and conflict, ethnic identity, and ethnic influence on domestic and foreign policy. Within these works, new information energized further research. To name just a few of the significant publications: Rudolph Vecoli and later John Bodnar countered Handlin's view of the immigrants being uprooted; Milton Gordon outlined the various stages of assimilation and opened a long-term discussion of how groups adapt to a new culture; Samuel Bailey wrote about Italian immigrants in New York and Buenos Aires; Donna Gabaccia analyzed the chain migration between Sicily and Elizabeth Street in New York; Jay Dolan studied the immigrant church; George Pozzetta and Gary Mormino looked at ethnic cooperation in Ybor City, Florida; and Ronald Bayor looked at the conflict found among European ethnic groups in New York. Ethnic identity has been a focus of sociologists such as Mary Waters and Richard Alba and historians such as Joshua Zeitz. Frederick Luebke and many other historians have studied foreign policy and ethnic influence. Many aspects of America's ethnic past and present found substantial exploration.[4] Along with the formation in the 1960s of what became the Immigration and Ethnic History Society, the publication of the *Harvard Encyclopedia of American Ethnic Groups* in 1980, and the appearance of the *Journal of American Ethnic History* (*JAEH*) in 1981, the field took on a more systematic methodology and a formal discipline among scholars.[5] However, certain topics remained understudied, even within the white European migration model. The role of women immigrants persisted as a largely neglected topic until the 1970s. The increasing public recognition of gender as an important analytic focus opened this aspect of immigration and ethnic history to further inquiry. Scholarship benefited from such works as *The Jewish Women in America* (1976);

The Italian Immigrant Woman in North America (1978); and, most significantly, Hasia Diner's *Erin's Daughters in America* (1983).[6] Importantly, studies of women in Mexican and Asian ethnic groups also appeared. However, in a 1991 Forum essay in *JAEH*, Donna Gabaccia could still write of the marginalization of immigrant women in the historical literature. As she pointed out, it is not that a lot of works in women's immigration history are unavailable or unstudied but rather that the field sat on the margins of so many disciplines and subfields that a synthesis noting its place in the body of literature was difficult.[7] Yet it has been clear since the 1980s that women's immigration fits solidly and importantly within the context of migration history.

But in writing about marginalization, the non-white peoples of American immigration have been most overtly left out of the history. In considering melting pot concepts, so long the myth of American life and still accepted by many nonscholars, a place for color never existed—for African Americans, Asian Americans, Latino Americans, or Native Americans. Perhaps the consensus approach of the 1950s that the American people were a united, conflict-free entity, defined by democratic beliefs rather than race, obscured the reality. Although multitudes of books and articles appeared about slavery and Jim Crow, race riots, and lack of citizenship rights, little scholarship emerged that placed each particular group's history into the American story beyond discrimination, ghettoization, conflict, conquest, and fear. Ellis Island signified the American immigration story, not Angel Island, where mostly Asians entered. The turning to that minority history opened up new questions fortified by the heavy non-white immigration that the United States experienced since the 1970s and the prospect of whites becoming a minority by 2050. Among the major sending countries now are China, South Korea, Mexico, El Salvador, and Nigeria, rather than Italy, Poland, or Russia.

This *Handbook* is designed to consider America's immigration and ethnic history within its full racial and ethnic unfolding and to analyze the substantial impact of the newest Americans as well as to understand the history and scholarship that came before the 1965 act. Which old questions must be asked again, and what new questions are needed? Where is the research going, and what topics will future scholars likely research for an understanding of the new population dynamics?

Immigration has always been a challenging subject for historians and sociologists as well as for the general public. Some questions have been persistent. All who research U.S. immigration and ethnicity still grapple with the question posed by eighteenth-century French immigrant writer St. John de Crèvecouer: "What, then, is the American, this new man?" This query constituted a difficult one in the eighteenth century; by the twenty-first century, with more religious, linguistic, nationality, and racial backgrounds evident in the United States, the inquiry takes center stage for understanding who we are. Furthermore, as the years have passed, Americans have tried to comprehend the assimilation process. Was a melting pot the way to describe what occurred, or perhaps was it a multicultural salad bowl with each part retaining its identity but still seeing itself as an element of the whole? But if multiculturalism is the norm, what becomes of the motto "E Pluribus Unum" ("Out of Many, One") found on the Great Seal of the United States, on U.S. currency, and on the President's Seal.

Concern with fragmentation of the American mosaic has reemerged as an issue among the public as well as among scholars. Arthur M. Schlesinger Jr., while supporting multicultural education, worried about a simplistic, yet defining, ethnic interpretation of American history, especially if embodied in school curricula. He wrote in 1991 in relation to a New York Commissioner of Education report on syllabus reform that this approach "will only increase the fragmentation, resegregation, and self-ghettoization of American life. The bonds of national cohesion in the republic are sufficiently fragile already." In a 1992 statement, Schlesinger feared that "the cult of ethnicity has reversed the movement of American history, producing a nation of minorities—or at least of minority spokesmen—less interested in joining the majority in common endeavor."[8] Do ethnic groups still see themselves as American or only as hyphenated Americans, or perhaps as part of a panethnic entity (e.g., all Asians seeing themselves as one group)? During high immigration times, anxiety about splits within America based on the country's many ethnic, religious, and racial groups has appeared along with the larger issue of assimilation. New groups that are not the traditional immigrants to America have intensified these discussions. Michael Novak, in his *Rise of the Unmeltable Ethnics* (1972), inspired and reflected such unease in a book written for a nonscholarly audience during the white ethnic revival of the 1970s as well as in response to the Black Pride movement that arose during the civil rights crusade.[9]

A concern with fragmentation has also arisen as a result of the proliferation of ethnic museums. Other than the Ellis Island and Angel Island museums, as Steven Conn notes, many museums commemorate one group, and visitors to that museum are from that group. The ethnic-specific museums actually follow the early writings of historians, telling the story of the accomplishments and the value of that group to America. The emphasis is on that group's worth as an acknowledgment of its acceptance. But these museums could also be an indication of less fragmentation as groups move into the American mainstream and long for their past heritage. Can the desire for ethnic museums be a sign of assimilation?

Scholarship has concentrated not only on what the immigrants became but also on what cultural traits they brought to the New World. Were the immigrants uprooted from their ancestral homes, leaving everything behind, as earlier writings suggested, or were they transplanted, bringing many aspects of their culture with them while adapting to the American environment as well? But then, the question must be asked whether all immigrants had the same experience and how these specific group assimilations took place, if at all.

Intermarriage, whose rates have recently increased substantially across ethnic, religious, and racial boundaries, must be analyzed in regard to assimilation as well as determining how to define who is an American. Is intermarriage the forerunner of a post-racial society; does it matter which groups are intermarrying; and what does this say about group identity in the future? With more immigration and with changing attitudes toward mixed religious, racial, and ethnic marriages, the understanding of background differences among Americans is more complicated than earlier. Even the

U.S. census has recognized mixed ancestry, but what that term means is not exactly clear and goes back to Crèvecouer's original statement.

Nativism has also been a constant issue in American life and academic studies. While native-born white Protestant Americans feared large-scale European migrations from Ireland and from southern and eastern Europe in the nineteenth and early twentieth centuries, it is the immigration, both documented and undocumented, from Asian, African, Latin American, and Caribbean nations since the passage of the 1965 immigration act that has sparked anti-immigrant reactions in present times. Nativism and anti-immigrant attitudes had many sources, mainly based on concerns about job competition, crime, disease, increasing poverty, radicalism or terrorism, religious and cultural differences, and a sense of invasion by racially inferior peoples who would outbreed the real Americans of Anglo-Saxon backgrounds, or by those who would not understand American democratic principles. The overall fears rested on the assertion that America would decline economically, culturally, and biologically according to the pseudoscience of eugenics, which considered these newcomers as racially unfit. Such opinions found expression throughout American history, even though the colonial period saw a mix of races, religions, and nationalities in its population.

Madison Grant, in *The Passing of the Great Race* (1916), warned against the new immigrant tide of southern and eastern Europeans who were weakening and changing America. Recent proponents of historical nativism include Patrick Buchanan, who similarly warns of the new immigrant tide of Third World immigrants who "are living off public services, and many are going into crime." He cautions that "the great American Melting Pot is not melting, as once it did."[10]

The introduction of Muslim immigrants into American life has brought all the old fears to the fore, especially after September 11. The apprehension of French Catholics in the eighteenth century and of Irish Catholics in the nineteenth and twentieth centuries has been revisited on Arabs and other Muslims in the twenty-first century. Gary Gerstle refers to this anti-Muslim attitude as a resurgence of religious nationalism. Although eugenics has been discredited, the science of genetics may still play a role in immigration debates. In a desire to explain human behavior through nature rather than nurture, a genetic test for entry into the United States could be a future scenario. Some scientists write of a genetic predisposition to crime or disease. New fields are developing along these lines, and that indicates future controversy over who is eligible for entry into the country.

As more non-white people have immigrated to the United States, historians and sociologists have taken a closer look at previous migrations in regard to who was considered white by law and custom, who was allowed to attain citizenship, and what has been the role of identity politics, which is based on the particular ethnic or racial group or on a multiethnic coalition. The new scholarship on "whiteness" is now a major theme of the field. Scholars such as David Roediger, Matthew Jacobson, Thomas Guglielmo, and Russell Kazal introduced a discussion regarding the initial treatment of white versus non-white immigrants. Italian, German, and other European immigrants benefited from their racial placement within the white category. Although these scholars have at times understated anti-immigrant hostility toward white groups, their overall assessment that white immigrants received a more favorable reception than immigrants of color is correct. The other judgment of these historians that European immigrants eventually coalesced into a white category, thereby removing most traces of their specific pre- and post-migration cultures is less evident. These scholars contend that only a "symbolic ethnicity" remains, which has little meaning within a group's life. However, a tendency still exists for Italians, Jews, and other European migrants to view themselves in both ethnic and racial (white) terms. Growing evidence exists of a continuation of ethnicity within the white grouping. One important work is Jordan Stanger-Ross's book, *Staying Italian*, which discusses the continuation of an Italian identity in postwar Toronto and Philadelphia. Ethnicity did not disappear but continued to shape lives.[11]

The United States has had a love-hate relationship with its immigrants.[12] Federal legislation since 1882 has tried to regulate or impede immigration through quotas and other laws. Race and nationality often determined eligibility for entry into America. The 1882 Chinese Exclusion Act, for example, was meant to prevent Chinese immigration into the United States, but western state legislatures also passed laws to deny rights to those born in China although already living in America, such as owning land. Legislation in the 1920s severely curtailed immigration from largely Catholic, Eastern Orthodox, and Jewish parts of Europe.[13] On the surface, it appeared that Congress wanted mainly white Protestants from northern and western Europe as immigrants. These attitudes were evident in large-scale nativist movements that worked to deny entry, citizenship, and voting rights to the "others." The Alien and Sedition Acts of 1798, which indicated early suspicions of foreigners, the Know Nothings of the 1850s, the American Protective Association and Immigration Restriction League of the 1890s, the Ku Klux Klan of the 1920s, and the white supremacist and anti-immigrant groups active today reveal a continued hostility and distrust of immigrants.[14] Anti-immigrant targets in the past consisted of Catholics and, to a lesser extent, Jews, but in contemporary America, the targets are primarily Arab Muslims and Hispanics. The racist aspects of America's past are revealed as well in colonial conquests and the role of racism in dealing with foreign non-white groups.

Yet clearly, the election of Barack Obama illustrates the other trend: an acceptance that was impossible until very recently. Acceptance was always part of the equation. Laws allowing refugees, war brides, and family members of those already in the United States to enter the country expanded the immigration numbers regardless of the restrictionists' desires. Citizenship for aliens serving in the U.S. armed forces further opened up that opportunity. Even the harsh national quotas acts in the 1920s allowed easy entry for Western Hemisphere immigrants. As the United States moved during the twentieth century from being an isolationist country to one engaged with the world, the laws became less harsh. Vying with the Soviet Union for the allegiance of Third World nations, the United States became more willing to accept previously excluded immigrants. The Chinese Exclusion Act repeal in 1943, when China was an ally in World War II, illustrates this shift. Most importantly, the Immigration and Nationality Act of 1965 eliminated discriminatory nationality quotas. The law allowed, through family unifica-tion and skill preferences, the entry of larger numbers of immigrants from Asia, Latin America, and Africa. The Immigration Reform and Control Act of 1986, which created an amnesty program for undocumented immigrants, further showed a generosity of the American people propelled by the need of labor on their farms and in their factories and a desire to finally end the illegal immigration issue.

The 1965 Act brought large-scale immigration to the American South for the first time. Always defined in black-white terms, the arrival of Asians, Hispanics, and Africans changed the definition, even though all the "new" groups have been in the South for many years, even centuries. But these were not Africans coming as slaves but as nation-ality groups moving from a postcolonial Africa. Hispanics came from South America as well as the Caribbean, and the new Asian immigrants showed a greater diversity than the Chinese who had settled in Mississippi in the nineteenth century. Not only the variety but also the numbers indicated a different situation than before. The impact on regional demographics, politics, culture, and racial identities has been profound.

What's next? Will the non-white immigrants merge into a black panethnic grouping? Will the churches, in this southern Bible belt of the United States, be able to adjust to and absorb these new people? What impact will multiculturalism have on Southern culture? How will the strong restrictionist attitudes evident in southern states such as Alabama and Georgia shape the future of ethnicity and race in this region? The 1965 Act brought the most changes to this part of the country and forced blacks and whites, particularly politicians, to change their focus from only issues that pertained to their groups.

Even with the 1965 Act, congressional deliberations included racial and ethnic con-siderations. Congress intended to allow more European immigrants, especially from such countries as Italy, to emigrate as nonquota family reunification immigrants. In their discussions over the 1965 legislation, members of Congress gave little thought to the possibility that the legislation would open the gates widely to Third World non-white immigrants. This law and the new immigrants, documented and undocumented, arriving from south of the border, inspired spirited debates once again about the future makeup of the country, the porous borders, the declining white majority in the United States, and the crime, poverty, employment issues evident in other periods of large-scale immigration. The American people were generally more accepting of immigrants than in earlier times, but resentments and hostility, even to the point of border mili-tias and draconian anti-immigrant laws in Arizona, Alabama, and Georgia contin-ued. The Dream Act is one example of the American split personality on immigration. The act proposed to provide citizenship to those brought to the United States at a very young age by their illegally entering parents. This special migrant category consisted of Americans who spoke English, went to college, and served in the armed forces. Some had never been to the Old Country and knew little of its culture. The Dream Act's failure in Congress, the subsequent outcry from pro-immigrant voices, and President Obama's efforts to allow these immigrants to stay and flourish indicated the persistence of the love-hate relationship. But what really changed? Was America becoming a different place? Were these new immigrants so unlike those in previous centuries?

Another consistent pattern has been the ethnic and racial group impact on U.S. foreign policy. Irish, Jewish, Cuban, and eastern European Americans have long exerted such an influence. Lobbying Congress concerning old world problems and interactions with the United States persist into the twenty-first century. In contemporary America, as immigrants arrive from new areas, issues such as transnationalism, dual citizenship, panethnicity, and improved communication with the former country have enhanced the ties and enabled the influence. But this has not been true for all groups, even some of the newer ones. The concern with terrorism and the tensions regarding Muslim immigrants have again raised the issue of foreign ties and divided loyalties. Although not yet on the level of the broad-based attacks on hyphenated Americans during World Wars I and II, the potential is there. Any new terrorist attack in the United States perpetrated by American citizens with ancestral ties to Muslim countries or by foreign nationals will make many Americans more wary of any semblance of dual loyalties.

Some other patterns have remained the same in present-day America but with variations. Chain migration, defined as immigrants following the migratory pattern of predecessors from villages to specific areas of the United States, still exists. As with the Irish, Germans, Jews, Italians, and others, contemporary immigrants migrate to certain areas that place them together in particular cities and neighborhoods. Ethnic enclaves rarely consisted of a majority of one group, so ethnic and racial interactions occurred often but not always amicably. Conflict, particularly if a racial factor existed, was frequent. The experience of earlier years is not directly repeated today as attitudes toward even racial "others" have changed. For example, Atlanta was once a city of highly contentious neighborhoods and conflicted groups, so much so that street names were changed to make it appear that whites and blacks did not live on the same street. Yet evidence is available in the twenty-first century to indicate racially mixed areas that have not experienced white flight or mob violence. New immigrants have moved to all parts of the city with little friction evident.

Economics remains a strong driving force for immigration along with issues such as war and religious persecution. People come to make their lives better, even if they have to migrate illegally. Migration from America's southern border declined as a recession took hold during the early twenty-first century. During the Great Depression, immigration declined as well, with more people leaving the country than entering. When the immigrants arrived, in any period, the first priority became securing a job. Each group found their employment niche. Irish and Germans, like present-day Chinese, Koreans, and Dominicans, found work in certain fields: Koreans opened fruit and vegetable stores, Chinese entered the garment industry, and Dominicans found jobs in the building trades. And immigrant workers have mobilized into unions much like earlier immigrants and have moved the unions—although they are much weaker than their organizational ancestors—into a pro-immigration stance. New immigrants' effect on various cities and neighborhoods is striking: Cubans have revitalized Miami as a gateway to Latin American business; Koreans have moved into cities like New York and Los Angeles as merchants helping to bring business back to declining neighborhoods.

Other similarities and differences exist as well between former and present immigrants. European immigrants, according to prevailing scholarship, coalesced into a Euro-American grouping with a dwindling sense of specific ethnicities, essentially a panethnic entity. If this has happened, although some questions remain as to when and how completely it occurred, does it mean a similar trajectory for non-whites. If so, what meaning will this have for assimilation, for political coalitions, for power sharing.

Southern and eastern European immigrants, although not always desired, did enter the United States as legally white and therefore were allowed all the citizenship rights given to the American white majority. These groups may have been shunned and looked at as not quite white, as in-between people, but no legal challenges occurred to contest their racial status. Their "whiteness" gave them a privileged status and set the non-white groups into a separate, more feared and less mobile position. White panethnicity was all about power and acceptance. In the latter half of the twentieth century, immigration policy made clear distinctions between white Cubans and black Haitians, indicating the continued reification of whiteness. Scholars need to study whether this racial split continued. While a panethnic Hispanic group is evident, nationality and perhaps racial splits are visible. Will white Hispanics eventually identify mainly as whites, following the European example? Whiteness is certainly still a privileged category. Will black Hispanics totally fall into the African American category and identify in that way? West Indian blacks indicate that this identification is already happening. Nigerians and other Africans present still another aspect of a black panethnic grouping. How intermarriage will affect various groups' identity in the future is unknown.

Religion is also a major marker in American life. The arrival of Muslims, Buddhists, and Hindus has complicated the usual acceptance of the Protestant, Catholic, and Jewish religious identification of Americans.[15] New groups have been marginalized and have been the victims of religious persecution. The terrorism threat has led to greater nonacceptance of Muslims, and particularly for Arab Americans among them. This reaction is revealed in the opposition to the building of mosques and the attacks on those, such as Sikhs, who look like they might be Muslims. As with earlier hostility, the persecuted, as in the case of Catholics, have had to make a strong effort to be recognized as loyal citizens not subject to any foreign dictates. America's changing religious makeup and the strong religiosity that has found its way into politics suggests a future in which the new immigrants and their unfamiliar beliefs will have to find a place in the American religious hierarchy. At what point Muslims will be accepted into the Protestant, Catholic, Jewish categorization of the American people as a fourth grouping will be an important future issue. World events, transnationalism, changing demographics, and political involvement will determine whether Muslims will have the same difficult path as nineteenth-century Catholics in winning acceptance.

Ethnic succession has long been an accepted way of understanding immigration mobility, especially in relation to crime, but a straight-line succession never occurred.[16] The new immigration reveals the long-known interethnic aspects of organized crime as well as the continuation of older groups in the "business." The public's prevailing wisdom stated that one group followed a previous one up the ladder as, supposedly, the

Irish were replaced by the Italians and later by Russian, Jamaican, and other, newer groups. The lack of attention to minority gangs in historical writing makes it appear that they just arrived due to succession but many were already active; however, the focus was on the white ethnic criminal activities.

Education and the cultural values immigrants brought with them appeared to be the main factor in upward occupational mobility. The concept of model minorities with a focus on Jews, Chinese, and Japanese explained for some analysts why certain groups emerged as high achievers.[17] But what is the link between culture and occupational mobility? What roles do premigration skills, discrimination, and class levels play? Ample evidence now exists to answer this question as new and poorer groups of Asians have emigrated to the United States as well as new migrants from Africa.

America's ethnic past reveals the importance of ethnic political mobility and the accession to power. Chicago and New York represented prime examples of cities with strong ethno-political histories.[18] Boss Tweed, Tammany, Fiorello La Guardia's ethnic appeals to Italians and Jews, Mayor Ed Koch's and Mayor Richard Daley's ethnic coalitions in New York and Chicago, and the election of Mayor Harold Washington in Chicago in 1983 and the ethnic and racial conflict that prevailed shaped the cities' politics. Ethnic bosses and reformers, ethnically and racially split tickets, and politicians making the rounds of ethnic neighborhoods and eating the appropriate foods are all part of American history. Does this political style still exist? Have the new groups taken part in the usual political power coalitions that have perhaps brought them to the fore of city politics? Various factors are involved: immigration numbers and, more important, naturalization rates, leadership elements willing to challenge the power structure, and the inclination of the established groups to make room for newcomers. Traditionally, entrenched ethnic and racial groups do not share power unless they are forced to do so. Having to share depends on the new group's voting strength and any threat of a breakaway from the party in charge. History tells us that the group in power will try to stay there as long as possible and will, if needed, bring some individuals from the new ethnic group into the ranks. This scenario played out in New York when the Irish-controlled Tammany allowed some Jews initially and then some Italians to stand with them on the ticket.[19] New ethnic involvement usually occurred but remained a slow process. At times, this struggle involved minority against minority groups. In New York, Dominicans have tried to win a congressional seat in a district including Harlem held by an African American and so far have failed. In other parts of the country, discrimination and efforts to prevent political organizing have stymied inclusion, but the Voting Rights Act of 1965 opened up political mobilization for blacks in the South and Hispanics in the Southwest. Political bosses of some of the newer groups have already emerged. Given the Chicago and New York historical experience, one can say that the prospects for a return to ethnic coalitions and boss politics can easily occur. Miami is a good example of racial and ethnic coalitions that formed between various Latino groups, blacks, and whites during the period after Cuban immigration.

One significant change evident in politics and assimilation is the easier communication immigrants now have with their ancestral homes. Previous generations of scholars relied

on immigrants' letters back and forth to the Old World as a way to determine acculturation, assimilation, and dual identities.[20] Immigrant letters have become the emails, videos,
and other forms of instant communication that are available today. Not only does this type
of communication make it difficult for historians to secure a lasting impression of immigrant life, but it affects national ties as well. Chat rooms, websites, and Skype have played
a role in the ethnic profiling used to identify terrorism suspects. Having the government
monitor this messaging is a new aspect of immigrant oversight not readily evident in earlier times. Modern communication removes the distance in time from old world contacts. It thereby helps maintain those ties at a stronger level and keeps immigrants fully
involved, if they desire, in the family matters and politics of their ancestral homes.

Instant communication may also affect the linguistic abilities of new immigrants.
Closeness to former countries either through travel or the Internet is perhaps allowing
a flourishing of foreign languages but alongside a continued effort to learn English. The
futility of the "English Only" movement, still present and an indication of hostility to
immigrants, is that it was never necessary. Americans benefit from a bilingual nation in
which communication with the rest of the world is made easier.

Another contemporary factor is that previous scholars for the most part wrote during periods when immigration into the United States was low. Beginning in the 1970s,
historians and sociologists could view the immigrant tide as it arrived in America, as it
adjusted to the new country, as it maintained a transnational aspect, and met with resistance from nativists. Not since the Chicago School studied immigration in the 1920s did
scholars have this opportunity.

The immigration and ethnic history field is at the point of new inquiries and further
analysis of the role of race and ethnicity in American life. The most recent books and
articles reveal, as do the essays in this *Handbook*, that this scholarship has moved further
from the initial chroniclers than any historian would have expected in the field's early
days. Recent JAEH articles focus on multiethnic and transnational identities, for example, Chinese Mexicans; the interconnections between race, ethnicity, gender, class, and
national identity; new refugees in the United States; African American women; Arab
Americans and Islam; and borderland studies. Single histories of specific ethnic groups
can still be found, but the analysis is more nuanced.

NOTES

1. Books by Theodore Blegen: *Norwegian Migration to America: 1825–1860* (1931); *Norwegian Migration to America: The American Transition* (1940); books by Carl Wittke: *Refugees of Revolution: The German Forty-eighters in America* (Philadelphia: University of Pennsylvania Press, 1952); *The German-Language Press in America* (University of Kentucky, 1957); *The Irish in America* (Louisiana University Press, 1956); *We Who Built America: The Saga of the Immigrant* (New York: Prentice Hall, 1940).
2. Oscar Handlin, *Boston's Immigrants, 1790–1880: A Study in Assimilation* (Cambridge: Harvard University Press, 1941); *The Uprooted: The Epic Story of the Great Migrations That Made the American People* (New York: Little Brown, 1951).

3. Paul Spickard, *Almost All Aliens: Immigration, Race, and Colonialism in American History and Identity* (New York: Routledge, 2007), 10.

4. Rudolph Vecoli, "Contadini in Chicago: A Critique of The Uprooted," *Journal of American History*, 51 (3) (December 1964): 404–417; John Bodnar, *The Transplanted: A History of Immigrants in Urban America* (Bloomington, IN: Indiana University Press, 1985); Milton Gordon, *Assimilation in American Life* (New York: Oxford University Press, 1964); Samuel Baily, *Immigrants in the Land of Promise: Italians in Buenos Aires and New York City, 1870–1914* (Ithaca, NY: Cornell University Press, 1998); Donna Gabaccia, *From Sicily to Elizabeth Street: Housing and Change Among Italian Immigrants, 1880–1930* (Albany, NY: State University of New York); Gary R. Mormino and George E. Pozzetta, *The Immigrant World of Ybor City: Italians and Their Latin Neighbors, 1885–1985* (Urbana: University of Illinois Press, 1987): Ronald H. Bayor, *Neighbors in Conflict: The Irish, Germans, Jews and Italians of New York City, 1929–1941* (Baltimore: The Johns Hopkins University Press, 1978); Mary Waters, *Ethnic Options: Choosing Identities in America* (Berkeley: University of California Press, 1990); Richard Alba, *Ethnic Identity: The Transformation of White America* (New Haven, CT: Yale University Press, 1990); Joshua Zeitz, *White Ethnic New York: Jews, Catholics, and the Shaping of Postwar Politics* (Chapel Hill: The University of North Carolina Press, 2007); Frederick Luebke, *German Americans and World War I* (DeKalb: Northern Illinois University Press, 1974).

5. Stephen Thernstrom, ed., *Harvard Encyclopedia of American Ethnic Groups* (Cambridge: Harvard University Press, 1980).

6. Charlotte Baum, Paula Hyman, and Sonya Michel, *The Jewish Woman in America* (New York: Dial Press, 1976); Betty Boyd Caroli, Robert F. Harney, and Lydio F. Tomasi, *The Italian Immigrant Woman in North America*, Proceedings of the Tenth Annual Conference of the American Italian Historical Association (Toronto: The Multicultural History Society of Ontario, 1978); Hasia Diner, *Erin's Daughters in America: Irish Immigrant Women in the Nineteenth Century* (Baltimore: The Johns Hopkins University Press, 1983).

7. Donna Gabaccia, "Immigrant Women: Nowhere At Home?," *Journal of American Ethnic History* 10 (4) (Summer 1991): 61–87.

8. Arthur Schlesinger, Jr., quoted in Ronald H. Bayor, ed., *The Columbia Documentary History of Race and Ethnicity in America* (New York: Columbia University Press, 2004): 896–899.

9. Michael Novak, *Rise of the Unmeltable Ethnics* (New York: Macmillan Publishing Company, 1972).

10. Buchanan, quoted in Bayor, *Columbia Documentary*, 868.

11. David R. Roediger, *The Wages of Whiteness: Race and the Making of the American Working Class* (London: Verso, 1991); Matthew Frye Jacobson, *Whiteness of a Different Color: European Immigrants and the Alchemy of Race* (Cambridge, MA, Harvard University Press, 1999); Thomas Guglielmo, *White on Arrival: Italians, Race. Color, and Power in Chicago, 1890–1945* (New York: Oxford University Press, 2004); Russell Kazal, *Becoming Old Stock: The Paradox of German-American Identity* (Princeton: Princeton University Press, 2004); Herbert Gans, "Symbolic Ethnicity: The Future of Ethnic Groups and Cultures in America," *Ethnic and Racial Studies* 2 (January 1979): 1–20; Ronald H. Bayor, "Another Look at 'Whiteness': The Persistence of Ethnicity in American Life," *Journal of American Ethnic History*, 29 (1) (Fall, 2009): 13–30; Jordan Stanger-Ross, *Staying Italian: Urban Change and Ethnic Life in Postwar Toronto and Philadelphia* (Chicago: The University of Chicago Press, 2009).

12. For the best work on the American split personality toward immigrants, see Gary Gerstle, *American Crucible: Race and Nation in the Twentieth Century* (Princeton: Princeton University Press, 2002).

13. Roger Daniels, *Guarding the Golden Gate: American Immigration Policy and Immigrants Since 1882* (New York: Hill and Wang, 2004).

14. Still the best book on hostility toward immigrants is John Higham, *Strangers in the Land: Patterns of American Nativism, 1860–1925* (Rutgers, NJ: Rutgers University Press, 1955).

15. Will Herberg, *Protestant—Catholic—Jew: An Essay in American Religious Sociology* (reprint ed. University of Chicago Press, 1983).

16. Humbert Nelli, *The Italians in Chicago: A Study in Ethnic Mobility* (New York: Oxford University Press, 1970); Humbert Nelli, *The Business of Crime: Italians and Syndicate Crime in the United States* (Chicago: University of Chicago Press, 1981); Robert Rockaway, *But He Was Good to His Mother: The Lives and Crimes of Jewish Gangsters* (New York: Gefen Publishing House, 2000); Jenna Weissman Joselit, *Our Gang: Jewish Crime and the New York Community, 1900–1940* (Bloomington, IN: Indiana University Press, 1983).

17. Thomas Kessner, *The Golden Door: Italian and Jewish Immigrant Mobility in New York City, 1880–1915* (New York: Oxford University Press, 1977); Sherry Gorelick, *City College and the Jewish Poor: Education in New York City, 1880–1924* (Rutgers, NJ: Rutgers University Press, 1981); John Bodnar, Roger Simon, and Michael Weber, *Lives of Their Own: Blacks, Italians, and Poles in Pittsburgh, 1900–1960* (Urbana, IL: University of Illinois Press, 1983).

18. Thomas Kessner, *Fiorello H. La Guardia and the Making of Modern New York* (New York: McGraw-Hill, 1989); Leo Hershkowitz, *Tweed's New York: Another Look* (New York: Anchor Press, 1977); Adam Cohen and Elizabeth Taylor, *American Pharaoh: Mayor Richard J. Daley* (New York: Little, Brown, and Company, 2001).

19. Ronald H. Bayor, *Neighbors in Conflict: The Irish, Germans, Jews, and Italians of New York City, 1929–1941* (Baltimore: The Johns Hopkins University Press, 1978).

20. See, for example, David Gerber, *Authors of Their Lives: The Personal Correspondence of British Immigrants to North America in the Nineteenth Century* (New York: New York University Press, 2008); Walter Kamphoefner, Wolfgang Helbich, and Ulrike Sommer, *News from the Land of Freedom: German Immigrants Write Home* (Ithaca, NY: Cornell University Press, 1993).

CHAPTER 1

....

THE IMPACT OF IMMIGRATION LEGISLATION

1875 to the Present

....

DAVID M. REIMERS

BEFORE 1875, Congress was content to leave immigration issues to the states. Beginning in 1819, the federal government provided for the counting of newcomers, but otherwise, state laws regulated the flow. However, in 1849, when the Supreme Court (*The Passenger Cases*) struck down state laws declaring that immigration regulation was a federal matter, Washington legislators began to construct a uniform system beginning in 1875 with enactment of the Page Act. That law, which was aimed at Chinese, barred the admission of prostitutes and had little impact on immigration. Several years later, responding to a growing hostility toward Chinese immigrants, especially in California, Congress passed the first of many laws affecting immigration and providing for the building of a bureaucracy to control the entrance of immigrants. In doing so, legislators attempted to create a nation based on ethnicity and nationality.[1] The attempt was, in Aristide Zolberg's words, *A Nation by Design: Immigration Policy in the Fashioning of America.*[2] It is also important to point out that the legislation often led to unintended results.

The first immigrants to be barred were Chinese laborers. Thousands of Chinese men (and a few women) headed to America after hearing of the discovery of gold in 1849 in California, where they at first experienced little hostility. The Chinese called California "the Gold Mountain." But as the thousands of miners from other parts of the United States, Australia, and Europe found that their dreams of vast wealth were not being fulfilled, they turned their frustrations against Chinese. White Californians passed laws to penalize Chinese miners and drive them from the mines. Nor were Chinese immigrants welcome elsewhere in the West, where they faced riots and forced removal.[3]

It was not economics alone that led to their exclusion. The rising tide of white racism during the late nineteenth century added to the hostility toward all Asians, not simply the Chinese immigrants. Proponents of this racism insisted that all Asians were inferior to white Americans and could never be assimilated into American society.[4]

Not content with ridding the mines and other occupations of Chinese immigrants, white Californians, with the support of the rest of the nation, persuaded Congress to enact the Chinese Exclusion Act in 1882, which banned the entrance of Chinese laborers to the country for a period of ten years. Legislators then extended the law and made it permanent in 1903. Not all Chinese were barred.[5] Diplomats, students, and temporary visitors were eligible for entrance, and so were merchants and their wives. However, the federal government made it very difficult for merchants and their wives to enter. Eventually, most of them who landed at Angel Island in San Francisco harbor were approved by the inspectors, but they had to wait many weeks and even months before convincing authorities that they were entitled to live in the United States.[6]

There was another way for Chinese to enter the country. Legislation barred Chinese immigrants from becoming citizens, but the San Francisco earthquake destroyed naturalization and other records, and many Chinese men then claimed that they had been born in the United States and that under the provisions of the Fourteenth Amendment they were United States citizens. Some returned to China and then announced the birth of a child (usually a male) who were American citizens by virtue of being the child of a U.S. citizen. Often, these were not in fact their children but were persons who purchased their papers from the returning "citizen." Years later, these "paper sons" showed up at Angel Island, and most were able to convince authorities that they were indeed American citizens. After World War II, the federal government instituted a legalization program that enabled thousands of the "paper sons" to become legal immigrants.[7]

Because so many more men than women entered the United States, the Chinese settlers remained essentially a bachelor society, and not until the Chinese Exclusion acts were repealed in 1943 did the Chinese neighborhoods begin to develop family-oriented communities. When several thousand Asian Indian men arrived after 1900, they too experienced intense hostility and violence, even though their numbers were small. Most of them eventually settled in California where they worked as farm laborers. Congress banned further Indian immigration in 1917.[8] Few Indian women had arrived before that date, and roughly half of the Indians married Mexican women.[9]

Congress faced a more difficult task in barring immigrants from Japan, which was in the process of economic development. Japanese immigrants began to arrive in the 1880s, first in Hawaii as agricultural workers and then the West Coast of the United States. Japan was becoming an industrial nation and had demonstrated its military power in the Russo-Japanese War of 1904. The Hearst press proclaimed that Japan represented a "yellow peril," a military threat to the United States; some extremists even insisted that Japanese immigrants were soldiers in disguise. The San Francisco Board of Education added to the growing tension between the two nations by announcing its intention to segregate Japanese pupils in the schools. When Japan protested, President Theodore Roosevelt managed to negotiate a "Gentlemen's Agreement" (1907-1908) between the United States and Japan. Japan agreed to stop its unskilled immigrants from immigrating to America, and, in return, Roosevelt used his influence to halt the segregation of Japanese students in San Francisco's schools.[10]

The agreement did not cover women, and many Japanese immigrants married women in Japan by proxy. Called "picture brides" because most of the men had never met their future wives, this migration of women contributed to the making of a family-based Japanese community. In the 1920s, Congress halted the practice of "picture brides" and barred practically all Asians from entering the United States. Korea, then a colony of Japan, was included in the Gentlemen's Agreement, but the number of Koreans migrating to the United States was only a few thousand.[11]

According to the 1870 naturalization law, only "whites" and persons of African descent could become citizens by way of naturalization, which set the stage for excluding Asians. In 1895 in the Gee Hop case, a federal court held that Chinese were not white. Dozens of cases followed until the Supreme Court in the 1920s held that Japanese (*Ozawa v. United States in 1922*) and Indians (*United States v. Thind in 1923*) were not white.[12] Congress simply banned immigration of "aliens ineligible for naturalization." Filipinos came from an American colony and were not considered to be "aliens"; rather, they were considered to be "nationals." When over 100,000 Filipinos arrived on the West Coast or Hawaii after other Asians were being barred, they immediately encountered nativism. Congress responded by granting them a quota of only fifty annually. When the Philippines received independence, Filipinos, along with other Asians, were to be excluded from entering the United States.[13]

Shortly after passing the Chinese Exclusion Act of 1882, Congress enacted other laws to bar immigrants. Thus, persons likely to become a public charge, those with loathsome diseases, anarchists, and others considered undesirable found the Golden Door shut. However, the vast majority of immigrants passed through screening at Ellis Island in New York City's harbor. Only 2 percent were rejected because of the limits that had been enacted. The favorite scheme of those wanting severe limits was a literacy test that would ban all persons over age 16 who were not literate in some language. It was hoped that such a test would substantially cut the numbers from southern and eastern Europe. However, Presidents Grover Cleveland, William Howard Taft, and Woodrow Wilson vetoed the literacy test; and finally, in 1917, Congress passed the measure over Wilson's veto. Immigration fell radically during World War I, so it was not known how much this test would have slowed immigration. In 1920, however, over 800,000 newcomers arrived, and many in Congress became alarmed and believed the literacy test would not slow immigration. By then, reports circulated that millions of Europeans were planning to immigrate to America.

As a result, legislators passed the first of the quota laws.[14] The 1921 law said that European nations would be limited to three 3 percent of the foreign-born of their nationality according to the 1910 census. This quota would have allowed about 350,000 persons to migrate to the United States. Not satisfied with this drop, Congress amended the law to limit the number to 2 percent as of the 1890 census data. Because so few southern and eastern European immigrants had settled in the United States before 1890 they had few foreign-born persons of their nationality in residing in the United States in

1890. This meant that the quotas for the European nations in those regions were very small. Congress extended the law several times until the Johnson-Reed Act went into effect in 1929; the national-origins quotas set forth in this act lasted until 1965. Under the act, a limit of roughly 150,000 persons from European nations were entitled to a number based on their nation's share of that number of the white population according to the 1920 census. The nations of northern and western Europe—Ireland, Great Britain, and Germany—were permitted about three-quarters of the slots. Although using the total white (foreign- and native-born) population and the 1920 census did increase the number of southern and eastern Europeans compared to using the 1890 census, doing so still had a drastic impact upon immigration. Italy, for example, had sent 300,000 immigrants to America several times before World War I, but the new quota for Italy was less than 6,000. Some nation's quotas were under 100 annually, so legislators allowed a minimum of 100 to all countries affected by the national-origins system. Few African nations were independent by the 1920s, and Congress gave them each an allotment of 100. The prior bans on Asians were maintained in the new system.[15] Such reductions were extreme, and that was precisely what Congress wanted. Immigration totaled only 700,000 persons from 1930 to 1945.[16]

The Johnson-Reed Immigration Act granted a nonquota status to persons from the Western Hemisphere, largely for economic reasons. Railroad and agricultural employers depended upon workers from the Western Hemisphere, mainly from Mexico, and these interests managed to keep the nonquota status for the hemisphere. Proponents of Mexican immigration also claimed that Mexicans would be temporary laborers who would return home after the crops were picked.[17] If Mexicans did not get the message, during the Great Depression, local, federal, and state governments sent them back to Mexico. Many Mexicans, who saw the hand writing on the wall, returned to their home country on their own.[18]

A little-noticed provision in the law was the nonquota status granted to certain professionals, artists, singers, and wives and children of United States citizens. The provision for exemption for wives and children would eventually become important after World War II, but it was little noticed and little discussed at the time. In 1928, Congress added husbands and children of United States citizens to the nonquota status.

During World War II and the decade following, Congress began to ease the harsh restrictions enacted against Asians and Europeans. As a gesture to a wartime ally, in 1943, Congress repealed the Chinese Exclusion acts and granted China a small quota of 105. In 1946, India and the Philippines also received small quotas. The enactment of War Brides legislation in 1945 opened the Golden Door a bit and was amended to include Asian women.[19] Special laws also made it possible for many refugees and displaced persons to become immigrants.[20]

These laws eroded the national-origins provisions. About two-thirds of immigrants during the period 1943 to 1964 were entering outside the quotas. About half of these were from the Western Hemisphere, and half of the European immigrants were nonquota: the national-origins system was not functioning as intended. Before Congress enacted a new system in 1965, lawmakers enacted a major bill, the McCarran-Walter

Immigration Act of 1952. This law represented an attempt by Congress to hold firm to the national-origins system while making a few reforms in national origins. The legislators kept national origins as the basic immigration system for the Eastern Hemisphere and limited the migration of people from the British colonies in the West Indies who had been using Britain's quota to come to America. McCarran-Walter put an annual ceiling of 100 on Jamaica and Trinidad and Tobago.[21] This quota remained after independence came to those two countries, but all other nations of the Western Hemisphere had no numerical quota. The McCarran-Walter Act also contained many provisions on security that were based on the belief that many persons sympathetic to communism might come to America.[22]

However, the law did contain a few reforms. Asians were now given small quotas (and a total annual ceiling of 2,000) and the right of naturalization. This provision was of special concern to Japanese immigrants, many of whom had lived most of their lives in the United States. A second provision of liberalization dealt with family members of United States citizens. The provision for female U.S. citizens who wanted to sponsor their family members had to have been married before 1928; but no such deadlines was imposed on similar males. Congress did change the dates several times for women, but these changes still lagged behind that of men. Therefore, Congress simply equalized the dates when it provided for the spouses and children (not simply husbands or wives) of United States citizens. At the time, this appeared to be a minor change. Most of those admitted as family members of citizens in the immediate postwar years were women married to American servicemen, and, by 1950, their numbers were not large. Refugee policy was left largely untouched in the 1952 act, which meant that it would be necessary to enact special laws in the future to admit refugees.[23]

Yet, even as the Immigration Act of 1952 went into effect, it was criticized by Presidents Harry S. Truman and Dwight David Eisenhower. Both presidents believed that low quotas discriminated against southern and eastern Europeans. They wanted to admit more refugees from that region in Europe, but the national origin quotas limited the opportunity to do so. Congress had passed Displaced Persons acts in 1948 and 1950 to admist 400,000 Europeans, but the President believed additional action was required. Congress, although with some reluctance, passed another refugee act in 1953, admitting about 200,000 persons, and then permitted 38,000 refugees from the failed Hungarian Revolution of 1956 to enter. Moreover, several thousand Chinese were accepted under separate laws. With the victory of liberals and Lyndon Johnson in 1964, the stage was set for a new immigration system to replace the national origins quotas. In 1965, Congress responded when it enacted the Hart-Celler Act.

The Hart-Celler Act abolished national origin quotas for the Eastern Hemisphere and replaced them with a preference system based mainly upon family unification. The act also had provisions for refugees and persons with skills needed in the United States. The total of persons for the Eastern Hemisphere allowed to immigrate was 170,000, with all nations to receive the same allotment of 20,000, excluding immediate family members of U.S. citizens. Immediate family members were defined as spouses, children, and parents of adult U.S. citizens. Thus, the group exempt from national limits now included parents. Legislators paid little attention to adding parents to the exempt categories. In 1963, for example, wives of United States citizens totaled 17,590, husbands 6,035, and children 6,981.[24] It was thought that only a few thousand more would enter as parents.

By using family unification as the basis of the new policy, the lawmakers believed that most of the newcomers would come from Europe, especially southern and eastern Europe, with perhaps a few thousand more coming from Asia. Indeed, the largest preference was for brothers and sisters of U.S. citizens, prompting some to label the law "the brothers and sisters act." Congress was made aware that Italy especially had a huge backlog of persons awaiting visas under the limited quotas of national origins.

Another preference was for immediate family members of immigrants already in the United States. The mood of the restrictive 1920s was being replaced by a belief that people from all parts of Europe should have the same quota. Leaders who were part of the movement to repeal national origins quotas believed that Greeks, Italians, and Portuguese should be able to migrate in larger numbers. Indeed, the new flow did benefit these nations during the first years of the program initiated by the Hart-Celler Act.[25]

Because of the marriage of United States citizens to foreign-born Asians and the flow of refugees after 1945, immigration from Asia increased, reaching 20,000 in 1965—not the 2,000 ceiling that had been established under the McCarran-Walter Immigration Act. Lawmakers did not foresee that immigrants who used the preferences for those with skills in demand (20 percent of the total) would use their status in the United States to bring their relatives to America. Highly educated Taiwanese, Filipinos, Indians, and later Africans were able to become immigrants under the new law; by the 2000s, Asian immigration accounted for more than 200,000 immigrants annually. Educated Asians eager to come to America—sometimes as students before petitioning for an immigrant visa—were the major groups to use the occupational categories. The changes occurred at the same time that Germans and British no longer wanted to settle in America; by the 1960s, war-torn European economies had improved substantially, and some were experiencing shortages of labor. It should also be noted that as African nations became independent, they were entitled to the 20,000 quota.[26]

While the law certainly liberalized immigration from Asia and Africa, it placed for the first time a ceiling of 120,000 on the Western Hemisphere. The Johnson administration had not suggested such a limit, but key figures in the House and especially the Senate won the new limit as a trade-off for ending national origin quotas. Congress established a Western Hemisphere Commission to report in 1968 on whether to have such a limit. The report made clear that its members wanted Hispanic immigrants to be limited, and it recommended a ceiling be put into place. The commission did not even mention Canada.[27] This ceiling did not contain a nation limit or a preference system, but Congress created a worldwide immigration system in 1979 by combining both hemispheres and setting a total quota of 290,000 with a uniform preference system.[28]

When signing the Immigration Act of 1965, President Johnson remarked: "This is not a revolutionary bill. It does not affect the lives of millions. It will not reshape the structure of our daily lives, or add importantly to our wealth and power . . . The days of unlimited immigration are past. But those who come will come because of what they are–not because of the land from which they sprung."[29]

The president was wrong about the impact of the bill, largely due to chain migration and the growing contacts between nations of the world. Yet in the second part of his 1965 speech, the President Johnson indicated that the United States would continue to admit refugees from Cuba, a migration that had begun in 1959. Presidents, beginning with Dwight Eisenhower, used the "parole" power to admit refugees. This power was inserted into the 1952 act, but it was meant to apply to individual cases and in emergencies, such as someone becoming ill off the coast of the United States. President Eisenhower used the parole power to admit more than 30,000 Hungarians who had escaped the failed revolution of 1956. He then used it again when the Cubans began to flee their country. Presidents believed that these Cuban newcomers were not to be counted as part of the Western Hemisphere limit. Then, in 1965, Cuban Prime Minister Fidel Castro said he would once again allow Cubans to go to America. Signing the law in 1965, President Johnson said that all Cubans were welcome, thus emasculating the Hart-Celler Act the very day he signed it.[30] The next year, Congress agreed that all Cubans were welcome and passed the Cuban Adjustment Act.

Moreover, U.S. presidents continued to employ the parole power to admit thousands of refugees beyond the 6 percent provision of the Hart-Celler Act (10,200 and 17,400 under the worldwide ceiling). When several hundred thousand South Asians fled after the communists won control of Vietnam in 1975, the United States accepted them. Often, the refugees were admitted in haste under chaotic conditions. Congress moved in 1980 to develop a more coherent refugee policy, which focused on increased numbers and programs to aid the refugees. The 1980 Refugee Act not only set in motion a program to aid refugees, but it also set the "normal" flow at 50,000; but this number, too, would be exceeded in the future.[31] After that date, administration officials spoke with key members of Congress to determine refugee admissions, but in reality, the executive branch determined the number of refugees to be admitted.[32]

Another provision of the 1980 law was for 5,000 places for those seeking asylum. Refugees were admitted from another country while asylum was to be granted to persons already in the United States who could prove, on an individual basis, that they had a "well founded fear" of persecution if they were deported to their homeland. This number, too, proved to be inadequate, and by the 2000s, twice that number were being granted asylum.[33]

Yet it took still other measures to weaken the Western Hemisphere limits. The ceiling made it difficult for Mexicans to head north, because now Mexico had a limit of only 20,000, excluding immediate family members of U.S. citizens. At the same time that the Hart-Celler Act was passed, a temporary worker program, the Bracero Program, ended. That program had been in existence since World War II and had ultimately resulted in several million Mexicans coming to the United States to labor temporarily in agriculture. With the end of the possibility of becoming a bracero to work in America and the new limit set for the Western Hemisphere, many Mexicans decided to cross the border illegally. This was not the first such movement. In the late 1940s and early 1950s, undocumented immigration from Mexico had increased. A large-scale federal effort in 1954, called "Operation Wetback," had resulted in over 1 million persons being returned to Mexico.[34] The next year, the Immigration and Naturalization Service (INS) assured the nation that the border was now "secured."

The new flow of undocumented immigrants after 1965 demonstrated how wrong the INS was. By the 2000s, it was estimated that one-half of all farm workers in the United States were illegal aliens. Yet most Mexicans headed for the cities of America, in search of jobs in landscaping, construction, hotels, motels, and restaurants and as day laborers and household workers. As the numbers of those trying to enter increased, Congress was once again faced with an immigration problem: how to halt this influx. In the early 1980s, legislators had debated a number of schemes, but no easy consensus emerged. Clearly, they would have to find some way to compromise in passing what became the Immigration Reform and Control Act (IRCA). Hispanic groups wanted amnesty for undocumented immigrants as did a number of ethnic and religious groups and some business leaders. On the other side stood organizations such as the Federation for American Immigration Reform (FAIR) and small environmental organizations that wanted tough measures for deporting illegal immigrants and denying them the right to work. According to the "Texas Proviso" in the McCarran-Walter Immigration Act, employing illegal aliens was not a crime, although transporting them was. The final deal that Congress reached by a close vote and which President Ronald Reagan signed into law in 1986, provided for amnesty for undocumented persons who had lived in the United State before January 1982 and had remained there after that date. In return for amnesty, Congress made it a crime for employers to knowingly hire persons without proper documents. The catch in the law was how to prove that the employers who hired illegal aliens had actual knowledge that these employees lacked documents to be in the United States legally. A long list of such documents, such as birth certificates, green cards, social security cards, and other government papers or cards, could be offered as proof of legal residence, and employers simply had to say they looked at the documents, even though many were fraudulent. Moreover, Congress did not provide for enough INS agents to raid businesses that were suspected of employing illegal workers. Raids on businesses were infrequent until 2006 when the administration of President George W. Bush stepped up internal enforcement of the immigration laws, a practice also followed by President Barack Obama.

At the last minute, Congress also granted amnesty for persons who had labored in agriculture for periods of four months between 1984 and 1985. The Congressional Budget Office estimated that only 200,000 or 300,000 persons would be covered by this act. The eventual number of individuals who were granted amnesty under this Special Agricultural Worker (SAW) provision was 1.1 million. Most observers believed that the SAW program was riddled with fraud. The INS lack sufficient personnel to carefully screen the regular amnesty program, and the agency was overwhelmed with applications under SAW.[35]

Moreover, Congress voted to provide funds for special programs to states in order to aid persons in adjusting their status to regular immigrants. This last provision assisted many undocumented aliens to become immigrants and later citizens who could then sponsor their relatives above the limits of the preference categories. By 2010, over one-third of those receiving amnesty had become citizens.[36]

Moreover, the amnesties themselves produced other problems. Persons who were granted amnesty and who had close family members who were not in the United States in January 1982 would have to wait for visas for their families, even though some of the preferences were backed up for several years. Congress later moved to allow those in the homeland to join their now legal families in the United States.

In short, IRCA left many issues unresolved. And it did not solve the problem of illegal immigration. Persons still wanted to come to the United States after 1986. Some were trying to escape civil wars in Nicaragua, El Salvador, and Guatemala or to escape economic difficulties in Mexico and throughout Central America. Many applied for asylum, but few were able to convince immigration officials of the merits of their case.[37] Western Hemispheric undocumented immigrants were not the only ones arriving after 1986. In the 1990s, there was an increase in undocumented immigrants from China, many of whom were smuggled in by boat; others were dropped off in Mexico and then crossed the border from there into the United States.[38]

Unauthorized immigrants also came from nations besides Mexico and China, mostly on tourist visas or temporary visas for tourism or legal short term employment, and simply stayed on after their time limit had expired. By 2010, immigration authorities estimated that these "visa abusers," as they were called, constituted roughly 40 percent of the 11 million undocumented persons living in the United States that year. Moreover, the backlog for some preference categories was as long as ten years. It is thus easy to see why many decided to settle in the United States without proper papers.

Precise estimates of the size of the undocumented have differed and have often been the source of considerable debate about their impact upon Americans. It appeared that the undocumented population grew slowly but steadily after 1982. Immigration authorities in 2000 estimated the figure to be 8.5 million and 11.6 million in 2008, only to decrease when the recession of that year began to an estimated 10.8 million in 2009. Government officials and scholars estimated the number in 2012 to 11.4 million. One provision of IRCA that was minor at the time but that later became a part of future law was the lottery. Some Irish leaders had criticized the Hart-Celler Act because they believed that the new law would make it difficult for the Irish to immigrate to the United States. Before the Hart-Celler Act, Ireland had the third largest quota and faced easy rules to immigrate to America. Between 1940 and 1970, more than 100,000 Irish had come to the United States, but the numbers began to plunge in 1968 when the Hart-Celler Act was fully in operation. Complicating the issue was the Irish economy, which was providing many jobs during the 1960s. But when their economy worsened, many Irish looked to America, as generations before them had done. However, the new rules made such migration more difficult. As a result, in the late 1970s and 1980s, many young Irish men and women came on tourist visas and simply remained after their visas expired. These "New Irish," as they called themselves, found jobs with relative ease, in construction for men and as household workers for women.[39]

The New Irish organized and lobbied lawmakers to change immigration laws to make it possible to legalize their status. In response, Congress included in IRCA a one-time lottery for 10,000 places. The Irish in Ireland and America were well aware of this provision—though many others were not—and they flooded the INS with applications; the Irish won 40 percent of the slots. The lottery—or "Diversity Visas" (DVs), as it was known—was repeated and was then made part of the Immigration Act of 1990. That law provided for 40,000 annual visas to be determined by lottery for three years and, without mentioning Ireland by name, reserved 40 percent of the places for Irish immigrants. The 1990 provision was increased to 55,000 places after three years and eventually was set at 50,000. The Irish advantage held for only the first three years.[40] The situation was ironic because just at the time the lottery became part of immigration policy, the Irish economy improved and was being called the "Celtic Tiger." As a result, few Irish wanted to migrate, at least not until the meltdown of the Irish economy, beginning in 2008.

But for other nations, the lottery was a boon. The INS ruled that to be eligible for the lottery, a nation had to have sent fewer than 50,000 (or 10,000 annually) persons over the last five-year period. All nations in Africa were eligible, and Africa was granted 40 percent of the DVs. Nations such as Bangladesh also gained many immigration DVs. In 2012, for example, 3049 DVs went to Bangladesh, while 2,672 went to the African nation of Nigeria.

The DVs were not the only change in the Immigration Act of 1990. Business groups had been vocal for years about their belief that the United States needed to import more immigrants with skills that were in demand in the United States, such as persons with advance degrees, computer technicians, and internet specialists. They won their case when Congress increased the number of occupation visas from 54,000 to 140,000. Congress also provided for a temporary worker program for highly skilled occupations in demand in the United States. The number of this type of visa was originally 65,000, but it was raised in 1998 to 115,000 before falling back to 65,000 several years later. The temporary workers under this program (H-1B) were admitted for a term of three years, but that visa could be renewed. Moreover, at the end of the term, many employers were able to sponsor these H-1B workers as regular immigrants.[41]

After 1990, immigration grew to the highest levels in any two-decade period, amounting to 20 million from 1990 to 2010. The flow was particularly heavy from Asia, the Middle East, Mexico, and Central America. In 2012, Mexican immigration was higher than the next two nations combined. In 2009, for the first time since the new nation was formed, immigration from Africa was larger than that of Europe. From Africa, the figure was 127,060, and from Europe, it was 105,398. In 2010, immigration from Africa dropped to 101,355, but Europe fell as well, to 88,743. Although Congress wanted to increase immigration after the days of the McCarran-Walter Act, it is doubtful, at best, that legislators realized that the laws they had passed would open the Golden Door so wide. The Hart-Celler Act, IRCA with its amnesty, and the Immigration Act of 1990 (which increased immigration 35 percent) certainly explain much of the increase in immigration to America as does the collapse of communism in Europe, which opened the possibility of immigration from eastern Europe. Yet by 2000, immediate family members of U.S. citizens accounted for more than 40 percent of all immigrants, an exemption dating back to the Chinese Exclusion Act of 1882 that allowed the wives of Chinese merchants to immigrate to the United States. In 2012, immediate family members accounted for 478,780 of the total immigration number of 1,031,631 As noted, the Johnson-Reed Act gave nonquota status to wives and children of United States citizens, and the McCarran-Walter Act equalized the nonquota status of men and women when it included all spouses and children. The Hart-Celler Act added parents to those persons who could arrive over the 20,000 limit, which all nations possessed. As noted, few in Congress believed this was a great change, but in some years after 2000, parents of adult United States citizens accounted for more than 100,000 newcomers. In 2012, for example, they totaled 124,230. It is important to note that there was a substantial backlog of greater than 4 million waiting for green cards to get into America. In 2008, the backlog in the preference category of unmarried adult children of United States citizens in China, as opposed to minor children, was for six years. It was the same for India, but for Mexico, there was a fifteen-year wait.

These figures were for legal immigration. How many were illegal is not known precisely. Mexico accounted for more than one-half of all unauthorized immigrants. As immigration grew, especially undocumented immigration, organizations and politicians pushed to cut immigration, especially the undocumented population. Californians passed a referendum (Proposition 187) in 1994 that denied most economic benefits to illegal aliens. The proposition included schools; however, the Supreme Court in 1980 had already ruled that schools could not deny admission to undocumented aliens. Court cases in California led to Proposition 187 being declared unconstitutional. Yet proponents of cutting immigration were heartened by the vote and the sweeping Republican victory in 1994.[42]

Congress responded in 1996 with laws cutting the benefits of immigrants and provided for increased deportation of immigrants, both legal and illegal. At first, these restrictions did not lead to a massive deportation of immigrants. However, the federal government steadily increased deportation, which by 2010 reached nearly 400,000. Immigration authorities deported thousands for relatively minor criminal offenses or because they lacked legal status and were caught in a raid of businesses that hired illegals. Some of those who were deported were guilty of serious criminal offenses.[43]

The passage of Proposition 187 and the provisions limiting immigrant benefits had the unintended effect of influencing many immigrants to become United States citizens in order to vote and to be eligible for all of the benefits that U.S. citizens enjoyed. In 1992, 342,238 persons applied for naturalization, but in 1996, the number of applicants was more than 1 million. That number topped 1 million several years after 2000. Immigration authorities could not process all of these petitions quickly, and a backlog developed.[44]

It is also important to realize the many households had both legal and illegal immigrants. Thus, some undocumented parents lived with their children who were American citizens because of the Fourteenth Amendment; they were therefore entitled to some welfare benefits. Congress later modified the restrictions, and several states picked up the slack.

In spite of the new provisions cutting the benefits of immigrants, Congress did not decrease the actual number of immigrants, although deportation grew after 1996. Instead, the debate about immigration centered on undocumented immigrants, and especially Mexicans. Opponents of a liberal immigration policy used many of the old arguments about immigration. Immigrants, they declared, used welfare, depressed wages, took jobs from Americans, were often criminals, hurt the environment, and placed economic burdens on local communities. Large numbers of Hispanic immigrants were seen as a threat to American values and were pushing the nation to become multicultural, with pockets of persons who did not join the American mainstream. Finally, opponents claimed that some undocumented immigrants were tied to the drug trade along the U.S.-Mexican border.[45] To counter these arguments, Hispanic and pro-immigrant groups, such as the National Immigration Forum, joined with businesses to urge a liberal policy.[46]

As important as these issues were, a new concern arose after the events of September 11, 2001, when New York City's World Trade Center was destroyed and the Pentagon damaged. Because several of the terrorists responsible for these events lacked legal status and had crossed American borders easily, politicians called for tighter border control, especially along the 1,900-mile border between the United States and Mexico.[47]

Congress placed tighter restrictions on persons coming from the Middle East and from Islamic nations.[48] But legislators could not agree on how to halt the influx of immigrants from the southern border. In 2006 and 2007, the House and Senate tried to reach an agreement about illegal immigration. Proposals in the House were particularly harsh and would even penalize persons, including ministers and priests, who aided illegal immigrants in any way. Many in the Senate endorsed a large-scale temporary worker program and the possibility of immigrant status for these workers after a few years. Yet the Republican-controlled House of Representatives was not open to such suggestions, and some Republican leaders believed that a large-scale temporary worker program leading to legalization was nothing more than a repeat of the amnesty of IRCA, which they insisted had not deterred people from trying to enter America without proper documentation.[49] In spite of his 2008 campaign promises, President Obama did not make immigration reform a high agenda.[50]

However, following the 2012 election the Senate enacted an immigration law that covered many areas. It did provide for more border security, but it did make some changes to induce more highly skilled immigrants to come to America, and it increased the temporary worker programs. It also tackled the difficult problem of undocumented immigrants. For those without proper papers the Senate bill provided for an path to legalization and eventual citizenship. The bill was almost immediately rejected in the House and immigration reform appeared dead for the immediate future.

In the end, the debates led to more deportations and tighter security along the southern U.S. border. During the 1990s, the INS had conducted two special programs to stem the flow of persons crossing the border. In Operation Hold the Line, the INS stationed agents in a large line across along the El Paso, Texas, border with Mexico. And Operation Gatekeeper strengthened the border south of San Diego by increasing the number of agents and using flood lights at the known crossing spots. These two programs had little impact, as "coyotes" (the term for smugglers of unauthorized immigrants) simply moved to other crossing spots. One of the major crossing areas was the Arizona border, with its high temperatures in the summer. Hundreds of people have perished in those attempted desert crossings.[51]

Author George Ramos described one of the worst tales of death in 2003. Seventy-three undocumented immigrants were loaded into a truck after crossing the border into the United States. Their destination was Houston, Texas. However, they never got there. The driver locked them in the back of the truck, even though the temperature was extremely hot. The driver did give them some water but then abandoned the truck. When the truck was discovered, nineteen people (including a 5-year-old child) had already died, and the other passengers experienced heat exhaustion. Authorities found the driver and the other persons responsible for crossing the border and successfully prosecuted them.[52]

Congressional proponents of tough restrictions insisted that special deportation and security programs were inadequate to halt undocumented immigration. They urged that the Department of Homeland Security's (which replaced the INS after the events of 9/11) border patrol be increased substantially and that new technologies be utilized along the border. Although the House and Senate could not agree on legalization or temporary workers, they could agree on more agents and walls. At the time of IRCA, the INS employed 3,000 agents along the border; by 2014, the number of agents was 20,000. The two legislative bodies also agreed on proposals for new and more walls along the border. They provided funding for 700 miles of wall separating the United States and Mexico. However, the building of walls within a year ran into funding problems and proved to be too costly to complete. As a result, Congress halted construction in 2010. Congress also provided a "virtual" wall of lighting, motion detectors, and increases in the number of helicopters and jeeps to patrol the border. This also proved to be too costly. Construction of the "virtual" wall was also halted.[53]

Proponents of tough border controls pointed to the fact that the number of people trying to cross into the United States dropped from roughly 1 million to 750,000 annually from 2007 to 2009. In 2010, only 500,000 were intercepted at the border. However, the economy surely played a role in the decrease as the United States plunged into recession in 2008. For many Hispanics, the recession began in 2007 because so many jobs dried up in the construction field, which was one of the main employers of Latino workers. Some officials also believed that the new tough policies made many undocumented persons uneasy about returning home because it was so difficult to cross again back into the United States.[54]

Although most of the discussion focused on the border, a related problem was the fact that so many of the people—as high as 40 percent—entered the United States as visitors, temporary workers, or students and simply remained when their visas expired.[55] Even with tighter controls after the events of 9/11, the federal government could not keep track of many who entered and supposedly left.[56] Stronger measures to ensure that employers complied with the law against hiring illegal aliens no doubt did make many employers cautious of hiring illegal immigrants. But "visa abusers" were usually not caught and deported.

As of this writing, it does not appear that Congress will pass major legislation on immigration in the near future. The fate of the Dream Act is a case in point. This proposal would have granted legal status to undocumented children who were brought into the United States at a young age by their parents. Those who had finished high school and were in college or were in the military could receive adjustment of their status. Before the election of 2010, the bill passed the House but failed in the Senate, and its prospects for adoption were considerably less after the election of that year.[57]

Because the federal government has been unable to stem the tide totally, many states and even local communities have enacted their own laws. Actually, states were active even after the federal government took over policing immigration with the passage of the Page Act of 1875. Around the turn of the twentieth century, states began to require citizenship to receive professional licenses. Moreover, states began to restrict the ballot to America citizens. Finally, the movement to make English the official language was largely a state issue, even though the English-only laws are rarely enforced. These issues have not been studied carefully, but states will probably become more involved with immigration policies. After 2007 several thousand bills were introduced in state legislatures, though only a few became law.[58] These covered driver's licenses (complying with federal standards), employment, access to hospitals and schools, the use of English only for government documents, cooperating with the federal government in deportation cases, and welfare benefits. Arizona passed the toughest of these laws, permitting police officers to question the immigration or citizenship status of people they stop for other violations, like speeding, and suspect are in the country illegally. Yet Maryland enacted its version of the Dream Act, permitting illegal aliens to attend state institutions of higher education and by 2014 18 states had similar Dream Acts. Utah established a temporary worker program for undocumented aliens.[59] The federal government did work with some state and local governments in utilizing local law enforcement agencies to report to immigration authorities if they found persons who were in the United States illegally and were guilty of crimes. But many local governments did not cooperate with the federal government, nor did it appear that all states would work with the federal agencies on these immigration issues.[60]

Assessing the impact of immigration is difficult, although some trends seem certain to continue. The changing religious pattern of America has been receiving attention, as it should. Diana Eck subtitled her book, "How a 'Christian Country' Has Become the World's Most Religiously Diverse Nation."[61] Koreans have rented or purchased dying churches and brought them new life. As for Catholicism, two scholars were blunt: "Except for the timely arrival of large numbers of Latino immigrants, the future of the American Catholic Church might appear bleak."[62]

Other impacts of the new immigration are more difficult to assess. The impact of economics is perhaps more noticeable. Many immigrants of the last thirty years have been highly educated and professional. The number of foreign students dropped after 9/11, but it recovered, and in 2012–2013, roughly 700,000 foreign students were enrolled in American colleges and universities. India and China alone each send 100,000 students to America in that academic year. Traditionally, many highly educated foreign students have immigrated to the United States, especially students in the sciences and engineering. Other nations are attempting to recruit the immigrant elite, but for the next few years, it appears that educated immigrants will continue to immigrant to the United States. Because so many Mexicans, Central Americans, and some refugees from the Vietnam War lack skills, they will continue to find employment in agriculture, in hotels and motels, as car washers, and as household workers and day laborers. But how long these trends will continue is hard to predict, especially in view of the American economy.

In politics, the Hispanic vote has been growing and has become important in states such as California, Florida, and Texas. Except for Cubans in Florida, the Latino voter favors the Democratic party. Yet as issues of employment, border fences, and undocumented aliens remain important, the Democratic Party cannot always count on Hispanic support. Moreover, voting is tied to naturalization, and Mexico has one of the lowest naturalization rates. Hispanics and some Democrats have put pressure on President Obama to stop deporting marginal cases or illegals and concentrate on deporting those convicted of serious offenses. They have pointed out that one difficulty is deporting persons who have children born in the United States and hence are citizens. It is estimated that over 1 million children live in families where at least one member is undocumented. Should the children be deported along with their parents? Some scholars, including authorities in the federal government, believe that persons of European heritage will be only one-half of the American population by 2050. Given the interracial and interethnic mixing (including intermarriage), what the nation will be in forty years is not known; it is probably best that historians not make rash predictions about forty years in the future. Congress could change the laws, and violence throughout the world could lead to large refugee flows to upset predictions.

However, groups that have not been studied may warrant closer attention. The change in laws has opened the door to Africans and Asians. We have only limited studies of the new African migration and some Asian groups. While Chinese and Indians have been the focus of growing investigation, Pakistanis and Bangladeshi have not drawn attention. The growing African communities also deserve study. Sociologists and anthropologists have begun to look at these communities, but much more work remains to be done. Probably the most neglected groups are the immigrants from South America. We know a great deal about immigration from Mexico and Central America, but little of South Americans in the United States. If the patterns of growth continue, they will be added to growing multicultural American society.

Notes

1. Erika Lee, *At America's Gates: Chinese Immigration During the Exclusion Era, 1882–1943* (Chapel Hill: University of North Carolina Press, 2005). For the rise of the bureaucracy, see especially Lucy E. Salyer, *Laws Harsh as Tigers: Chinese Immigrants and the Shaping of Modern Immigration Law* (Chapel Hill: University of California Press, 1995).
2. Aristide R. Zolberg, *A Nation by Design: Immigration Policy in the Fashioning of America* (Cambridge: Harvard University Press, 2006).
3. For a discussion of violence against the Chinese, see Jean Pfaelzer, *Driven Out: The Forgotten War Against Chinese Americans* (New York: Random House, 2007).

4. John Higham's work remains a classic. See John Higham, *Strangers in the Land: Patterns of American Nativism*, 2d ed. (New Brunswick: Rutgers University Press, 1988), but also Matthew Frye Jacobson, *Whiteness of a Different Color: European Immigrants and the Alchemy of Race* (Cambridge: Harvard University Press, 1998).

5. Lee, *At America's Gates*.

6. Ibid., 27–30.

7. Ibid., 203–207.

8. Joan M. Jensen, in *Passage from India: Asian Immigrants in North America* (New Haven: Yale University Press, 1988), covers the rising tide of opposition to and the eventual exclusion of Indians.

9. See Karen Leonard, *Making Ethnic Choices: California's Punjabi Mexican Americans* (Philadelphia: Temple University Press, 1992).

10. Roger Daniels, *Guarding the Golden Door: American Immigration Policy and Immigrants Since 1882* (New York: Hill and Wang, 2004), 41–45.

11. Bill Ong Hing, *Defining America Through Immigration Policy* (Philadelphia: Temple University Press, 2004), 41.

12. Ian F. Haney Lopez, *White By Law; The Legal Construction of Race* (New York: New York University Press, 1996), chap. 4.

13. Mae M. Nagi, *Impossible Subjects: Illegal Aliens and the Making of Modern America* (Princeton: Princeton University Press, 2004), chap. 3.

14. There are several good studies of the Johnson Reed Immigration Act. See Zolberg, *A Nation By Design*; Nagi, *Impossible Subjects*; and Desmond King, *Making Americans: Immigration, Race, and the Origins of Diverse Democracy* (Cambridge: Harvard University Press, 2000).

15. King, *Making Americans*, chap. 7.

16. Unless otherwise indicated, all figures in this chapter come from the *Statistical Yearbooks* of the Department of Homeland Security (formerly the Immigration and Naturalization Service).

17. A good discussion of the migration of Mexican workers in the 1920s is Mark Reisler, *By the Sweat of Their Brow: Mexican Immigrant Labor in the United States, 1900–1940* (Westport, CT: Greenwood Press, 1976).

18. Daniels, *Guarding the Golden Door*, chap. 3.

19. Ibid., chap. 4.

20. Carl Bon Tempo, *Americans at the Gate: The United States and Refugees During the Cold War*, (Princeton: Princeton University Press), chaps. 2, 3.

21. Bill Ong Hing, *Defining America Through Immigration Policy* (Philadelphia: Temple University Press, 2004), chap. 5.

22. Regarding the tight security, see Gil Loescher and John A. Scanlan, *Calculated Kindness: Refugees and America's Half-Open Door, 1945–Present* (New York: The Free Press, 1986).

23. Bon Tempo's *Americans at the Gate* is especially informative on these acts. See chaps. 2, 3.

24. David M. Reimers, *Still the Golden Door*, 2d ed. (New York: Columbia University Press, 1992), chap. 3. Other accounts of the law can be found in Ngai, *Impossible Subjects*; Zolberg, *A Nation By Design*; and Daniels, *Guarding the Golden Door*.

25. Economic conditions had improved considerably in Europe by the late 1970s to the extent that many fewer persons were eager to migrate to the United States.

26. Reimers, *Still the Golden Door*, 69–76.

27. Commission on Western Hemisphere Immigration (Washington, DC: Government Printing Office, 1968).
28. Ngai, *Impossible Subjects*, 261, asserts that the decrease for the Western Hemisphere was 40 percent. However, the actual numbers before the Hart-Celler Act limited the Western Hemisphere averaged 110,000 yearly from 1946 to 1964. Only in the years just before 1965 did the figures grow rapidly. Ibid.
29. Quoted in Daniels, *Guarding the Golden Door*, 135.
30. See Bon Tempo, *Americans at the Gate*, chap. 5.
31. A general account of refugees and refugee policy can be found in David W. Haines, *Safe Haven? A History of Refugees in America* (Sterling, VA: Kumarian Press, 2010).
32. Susan Martin, *A Nation of Immigrants* (New York: Cambridge University Press, 2011), chap. 11.
33. It should be noted that most applications for asylum were rejected.
34. Kelly Lytle Hernandez, *La Migra: A History of the U.S. Border Patrol* (Berkeley: University of California Press, 2011), chaps. 8, 9. The best overall account of Mexican-United States relations and the border is Douglas Massey, Jorge Duran, and Nolan J. Malone, *Beyond Smoke and Mirrors: Mexican Immigration in an Era of Economic Integration* (New York: Russell Sage Foundation, 2002).
35. Martin, *A Nation of Immigrants*, 210–219.
36. For an early study of IRCA, see Frank D. Bean, Georges Vernez, and Charles Keely, *Opening and Closing the Doors: Evaluating Immigration and Control* (Washington, DC: The Urban Institute, 1989).
37. Fewer than 10 percent of Central Americans were granted asylum. But later, the courts and Congress, in enacting the Nicaragua and Central American Relief Act in 1997, forced officials to grant permission to many more so they could remain in the United States.
38. For the illegal Chinese, see Peter Kwong, *Forbidden Workers: Illegal Chinese Immigrants and American Labor* (New York: The New Press, 1997).
39. For the New Irish, see Linda Almeida, *Irish Immigrants in New York City, 1945–1995* (Bloomington: University of Indiana Press, 2001), which covers the diversity visas as well as the New Irish generally.
40. An excellent study of the Diversity Visa is Anna O. Law, "The Diversity Visa Lottery," *Journal of American Ethnic History* 21 (Summer 2002): 3–29.
41. Martin, *A Nation of Immigrants*, 215–219.
42. Zolberg, *A Nation by Design*, 402–418.
43. Two works critical of the deportations are Bill Ong Hing, *Deporting Our Souls: Values, Morality, and Immigration Policy* (New York: Cambridge University Press, 2006) and Kevin Johnson, *The "Huddled Masses" Myth; Immigration and Civil Rights* (Philadelphia: Temple University Press, 2004).
44. Zolberg, *A Nation by Design*, 402–432.
45. For an example of these arguments, see Congressman J.D. Hayworth, *Whatever It Takes: Illegal Immigration, Border Security, and the War on Terror* (Washington, DC: Regnery Publishing, Inc., 2006).
46. David M. Reimers, *Unwelcome Strangers: American Identity and the Turn Against Immigration* (New York: Columbia University Press, 1998), chap. 7.
47. Edward Alden, *The Closing of the American Border: Terrorism, Immigration, and Security Since 9/11* (New York: Harper/Collins, 2008).

48. Two basic books on the impact of the events of September 11, 2001, are Anny Bakalian and Mehdi Bozorgmehr, *Backlash: 911 and the Middle Eastern and Muslim Americans Respond* (Berkeley: University of California Press, 2009) and Alden, *The Closing of the American Border*.

49. Aaron Matgteo Terrazas, "Comprehensive Immigration Reform Eludes Senate, Again," *Migration Information Source*, July 16, 2007.

50. Ginger Thompson and Sarah Cohen, "More Deportations Follow Minor Crimes," *New York Times*, April 20, 2014.

51. See Massey et al., *Smoke and Mirrors*, for a discussion of the border conflicts.

52. Jorge Ramos, *Dying to Cross: The Worst Immigrant Tragedy in American History* (New York: Harper/Collins, 2005).

53. Muzaffar Chishti and Claire Bergeron, "Quiet Demise of the Virtual Fence," *Migration Informative Source*, Feb. 15, 2011.

54. For a good discussion of border policies, see Massey et al., *Smoke and Mirrors*.

55. Alden, *The Closing of the American Border*, 65–67.

56. An excellent discussion of the growth of immigration enforcement is Donald Kerwin, Doris Meissner, Muzaffar Chishti, and Clair Bergeron, "Immigration Enforcement in the United States: The Rise of a Formidable Machinery," *Migration Policy Institute* Jan., 2013.

57. David M. Herszenhorn, "Senate Blocks Bill for Young Illegal Immigrants, *New York Times*, Dec. 18, 2010.

58. *Migration Policy Institute*, "State Responses to Immigration," http://www.migrationinformation.org/datahub/statelaws_home.cfm.

59. Trip Gabriel, "Virginia Attorney General Opens In-State Tuition to Students Brought to the U.S. Illegally," *New York* Times, April 29, 2014, and Jeff Biggers, *State Out of the Union: Arizona and the Final Showdown Over the American* Dream New York: Nation Books, 2012). Most state laws attempted to be more restrictive about immigration.

60. Randy Capps, March R. Rosenblum, Chrstina Rodriguez, and Muzaffar Chishti, *Delegation and Divergence: A Study of the 287(g) State and Local Immigration Enforcement* (Migration Policy Institute, Jan. 2011).

61. Diana L. Eck, *A New Religious America: How a "Christian Country" Has Become the World's Most Religiously Diverse Nation* (New York: HarperCollins, 2001).

62. Robert D. Putnam and David E. Campbell, *American Grace: How Religion Divides and Unites Us* (New York: Simon and Schuster, 2010).

BIBLIOGRAPHY

Alden, Edward. *The Closing of the American Border: Terrorism, Immigration, and Security Since 9/11*. New York: Harper/Collins, 2008.

Almeida, Linda. *Irish Immigrants in New York City, 1945–1995*. Bloomington: University of Indiana Press, 2001.

Bakalian, Anny, and Mahdi Bozorgmehr. *Backlash 9/11: Middle Eastern and Muslim Americans Respond*. Berkeley: University of California Press, 2009.

Bon Tempo, Carl. *Americans at the Gate: The United States and Refugees During the Cold War*. Princeton: Princeton University Press.

Daniels, Roger. *Guarding the Golden Door: American Immigration Policy and Immigrants Since 1982*. New York: Hill and Wang, 2004.

Eck, Diana L. *A New Religious America: How a "Christian Country" Has Become the World's Most Religiously Diverse Nation*. New York: HarperCollins, 2001.

Haines, David W. *Safe Haven? A History of Refugees in America*. Sterling, VA: Kumarian Press, 2010.

Hayworth, J.D. *Whatever It Takes: Illegal Immigration, Border Security, and the War on Terror*. Washington, DC: Regnery Publishing, Inc., 2006.

Hernandez, Kelly Lytle. *La Migra: A History of the U.S. Border Patrol*. Berkeley: University of California Press, 2011.

Higham, John. *Strangers in the Land: Patterns of American Nativism, 1860–1925*. 2nd. ed. New Brunswick: Rutgers Press, 1988.

Hing, Bill Ong. *Defining America Through Immigration Policy*. Philadelphia: Temple University Press, 2004.

Hing, Bill Ong. *Deporting Our Souls: Values, Morality, and Immigration Policy*. New York: Cambridge University Press, 2006.

Jacobson, Matthew Frye. *Whites of a Different Color: Europeans and the Alchemy of Race*. Cambridge: Harvard University Press, 1998.

Jensen, Joan M. *Passage from India: Asian Immigrants in North America*. New Haven: Yale University Press, 1988.

Johnson, Kevin. *The "Huddled Masses" Myth; Immigration and Civil Rights*. Philadelphia: Temple University Press, 2004.

King, Desmond. *Making Americans: Immigration, Race, and the Origins of Diverse Democracy*. Cambridge: Harvard University Press, 2000.

Kwong, Peter. *Forbidden Workers: Illegal Chinese Immigrants and American Labor*. New York: The New Press, 1997.

Lee, Erika. *At America's Gate: Chinese Immigration During the Exclusion Era, 1882–1943*. Chapel Hill: University of North Carolina Press, 2003.

Leonard, Karen. *Making Ethnic Choices: California's Punjabi Mexican Americans*. Philadelphia: Temple University Press, 1992.

Loescher, Gil, and John A. Scanlan. *Calculated Kindness: Refugees and America's Half-Open Door, 1945–Present*. New York: The Free Press, 1986.

Lopez, Ian F. Haney. *White By Law: The Legal Construction of Race*. New York: New York University Press, 1996.

Martin, Susan F. *A Nation of Immigrants*. New York: Cambridge University Press, 2011.

Massey, Douglass S., Jorge Durand, and Nolan J. Malone. *Beyond Smoke and Mirrors: Mexican Immigration in an Era of Economic Integration*. New York: Russell Sage Foundation, 2002.

Nagai, Mae M. *Impossible Subjects: Illegal Aliens and the Making of Modern America*. Princeton: Princeton University Press, 2004.

Pfaelzer, Jean. *Driven Out: The Forgotten War Against Chinese Americans*. New York: Random House, 2007.

Putnam, Robert D., and David E. Campbell. *American Grace: How Religion Divides and Unites Us*. New York: Simon and Schuster, 2010.

Ramos, Jorge. *Dying to Cross: The Worst Immigration Tragedy in American History*. New York: HarperCollins, 2005.

Reimers, David M. *Still the Golden Door: The Third World Comes to America*, 2nd ed. New York: Columbia University Press, 1992.

Reimers, David M. *Unwelcome Strangers: American Identity and the Turn Against Immigration*. New York: Columbia University Press, 1998.

Reisler, Mark. *By the Sweat of Their Brow: Mexican Immigrant Labor in the United States, 1900–1940*. Westport, CT: Greenwood Press, 1976.

Tichenor, Daniel. *Dividing Lines: The Politics of Immigration Control in America*. Princeton: Princeton University Press, 2002.

Zolberg, Aristide R. *A Nation By Design: Immigration Policy in the Fashioning of America*. Cambridge: Harvard University Press, 2006.

CHAPTER 2

···

EUROPEAN MIGRATIONS

···

DIRK HOERDER

TRADITIONAL perspectives on European immigrants to America begin either with the migrants to Virginia or, more often, with the Pilgrim Fathers to what they came to call "New England." Their intensive historical writing established the long dominant "New England view" of American history. Recent scholarship has analyzed migrant arrival in transoceanic-imperial and transcontinental perspectives: Europe's empires competed about possession and settlement of the Americas, none negotiated with resident Native or First Peoples. Newcomers also arrived from "New Spain" and along the Pacific Coast.

IMPERIAL INTRUSIONS: EARLY SETTLEMENT IN NATIVE PEOPLES' CULTURAL SPACES

···

In transoceanic–imperial perspective, the first to claim possession of parts of Central and North America was the Spanish dynasty. Having established rule over all of Central and large parts of South America, in the 1540s it extended its claims northward ("Kingdom of New Mexico"). The first European or European-background settlers to arrive in the territory of the future United States were Spanish, including ethnic Basques, who founded St. Augustine (Florida)[1] in 1565 and Santa Fe in the region of the Pueblo peoples (New Mexico) in 1598. In the north, Basque and Bristol fishing vessels reached the Newfoundland banks and coasts. From imperial France, merchants established a post in Tadoussac on the St. Lawrence River in 1599 to trade with the Montagnais people for furs; colonial administrators founded Port Royal as an Atlantic harbor on Micmac land in 1604 (Acadia, now Nova Scotia) and Quebec City in 1608 in a region of Algonquin-speaking peoples. Over time, the French North American settlement comprised Acadia, New France, and the vast region of the Mississippi (Louisiana Territory) to New Orleans (1718). From there it continued to the Caribbean colonies.

From England, claiming and settling began with large royal land grants to wealthy individuals of rank or capital-raising chartered merchant companies. First attempts to settle at Roanoke Island, 1584–1602, proved as unsuccessful as the earlier ones of the Spanish at Pensacola, 1559, and the French at Quebec, 1534. To achieve sufficient capitalization for colonization ventures, two merchants' companies, London and Plymouth, were chartered in 1606 and the first settlers arrived in Virginia in 1606 and in Maine in 1607. From the Plymouth Company, the Puritan settlements of Pilgrim fathers, mothers, children, and servants emerged, a migration in stages that involved a stay in Leiden, Netherlands. Afraid—like many later migrants—to lose their culture in the highly urbanized Dutch society, the pilgrim families sailed for the wilderness. In the Mayflower agreement they established hierarchies of rule (the traditional aspect) by compact of all (the innovative aspect). Subsequent royal charters and grants involved Lord Baltimore, whose Maryland became a shelter for Catholics; William Penn, who opened his lands to persecuted religious groups from continental Europe; and Georgia as a philanthropic endeavor for the "worthy poor." In the New York–Delaware region, Dutch and Swedish investors established New Amsterdam (1624) and New Sweden (1638), both later absorbed by the English. In the far North, the London-based "Company of Adventurers of England," the Hudson's Bay Company (1670), used venture capital to ship Scotsmen and Orkneymen as fur traders. These usually lived in consensual unions with Native women—a Native–Scottish métis population emerged.

To complete the global story of the European migrations: Along North America's Pacific Coast, Spanish fishing vessels sailed northward as far as British Columbia, and Russian vessels southward as far as San Francisco. Both established temporary settlements for fish-processing and reprovisioning of ships. The British East India Company, engaged in global competition with the Hudson's Bay Company, in 1793 sent ships under Capt. Vancouver from Asia across the Pacific to claim territory—Vancouver Island was named after him. To establish a fort and build ships for interisland transportation, he settled a small number of Chinese craftsmen and sailors.

The many colonial societies of the Atlantic Coast, the Gulf of Mexico's littorals, and the California shores thus were many-cultured from the beginning. Some migrants returned, others moved on, and the majority became "immigrants" (i.e. *permanent* new arrivals. Since from all cultures men predominated, many lived in unions with Native women, often in a consensual "marriage according to the customs of the country" but also in relationships involving sexual violence. Much of North America's population in the present thus has roots among First Peoples, a fact never accepted in the memory of whiteness-espousing Anglo America but conceptualized in Mexico in the 1920s and 1930s. With rhetorical flourish, the Minister of Education, José Vasconcelos, called Mexicans a "cosmic race" emerging through *mestizaje* from people of all continents (1925). In Cuba, historian and philosopher Fernando Ortiz provided a thoughtful and well-researched analysis of "transculturation" in 1940.

The creation of societies and peoples (ethnogenesis) by the newcomers from Europe with help from First Peoples displaced the latter and set in motion vast refugee migrations. It also involved large-scale input from African forced migrants; South Carolina's population temporarily had a black majority. Sexual violence against Black women resulted in mixed children, all whiteness-ideology notwithstanding. In an imperial socioeconomic perspective, the Southern mainland colonies' plantation regime was more a part of the circum-Caribbean slave societies than of the commercial and farming Northeast.

(Re-)Peopling the Colonies in the Eighteenth Century

Immigrant arrival, called "the peopling of North America" in a Euro-centric White perspective that negates the presence of—red or brown—First Peoples, was a process of "re-peopling."[2] The most comprehensive human-geography approach to the spaces of both first and second peoples is Donald Meinig, *The Shaping of America* (4 vols., 1986–2004), which covers the five centuries since 1492. In the first 150 years of settlement, the Spanish, from the south, unintentionally provided Native Peoples with horses and thus the Plains cultures emerged, while east of the Appalachians, the English, in cultural genocide, displaced Native Peoples except for those of the Iroquois Federation.

From imperial governments' and chartered companies' points of view, voluntary settlement (and, thus, return on investment) was slow; from settlers' interests, labor was scarce. To increase populations, poor men and women could migrate under indentures, others were sent as deportees, and—following the example of the Puritans—religious dissenters and refugees arrived. While much has been made of "convict" deportation, numbers were small and the offences often insignificant—theft of food or vagrancy: bureaucrats shipped out marginal people. Among early arriving men and women, mortality was high: in unsuitable lands and without shelter, illness was frequent, no midwives could attend women in childbirth, and gentlemen came without intent to work.

Under indentures came between one-half and two-thirds of all White English-, German-, and French-language immigrants before 1776. Indentures, usual in English labor relations of the time, provided poor men and women with passage in return for an agreement to work off the fare—they were bound laborers. Contracts required 3 to 7 years of service depending on the country of origin's laws. Thereafter, the "servants" redeemed their freedom (hence: "redemptioners") and, as after an apprenticeship, were expected to be able to begin an independent life as useful members of colonial societies. Poverty in Europe, an efficient labor market in the colonies, and postcontract self-determined lives explain why indentures were the most common way to emigrate.

Cost of passage was usually advanced by merchants or captains, but governments, speculators, and joint stock companies also involved themselves. English and Irish redemptioners tried to avoid being shipped to the Caribbean because of the high mortality. Those from the German areas had as a labor market the German-speaking religious refugees in Pennsylvania: compared with Europe, the region appeared as the "best poor man's country." But some were marched to the hinterlands for sale of their terms of service, and masters could sell indentured servants for their remaining years of service. Most worked in family agriculture and staple crop production, but skilled artisans came to urban labor markets. In plantation work, enslaved Africans came to replace bound Europeans. The indenture system ended in the 1820s.

Less than one-half of the early comers were "free" migrants, i.e. people who usually left under—often extreme—economic constraints but could afford the cost of passage. Men and women from the British Isles predominated, but those summarily called "Anglo Americans" were highly differentiated: The ethnically and linguistically diverse English-speakers included Anglicans and Dissenters, Protestant and Catholic Irish, Highland and Lowland Scots, Scots–Irish, and some Welsh. By 1700, the Crown's Caribbean and North American possessions counted some 270,000 inhabitants of British back-ground. Among the next cohort, about 260,000 British immigrants from 1700 to 1775, the majority were Irish, Scots ranked second, and 50,000 were English. More White and freer migrants came to the colonies in the seventeenth century than in the eighteenth century, when the ratio of European bound and African slave migrants increased. To the 1830s more Africans than Europeans reached the Americas as a whole. English and Scots also migrated to colonized Ireland; Scotland had migratory traditions to conti-nental Europe; and, following Oliver Cromwell's victories, Scottish prisoners were sent to Tangiers, Guinea, and the Americas. Clearances of land from tenants, commercializa-tion of agriculture, linen recessions, and crop failures added to the potential for emigra-tion. For the Irish, poverty, population increase, and English overlordship were push factors for multidirectional migration in the Americas to a region extending from the St. Lawrence to the La Plata rivers. These many-cultured English- and Gaelic-speakers needed to learn to get along with each other and to form a culture and institutions that would be called "Anglo America."

In addition to English-, French-, and German-language migrants, Walloons, Dutch, Swedes, and other Scandinavians came. Finns introduced log-cabin construction, often considered a quintessentially American contribution to material culture. Men and women from Minorca, Livorno, and Greece settled in Florida. Religious refugees included Pietists, Moravians, Huguenots, Mennonites, and Old Order Amish. Lutheran Palatines fled devastations of war and overcrowded crafts. At the destination, disap-pointing conditions sometimes prevented settlement and demanded involuntary sequential moves to better prospects. Migration peaked between 1760 and 1775 when about 15,000 came annually—the largest ethnocultural group of which were, in absolute numbers over the 15 years, 85,000 enslaved Africans. Interregional migrations made the colonies mobile societies: circuits to sell redemptioners, migration from New England to Nova Scotia, sale and forced migration of slaves, deportation and return of Acadians, the mass flight and emigration of Loyalists. The Declaration of Independence of thirteen of the North American colonies involved, among many other reasons, settlers' and spec-ulators' demand for land, indicating the readiness to migrate farther inland. In 1790, the U.S. population of 3.9 million consisted of English (49 percent), Africans mostly enslaved but a few free (20 percent), Germans and Scots (7 percent each), Scots-Irish, Irish, Dutch, French, Swedish, and Spanish.

CAESURA AND NEW PATTERNS: FROM THE AGE OF REVOLUTION TO INDUSTRIALIZATION

During the Age of Revolution and the unsettling warfare of Napoleon's imperial and dynastic regimes' antirevolutionary goals, migration slowed and, after 1815, several developments changed its patterns. First, a sequence of images about "America"—a mental construct rather than the United States as a state—emerged. In contrast to Europe's societies, the successful revolution created a discourse about "free" institutions; from the 1840s, the low price of farmland brought a belief in "free" land; and urban growth and post–Civil War industrialization translated into a view of a dynamic job-providing economy. Potential migrants, however, who had to invest all their savings for the passage, could not afford to trust broad imaginations but relied on emigrant letters' detailed information on the cost of land or job options. The "unlimited opportunities" cliché, a U.S.-created advertising slogan, never motivated migrants: By fall they had to have the first harvest in, a job had to be found within days after arrival.

Second, migration patterns in Europe changed: Around 1820, Tsarist authorities, resettling the South Russian Plains, ended recruitment of peasant families from the overpopulated southwestern German states. These, in consequence, changed direction and moved westward down the Rhine River and via Dutch ports to North America. At that time the U.S. military vacated land for settlers by pushing Native Peoples farther west to the Mississippi and beyond. In mid-1840s Ireland's British colonialism and the potato blight resulted in mass starvation: more than 1 million had to emigrate within 5 years. Third, shipping companies—English and Irish and, on the continent, Dutch and North German—facilitated emigration by organizing "package tours": From mid-century, migrants could buy tickets from place of origin to destination. In addition, state and port-city authorities regulated the migration business to avoid having middlemen exploit migrants to a degree that an impoverished transient underclass would get stuck in the transit cities. When in the 1870s steamers replaced sailing vessels, the crossing time fell from 6 to 12 weeks to 12 days or less. Tickets became ever cheaper and were often sent as "prepaid" tickets by earlier migrant kin and friends.

Fourth, once information flows and transport facilities made migration self-sustaining, migrants compared relative advantages on both sides of the Atlantic. Less rigorous social hierarchies and class barriers, the possibility to elect municipal officials and get responses from them (sometimes decried as "boss rule"), and the option to continue one's own language, religion, and food habits in ethnic communities became pull factors. Such cultural self-determination, for smaller peoples in European empires, was threatened or abolished by national homogenization policies, whether Russification, Germanization, or Habsburg-Austrianization. But, from the 1880s, in the United States, postmigration ethnocultures would also come under attack. Americanization drives attempted to push newcomers to Anglo-conformity.

In terms of gender, a fifth aspect emerged: Women, who accounted for about 40 percent of the total migration to the 1920s and for 50 percent from the 1930s, noticed the less restrictive gender relations and role ascriptions in North America. They had high rates in labor market participation, if married because men's wages did not feed families and, if single, to achieve some independence. Their letters and prepaid tickets brought over other women, just as men usually brought over other men. They worked on farms, in domestic service, and in factories—in addition to the reproductive labor in families.

To summarize, from 1815 a migration system connected the Atlantic economies within which, to mid-20th century, some 60 million moved: 33 million to the United States, 5 million to Canada, and 6.5 and 4.5 million to Argentina and Brazil, respectively—the continent's four frontier societies. Three million moved to other American areas and 8 million to other global destinations. The Atlantic system, in global perspective, was one of several migration systems: the European Russia–Siberian, the Southern Chinese and distinct North China–Manchuria, the Indian–Southeast Asian, and, in addition, macro-regional internal systems within Europe (74 million) and the Americas (35 million), as well as in China, Southeast Asia, sub-Saharan Africa, and the Eastern Mediterranean–West Asia region. Many migrants pursued multiple trajectories—only some emigrated/immigrated only once and permanently: From North America an estimated 7 million returned to Europe—they had come as temporary workers ("guestworkers" to use the problematic modern term). In family strategies of risk diversification, they had been "delegated" to migrate and send money back. Their remittances helped family members staying behind to re-achieve a sustainable family economy and thus avoid migration.

Europe's Societies and Economies of Origin: The Frame of Migration Decisions

In the "delayed" nineteenth century—from the end of the Napoleonic/anti-Napoleonic wars in 1815 to the beginning of World War I in 1914—tens of millions of men and women made the decision to depart, a majority bound for the United States. Europe's old elites and dynastic states had reestablished a reactionary social order, with only Switzerland and the Netherlands being exceptions. Economic innovation and growth were slow and demographic growth was fast in all societies except France. Taxes and tithes ate into people's meager incomes and food intake, and rigorous norms and stratification prevented realization of human potential. The hold of the Church declined when men and women secularized their hopes: Rather than waiting for paradise after death, they could attain a better world by geographic relocation in their lifetime. The hold of the state, on the other hand, was tightened: The construction of bloodline nations and essentialist national identities began. At the beginning of the nineteenth century, national consciousness emerged, positively, as an awareness of local people's cultures (as opposed to the delocalized culture and power of the noble orders); It then became a nationalist instrument to oppress "minorities" (who usually were majorities on their historic territories) and labor migrants of other cultures in the empires and nation-states. Finally, it brought chauvinist expulsion of "others" and expansionist wars. People decided to leave for economic reasons—often a question of mere survival; for social reasons—ossified hierarchical structures; and cultural reasons—oppression of working-class cultures and whole ethnocultural groups and, as regarding women, to reduce gender inequalities.

The migration from Europe, even of those who had indentured themselves, was "free" but decisions were made within severe constraints—There were few options for sustainable lives and secure family economies; for the lower classes, there were few chances for an education and few options to rise on the social scale; and, for young men, the draft into the dynastic armies, and for women, marriage without the need for a dowry, played roles. In some regions, Eastern Germany, for example, by mid nineteenth century, landlords still had the right to refuse permission to young people to marry. One of the advantages of France's egalitarian revolutionary thought was the stepwise abolition of serfdom in Europe, last—in 1861—in Russia.[3] Men and women could move more easily, and, from the 1830s, railroad construction began to facilitate mobility.

At first, mainly West Europeans migrated through the Dutch and German North Sea ports, then North Europeans came from Baltic and Scandinavian ports. Migrants came from clearly defined regions, characterized by demographic and economic factors, rather than from nation-states—"Palatines" rather than "Germans." Regions of departure expanded to East Central Europe, to the eastern Tsarist Empire. From the latter departed mainly Ashkenazi Jews with their German-Yiddish language and Ukrainians as well as the descendants of some earlier religious refugees who lost their ethnoreligious privileges. At the same time, people began to leave Mediterranean Europe, especially Italy. The East Europeans came as transit migrants through the German Reich and the South Europeans mainly through Italian ports. From among the latter, the largest groups were Southern Italians, but Greeks and Lebanese also migrated. Transregional and translocal information connections (rather that statewide transnational ones) informed people staying behind of labor market options in the United States, permitted consolidation of their family economies by remittances, or supported class and ethnic struggles for better societies in Europe. When the reactionary German government outlawed the social democratic party, its clandestine survival depended on support from emigrant workingmen and women; when the Habsburg government deprived Slovaks of their press and higher education, more Slovak newspapers were printed in the United States than in the inhospitable home. On the other hand, funds were also transmitted to the United States: emigrant children received their inheritances when parents died, and to 1872, more funds were thus transmitted to the United States than back to Europe.

The emphasis on nation-state identity and obligation—military service and bearing of children—overlooks the nations' exclusionary practices: poor peasants, working classes, women, and minorities were not granted full membership. Some were encouraged/pressured to depart, and small numbers were actively expelled. In economic, labor market, terms, potential migrants could select destinations in Europe: the Irish went to England and the Scottish Lowlands; Slovaks and Rumanians went to Budapest. Russian Orthodox or Jewish migrants went to St. Petersburg and Odessa, and Poles and Germans went to the Ruhr District. Such moves provided them with jobs but not with more open social and cultural frames. To the 1880s intra-European labor markets were concentrated in industrial "islands" rather than whole societies.

The mass transatlantic migration, at first, involved mainly peasant families heading for farmland in the Midwest and the rest of the Prairies and (Canadian) Plains. Others headed for the plains of South Russia, Argentina, and Australia—all set out to produce grain for local and worldwide markets. In result, the world market prices for grain collapsed in the 1870s and 1880s, forcing millions of families off marginal lands into migration—migration to urban factory jobs since farmlands were settled. The "proletarian mass migration" from the late 1860s, on the push side, was the result of these constraints. On the pull side, the U.S. economic growth in general and, in particular, expansion of specific regional industries and local factories created a high demand for labor. Without migrant arrival, growth would have had to slow.

The macro-economic changes, emerging both from millions of individual or family decisions to migrate and from capital investment in industrialization and mining, in turn changed the parameters for decision-making. In the first half of the nineteenth century, a peasant family would sell their possession, migrate as a family, and attempt to recommence lives in agriculture—just as the Puritans had attempted to replicate a certain kind of religious life. Industries, in contrast, needed individual workers. Thus, single young men and women migrated, and some would later bring in family members or spouses. For this mass migration, states or nations had only a limited role; emigration was—with some restrictions—free or uncontrolled, and so was entry into the United States. From 1882, when "Orientals" were being totally excluded on the West Coast (after a first law in 1875 that targeted women), a few minor categories of Europeans were also barred.

Thus, macro-societal and macro-economic frames induced tens of millions of family and individual deliberations and decisions. Departures created a migration discourse in regions of origin and a migration business along the routes. Even if migrants departed with an intention to return, the sum total of these decisions created the Atlantic migration system and made the United States one of America's immigration countries. Neither the settlement of the Prairies nor the growth of East Coast and Chicago industries could have occurred in the form they took without the some 30 million men and women—not counting French-Canadian and English-Canadian migrants, people from Asia, and men and women from Mexico.

ETHNOCULTURAL GROUPS, GENDER, AND CLASS IN THE UNITED STATES, 1815–1914

From 1790 to 1820, an estimated quarter of a million immigrants arrived, from 1820 to 1840 three quarters of a million, in the decade of the 1840s, 1.7 million, and in the 1860s, 2.6 million. From these gross figures, those returning to Europe would need to be deducted, but the U.S-as-an-immigration-country ideology precluded any awareness of departures, and they began to be counted only from 1908. Return was low when sailing times were long, but with steamship travel, rates of return increased to, on average, one-third of all arrivals around 1900. Rates of in-migration grew from 1.2 per 1,000 population in the 1820s to 9.3 per 1,000 in the 1850s; the foreign-born accounted for 9.7 percent of the total population in 1850. Numbers of migrants continued to increase, reaching between 14 and 15 percent of the total population from 1870 to 1910 and thereafter decreasing to 11.6 percent in 1930.

In the 1840s, one-third of the migrants came as farming families; by 1900, less than 5 percent were farmers—95 percent were, mostly single, young workingmen and -women moving in sequential migrations, according to the destinations given at Ellis Island, to relatives (79 percent) and acquaintances (15 percent).[4] Urban and industrial growth was far more important to immigration than the "frontier" and its closing. The emphasis on the West as a macro-region settled by European and internal migrants and allegedly shaping U.S. national character has negated the impact of the Southwestern frontier with interaction between Anglos and Mexicans, Hispanic, and European immigrants.[5] Migration was never transnational from a nation-state to the American nation but translocal and transregional from the place of birth/economic region of origin to a local destination in specific agricultural, urban, or industrial regions, an anchor point where acquaintances lived.

Before 1860, newcomers originated mainly from, first, the politically divided German-language area, then colonized Ireland, and finally the Scandinavian societies. Though, in retrospective from the 1880s, this "old immigration" appeared as racially desirable and culturally willing to adjust, and although badly needed as rural settlers and urban workers, all faced Nativist hostilities.

"Ethnic" groups, a problematic designation that assumes genetic similarity and might better be replaced by "ethnocultural groups," were not only heterogeneous as to regional and class origins and by gender and age. They also developed regional belongings in the United States: German or Swedish agriculturalists in the Midwest differed from the respective groups' workers in Eastern cities or in Chicago and from the emerging ethnocultural urban middle classes. Of the German Americans, many of those in Missouri and Texas became supporters of slavery, and many of those in Chicago and New York opposed wage slavery in socialist working-class organizations. These sociologically, politically, and culturally defined subgroups were in turn divided by gender and age. Immigrant women and men often formed separate organizations. Women had to struggle for a place of their own, and men—native and immigrant alike—simply created male spheres, whether pubs, clubs, or others. Some immigrant men were highly critical of the rights women had in the United States; women emphasized such rights in letters to sisters at home.

Irish migration (and death) emptied the colonized and, from 1845 to 1850, starvation-hit country: The population declined from 8.2 million in 1841 to 4.7 million in 1891. Of a total of 5.4 million overseas migrants, four-fifths came to "the U.S"—regional destinations like the New England textile factories demanding family labor in the 1830s and 1840s and, for men, vast infrastructural earthworks like the Erie Canal, then big and small cities along the East Coast and further inland for both women and men. Even if departing from small rural farms, the Irish did not have the funds to move West and farm again. Their Catholic faith and, in particular for the famine Irish, their extreme poverty and ill health from years of malnutrition made them targets for hate campaigns. Most men and women, with clearly divided gendered cultures due to developments in Ireland, remained in the working-class—they came with few resources and nativism hindered acculturation and integration. A virulent anti-immigrant attitude, similar to anti-Semitism, emerged.

From the late 1860s, U.S. industry expanded and demand for workers increased. The "scientific management"—in the 1870s in Carnegie's steel mills and subsequently generalized by engineer Frederick W. Taylor—reduced complex tasks to ever simpler, ever more repetitive parts of tasks. Thus, men and women from rural backgrounds, skilled agriculturalists, could be hired by factories as unskilled labor for jobs that required little training. The "disassembly lines" of the slaughterhouses and the mass production of textiles—both employing men and women—are cases in point both long before the oft-cited assembly line in automobile factories emerged and were staffed almost exclusively by men. Women would find work in factories for electrical appliances. Such job options were the pull factors for peasant men and women displaced and pushed by the global agrarian crisis. They entered labor market segments with no competition from Natives who shunned the 3-D sector—dirty, dangerous, and often degrading work. No labels or slogans like "golden door," "great opportunities," or "social ascent" capture the immigrant experience in the past or the present.

Internationalized labor markets, at the lower end of the pay-scale, provided the entry jobs for newcomers whose "otherness" turned out to be both a resource and a burden: As resource, it made them employable on arrival. As burden, it made them exploitable at the same time. Relieved to have a job, many immigrants felt that draft animals in the rural homes had been fed and sheltered better than were "free workers" in U.S. industries.[6] Their letters home, describing the working conditions, might have reduced propensity to cross the Atlantic. However, with the exception of Britain, industrialization in Europe took off a few decades later than in the northeastern United States—there were no jobs, yet. In Europe, wherever industrial development accelerated, transatlantic migration declined. More migrated within states or intracontinentally.

"New" immigrants arriving from the mid-1880s were mostly "East" and "South" Europeans, generic macro-regional designations that differ from the ethnoculturally specific designations of "Germans" or "Irish." Few Americans could differentiate between Czechs, Poles, Slovaks, Slovenes, Croats, Magyars, and others or the many Mediterranean cultures. In addition, an increasing number did not want to differentiate: The anti-immigrant attitudes of the 1840s came to include a racializing-racist streak. Racially, East Europeans were said to be dark, South Europeans were olive or swarthy, and Russian Jews could easily be singled out—none, the Irish included, were Anglo White. Although about 20 million came from 1885 to 1914 (23.5 million in the census decades 1880 to 1920), in view of economic growth their labor power was still insufficient. At the same time French and Anglo Canadians came (from the 1830s), Chinese (from mid-century), Japanese, and Filipinos and Sikhs—labeled generic "Orientals" or "Asians"—arrived, and, from the 1880s, Mexicans began to come often recruited by U.S. companies. The remaining demand for urban labor came from internal migration, African Americans from the South, and eastward-moving sons and daughters leaving European American family farms without enough land for growing families. U.S. citizens also emigrated, especially to Canada and Mexico, and—to repeat—about one-third of the migrants returned.

The largest group of arrivals, about 2 million, were Jews from Tsarist Russia, where they faced settlement restrictions to a region called "the pale," were barred from many occupations, and, from the 1880s, were subjected to pogroms. From a demographically fast growing population, one-third left within a few decades. In several respects they differed from other groups: Since the religion valued texts, literacy was far higher than among other groups; since persecution in Tsarist Russia increased, a lower ratio than from among other cultural groups returned. Most came from small towns, the *shtetl*, and since persecution hit indiscriminately, men and women came in equal numbers and brought their children. In general, the closer the gender ratio to 1:1, the easier was community and family formation. Thus, the group's sociological characteristics were assets. However, they came from extreme poverty; just after the turn of the century, each individual on average arrived with no more than of $12 (the "better-off" German migrants at that time came with $40) and, like other new immigrants, they faced informal segregation into low-cost housing in congested quarters (slums).

In a perspective of both cultural continuity and acculturation, most temporary migrants and immigrants settled by group in shared neighborhoods. Often decried as a "ghetto" or an "enclave," such communities cushioned the hard landing in an alien culture. Food habits and religious practices could be continued, language change could be extended over a generation or two, and, in the absence of any social security system, mutual aid societies sprang up. Fast adjustment was required at the workplace, but whole factory departments were staffed by people sharing a language other than English. For the second generation, the schools have been assumed to be the major Americanizing institution. However, compulsory attendance requirements in many states were low, and thus the role of the education system, important as it was, has been overemphasized. Public librarians bought foreign-language literature to draw in young people, hoping to introduce them in a further step to American literature. Consumption patterns served to Americanize material culture and everyday lives. Acculturation proceeded, in a simplified but not incorrect view, over three generations. Part of the sense, that the United States was a "free" country, emerged from the experience that the steps toward the new society were self-determined moves. The massive repression of workers' trade unions, on the other hand, made the U.S. appear as "unfree" and in need of deep-going reform. Given the state of European societies, however, a Europe-wide discourse in culturally specific expressions emphasized the greater options across the Atlantic: wakes for departing migrants in Ireland, a change from the greeting "next year in Jerusalem" to "next year in America" among Jews.

RACIALIZATION, ANGLO-CONFORMITY, AND MELTING POT—OR A TRANSNATIONAL AMERICA?

For many ideologues of whiteness and Anglo-conformity, the immigration of dark and swarthy peasants-turned-day-laborers or factory workers, often illiterate, seemed as subversive of the American race as that of peoples from Asia's many cultures on the Pacific Coast. The latter, excluded from 1875–1882, were recognizable by outer appearance and could easily be segregated. The former came in far larger numbers: For each individual from Asia, 100 Europeans arrived in 1890 and, phenotypically less different, they were more difficult to segregate. Considered "un-White," they also seemed "un American" and as such, racializers argued, should be kept out and those in the country needed to be Americanized. Recent research suggests that Asian exclusion may have been the testing ground for European exclusion.

Excluding legislation at first, applied only to criminals, paupers, the insane, and "other undesirables" (1882) and subsequently to contract laborers and persons entering for (alleged) immoral purposes. Much of this legislation was enforced "off-shore": German shipping companies, fearful of having to transport back rejected arrivals, instituted their own controls along the eastern border of the Reich where all transit migrants would enter. In Italian embarkation ports, U.S. consuls had the right to inspect migrants. Altogether no more than an estimated 5 percent were rejected. Still, Ellis Island, opened as the central entry station in 1892, was known as both "island of hope" and "island of tears." It was impossible for many migrants to understand on what ground anyone would be rejected. Who of them would know how trachoma, an eye disease, was different from another eye problem? As regards labor contracts: to have a contract, first, seemed to prove that the entrant was not "likely to become a public charge," a reason for rejection, and, second, since professional, skilled, and domestic labor could come with contracts, one person could enter, the next was rejected. Such "host/hostile" society accounting overlooks the fundamental economics that for each migrant, 16 years and older, the society of origin has assumed the cost of upbringing and schooling and the United States, like any other immigration country, not only received their human capital for free but also collected the taxes that, in the country of origin, should have supported the next cohorts' education. In some respects, migration is a subsidy paid by lesser-developed societies to more-developed ones. The—few—restrictions' impact, furthermore, was unequal by gender. A fear that women might be prostitutes or would be lured into prostitution meant that women coming on their own initiative were easily suspected of coming "for immoral purposes." In the legal sphere, the entry-gate remained almost open, but the entry-way was increasingly difficult to negotiate.

Stumbling blocks, placed in the way of migrants whether marginalization or racialization, slow their trajectory toward the new society. To them, integration becomes more difficult and costly; to the receiving society, the cost of enforcement increases. Repression is expensive, for men and women who want to pursue their life courses after migration, and for the societies that pay for the new institutions and agents of exclusion and control.

CLOSED DOORS AND DEPRESSION, 1917–1945

When, from August 1914, warfare in Europe stopped out-migration, many had been planning to leave. While fewer left from Western and West Central Europe in view of industrial and job growth, departures remained high in East Central, Eastern, and Southern Europe. Many of these migrants moved to larger cities in Europe or took them as intermediary stops to earn the fare for the next leg of the trip (migration in stages). Their plans were stalled. In the United States, immigrants from the axis power countries—who purposefully had left those states—saw themselves labeled as "enemy aliens."

The war years, after 1917, had different impacts on ethnocultural groups. It has been assumed to have led to the collapse of the German American community, but with the decline of German-background migrations since the early 1890s, the group institutions had begun to stagnate a decade earlier. For East European American groups and organizations, the peace negotiations provided the opportunity to influence U.S. foreign policy in support of claims for independent states. When Poland, foreign-ruled since 1795, was reestablished, several thousand Polish Americans returned to help build the new state. But, regardless of cultural background, most such groups had acculturated and stayed in the United States (or in Canada). The U.S. government shifted attention from racial to radical: Deeply fearful of the emergence of a different, socialist society in the new Soviet Union, it deported hundreds of avowed or suspected radicals ("Red Scare").

After the war, many Europeans whose departure had been delayed were ready to leave, and immigration, a mere 31,000 in 1918 (down from 1.06 million each in 1913 and 1914), briefly surged to 0.65 million in 1920. However, the reconversion crisis in the United States reduced job options, and from 1921, fewer migrants arrived. In the years before the Great Depression, immigration averaged only 210,000 annually. Europe's reconstruction and increasing American restrictions combined to reduce the Atlantic migration system to a phase of stagnation.

The connection almost came to a standstill under the Great Depression in conjunction with the restriction law of 1924, which became fully effective only in 1929. Average gross annual arrivals amounted to a mere 33,000 in 1931–1939—from which the departures need to be deducted. In 1932, more people left the United States than arrived. Migrants knew or assumed that in their country of origin they would be able to rely on more networks and, if from rural regions, to feed themselves. However, in a macroeconomic perspective, such return migration driven by economic crisis shifts the social cost of unemployment from the society of arrival to that of departure. In the United States (and, similarly, in Canada), the ratio of the foreign-born population in the total population leveled.

Political change in Europe should have increased migrants—the coming to power of fascism in Italy, Germany, and Spain. In particular from Germany, large numbers wanted to leave, Jews in particular, but also the politically persecuted, ethnocultural minorities like the gypsies and others. The fascist states made departure difficult and prohibited transfer of any assets, and entry-doors were closed. Though the potential refugees' plight was apparent, authorities in the Atlantic world professed obsession with administrative orderliness of admission. At the international refugee conference in Evian, France, July 1938, U.S. diplomats refused to agree to anything but establishing an Inter-Governmental Committee on Refugees to negotiate an end of the chaos of expulsions and proper procedures of property transfer. The latter would free receiving societies from the cost of supporting indigent Jews and others. In result, few could emigrate before the extermination program began. The United States, which had capacity to ship tens of thousands of German POWs to the United States, could find no vessels for Jews fleeing the Holocaust. In the words of one historian, the refugee-generating fascist states were surrounded by refugee-refusing democratic states.[7]

DISPLACED EUROPEANS AND THE END OF THE ATLANTIC MIGRATION SYSTEM

After 1945, as after World War I, a pent-up demand for emigration existed—many Europeans, including many from the aggressor states, considered the war-time years lost in their lives, saw the ruins around them, and wanted to restart their life-courses under better conditions. However, from Eastern Europe under Soviet control, emigration was difficult and, soon, not possible. Until 1947, the Allies did not permit German emigration. The "Displaced Persons," survivors of the Fascist extermination and labor camps, numbering more than 7 million in May 1945, were to be repatriated rather than permitted to choose a county. Many, however, no longer had home or family to return to, and others refused to return to their, now communist-ruled, countries. The traditional immigration countries, still in need of labor, began to select healthy workers from the camps and admit them under special programs—in the United States with a directive by President Truman. Admission began late in 1945 and lasted until 1951–1952 with the Refugee Relief Act in 1953 following. Just over 400,000 came—total admission figures are unclear given the various overlapping and changing categories of entry. Another special group to gain entry were "war brides," who as wives of American soldiers, received citizenship.

By 1948, with transport conditions improving, immigration resumed with annual arrivals in the range of 100,000, reaching 200,000 only in 1950 and 1952. In the early 1950s, it became obvious that West European economies recovered far faster than expected ("economic miracle") and that the post-war societies did provide life-course options. The East–West divide ("iron curtain"), on the other hand, precluded emigration from Eastern Europe, individuals' flight and with a brief exodus after the quashed Hungarian uprising in 1956 excepted. The facilitation of migration by the shift from ocean to air travel in the mid-1950s could not counter the decline of migration.

The Atlantic Migration System, operating since the sixteenth century and involving mass migrations in the delayed nineteenth century, after interruption and stagnation from 1914 to 1945, thus ended in the mid-1950s. In the next decades, annual emigration/immigration stood between 100,000 and 125,000. However, labor demand in Recovery Europe and in post-war America remained high, and in result, two new South–North migration systems emerged, sponsored by the respective governments. In Europe, the temporary labor migration of men and women ("guestworkers") from Europe's Mediterranean societies to countries/labor markets north of the Alps assumed large proportions from 1955 on and changed the ethnic composition of the receiving societies. In addition, with independence of most colonies, post-colonial migrants moved to the former colonizer countries, especially Britain, France, and the Netherlands, linked by language, transportation routes, and personal connections. In the United States, the supply of labor was recruited from Mexico under the government's "bracero program," also intended as a rotatory or "guest" working program. With—often U.S.-supported—right-wing dictatorships emerging in Central and South America, large refugee migrations, transiting Mexico, also targeted the United States. The two new systems are functionally comparable to Europe-to–North America mass migrations of the nineteenth and early twentieth centuries.

CONTINUING CONNECTIONS

The end of the Atlantic Migration System does not imply the end of migratory connections and cultural exchange. Special groups—student exchanges and mobile managerial personnel in multinational business—continue to move back and forth. Rather than turning into immigrants, many remain mobile cosmopolitans. After the war, European labor migrants from Italy and Portugal continued to come for two decades but changed destination: they moved to Canada. In the present, while the flexibility of U.S. labor markets and social hierarchies are still attractive compared with Europe, the health insurance and social security systems are more attractive in Europe. All of this figures in migrant decision-making. In a global perspective, the end of racial quotas in 1965 (preceded by Canada in 1962) shifted migration to transpacific routes—the quantity of travel surpassed transatlantic routes from the mid-1980s. The collapse of the socialist bloc in 1989 and the crumbling of the "iron curtain" did not result in the tabloid press– and pundit-predicted new mass migration from Europe. People still move translocally to kin and acquaintances, and thus the only sizable new migration was that of Poles to the Polish American diaspora. The European-background segment of the U.S. population is shrinking in comparison to groups of other backgrounds. Just as Puritan and, subsequently Anglo Northeast Coast culture was changed by immigrants from continental Europe from an (imagined) "New England" to a Euro America, the immigration from the many cultures of Spanish America and Asia as well as, recently from Africa, will change the present—regionally very diverse—U.S. culture to a more cosmopolitan one. But calls to stop the "new new migration" echo a caricature showing a group of Native People seeing the Mayflower approach, and ordering it to head back, commenting that those on board are coming undocumented.

SCHOLARSHIP ON EUROPEAN MIGRANTS

Though migrants of many cultures built America, U.S. historians have, for long, pursued an Anglo-centric master narrative and relegating early migrants of languages other than English as well as all later immigrants into slots of "ethnics" and "immigrants." In this interest-driven, partial and partisan interpretation, immigrants were said to be uprooted or, if carrying old-world traits, having to drop their "cultural baggage." Few scholars had any language other than English and thus could not study cultures of origin and migrants' socialization prior to arrival. This "Ellis Island" view of immigrants left backgrounds nebulous and considered newcomers as uncouth and uneducated.[8]

From the arrival of the "new immigrants" form Eastern and Southern Europe, social issues (often labeled "problems") induced reformers and social workers from New York to Chicago to investigate their living conditions. The reform-minded women of Chicago's Hull House, a support center for migrants, collected data to induce state legislatures and the U.S. Congress to pass protective legislation to help women and immigrants. Prominent were Jane Addams, a founding member of the American Sociological Association, and Sophonisba Breckinridge, Edith Abbott, and Florence Kelley among others who turned to economics to contextualize poverty, class, and migration. These scholar-reformers, the Chicago Women's School of Sociology,[9] connected transnationally to European reform thought and practice. They resided in "settlement houses" in immigrant neighborhoods to collect data and improve living conditions. Another early scholar, Emily Greene Balch of Wellesley College, in her *Our Slavic Fellow Citizens* (1910), paid attention to the cultures from which migrants came.

The most-cited research emerged at the University of Chicago's (Men's) School of Sociology who, as assimilationists, asked: How could migrants be changed so as not to pose a threat—assumed to exist—to societal structures? Robert E. Park and colleagues, sharing prejudices of the time, considered ethnics or "races" and people of other skin color less developed. Their incorporation into the White Anglo (and male) society would require government Americanization projects. Compared with exclusionist ideologies, their assimilation approach reached integration-minded educators through the Carnegie-funded "Americanization" series. Somewhat less Anglo American centered than Park was ethnologist William I. Thomas, whose internal migration from the rural Plantation South through mid-sized towns to the metropolis of Chicago made him aware of regional differences. Jointly, Thomas and the Polish philosopher and sociologist Florian W. Znaniecki developed a cultural anthropology approach of societally embedded meanings of empirical data and a "life history" or biographical approach to migrant culture. Like Jane Addams and Emily Balch, they viewed men's and women's lives in the double relation of culture of origin and receiving culture.[10]

Though the Chicago Men's School became the internationally most-cited interpretation of assimilation, research and conceptualizations in other countries were far more differentiated. In Brazil, sociologist Gilberto Freyre argued that the mixing (*mestiçagem*) of migrants from Europe and Africa with Natives Peoples in processes of ethnogenesis established a new, culturally richer people. In many-cultured Cuba, Fernando Ortiz, in a comprehensive societal approach, conceptualized transculturation as everyday cultural fusion through human agency in power hierarchies and economic frames. In the United States of Mexico, to counter the "Yankee" ideology of white superiority, José Vasconcelos proclaimed a Mexican "cosmic race" as a fusion of migrants from all continents. In bicultural Canada, Everett Hughes and Helen MacGill Hughes teaching in Montreal, Canada, and critical of assimilation studies, argued that no receiving society sets only one national frame as reference for immigrant acculturation but offers options defined by region, urbanization, class, and gender. In Poland, the highly developed anthropology researched emigration contexts in rural regions. All of these scholars were part of a transatlantic community of researchers.[11]

The U.S. node of cultural research was not the University of Chicago but Columbia University with its renowned anthropology department where migrant scholars like Franz Boas from Germany and Bronisław Malinowski from Poland worked. A smaller "Minnesota School" (Theodore Blegen and George Stephenson) concentrated on the region's Scandinavians and Germans and emphasized the cultural background in the "old world" and, in a life-history approach connected premigration and postmigration cultures. With focus on Mexican migration, Manuel Gamio, renowned anthropologist from Mexico at Columbia University, interviewed migrants and discussed their transregional moves and transborder lives. Combining regional economies and national legal frames, political economist Paul S. Taylor (University of California) also studied the role of Mexican migrants in the United States. The most sophisticated study on acculturation, Caroline Ware's sensitive research (Columbia University) focused on intergenerational and interethnic life in Greenwich Village, New York. Recognizing that the United States was a society of immigrants, the Social Science Research Council established a Committee on Scientific Aspects of Human Migration in the 1920s, chaired by Edith Abbott.

None of these studies received the public attention and political acclaim of the Chicago Men's "assimilation" paradigm, which was reinforced by 1940s' research in the discursive frame set by the arrival of the "displaced persons" from fascist and wartime labor camps. These men and women had, indeed, been torn form their roots. "The Uprooted," however, became the catchword for self-willed migrants in general. Only from the 1970s did a far more inclusive, generation of scholars transform the terminology from "uprooted" into "transplanted." Since then, the study of immigration, in-migration, refugee admittance, family strategies, return migration—in conjunction with the integrative and comprehensive historiography on the United States as one, if regionally diverse, gendered society—has provided a balanced analysis of the role of migrants and the frames of institutions and grids of meaning of public discourses into which newcomers had to insert themselves, changing them by their presence and participation. In this reconceptialization, European-origin Americans played a contributing role.

NOTES

1. For easy understanding all geographical references will be to place-names imposed, usually at a later point in time, by the British or the Anglo Americans.
2. Bernard Bailyn, *The Peopling of British North America: An Introduction* (New York, 1986); R. Cole Harris, *The Resettlement of British Columbia. Essays on Colonialism and Geographical Change* (Vancouver: UBC Press, 1997), esp. 137–160, 250–275.
3. In the United States, bondage lasted longer; legally, slavery was ended in 1863, in practice after 1865—only to be replaced by the lynch regime.
4. Detailed statistical data are accessible in *Historical Statistics of the United States* (multiple editions, now available in the internet) and in the U.S. Senate, Immigration [Dillingham] Commission's *Reports of the Immigration Commission*, 41 vols. (Washington, D.C., 1911–1912).
5. Frederick J. Turner, *The Frontier in American History* (New York: Holt, 1920); Herbert E. Bolton, *The Spanish Borderlands: A Chronicle of Old Florida and the Southwest* (New Haven, Conn.: Yale University Press, 1921).
6. Dirk Hoerder, ed., *"Struggle a Hard Battle"—Essays on Working-Class Immigrants* (DeKalb, Ill.: Northern Illinois University Press, 1986).
7. Michael R. Marrus, *The Unwanted. European Refugees in the Twentieth Century* (Oxford, 1985).
8. Dirk Hoerder, "Historians and Their Data: The Complex Shift from Nation-State Approaches to the Study of People's Transcultural Lives," *Journal American Ethnic History* 25.4 (Summer 2006), 85–96.
9. Patricia Madoo Lengermann and Jill Niebrugge-Brantley, *The Women Founders: Sociology and Social Theory* (New York: McGraw Hill, 1998 [new edition 2008]), created the apt designation, p. 1.
10. Christiane Harzig, Dirk Hoerder with Donna Gabaccia, *What Is Migration History?* (Cambridge: Polity, 2009), 53–86.
11. Freyre, *Casa-grande e senzala* (1935); Vasconcelos, *Raza cósmica* (1925); Ortiz, "Del fenómeno de la transculturación y su importancia en Cuba" (1940); Hughes and MacGill Hughes, *Where Peoples Meet: Racial and Ethnic Frontiers* (1952).

BIBLIOGRAPHY

Archdeacon, Thomas J., *Becoming American. An Ethnic History* (New York: Free Press, 1983).

Bodnar, John, *The Transplanted. A History of Immigrants in Urban America* (Bloomington, Ind.: Indiana University Press, 1985).

Daniels, Roger, *Coming to America. A History of Immigration and Ethnicity in American Life* (New York: HarperCollins, 1991, rev. ed. 2002).

Gabaccia, Donna R., *From the Other Side. Women, Gender and Immigrant Life in the U.S. 1820–1990* (Bloomington, Ind.: Indiana University Press, 1994).

Gabaccia, Donna R., *Immigration and American Diversity. A Social and Cultural History* (Malden, Mass.: Blackwell, 2002).

Harvard Encyclopedia of American Ethnic Groups, ed. Stephan Thernstrom (Cambridge, Mass.: Harvard, 1980)

Harzig, Christiane, ed., *Peasant Maids, City Women. From the European Countryside to Urban America* (Ithaca: Cornell, 1997).

Hoerder, Dirk, ed., *Labor Migration in the Atlantic Economies. The European and North American Working Classes During the Period of Industrialization* (Westport, Conn.: Greenwood, 1985).

Hoerder, Dirk, Inge Blank, and Horst Rößler, eds., *Roots of the Transplanted*, 2 vols. (Columbia, N.Y./Boulder, Colo.: East European Monographs, 1994).

Hoerder, Dirk, and Nora Faires, eds., *Migrants and Migration in Modern North America: Cross-Border Lives, Labor Markets, and Politics in Canada, the Caribbean, Mexico, and the United States* (Durham: Duke, 2011).

Isajiw, Wsevolod W., *Understanding Diversity. Ethnicity and Race in the Canadian Context* (Toronto: Thompson, 1999). [This sociological analysis of acculturation is equally applicable to the United States and other societies.]

Marrus, Michael R., *The Unwanted. European Refugees in the Twentieth Century* (Oxford: Oxford, 1985).

Meinig, Donald W., *The Shaping of America: A Geographical Perspective on 500 Years of History*, 4 vols. (New Haven, Conn.: Yale University Press, 1986–2004).

Moya, José, and Adam McKeown, "World Migration in the Long Twentieth Century," in Michael Adas, ed., *Essays on Twentieth-Century History* (Philadelphia: Temple, 2010), 9–52.

Nugent, Walter, *Crossings. The Great Transatlantic Migrations, 1870–1914* (Bloomington, Ind.: Indiana University Press, 1992).

Olson, James S., and Heather Olson Beal, *The Ethnic Dimension in American History* (4th ed., New York: Wiley-Blackwell, 2010).

Takaki, Ronald, *A Different Mirror. A History of Multicultural America* (Boston: Little, Brown, 1993).

Tanner, Helen Hornbeck, ed., Janice Reiff, John H. Long, Dirk Hoerder, Henry F. Dobyns, assoc. eds., *The Settling of North America. The Atlas of the Great Migrations into North America from the Ice Age to the Present* (New York: Macmillan, 1995).

CHAPTER 3

....

ASIAN IMMIGRATION

....

MADELINE Y. HSU

"Asian American" is a category of tremendous complexity and diversity that can encompass more than 40 different groups of people from geographic regions extending from the Middle East to East Asia who are of highly varied ethnic and cultural, political, religious, socioeconomic, legal, and educational statuses, affiliations, and degrees of acculturation. For example, in 2010 the U.S. Census Bureau offered Language Assistance Guides in 19 different Asian languages, including Bengali, Burmese, Cebuano, Chinese (Traditional and Simplified), Hindi, Hmong, Ilocano, Japanese, Khmer, Korean, Laotian, Malayalam, Tagalog, Tamil, Telugu, Thai, Urdu, and Vietnamese. Often collapsed into a celebratory stereotype as a "model minority," Asian Americans are associated with statistically demonstrable, comparatively high levels of educational attainment, household incomes, and white-collar and professional employment. Such numbers, however, mask the heterogeneity of Asian American populations which includes significant numbers mired in poverty, labor-intensive small family businesses, employment in service industries, and undocumented status. Now approximately 70 percent foreign-born, Asian American demographic and community attributes have been shaped in great part by immigration legislation and the economic fears and aspirations, domestic racial ideologies, and international relations objectives from which such laws emanate.

LEGAL FRAMEWORKS

....

The Immigration Act of 1965 (Hart–Celler Act) usually receives credit for the geometric growth in Asian population and diversity from just less than 1 million in 1960 to an estimated 16 million in 2009. These dramatic increases stemmed from liberalizations of immigration law that displaced discriminatory systems that had once sought openly to maintain a largely White, Anglo-Saxon Protestant population by allocating differential quotas based on race and national origins. The 1924 Johnson–Reed Act aimed to maintain America's racial and ethnic composition by using "scientific" methods to derive annual immigration quotas based on percentages of ethnic and national populations enumerated in past U.S. Census counts. By reaching back into the American past, such baselines heavily privileged immigration from Western and Northern European countries while severely limiting the entry of more recent arrivals such as Italians, Portuguese, and Greeks. The 1924 act built on earlier restrictions that severely limited Asian immigration such as the Chinese Exclusion Laws (1882–1943), the Gentlemen's Agreement of 1908 targeting Japanese, the 1907 Barred Zone Act imposing a no-immigration zone extending from East Asia to the Middle East, and the 1934 Tydings–McDuffie Act, which promised eventual independence to the Philippines and imposed a fifty-person annual immigration quota. In the 1924 Act, Congress took a further step by prohibiting altogether the entry of "aliens ineligible for citizenship," a legal category referring to Asians as defined by a body of laws dating back to the 1790 Nationality Act, which restricted rights to citizenship by naturalization by race to "free white persons." In 1952, Congress passed the McCarran–Walter Act, which only slightly improved immigration rights by granting entry quotas at symbolic levels to Asian nations. China's, for example, was 105. This law enacted nonquota entry for immediate relatives of U.S. citizens but, through the Asia-Pacific Triangle cap, tracked Asians by race to limit their total entries to 2000 per year. The chief advance of the McCarran–Walter Act was its removal altogether of racial considerations in access to naturalized citizenship. It was also the first general immigration law to prioritize employment-based preferences.

Under Asian Exclusion and the national origins quota systems, few Asians could immigrate to the United States. Most who did so were men in search of employment or business opportunities who left behind their families and communities which depended heavily upon their access to economic opportunities in the wealthier United States. In 1940, on the cusp of World War II, most of the ethnic Asian population were either immigrant men or American-born and of Japanese, Chinese, or Filipino ancestry. Continuing racialization of Asians as foreigners contributed to the internment of over 120,000 west coast Japanese Americans as "enemy aliens," even though the majority were U.S-born citizens, while Chinese, Filipinos, and Asian Indians enjoyed improved status through their association with allied forces. Nationalist China's role as America's chief friend in Asia contributed to the repeal of the Chinese exclusion laws in 1943, with Chinese becoming the first Asians to gain entry quotas and naturalization rights, to be followed in 1946 by Filipinos and Indians. Such acknowledgement of the need for Asian allies, however, did not greatly change opposition to entry and settlement by Asians in America although the symbolic reforms of the 1952 McCarran–Walter Act did permit some family reunifications.

Spurred by aspirations toward global leadership after World War II, a succession of U.S. presidents worked in coalition with congressional immigration reformers, and religious and ethnic organizations to break down racial preferences in immigration restriction in recognition of the harm such discriminatory quotas inflicted on American efforts to woo alliances among developing, decolonizing nations in Asia and Africa. The McCarran–Walter Act had passed over President Harry Truman's veto. He and his successors, Eisenhower, Kennedy, and Johnson, worked with congressional allies to pass a series of piecemeal laws that inflicted cracks in the protective immigration facade maintained by the 1924 and 1952 Immigration Acts by legislating for the race-blind, nonquota admission of military spouses and fiancées, transnational and biracial adoptees, and refugees from communism. In the first two cases, the ideological heft of rewarding military veterans and the imperative of family reunification overrode antimiscegenist fears to permit mixed-race families, which usually consisted of Asian women married to white or black servicemen and Korean, often biracial, children adopted by White parents. For example, between 1951 and 1956, the Korean War led to the entry of about 12,800 Koreans as nonquota immigrants including 6300 adopted "war orphans" and 6500 war brides,[1] numbers that far exceeded Korea's regular quota of 100. These new migration flows contrasted with the earlier predominance of male laborers and entrepreneurs to give a more feminine, childlike, and less-threatening cast to Asian immigration. Leading up to the transformations of 1965, America's extensive military presence in Asia meant that significant proportions of Japanese and Filipino immigration also consisted of war brides, while transracial adoptions would also feature prominently in the 1980s immigration of Vietnamese, although, since the early 1990s, China became the main source of international adoptees.

In the push to demonstrate America's multiracial egalitarianism while identifying new rationales for immigration restriction that might satisfy conservatives, labor organizations, and nativists, refugee legislation such as the 1948 Displaced Persons Act, the 1953 Refugee Relief Act, and its 1957, 1958, and 1960 amendments and extensions emphasized shared political causes and humanitarian outreach even while implementing economic preferences that privileged individuals with skills needed in the U.S. economy. Emergency paroles of Hungarian (1956), Cuban (1960), and Chinese (1962) refugees laid the terrain for emergency admission of about 100,000 Vietnamese in 1975 while underscoring the incapacities of the quota system to serve Cold War America's political needs. Such feints in immigration law and administration admitted nonquota Asian immigrants at levels that exceeded quota entries by thousands each year. Nonetheless, census data reveals an all-time low of 32 percent foreign-born Asians in 1960.[2]

The 1965 Immigration Act dramatically shifted this balance, although Congress originally intended the law to maintain America's ethnic composition even as it removed the egregiously discriminatory quotas. The chief conserving mechanism was to be a preference system that favored family reunifications in which immediate relatives of U.S. citizens enjoyed nonquota entry rights while four preference categories went to more distant relatives such as siblings, adult unmarried children, and the immediate family of permanent residents. Through even distribution of 20,000 person immigration caps for each country in the Eastern Hemisphere, Congress sought to demonstrate America's democratic principles while advancing its economic interests with two employment preferences for professionals, artists, and scientists of "exceptional skills" and skilled and unskilled workers in areas with short supply as designated by the Department of Labor. One preference favored refugees. Contrary to congressional expectations, which anticipated only a 5-year surge in Asian immigration through family reunifications, lack of economic opportunities and political instability propelled dramatic and steady increases in Asian immigration, which by the 1990s comprised about one-third of the U.S. total.[3] Through chain migration and patient use of the family reunification categories, entire extended Asian family groups managed to settle permanently in the United States. Asians of nationalities that once had only a trace presence in the United States, such as India, South Korea, Taiwan, Thailand, Pakistan, Bangladesh, Indonesia, Sri Lanka, Malaysia, and Burma, could initiate migration chains through the skilled labor and employment preferences, immigrate as complete family units, and later bring their extended families. Although widely viewed as a liberalizing measure, the 1965 Act had intended to increase annual entries by only about 50,000, but the bulk of documented immigration now originated from developing nations in Central and South America, the Caribbean, and Asia rather than Europe. In telling contrast, the numbers of Japanese immigrants has dropped because Japan's rapid economic growth and political stability provide fewer reasons to leave home.

Since 1965, the Philippines has been the biggest source of Asian immigrants, both legal and undocumented. The twin quagmires of a corrupt political system and a stagnant economy have made the Philippines highly dependent on the export of contract labors, as domestic servants, construction workers, caregivers, musicians, and prostitutes to wealthier countries in Asia, the Middle East, Oceania, and North America. The long history of American influence in the Philippines, extending to the colonial era inculcation of American-educated *pensionado* elites and schools that taught U.S. history and English, have primed Filipinos to seek opportunities to gain access to the relative wealth and possibilities of coming to the United States. Even after the Philippines gained independence, dense economic and military ties produced many pathways to the United States—through service with the U.S. military, marriage to American servicemen deployed in the Philippines, and employment with American firms. Medical personnel in particular have found many employment opportunities in the United States and in turn have initiated extensive family reunification chains. With the 1965 Act, Filipino immigration skewed sharply toward the professional and skilled ranks, in marked contrast to the largely working class composition of pre-World War II immigrants.

These kinds of employment preferences served as the basis for new chains of immigration after 1965 and were an acceleration of patterns begun during the 1950s in which international students were able to find jobs in the United States and resettle permanently, rather than be forced to return home. The Cold War fostered greater appreciation for educated Asian immigrants, particularly scientists and engineers, who could aid the United States in its space and nuclear arms races against the Soviet Union. The United States had become an international leader in scientific innovation through the 1930s and 1940s influx of brilliant Europeans fleeing chaos at home. During the 1950s and 1960s, Asian scientists joined their ranks, including highly visible successes such as the Nobel Prize–winning physicists T.D. Lee and C.N. Lee and the computer entrepreneur An Wang, who forcefully demonstrated the utility of admitting immigrants on the basis of skills and aptitudes rather than race. The United States also confronted the reality that Chinese scientists leaving the United States would end up working for the communist side, as did Qian Xuesen, who is widely considered the father of China's missile program.

In this competition for talent, and despite the tiny quotas of the McCarran–Walter Act, the Immigration and Naturalization Bureau actually approached some prominent successes such as Wang in 1955 to offer them citizenship and a secure place in the United States, rather than forcing them to leave. These most successful of American Ph.D.s laid a path followed by an estimated 75 to 95 percent of less-visible but well-educated students from Taiwan, Korea, and South Asia who managed to find work in the United States and through legal and administrative accommodations, found ways of converting their student visas to permanent residence and eventually citizenship. By the mid-1960s, this migration flow was serious enough to generate an outcry against the "brain drain" of valuable, educated elites from struggling developing nations to the industrialized first world. An estimated 25,000 Filipino nurses immigrated between 1966 and 1985. By 2000, fully 18 percent of New York City's registered nurses were Filipino.[4] The growing visibility of educated professional and white collar Asian immigrants, even those who suffered downward mobility or could not find commensurable employment and turned to running small businesses such as restaurants, grocery stores, motels, liquor marts, gas stations, laundries, and nail salons, contributed to improving impressions of this population.

Moving toward Multiculturalism

Cultural and social transformations accompanied post-World War II moves toward celebrating at least the image of a more multicultural and multiracial American society. Popular movies and novels celebrated Asian ethnic experiences as equally valid narratives of American life in memoirs such as *Nisei Daughter* (1953) by Monica Sone, *Fifth Chinese Daughter* (1945) by Jade Snow Wong, and the C.Y. Lee novel (1957), Rogers and Hammerstein Broadway musical (1958) and movie (1961) "Flower Drum Song." Moving America toward a greater embrace of cosmopolitanism, high-profile films depicted as initially fraught, but ultimately friendly and mutually beneficial the extension of American influence into Pacific worlds through popular depictions such as "Teahouse of the August Moon" (1956), "Sayonara" (1957), "The World of Suzie Wong" (1960), "The King and I" (1956), the James Michener Pulitzer-winning book *Tales of the South Pacific* (1947), and its Pulitzer Prize–winning stage and film adaptations by Rogers and Hammerstein, "South Pacific" (1949 and 1958). At least several of these productions advocated for interracial romance, although almost always between a white leading man and an Asian female costar. The martial arts superstar Bruce Lee burst into the American consciousness through five films released between 1971 and 1978 and, before dying young at age 33 in 1973, had become an iconic symbol of Asian masculinity. Asian spirituality also gained inroads into American culture through the growing appeal of religious philosophies and practices propagated by celebrity figures such as the Zen monk and author, D.T. Suzuki, who taught in the United States from 1951 until 1957, and the Maharashi Mahesh Yogi, guru to the Beatles and Mia Farrow.

Even as their community was undergoing dramatic transformation, a generation of American-born Asians became active in the national upheaval of the Civil Rights movement. Inspired by the Black Power movement and drawing primarily from college-educated Chinese, Japanese, and Filipinos, the Yellow Power movement transcended their middle-class socioeconomic status to identify strongly with urban working-class struggles around health, educational access, residential overcrowding, employment conditions, and youth delinquency and drawing connections between minority marginalization in the United States and imperialism overseas through projects like the Third World Liberation Front, anti–Vietnam conflict protests, opposition to Ferdinand Marcos's regime of martial law in the Philippines, the Diaoyutai Islands sovereignty disputes, and the campaign to save the International Hotel. In 1969–1970, a coalition of black, Chicano, and Asian American students at San Francisco State College (now University) and the University of California at Berkeley enacted the Third World Strike, resulting in the establishing of ethnic studies programs, improved admissions, and hiring of faculty and offering of courses more inclusive of communities of color. Despite such advances, the 1982 baseball bat-beating and murder of Vincent Chin in Detroit by unemployed auto factory workers who mistook him for Japanese alarmed and mobilized a broader swathe of Asian Americans to their continuing racialization as foreigners and the hostility directed at economic competition, then associated with the growing economy of Japan. The killers received only probation and served no jail time, compelling a national movement demanding their trial at the federal level for violations of Chin's civil rights in a race-based crime. Almost concurrently, the Japanese American Citizens League, aided greatly by Asian American Congressional representatives such as Senator Daniel Inouye from Hawaii and California's Norman Mineta, pursued redress for the internment of Japanese Americans culminating in a formal apology from President Reagan in 1988 and restitution of $20,000 to each surviving internee.

The civil rights era also fostered artistic endeavors by Asian Americans seeking to explore and explicate their histories and culture. Maxine Hong Kingston's highly original memoir *Woman Warrior* (1976) about her childhood in a Stockton laundry and the powerful storytelling of her mother brought her the National Book Award but also sharp criticism from a group known as the Big Aiiieeeee boys headed by noted playwright and author Frank Chin, for negatively portraying Asian Americans, particularly men, and pandering to white audiences. Seeking to identify and celebrate "authentic" Asian American voices, *The Big Aiiieeeee!* anthology included writings from overlooked earlier and contemporary writers such as Sui Sin Far, John Okada, Milton Murayama, Hisaye Miyamoto, Michi Weglyn, and Wing Tek Lum. This group has been most skeptical of those Asian American writers receiving the greatest general acclaim, such as Kingston, the bestselling Amy Tan, or David Henry Hwang, who won a Tony and Drama Desk Award in 1988 for his play, "M. Butterfly," a potent reworking and critique of Puccini's Orientalist opera based on a real-life espionage scandal. Despite a sometimes ambivalent reception by Asian American scholars and writers, Tan's success demonstrated to publishers the viability of Asian American–themed books and opened doors for scores of other Asian American authors such as Bharati Mukherjee, Gish Jen, Susan Choi, Don

Lee, Ruth Ozeki, David Wong Louie, Lisa See, Karen Tei Yamashita, Jhumpa Lahiri, Chang-rae Lee, Ha Jin, and Monique Truong. American tastes for Japanese, Chinese, Indian, Vietnamese, and Korean foods provide another indicator of inclusion into American multiculturalism.

Asian American integration can be measured in the notable successes of artists such as the architect I.M. Pei, the designer Vera Wang, the artist Nam June Paik, and the sculptor Ruth Asawa whose output can be described as universalistic and not characterized by ethnic or cultural traits. Film directors such as Wayne Wang, Justin Lin, Cary Fukunaga, and Ang Lee are not restricted to Asian American–themed films and have helmed mass audience Hollywood vehicles as well as art-house films, with Lee becoming the first ethnic Asian director to win an Academy Award for his adaptation of Annie Proulx's gay-themed "Brokeback Mountain" in 2005. Many American moviemakers now imitate the stylistic and narrative innovations of thriving cinema industries based in Hong Kong, South Korea, Japan, and India's Bollywood. However, the controversy that erupted surrounding the selection of Maya Lin as designer for the Vietnam Veterans Memorial in a blind submission process in 1979 served as a stark reminder that many Americans had difficulty separating Asian Americans from the United States's abortive military project overseas.

HISTORICAL LEGACIES

America's expensive, protracted, and partially covert anticommunist projects in the Southeast Asian peninsula generated new migration flows of Vietnamese, Cambodians, and Laotians whose homes and livelihoods were destroyed by the extreme political struggles. America's bitter loss of the deeply divisive Vietnam conflict attached particularly complicated and powerful layers of guilt, obligation, ambivalence, hostility, and amnesia to the influx of almost 1 million refugees who arrived in several waves propelled by continuing upheaval and violence in homelands whose turmoil had been exacerbated by American interference. In May 1975, the imminent fall of Saigon led President Gerald Ford to order the emergency parole of 130,000 refugees. This first wave of Vietnamese included the better educated and more westernized, those most closely affiliated with American personnel and programs in Vietnam. Later waves were less equipped to adapt to American lives and included those fleeing neighboring Laos and Kampuchea, which had fallen to extremist Communist regimes seeking to purge urban, westernized, and capitalist-influenced residents. Hmong tribesmen from the highlands of Laos had been recruited to aid U.S. covert activities in Vietnam. With the withdrawal of American forces, they were forced to depart as well. Camps in neighboring Thailand provided temporary residence to the tens of thousands of later waves of Hmong, Lao, Khmer, and Vietnamese seeking escape by land, while those with slightly more resources turned desperately to escape by sea and, if fortunate, ended up in camps in Hong Kong, Guam, and the Philippines. Countries such as Canada, Australia, and the United States provided permanent homes for some of this outflow. The U.S. government continued to devote resources to Southeast Asian refugee resettlement but weighed its responsibility to former allies against domestic resentment for the newcomers. To minimize local impact of these large influxes of Asian refugees, the U.S. government first located them in military bases and funded voluntary civilian agencies to help manage their release and integration into American settings, and required that refugees line up jobs and sponsors before they could be released. The 1980 Refugee Act regularized these processes in recognition that these outflows would be ongoing, while the 1987 Amerasian Homecoming Act legalized the entry of mixed-race children fathered by U.S. military personnel despite the lack of official relations with the government of Vietnam. This legislation indicates the responsibility felt by the United States to Southeast Asians influenced by the American presence, as do the millions spent in resettlement costs. Despite programs to distribute refugees across the United States, California has become home to about 40 percent, with 10 percent settling in Texas. Unexpectedly, about 40 percent of Hmong have chosen Minnesota as their new home, while others have settled California's Central Valley in order to return to farming. More accustomed to farming and hunting, many among these refugee populations are otherwise ill-suited to life in an industrialized and service economy with high percentages remaining trapped on welfare, seeking a return to former livelihoods, or opening low-capital, low-skill businesses such as nail salons and doughnut shops. Despite government efforts, the settlement of refugees has been marked by occasional violence and outbursts, such as the 1979 burning of Vietnamese fishing boats by competitors in Seadrift, Texas. By 2010, high levels of family reunification immigration made Vietnamese the fifth largest ethnic Asian community.

Significant numbers of Asians live in the United States as undocumented immigrants who overstay tourist, student, or temporary work visas, have their political asylum status run out or sneak across borders. The Philippines is among the top 10 of countries sending illegal immigrants, while New York's Chinatown, now the biggest in the United States, features many businesses and organizations formed by Fujianese Chinese, who have to find alternative means of coming to America due to their lack of family ties or employment qualifications. The 1993 accidental grounding of the *Golden Venture* freighter off the coast of Rockaway Beach in New York drew widespread publicity to the high debts and arduous risks Fujianese were willing to undertake to come to America only to labor in an underground economy of restaurants and textile factories. Some have managed to work their way up to business ownership after paying off debts ranging from $25,000 to $50,000, revealing the relatively lax enforcement of immigration restrictions toward some Asians on America's eastern and northern borders. Although Asian undocumented immigrants attract less ire than their Latino counterparts, since 9/11, the intensifying crackdowns on undocumented immigrants have implicated many Asians as well.

By the late twentieth century, Asian immigrants received more attention as examples of successful settlement than as threats to the United States. According to Sucheng Chan in 1991, since 1965, about 2 million Asian immigrants arrived through quota entries, 2 million as nonquota family members, and 1 million as nonquota refugees, and about

800,000 arrived on temporary visas for students, tourists, and businessmen but were able to adjust their status to permanent residents.[5] Since the 1980s, one-third of engineers and medical personnel have come from abroad, mostly from Asia and places like India, China, Taiwan, and the Philippines. Over 60 percent of immigrants from India and Taiwan report having bachelor's degrees.[6] According to 2009 census data, 50 percent of single-race Asians aged 25 and older had a bachelor's degree or higher level of education compared with 28 percent of all Americans aged 25 and older overall. Twenty percent of single-race Asians had a graduate or professional degree compared with 10 percent of the general population.[7] These impressive statistics should be weighed, however, against the predominance of foreign-born, which in 1980 became the majority of Asian Americans, and the selection processes imposed by immigration criteria that favor those with family ties, which constitute the majority of Asian immigrants, or those with needed skills such as computer software engineers and Chinese restaurant chefs. For example, most recipients of H1-B temporary worker visas for the information technology industry are Indian.

Post-1965 immigration has produced new community formations that are sometimes called ethnoburbs, a term coined by the geographer Wei Li. Affluent, educated, professional Asian Americans have been settling in suburban areas such as Monterey Park, Fremont, Rowland Heights, Daly City, and Flushing and making highly visible changes in terms of business establishments, places of worship, public signage, housing stock, and attendance in schools. Although a far cry from the crowded urban ghettos marked by poverty, disease, crime, and low educational attainment earlier associated with new immigrants, suburban Asian American communities have attracted some resentment in the form of proposals for English-only signage and restrictions on residential zoning laws.

Since the 1980s, the largest communities are ethnic Chinese (which includes immigrants from the PRC, Hong Kong, Taiwan, and a diasporic population from Southeast Asia and Central and South America), Filipinos, South Asians, Koreans, and Vietnamese, with Japanese falling to sixth in numbers. In 2009, there were 3.8 million ethnic Chinese in the United States, followed by 3.2 million Filipinos, 2.8 Asian Indians (including Indians, Pakistanis, Sri Lankans, Bangladeshis, Burmese, Nepalese, Indo-Africans, and Indo-Caribbeans), 1.7 million Vietnamese, 1.6 Koreans, and 1.3 million Japanese [these estimates include those who reported a specific Asian group alone, and those who reported an Asian group in combination with one or more other Asian groups or races].[8] Most Asian immigrants still choose either California or New York as their destination, followed by Texas and New Jersey. Hawaii and Illinois round out the top six states with the highest Asian American populations with Hawaii being the only majority Asian state. West Virginia has the smallest number and percentage of Asian population. Asian Americans now have access to a broader array of white-collar, professional, and technical employment options across the country and have settled in areas with strong job growth such as Atlanta, Austin, Chicago, Houston, and Las Vegas.

In 2009, 49 percent of civilian-employed, single-race Asians worked in management, professional and related occupations, such as financial managers, engineers, teachers, and registered nurses; 17 percent worked in service occupations, 22 percent in sales and office occupations, and 10 percent in production, transportation, and material moving occupations. Despite the high levels in white-collar and professional occupations, many Asian Americans have experienced a glass-ceiling that limits access to management positions. A 1995 study by Chinese for Affirmative Action found Asians underrepresented in executive, management, and administrative positions in areas including business services, finance, communications, and retail trades. During the 1970s and 1980s, high numbers of Asian engineers and scientists in research firms did not translate into equally high representation in management ranks. The 1990 Census revealed that 20 percent of scientists and engineers in Silicon Valley were Asian immigrants but that only 15 percent had attained management ranks compared with 26 percent of whites. A partial outcome of this discrimination was the many Asians who began their own businesses, a disproportionately high 20 percent of all Silicon Valley firms founded between 1995 and 1998.[9]

Statistics concerning median household incomes also skew toward the overly positive. In 2009, the median household income for Asian Americans was $68,780, the highest national average. However, these figures differed considerably by Asian group. At the high end, the median for Asian Indian households was $90,429 compared with $46,657 for Bangladeshis.[10] Such statistics present levels of success that obscure the reality that in many Asian American households, more earners contribute to overall income and the higher cost of living faced by many residing in expensive states such as California, New York, and Hawaii. The relatively high rate of Asian Americans living in poverty is not so well known, although at 12.5 percent in 2009, it was higher than that of non-Hispanic whites at 9.4 percent, but lower than that for blacks at 25.8 percent and for Hispanics at 25.3 percent.[11]

High levels of business ownership also clouds understandings of the levels of economic attainment by Asian Americans. There were 1.6 million Asian-owned businesses in 2007 with receipts totaling $513.9 billion.[12] Entrepreneurship is frequently associated with economic success, but for many Asian Americans, this toehold into the middle class comes with heavy costs. Quite a few Silicon Valley entrepreneurs, most notably Jerry Yang of Yahoo, have become well-known successes at the cutting edge of the computer and dotcom boom. However, most Asian American businesses are small, family-run affairs that do not involve innovation and absorb considerable unpaid, family labor such as restaurants, grocery stores, motels, gas stations, and nail salons. In 1997, for example, the average Asian Pacific American–owned company had receipts of about $336,000, compared with a national average of $410,000, with 28 percent earning less than $10,000 in sales. And 71 percent of Asian Pacific American–owned businesses were sole-proprietorships.[13] Nonetheless, immigrant parents working 15-hour days in an unsafe corner liquor store have managed to send children to college and provide them with credentials that will ensure their escape into white-collar and professional work.

The limits on economic attainment in the United States in combination with economic developments in Asia have modified migration flows since the 1990s. Rising levels of prosperity and stability in formerly developing economies in Hong Kong, Taiwan,

South Korea, the PRC, and Singapore have spurred circular migration flows. As in the past, many international students come from Asia with the PRC, India, South Korea, and Taiwan among the top five senders of students at both graduate and undergraduate levels of study. For example, in the 2009–2010 academic year, of a total of 690,923 international students, 127,628 came from China, 104,897 from India, and 72,153 from Korea.[14] Some U.S. institutions now set out to recruit students from affluent Asian countries who will pay full tuition rates. In another contrast with past patterns, more graduates are returning to comparably lucrative jobs in major global cities such as Hong Kong, Beijing, Shanghai, Taipei, Singapore, and Seoul rather than remaining in the United States. A parallel development is the return of experienced and networked Silicon Valley engineers who use their bicultural capacities and contacts to establish firms in the emerging, and therefore now more profitable, technological zones in places like the Hsinchu Science Park in Taiwan, Zhongguancun near Beijing in China, and Bangalore in India. The brain drain is reversing to become something of a brain, and capital, exchange. Asian students arrive at even younger ages in what has come to be called the parachute kid phenomenon, in which affluent parents from Taiwan, South Korea, and the PRC send teenaged children on their own away from pressure-cooker educational systems to study in American schools at costs of about $40,000 per year. If the plan works out, the children attend university in the United States and then graduate with a choice of whether to return home to work or to remain.

The high visibility of growing levels of Asian American prosperity and attainment bring benefits that nonetheless fail to fully erase historical exclusions and fears The model minority stereotype and high visibility of Asian students on the campuses of highly selective universities such as UCLA, UC-Berkeley, and the Ivy League schools evoke praise for family values and work ethics while also incurring resentments and mockery against academic competition with stereotyped overachievers and poorly socialized science and math "nerds." Less visible are the majority of Asian American college students enrolled in community colleges where they take longer and are less likely to graduate. The growth of Asian economies compels both admiration and fear as well. Japan's emergence as a leading manufacturer of autos and small electronics during the 1980s enhanced the attractions of eating sushi even as it provoked jingoistic campaigns to "buy American." China's growing economic clout since the 1990s in conjunction with its still-communist government and willingness to exert authoritarian power has made it the leading Asian contender to be America's number one foreign enemy. Such leftover tensions from the Cold War contributed to the United States's decision to grant asylum to Chinese students after the 1989 Tiananmen massacre and to those claiming refuge from the PRC's one-child policy.

Despite continuing racialization as foreigners, relatively small numbers, and high percentages of immigrants who must wait several years before becoming qualified to vote, Asian Americans have been gaining elected office. In 2008, 48 percent of Asians turned out to cast a total of 3.4 million votes.[15] Although it took San Francisco until January 2011 to install its first Asian American mayor, Edwin Lee, who gained the position by appointment, the first Asian American to win national, elected office did so in 1956 soon after Asians gained naturalization rights. Dalip Singh Saund served in the House of Representatives 1957–1963 representing the 29th District in California. When Hawaii gained statehood in 1959, it became the only majority Asian state with representation to reflect its population. It sent to Congress the first two Asian American senators, Hiram Fong and the second longest serving senator, Daniel Inouye, who had been able to leverage his seniority to advocate for Asian American causes. The 1990s witnessed significant inroads by Asian Americans in national politics by those who gained elected national office in states other than California or Hawaii. In 1996, third-generation Gary Locke became governor of Washington State, completing a classic immigrant tale of family ascendance from houseboy, to laundry worker and World War II veteran, to lawyer, public servant, and national leader. Locke's campaign success ran concurrently with the campaign finance scandal besetting Bill Clinton's reelection campaign in which Asian and Asian American donors were widely accused of making illegal political contributions to leverage policies economically advantageous for the PRC. In the twenty-first century, Asian American politicians have made further inroads serving both political parties. The George W. Bush Cabinet included Elaine Chao and Norman Mineta, while Barack Obama's featured Locke, Stephen Chu, and Mineta once again. In the 2010 U.S. Congress, nine House representatives acknowledged Asian American ancestry, as did three Senators including both of Hawaii's and John Ensign from Nevada. In 2008, two Asian Indians, Nikki Haley and Bobby Jindal, became governors in South Carolina and Louisiana, respectively. Electoral success has come to Asian Americans regardless of region and demographics, suggesting the many pathways to mainstream acceptance that now exist.

Despite these successes, recent events reveal that undercurrents of anti-Asian hostility can readily emerge in times of crisis. The 1996 Campaign Finance Scandal targeted ethnic Asian donors for criticism and public vilification in what is generally a corrupt and money-driven system for buying influence. The problem of improper donations by some Asian donors was magnified, however, by the unproved but widely publicized charge that they were efforts to enhance PRC influence in American political processes. This willingness to associate Asian Americans politically with economically competitive and possibly hostile ancestral homelands is an ugly echo of the World War II internment of Japanese. In 1999, a particularly ugly episode of racialization as foreign enemies occurred with the drummed-up espionage case leveled at Wen Ho Lee, a Taiwanese American scientist working at the Los Alamos National Laboratory and accused of leaking cutting-edge, nuclear missile technology to the PRC. A flurry of media-led paranoia, spearheaded by the *New York Times*, led the Clinton White House, which was fearful of being seen as "soft" in dealings with China, to prosecute a case against Lee that ignored the unlikelihood that a Taiwanese American would aid the PRC and the lack of evidence that any critical information had actually been leaked. However, the political and media firestorm led to Lee being placed in solitary confinement while awaiting trial for 56 counts of mishandling information. When the case inevitably unraveled, the presiding judge actually apologized to Lee, who in 2006 won a civil case against the federal government and five media organizations. Although the tragedies of September 11,

2001, have diverted American attention away from China to new threats in the form of international, Muslim terrorist networks, anti-Islamicist campaigns and profiling have brought into its net many South Asians and Asian Muslims alike. In this much vaunted nation of immigrants, we still struggle with whether, and how, to embrace those whose faces do not mirror our own.

Recent projects in Asian American studies seek to unpack twenty-first century manifestations of racial inequalities and exclusionary practices of the American nation-state. Most recently, cultural critics have situated the post 9/11 security state in longer histories of religious intolerance, the eroding of civil rights in the face of expanding federal authority claiming national security needs, and American imperialism abroad. To better understand the uneven inclusion of Asians, rather than their exclusion, some historians explore Asian migration as embedded in international relations projects and the emergence of global systems of capitalism. Both historians and literary scholars seek to complicate received, racial binaries of black and white or Asian and white by comparing the trajectories and racialization of African American, Latino, and Native Americans with that of East and South Asian Americans. Another key project extends the chronology and region of Asian American studies by decentering North America to conceptualize migrations and historical connections hemispherically to include flows through Central and South America and the Caribbean that became systematized with the Spanish empire. All of these approaches seek to explicate how Asian Americans can be considered simultaneously exemplary immigrants and perpetually foreign threats.

NOTES

1. Lai, Eric and Arguelles, Dennis, eds., *The New Face of Asian Pacific America: Numbers, Diversity, and Change in the 21st Century* (*AsianWeek* with UCLA Asian American Studies Center Press, 2003), 58. Cited hereafter as Lai and Arguelles.
2. Lai and Arguelles, 9.
3. Ibid,. 24.
4. Ibid., 232.
5. *Asian Americans: An Interpretive History* (Boston: Twayne Publishers, 1991), 147.
6. Lai and Arguelles, 13.
7. See [http://factfinder.census.gov].
8. See 2009 American Community Survey, [http://factfinder.census.gov].
9. Lai and Arguelles, 236.
10. See 2009 American Community Survey, [http://factfinder.census.gov].
11. See Income, Poverty, and Health Insurance Coverage in the United States: 2009, [http://www.census.gov/newsroom/releases/archives/income_wealth/cb10-144.html].
12. See [http://www.census.gov/newsroom/releases/archives/economic_census/cb10-107.html].
13. Lai and Arguelles, 243.
14. Tamar Lewin, "China Surges Past India as Top Home of Foreign Students," *New York Times* November 15, 2010.

BIBLIOGRAPHY

Ancheta, Angelo. *Race, Rights, and the Asian American Experience* (Piscataway: Rutgers University Press, 2006).

Brooks, Charlotte. *Alien Neighbors, Foreign Friends: Asian Americans, Housing Reform, and the Transformation of Urban California* (Chicago: University of Chicago Press, 2009).

Haney-Lopez, Ian. *White by Law: The Legal Construction of Race* (New York: New York University Press, 2006).

Hing, Bill Ong. *Making and Remaking Asian America through Immigration Policy, 1850–1990* (Palo Alto, CA: Stanford University Press, 1993).

Klein, Christina. *Cold War Orientalism: Asia in the Middle-Brow Imagination* (Berkeley: University of California Press, 2003).

Kurashige, Lon and Murray, Alice Yang, eds. *Major Problems in Asian American History: Documents and Essays* (Boston: Houghton Mifflin, 2002).

Lee, Erika and Yung, Judy. *Angel Island: Immigrant Gateway to America* (New York and London: Oxford University Press, 2010).

Maeda, Daryl. *Chains of Babylon: The Rise of Asian America* (Minneapolis: University of Minneapolis Press, 2009).

Ngai, Mae. *Impossible Subjects: Illegal Aliens and the Making of Modern America* (Princeton, NJ: Princeton University Press, 2004).

Okihiro, Gary. *The Columbia Guide to Asian American History* (New York: Columbia University Press, 2001).

Prashad, Vijay. *The Karma of Brown Folk* (Minneapolis: University of Minnesota Press, 2000).

Takaki, Ronald. *Strangers from a Different Shore: A History of Asian Americans* (Boston: Little, Brown, 1998).

Wu, Frank. *Yellow: Race in America Beyond Black and White* (New York: Basic Books, 2002).

Zia, Helen. *Asian American Dreams: The Emergence of an American People* (New York: Farrar, Straus and Giroux, 2000).

CHAPTER 4

··

LATINO IMMIGRATION

··

MARÍA CRISTINA GARCÍA

In 2017, the U.S. Census Bureau reported that 57.5 million people, or 17.8 percent of the general population, were of "Hispanic" or "Latino"[1] origin—up from 14.5 million in 1980—making Latinos the fastest-growing population in the United States.[2] These figures did not include the 3.8 million residents of the commonwealth of Puerto Rico, who are U.S. citizens and can travel unhindered to the United States; nor did it include the undocumented population from Latin America working and studying in the United States; nor did it take into account the victims of trafficking—many of them children— who are brought to the United States to work in the sex trades, in servitude, or as drug runners. Accounting for these other populations would bring the total number of Latinos closer to 65 to 70 million people. For three decades, the U.S. news media has euphemistically referred to these demographic changes as the "browning of America" and "*la Reconquista*" (the "reconquest"), alerting the nation to the cultural, political, and economic consequences of continued immigration from Latin America. The Census Bureau, in turn, projects that with continued immigration and natural increase, the Latino population will reach 102.6 million by 2050. Such speculations and projections have elicited fear and an anti-immigrant backlash across the country: a discourse that, in some ways, mirrors the anti-immigrant mood in the United States at the turn of the twentieth century that produced some of the most restrictive immigration laws in our national history.

Latinos are framed as recent arrivals to the United States in part because over half of those who identify as "Hispanic" or "Latino" today were born outside the United States. Consequently, it is easy to forget that the roots of this population lie in the colonial era and that Hispanics/Latinos have played a key role in nation building for centuries. Decades before the English established their first colonial settlements at Jamestown and Plymouth, the Spanish had settled in the territories that are now the states of Florida and New Mexico. By the time the Declaration of Independence was signed in 1776, a network of Spanish settlements, missions, and presidios extended from the Florida peninsula to California. The Spanish/Latino origins of the United States are evident in the names of cities, geographic landmarks, and botanical species, as well as in the nation's cultural pageants, food, folkways, and lexicon. But because the United States as a political entity emerged out of the English colonies on the Eastern Seaboard, this history was downplayed or obscured for generations. Indeed, until fairly recently, U.S. history textbooks reflected an "east-of-the-Mississippi" bias and equated all things "American" with Northern and Western European.

Further complicating this history is the fact that the terms "Hispanic" and "Latino"—although convenient terms in political and popular discourse—mask the very different experiences and histories of the various constituent groups. Some Latinos are first-generation immigrants to the United States, while others trace their families' presence in the United States as far back as the seventeenth and eighteenth centuries. Some have come to the United States as immigrants, and others as refugees, exiles, or guest workers. Yet others are the descendants of people who were conquered and colonized. Racially they may identify as white, black, Asian, indigenous, or multiracial. The majority are at least nominally Roman Catholic, but Latinos are also mainline, evangelical, and Mormon Protestant, Jew, Muslim, Buddhist, and believers in syncretic religions such as *santería*. Their life experiences have varied, shaped by factors such as citizenship and political status, race and indigeneity, class and labor, gender and sexuality, religion, and the region of the country in which they have settled. In sum, Latinos reflect the diversity of the countries from which they trace their ancestry and the diversity of the communities in which they settle here in the United States. Even the ways they speak Spanish and English are different, reflecting the national and regional variations of the Spanish and English languages. Over 34 million Latinos 5 years of age and older speak Spanish at home, arguably making the United States the third-largest Spanish-speaking nation, but Census records also show that with each passing generation English replaces Spanish as the home language, as has happened for other immigrant groups to the United States. Consequently, it is not unusual for many self-identified Latinos to be monolingual English speakers. In addition, thousands of the immigrants categorized as "Hispanic" by U.S. institutions are native people who speak their indigenous languages rather than Spanish.

My goal in this essay is to provide a very brief history and profile of this large and diverse "Hispanic" or "Latino" population in the geographic and political space we call the United States of America. While many migrated and/or became "Americans" due to forces beyond their control—empire, war, revolution, environmental disaster—their story is one of agency, courage, and resiliency. More important, their presence and participation in U.S. society teaches us that to be American is also to be *Americano*: a citizen of a region or hemisphere and not just a nation-state.

ORIGIN STORIES

Mexican Americans, the largest of the Hispanic/Latino groups at 64 percent, have one of the longest histories in the United States and represent several models of accommodation to U.S. society: the first became Americans by conquest when territory was acquired from Mexico as a result of the Texas revolution (1836), the Mexican War (1846–1848), and the Gadsden Purchase (1854), but since the mid nineteenth century, Mexicans have migrated across the United States–Mexico border as refugees, immigrants, and contracted labor.

In nineteenth-century newspapers, journals, travel diaries, and fiction, Americans rationalized their political and economic domination of the newly acquired territories by portraying Mexicans as the descendants of two inferior cultures that could not be trusted to understand or participate in democratic institutions or to take full advantage of the vast riches of the Western territories. Consequently, while the Treaty of Guadalupe Hidalgo and the Protocol of Queretaro theoretically guaranteed Mexicans in the conquered territories the rights and privileges of U.S. citizenship, during the second half of the nineteenth century, the *tejanos*, *californios*, *hispanos*, and others of Spanish–Mexican descent struggled to defend and assert those rights. As Americans settlers moved into these newly acquired territories, they clashed with the Mexican and indigenous inhabitants over land and water rights and over political control. State and territorial governments appointed land commissions to adjudicate the Spanish–Mexican land grants and titles. Some cases took over a decade to decide, and in the meantime landholders had to pay for legal representation, interpreters, and other assorted court costs. They also had to defend their lives and property from those who sought to acquire their land by more violent means. Even when the land commissions ruled in their favor, the high cost of litigation often forced families to sell part or all of their land. In some communities, merchants, bankers, lawyers, and politicians conspired to raise taxes, increase foreclosures, and bar access to goods, resources, and services, all in an effort to drive the Mexican inhabitants from their farms, ranches, and businesses, and prevent them from holding political office. In some areas, most notably Texas, vigilante groups and agents of the state also used lynching as a form of social control. Exemplifying the devastating consequences of these practices was the prominent *californio* statesman, General Mariano Vallejo, one of the eight *californios* who participated in the state's constitutional assembly. In 1846, at the beginning of the United States–Mexico War, his estate was estimated at 175,000 acres; by the time of his death in 1890, his homestead was a mere 200 acres.

Even those who were able to retain their property into the twentieth century found it difficult to compete in the changing capitalist economy of the Southwest that relied on private enclosure rather than communal grazing lands and on large-scale commercial agriculture and ranching rather than subsistence farming. State and territorial governments also played a role in the confiscation of land, seizing communal grazing lands, most notably in New Mexico and Arizona, to establish state or federal park lands or to give acreage as entitlements to railroad companies and other private interests. With the loss of land came a further loss of influence, respect, and prestige in a society that already devalued all things Mexican. Discriminatory hiring practices and limited educational opportunities resulted in Mexican Americans becoming concentrated in unskilled or semiskilled labor and excluded from managerial positions and membership in skilled trade unions, as well as the professions. Literacy tests and poll taxes prevented the majority of Mexican Americans (and, later, other Latinos) from exercising an effective political voice until well into the twentieth century, when the 1960s Civil Rights legislation finally abolished many of these practices. Segregation in housing, education, and public areas such as theaters, restaurants, pools, and even churches and cemeteries was enforced by custom if not by law. Elite families were sometimes able to protect their economic and political interests by aligning themselves through marriage, most commonly by marrying their daughters to influential members of the "Anglo-American" community. In New Mexico, for example, elite *hispanos* used such connections and were appointed to political office and other influential positions well into the twentieth century. But in most areas of the Southwest, the odds were against people of Mexican descent. From 1900 to 1953, only two Tejanos were elected to the Texas state legislature, both from the border city of Brownsville that had a majority Mexican American population. Likewise, in California, no Mexican Americans were elected to the state assembly from the 1880s to 1962.

Nineteenth-century Mexican American history, then, chronicles this loss of land and status, but it also chronicles the many ways that Mexican Americans tried to empower themselves in a society that limited their opportunities. Mexican Americans used the courts to assert their political and economic rights in a changing society, and when these forums for legal redress failed them, they forcefully defended their families and communities. During the period of 1850 to 1920, for example, "social bandits" like Juan Nepomucena Cortina, Catarino Garza, Tiburcio Vasquez, and Gregorio Cortez and groups like *las Gorras Blancas* challenged the individuals and institutions responsible for their displacement. This "lawlessness" was celebrated in folklore, especially the ballads known as *corridos*. "Rebellions" such as the 1857 Cart War, the Salt Wars of the 1870s, and the Plan de San Diego (1915–1917), as well as the labor strikes in factories, agricultural fields, mines, and other industries during the late nineteenth century, challenged the stereotypes of Mexican Americans as a docile population willing to accept the fate that others had prescribed for them.

Given these social realities for Mexican Americans (and other racial and *racialized* minorities), it may be hard to imagine that immigrants would have willingly migrated to the United States during the late nineteenth and early twentieth centuries, yet hundreds of thousands of Mexicans, Cubans, and Puerto Ricans, of different races and social classes, fled political upheaval and economic displacement in their countries and took their chances in the United States. The transportation networks established by railroad and steamship companies facilitated this migration because it made travel easier and more affordable. Big Business also played a role in their migration, actively recruiting them to work in factories, farms, mines, and ports, especially after 1882, when Congress passed the first of a series of immigration acts designed to restrict the entry of "undesirables" from Asia and, later, Eastern and Southern Europe. Needing an abundant flow of cheap labor, U.S. businesses turned to Latino immigrant workers since the Americas were exempt from the restrictive quotas established by immigration law.

In Mexico, the economic policies of the Porfirio Diaz regime (1876–1910), and the subsequent Revolution (1910–1920), resulted in the migration of over a million Mexicans to the borderland states, their migration facilitated by the expansion of railroads into Mexico during the "*Porfiriato*," and the reality of a poorly patrolled border. Towns such as San Antonio, Los Angeles, and El Paso tripled in size because of the refugee population. Many of the new arrivals considered themselves exiles and hoped to return to their country once political conditions stabilized. As they waited to return, they established businesses, created cultural organizations to celebrate *mexicanidad,* and published Spanish-language newspapers to keep their countrymen informed of political developments in Mexico, as well as to interpret the social realities in their host country. Over time, these refugees and exiles established ties to the United States despite their original intentions.

By 1930, then, the Southwest had a diverse population of Mexican Americans. Some had been "Americans" for several generations; others were more recent immigrants and refugees. Yet others were transnational workers who moved back and forth across the border with ease, spending part of their working lives in each country (a practice that continued well into the late twentieth century, until an increasingly militarized border made such movement difficult).

Like the Mexicans, Cubans were drawn to the United States for a variety of political and economic reasons. As early as the eighteenth century, Cuban merchants came to the United States to conduct trade or business and they established residences and businesses in port cities such as Boston, New York, Philadelphia, New Orleans, Wilmington, and Baltimore. By the nineteenth century, the *criollo* elites of Havana, Trinidad, Cienfuegos, and Santiago de Cuba routinely sent their children to boarding schools and colleges and universities in the United States rather than to Europe, recognizing that their country's future was tied more to North America than to Europe. *Criollos* traveled back and forth across the Florida straits with ease, intermarried with prominent American families, and adopted U.S. citizenship to protect their economic interests in both countries. Some even became vocal advocates for Cuba's annexation: a cause that was weighed carefully by various American political administrations until the Civil War.

A larger and more diverse population migrated from Cuba after the failure of the Ten Years' War (1868–1878) and the *Guerra Chiquita* (1879–1880). These wars that tried to secure Cuban independence from Spain devastated Cuba's colonial economy. Displaced workers, both black and white, found employment in the expanding tobacco and cigar industry in the United States and helped to turn Florida, Louisiana, and New York into important centers of production. By 1895, distinct Cuban worker communities existed in Key West, Tampa, Martí City (Ocala, Florida), Jacksonville, New Orleans, and New York City. Tampa and its cigar factory district, Ybor City, had the largest concentration of workers and became the heart of the Cuban expatriate community.

Many of Cuba's—and Puerto Rico's—most prominent nineteenth-century intellectuals and revolutionary leaders spent part of their adult lives in self-imposed or forced exile in the United States, among them Jose Martí, Calixto Garcia, Ramón Emeterio Betances, Eugenio María de Hostos, Lola Rodríguez de Tío, and Sotero Figueroa. It was in the United States that philosopher and journalist Jose Martí published his most influential essays about race, labor, the United States, and the Americas; and it was in the United States that he founded the *Partido Revolucionario Cubano* (Cuban Revolutionary Party) to unite Cubans of different races and classes in a common struggle and under a common vision for Cuba. Cubans and Puerto Rican exiles together debated what independence might look like for their respective countries, raised funds for the armies and supplies needed for war, and debated the contours of a post-independence Antillean confederation that might protect them from the reach of the "colossus of the North." In one of her most famous poems, the poet and exile Lola Rodríguez de Tío aptly described the Puerto Rican and Cuban revolutionary causes as "two wings of the same bird."[3]

American involvement in the final months of the Cuban War of independence (1895–1898) changed the outcome of the war and forever altered the nature of sovereignty for Cuba and Puerto Rico. Although the 1898 Teller amendment required American military withdrawal from Cuba (which occurred in 1902), the Platt amendment (1903) granted the United States the power to intervene in Cuban affairs if deemed in the Cubans' political interest—a right the United States exercised on several occasions until the amendment was abrogated in 1934. Puerto Ricans' aspirations for independence were dashed altogether when the United States established a protectorate. Puerto Ricans were left in political limbo, neither citizens of the United States nor citizens of an independent sovereign nation, until Congress passed the Jones Act of 1917 that finally gave the Puerto Ricans U.S. citizenship. Since 1917, Puerto Ricans who have migrated to the continental United States have done so as U.S. citizens, exempt from visas and quotas. The 1917 Jones Act also made Puerto Ricans immediately eligible for the military draft, and 18,000 Puerto Ricans served as members of the American armed forces during World War I, most of them in racially segregated units in Europe or stationed at the Panama Canal.

Americans conducted a radical restructuring of their protectorate's agricultural production in a campaign to "modernize" the Puerto Rican economy, and in the process created a disposable population. U.S. sugar companies established plantation-style agriculture, displacing small farmers from their lands, and making coffee, tobacco, and the production of other staple crops less important. Sugar production offered employment for a few months of the year, and many of those who could not find employment in the fields and sugar mills migrated to coastal towns such as San Juan and Ponce in search of employment in service industries or in the island's small manufacturing sector. Others migrated as seasonal labor to Cuba, El Salvador, and the Dominican Republic. Over 6000 went to Hawaii (then a U.S. territory) during the first decades of the twentieth century as contract labor on sugar cane plantations, but the largest number of migrants went to the continental United States. By 1920, the U.S. census reported residents of Puerto Rican heritage in 45 states. Puerto Rican men and women worked in garment and cigar factories, on the docks and shipyards, and on the construction and maintenance crews that built the infrastructures of American cities.

Migration from Cuba also continued. Because of the short distance between the two countries, and the higher wages across the Florida straits, it was not uncommon for

Cuban workers to spend at least part of their adult working lives working in the United States. Records show that from 1920 until the eve of the revolution of 1959, an estimated 130,000 Cubans migrated to the United States, although these figures are probably an undercount. They came from all different classes, motivated by a variety of political and economic concerns, and most migrated with the intention of one day returning to their homeland to enjoy the hard-earned fruits of their labor. Joining these transnational workers were thousands more who came temporarily to the United States to vacation, to study, to invest, or to transact business, all contributing to the Cuban presence in the United States.

The Great Depression of the 1930s temporarily stopped migratory flows to the United States, and had particularly devastating consequences for ethnic minorities in the United States. Mexican Americans and other Latinos, as well as African Americans and Asians, were usually the first fired from the workforce as a last ditch effort to preserve as many jobs as possible for white male heads of households. In many communities, Latinos and African Americans were barred from receiving charitable assistance or from participating in New Deal projects in order to preserve limited resources for whites. Thousands of Mexicans (and Mexican Americans) were "repatriated" by the U.S. government as part of a government campaign to rid the country of "foreigners" who many erroneously claimed were taking jobs away from Americans. State and federal officials working with local settlement houses, church groups and civic associations, as well as with Mexican consulates in the United States, pressured Mexican nationals to return to their homeland with the promise of land and jobs in northern Mexico that in many cases never materialized. Thousands of others were forcefully rounded up and transported across the border, sometimes without any regard for citizenship. Over half a million persons of Mexican origin are believed to have been repatriated or deported during the 1930s. Many were U.S. citizens and the American-born children and spouses of Mexican nationals.

The Great Depression, like other economic downturns before and after, inhibited migration from the Americas, but when the economy entered a period of recovery, immigration was encouraged once again if only to provide a cheap, abundant, and exploitable workforce. The labor shortages created by World War II led to the creation of the Mexican Farm Labor Program Agreement, popularly known as the "bracero program." Over the next two decades, the United States negotiated various bracero agreements with the Mexican government, and by the time the program was terminated in 1964, approximately 4.6 million Mexican workers had been brought in to work temporarily in the United States, primarily in agriculture. Thousands of Puerto Ricans and Filipinos were also brought in as wartime contract labor. When bracero contracts failed to produce enough cheap labor, growers colluded with agents of the state to keep the border open so that workers could cross over into the United States.

World War II was transformational for the Latinos and Latinas living in the United States. High-paying, high-prestige skilled jobs in factories and war industries suddenly became open to Latinos and Latinas who remained on the home front. Thousands of Mexican Americans left the southwest and relocated to industrial centers in the

Midwest and Great Lakes region to take advantage of these higher-paying jobs. With higher salaries came a higher standard of living: the opportunity to buy better homes, automobiles, and consumer goods—and the opportunity to be trained in marketable skills that might be used after the war.

However, it was through their military service that Latinos experienced and exerted the greatest impact. Latinos have a long history of military service for the United States, from the Civil War to the present, but their participation in World War II was up to that point unparalleled. Roughly three-quarters of a million Latinos enlisted or were drafted to serve in the armed forces during World War II, the vast majority of them of Mexican ancestry. They distinguished themselves in battle. Mexican Americans, for example, served in both the Atlantic and Pacific arenas and earned more Medals of Honor and other military commendations in proportion to their numbers than any other ethnic group. The Puerto Rican 65th Infantry Regimen, "the Borinqueneers," an all-volunteer unit, served valiantly in North Africa, Italy, and France. Women also distinguished themselves in military service, primarily as nurses and support staff, but they were also recruited to serve in the Women's Army Corps (WAC) as linguists, interpreters, and cryptologists. This participation was largely ignored until scholars at the University of Texas at Austin established an oral history project to collect the stories of the men and women who served in World War II and other wars.[4]

These stories reveal that Latinos were profoundly affected by the experience of serving overseas. Military service provided them with their first opportunity to leave their segregated communities and glimpse what full citizenship might mean. Wherever they were stationed, local townspeople regarded them as just another group of American GIs. They were not asked to enter restaurants through back doors or to sit at segregated lunch counters. Nor were they forced to sit in theater balconies reserved for people of color or in the segregated rows of seats on public transportation. When they returned to the United States, the GI Bill allowed many to attend college or vocational schools for the first time or have access to loans for homes and businesses. However, as veterans of previous wars discovered, military service did not guarantee respect and appreciation once they returned home. When the body of Private Felix Longoria of Three Rivers, Texas, was sent home for burial, for example, his family was denied the use of the town's only funeral home. Medal of Honor winner Macario García was denied service by a diner in his hometown of Sugarland, Texas.

Not surprisingly, it was this World War II generation that was at the forefront of the decisive Civil Rights battles of the 1950s and 1960s. In the years following the war, legal cases such as *Mendez v. Westminster* (1946) and *Delgado v. Bastrop* (1948) successfully challenged the segregation of Mexican American children in public schools in California and Texas, respectively; Supreme Court cases *Hernández v. the State of Texas* (1954) challenged the exclusion of Mexican Americans from juries; and *Escobedo v. Illinois* (1964) addressed criminal procedure and affirmed the right to counsel. The hegemony of older civil rights organizations like the League of United Latin American Citizens (LULAC, founded in 1929) was challenged by the newer political organizations of the post-war years such as the Mexican American Political Association (MAPA) and the Political Association of Spanish-Speaking Organizations (PASSO), among many others, that also encouraged voter registration, voting, and the election of Mexican Americans to public office. By 1964, five Mexican Americans had been elected to the U.S. Congress (four to the House of Representatives and one to the Senate), at the time the largest electoral representation of Mexican Americans in national politics in the twentieth century.

Despite the advantages that theoretically came with U.S. citizenship, Puerto Ricans faced as many challenges as Latino/a immigrants, in part because of the changing economy of the Northeast in the final decades of the twentieth century. By the 1950s, grassroots leadership in the Puerto Rican community tried to tackle a host of problems, from the exceptionally high dropout rates among students to the need for vocational and language training to retool workers for the changing U.S. labor market. Scores of young, idealistic, and bilingual graduates of universities and professional schools created organizations to advocate on their behalf, among them the Puerto Rican Association for Community Affairs (PRACA), the Puerto Rican Forum, ASPIRA, the Puerto Rican Family Institute, and the Puerto Rican Legal Defense and Education Fund. The educator Antonia Pantoja played a key role in the creation of many of these organizations.

Enormous transformations were also under way in the commonwealth of Puerto Rico in the post-war period. In 1948, under pressure from the United Nation's decolonization campaign, the United States finally permitted Puerto Ricans to elect their own governor. Luis Muñoz Marín, the head of the *Partido Democrático Popular* (PDP), was elected that year; and 4 years later, Puerto Ricans drafted the constitution of their *estado libre asociado* (literally, "free associated state") or commonwealth government. Muñoz Marín, who served four terms as governor, oversaw a comprehensive economic development program popularly known on the island as Operation Bootstrap. The Puerto Rican government lured hundreds of U.S. companies to the island through Sections 931 and 936 of the federal tax code, which offered tax exemptions to subsidiaries of U.S. companies. The island's ports and transportation and communication networks were developed in preparation for the projected increase in production and trade. By the 1970s, Puerto Rico had became one of the top revenue-producers for American companies in Latin America, but Muñoz Marín's goal of diminishing poverty on the island had less spectacular results. For those fortunate enough to find employment in factory towns, incomes and living standards improved. But a large number of those who migrated to the towns and cities in search of steady employment never found the opportunities they sought, and instead capitalized on the new post-war airline routes (and installment credit) that linked San Juan to New York.

By 1960, over 1 million Puerto Ricans had traveled to the United States as part of this post-war "Great Migration." New York City was once again the most popular destination for workers (inspiring the nickname "Nuyoricans" for this population), followed by Chicago, Philadelphia, and Camden, New Jersey. Migration to the Northeast became so institutionalized that the "Migration Division" of the commonwealth's Department of Labor established offices in New York City and Camden to provide referral services on housing and social services to Puerto Rican migrants, as well as to serve as a clearinghouse of information about the island and its population to potential employers, business investors, and labor unions. The growth and concentration of this population in New York City in a relatively short period of time generated controversy and tension, and citizens' groups unsuccessfully lobbied to restrict further migration from the island. As early as 1949, the mayor's office established an advisory committee on "Puerto Rican affairs" to improve community relations. The Great Migration inspired the popular Broadway musical *West Side Story* (made into a Hollywood film in 1961), which even today, despite its one-dimensional portrayals, continues to be the dramatic work most associated with Puerto Ricans in the United States.

The most important victories for Latinos in the arena of civil rights came in the late 1960s and the 1970s, through a series of events collectively known as *El Movimiento* or the Chicano Movement in the Southwest, and the "Puerto Rican Movement" in the Northeast.[5] A new generation of Mexican American activists re-appropriated the terms "Chicano" (which for previous generations had been a pejorative) and *la raza* and drew on Mexican and indigenous symbols and mythology, to signify their new cultural identity and political consciousness. To identify as "Chicano" or "Chicana" meant that one was politically and culturally aware and committed to social justice. Inspired by the Black Civil Rights and Black Power Movements, young Chicano activists held rallies, sit-ins, "blowouts," and other mass demonstrations to call local, state, and national attention to the disparities in poverty, the high educational dropout rates, and the workplace discrimination faced by Mexican Americans and other racial and ethnic minorities.

A number of individuals and organizations were at the forefront of the civil rights struggles of the 1960s and 1970s, although not all of them readily identified as "Chicano/a." Cesar Chávez, Gil Padilla, and Dolores Huerta organized the National Farmworkers Association in California (later renamed the United Farm Workers) to advocate for better wages and working conditions for the agricultural workers of California and other parts of the Southwest. Reies López Tijerina and the *Alianza Federal de Mercedes Libres* occupied Kit Carson National Forest and the county courthouse at Tierra Amarilla, both in New Mexico, to call attention to the intense poverty that was the legacy of land loss. Rodolfo "Corky" González and the Denver-based Crusade for Justice organized a national conference for Chicano youths in 1969 that drafted the *Plan Espiritual de Aztlán* to articulate the goals of Chicano activism in the next decade. Chicano college students founded organizations like the Mexican American Youth Organization (MAYO) and the *Movimiento Estudiantil Chicano de Aztlán* (MEChA) to call for educational reforms including a new curriculum that would incorporate the histories of racial and ethnic minorities, create Chicano Studies programs in colleges and universities, and hire Chicano/a teachers and administrators. José Ángel Gutiérrez and Mario Compean founded a political party, La Raza Unida Party, in 1970 to make the political system more responsive to the needs and concerns of the Mexican-origin population. LRUP's first national convention drew over 1500 participants; and in the 1972 Texas gubernatorial election, the LRUP candidate received 6 percent of the popular vote, a significant accomplishment for a third party less than 2 years old.

Puerto Rican organizations with a more radical agenda emerged in New York City and Chicago during the 1960s and 1970s, inspired by the national liberation movements around the world and the civil rights struggles of other racial and ethnic communities at home. At the core of the Puerto Rican Movement were eight organizations: the Young Lords, the Puerto Rican Socialist Party U.S. branch, El Comité–Puerto Rican Nationalist Left Movement (MINP), the Puerto Rican Student Union, the Movement for National Liberation, the Armed Forces for National Liberation (FALN), the Nationalist Party, and the Puerto Rican Independence Party. Most of these organizations focused on both U.S. and Puerto Rican island politics, but their goals and strategies varied according to their self-identification. For some groups, it was their *nationhood* as *puertorriqueños* that was most important, and thus they dedicated their energies to working for Puerto Rican independence. For others it was their status as members of an ethnic/racial minority in the continental United States that they felt deserved the most attention, and these organizations concentrated on issues such as discrimination and poverty in their local communities.

The Young Lords is perhaps the best example of an organization that fused both causes. This political organization was founded in Chicago in the 1960s, drawing its membership from the second-generation children of Puerto Rican agricultural work-ers who had settled in the immigrant enclaves of Chicago. Inspired by Fred Hampton of the Black Panthers, José "Cha Cha" Jimenez took on the political education of the youths associated with the Young Lords. Among their first activities were protests against urban renewal that would lead to the destruction of traditional Puerto Rican neighborhoods in Chicago. Their successes and failures in political activism inspired other Puerto Rican youths, and over the next decade, chapters of the Young Lords emerged in New York and other major cities. The Young Lords called attention to issues ranging from police brutality to the lack of affordable housing and health care. The organization also provided a number of services to its communities including street cleanup campaigns, legal aid and health clinics, and public information sessions. At the same time, it worked with pro-independence groups on the island, such as the Puerto Rican Nationalist Party, to demand an end to Puerto Rico's colonial relation-ship with the United States, which they argued contributed to the poverty of Puerto Ricans on and off the island.

The idealism of the Chicano and Puerto Rican Movements was hard to sustain, how-ever, especially when these various organizations came under the FBI's surveillance. Under pressure, infighting became common and members disagreed about goals and strategies. Many of the organizations at the forefront of the Chicano and Puerto Rican Movements eventually disbanded and their members dispersed, some in disillusion-ment and frustration, others to take advantage of the new opportunities generated by their activism. However, the Chicano and Puerto Rican activism of the 1960s and 1970s did result in significant opportunities for a new generation of Latinos. The emergence of bilingual education programs to help children stay in school, the hiring of Latino fac-ulty and administrators, the growing political clout of Latino constituencies, the elec-tion of Latinos to public office, the rise of new political and cultural institutions, and the emergence of Chicano, Puerto Rican, and Latino studies programs at colleges and universities across the country are all part of the legacy of this period of activism.

THE POST-1965 MIGRATION

Immigration scholars have written that the Immigration and Nationality Act of 1965, passed by Congress to abolish the restrictive national origin quotas in place since the 1920s, had the unintended consequence of increasing the number of immigrants from Latin America and Asia rather than Europe. The 1965 Act might have created a bureaucracy that *facilitated* the immigration of Latin American immigrants to the United States, but it did not cause the migration. In the global Cold War—in the struggles for the "hearts and minds" of the developing world—hundreds of thousands of *latinoamericanos* were displaced by revolutions, insurgencies, and counter-insurgencies. Others were displaced by economic "development" programs that, in reality, privileged only a small sector of their populations. Yet others were displaced by environmental disasters: droughts, hurricanes, flooding, earthquakes. For some of these displaced persons, it was their countries' historic ties to the United States that made the latter a logical destination for temporary or permanent settlement. But the United States was not the only country that received immigrants. Americans tend to think of Latin America as immigrant producing nations, but these nations have a long tradition of accommodating immigrants as well. It is also important to note that not everyone who travels to the United States has stayed; some countries have a long migratory tradition to the United States and workers spend part of their lives living and working in the United States, to return to their countries with the profits of their labor.

In the case of migration to the United States, some national groups have had an easier time legally migrating to the United States than others. Congressional acts such as the 1966 Cuban Adjustment Act, the 1980 Refugee Act, and the 1990 Immigration Act, for example, prioritized certain groups over others and exemplify how politicized immigration policy can become.

The majority of the 1.7 million Cuban Americans currently in the United States, for example, arrived after 1959, the year Fidel Castro's revolutionaries assumed total control of the Cuban government and created a Marxist state. The Cubans who arrived during the 1960s and 1970s were perhaps the most privileged of the post-1965 Latino immigrants. Though diplomatic and trade relations were severed between Cuba and the United States shortly after Fidel Castro took power, the United States facilitated the entry of almost half a million Cuban refugees through "freedom flights," visa waivers, and parole status. The Cuban refugees became for Americans powerful symbols during the Cold War of the clash between democracy and authoritarianism, and the government facilitated the entry of not just middle-class professionals but also office and factory employees, artisans, and skilled and semi-skilled laborers. The 1966 Cuban Adjustment Act allowed for the permanent resident status and naturalization of those paroled into the United States, and the Cuban Refugee Program (CRP) was the most generous immigrant assistance program known up to that point.

The popular media has celebrated Cubans as the most successful Latino immigrant group, and Miami as home to the wealthiest Latino business community. As early as 1980, Cubans exhibited the highest income and educational levels of the three largest Latino groups, levels that were only slightly below the national average. Miami is now home to one of the wealthiest Latino business communities in the nation, and regarded as the "Gateway to the Americas." If the Cubans as a group are economically successful, however, it is due as much to the government's investment in their future as to the entrepreneurial spirit of the middle and working classes. The Kennedy and Johnson administrations invested in their economic future through the job retraining programs of the Cuban Refugee Program, assisting thousands to retool for the U.S. economy and rebuild their lives in the United States.

Subsequent arrivals from Cuba were not as fortunate as those who arrived during the 1960s and 1970s. The Cubans who arrived as part of the 1980 Mariel Boatlift and the 1994 *balseros* (rafters) migration, for example, did not have access to the benefits of the Cuban Refugee Program, nor did they enjoy the status and respect that often comes with the designation of "Cold War refugee." Instead, they were stigmatized by the U.S. new media, and even their own compatriots in the United States. However, the fact that these new arrivals were allowed to remain in the United States despite the absence of proper papers or documentation, when other Latinos in similar circumstances are routinely deported, reflects how Cuban immigration has been prioritized even in the post– Cold War era.

Those who fled rightist regimes that were allies of the United States had much more difficulty prying open the door to the United States. During the 1970s, thousands of Brazilians, Uruguayans, *Argentinos*, and Chileans tried to escape the military dictatorships in their homelands. Most of them did not fit the United States' general profile of refugees because they were fleeing governments regarded as strong allies of the United States, and therefore did not attract the sympathy of Cold War–minded politicians in Congress. Consequently, the numbers of refugees from South America admitted to the United States during the 1970s were comparatively small. Other countries, most notably Canada, had a better record of accommodating those fleeing rightist regimes.

Such was the case with the Chileans who fled their homeland after September 11, 1973, when General Augusto Pinochet overthrew the democratically elected Socialist government of Salvador Allende. Thousands of Allende supporters were imprisoned, raped, and tortured, and over 3000 were executed or made to disappear. Thousands more took refuge in foreign embassies in the capital city of Santiago or crossed the border into neighboring countries. The United Nations High Commissioner for Refugees (UNHCR) and other international nongovernmental organizations (NGOs) tried to negotiate the release of those detained in Pinochet's prisons, and by 1979 some 30,000 Chilean refugees had been resettled throughout Europe and Latin America. The United States resisted creating a refugee or resettlement program like that created for the Cubans for fear that the Chileans' leftist politics might pose a security threat. When the international media's coverage of the human rights abuses in Chile cast into light the United States' role in arming and supporting the Pinochet dictatorship, the pressure from domestic advocacy groups increased and eventually forced the U.S. government to enact a limited parole program for a select number of Chilean dissidents: those who agreed to sign a declaration of nonintervention in the political affairs of the United States, and who agreed to reimburse the U.S. government for travel expenses once they became economically self-supporting. By 1977, however, only 1100 Chileans had resettled in the United States. Similarly, Argentines fleeing the "Dirty War" (1976–1983) in their country found limited opportunities for migration to the United States, despite the overwhelming evidence of human rights abuses. Between 15,000 and 30,000 people are believed to have become *desaparecidos* ("the disappeared") at the hands of the military junta in Argentina during this period, and yet only a few thousand found refuge in the United States. It was not until the 1990s that a new generation of *Chilenos* and *Argentinos* migrated to the United States in larger numbers, partly in response to economic pressures.

Perhaps the best example of how politicized immigration and refugee policy became during the Cold War era—and the importance of domestic advocacy networks in securing protection for immigrants—can be seen in U.S. responses to the Salvadorans, Guatemalans, and Nicaraguans who migrated during the 1980s and 1990s. The majority of the Central Americans who sought refuge in the United States during this period arrived without papers and did not qualify for asylum in the United States under the terms of the recently passed 1980 Refugee Act since most fled a generalized climate of violence rather than individual persecution. The Reagan and Bush administrations argued that this was an economically driven migration because to do otherwise would be to admit that the countries that they were supporting with billions of dollars were repressing their own citizens. Consequently, during the 1980s, not more than five percent of Salvadoran and Guatemalan asylum applications were successful.

However, a vocal segment of the U.S. population challenged U.S. refugee policy, in part as a means of protesting U.S. foreign policy in Central America. These advocates argued that the United States had a legal obligation to protect those displaced by war based on the international conventions to which the United States was a signatory, and a moral obligation to do so because of the role the United States had played in supporting the corrupt military regimes that had displaced the Central Americans from their homes. Much of this popular advocacy focused on the campaign to win a temporary protected status for Central Americans that would allow them to remain legally in the United States until conditions improved in their homeland and they could return home. Across the country Americans mobilized in support of the Central American immigrants. Community groups along the United States–Mexico border provided them with shelter, medical attention, and legal and psychological counseling. By the mid-1980s, thousands of Americans were engaged in one of the most important acts of civil disobedience of the late twentieth century—the sanctuary movement—a grassroots resistance movement that protested U.S. policy through the harboring and transporting of refugees across the United States and Canada.

The struggle to secure legal protection for the Central American immigrants lasted over a decade and required sustained litigation. Abuses at the detention centers where Central Americans were housed prompted numerous lawsuits.[6] U.S. judges hearing these cases ruled in favor of the Central American plaintiffs and ordered the Immigration and Nationality Service (INS) to inform detainees of their right to petition for asylum, to meet with legal counsel, and to have their legal rights explained in Spanish and English. According to the courts, no one could be deported or coerced to sign voluntary departure forms without being informed of these rights. These decisions did little to halt the deportation of Central Americans, however. A shift in policy did not occur until the early 1990s. In 1991, a class-action lawsuit filed by 80 religious and refugee assistance groups (*American Baptist Churches in the USA, et al. v. Edwin Meese III and Alan Nelson*) was finally settled and allowed Salvadorans and Guatemalans who had entered the United States before 1991 to receive new asylum hearings. In a parallel development, Congress passed the omnibus Immigration Act of 1990, which included a provision for Temporary Protected Status (TPS). Through TPS and the new asylum adjudication process, Salvadorans and Guatemalans had more opportunities through which to negotiate their legal stay in the United States. Nicaraguan immigrants, in turn, won a major victory in 1997 when Congress passed the Nicaraguan Adjustment and Central American Relief Act (NACARA) which offered suspension of deportation to Nicaraguans and other Central American groups if they met certain conditions. For sanctuary workers, legal counsel, and all those involved in the protests of the 1980s, these developments were a significant victory, and demonstrated the importance of advocacy networks in shaping the contours of immigration policy.

LOOKING TO THE FUTURE

The immigrants who have migrated from Latin America in the post-1965 period have diversified the Latino population and complicated what we understand as Latino history. Some have migrated as political refugees or exiles from rightist or leftist regimes; others are more traditional immigrants and sojourners, migrating alone or as part of family units, trying to improve their economic prospects. Some, like the Cubans and Mexicans, come from countries that have a migratory tradition to the United States, while others, like the Dominicans, the Central Americans, and recent arrivals from Brazil, Venezuela, Paraguay and Colombia, and have established new migratory traditions. They are the pioneers, establishing the networks that will lead others to follow in their footsteps.

The political and economic realities in the Americas continue to produce a large migration of workers who seek opportunities in the United States and other developed economies, either as immigrants or guest workers. The waiting period for a "green card" or a temporary workers' permit in the United States can be long, however, especially if one does not have relatives, employment, or skills necessary to the U.S. economy.

The fees for filing are expensive and the bureaucracy is difficult to navigate. For some, crossing the border or overstaying a tourist or student visa and working illegally in the underground economy is the only prospect. Over the past two decades—and especially since 9/11—this has become increasingly difficult to do, however, because immigration has been framed as one of the threats to national security, U.S. borders have become more militarized and the immigration bureaucracy more cumbersome. But it is not impossible. Overstaying one's visa is still the most common way to become an undocumented immigrant.

Ironically, as the United States seeks to control the movement of peoples across its borders, it has negotiated a record number of free trade agreements providing for the unrestricted movement of goods and capital, which have generated billions of dollars in corporate revenues. Americans generally support free trade but they do not want the workers that are displaced by free trade policies. The state relies increasingly on detention and deportation as tools for managing migration, and multilateral agreements now facilitate the sharing of information, technology, and personnel to assist in these efforts. However, decades of ineffective measures have demonstrated the difficulties of controlling migration. Restrictions on visas, fines on airlines and shipping companies, increased border security, criminal penalties on smugglers, streamlined detention and deportation procedures, and multinational crackdowns on undocumented labor may temporarily reduce the number of immigrants and refugees in a given year, but only until new entry points, transportation networks, and legal loopholes are created or identified. As long as regional economies offer such vastly different opportunities, professionals and workers will seek to improve their life chances elsewhere.

Latinos have become the largest minority group in the United States. They have transformed urban, suburban, and rural areas not only in traditional population centers such as California, Texas, Florida, and New York but also "new destinations" such as Georgia, North Carolina, and Oregon. American corporations cater to this multibillion-dollar market, while politicians try either to engage them, or conversely, curtail their potential influence depending on whether they are viewed allies or threats. At the same time, Latinos continue to exert significant influence on their countries of origin through remittances and even direct political participation, exemplifying the transnationalism that so intrigues social scientists. Latinos, the majority of whom are first-generation immigrants, generate billions of dollars in remittances each year. These remittances—$10 billion annually to Mexico alone—constitute one of the principal sources of income for many countries in the Americas. Several Latin American countries now allow immigrants in the United States to participate in their electoral processes, and Latin American presidential candidates today campaign in Miami, New York, and Los Angeles as readily as they do in Managua, Santo Domingo, or Mexico City. The Mexican state of Michoacán even designates one seat in its legislature as the "migrant seat," to represent Mexicans abroad.

Continued immigration from Latin America means that a significant percentage of the Latino population will continue to be first generation with emotive ties to their countries of origin, and perhaps more opportunities for maintaining those ties over a longer period of time. These transnational behaviors do not mean that Latinos refuse to assimilate to the United States or pose a threat to the social fabric, as some have argued. Studies show that over time Latinos generally adapt and segmentally assimilate to the United States in ways similar to immigrants who have come before them. Their experiences demonstrate that adopting an "American" identity does not mean forfeiting ties to the country of origin. Latinos may help us broaden our understanding of what it means to be American: a citizen with responsibilities not just to a nation-state but a hemisphere. *Americanos broadly defined.* Perhaps the more important question to consider as we enter the second decade of the twenty-first century is whether U.S. society will allow Latinos opportunities for a fully engaged citizenship or whether they will occupy a liminal political or economic space with no country to claim them.

Those interested in Latino history will find it to be one of the most dynamic fields in the American academy today. Chicano Studies and Puerto Rican Studies programs were few back in the 1960s and 1970s, but these produced the foundational work that addressed the erasure of Hispanics/Latinos from the American historical narrative.[7] Over the past few decades, however, a generational shift has produced new programs and departments, some focused on the experience of newer or smaller groups such as the Dominicans or Cubans; others more broadly focused on a new interdisciplinary and transhemispheric field called "Latino Studies." Latinos do not fit easily into the classic American ethnic narrative, as this essay has hopefully demonstrated, so scholars of Latino history face two interrelated research and teaching challenges: they work to center the various Hispanic/Latino populations in the scholarship and teaching of U.S. history while also examining global, transnational, and cross-border issues and processes. The scholarship contributes to our understanding of the ways race and ethnicity affect the life chances and opportunities of immigrants and how marginalized peoples participate in democratic processes and claim membership. But the scholarship also shows us the multiple ways that immigrants have maintained transnational connections across time and space, influencing their countries of origin through remittances, political participation and activism, investment, and cultural productions. Latino scholarship has also shaped the way we understand foreign policy and borders. Scholars of immigration and foreign policy, for example, draw on each other's work as the relationship between foreign policy decisions, population flows, and "ethnic" policy advocates is increasingly acknowledged and explored. Likewise, studies of the United States–Mexico borderlands have had enormous influence worldwide on the study of borders as geo-political constructions, cultural spaces, and as metaphors for hybridity and "in-betweenness." Latino Studies will continue to emphasize these particular thematic strengths in the years to come. The field is broad, vigorous, dynamic, and open to intellectual engagement.

NOTES

1. The term "Hispanic" was first used by the Census Bureau in the 1970s and has now become a common term of reference in U.S. popular culture. Since 1990 the terms "Latino"/"Latina" have also become increasingly popular, in part as a reaction to the term "Hispanic," which some feel was imposed by the government and/or privileges the Spanish ancestry of this population at the expense of its African and indigenous origins. However, studies show that most Hispanics/Latinos prefer to identify according to their national ancestry or ethnic or regional identification rather than one of these generic terms (e.g., those who trace their ancestry to Mexico usually identify as Mexican American or Chicano/Chicana, while those from Puerto Rico might identify as Boricua, *puertorriqueño*, or Puerto Rican).

2. In 2010, the wording of the Hispanic origin question differed from the 2000 Census. In 2000, the Census asked, "Is this person Spanish/Hispanic/Latino?" while in 2010, the Census asked, "Is this person of Hispanic, Latino, or Spanish origin?" For a more detailed explanation of the other differences in the Hispanic origin questions, see: U.S. Census, "The Hispanic Population: 2010" [http://2010.census.gov/2010census/data/].

3. Lola Rodríguez de Tío, "A Cuba," *Obras Completas* (San Juan, Instituto de Cultura Puertorriqueña, 1968), 319–321.

4. "Voces Oral History Project" [http://www.lib.utexas.edu/voces/]. The oral history project is under the direction of Professor Maggie Rivas-Rodríguez, School of Journalism, University of Texas at Austin. One of the publications to come out of this oral history project is: Maggie Rivas-Rodríguez, ed., *Mexican Americans and World War II* (Austin: The University of Texas Press, 2005). Due to the pressure exerted by Rivas-Rodriguez and her colleagues, documentary filmmaker Ken Burns revised his important PBS television series on World War II to include reference to underrepresented minorities.

5. Works on the Latino civil rights struggle and construction of citizenship include Francisco A. Rosales, *Chicano!: The History of the Mexican American Civil Rights Movement* (Houston, TX: Arte Público Press, 1996); Lorrin Thomas, *Puerto Rican Citizen: History and Political Identity in Twentieth-Century New York City* (Chicago: University of Chicago Press, 2010); and Andrés Torres and José E. Velázquez, eds., *The Puerto Rican Movement: Voices from the Diaspora* (Philadelphia: Temple University Press, 1998).

6. See, for example, including *Noe Castillo Núñez, et al. v. Hal Boldin, et al., Orantes-Hernández, et al. v. Smith, et al., El Rescate Legal Services, Inc., et al., v. Executive Office for Immigration Review, et al.,* and *INS v. Cardoza-Fonseca.*

7. Due to the prescribed word limit only one of these early texts was listed in the select bibliography: Rodolfo Acuña's *Occupied America*, first published in 1972 with the subtitle "*The Chicano Struggle Toward Liberation,*" is now in its 7th edition.

BIBLIOGRAPHY

Acuña, Rodolfo. *Occupied America: a history of Chicanos.* 7th ed. (New York: Pearson Longman, 2010).

Burgos, Adrian J. *Playing America's Game(s): Baseball, Latinos, and the Color Line* (Berkeley: University of California Press, 2007).

Duany, Jorge. *Blurred Borders: Transnational Migrations between the Hispanic Caribbean and the United States* (Chapel Hill: University of North Carolina Press, 2012).

García, María Cristina. *Havana USA: Cuban Exiles and Cuban Americans in South Florida, 1959–1994* (Berkeley: University of California Press, 1996).

García, María Cristina. *Seeking Refuge: Central American Migration to Mexico, the United States, and Canada* (Berkeley: University of California Press, 2006).

Gómez, Laura E. *Manifest Destinies: The Making of the Mexican American Race* (New York: New York University, 2007).

Guridy, Frank. *Forging Diaspora: Afro-Cubans and African Americans in a World of Empire and Jim Crow* (Chapel Hill: University of North Carolina Press, 2010).

Gutiérrez, David G. *Walls and Mirrors: Mexican Americans, Mexican immigrants, and the politics of Ethnicity* (Berkeley: University of California Press, 1995).

Hernandez, Kelly Lytle. *Migra!: A History of the U.S. Border Patrol* (Berkeley: University of California Press, 2010).

Hoffnung-Garskof, Jesse. *A Tale of Two Cities: Santo Domingo and New York after 1950* (Princeton: Princeton University Press, 2008).

Matovina, Timothy. *Latino Catholicism: Transformation in America's Largest Church* (Princeton: Princeton University Press, 2011).

Mize, Ronald and Swords, Alica. *Mexican Labor for North American Consumption: From Braceros to NAFTA 1942–2009* (Toronto: The University of Toronto Press, 2011).

Portes, Alejandro and Rubén G. Rumbaut. *Immigrant America: a portrait.* 3rd ed. (Berkeley: University of California Press, 2006).

Rosales, Francisco A. *Chicano!: The History of the Mexican American Civil Rights Movement* (Houston, TX: Arte Público Press, 1996).

Thomas, Lorrin. *Puerto Rican Citizen: History and Political Identity in Twentieth-Century New York City* (Chicago: University of Chicago Press, 2010).

Torres, Andrés and José E. Velázquez, eds. *The Puerto Rican Movement: Voices from the Diaspora* (Philadelphia: Temple University Press, 1998).

CHAPTER 5

....

AFRICAN AMERICAN MIGRATION FROM THE COLONIAL ERA TO THE PRESENT

....

JOE W. TROTTER

MIGRATION has been an enduring theme in African American history. Yet, during the first 250 years of the nation's history, the vast majority of African people entered the New World primarily as enslaved or "forced migrants." They moved from one agricultural region to another. During the colonial era, the first generation moved from West Africa to the staple-producing areas of the Upper and Lower South. In the wake of the American Revolution and the rise of the new republic, enslaved people migrated from the Upper South tobacco area to the booming cotton-producing Deep South states. Following the Civil War and the advent of emancipation, coerced migration gradually gave way to the "voluntary" movement of African Americans from farm to city. By the mid-20th century, the Great Migration from rural to urban America resulted in the transformation of African Americans into a predominantly city people. While massive black population movements disrupted established cultural, political, and social relations, migration also gave rise to new forms of family, community, and political struggles for full citizenship rights. Despite the persistence of significant internal cultural, ideological, and social conflict, African Americans forged dynamic political movements designed to secure their own freedom. Their efforts not only ended the system of slavery and later Jim Crow but also helped to transform America into a broader and more inclusive democracy, including the liberalization of U.S. immigration policies.[1]

Coerced and voluntary forms of black migration had deep roots in the soil of precolonial West Africa. The medieval expansion of the trans-Saharan trade network and the advent of Islam opened the door to massive population movement in the region, including an extensive trade in human beings across the desert. Some 3.5 million Africans entered North Africa and the Mediterranean world as slaves between 900 and 1400 CE.[2] But the arrival of Europeans opened a new and more coercive chapter in the history of black migration. An estimated 11 million Africans entered the New World under the impact of the international slave trade. Africans endured not only a painful separation from their homeland but also the infamous "Middle Passage" across the Atlantic. Predominantly young men in their prime working years (supplemented by a few women and children), enslaved Africans traveled to the New World under armed guards in the holds of tightly packed, disease-ridden, and violent ships. Some 2 million Africans lost their lives at sea, devoured by the ever-present sharks that traveled in the wake of slave ships. Even as Africans endured some of the most destructive conditions of human bondage, they gradually forged bonds with their "shipmates." These bonds would enable them to begin the process of bridging the gap between various African ethnicities and forging a New World African American culture and forms of resistance, including revolts, mutinies, and plots to revolt.[3]

Most Africans bound for the New World entered the European-controlled plantation regions of Latin America and the Caribbean. Only about 5 percent, or 300,000 Africans, arrived in British North America, mainly via the West Indies. Men outnumbered women and children, and the number of deaths greatly exceeded births. By the 1730s and 1740s, however, as the demographic balance between men, women, and children improved, African Americans gradually made the transition to a self-sustaining population. The black population rose to an estimated 600,000 people by the end of the American Revolution, nearly double the number of all Africans who reached North America during the era of the Atlantic slave trade. For a brief moment, between 1619 and 1660, Africans shared an unfree status with white indentured servants. Some first-generation Africans gained their freedom, purchased land, married, raised families, and imported their own servants. By the early 1700s, however, in both the North and South, colonial law declared African people slaves "durante vita" or slaves "for life," while ensuring the eventual freedom of white indentured servants.[4]

Significant numbers of blacks arrived in the northern colonies, but the agricultural staple-producing areas of the Upper and Lower South claimed the bulk of enslaved Africans. Fewer than 100,000 of these blacks lived and worked outside the plantation South. Black people not only cultivated the principle cash crops—tobacco, rice, sugar, and indigo—but also cleared land and prepared plantations for cultivation and human habitation. Although colonial cities served primarily as suppliers of slave labor to nearby plantations and farms, enslaved people also lived and labored in the seaport cities of New York, Boston, Philadelphia, Charleston, New Orleans, and Savannah. In addition to work as general laborers, domestic, and personal servants, urban blacks worked in the households, shops, and businesses of merchants, landowners, and artisans.[5] Advertisements for the sale of slaves frequently stressed the skills of black artisans as bricklayers, plasterer, blacksmiths, and coopers among many other craftsmen. In 1763, the *New York Gazette* advertised, "A Negro Man to be sold by Samuel Dunnscomb in New-Street, he is about 32 years of Age, understands most of the Cooper's Business . . . He has been some Voyages to Sea."[6]

Under the impact of the American Revolution, the rise of the "Cotton Kingdom," and the dramatic expansion of the international textile industry, an estimated 1.5 million blacks moved under the force of the whip from the Upper South to the Lower

South. As tobacco and, to some extent, rice declined as profitable cash crops, a variety of forces stimulated the emergence of cotton as the nation's major engine of economic growth. The cotton gin revolutionized the labor-intensive process of separating the cotton fiber from its seed, while the adoption of new spinning and weaving machines transformed the textile industry into a mass producer of cotton fabrics. These technological developments paved the way for escalating demands for slave labor in the cotton fields. In 1830, an able-bodied male slave sold for about $350 in the Chesapeake region; three decades later, the price of a male slave had increased in the Deep South to between $1500 and $2000. African people not only picked cotton and transported it to the expanding gin houses, they also cut down trees, uprooted tree stumps, burned brush, and transformed overgrown land into places fit for cultivation and human settlement. They built "big houses," slave quarters, barns, tool sheds, barrels, stables, and gin houses. Cotton production rose from fewer than 300,000 bales in 1820 to nearly 4.5 million bales in 1860. Slave labor not only fueled the spread of the cotton fields in the South but also spurred the growth of the textile industry in New England and abroad.[7]

The domestic slave trade gave rise to a new nineteenth-century "Middle Passage" in African American migration history. As Deep South planters cleared and opened increasing acres of cotton land, their Upper South counterparts perceived the transport and sale of slaves to the Deep South as a new financial bonanza. In addition to the proliferation of small trading companies, large slave-trading firms—Austin Woolfolk of Baltimore; Seth Woodruff of Lynchburg; and Franklin and Armfield of Alexandria, Virginia—established their own sales and marketing forces; purchased their own slave ships; built their own warehouses and holding facilities; and developed aggressive advertising campaigns designed to move enslaved Africans from the Upper to Lower South.[8] In his narrative of life as a slave, Henry Bibb described the beginning of his journey from Kentucky to New Orleans after serving time in a slave prison:

> "One Sabbath morning Garrison [the slave trader] . . . called us up to an anvil block, and the heavy log chains which we had been wearing on our legs during three months, were cut off. . . . The hand-cuffs were then put on to our wrists. We were coupled two and two—the right hand one to the left hand of another, and a long chain to connect us together. . . . We marched off to the river Ohio, to take passage on board the steamboat Water Witch."[9]

During the 1830s, one visitor described conditions on the inland waterways in terms reminiscent of earlier conditions on the high seas:

> "The hold was appropriated to the slaves, and is divided into two apartments. The after-hold will carry about eighty women, and the other about one hundred men. On either side [of the hold] were two platforms running the whole length; one raised a few inches, and the other half way up the deck. They were about five or six feet deep. On these the slaves lie, as close as they can be stowed."[10]

Unlike the earlier Atlantic "Middle Passage," more blacks reached the Deep South via overland caravans than by sea or the inland Mississippi, Ohio, Missouri, and Alabama rivers. Using livestock halters, iron neck collars, leg chains, and padlocks, slave traders and their various assistants marched African people, sometimes numbering over 50 people, on foot across rough terrain for miles each day over several weeks until they reached their destination. In his narrative of life as a slave, Charles Ball described the coffle of over 50 slaves that brought him to the Deep South. The women, he said, "were tied together with a rope, about the size of a bed cord, which was tied like a halter round the neck of each; but the men . . . were very differently caparisoned. A strong iron collar was closely fitted by means of a padlock round each of our necks. A chain of iron about a hundred feet long was passed through the hasp of each padlock, except at the two ends, where the hasps of the padlocks passed through a link of the chain. In addition to this, we were handcuffed in pairs." Other enslaved people made the journey south via rail. In 1856, according to a northern visitor to the South, Lyman Abbott, "every train going south" had 20 or more slaves on board.[11]

Small but important streams of immigration from overseas supplemented the larger Upper-to-Lower South movement of black people. Between the American Revolution and the 1808 termination of the Atlantic slave trade, an estimated 100,000 Africans entered the United States. After 1808, another 54,000 Africans entered the country via the underground smuggling trade. As late as 1859, the *Clothilde*, the last known slave ship to dock in a U.S. port, transported nearly 130 West African men, women, and children to Mobile, Alabama. Other blacks entered the United States from the Caribbean when the Haitian Revolution drove French slaveholders off the island.[12]

In order to maximize the use of slave labor year round, planters allowed growing numbers of rural blacks to move into cities to work under the "hiring out" system. Enslaved people entered contracts with employers in exchange for a set return on their labor to owners. After meeting their obligation to owners, some enslaved people saved enough money to purchase themselves and other family members. The flexibility of the hiring out system also provided an opportunity for fugitives to elude capture. By the late antebellum years, fugitives also joined the expanding underground railroad network to the free states of the North. The free black population rose from 60,000 in 1790 to nearly a half million by 1860. Over one-third of southern free blacks and the majority of their northern brothers and sisters lived in cities, while only 5 percent of slaves, 15 percent of southern whites, and about 40 percent of northern whites claimed urban residence. By the 1850s, New Orleans (27,000), Charleston (23,000), New York (14,000), and Philadelphia (11,000) had the largest concentrations of urban blacks, mainly slaves in the urban South and free blacks in the North. In both the North and South, unlike the plantation and farm, women who lived and worked in the households of white families made up the majority of antebellum black urbanites.[13]

In the wake of the Civil War and emancipation, voluntary migration gradually supplanted forced migration as the major engine of black population movement. Scores of freedmen and women moved to southern and northern cities seeking loved ones separated during the era of slavery and the perils of Civil War. In October 1867, ex-slave Elizabeth Low of Washington, D.C., asked the Freedmen's Bureau to help her reclaim her daughter, Harriet, from a former slave-owner in Fredericksburg, Virginia. A year earlier, Henry Plummer traveled from Baltimore to New Orleans to locate his sister, Sarah Miranda Plummer. An advertisement in the *Colored Tennessean* offered a "$200 Reward" for the return of "our daughter, Polly, and son, Geo. Washington . . . to Nashville, or get word to us of their whereabouts, if they are alive." Caroline Dodson's mother also promised a reward for "any information" on the location of her daughter. During the war, slave owners had sold Caroline from Nashville, Tennessee, to Atlanta, Georgia. After moving to Utica, New York, another ex-slave Samuel Dove searched "for his mother, Areno, his sisters Maria, Neziah, and Peggey, and his brother Edmond." The slave trade had scattered family members to various parts of Virginia and Tennessee, including Richmond and Nashville. "Every mother's son," a Freedmen's Bureau official reported, "seemed to be in search of his mother; every mother in search of her children."[14]

The percentage of all blacks living in cities rose from less than 10 percent at the end of the Civil War to over 25 percent by World War I. Similar to the antebellum years, most early emancipation era migrants were black women bound for work in the households of white urban elites.[15] At the same time, the number of black men also increased. Partly because migrants like P.B.S. Pinchback, former governor of Louisiana, and the educator Fannie Jackson Coppin of New Orleans expressed increasing dissatisfaction with the Jim Crow system by moving to the urban North, some contemporary observers and scholars referred to this population movement as the migration of the "talented tenth," but the vast majority of pre-World War I migrants were members of the poor and working class. They came mainly from the Upper South states of Virginia, Maryland, and Kentucky.[16]

Although blacks moved steadily toward cities after the Civil War, it was the inter-war years that ushered in the Great Migration. Between World War I and the end of World War II, an estimated 3 million black people left the rural and urban South for cities of the North and West. Black migration to southern cities also increased, but most southern cities reported a decline in the percentage of blacks in the total population. Compared with the pre-World War I years, young men, roughly ages 21 to 44, dominated the migration stream. They came mostly from the Deep South states and entered the urban–industrial workforce, where young women found far fewer opportunities for employment.[17]

In both urban and rural areas, disfranchisement, mob violence, institutional segregation, and economic discrimination transformed the South into new sources of African American labor for the urban–industrial economy. As migration historian Isabel Wilkerson notes, African Americans "did not cross the turnstiles of customs at Ellis Island. They were already citizens. But they were not treated as such. Their every step was controlled by the meticulous laws of Jim Crow, a nineteenth century minstrel figure that would become shorthand for the violently enforced code of the southern caste system."[18] Simultaneously, the decline of European immigrants opened up new industrial opportunities in the urban North and West. In the decade and a half before World War I, over 12 million immigrants had entered the United States. Between 1914 and 1918, however, the number of immigrants arriving each year steadily dropped from 1 million to only 110,000. Another 100,000 European-born Americans returned to their countries of origin.[19] At the same time, African Americans living in cities rose from under 30 percent before World War I to nearly 60 percent by the late 1940s. Midwestern and West Coast cities experienced the most dramatic black population growth. Whereas the number of blacks moving to New York and Philadelphia trebled during the 1910s and the 1920s, Chicago's and Detroit's black populations increased more than fivefold during the same period. By the end of World War II, the number of southern blacks moving to Los Angeles and San Francisco nearly matched the number moving to the leading cities of the urban Midwest.[20]

While a variety of national and global socioeconomic and political factors stimulated twentieth-century black population movement, African Americans also organized their own movement into urban–industrial America. They devised their own complex communications network and channeled their own journeys into cities. In addition to an expanding chain of family and friends, their network included railroad employees, particularly the expanding ranks of black porters on sleeping cars; porters gathered and dispensed valuable information on jobs and living conditions outside the rural South. Other dimensions of the black communications system included northern black weeklies like the *Chicago Defender* and the *Pittsburgh Courier*; migration clubs that negotiated lower group rates for railroad tickets for prospective migrants; and the proliferation of national conventions among black churches, fraternal orders, and social clubs. Black women played a key role in the building and maintenance of these networks. They not only took the lead in helping to organize national black conventions but also initiated extensive letter-writing efforts to connect prospective migrants with relatives, friends, jobs, and housing in the industrial city. In a letter to a northern branch of the National Urban League, a woman wrote from South Carolina that she had "two grown sons" and wanted "to settle down somewhere north . . . wages are so cheap down here we can hardly live." By gathering careful information on life at points of destination, southern African Americans expressed increasing optimism with the prospects of improving their condition through interregional movement. Accordingly, they often described the Great Migration in biblical terms as, "The Promised Land," "Going to Canaan," and "Flight from Egypt." In letters back home, they reinforced these very positive perspectives on life in the urban North. As one migrant put, "Up here, a man can be a man."[21]

Industrial job opportunities reinforced their optimism for a better life in the urban North. During World War I and again during the economic expansion of the mid-1920s, African American men, and to some extent women, gained increasing access to jobs in meatpacking, auto, steel, shipbuilding, and other mass production industries. Although African Americans entered jobs at the floor of the industrial economy, they earned nearly twice as much as they earned in southern agriculture and urban areas, where employment on farms and plantations averaged between $1 and $3 per 12-hour day. In Philadelphia, African Americans found their most significant employment opportunities with the Pennsylvania Railroad, the Midvale Steel Company, and the Sun Shipyards, on the city's south side. The Pennsylvania Railroad hired over 1100 black maintenance-of-way men in 1916, while the Midvale Steel Company reported 4000 African American workers on its payroll in 1917. At the Sun Shipyards, black workers soon reached over 50 percent of the total work force. Other major Philadelphia firms employing black workers included the Atlantic Refinery, Franklin Sugar, Westinghouse, and Disston Saw.[22]

In Pittsburgh and Western Pennsylvania, the U.S. Steel Homestead works, the Jones and Laughlin Steel Company, and Carnegie Steel hired increasing numbers of black workers. African Americans rose from only about 3 percent of the steel industry workforce in 1910 to over 20 percent by the end of World War I.[23] Some companies—Oliver Iron and Steel, Pittsburgh Forge and Iron, and A. M. Byers, among others—hired black workers for the first time. In Chicago, such manufacturing firms as Swift, Armour, Pullman, International Harvester, and others also added increasing numbers of blacks to their payroll. Concentrated mainly in Kansas City, St. Louis, and Chicago, black workers in the nation's meatpacking industry rose from less than 6000 in 1910 to nearly 30,000 in 1920. In Kansas City, one contemporary observer reported, "There is no other large employer of Negroes in Kansas City which treats colored workers with more consideration than does the Armour Packing Company."[24]

Beginning with a smaller percentage of black workers in industrial jobs than Philadelphia, Pittsburgh, Cleveland, and other northern cities before World War I, Detroit surged to the forefront of black industrial workers nationwide by the mid-1920s. As early as May 1917, the Packard Company employed 1100 African American workers, but the Ford Motor Company soon gained a reputation as the city's and nation's most progressive employer of black workers. Ford's black work force rose from only 50 employees in 1916 to nearly 1700 by war's end. Ford also offered blacks a broader range of production and supervisory opportunities than did other companies. A reporter for the *Associated Negro Press* later recalled, "Back in those days [1920s and early 1930s] Negro Ford workers almost established class distinctions here . . . the men began to feel themselves a little superior to workers in other plants . . . 'I work for Henry Ford'; was a boastful expression."[25]

Whereas black men experienced a dramatic reversal of their numbers from domestic service and general labor jobs to the industrial sector, black women experienced only modest increases in manufacturing employment. Nonetheless, during the labor shortages of World War I, black women employed in industrial firms increased by nearly 75 percent from an estimated 68,000 in 1910 to 105,000 in 1920. In Philadelphia, nearly 300 black women had entered the garment trades in 1910 as strikebreakers. World War I and a postwar strike in 1921 brought another 1000 black women into the city's garment makers' work force. In 1917, some 500 black women entered the garment industry of Chicago as strikebreakers. According to economists Sterling Spero and Abram Harris, "This strike was largely lost through the employment of colored labor and when it ended . . . Negro girls found permanent places in the trade." In Chicago, between 1910 and 1920, black women classified as factory operatives increased from about 10 to 15 percent of all black women workers. In New York, the number of black apparel workers rose to an estimated 3000 in 1925 and to 6000 in 1927.[26]

What some historians call the Second Great Migration brought another 3 million African Americans from the South to the urban North and West after World War II. The percentage of all blacks living in cities rose from just over 50 percent during the 1940s to over 80 percent by the 1970s. Almost half of the African American population now lived in the urban North and West. Nearly 140,000 black people from Barbados, Jamaica, Trinidad, and other Caribbean islands had moved to urban America during the inter-World War year, but their numbers would increase slowly until passage of a new immigration law in 1965.[27]

Postwar African American migrants moved primarily to large cities where black people had already established their own neighborhoods and networks of support. When Ruby Daniels moved from Clarksdale, Mississippi, to Chicago in 1946, she followed the lead of her aunt Ceatrice who had moved there during the war years. In 1957, when her sister passed away in Eustis, Florida, Inez Starling and her husband, George, brought her sister's teenage daughter to Chicago to live with them. Robert Joseph Pershing Foster moved from Monroe, Louisiana, to Los Angeles during the 1950s; he soon vowed to return South only "to get as many of his loved ones from Monroe to move out to California" as possible. Monroe migrants to the Bay Area included the families of such luminaries as Huey P. Newton, later founder of the Black Panther Party, and future hall of fame Celtic professional basketball player Bill Russell. While major rail lines continued to bring black people to the nation's large metropolitan areas, the rapid expansion of the federal highway system, automobile production, commercial bus lines, and moving companies supplemented the migration of blacks via rail.[28]

The rapid technological and economic transformation of southern agriculture reinforced the flow of black people out of the South in the years after World War II. Federal agricultural assistance programs, initiated during the New Deal years, strengthened the hand of southern segregationists and weakened the economic foundation of black life in the South. The U.S. Department of Agriculture paid landowners to withhold acreage from production, presumably to drive up the price of cotton, but such programs allowed landlords to greatly reduce the tenant work force. Consequently, sharecroppers lost their portion of agricultural subsidy payments and slipped down the tenure ladder into the category of hired "wage hands." Mechanical cotton pickers, tractors, herbicides, and other technological and scientific innovations also reduced the demand for manual labor. Within the 6-year period between 1958 and 1964, the proportion of all Mississippi Delta cotton harvested by mechanical cotton pickers rose from 27 to 81 percent. As the mechanical cotton picker spread into 17 cotton-producing counties of Arkansas during the 1950s, the number of tenant farmers dropped from 21,000 to about 6500. Farm wage workers found it even more difficult to make a living than their sharecropping counterparts.[29]

Displaced black sharecroppers and low-wage farm hands moved into nearby southern cities and towns in rising numbers. From there, thousands made their way to the urban North and West. African Americans also migrated into cities from the southern Appalachian coalfields of Virginia, Kentucky, West Virginia, Tennessee, and Alabama. The collapse of the bituminous coal industry, a significant employer of black workers in the Appalachian South, precipitated the increasing out migration of black workers and their families from the coal towns. Technological changes like the mechanical coal loader figured prominently in the reduction of demand for workers in the coal industry. In his recollections of life in the coal mines of West Virginia, the veteran miner Robert Armstead later described how coal-loading machines displaced increasing numbers of handloaders. "With giant, crablike arms, the coal-loading machine, or loader, scooped the coal up onto its belt-type surface. The belt tumbled it back out of the way, usually onto the bottom or into empty cars . . . Some timbermen, trackmen, and loaders kept their jobs, but the mining machines created massive layoffs. Every two or three months, three hundred or more men got laid off." In West Virginia, for example, the number of black coal miners declined steeply from nearly 35,000 during the 1940s to only about 3000 in 1970.[30]

The relationship between technological change and black labor migration was by no means a simple process. In 1946, Harris P. Smith, an agricultural engineer at Texas A&M, observed the huge outmigration of black workers from the cotton belt and concluded, "Instead of the machines displacing labor, they were used to replace the labor that had left the farm." Nate Shaw found it difficult to adapt to the tractor, but his sons embraced the new technology and stayed on the land longer than some other blacks who moved north.[31] In West Virginia, Robert Armstead witnessed the shrinking coal mine labor force but later became an operator of the mechanical coal loading machine and stayed in the coal fields. As he put it, "I aspired that someday, if I worked long enough in the coal mines, I could attain one of those positions with a higher hourly rate. . . . Before long, one of the loading-machine operator positions opened up. I applied for it and got the job."[32] But most black coal miners and their families joined the second Great Migration of blacks to the urban North and West. In his memoir of a black coal mining family, retired social worker and special education teacher Otis Trotter underscored the bittersweet journey of his family from a West Virginia coal town to life in Newcomerstown, a small town in eastern Ohio just south of the Canton-Massillon area. "After saying our good byes to friends and neighbors, we all got in the cars [pulling U-Hauls] and headed up the hill and down the road towards a future in Ohio that we hoped would be brighter."[33]

Despite proximity to the declining cotton, tobacco, rice, and coal fields of the South, southern cities attracted fewer rural-to-urban black migrants than their northern and western counterparts. Between 1940 and 1950, for example, the black population of Atlanta, New Orleans, Birmingham, and Memphis increased by no more than 10 to 22 percent, while that of northern cities like Detroit, Cleveland, and Philadelphia rose by

50 to 100 percent. Migration accounted for the bulk of black population growth outside the South, while natural increase made up over 95 percent of black population growth in southern cities. The upper South and border cities of Washington, DC, Baltimore, Louisville, and St. Louis experienced higher black population growth than Deep South cities, but natural increase rather than migration also accounted for the bulk of this expansion. In his recent study of black migration to Louisville, historian Luther Adams illuminates the unique dimensions of black population movement to this upper South city. Adams places the notion of "home" or what he describes as a powerful African American commitment to life in the South at the center of his analysis. In his view, while most southern black migrants might have moved to the urban North and West as acts of liberation and self-transformation, others moved to Louisville for similar reasons. Unlike most other southern states, Kentucky enfranchised black citizens following the Civil War, established fewer Jim Crow statutes, and for Louisville recorded fewer incidents of mob violence and lynching than elsewhere in the state and South.[34]

Post–World War II migrants later vividly recalled a broad range of motives for moving out of the South after World War II. Following interviews with more than twelve hundred migrants about their migration decision, Isabel Wilkerson noted, "It was not one thing; it was many things, some weighing more heavily in one migrant's heart than another but all very likely figuring into the calculus of departure." In interviews with Wilkerson and numerous other oral historians, African Americans accented profound dissatisfaction with the segregationist system in their decisions to move. In 1947, David Blakely left his home in Pensacola, Florida. He moved first to Manhattan and then to Pittsburgh in 1948. Similar to many migrants of the first wave of the Great Migration, Blakely later recalled, "I left [Pensacola] because I was tired of not being able to vote and not being treated like a human being."[35]

In April 1945, the Silver Meteor, part of the East Coast Seaboard Airline Railroad system, took George Swanson Starling from his home in Eustis, Florida, to New York City. Starling departed his hometown following threats on his life. Under his leadership and a small cohort of other black labor activists, black orange grove workers had organized and demanded higher pay and better working conditions from grove owners. Company officials and law officers made it clear that Starling would be lynched if he remained in the area. On the Monday after Easter in 1953, the physician Robert Joseph Pershing Foster departed Monroe, Louisiana, for Los Angeles. Pershing Foster had turned down his brother's plea to remain in Monroe. His brother, also a physician, wanted Robert to remain and help build a family medical practice serving Monroe's sizable black community. Pershing Foster later recalled moving to Los Angeles because he did not want to practice medicine behind the cotton curtain. He "did not want to be paid with buttermilk or the side of a freshly killed hog and did not want to deliver babies in somebody's kitchen."[36]

Some blacks continued to leave the South, reminiscent of fugitives on the antebellum underground railroad. In 1963, Eddie Eason, recalled eluding the grip of a Mississippi Delta plantation owner. One day the "boss man" put a Winchester rifle to Eddie's head for daring to go to a doctor for treatment of a serious injury on the job. "We were still in slavery, like," he said. During the next 3 years after the incident over medical treatment, Eason quietly saved enough money to purchase bus tickets for himself, his sister, and her two children. As he recalled, "You didn't talk about it or tell nobody . . . You had to sneak away." In February 1958, Arrington High escaped from Mississippi via Alabama in a coffin that traveled 15 hours by train to Chicago. Five months earlier, authorities had confined the 44-year-old husband and father of four children to an insane asylum for challenging the system of white supremacy in his newspaper, the *Eagle Eye*.[37]

By the opening years of the twenty-first century, a variety of local, national, and global forces had set in motion several new trends in black migration history. First and perhaps most important, by the mid-1970s the Great Migration of the twentieth century had run its course. For the first time in the nation's history, more blacks moved from the urban North and West to the South than vice versa. Before the 1970s, no more than about 15,000 blacks joined the counterstream of northern migration to the rural South. During the 1970s and 1980s, the number of blacks moving North to South rose to nearly 50,000 each year. Over the first half of the 1970s, an estimated 2.2 million people, blacks and whites, left the South, while another 4.1 million moved into the region from elsewhere. Nearly as many left and moved in during the second half of the 1970s. By the final decade of the twentieth century, the South claimed over 500,000 African Americans from the urban North. Northern black migration to the South included some 210,000 former residents who had left the region during the era of the Great Migration.[38]

Why did northern blacks move back South in rising numbers? In her pioneering study of the phenomenon, anthropologist Carol Stack aptly concluded, there were as many stories as there were migrants—"ailing grandparents, a dream of running a restaurant, a passion for the land, a midnight epiphany, rumors and lies, weariness, homesickness, missionary vision, community redemption, fate, romance, politics, sex, religion." People often told Stack their stories in terms of "pushes and pulls, disequilibriums both personal and historical that perturbed the heart until the feet hit the road." In Stack's view, the resolve to return home was not "primarily an economic decision but rather a powerful blend of motives" as "bad times back home" could "pull as well as push" people located in a broad orbit of family connections and commitments.[39]

While northern blacks moved South for a complex combination of personal, cultural, political, and economic considerations, the exodus escalated as the material foundation of African American life slowly disappeared with the demise of the industrial economy in the urban Northeast and Midwest. During the 5 middle years of the 1980s, the industrial Northeast and Midwest lost nearly 10 million jobs through plant closings, technological innovations, or movement of major manufacturers to overseas locations. In Pittsburgh and other steel-producing centers of the nation, the heavy metals industry had nearly disappeared by the turn of the twentieth century. In rapid succession, U.S. Steel closed its great blast furnace and mill plants at Homestead, Duquesne, McKeesport, and Clairton, to name a few. The city of Pittsburgh's black population declined from over 105,000 in 1970 to 94,000 during the 1990s. Nationwide, whereas nearly 33 percent of all workers found manufacturing jobs in 1960, that figure had plummeted to no more than 10 to 14 percent by 1990. Northern urban blacks bore the brunt of deindustrialization as their unemployment figures remained double those of whites and the proportion of blacks living in metropolitan poverty areas rose from nearly 33 percent in 1970 to about 50 percent by the early 1990s. At the same time, the southern and western Sunbelt emerged as new growth areas with expanding employment opportunities. Although characterized by jobs with substantially lower wages, the lack of union representation, and greater workplace inequities than those of the declining northern industrial sector, the southern economy appealed to a growing number of young workers suffering high rates of unemployment above the Mason-Dixon line.[40]

Not all reverse migrants took low-end jobs in the Sunbelt economy. Whereas the Great Migration included disproportionally large numbers of blacks with high school education or less, the late twentieth-century migration to the South included substantial numbers of young college-educated black professional and business people. In the spring of 1990, the *Wall Street Journal* carried a special story on the "reverse exodus" of middle-class blacks from ailing industrial centers in the Northeast and Midwest to booming Sunbelt cities like Atlanta, Houston, and San Antonio. Compared with the urban North, one bank executive moved to Atlanta, he said, because the city offered more opportunities to work in "revenue generating jobs" and influence "the bottom line" in corporate offices with higher ratios of blacks to whites. In Pittsburgh, Ralph Proctor, director of a major social service institution for urban youth on the city's East Side, identified racial discrimination in the context of deindustrialization as a major reason that young people left the region: "There was nothing here for them so they left because of discrimination."[41] Many of the Great Migration era migrants had maintained ongoing contact with the South of their birth, but they also determined to transform the land of their birth upon return. When Eula and her husband, Al Grant, returned to Burdy's Bend in 1979, she informed her parents that "in every stranger she'd met in New York she'd planted a bit of Burdy's Bend, and now, back in the country, it was time to instill a touch of the wider world in the people here." Within a 3-year period, Eula Grant had helped to spearhead the formation of a new tax-exempt nonprofit organization called Holding Hands. This organization expanded the range of social services available for black people in this rural area.[42]

Along with the conditions precipitating the massive movement of African Americans from North and West to South, new federal immigration policies also transformed the dynamics of late twentieth-century black population movements. In 1965, the Hart-Celler Immigration Act demolished the old ethnically and racially discriminatory quota system of immigration that favored selected northern and western European countries over the rest of the world. The new law opened the door for growing numbers of immigrants from Asia, Latin America, the Caribbean, and Africa. By the turn of the twenty-first century, African immigrants had increased to over 640,000, making up about 7 percent of the total black population. The vast majority of Africans came from Nigeria, Guinea, Ethiopia, Liberia, Sudan, Somalia, and Sierra Leone. At the same time, some 2 million blacks emigrated from former British, French, and Spanish colonies in the Caribbean. As these groups obtained

U.S. citizenship over time, they also took advantage of the nation's family-sponsored immigration policy and reinforced the flow of new people of African descent into the United States.[43]

Patterns of African and Caribbean immigration into the United States exhibited certain similarities as well as profound differences. Both groups included a mix of voluntary migrants and refugees, but migrants from the former British colonies of Jamaica, Barbados, Antigua, and others came voluntarily, while disproportionately larger numbers of blacks from Haiti, Cuba, Nicaragua, and El Salvador entered the country as refugees. Civil wars in Nigeria, Ethiopia, Rwanda, Sierra Leone, Liberia, and Sudan also precipitated an increase in refugees to the United States. Most black immigrants were able-bodied men and women ages 25 to 50, but Caribbean women outnumbered men 100:85, while African women outnumbered men 140:100. Moreover, whereas Caribbean blacks represented diverse local Creole languages as well as French, English, Spanish, and Dutch, African migrants brought experience with the tongues of European colonizers as well as their own indigenous ethnic and nationality group languages. These included, for example, the languages of the Igbos, Yorubas, and Hausas of Nigeria, and the Ewe, Fante, and Akan of Ghana.[44]

Partly because U.S. immigration law privileged the admission of well-educated professional immigrants over general laborers, the late twentieth and early twenty-first century immigration attracted more African people from middle-class and elite backgrounds than earlier immigration streams. As such, these immigrants, as historian Ira Berlin notes, "arrived with knowledge, money, and connections." In his introduction to a revealing collection of essays on the African diaspora, Africanist Isidore Okpewho underscored the class dimension of the recent African migration to the United States. Before moving to the United States, Okpewho had taught at the University of Ibadan, where he and his wife started their family. He eventually moved his family to the United States, where he teaches on the faculty of a major northeastern university. Not only did his children gain access to an excellent education in the United States, but they soon embarked on their own professional careers.[45]

For their part, refugees not only entered the country with few material resources at their disposal but also often struggled to overcome more violent and disruptive events that had rendered them homeless in their own countries. Thousands of late twentieth-century Ethiopian, Igbo Nigerian, Somalian, Liberian, and Sudanese immigrants to the United States recall stories of suffering and despair that preceded their forced migration from their homelands. One of the most widely broadcast recent tales of forced migration involves the experiences of young male children, dubbed the "Lost Boys of Sudan." Following years of attacks on the southern region of Sudan, government forces drove hundreds of thousands of people from their homes and precipitated a mass march of some 20,000 young males from their homeland to a refugee camp in Kenya. Acik Ateng Nai, one of the survivors selected for asylum in the United States, later recalled his ordeal in the Sudan as well as his early encounter with life in America. After landing in the United States, Nai spent a period of time on the federal food stamp program, supplemented by support from a Catholic charity organization. He eventually studied for his

GED and acquired a general labor job with a big box retailer as he prepared to take the next steps toward acquiring U.S. citizenship.[46]

The new immigration from Africa and the Caribbean posed fundamental issues for large metropolitan black communities. In her close study of West Indian migration to New York, anthropologist Nancy Foner concludes, "For West Indian New Yorkers of African descent, being black is the 'master status' that pervades and penetrates their lives. This was true in the past and continues to be true today." In Foner's view, New York's Caribbean community suffered from the tendency of American whites to classify them as members of the existing African American community, giving little credence to their claims to cultural distinctiveness. African immigrants articulated a similar frustration with the prevailing white presumption of African identification with African Americans. When one African immigrant arrived in the United States from Togo via Europe, he soon remarked with some aggravation, "In Germany, everyone knew I was African. Here, nobody knows if I'm African or American." Under these circumstances, some black Americans resented the effort of Caribbean and African blacks to accent their distinctiveness rather than identify with the culture, politics, and aspirations of African Americans. Following a public radio broadcast regarding the meaning of the Emancipation Proclamation, historian Ira Berlin was taken aback by the response to his presentation by a group of Caribbean and African immigrants or children of immigrants—"Almost all had been born outside the United States—two in Haiti, one in Jamaica, one in Britain, and three others in Africa, two in Ghana, and one, I believe, in Somalia. Others may have been children of immigrants."[47]

The group insisted that the saga of Abraham Lincoln, the Civil War, and emancipation of enslaved black Americans was not their history. Although this group had embraced America as their country through immigration, naturalization, and even birth for some, their vision of their own history was at odds with that of most African Americans. For their part, African Americans sometimes reacted by mistreating the newcomers. As late as 2005, an article in the black *New Amsterdam News* noted that some of the city's 4400 Africans had been "routinely targeted and singled out for discrimination and abuse" by Harlem's black community. When a black woman killed an East African man in Seattle, Washington, in the summer of 2006, a group of African leaders declared, "These people [African Americans], they do not like us; that is why they kill us."[48]

While such conflicts divided African Americans from both Africans and Afro-Caribbeans, the dynamics of racial discrimination within the U.S. social order called such internal conflicts into question. In February 1999, when four New York City police officers killed an unarmed Guinean immigrant Amadou Diallo in his apartment building, the African and African American community came together to discuss their common vulnerability in a continuing highly racialized and unequal American urban social order. The killing of Diallo, an educated member of the middle class in his home country, also underscored the leveling of class as well as ethnic and nationality distinctions in the U.S. racial system. As suggested by the experiences of Isidore Okpewho and Acik Ateng Nai, immigrant communities in the United States were divided by class and status as well as by nationality and ethnic backgrounds. But Diallo's death challenged both class and ethnic boundaries among diverse people of African descent. Manthia Diawara, a New York University professor of African descent, highlighted the way Diallo's death undercut certain fundamental assumptions about difference within the shifting late twentieth-century African American community:

> "Just as my success story in America could have been his, the tragedy that had befallen him could have been mine, as a black man in America—albeit an African. Little do the Amadou Diallos of the world know that the black man in America bears the curse of Cain, and that in America they, too, are considered black men, not Fulanis, Mandigos, or Wolofs. They cut Amadou Diallo down like a black American, even though he belonged to the Fulani tribe in his native Guinea. There is a lesson here for all of us to learn."[49]

Each era of massive black population movement disrupted established patterns of African American cultural, economic, and political life. Forced migration of Africans to the Americas not only permanently separated millions of Africans from their families and communities in the Old World, but also depopulated and transformed the West African homeland, making it a different place from the one that New World blacks departed. In varying degrees, similar processes of change marked the mass movement of blacks during the nineteenth and twentieth centuries. In each era of massive black population movement and social disruption, however, people of African descent forged bonds with each other and created new families and forms of community. These new forms of solidarity also established the foundation for the fight against slavery during the colonial and antebellum years and the struggle against Jim Crow during the late nineteenth and twentieth centuries. The African American struggle for freedom and full citizenship rights culminated in the rise of the twentieth-century Modern Black Freedom Movement. The Civil Rights and Black Power movements demolished the system of Jim Crow and established the groundwork for the rise of a more inclusive multiracial nation, best symbolized by the election of Barack H. Obama as the first U.S. president of African descent.[50]

By the opening years of the twenty-first century, a variety of local, national, and global forces had set in motion several new trends in black migration history. Contemporary scholars are hard at work forging new research agendas to bring these trends and their broader implications to light.[51] While existing research illuminates African American return migration to the small town and rural South, we know far less about late twentieth-century black migration (not all returnees) to large metropolitan regions of the South, including the major Sunbelt cities. Scholars are giving increasing attention to the diverse waves of post Hart-Celler immigration of Caribbean and African immigrants into the United States, but work on the second generation remains underdeveloped. There were significant contextual and substantive differences between the two periods. The first generation entered the country in the wake of the Modern Black Freedom Movement and the expanding and more liberal U.S. immigration policy; the second generation confronted a retrenchment of Civil Rights era initiatives and, more recently, the deleterious impact of 9/11 and the advent of the Patriot Act and Homeland Security measures. In addition to numerous case studies covering a wide-range of groups at different points in time, we also need new comparative research, with varied foci. Such comparative scholarship might examine the same group for different cities; multiple groups within the same city; or particular dimensions of the migration experience—work, residence, community-building, political engagement—across two or more generations. Among other possible subjects, research along these distinct but overlapping topics will broaden and deepen our understanding of black migration in historical perspective.

NOTES

1. Ira Berlin, *The Making of African America: The Four Great Migrations* (New York: Viking, 2010); Peter M. Rutkoff and William Scott, *Fly Away: The Great African American Cultural Migrations* (Baltimore: John Hopkins University Press, 2010); James N. Gregory, *The Southern Diaspora: How the Great Migrations of Black and White Southerners Transformed America* (Chapel Hill: University of North Carolina Press, 2005); David M. Johnson and Rex R. Campbell, *Black Migration in America: A Social Demographic History* (Durham: Duke University Press, 1981).

2. William D. Phillips, Jr., *Slavery from Roman Times to the Early Transatlantic Trade* (Minneapolis: University of Minnesota Press, 1985), p. 87; Catherine Coquery-Vidrovitch (translated from French by Mary Baker), *The History of African Cities South of the Sahara: From the Origins to Colonization* (Princeton, NJ: Marcus Weiner Publishers, 2008), pp. 100–126.

3. John Thornton, *Africa and Africans in the Making of the Atlantic World, 1400–1800* (New York: Cambridge University Press, 1992, 1998, 2008), pp. 43–71; Alexander X. Byrd, *Captive and Voyagers: Black Migrants Across the Eighteenth Century British Atlantic World* (Baton Rouge: Louisiana State University Press, 2008), pp. 2–3, 14–15; Marcus Rediker, *The Slave Ship: A Human History* (New York: Viking, Penguin Group (USA) Inc., 2007), pp. 5, 115, 347.

4. Ira Berlin, *Many Thousands Gone: The First Two Centuries of Slavery in North America* (Cambridge, MA: The Belknap Press of Harvard University Press, 1998), pp. 1–28; Michael L. Coniff and Thomas J. Davis, *Africans in the Americas: A History of the Black Diaspora* (New York: St. Martins Press, 1994), pp. 29–30, 46–69; David Eltis, *The Rise of African Slavery in the Americas* (Cambridge, United Kingdom: Cambridge University Press, 2000), pp. 29–84; A. Leon Higginbotham, Jr., *In the Matter of Color: Race and the American Legal Process, the Colonial Period* (New York: Oxford University Press, 1978), pp. 26–47, 61–68; Horton and Horton, *In Hope of Liberty*, pp. 10–11; Edmund S. Morgan, *American Slavery, American Freedom: The Ordeal of Colonial Virginia* (New York: Norton and Company, 1975), pp. 94–95, 295–315.

5. Leslie M. Harris, *In the Shadow of the Plantation: African Americans in New York City, 1626–1863* (Chicago: University of Chicago Press, 2003); James Oliver Horton and Lois E. Horton, *In Hope of Liberty: Culture, Community, and Protest Among Northern Free Blacks, 1700–1860* (New York: Oxford University Press, 1997), pp. 4–7, 10; Gary B. Nash, *Forging Freedom: The Formation of Philadelphia's Black Community 1720–1840*

(Cambridge: Harvard University Press, 1988), pp. 11–12,14–15; Lawrence H. Larsen, *The Urban South: A History* (Lexington: The University Press of Kentucky, 1990), p. 9; Betty Wood, *Slavery in Colonial Georgia, 1730–1775* (Athens: University of Georgia Press, 1984) pp. 61–63, 75, 83–85, 220, n. 21; Peter H. Wood, *Black Majority: Negroes in Colonial South Carolina From 1670 Through the Stono Rebellion* (New York: W.W. Norton & Company, 1974), pp. 142–166.

6. Philip S. Foner and Ronald L. Lewis, ed., *The Black Worker to 1869, Volume 1* (Philadelphia: Temple University Press, 1978), p. 9.

7. Peter Kolchin, *American Slavery, 1619–1877* (New York: Hill and Wang, 1993), pp. 96–139; James Oakes, *Slavery and Freedom: An Interpretation of the Old South* (New York: Alfred A. Knopf, 1990), pp. 22–24, 143–144; Harold D. Woodman, *Slavery and the Southern Economy: Sources and Readings* (New York: Harcourt, Brace and World, 1966), 1–18, 66–94.

8. Michael Tadman, *Speculators and Slaves: Masters, Traders, and Slaves in the Old South* (Madison: University of Wisconsin Press, 1989), pp. 3–25.

9. "Narrative of the Life of Henry Bibb: An American Slave," in Gilbert Osofsky, ed., *Puttin' On Old Massa* (New York: Harper and Row Publishers, 1969), pp. 112–113.

10. Tadman, *Speculators and Slaves*, p. 81.

11. Tadman, *Speculators and Slaves*, pp. 2–25, quotes, 73, 77; Michael A. Gomez, *Exchanging Our Country Marks: The Transformation of African Identities in the Colonial and Antebellum South* (Chapel Hill: University of North Carolina Press, 1998), pp. 22–27, 175.

12. Allan Kulikoff, "Uprooted Peoples: Black Migrants in the Age of the American Revolution, 1790–1820," in Berlin and Hoffman, ed., *Slavery and Freedom in the Age of the American Revolution*, p. 146; Sylviane Anna Diouf, *Dreams of Africa in Alabama: The Slave Ship Clotilda and the Story of the Last Africans Brought to America* (New York: Oxford University Press, 2007); Tadman, *Speculators and Slaves:*, pp. 2–25; Gomez, *Exchanging Our Country Marks*, pp. 20–21, 175; Nathalie Dessens, *From Saint—Domingue to New Orleans: Migration and Influences* (Gainesville: University of Florida Press, 2007), pp. 11–45.

13. Ira Berlin, *Slaves Without Masters: The Free Negro in the Antebellum South* (New York: Free Press, 1974), pp. 29–35, 46–47, 136–137, 176–178; Leon Litwack, *North of Slavery: The Negro in the Free States, 1790–1860* (Chicago: University of Chicago Press, 1961), pp. 7–11; Leonard P. Curry, *The Free Black in Urban America, 1800–1850* (Chicago: University of Chicago Press, 1981), 1–14, 245–257; Claudia D. Goldin, *Urban Slavery in the American South, 1820–1860* (Chicago: University of Chicago Press, 1976), pp. 12, 51–55; Lawrence H. Larsen, *The Urban South: A History* (Lexington: The University Press of Kentucky, 1990), pp. 24–25; Richard Wade, *Slavery in Cities: The South, 1820–1860* (New York: Oxford, 1964), pp. 327–328; Joe William Trotter, Jr., *River Jordan: African Americans Urban Life in the Ohio Valley* (Lexington, KY: University Press of Kentucky, 1998), pp. 24–51.

14. Kate Masur, *An Example for All the Land: Emancipation and the Struggle Over Equality in Washington, D.C.* (Chapel Hill: University of North Carolina Press, 2010), pp. 75–76; Herbert G. Gutman, *The Black Family in Slavery and Freedom, 1750–1925* (New York: Pantheon Books, 1976), pp. 364–365; Leon F. Litwack, *Been in the Storm So Long: The Aftermath of Slavery* (New York: Vintage Books, 1979), p. 232.

15. Elizabeth Clark-Lewis, *Living In, Living Out: African American Domestics in Washington, D.C., 1910–1940* (Washington, D.C.: Smithsonian Institution Press, 1994), pp. 1–7. This pattern of domestic service for black women urbanites would only slowly breakdown in the years after World War II, see Lisa Krissoff Bochm, *Making a Way out of No Way: African American Women and the Second Great Migration* (Jackson: University of Mississippi Press, 2009).

16. See Joe William Trotter, Jr., ed., *The Great Migration in Historical Perspective: New Dimensions of Race, Class, and Gender* (Bloomington: Indiana University Press, 1991), pp. 112–113 and 8–9; Carter G. Woodson, *A Century of Negro Migration* (1918; reprt. New York: Russell and Russell, 1969), pp. 2–7.

17. Gregory, *The Southern Diaspora*, pp. 14–15; Johnson and Campbell, *Black migration in America*, pp. 44–70; Trotter, Jr., ed., *The Great Migration in Historical Perspective*, pp. 1–21.

18. Isabelle Wilkerson, *The Warmth of Other Suns: The Epic Story of America's Great Migration* (New York: Random House, 2010), pp. 9–10.

19. Johnson and Campbell, *Black Migration in America*, pp. 71–72.

20. Berlin, *The Making of African America*, p. 152–200; Wilkerson, *The Warmth of Other Suns*, pp. 8–15; Rutkoff and Scott, *The Great African American Migration*, pp. 11–14; Gregory, *The Southern Diaspora*, pp. 11–41; Johnson and Campbell, *Black Migration in America*, pp. 71–113, 132, 158.

21. James R. Grossman, *Land of Hope: Chicago, Black Southerners, and the Great Migration* (Chicago: The University of Chicago Press, 1989), pp. 187–199; Allan Spear, *Black Chicago: The Making of a Negro Ghetto, 1890–1920* (Chicago: The University of Chicago Press, 1967), pp. 151–152d; Peter Gottlieb, *Making Their Own Way: Southern Blacks' Migration to Pittsburgh, 1916–30* (Urbana: University of Illinois Press, 1987), pp. 90–93; Joe William Trotter, Jr., *The African American Experience* (Boston: Houghton Mifflin Company, 2001), p. 385.

22. Walter Licht, *Getting Work: Philadelphia, 1840–1950* (Cambridge: Harvard University Press, 1992), pp. 46–47; Theodore Kornwiebel, Jr., *Railroads in the African American Experience: A Photo Journey* (Baltimore: The Johns Hopkins University Press, 2010), pp. 52–53; Philip Scranton and Walter Licht, *Work Sights: Industrial Philadelphia, 1890–1950* (Philadelphia: Temple University Press 1986), pp. 203–204, 244–246; Lester Rubin, *The Negro in the Shipbuilding Industry* (Philadelphia: University of Pennsylvania Wharton School of Finance and Commerce, Report No. 17, 1970), p. 46.

23. Dennis C. Dickerson, *Out of the Crucible: Black Steelworkers in Western Pennsylvania, 1875–1980* (New York: State University of New York Press, 1986), pp. 21–22, p. 45; Gottlieb, *Making Their Own Way*, pp. 90–93; John Hinshaw, *Steel and Steelworkers: Race and Class Struggle in Twentieth Century Pittsburgh* (Albany: State University Press of New York, 2002), pp. 35–38; Joe William Trotter, Jr., "Reflections on the Great Migration to Western Pennsylvania," *Pittsburgh History* (Winter 1995/96), pp. 153–158.

24. Roger Horowitz, *"Negro and White, United and Fight!": A Social History of Industrial Unionism in Meatpacking, 1930–80* (Urbana: University of Illinois Press, 1999), pp. 87–88; Walter A. Fogel, *The Negro in the Meat Industry* (Philadelphia: University of Pennsylvania Wharton School of Finance and Commerce, Report No.12, 1970), pp. 46–47; Rick Halpern, *Down on the Killing Floor: Black and White Workers in Chicago's Packinghouses, 1904–54* (Urbana: University of Illinois Press, 1997), pp. 47–48; Rick Halpern and R. Horowitz, *Meatpackers: An Oral History of Black Packinghouse Workers and Their Struggle for Racial and Economic Equality* (New York: Monthly Review Press, 1999), pp. 3–10; Grossman, *Land of Hope*, pp. 187–199; Spear, *Black Chicago*, pp. 151–152.

25. Richard Walter Thomas, *Life for Us Is What We Make It: Building Black Community in Detroit, 1915–1945* (Bloomington: Indiana University Press, 1992), pp. 29–30; August Meier and Elliot Rudwick, *Black Detroit and the Rise of the UAW* (New York: Oxford University Press, 1979), pp. 15–16; Victoria W. Wolcott, *Remaking Respectability: African American*

Women in Interwar Detroit (Chapel Hill: University of North Carolina Press, 2001), pp. 78–81.

26. Jacqueline Jones, *Labor of Love, Labor of Sorrow: Black Women, Work and the Family from Slavery to Freedom* (New York: Basic Books, 1985), pp. 166–180; Sadie Tanner Mossell Alexander, "Negro Women in Our Economic Life," *Opportunity* 8 (July 1930), pp. 201–203, cited in Bevely Guy-Sheftal, *Words of Fire: An Anthology of African American Feminist Thought* (New York: New Press, 1995), pp. 97–98, online version, consulted January 27, 2011; Kusmer, *A Ghetto Takes Shape*, pp. 74, 200–201; Phillips, *AlabamaNorth*, pp. 72, 75–76; Spear, *Black Chicago*, pp. 151–158; Elaine G. Wrong, *The Negro in the Apparel Industry*, (Philadelphia: University of Pennsylvania, Wharton School, Report. No. 31), pp. 31–32.

27. Gregory, *The Southern Diaspora*, pp. 14–17, 32, 143–146; George A. Davis and Fred O. Donaldson, *Blacks in the United States: A Geographic Perspective* (Boston: Houghton Mifflin, 1975), p. 49; Berlin, *The Making of African America*, pp. 155–156; Johnson and Campbell, *Black Migration in America*, pp. 106, 115–117, 127–132. 155–162; Wilkerson, *The Warmth of Other Suns*, pp. 217–218; Irma Watkins-Owens, *Blood Relations: Caribbean Immigrants and the Harlem Community, 1900–1930* (Bloomington: Indiana University Press, 1996), pp. 11–29; Nancy Foner, ed., *Islands in the City: West Indian Migration to New York* (Berkeley: University of California Press, 2001), pp. 3–10.

28. Gregory, *The Southern Diaspora*, pp. 14–17, 32, 143–146; Davis and Donaldson, *Blacks in the United States*, p. 49; Berlin, *The Making of African America*, pp. 155–156; Johnson and Campbell, *Black Migration in America*, pp. 106, 115–117, 127–132, 143–146, 155–162; Wilkerson, *The Warmth of Other Suns*, pp. 217–218, 356–358, 367, 441–444; Watkins-Owens, *Blood Relations*, pp. 11–29; Foner, ed., *Islands in the City*, pp. 3–10; Gunnar Myrdal, *An American Dilemma: The Negro Problem and Modern Democracy* (New York: Pantheon Books, Div. of Random House, 1962), pp. 186–187; Nicholas Lemaan, *The Promised Land: The Great Migration and How it Changed America* (New York: Vintage Books, 1992), pp. 52–53.

29. Raymond Wolters, *Negroes and the Great Depression: The Problems of Economic Recovery* (Westport: Greenwood Publishing Corporation, 1970), pp. 58–60; Johnson and Campbell, *Black Migration in America*, pp. 98–99, 140–142; Gregory, *The Southern Diaspora*, p. 33; Theodore Rosengarten, *All God's Dangers: The Life of Nate Shaw* (Chicago: University of Chicago Press, 1974), p. 517.

30. Robert Armstead, as told to S. L. Gardner, *Black Days, Black Dust: The Memoirs of an African American Coal Miner* (Knoxville: The University of Tennessee Press, 2002), pp. 64–65; Ronald Lewis, *Black Coal Miners in America: Race, Class, and Community Conflict, 1780–1980* (Lexington: University of Kentucky Press, 1987), pp. 167–193; Keith Dix, *What's a Coal Miner to Do?: The Mechanization of Coal Mining* (Pittsburgh, PA: University of Pittsburgh Press, 1988).

31. Wilkerson, *The Warmth of Other Suns*, pp. 534–535; Rosengarten, *All God's Dangers*, p. 488.

32. Armstead, as told to Gardner, *Black Days, Black Dust*, pp. 98–99.

33. Otis Trotter, *From Vallscreek to Highland Creek: A Memoir of Medicine, Family Struggle and Race* (ms. in author's possession, 2010), p. 32.

34. Karl E. Taeuber and Alma F. Taeuber, *Negroes in Cities: Residential Segregation and Neighborhood Change* (Chicago: Aldine Publishing Company, 1965), p. 119; Luther Adams, *Way Up North in Louisville: African American Migration in the Urban South, 1930–1970* (Chapel Hill: University of North Carolina Press, 2010), pp. 38–40.

35. Wilkerson, *Warmth of Other Suns*, pp. 534–535; Joe W. Trotter and Jared N. Day, *Race and Renaissance: African Americans in Pittsburgh Since World War II* (Pittsburgh: University of Pittsburgh Press, 2010), p. 46.

36. Wilkerson, *The Warmth of Other Suns*, pp. 172–173, 186–189, 192.
37. Ibid., pp. 220–221, 351–356.
38. Carol Stack, *Call to Home: African Americans Reclaim the Rural South* (New York: Basic Books, 1996), pp. xii–xiv, 6–8; Gregory, *The Southern Diaspora*, pp. 321–322.
39. Carol Stack, *Call to Home: African Americans Reclaim the Rural South* (New York: Basic Books, 1996), pp. xii–xiv, 6–8; Gregory, *The Southern Diaspora*, pp. 321–322.
40. Joe W. Trotter and Jared N. Day, *Race and Renaissance: African Americans in Pittsburgh Since World War II* (Pittsburgh: University of Pittsburgh Press, 2010), pp. 141–146; James S. Hirsch and Suzanne Alexander, "Reverse Exodus: Middle Class Blacks Quit Northern Cities and Settle in the South," *Wall Street Journal*, May 22, 1990; Trotter, *The African American Experience*, pp. 604–608.
41. Trotter and Day, *Race and Renaissance*, pp. 141–146; Hirsch and Alexander, "Reverse Exodus: Middle Class Blacks Quit Northern Cities and Settle in the South," *Wall Street Journal*, May 22, 1990; Trotter, *The African American Experience*, pp. 604–608.
42. Stack, *Call to Home*, pp. xii–xiv, 6–8, 140–141; Gregory, *The Southern Diaspora*, pp. 321–322.
43. Paul Spickard, *Almost All Aliens: Immigration, Race, and Colonialism in American History and Identity* (New York: Routledge, 2007), pp. 382–385; Berlin, *The Making of African America*, pp. 207–208; Nancy Foner and George M. Fredrickson, ed., *Not Just Black and White: Historical and Contemporary Perspectives on Immigration, Race, and Ethnicity in the United States* (New York: Russell Sage Foundation, 2004), pp. 1–19; Dennis Wepman, *American Experience: Immigration* (2002; reprt. New York: Facts on File, 2008), pp. 308–317, 336–351.
44. Berlin, *The Making of African America*, pp. 206–207.
45. Isidore Okpewho and Nkiru Nzegwu, ed., *The New African Diaspora* (Bloomington: Indiana University Press, 2009), pp. 25–26; Spickard, *Almost All Aliens*, pp. 382–384; Berlin, *The Making of African America*, pp. 210–211.
46. Spickard, *Almost All Aliens*, pp. 382–384.
47. Foner, *Islands in the City*, pp. 10–11; Spickard, *Almost All Aliens*, p. 385; Berlin, *The Making of African America*, pp. 1–2.
48. Berlin, *The Making of African America*, pp. 1–2, 222–223.
49. Spickard, *Almost All Aliens*, pp. 385–386.
50. Peniel Joseph, *Dark Days, Bright Nights: From Black Power to Barack Obama* (New York: Basic Civitas Books, Perseus Books Group, 2010).
51. Foner, *Islands in the City*, pp. 16–20; Amadu Jacky Kaba, "Africa's Migration Brain Drain: Factors Contributing to the Mass Emigration of Africa's Elite to the West," in Okpewho and Nzegwu, ed., *The New African Diaspora*, 109–123; Foner and Fredrickson, ed., *Not Just Black and White*, pp. 1–19; Stack, *Call to Home*, pp. xii–xix, 6–8; Gregory, *The Southern Diaspora*, pp. 1–41.

BIBLIOGRAPHY

Berlin, Ira. *Slaves Without Masters: The Free Negro in the Antebellum South* (New York: Free Press, 1974).
Berlin, Ira. *The Making of African America: The Four Great Migrations* (New York: Viking, 2010).
Boehm, Lisa Krissoff. *Making a Way Out of No Way: African American Women and the Second Great Migration* (Jackson: University of Mississippi Press, 2009).

Byrd, Alexander X. *Captive and Voyagers: Black Migrants Across the Eighteenth Century British Atlantic World* (Baton Rouge: Louisiana State University Press, 2008).

Clark-Lewis, Elizabeth. *Living In, Living Out: African American Domestics in Washington, D.C., 1910–1940* (Washington, D.C.: Smithsonian Institution Press, 1994).

Foner, Nancy, ed., *Islands in the City: West Indian Migration to New York* (Berkeley: University of California Press, 2001).

Foner, Nancy and George M. Fredrickson, ed., *Not Just Black and White: Historical and Contemporary Perspectives on Immigration, Race, and Ethnicity in the United States* (New York: Russell Sage Foundation, 2004).

Gregory, James N. *The Southern Diaspora: How the Great Migrations of Black and White Southerners Transformed America* (Chapel Hill: University of North Carolina Press, 2005).

Harris, Leslie M. *In the Shadow of the Plantation: African Americans in New York City, 1626–1863* (Chicago: University of Chicago Press, 2003).

Horton, James Oliver and Lois E. Horton, *In Hope of Liberty: Culture, Community, and Protest Among Northern Free Blacks, 1700–1860* (New York: Oxford University Press, 1997).

Johnson, David M. and Rex R. Campbell, *Black Migration in America: A Social Demographic History* (Durham: Duke University Press, 1981).

Nash, Gary B. *Forging Freedom: The Formation of Philadelphia's Black Community 1720–1840* (Cambridge: Harvard University Press, 1988).

Okpewho, Isidore and Nkiru Nzegwu, eds., *The New African Diaspora* (Bloomington: Indiana University Press, 2009).

Rediker, Marcus. *The Slave Ship: A Human History* (New York: Viking, Penguin Group [USA] Inc., 2007).

Rutkoff. Peter M. and William Scott, *Fly Away: The Great African American Cultural Migrations* (Baltimore: John Hopkins University Press, 2010).

Spickard, Paul. *Almost All Aliens: Immigration, Race, and Colonialism in American History and Identity* (New York: Routledge, 2007).

Stack, Carol. *Call to Home: African Americans Reclaim the Rural South* (New York: Basic Books, 1996).

Tadman, Michael. *Speculators and Slaves: Masters, Traders, and Slaves in the Old South* (Madison: University of Wisconsin Press, 1989).

Thornton, John. *Africa and Africans in the Making of the Atlantic World, 1400–1800* (New York: Cambridge University Press, 1992, 1998, 2008).

Trotter, Joe William, Jr. ed., *The Great Migration in Historical Perspective: New Dimensions of Race, Class, and Gender* (Bloomington: Indiana University Press, 1991).

Watkins-Owens, Irma. *Blood Relations: Caribbean Immigrants and the Harlem Community, 1900–1930* (Bloomington: Indiana University Press, 1996).

Wilkerson, Isabelle. *The Warmth of Other Suns: The Epic Story of America's Great Migration* (New York: Random House, 2010).

Wood, Peter H. *Black Majority: Negroes in Colonial South Carolina From 1670 Through the Stono Rebellion* (New York: W.W. Norton & Company, 1974)

Woodson, Carter G. *A Century of Negro Migration* (1918; reprinted New York: Russell and Russell, 1969).

CHAPTER 6

....

EMANCIPATION AND EXPLOITATION IN IMMIGRANT WOMEN'S LIVES

....

DONNA R. GABACCIA

BECAUSE the United States celebrates itself as a beacon of freedom and liberty, it would indeed be surprising if emancipation was not a central theme in histories of immigrant women. Still, as the origins of America's immigrants have changed, so has the assumption that migration to the United States necessarily offers emancipatory opportunities to immigrants in general or to women immigrants in particular. Studies of Asian, Caribbean, and Latin American migrants more often document how racial ideologies have forced migrant men and women into the worst jobs and living conditions while denying them opportunities for justice, welfare, and self-expression that are available to white Americans or immigrants from Europe.[1] Exploitation and discrimination on the basis of race are as central to histories of American immigrant women as empowerment and agency.

This essay briefly surveys the central and fundamental tension between agency and inequality in the lives of American immigrant women from the eighteenth century to the present. It focuses exclusively on the foreign-born, with occasional references to immigrants' American-born children. Immigrants are defined inclusively as foreigners who enter North America to live or work for a year or longer, regardless of motivations, degree of choice, or intention to settle. Popular discourse increasingly reserves the label immigrant for foreigners who migrate voluntarily and permanently in search of work. But it is not obvious that immigrant children or even all adult, married women immigrated voluntarily or that they were motivated by dreams of work; nor was this true of refugees or labor migrants seeking work before a return to their homelands. Today, thousands of international students enter the United States with no initial intention to settle. A broad definition of "immigrant" allows readers to consider the many possible balances of exploitation and emancipation in female lives.

No other country in the world so prides itself for offering opportunities to immigrants as the United States. Modernity, economic opportunity and liberty constitute the central features of the so-called immigrant paradigm of American history, expressed in the metaphor of a welcoming "nation of immigrants."[2] A gendered perspective seems implicit in that paradigm: one of the defining characteristics of American modernity has been its elevation of the status of women. Since the nineteenth century, Americans have especially defined their gender ideals as "modern"—unlike the "traditional" patriarchy in foreign lands.[3] In the most recent version of this contrast, immigration releases women from male domination through wage-earning, exposure to American individualism, access to education and civil rights, and increased levels of participation in public life.

Whether in the eighteenth century or today, both emancipation and exploitation have been gendered and are the product of the gendered exercise of power by foreign- and native-born men and women. Immigrants' frequent resistance to the Americanization of gender relations does not reproduce older forms of patriarchy but rather creates new practices that are reactions to American gender prescriptions. Those reactions can enhance immigrant women's agency while simultaneously making them appear to Americans as less modern or as more dominated by men than American women. Americans' attention to immigrant women's exploitation by immigrant men in turn makes American forms of gender inequality almost invisible.

COLONIAL NORTH AMERICA AND THE NEW AMERICAN REPUBLIC, 1565–1820

Although Europeans and Africans traveled long distances to settle in colonial North America and both groups worked hard after arrival, relatively few traveled voluntarily or to seek work. Most Africans were slaves; the largest groups of Europeans were either religious refugees or indentured servants who signed away their liberty to seek work. Only with much imagination and denial can one view their migrations as emancipatory.

Had they been disposed to adopt native customs (which they were not), European women might have achieved increased agency, as some of the narratives of "white Indians" (Europeans who adopted Indian culture) suggest.[4] European immigrants instead transplanted many of their more hierarchical forms of patriarchy, in which power emanated ultimately from male monarchs or from a God imagined as male. Fatherhood, ownership of land and other forms of wealth, the right to sign contracts, and religious and political leadership produced power for males and excluded almost all females, all children and servants (regardless of sex), and, of course, slaves from the exercise of power. For the British, Germans, French, and Spanish, patriarchy often literally meant the rule of fathers; married women were absorbed juridically by their husbands under the principle of coverture.[5] Among Pilgrim refugees, women were equal to men in the eyes of God, but on earth, cheerful subordination of women, children, and servants to male authority was expected, if not always realized.[6] As Christians, most Europeans feared the negative example of the sinful Eve, fueling the infamous witch persecutions in Europe and colonial New England.[7] Parents usually arranged the marriages of young women, and by the eighteenth century American women—whether foreign- or native-born—were known in Europe for their high fertility and large families.[8] Older women, widows, and the wives of wealthy men could at times head households, own and manage property, command the labor and respect of men, and even—as did Eliza Lucas Pinckney in South Carolina—engage in business or intellectual pursuits.[9] But for most migrant females from Europe, life in America brought only a continuation of hard physical labor within male-headed households.

And, of course, there was no emancipation for African slaves. Given their large numbers in places such as coastal Carolina and Georgia, Africans managed to reproduce some familiar customs and, tellingly, many of these were related to female work, such as cooking, agricultural techniques, and basket-making.[10] As slaves, Africans could not easily reproduce other common West African customs such as female responsibility for agricultural work, house building, and marketing. European slave owners believed initially that men made the best fieldworkers. Gender mattered even in slave communities, however. Relatively more females worked in and around the homes of their owners; in slave cabins, the care of children might be shared but was nevertheless women's work.[11] Slave fathers were not patriarchs, and marriage between slaves had no legal foundation: owners could and did separate mothers and children and husbands and wives.[12]

At most, small numbers of European women and even smaller numbers of African slave women could translate their own relative scarcity—for males outnumbered females as slaves[13] and as servants—into more comfortable material arrangements through liaisons with more powerful white men. (Only among redemptioners and religious refugees in New England, who migrated in family groups, were sex ratios relatively balanced.[14]) The imbalance of males and females exerted tremendous sexual pressure on females once they reached puberty, and the vulnerability of female slaves and European servants to unwanted male sexual attentions increased with migration, especially to the southern colonies. Young slaves and servants were particularly vulnerable to rape and abuse; servants who became pregnant during their indenture had to serve extra years.[15] Almost all European women ultimately married, at younger ages than in Europe, while American slaves became the only self-reproducing slave population in the Americas.[16]

After 1776, a newly independent American government guaranteed easier naturalization for European migrants and prohibited the slave trade. These changes generated few new liberties for immigrant females. Enslaved women remained slaves, and the practice of indentured servitude waned only slowly over the next half century. American republicanism did include a critique of patriarchy, or at least of rule by property-owning fathers: by the 1830s, all adult American males enjoyed the right to vote. However, for married females, as for children, citizenship remained derivative; it was a father's or husband's prerogative to decide if and when to acquire American citizenship, just as it was a male prerogative to vote and to represent the interests of a unified family in the political realm. [17] At most, women born in Europe and recently arrived might hope to earn respect as "republican mothers" by raising children who valued American independence and the rights of adult white man. [18] Overall, coercion and submission to male authority, not emancipation, seem the main theme of colonial era migrations.

Immigrant Women as Rural Settlers, 1820–1890

Both American gender ideologies and the scale and origins of immigration to the United States changed dramatically after 1820. An elaborate cult of domesticity (sometimes also called the cult of true womanhood) now portrayed Anglo-American women as occupying an exalted status as managers of a separate, domestic sphere. There, they nurtured superior cultural values (e.g., love and cooperation) while male family members spent their days in the competitive, harsh, and grubby public world of wage work and politics.[19] By 1890, when the U.S. Census Bureau proclaimed the end of the frontier, millions of girls and women from Great Britain, Ireland, German-speaking Central Europe, and Scandinavia had encountered this cult of domesticity in rural areas and small towns, especially in the northeast, Midwest, and Pacific Coast. So long as American womanhood was defined through domesticity, any new liberties to be gained by females through migration to the United States were tied mainly to marriage, not individual autonomy.

These liberties are, however, worth enumerating. For one, coercion no longer drove European migration in North America or placed new arrivals directly under the rule of a wealthier male stranger or master. Male and female migrants increasingly chose to travel to rural areas, where they could usually work for themselves, within families, as independent farmers or operators of small businesses. Europeans' new willingness to migrate originated in complex changes that affected large numbers of young people in Europe. The spread of commercial agriculture and emerging industries during a period of rapid population growth meant that many adolescents in peasant and artisanal households could no longer be gainfully employed in family work groups. They were "freed" to work for wages outside their families but that freedom carried with it the constant threat of downward mobility, loss of social status, and poverty.[20] Without access to an inheritance or, even, in some parts of Germany, the right to marry without property, migration to nearby cities, factories, and America became attractive and competing options, especially for those concerned about the education of their future children.[21]

The anticipation of migration and life in the United States also allowed young men and women greater agency in choosing their marriage partners. Settler migrations were more gender balanced—hovering around 40 percent—than the colonial era migrations. Since Western territories in America also attracted disproportionate numbers of males, the United States became known in Europe as a country where women could easily find and choose a spouse for themselves, luring unmarried young women to join friends or family members in America.[22]

Still, most adult women and almost all preadolescent children who migrated to rural areas moved within family groups or as parts of migratory "chains," following their previously departed fathers and husbands. And, with the exception of the Irish, those who arrived single, also generally married soon after arrival. Forming a family was itself a major incentive to migrate, as was the recreation of at least some elements of a disappearing rural European way of life. In America, fathers again organized and worked with family work groups; the home and the workplace were not separate for most immigrant farmers or in most immigrant small businesses. Wives and children provided much unpaid labor in both sites: German, Dutch, and many Scandinavian daughters and wives routinely worked in the barn and fields. [23] That work was no longer routine for American farm wives and daughters influenced by the cult of domesticity, with the result that Americans perceived immigrant women working in the fields as evidence of their exploitation by fathers and husbands.

Immigrants were also less involved in the Protestant Second Great Awakening, which contributed to the American cult of domesticity by substituting new stereotypes of morally pure and spiritual females, resistant to the temptations of sex and alcohol, for older images of female temptresses or "Eves."[24] Women's supposedly greater spiritual commitments allowed Protestant American women to carve out new forms of public activism within their religious communities. Without the state support for religious institutions, which had been common in Europe, immigrant Protestant and Jewish women soon emulated American Protestant women, especially in becoming the main fund-raisers for their religious communities. Immigrant and American women, whether in the countryside or in the city, formed sewing, self-help, and missionary societies that hosted annual fund-raising bazaars.[25] In urban settings, female-financed and female-staffed homes for aging immigrants also enhanced female opportunities for a kind of public leadership that even Americans deemed appropriate.[26]

Among German and Irish Catholics, transatlantic migration also encouraged both the rapid expansion and transformation of Catholic sisterhoods from groups of cloistered women devoted mainly to prayer into dynamic agents of community service. Celibate nuns could migrate as parts of sisterhoods to immigrant communities where they taught the young and cared for the sick and old.[27] Long before the first generation of college-educated American women resisted the "family claim" (as Jane Addams would later call it) to develop professional service careers as unmarried women, Catholic women in sisterhoods became leaders, managers, and staff in immigrant Catholic hospitals, parochial schools, and even women's colleges.[28] They fulfilled Catholic expectations of female self-sacrifice and service, rejected American domesticity, lived in all-female groups, and prospered despite remaining unmarried. As with Protestant ministries and the Jewish rabbinate, however, the Catholic priesthood remained closed to women.

American Protestants nevertheless perceived Catholic nuns as symbols of the backwardness of an alien and oppressive religion. A prurient genre of Anglo-American anti-Catholic literature even portrayed cloistered sisters—an increasingly rare type in the

United States—as sexually enslaved by lascivious and vicious male priests. One of the most violent xenophobic attacks on foreigners in nineteenth-century America was the 1836 burning of a Catholic convent and school in Charlestown, Massachusetts; its male attackers insisted the convent lured American women into servitude.[29]

Nor were women in the fields and Catholic sisterhoods the only cases where Americans perceived immigrant women as vulnerable to immoral immigrant men. In rural Ireland, young men and women had enjoyed an easy camaraderie, dancing and consuming alcohol beverages without producing high rates of premarital pregnancy or social stigma. Americans were as shocked to note such sociability as they were to observe entire German families drinking together on Sundays. Distrust worked in both directions: immigrant men pointed to the supposedly leisurely domestic lives of "lazy" American women and warned their daughters against such indolent role models. Some immigrant men saw the emergence of an American feminist movement demanding property and other civil rights, including the suffrage, as further evidence that America was an unnatural country where women ruled and men worked "like slaves" to support idle females. [30] With female behavior subject to such different interpretations, immigrant women's lives and loyalties remained under close scrutiny by both Americans and immigrant men. Immigrant women's small, new liberties must be balanced against the contradictory pressures such gendered scrutiny imposed.

WOMEN AND THE PROLETARIAN MASS MIGRATIONS, 1820–1924

Nor was such scrutiny limited to rural areas. Both at the borders of the United States and in their lives as urban dwellers and wage workers, immigrant women faced obstacles to acceptance from both American gender ideologies and the gendered dictates of scientific racism. Again, American assumptions about gender and race worked to limit the emancipatory consequences of the small, new liberties that females enjoyed as migrants. Female wage-earning could not guarantee female autonomy, although it did underwrite improved standards of living for immigrant families. And even when immigrant women embraced urban domesticity and motherhood, as most expected to do, they set off alarm bells for nativists.

Despite racist American assumptions to the contrary, the immigrants who traveled to the United States in search of waged work did not differ dramatically from those who settled in rural America. They, too, came from societies in transition, affected by the same forces that produced migrations to rural America; often, however, they could mobilize fewer resources than the migrants who traveled to the West.[31] By the latter decades of the nineteenth century, societies in transition included southern and eastern Europe, Mexico, China, Japan, and Korea, triggering racist fears and nativist demands for immigration restriction. As costs of international travel declined and the American frontier "closed," young people in these changing societies devised new strategies for migration. The industrializing American economy generated a highly gendered job market where demand for male labor in agriculture, mining, and industry outstripped demand for female wage-earners. In Mexico, China, Greece, and Italy, young people married with the common expectation that husbands and, later, growing sons would work temporarily in America—often in precarious jobs in construction or commercial agriculture—while women remained behind to grow food and raise children, sometimes within multigenerational households.[32] As a result, women's representation among immigrants fell to only 30 percent after 1890. In American cities, jobs for women were more plentiful and female immigrants slightly outnumbered males. Refugees from famine-era Ireland in the 1850s, Czarist Russia in the 1880s, and Korea and revolutionary Mexico after 1900 were gender balanced but impoverished and arrived in desperate need of waged work.[33]

Americans often looked askance at the immigrant seekers of wages, suggesting the newcomers were racially unprepared for independent pioneering in the west. Already in the 1830s, Americans claimed immigrant "paupers" drained charity coffers; by the 1890s, they feared immigrants who might take their jobs. Wage-earning and urban life thus became markers of threatening racial inferiority.[34] Across the nineteenth century, the U.S. Congress passed an accumulating list of restrictions. Aimed at supposedly immoral and coerced Chinese immigrants, the earliest restrictions denied entry to prostitutes and contract laborers. After 1882, Chinese laborers (and, through derivative nationality, their wives and children) were excluded. Rates of detention and deportation of women traveling alone or with dependent children increased after the United States excluded anyone who might become "a public charge" (by applying for charity support). At the same time, U.S. immigration law sought to protect heterosexual men's right to a wife: wives and dependent children of Europeans did not count toward the low "quotas" imposed by law on southern and eastern Europeans in 1924. Female immigrants did not enjoy the same rights to "re-unify" families; neither did Asian males. Foreign-born females of European origin gained the individual right to naturalize individually in 1922, but those from Asia waited until the 1940s.[35] At the American border, race and gender placed clear limits on female agency.

Once in the United States, both female wage-earners and immigrant mothers upset American notions of gender and race. Most women who migrated to the United States expected to work, with or without wages. Immigrant women took jobs that few American women wanted, largely in domestic service and in factories. Unlike African-American women (who worked as servants in the south), immigrant servants lived in the homes of their employers: their wages could not support independent residence. Young Irish women nevertheless saw advantages in the arrangement: with no rents to pay, they could stretch low wages to send remittances home or choose between discretionary spending (American clothing, for example) or saving.[36] Irish, Scandinavians, and Germans viewed domestic service as appropriate employment for unmarried females but others viewed domestic work less positively: Jewish and Italians preferred factory work while living with their own families.[37] For the Asian domestic servants of the West, domestic service proved particularly exploitative.[38]

Young immigrant women working in canneries and garment or textile factories also earned wages too low to support independent residence. The hours of factory operatives were not as long as those of servants, but working conditions were dangerous and dirty. While young unmarried women workers escaped supervision by family members, they submitted instead to close surveillance and factory discipline. Still, many expressed excitement about industrial work, either because it introduced them to a wider world or created opportunities for sociability with men and women of their own age. Marriage, not wage-earning, promised release and increased autonomy. Wage-earning widows, wives and mothers, and older unmarried women, by contrast, experienced factory work mainly as necessary, draining drudgery.[39] Immigrant females working in commercial and family-based agriculture on the West Coast also seemed unified in their negative view of the labor required.

Wage-earning allowed urban women to enjoy some choices as consumers.[40] For Asian and Jewish immigrants, attending public school or night school after work also opened new doors. By the early years of the twentieth century, the ideal of romantic love spread rapidly through popular American culture, and young urban women also gained autonomy in choosing marriage partners, even in groups with strong traditions of arranged marriage in Europe or Asia.[41]

Once married, immigrants, much like their white American counterparts, avoided work outside the home—not because it violated the cult of domesticity but because it increased women's already heavy burden of domestic chores. With husbands earning very low wages, immigrant wives nevertheless earned wages at higher rates than native whites (although not at the much higher rates of native black wives). In American cities and in the commercial agriculture of California, Asian and European immigrant wives transformed their domestic work into meals and laundry service for paying male guests. Wives and mothers undertook industrial work at home by sewing garments and cracking or packing nuts, or they helped to operate family-run laundries, restaurants, or grocery stores.[42] With their children assistants, the clear line between public and domestic realms became muddy in such homes.

At a time when fertility among American women was falling rapidly, immigrant mothers garnered negative attention for their large families, for their supposedly ignorant habits of childcare, and for the threat both posed to the survival of a racially pure Anglo-Saxon American nation.[43] Sympathetic American school teachers, social workers, and nurses worried over the toll of heavy work loads and frequent pregnancies on immigrant women but their solution—American-style domesticity, with work removed from the home, and children in school—seemed unimaginable to most immigrants. The cult of domesticity rested on a material basis—a "family wage"—that few immigrant men earned.[44] Paradoxically, Americans also worried about immigrant mothers remaining "isolated" in their homes, unable to learn about American domestic practices or the English language. Such oppressed and ignorant mothers, racists argued, could not rear children prepared for the demands of modern life or democracy.[45]

Female agency was not determined exclusively by wage-earning and domesticity. Like their rural counterparts, urban women sometimes became activists within their own communities, often through Christian or Jewish religious organizations exclusively for women or through female "auxiliaries" to male fraternal, mutual aid societies. They extended their domestic and maternal duties into distinctive "ethnic public spheres." The most significant public expressions of female power were realized through workplace mobilizations and strikes. While few immigrant women were attracted to the American suffrage movement, they produced feminisms—often maternalist, separatist, and ethnic-communal in orientation—of their own.[46] The public activism of immigrant women emerged from family and communal commitments; they did not reject the "family claim" or (with rare exceptions) critique the cult of domesticity. In American eyes, then, they remained under the domination of men.

IMMIGRANT WOMEN SINCE 1924

As immigration dropped to its historical nadir under the impact of restrictive legislation, the origins of immigrants arriving in the United States began to change: more migrants came from the Americas and fewer from Europe. Passage of a new immigration law in 1965 resulted in new increases in migration; by 2000, Mexicans[47] constituted 40 percent of all recent arrivals, with large numbers of Asians and other Latin Americans[48] and smaller numbers from Africa[49] and the Middle East. Americans' understanding of gender relations also changed dramatically. White American women began working for wages in increasing numbers after 1960, and a minority now also pursued life-long professional careers. Women's growing presence in the labor market reflected the expansion of the service sector—female service and clerical jobs. As women left their homes to work, they increased demand for women workers who would provide meals, childcare, and elder care. Both the Civil Rights Movement and a new American feminist movement challenged the cult of domesticity by advocating greater equality not only in the public world but also in the most personal and intimate realm of domestic, familial, and sexual relationships. The "juggling" middle-class wife, mother, and wage-earner, along with the sexually "liberated" young unmarried woman, increasingly defined Americans' understanding of female emancipation—although a vocal minority of "born again" American Protestants soon contested those ideals.

At the border, a new set of restrictive rules created preferences for highly skilled workers, refugees, and those joining or "unifying" family members. Ostensibly race and gender neutral, they were nevertheless accessed differently by males and females. While scholars became fascinated with the women who migrated independently as job-seekers or "pioneering" mother wage-earners,[50] most adult women and girls entered the United States in the 1970s with visas for family unification. Countries with U.S. military bases have sent disproportionately large numbers of "brides" to the United States since the 1940s.[51] With the exception of nurses, none of the occupations identified as eligible for high-skill visa preference had been traditionally performed by women. International students and refugees, by contrast, were more gender balanced.[52] Overall, females were half of all migrants already in the 1930s; the migrant population was close to gender balance at the turn of the twenty-first century.

Gender and sexuality continue to matter at the border. Immigration restriction encouraged the proliferation of businesses that exploited those they assisted (for a fee) in crossing borders illicitly; for women and children, the result was sometimes sex trafficking.[53] Women continue to face particular difficulties in claiming asylum in the United States,[54] and until 2013 the United States ignored nonheterosexual family and marriage relations at the border. [55]

Confronting Americans' own changing and complex notions of gender, foreign-born women now formed a diverse population that included refugees, unskilled, clerical, and highly educated professional labor migrants, as well as international students and stay-at-home mothers.[56] Many have observed the "bifurcated" nature of the immigrant population; both very poorly educated (sixth grade education) and very highly educated (postgraduate degrees) women are more common among female immigrants than in the native female population. By contrast, immigrants' private, domestic, and sexual behaviors remain the focus of negative scrutiny. Old fears of prolific immigrant mothers and their need for public "welfare" financial support especially focus on immigrant women from Latin America and on refugee women from Asia: as neoliberal critiques of the American welfare state developed in the 1980s, foreign-born mothers and African-American "welfare queens" symbolized the drain that working-class women placed on public coffers and white tax payers. The fact that most immigrant women worked for low wages for American employers did not prevent Congress from passing laws to exclude them from most forms of welfare support.[57] Nor did it prevent wild proliferation of rumors about women crossing the border illegally to give birth to "anchor babies." Careful studies by social scientists however repeatedly showed that immigrant women's fertility declined sharply with migration to the United States and did not much surpass that of American citizens.[58]

For immigrant daughters, an American youth culture characterized by open, casual sexuality poses other challenges. Whether as Filipinas in California, Somali in Minneapolis, or Dominicans in New York, some young immigrants simply declare, "We don't sleep around like the white girls do."[59] Even virginity and modesty become signs, to some Americans, at least, of daughters' subordination to patriarchal immigrant fathers. Americans worry over female subordination whether expressed in the covered heads of Muslim women or in occasional, but shocking stories of honor killings.[60] But there is no evidence that marital or family violence is more common among immigrants than among Americans.[61] And some evidence even points toward foreign-wives gaining greater power within their marriages through migration.[62]

For females from communally oriented societies, the American expectation that they will develop autonomous "identities" is itself a challenge of contemporary American life. Even sympathetic scholars suggest that American individualism is the only way for immigrant females to develop a "real self."[63] By contrast, immigrant women's mobilization as public activists—in their workplaces, through their communities—gets small attention, especially compared with women's transnational networks and persisting ties to their foreign homelands.[64]

Despite fundamental changes in both immigrants' origins and culture and America's gender ideologies, immigrant females continue to be constructed as different from American women. Some adaptation to and acceptance of "modern" and American-gendered relations and identities still seem necessary, even in the current age of multiculturalism, if foreign-born women are to find acceptance. Americans' fears about immigrant fertility, family orientation, and domesticity persist in making immigrant women seem both less modern and more subordinate to the males of their own families and communities who, in turn, are considered more patriarchal than American males. These negative concerns, however, focus almost exclusively on working-class women, ignoring the many middle-class and high-achieving immigrants that U.S. immigration law prefers. Today, it is not immigrant women's wage-earning that makes them problematic to Americans but rather their poverty and domesticity. And it is in that poverty, of course, that one must assess the balance of autonomy that immigrants gain through migration against the exploitation they continue to suffer as racialized domestic and industrial workers in the American economy.

CONCLUDING THOUGHTS

If nothing else, this survey of the gendered consequences of migration for female immigrants should convince readers that "emancipation" and "exploitation" are blunt analytical terms: relations of gender in education, families, marriages, workplaces, communities, and American institutions do not all change together or in tandem with changes in gender ideology. Any change in gender ideology or practice can be, and typically has been, understood differently by immigrant and American women. Scholars will never have simple, empirical, measures of patriarchy, racism, exploitation, or emancipation that are cross-culturally valid. Similarly, the gendered meanings of modernity and tradition can be difficult to define, let alone to define cross-culturally.

Still, by taking into account both the structure and motivations of differing forms of international migration and by carefully contextualizing female lives and gender ideologies in sending and receiving countries, readers should be able to see the kinds of gendered opportunities that migration to the United States opened or precluded. By many measures, the United States itself has not yet achieved gender equality, and the jobs most traditionally held by womens are now often held by racialized immigrants from Latin America and, to a somewhat lesser extent, Asia.

Since at least the colonial era, opportunities for immigrant women from Europe to expand their own sense of personal autonomy and agency have repeatedly surpassed similar opportunities for immigrant women from Asia, Latin America, Africa, or the Caribbean. Inequalities between refugee Europeans, European servants, and African slave women were especially large in the colonial era. Yet despite American efforts to purge public policy of the legacy of scientific racism, late twentieth-century discussions of immigration suggest that the gendered consequences of racism persist in, for example, the heavy concentration of Latina and other immigrants in low-paid service work, especially as domestic servants. By recognizing how gender inequality has operated in immigrant women's lives, we can see exploitation as a product of both the confrontation of immigrant and American forms of patriarchy and the troubled American history of racism. Future research that acknowledges the differential impact of both American racism and gender ideology should begin to undermine the longstanding assumption that immigrant women's main enemies are the patriarchs of their own communities.

Notes

1. See critique of the "Ellis Island" immigration historians by Paul Spickard, *Almost All Aliens: Immigration, Race, and Colonialism in American History and Identity* (New York: Routledge, 2007). More consistent attention to gender and race can be found in Evelyn Nakano Glenn, *Unequal Freedom: How Race and Gender Shaped American Citizenship and Labor* (Cambridge, Mass: Harvard University Press, 2002).

2. Donna R. Gabaccia, "Is Everywhere Nowhere? Italy's Transnational Migrations and the Immigrant Paradigm of American History," Special Issue on Transnational History, *Journal of American History*, 86, 3 (December 1999): 1115–1134.

3. Donna R. Gabaccia, *From the Other Side: Women and Gender in American Immigrant Life, 1820–1990* (Bloomington: Indiana University Press, 1994). In the endnotes to this essay, I try to call attention to newer works on immigrant women, written after this 1994 publication.

4. James Axtell, "The White Indians of Colonial America," *The William and Mary Quarterly*, 3rd Series, 32, 1 (January, 1975): 55–88.

5. Steven M. Ozment, *When Fathers Ruled: Family Life in Reformation Europe* (Cambridge, Mass.: Harvard University Press, 1983).

6. Carol Berkin, *First Generations: Women in Colonial America* (New York: Hill and Wang, 1997); Laurel Thatcher Ulrich, *Good Wives: Image and Reality in the Lives of Women in Northern New England, 1650–1750* (Oxford: Oxford University Press, 1983); Kathleen M. Brown, *Good Wives, Nasty Wenches, and Anxious Patriarchs: Gender, Race and Power in Colonial Virginia* (Chapel Hill: Institute of Early American History and Culture and University of North Carolina Press, 1996).

7. Marianne Hester, "Patriarchal Reconstruction and Witch Hunting," in *Witchcraft in Early Modern Europe: Studies in Culture and Belief*, ed. Jonathan Barry, Marianne Hester and Gareth Roberts (Cambridge: Cambridge University Press, 1996), pp. 288–306.

8. Michael R. Haines and Richard H. Steckel, *A Population History of North America* (New York: Cambridge University Press, 2000).

9. *Letterbook of Eliza Lucas Pinckney, 1739–1762* (Columbia, SC: University of South Carolina Press, 1997).

10. Joseph E. Holloway, ed. *Africanisms in American Culture* (Bloomington: Indiana University Press, 1990).

11. Jennifer Lyle Morgan, *Laboring Women: Reproduction and Gender in New World Slavery* (Philadelphia: University of Pennsylvania Press, 2004).

12. Frances Smith Foster, '*Til Death or Distance do Us Part: Love and Marriage in African America* (New York: Oxford University Press, 2010).

13. David Eltis, "The Volume, Age/Sex Ratios, and African Impact of the Slave Trade: Some Refinements of Paul Lovejoy's Review of the Literature," *The Journal of African History*, 31, 3 (1990): 485–492.

14. Allen Kulikoff, *Tobacco and Slaves: The Development of Southern Cultures in the Chesapeake, 1680–1800* (Chapel Hill: University of North Carolina Press, 1986).

15. Sharon V. Salinger, "*Colonial Labor in Transition*: The Decline of Indentured Servitude in Late Eighteenth-Century Philadelphia," *Labor History*, 22 (1987): 183–191.

16. Russell R. Menard, *Migrants, Servants and Slaves: Unfree Labor in Colonial British America* (Aldershop: Ashgate, 2001).

17. Marian L. Smith, "'Any Woman who is Now or May Hereafter be Married': Women and Naturalization, ca. 1802–1940, Part I," *Prologue Magazine*, 30, 2 (Summer 1998): 146–153.

18. Linda Kerber, "The Republican Mother: Women and the Enlightenment—An American Perspective," *American Quarterly*, 28, 2 (1976): 187–205.

19. Barbara Welter, "The Cult of True Womanhood, 1820–1860," *American Quarterly*, 18, 2 (Summer 1966): 151–174.

20. Wally Seccombe, *Weathering the Storm: Working-Class Families from the Industrial Revolution to the Fertility Decline* (London: Verso, 1993).

21. On the relation of language, education, and autonomy, see Suzanne Sinke, *Dutch Immigrant Women in the United States, 1880–1920* (Urbana: University of Illinois Press, 2002); and David Fitzpatrick, "A Share of the Honeycomb: Education, Emigration and Irishwomen," *Continuity and Change*, 1, 2 (1986): 217–234.

22. Suzanne Sinke, "Migration for Labor, Migration for Love: Marriage and Family Formation across Borders," *OAH Magazine of History*, 14, 1 (Fall 1999): 17–21.

23. Studies of rural immigrant women include Sinke, *Dutch Immigrant Women*; Betty A. Bergland et al, *Norwegian American Women: Migration, Communities and Identities* (St. Paul, Minn.: Minnesota Historical Society, 2011); Robyn Burnett and Ken Luebbering, *Immigrant Women in the Settlement of Missouri* (Columbia: University of Missouri Press, 2005); and Linda Schelbitzki Pickle, *Contented Among Strangers: Rural German-Speaking Women and their Families in the Nineteenth-Century Midwest* (Urbana: University of Illinois Press, 1996).

24. Nancy F. Cott, "Young Women in the Second Great Awakening in New England," *Feminist Studies*, 3, 1/2 (Autumn 1975): 15–29.

25. Irene Haderle, "Women and Lay Activism: Aspects of Acculturation in the German Lutheran Churches of Ann Arbor, Michigan, 1870–1917," *Michigan Historical Review*, 25, 1 (1999): 25–43; Jenna Weissman Joselit, "The Special Sphere of the Middle-Class American Jewish Woman: The Synagogue Sisterhood, 1890–1940," in *The American Synagogue: A Sanctuary Transformed*, ed. Jack Wertheimer (Cambridge: Cambridge University Press, 1987).

26. Christiane Harzig, "The Ethnic Female Public Sphere: German-American Women in Turn-of-the-Century Chicago," in *Midwestern Women: Work Community and Leadership at the Crossroads*, ed. Lucy Eldersveld Murphy and Wendy Hamand Venet (Bloomington, IN: Indiana University Press, 1997), 141–157.

27. Suellen Hoy. "The Journey Out: The Recruitment and Emigration of Irish Religious to the United States, 1812–1914," *Journal of Women's History*, 6, 4/7, 1 (Winter/Spring 1995): 64–98.

28. Yvonne McKenna, *Made Holy: Irish Women Religious at Home and Abroad* (Dublin: Irish Academic Press, 2006); Bernadette McCauley, *Who Shall Take Care of Our Sick? Roman Catholic Sisters and the Development of Catholic Hospitals in New York City* (Baltimore: Johns Hopkins University Press, 2005); and Cynthia Russett, ed., *Catholic Women's Colleges in America* (Baltimore and London: Johns Hopkins University Press, 2002).

29. Nancy Lusignan Schultz, *Veil of Fear: Nineteenth-Century Convent Tales by Rebecca Reed and Maria Monk* (West Lafayette, Ind.: Purdue University Press, 1999).

30. Gabaccia, *From the Other Side,* pp. 110–111.

31. John Bodnar, *The Transplanted: A History of Immigrants in Urban America* (Bloomington: Indiana University Press, 1985).

32. Linda Reeder, *Widows in White: Migration and the Transformation of Rural Italian Women, Sicily, 1880–1920* (Toronto: University of Toronto Press, 2003).

33. Donna R. Gabaccia, "Women of the Mass Migrations: From Minority to Majority, 1820–1930," in Dirk Hoerder and Leslie Moch, eds., *European Migrants: Global and Local Perspectives* (Boston: Northeastern University Press, 1996), pp. 90–111.

34. Daniel Bender, *American Abyss: Savagery and Civilization in an Age of Industry* (Ithaca: Cornell University Press, 2009).

35. Martha Mabel Gardner, *The Qualities of a Citizen: Women, Immigration, and Citizenship, 1870–1965* (Princeton: Princeton University Press, 2005); Eithne Luibheid, *Entry Denied: Controlling Sexuality at the Border* (Minneapolis: University of Minnesota Press, 2002); Eithne Luibheid and Lionel Cantu, Jr., eds., *Queer Migrations: Sexuality, U.S. Citizenship and Border Crossings* (Minneapolis: University of Minnesota Press, 2005); and Margot Canaday, *The Straight State: Sexuality and Citizenship in Twentieth-Century America* (Princeton: Princeton University Press, 2009). See also Deirdre M. Moloney, "Women, Sexual Morality, and Economic Dependency in Early U.S. Deportation Policy," *Journal of Women's History,* 18 (2006): 95–122; Eileen Boris, "On the Importance of Naming: Gender, Race, and the Writing of Policy History," *Journal of Policy History,* 17 (2005): 72–92; and Jeanne D. Petit, *The Men and Women We Want: Gender, Race, and the Progressive Era Literary Test Debate* (Rochester: University of Rochester Press, 2010).

36. Margaret Lynch-Brennan and Maureen O'Rourke Murphy, *The Irish Bridget: Irish Immigrant Women in Domestic Service in America, 1840–1930* (Syracuse: Syracuse University Press, 2009). Most scholarly work on immigrant domestic servants was published in the 1980s and 1990s; see Gabaccia, *From the Other Side.*

37. Gabaccia, *From the Other Side,* pp. 48–50.

38. Evelyn Nakano Glenn, *Issei, Nisei, War Bride: Three Generations of Japanese American Women in Domestic Service* (Philadelphia: Temple University Press, 1986).

39. Recent studies of immigrant women workers include Carol Lynn McKibben, *Beyond Cannery Row: Sicilian Women, Immigration, and Community in Monterey, California, 1915–1999* (Urbana: University of Illinois Press, 2006); Miriam Cohen, *Workshop to Office: Two Generations of Italian Women in New York City, 1900–1950* (Ithaca: Cornell University Press, 1993); Vicki Ruiz, *From Out of the Shadows: Mexican Women in Twentieth Century America* (New York: Oxford University Press, 1998).

40. Nan Enstad, *Ladies of Labor; Girls of Adventure: Working Women, Popular Culture, and Labor Politics at the Turn of the Twentieth Century* (New York: Columbia University Press, 1999).

41. Randy D. McBee, *Dance Hall Days: Intimacy and Leisure among Working-Class Immigrants in the United States* (New York: New York University Press, 2000).

42. Diane C. Vecchio, *Merchants, Midwives, and Laboring Women: Italian Migrants in Urban America* (Urbana: University of Illinois Press, 2006). See also Rose Laub Coser, Laura S. Anker and Andrew J. Perrin, *Women of Courage: Jewish and Italian Immigrant Women in New York* (Westport, Conn.: Greenwood Press, 1999).

43. Katrina Irving, *Immigrant Mothers: Narratives of Race and Maternity, 1890–1925* (Urbana: University of Illinois Press, 2000).

44. Eileen Boris, *Home to Work: Motherhood and the Politics of Industrial Homework in the United States.* (Cambridge and New York: Cambridge University Press, 1994).

45. Irving, *Immigrant Mothers.*

46. Hadassa Kosak, *Cultures of Opposition: Jewish Immigrant Workers, New York City, 1881–1905* (Albany: State University of New York Press, 2000); Jennifer Guglielmo, *Living the Revolution: Italian Women's Resistance and Radicalism in New York City, 1880–1945* (Chapel Hill: University of North Carolina Press, 2010); Donna R. Gabaccia and Franca Iacovetta, *Women, Gender and Transnational Lives: Italian Workers of the World* (Toronto: University of Toronto Press, 2002). See also Angela Pienkos and Donald Pienkos, *"In the Ideals of Women is the Strength of a Nation": A History of the Polish Women's Alliance of America* (New York: Columbia University Press, 2003).

47. Among recent studies of immigrant women from Mexico, see Vicki L. Ruiz, *Out of the Shadows*; Ruiz and John R. Chavez, *Memories and Migrations: Mapping Boricua and Chicana Histories* (Urbana: University of Illinois Press, 2008); Ruiz Virginia Sanchez Korrol, eds., *Latinas in the United States: A Historical Encyclopedia* (Bloomington: Indiana University Press, 2006); Denise A. Segura and Patricia Zavella, eds., *Women and Migration in the U.S.-Mexico Borderlands: A Reader* (Durham: Duke University Press, 2007).

48. Sylvia Duarte Dantas DeBiaggi, *Changing Gender Roles: Brazilian Immigrant Families in the U.S.* (New York: LFB Scholarly Publishing, 2002); Cheris Brewer Current, *Questioning the Cuban Exile Model: Race, Gender and Resettlement, 1959–1979* (New York: LFB Scholarly Publishing, 2010).

49. John A. Arthur, *African Women Immigrants in the United States: Crossing Transnational Border* (New York: Palgrave Macmillan, 2009).

50. Sheba Miriam George, *When Women Come First: Gender and Class in Transnational Migration* (Berkeley: University of California Press, 2005). For the global feminization of migration, see Stephen Castles and Mark J. Miller, *The Age of Migration; International Population Movements in the Modern World* (New York: Guildford Press, 1998).

51. Philip E. Wolgin and Irene Bloemraad, "Our Gratitude to Our Soldiers': Military Spouses, Family Re-Unification, and Postwar Immigration Reform," *Journal of Interdisciplinary History,* 41 (2010): 27–60; for the sometimes difficult lives of intermarried war brides, see Ji-Yeon Yuh, *Beyond the Shadow of Camptown: Korean Military Brides in America* (New York: New York University Press, 2002).

52. Marion Houstoun, R.G. Kramer and J.M. Barrett, "Female Predominance in Immigration to the United States since 1930: A First Look," *International Migration Review,* 18, 4 (1984); 908–963.

53. Dina Francesca Haynes, "Used, Abused, Arrested and Deported: Extending Immigration Benefits to Protect the Victims of Trafficking and to Secure the Prosecution of Traffickers," *Human Rights Quarterly,* 26 (2004): 221–272.

54. Connie G. Oxford, "Protectors and Victims in the Gender Regime of Asylum," *NWSA Journal*, 17 (2005); 18–38; T.S. Twibell, "The Development of Gender as a Basis for Asylum in the United States Immigration Law and Under the United Nations Refugee Convention: Case Studies of Female Asylum Seekers from Cameroon, Eritrea, Iraq and Somalia," *Georgetown Immigration Law Journal*, 24 (2010): 189–309; Sara Zeigler and Kendra B. Steward, "Positioning Women's Rights within Asylum Policy: A Feminist Analysis of Political Persecution," *Frontiers: A Journal of Women Studies*, 30 (2009): 115–142.

55. Eithne Luibheid, "Sexuality, Migration, and the Shifting Line between Legal and Illegal Status," *GLQ: A Journal of Lesbian and Gay Studies*, 14 (2008): 289–315.

56. Pierrette Hondagneu-Sotelo, ed., *Gender and U.S. Immigration: Contemporary Trends* (Berkeley: University of California Press, 2003); Susan Pearce, Susan C. Elizabeth, J. Clifford, and Reena Tandon. *Immigration and Women: Understanding the American Experience* (New York: New York University Press, 2011).

57. Lynn Fujiwara, *Mothers without Citizenship: Asian Immigrant Families and the Consequences of Welfare Reform* (Minneapolis: University of Minnesota Press, 2008); Lisa Sun-Hee Park, *Entitled to Nothing: The Struggle for Immigrant Health Care in the Age of Welfare Reform* (New York: New York University Press, 2011).

58. Ann I. Gluster, *Fertility Patterns of Native- and Foreign-Born women: Assimilating to Diversity* (New York: LFB Scholarly Publishing, 2003); Emilio A. Parrado and S. Phillip Morgan, "Intergenerational Fertility among Hispanic Women: New Evidence of Immigrant Assimilation," *Demography*, 45 (2008): 651–671.

59. Yen Le Espiritu, "We Don't Sleep Around like White Girls Do": Family, Culture and Gender in Filipina American Lives," *SIGNS*, 26, 2 (2001): 415–440.

60. On the complex meaning of the head scarf or "veil," see Jamillah Ashira Karim, *American Muslim Women Negotiating Race, Class, and Gender within Ummah* (New York: New York University Press, 2009).

61. Margaret Abraham, *Speaking the Unspeakable: Marital Violence among South Asian Immigrants in the United States* (New Brunswick: Rutgers University, 2000); Hoan N. Bui, *In the Adopted Land: Abused Immigrant Women and the Criminal Justice System* (Westport, Conn.: Praeger, 2004).

62. Emilio A Parrado, Chenoa A. Flippen and Chris M. McQuiston, "Migration and Relationship Power among Mexican Women," *Demography*, 42 (2005): 347–372.

63. Inn Sook Lee, *Passage to the Real Self: The Development of Self Integration for Asian American Women* (Lanham: University Press of America, 2009); Jenny Hyun Pak, *Korean American Women: Stories of Acculturation and Changing Selves* (New York: Routledge, 2006); Carolyn Chen, "A Self of One's Own: Taiwanese Immigrant Women and Religious Conversion," *Gendered Society*, 19 (2005); 336–357.; Park Keumjae, *Korean Immigrant Women and the Renegotiating of Identity: Class, Gender and the Politics of Identity* (El Paso: LFB Scholarly Publishing, 2009); Tom Stritikus and Diem Nguyen, "Strategic Transformation; Cultural and Gender Identity Negotiation in First-Generation Vietnamese Youth," *American Educational Research Journal*, 44 (2007): 853–895.

64. On workplace activism see Carolina Bank, *Transnational Tortillas: Race, Gender, and Shop-Floor Politics in Mexico and the United States* (Ithaca: ILR Press, 2008); Miriam Ching Yoon Louie, *Sweatshop Warriors: Immigrant Women Workers Take on the Global Factory* (Cambridge, Mass: South End Press, 2001). On religious activism, see Glenda Tibe Bonifacio and Vivienne S.M. Angeles, *Gender, Religion, and Migration: Pathways of Integration* (Lanham: Lexington Books, 2010). From the rich literature on women's transnational

(and often familial) ties, see Silvia Dominguez and Amy Lubitow, "Transnational Ties, Poverty, and Identity: Latin American Immigrant Women in Public Housing," *Family Relations*, 57 (2008): 419–430; Luiz Maria Gordillo, *Mexican Women and the Other Side of Immigration: Engendering Transnational Ties* (Austin: University of Texas Press, 2010).

BIBLIOGRAPHY

Asian Women United of California. *Making Waves: An Anthology of Writings by and about Asian American Women* (Boston: Beacon Press, 1989).

Gabaccia, Donna R. *Seeking Common Ground: Multidisciplinary Studies of Immigrant Women in the United States* (Westport, Conn.: Greenwood Press, 1992).

Gabaccia, Donna R. *From the Other Side: Women and Gender in American Immigrant Life, 1820–1990* (Bloomington: Indiana University Press, 1994).

Gardner, Martha Mable. *The Qualities of a Citizen: Women, Immigration, and Citizenship, 1870–1965* (Princeton: Princeton University Press, 2005).

Harzig, Christiane, ed. *Peasant Maids, City Women: From the European Countryside to Urban America* (Ithaca: Cornell University Press, 1997).

Hondagneu-Sotelo, Pierrette, ed., *Gender and U.S. Immigration: Contemporary Trends* (Berkeley: University of California Press, 2003).

Kleinberg, S.J., Boris, Eileen and Ruiz, Vicki, eds. *The Practice of U.S. Women's History: Narratives, Intersections and Dialogues* (New Brunswick: Rutgers University Press, 2007).

Lamphere, Louise. *From Working Daughters to Working Mothers: Immigrant Women in a New England Industrial Community.* (Ithaca: Cornell University Press, 1987).

Luibheid, Eithne *Entry Denied: Controlling Sexuality at the Border* (Minneapolis: University of Minnesota Press, 2002).

Neidle, Cecyle S. *America's Immigrant Women* (Boston: Twayne Publishers, 1975).

Pearce, Susan C. Clifford, Elizabeth J., and Tandon, Reena. *Immigration and Women: Understanding the American Experience* (New York: New York University Press, 2011).

Ruiz, Vicki L. and DuBois, Ellen Carol, eds., *Unequal Sisters: A Multicultural Reader in U.S. Women's History.* 3rd ed. (New York: Routledge, 2000).

Ruiz, Vicki L. and Korrol, Virginia Sanchez, eds., *Latina Legacies: Identity, Biography, and Community* (Oxford: Oxford University Press, 2005).

Seller, Maxine Schwartz, ed. *Immigrant Women.* 2nd ed. (Albany: State University of New York Press, 1994).

Weatherfod, Doris. *Foreign and Female: Immigrant women in America, 1840–1930* (New York: Schocken Books, 1986).

Zinn, Maxine Baca and Dill, Bonnie Thornton, eds., *Women of Color in U.S. Society* (Philadelphia: Temple University Press, 1994).

CHAPTER 7

....

PROTECTING AMERICA'S BORDERS AND THE UNDOCUMENTED IMMIGRANT DILEMMA

....

DAVID G. GUTIÉRREZ

ILLEGAL migration and the attendant growth of a huge population of unauthorized persons within the territorial boundaries of the United States have been hot-button political issues for decades, but with the onset of the deep recession of the early twenty-first century, these questions have become even more heated and divisive. Although the circulation of technically unauthorized persons within U.S. territory has been a consistent feature of American life since the early national period, the explosive growth of unlawful residents from approximately 600,000 in the 1970s to an estimated 11 to 12 million by 2006 has provoked a running debate on U.S. immigration and citizenship policy that rivals the intense debates over similar questions that have roiled American politics for generations.[1] In the first decade of the current century, the debate over the dual issues of border security and the unauthorized presence of millions of people has intensified to the extent that critics are now demanding the implementation of a broad range of draconian measures. These include the mass deportation of illegal residents (and presumably, therefore, many of their U.S.-citizen children as well), criminal prosecution of anyone providing any kind of aid or sanctuary to unauthorized persons, and, at the extreme, a rethinking of the very basis of citizenship through the repeal of the birthright citizenship provision of the Fourteenth Amendment to the Constitution of the United States.

Although space limitations make it impossible to provide a detailed survey of the long history of these complex issues, this chapter will provide a broad overview of the evolution of the debate over unauthorized migration and border control. The chapter focuses in particular on the heart of the ongoing controversy—the historical tension and antagonism between those who have advocated strict policies of immigration restriction and border enforcement versus those who, mainly for economic reasons, have exhibited a much higher toleration for the presence of foreigners of all legal statuses. Given that economically driven migration will likely remain a constitutive feature of global capitalism into the foreseeable future, the chapter suggests that the vexed questions of border enforcement and the presence of unlawful residents will continue as two of the most divisive issues in modern U.S. politics.

CITIZENSHIP, CAPITALISM, AND PROBLEMATIC BORDERS

The intensity of the debate over unauthorized migration and border enforcement policy over the past four decades has tended to obscure the fact that these controversies have their origins in some of the basic contradictions associated with the creation of the United States as an independent nation and, more generally, with the emergence of the nation-state as the dominant form of sociopolitical organization in the modern world system. Indeed, dating from the dawn of the Industrial Revolution to the present day, participation of individual nations in an increasingly intertwined transnational market economy—and the more or less continuous global circulation of economically motivated migrants and immigrants that has been a defining characteristic of capitalism from the outset—rather glaringly exposed the myth of distinct and homogeneous peoples occupying hermetically sealed sovereign territory from time immemorial.

In the case of the United States, the evolution of the institution of national citizenship provides another clear example in which the so-called "container theory" of the nation does not easily mesh with the actual historical record.[2] Indeed, even a cursory review of the organizational logic underlying the development of national citizenship in the United States makes clear that formal membership in the early republic (that is, full rights-bearing status) was, from the outset, imagined as the exclusive and privileged purview of a fraction of the actual inhabitants of the new nation. Thus, whereas one will search in vain for an affirmative definition of citizenship in the text of the Constitution, evidence abounds of the framers' clear sense of what citizenship was *not*. In Article I, for example, the exclusion of native peoples from membership; the slave trade and fugitive slave clauses; the infamous "three-fifths" clause regarding the census enumeration of slaves; and the strongly gendered, white-male-centered language of the entire text all clearly, if indirectly, demarcated groups that were from the beginning considered to be outside the embrace of both actual and potential citizenship. In short, citizenship in the early republic was at least tacitly defined against a shadowy but vast body of inhabitants who, while recognized as permanent features of the new national landscape, were nevertheless imagined to be beyond the pale of formal membership in the polity. This system of exclusion was so extensive that some scholars estimate that citizenship may well have been limited to only about 20 percent of the actual population of the young republic.[3]

It is not surprising, therefore, that the logic of privilege, exclusion, and sharp racial and gender boundaries that lay at the heart of the nation's original political community was also expressed in the United States' first laws regulating immigration and naturalization. On one level, the nation's first federal statute on naturalization, the Naturalization Act of March 26, 1790 (1 Stat. 103), provided a very liberal two-year waiting period for applicants for citizenship. But the nation's first naturalization law also extended the country's conservative founding principles by limiting access to citizenship exclusively to "free white [male] person[s]." This male-gendered and racially exclusive definition remained the de facto baseline requirement for naturalized citizenship until the end of the Mexican War in 1848 (when the first small number of "mixed race" Mexican Americans in the newly annexed Southwest became U.S. citizens under the terms of the Treaty of Guadalupe Hidalgo) and the Fourteenth Amendment (ratified in 1868) extended citizenship to all of those born in U.S. territory. In rudimentary form, the Naturalization Act also provided a rough template regarding those who were considered "legal" residents of the nation and therefore also those who were not.

In theory, the racially based and gendered restrictions on access to citizenship might well have been expected to contribute to the eventual emergence of a more homogeneous society over time. However, despite the clear preference for just this outcome among many of the framers, from the outset, advocates of highly selective immigration policies were often stymied by other powerful interests who, for economic reasons, sought to encourage more or less free flows of immigrants across the nation's borders. Despite the fact that the supporters of this position usually held racial views that were virtually identical to those of their opponents, they considered the settlement and broader circulation of immigrants vital to the development of the nation's territory and natural resources. Consequently, they either pushed for lenient immigration and naturalization policies—or simply encouraged the maintenance of laissez-faire approaches to these questions. Over the first half of the nineteenth century, proponents of substantially open borders generally prevailed, their position bolstered by the addition of vast new expanses to the national domain through the Louisiana Purchase (1803), the admission of new states from the old Northwest Territories (1803–1847), and the addition of territory seized in the Mexican War (1846–1848).

This is not to suggest, however, as some have, that the period between the early republic and the Civil War represented an era of completely "free" immigration. To the contrary, recent scholarship has revealed an intricate meshwork of state and local statutes that emerged over the course of the late eighteenth and early nineteenth centuries. These statutes varied depending on locale, but in general, the first local immigration laws were designed to discourage or restrict the entry and/or naturalization of a variety of persons deemed undesirable (that is, above and beyond extant racial criteria). These persons included criminals, the physically or mentally infirm, the elderly, and, especially, the destitute (or, to use the increasingly common parlance of the time, those who were seen as "likely to become a public charge").[4] Even so, at this point, most state and local immigration laws were directed not toward individual immigrants but rather toward those who facilitated the immigration process through recruitment or conveyance. Thus, in effect, over much of the nineteenth century, rather than being a direct responsibility of the federal government, national immigration policy was indirectly administered at state and local levels by shipping and transport companies, ship's captains, labor recruiters and agents, and other intermediaries who bore much of the burden of immigration regulation.[5]

However, as the pace of U.S. economic growth (and the expansion of global capitalism more generally) accelerated over the course of the nineteenth century, American employers continued to look abroad for labor. Beginning in the 1840s and increasing sharply after the Civil War, American development was increasingly fueled by the labor of immigrants and their children. The structural use of immigrant labor was not unique to the United States at this time. Indeed, following the abolition of slavery, whether "free" and volitional, coerced or conscripted (as with the infamous "coolie trade"), or formally recruited and contracted, imported immigrant or migrant labor had become the norm in the developing world, and the citizenship status of such workers and the "legality" of these practices were seldom questioned. It is also crucial to note here that although much of this massive global circulation of human beings was unidirectional and permanent, one-quarter to one-third (and for some groups, much more) of gross transnational population flows between the 1840s and the 1940s were temporary or circular. Sojourners, who essentially circulated in the interstices of national citizenship systems for periods ranging from months to years, were (and remain) a vital component in the expansion of global capitalism and represented another prime example of the way the market forces unleashed by global capitalism were not contained by fixed national borders.[6]

The continual mixing of populations of very different statuses was particularly evident in the United States in the period of its most intensive industrialization, roughly from the 1870s to the onset of the Great Depression. Again, reflecting the seemingly inexhaustible demand for labor in the United States, the continuous ingress of immigrants played a key role in both economic development and population growth. For the entire period between 1860 and 1930, the officially acknowledged foreign-born population of the country ranged from a low of about 13 percent of the total U.S. population (in 1860) to a high of nearly 15 percent in 1910—and this did not include an unknown but surely sizable number of foreigners who had landed without documentation. In that era, immigrants and their children (who, not coincidentally, also by now constituted pluralities if not outright majorities in most major American cities) became a structurally embedded feature of the workforces of virtually all basic industries. Immigrant labor filled the vast majority of low-skilled or unskilled jobs, but highly skilled immigrants and sojourners also played key roles in the developing economy.[7] Eager to employ skilled workers for their expertise and unskilled workers for their willingness to do physically demanding and often hazardous work for low pay (and not, incidentally, because of their tenuous legal and social status), employers relied on immigrants as a reserve labor supplement to native workers wherever and whenever they could.

BORDER ENFORCEMENT AND
THE PRODUCTION OF "ILLEGALITY"

The global circulation of immigrants in this era inevitably created social tensions and eventually generated similar kinds of reactions in immigrant-receiving societies around the world.[8] In the United States, as the volume and composition of the vast throng of immigrant and sojourner populations increased—and the ability of local and state authorities to manage the initial entry and subsequent integration of immigrants was gradually overwhelmed—powerful anti-immigrant sentiments began to emerge at both the grass-roots and elite levels. The earliest expression of anti-immigrant sentiment was directed at Irish-Catholic immigrants in the 1840s and 1850s, but American nativism reached an unprecedented level of virulence against Chinese immigrants in the decades following the California Gold Rush. Rooted partly in racism and xenophobia, partly in concern about the rapidity of economic, demographic, and cultural change, and in no small part in growing anxiety among self-defined white native workers about immigrants' negative impact on wages, working conditions, and unionization efforts, different nativist movements emerged and subsided in national politics for the rest of the century.

The virulence of anti-immigrant sentiment after the Civil War finally forced Congress into the immigration policy arena. The legislative branch was further pushed in this direction by the important Supreme Court ruling, *Henderson v. Mayor of New York*, 92 U.S. 259 (1875). Building on the logic of the precedents set in an earlier set of suits known as the *Passenger Cases*, the Court ruled in *Henderson* that contrary to a long history of local control over immigration policy, state and local regulation of immigration was an unconstitutional infringement of Congress's plenary authority to regulate foreign commerce. The Court's ruling set the stage for a period of unprecedented legislative action by Congress.

The first major federal immigration legislation passed by Congress was the Chinese Exclusion Act of 1882 (22 Stat. 58), which barred further Chinese immigration for a period of ten years. But over the next several decades, subsequent Congresses passed a series of progressively more restrictive laws targeting a growing list of undesirable immigrants, including the diseased, the mentally infirm, convicts, polygamists, paupers, prostitutes, anarchists and other political radicals, and others. However, the capstone of this era of reform was the Johnson-Reed Immigration Act of 1924. Passed with broad bipartisan support, this sweeping statute (43 Stat. 669) established a highly exclusionary national-origins quota system (which completely banned further immigration from Asia and severely limited immigration from anywhere other than northern and western Europe); expanded the grounds on which individuals could be deported and/or denaturalized; eliminated a statute of limitations on prosecution for unlawful residence; and, for the first time, created a federalized Border Patrol. A companion law passed several years later (45 Stat. 1551 (1929)) made it a misdemeanor to enter U.S. territory without immigration inspection.

Over the short run, the onset of the Great Depression and the Second World War probably did more to curb previous patterns of mass migration to the United States than did restrictive legislation, but on a more general plane, the move toward immigration restriction and more stringent border control between the 1880s and the 1920s had the effect of sharpening and hardening what, until that time, had been fairly fluid distinctions between citizens and noncitizens in American society. Prior to this time, many jurisdictions had fairly flexible policies regarding the legal status of noncitizens. Indeed, until the practice came to an end in the 1920s, at least twenty-two states allowed white male noncitizens to vote in various combinations of local, state, and even federal elections.[9]

With the advent of the new legal regime, however, this changed dramatically, with the distinction between those with citizenship and those without becoming a bright line. As one historian has noted of this key transition: "Because illegal entry is a concomitant of restrictive immigration policy, the quota laws stimulated the production of the illegal alien and introduced that problem into the internal spaces of the nation . . . The [new regulatory] system shifted to a different, more abstract register, which privileged formal status over all else. It is this system that created what we today call the 'undocumented immigrant.' "[10]

It is important to keep in mind here, however, that while noncitizens had clearly become more vulnerable after the 1920s, the emergence of the modern American immigration and border enforcement regime did little to alter the continuing tension between advocates of border interdiction and employers who continued their pursuit of cheap labor—a fact that became abundantly clear once the Depression came to an end. Once the United States entered the Second World War, U.S. employers anticipated imminent labor shortages, particularly in agriculture and food and fiber processing. With their former sources of foreign labor closed off, American employer lobbies immediately pressured the State and Labor Departments to make arrangements with the Mexican government to explore the reimplementation of a labor importation program that had been tried on a smaller scale during World War I. In bilateral negotiations, the Mexican government acceded to this request, but only after insisting that any of its citizens contracted to work in the United States be guaranteed transportation to and from Mexico, a fair wage, decent food and housing, and basic human rights protections. After hammering out the details in the spring of 1942, the two governments announced the creation of the Emergency Farm Labor Program. Soon dubbed the "Bracero Program" (for a Spanish colloquial term for manual laborer), the program not only reopened the southern border to Mexican labor but, more significantly, reinstituted the use of immigrant workers in the U.S. economy.

The initial scale of the agricultural labor scheme remained fairly modest through the war years, with an average of about 70,000 contract laborers working in the country each year during the war. But over time, the program, which was extended by various means after the war, had the effect of priming the pump for the much more extensive use of such workers. By 1949, the number of imported contract workers had jumped to 113,000 and then, between 1950 and 1954, averaged more than 200,000 per year. During the peak years of the program between 1955 and 1960, an average of more than 400,000 laborers (predominantly from Mexico but augmented by smaller numbers of Jamaicans, Bahamians, Barbadians, and Hondurans as well) were employed in the United States.[11]

More important, it soon became apparent that the implementation of this new guest-worker program stimulated a concomitant influx of workers from Mexico and else-where who had entered the country without authorization as news of the availability of work traveled through the communication networks established by the foreign workers themselves. Again, there was nothing particularly novel about this—significant surges of clandestine entry were seen during the Chinese exclusion era, during the first experiment with Mexican contract labor during World War I, and, more generally, with the chain- and circular-migration patterns that previously had brought tens of millions of Europeans to the United States. However, the essential difference between the earlier forms of labor circulation and that of the 1940s and beyond was how much of it was now officially unsanctioned and thus "illegal." In short, although noncitizen foreign workers of all statuses continued to perform almost exactly the same work immigrants had performed for more than 100 years, the new regulatory framework technically transformed many of the latest generation of immigrant workers into "illegal aliens" subject to expulsion at any time. The change was clearly reflected in apprehension statistics of the period: apprehensions of unauthorized immigrants (again, mainly from Mexico but increasingly from other places as well) rose dramatically from a negligible number in 1940 to more than 91,000 in 1946, nearly 200,000 in 1947, and more than 500,000 by 1951.

As always, the postwar circulation of unauthorized workers suited both employers, who sought to avoid the red tape and higher costs associated with participation in the formal labor importation program, and would-be braceros, who were unable to secure contracts through official means. For both employers and employees habituated to this kind of exchange, this was simply business as usual. Indeed, the mutual economic incentives for unsanctioned entry (bolstered by ever more sophisticated and economically lucrative smuggling, communication, and document-forging networks) increased so much in this period that it is estimated that at different times, the ratio of unauthorized workers to legally contracted braceros was at least two-to-one and, in some cases, was even higher in specific local labor markets. That the use of unauthorized labor had once again become a systemic feature of the U.S. economy is further reflected in the fact that over the twenty-four years of the Bracero Program, the estimated number of unauthorized persons apprehended—nearly 5 million—was roughly equivalent to the total number of official contracts issued.

The Ambivalence of Immigration and Border Control Policy after World War II

The use of unauthorized workers on this scale eventually provoked a fierce response as labor unions, religious groups, philanthropic organizations, and civil rights activists demanded an end to both the Bracero Program and the widespread abuse by American employers of undocumented workers. But, as always, the economic and political interest groups that had long supported the use of such labor continued to push back against reform efforts. Indeed, while there is no question that the legal regime erected earlier in the century had greatly increased the risks associated with unlawful entry, the law functioned not so much as a way to end the employment of unauthorized workers but as a mechanism that ensured both their availability to employers and their vulnerability under American law.[12]

The bald cynicism underlying much of immigration and border control policy after the 1920s could be seen in a variety of ways. For example, the fact that the Immigration Act of 1924 had pointedly *excluded* from restriction potential immigrants from the Western Hemisphere demonstrated both the persistent power of employer lobbies (which had worked aggressively behind the scenes to gain the hemispheric policy exemption) and the likelihood that employers would return to the use of foreign labor once the economy recovered. A second important indicator of the ambivalent nature of immigration and border control policy at this time was the anemic support given to the Border Patrol and the larger immigration and naturalization bureaucracy from their inception. Indeed, much as the heated rhetoric of the current immigration debate often serves to deflect attention from the marked ineffectiveness of extant policy in preventing the growth of a huge unauthorized population, the creation of a border enforcement bureaucracy between the 1890s and 1920s was designed, at least in part, to provide the *appearance* of concerted action while masking the relative paucity of resources actually devoted to the task of "securing" the border. For example, when the first Bureau of Immigration was created in 1891, Congress appropriated resources sufficient to fund only twenty-four border inspection stations to police more than 5,000 miles of the United States' land borders with Canada and Mexico. Between 1924 and 1926, border enforcement efforts increased substantially, with the Border Patrol's administrative and enforcement staff growing to 700 and its budget rising to $1.5 million annually. But virtually all of these still-thin assets were deployed on the southern border. In the meantime, the 3,000-mile-long Canadian frontier remained practically unmanned except for official ports of entry—despite the fact that unauthorized Asian and European immigrants regularly used the northern border as a gateway.[13]

During the Bracero era, the cynicism underlying U.S. immigration and labor policies was even more apparent. Nothing exemplified this more than two of the most notorious policy developments of the period—the enactment of the so-called "Texas Proviso" in 1952 and "Operation Wetback" in 1954. As the scandal over the widespread use of unauthorized labor grew in the early 1950s, a growing coalition of labor and civil rights activists insisted that the best way to curb it was to impose legal sanctions on employers who hired such workers. However, once again, employers' lobbies and their congressional allies stymied virtually all meaningful efforts in this direction. When a liberal congressional coalition tried to pass a measure that made it illegal to "harbor, transport, and conceal" illegal workers in 1951–1952, Texas agricultural interests convinced their delegation and, eventually, a majority in Congress to pass the infamous Texas Proviso instead. The proviso's authors feigned cooperation by acquiescing to some minor anti-smuggling features of the larger bill but brushed away the employer-sanctions measure by inserting language into the bill that decreed that employment of unauthorized workers was not to be considered "harboring."[14]

Operation Wetback was an even more egregious example of the general cynicism of U.S. immigration, border control, and labor policies during this period. Although the Texas Proviso had essentially provided a free pass to American employers who continued to use unauthorized workers, the public outcry about the rapidly growing undocumented population eventually forced immigration enforcement officials to take action. Once again caught between the wishes of regional employers and increasing political pressure in Washington, INS commissioner Joseph Swing decided to stage a spectacular show of force in the western states that regularly employed the largest numbers of unauthorized workers. In the summer and fall of 1954, the INS massed personnel and resources in different spots along the U.S.-Mexico border in a highly publicized campaign to apprehend and repatriate suspected undocumented persons (again, the northern border remained almost completely ignored). Within weeks, the INS announced that it had physically repatriated hundreds of thousands of unauthorized persons, nearly all of them Mexicans. But beyond this, the INS suggested that the highly visible workplace and neighborhood raids had also pressured untold numbers of other unlawful residents to depart the country "voluntarily."

The INS's combined strategy of coercion and physical removal proved to have a number of advantages. The large repatriation numbers announced by the INS seemed to assuage those who wanted to see strict control of the border. The INS purported to have expelled well more than 1 million unauthorized persons, a significant increase from the 526,000 apprehensions reported in 1952 and the 885,000 claimed in 1953. In addition, INS officials argued that the unknown number of voluntary departures that occurred under the border sweeps had saved the government the expense of mounting formal deportation proceedings. More important, the apparent success of Operation Wetback also allowed the Immigration Service to tout what it claimed were the long-term effects of its campaign. At the end of the operation, INS officials went so far as to proclaim that "the so-called 'wetback' problem no longer exists . . . The border has been secured."[15]

In hindsight, it is difficult to judge how much of the INS's rosy assessment of the death of the "wetback problem" reflected a dramatic shift in hiring patterns and a steep decline in unlawful entries or simply an extension of its ongoing public relations campaign. Most conventional historical portrayals of the aftermath of Operation Wetback have largely accepted the INS's account of events, but it strains credulity to believe that historical trends that had seen millions of unauthorized immigrant workers working alongside legally contracted ones were suddenly reversed in the face of a concerted unilateral policy intervention by U.S. immigration authorities. It is much more likely that as bracero contracts increased during the peak years of the program, the demand for unauthorized workers lessened but never disappeared.

This basic fact of economic life was confirmed with the end of the Bracero Program in 1964 and the overhaul of the extant U.S. immigration system the following year. Although the number of formal bracero contracts gradually declined until the program's end in 1964, there is no indication that the demand for labor in occupations in which undocumented workers toiled had dropped appreciably. Again, given historical trends, it is much more likely that as the program wound down, braceros were simply replaced by unauthorized workers (or, after their contracts expired, simply became unauthorized workers themselves). In any case, border apprehensions began to rise again almost immediately after the guest-worker program's demise. Whereas the INS reported apprehending an average of 75,000 unauthorized workers per year in the nine years between Operation Wetback and the end of the Bracero Program, apprehensions surpassed 100,000 again in 1965 and continued to rise sharply thereafter. The passage of the Immigration and Nationality Act (INA) Amendments that same year (79 Stat. 911) almost certainly exacerbated this trend. Although the new law finally scrapped the national origins quota system, for the first time in history, the INA imposed a hemispheric ceiling of just 120,000 legal immigrants per year. Later adjustments in the law further lowered the number of visas available in Western Hemispheric nations.

The 1973 Arab oil embargo further disrupted the American labor market and eventually helped lay the foundations for an even greater influx of unauthorized workers. The extended period of simultaneous contraction and inflation that followed the 1973 crisis—and the neoliberal economic reforms that were instituted in response—signaled a massive reorganization of work and production processes that in many ways continue to the present day. This ongoing restructuring was regionally and temporally uneven, but across the economy, the general trend was toward a contraction of comparatively secure high-wage, high-benefit (often union) jobs in the manufacturing and industrial sectors and a corresponding growth of increasingly precarious low-wage, low-benefit, often nonunion jobs in the expanding service and informal sectors of a transformed economy. In addition, the protracted crisis and policy responses that followed also paved the way for a steady degradation in public health, education, and welfare expenditures that eventually put a growing number of working-class citizens under even more economic pressure at a time when real wages remained static or actually declined in many sectors. In the international arena, the deepening global debt crisis and austerity measures imposed on many developing countries over this same period by the World Bank and International Monetary Fund set the stage for even more drastic economic restructuring and displacement abroad.

On another front, the effects of these interlocking trends were further intensified by ongoing neoliberal "free trade" negotiations designed to reduce trade barriers and foster greater regional economic integration. In the United States, the two signal developments in this area—the ratification of the North American Free Trade Agreement (NAFTA) in 1994 and a similar initiative, the Central American Free Trade Agreement (which is gradually being implemented with several Central and South American nations)—have been tremendously successful in increasing trade between the signatories. But at the same time, these agreements also provided the means for U.S.-based firms to export parts of their production processes to comparatively low-wage and laxly regulated economies while downsizing production capacities (and shedding higher-wage, often unionized labor) within the borders of the United States.

Together, these structural changes laid the foundations for an intensification of two trends that have come to define the U.S. economy at the turn of the twenty-first century: the downsizing and outsourcing of production processes that were once based in the United States and a concomitant trend toward what might be called labor "insourcing" of ever larger numbers of both authorized and unauthorized immigrants.

The stunning result of structural reshaping of the economy has been an unprecedented explosion of the unauthorized population in the United States. Again, although INS apprehension statistics must be considered rough proxies for the actual growth of the unauthorized population, the trend after the mid-1960s was unmistakable. The INS reported apprehending between 100,000 and 200,000 unauthorized individuals annually in the period 1965 through 1968, but after 1970, the number of apprehensions shot up, reaching 400,000 in 1971, 500,000 in 1972, and 600,000 in 1973, and continuing on this steep upward trajectory thereafter. By the late 1970s and into the 1980s, apprehensions hovered between 800,000 and 1 million per year, reaching a peak of more than 1.6 million in 1986. Although apprehensions dipped sharply for a short time after passage of the Immigration Reform and Control Act (IRCA) of 1986 (discussed further below), they continued their rise again in the 1990s to well more than 1 million per year. One should note again that apprehension statistics actually tended to understate the magnitude in the growth of the unauthorized population since most migration scholars agree that somewhere between 40 and 50 percent of all persons not legally in the country are individuals who did not cross the border illegally but rather have overstayed valid tourist, student, or other visas. Thus, although illegal immigration has come to be perceived primarily as a "Mexican problem," Mexicans accounted for about 56 percent of the estimated total in 2005—with the remaining 44 percent, many of them visa violators, coming from virtually every other nation in the world.

Although such estimates are always tenuous, demographers believe that in aggregate, the unauthorized population of the country rose from approximately 3 million in 1980 to about 5 million by the mid-1990s, reached an estimated 8.4 million by 2000, and peaked at between 11 and 12 million (or about 4 percent of the total U.S. population) before turning downward after the financial crisis of 2008–2009. With much of the global economy in a sustained slump since then, the unauthorized population is estimated to have dropped by at least 1 million since 2009.[16]

THE POLICY RESPONSE

Against this unprecedented surge of unauthorized migration and socio-demographic transformation, budgets and personnel devoted to border enforcement and repatriation have skyrocketed. As recently as 1971, the U.S. government spent less than $70 million for border policing, which was smaller than the law enforcement budgets of many U.S. cities. But by 1997, the INS budget had reached $1.7 billion, and continued upward, reaching $4.2 billion in 1999. Most of these new resources went into border enforcement activity, especially along the U.S.-Mexico border. In terms of personnel, the size of the Border Patrol doubled between the 1970s and 1980s and then doubled again in the 1990s.

In the wake of the terror attacks of September 11, 2001, the border enforcement apparatus was strengthened even more with the creation of the Department of Homeland Security (DHS), a sprawling umbrella organization with an annual budget of more than $37 billion. The INS was disestablished, with border security responsibilities being divided between two new entities, U.S. Immigration and Customs Enforcement (ICE) and U.S. Customs and Border Protection, operating with a combined annual budget in 2009 of more than $15 billion. Under this new organizational structure, the Border Patrol's budget also shot upward, growing to $400 million in 1992, reaching the $1 billion mark in 2000, and nearing $3 billion by 2009. With a current force of 20,000 personnel as of this writing, the U.S. Border Patrol is now the largest nonmilitary armed force within the U.S. government.

As border enforcement budgets and personnel have expanded over the years, policing efforts have gone through several permutations. In 1986, largely in response to growing public pressure to address the growing unauthorized population, Congress passed the Immigration Reform and Control Act (Public Law 99-603). Something of a policy hybrid, IRCA added substantially to the budget of the INS and Border Patrol and, after decades of failed attempts, finally mandated (weak) civil and criminal sanctions on individuals and firms that "knowingly" employed unauthorized workers. But in addition to an emphasis on punitive measures, IRCA also gave millions of unauthorized persons the opportunity to "regularize their status" by applying to the INS. More than 3 million individuals were legalized under provisions of the 1986 act.

While the legalization program of IRCA can be read as a belated acknowledgement of the reality of the permanent presence of unauthorized persons, both the liberal and punitive provisions of the new law obviously did little to stem the continuing illegal influx of immigrants. Indeed, if anything, due to the eroding economic and political conditions in Mexico, Central America, and other immigrant-sending regions, undocumented migration increased dramatically in the years following passage of IRCA. With public concern about the unauthorized population growing, members of Congress once again were forced to take action that made it appear, if nothing else, that the issue of border security was being systematically addressed. As we have seen, this led to an even greater investment in border interdiction and also to a series of even more punitive laws, including the Immigration Act of 1990 (Public Law 101-649).

Laws passed in the early 1990s further increased the size and scope of the Border Patrol and supported highly publicized border-interdiction campaigns such as "Operation Blockade" (later renamed "Operation Hold-the-Line") in El Paso, Texas (1993–1994); "Operation Gatekeeper" in the San Diego, California, border sector (1995–1996); "Operation Safeguard" in Nogales, Arizona (1996); and "Operation Rio Grande" (1997) in Texas's lower Rio Grande Valley. Although these initiatives were successful in diverting unauthorized migrants from crossing into the United States in these targeted sectors, migrants and smugglers simply plotted new and more dangerous routes across the border. While migrant fatalities increased as a result, the overall number of illegal entrants continued to rise right up to the great economic contraction of 2008.

Indeed, many migration scholars have noted that since the border policing efforts implemented in the 1990s made crossing the border more difficult and more expensive, they may well have contributed to the long-term growth of the resident unauthorized population because potential migrants dealt with rising opportunity costs by planning to stay in the United States longer than they would have otherwise, and because unauthorized migrants already in the United States could no longer circulate across the border as freely as they once did. In any case, the high public visibility of these issues compelled Congress to revisit immigration and border enforcement policy several more times in the 1990s, first with passage of the Illegal Immigration Reform and Immigrant Responsibility Act of 1996 (IIRIRA, Public Law 104-208) and later in that same year with the Personal Responsibility and Work Opportunity Reconciliation Act (Public Law 104-193). Again, both laws focused on deterrence of potential migrants at the border and the harassment of unauthorized persons already in the country, with the first directing even more resources to expanding the Border Patrol and physical barriers (like walls, fences, vehicle barriers, and stadium lighting) along the border, and both targeting unlawful residents (and their families) by making access to public services more difficult.

While it is difficult to pinpoint the exact causes of slowing rates of unauthorized migration since 2000, it is clear that the combination of heightened security measures and the ongoing recession have contributed to the steep declines. Apprehensions reported by ICE have dropped from a recent peak of nearly 1.64 million in 2000 to fewer than 450,000 in 2010.[17] Whether such declines continue if and when the economy recovers is an open question, especially given the increasingly integral role unauthorized workers have come to play in the economy.

Before the current economic contraction, patterns of immigrant labor in-sourcing had accelerated to the extent that immigrants of all legal statuses were filling jobs in the United States at a rate comparable to that of 100 years before. Indeed, although the ongoing recession has clearly suppressed the hiring of both native and foreign workers, recent data reveal just how much immigrants have become part of the fabric of American economic life. According to census data, as recently as 2007, highly skilled "legal" immigrants were essential to many key economic sectors, constituting fully 44 percent of all medical scientists, 37 percent of all physical scientists, 34 percent of all computer software engineers, 31 percent of all economists, 30 percent of all computer engineers, and 27 percent of all physicians and surgeons. With citizen members of the "baby boom" generation entering retirement in ever increasing numbers, demographers predict that pressure to recruit such high-skilled immigrants will continue to rise.[18]

In the vast occupational landscape below such elite professions, immigrant workers of all legal statuses (the census does not distinguish between "legal" and unsanctioned workers) are similarly structurally embedded in virtually every job category in the economy. As would be expected, more than half of all agricultural workers, plasterers, tailors, dressmakers, sewing machine operators, and "personal appearance workers" are immigrants. Beyond their well-known presence in these occupations, immigrants are estimated to constitute another 40 to 50 percent of all drywall workers, maids and housekeepers, and packers and packaging workers. In the next decile, immigrants comprise 30 to 40 percent of all roofers, painters, meat and fish processors, cement workers, brick masons, cooks, groundskeepers, laundry workers, textile workers, and dishwashers. Below this, immigrants of all statuses are estimated to hold another 20 to 30 percent of thirty-six additional occupational categories.[19] In addition, untold numbers of other noncitizens of all legal statuses toil in the vast and expanding reaches of the "informal" or unregulated "gray" and subterranean "black" market economies.[20] At the turn of the twenty-first century, employment of noncitizens was so pervasive that foreign workers are estimated to have accounted for one-half of all jobs created between 1996 and 2000. And overall, undocumented workers were estimated to constitute at least 16 percent of the total U.S. work force.[21]

As always, the economic dependence of the U.S. labor market on both "legal" and "illegal" immigrants has inevitably cemented and extended links of mutual dependence to immigrant-sending regions of the world and thus has also contributed to the continuing cycle of illicit movement into U.S. territory. Since the 1970s, the same kinds of social networks previously established by European, Asian, and Mexican labor migrants have been established by more recent migrants, thus expanding the ties of mutual dependence between immigrant-source and immigrant-receiving regions. The depth of this interdependence becomes clear when one considers the scale of remittances migrants of all statuses send to their countries of origin. Before the global economic contraction of 2008, when global remittances peaked, remittances constituted at least 26 percent of the GDP of Honduras, 18 percent of El Salvador's, 22 percent of Haiti's, 18 percent of Jamaica's, 13 percent of the Philippines', 12 percent of GDP of Nicaragua and 10 percent of Guatemala's. In 2007, Mexico alone received more than $24 billion in remittances from its citizens abroad. Another study notes that in 2003, 14 percent of adults in Ecuador, 18 percent of adults in Mexico, and an astonishing one in four adults in Central America reported receiving remittances from abroad.[22] In short, in-sourcing of unauthorized immigrant labor has become a deeply embedded structural feature of both the supply and the demand side of the unauthorized immigration equation and is, therefore, that much more difficult to arrest with unilateral policy interventions.

The brutal reality of these aspects of globalization has done little to mitigate what is an increasingly volatile and often deeply contradictory political environment—despite the ongoing investment in new border enforcement measures. The unprecedented massive mobilization in the spring of 2006 and beyond, now known as the immigrants' rights movement, represents one pole in the spectrum of public opinion. The protestors, many of them "illegally" in the country, have demanded recognition for the contributions they make to U.S. economic growth. By also insisting that noncitizens of all statuses have always been a permanent feature of American society, they have demanded both recognition of this fact and legislative action to "regularize their status" within some broadened framework of societal membership.[23]

Of course, on the other side of the rancorous debate, the perceived effrontery of unlawful residents making such rights claims fanned the flames of dissent among those who are infuriated not only with what they see as the unconscionable expansion of the nation's unauthorized population but, more generally, with the erosion of domestic living standards associated with the ongoing restructuring of the U.S. economy. Fears about the inexorable aging of the "white" citizen population and the rapid growth of a comparably youthful non-white population have tended to heighten resentment against the foreign-born and their children—and especially against those without legal status. The widespread sense that the federal government has not seriously enforced existing law has added to the frustration of those holding such views.

Consequently, in what is clearly the most dramatic recent development in the debate over immigration and border control policy, states and localities have entered the fray by enacting a range of measures designed to decrease local populations of unauthorized persons. Following precedents previously set by activists in California and elsewhere, localities such as Hazleton, Pennsylvania; Vista and Escondido, California; and at least 130 other American towns and cities have passed local ordinances that criminalize everything from hiring unauthorized day laborers, renting to unauthorized residents, and suspending business licenses of firms employing unauthorized workers to the public use of languages other than English. In addition, a number of states—perhaps most notoriously Arizona and, more recently, Indiana, Georgia, Alabama, and others—have debated and/or enacted a variety of measures designed to pressure unauthorized persons to leave state jurisdictions. In 2010 alone, states passed more than 300 such laws, including measures requiring local law enforcement officials, teachers, social workers, healthcare providers, private-sector employers, and others to verify the citizenship of any individual they encounter in their official duties or businesses—and make it a crime for noncitizens not to have documents verifying their legal status. Some have gone so far as to propose that unauthorized persons be prohibited from driving (or, for that matter, be barred from receiving any kind of state license), and that states not recognize the U.S. citizenship of infants born of unauthorized residents, regardless of the birthright citizenship provision of the Fourteenth Amendment. Federal courts have thus far tended to enjoin or strike down such statutes as violations of federal prerogative in immigration matters, but the future in this arena of immigration and citizenship politics remains uncertain.[24]

In stark contrast to most state and local anti-immigrant agitation, smaller humanitarian immigrants-rights movements (and even some legislation) have begun to emerge in some states and localities. For example, in the spring of 2011, the state of Utah passed a bill that would allow unauthorized workers to work in the state's own "guest worker" program. Other states—notably Texas, California, Maryland, and at least ten others— have passed or attempted to pass legislation making it possible for U.S.-born children of unauthorized persons to attend college paying in-state tuition. Such legislation also makes it possible for such students to receive financial aid. Patterned after the proposed federal "Dream Act"—which would provide legal status and a "path to citizenship" for otherwise law-abiding noncitizen youth who attend college or join the military—such measures are rooted in the proposition that most unauthorized residents are productive, taxpaying members of the community and, as such, should have access to at least a modicum of rights and tax-supported services. Based on the same logic, more than 100 cities have passed various kinds of "sanctuary" ordinances, pledging not to harass unauthorized persons or aid law enforcement officials in pursuit of such individuals.[25]

For its part, the immigration and border enforcement bureaucracy under the Obama administration has responded to the political pressure emanating from states and localities on two fronts. On the one hand, the Justice Department has filed a series of suits challenging the constitutionality of state- and locally based immigration and/or citizenship statutes. On the other hand, however, the DHS under Obama has dramatically stepped up internal enforcement efforts by significantly increasing workplace raids and audits against employers suspected of hiring unauthorized workers and encouraging all employers to be more scrupulous in utilizing the so-called E-Verify program, a decidedly imperfect computer system that, in theory at least, allows employers to verify an applicant's legal right to work. The Obama administration has also aggressively increased other enforcement efforts against unauthorized residents by emphasizing the so-called "Secure Communities Program" that allows local jurisdictions to check arrested individual's immigration status against federal databases. In addition, federal immigration officials have also engaged in a protracted campaign of neighborhood sweeps, detentions, and an unprecedented number of deportations. According to figures released by ICE, 380,000 noncitizens—most of them criminals but many of them not—were deported in fiscal 2009–2010 and another 393,000 in 2010–2011.[26]

Given the tremendously unstable state of the U.S. and global economies and the highly volatile state of the debate over border enforcement and undocumented immigration in the second decade of the century, it is impossible to predict even partial resolution to these festering controversies. Although the continuing precariousness of the economy may well lay the groundwork for the projection of more force on U.S. borders and an even more hostile climate for noncitizens already within U.S. territory, global economic trends will almost certainly continue to create incentives for the ongoing structural use and abuse of both officially authorized and unauthorized immigrant workers. Under these circumstances, it is likely that the historical debate over border enforcement and the status of unauthorized immigrants will persist into the foreseeable future.

NOTES

1. Obviously, the surreptitious nature of illegal migration and unauthorized residence requires that analysts develop best estimates on the actual number of unauthorized persons physically present within the United States at any one time. For contextual and methodological discussion of the numbers cited above, see Robert E. Warren and Jeffrey S. Passel, "A Count of the Uncountable: Estimates of Undocumented Aliens Counted in the 1980 United States Census," *Demography* 24 (3) (Aug. 1987): 375–393; Jeffrey S. Passel, *The Size and Characteristics of the Unauthorized Migrant Population in the U.S.: Estimates Based on the March 2005 Current Population Survey* (Washington, DC: Pew Hispanic Center, Mar. 7, 2006).

2. Although a number of scholars have used the term "container theory" to describe what is argued to be a flawed conceptualization of the political and social organization of the world system, it has perhaps been most closely associated with the work of the German sociologist Ulrich Beck. For a recent explication of the debate, see Ulrich Beck, "Cosmopolitan Realism: on the Distinction between Cosmopolitanism in Philosophy and the Social Sciences," *Global Networks: A Journal of Transnational Affairs* 4 (2) (Apr. 2004): 131–156.

3. For the contours of this contentious debate during the Constitutional era, see Madison Grant and Charles Stewart Davison, eds., *The Founders of the Republic on Immigration, Naturalization, and Aliens* (New York: Scribner's, 1928); Rogers M. Smith, *Civic Ideals: Conflicting Visions of Citizenship in U.S. History* (New Haven: Yale University Press, 1997). For two very different explorations of the use of "the other" as negative referents for defining U.S. citizenship, see Edmund S. Morgan, *American Slavery, American Freedom* (New York: Norton, 2003) and Bonnie Honig, *Democracy and the Foreigner* (Princeton: Princeton University Press, 2001).

4. The historical evolution of the public charge provision is discussed in Gerald L. Neuman, *Strangers to the Constitution: Immigrants, Borders, and Fundamental law* (Princeton: Princeton University Press), 23–31.

5. For thorough overviews and analyses of early immigration regulation, see Benjamin J. Klebaner, "State and Local Immigration Regulation before 1882," *International Review of Social History* 3 (3) (1958): 269–295; Gerald L. Neuman, "The Lost Century of American Immigration Law (1776–1875)," *Columbia Law Review* 93 (8) (Dec. 1993): 1833–1901. For estimations of the size of the citizen population at this time, see Jamin B. Raskin, "Legal Aliens, Local Citizens: The Historical, Constitutional, and Theoretical Meanings of Alien Suffrage," *University of Pennsylvania Law Review* 141 (4) (Apr. 1993): 1391–1470.

6. See Adam McKeown, "Global Migration, 1846–1940," *Journal of World History* 15 (2) (2004): 155–189; Dirk Hoerder, *Cultures in Contact: World Migrations in the Second Millennium* (Durham: Duke University Press, 2002).

7. See Kitty Calavita, *Immigration Law and the Control of Labor, 1820–1924* (London: Academic Press, 1984).

8. For discussion of the parallel development of restrictive immigration laws in different parts of the world at this time, see Aristide Zolberg, "International Migration Policies in a Changing World System," in *Human Migration: Patterns and Policies*, eds. William McNeill and Ruth Adams (Bloomington: Indiana University Press, 1978): 241–286; John Torpey, "States and the Regulation of Migration in the Twentieth-Century North Atlantic World," in *The Wall Around the West: State Borders and Immigration Controls in North America and Europe*, eds. Peter Andreas and Timothy Snyder (Lanham, MD: Rowman and Littlefield, 2000): 31–54; Charles A. Price, *The Great White Walls Are Built: Restrictive Immigration to North America and Australia* (Canberra: Australian National University Press, 1974); Triadafilos Triadafilopoulos, "Building Walls, Bounding Nations: Migration and Exclusion in Canada and Germany, 1870–1939," *Journal of Historical Sociology* 17 (4) (Dec. 2004): 385–427.

9. See Raskin, "Legal Aliens, Local Citizens"; Sarah Song, "Democracy and Non-Citizenship Voting Rights, *Citizenship Studies* 13 (6) (2009): 607–620.

10. See Mae M. Ngai, "The Strange Career of the Illegal Alien: Immigration Restriction and Deportation Policy in the United States, 1921–1965," *Law and History Review* 21 (1) (Spring 2003): 70, 77. See also Nicholas P. De Genova, "Migrant 'Illegality' and Deportability in Everyday Life," *Annual Review of Anthropology* 31 (2002): 419–447.

11. See U.S. Senate, Committee on the Judiciary, Report on the *History of the Immigration and Naturalization Service*, 96th Cong., 2d sess. (Washington, DC: U.S. Government Printing Office, 1980): 51, 57, 65.

12. See David G. Gutiérrez, "The Politics of the Interstices: Reflections on Citizenship and Non-citizenship at the Turn of the Twentieth Century," *Race/Ethnicity: Multidisciplinary Global Contexts* 1 (1) (Autumn 2007): 89–120; David G. Gutiérrez, "The Shell Game of Immigration Policy 'Reform': A Response to Dan Tichenor," *Labor: Studies in Working-Class History of the Americas* 5 (2) (Summer 2008): 71–76; David Gutiérrez, "The 'New Normal'? Reflections on the Shifting Politics of the Immigration Debate," *International Labor and Working-Class History* 78 (Fall 2010): 118–122.

13. See Andrew Graybill, *Policing the Great Plains: Rangers, Mounties, and the North American Frontier, 1875–1910* (Lincoln: University of Nebraska Press, 2007); Kornel Chang, "Enforcing Transnational White Solidarity: Asian Migration and the Formation of the U.S.-Canadian Boundary," in *Nation and Migration: Past and Future*, eds. David G. Gutiérrez and Pierrette Hondagneu-Sotelo (Baltimore: Johns Hopkins University Press, 2009): 169–194; Claudia Sadowski-Smith, "Unskilled Labor Migration and the Illegality Spiral: Chinese, European, Mexican *Indocumentados* in the United States, 1882–2007," in Gutiérrez and Hondagneu-Sotelo, eds., *Nation and Migration*: 277–302.

14. For the clearest account of the convoluted legislative maneuverings that led to the eventual enactment of the Texas Proviso, see Kitty Calavita, *Inside the State: The Bracero Program, Immigration, and the I.N.S.* (1992; repr., New Orleans: Quid Pro Quo Books, 2010): 71–77.

15. See U.S. Department of Justice, *Annual Report of the Immigration and Naturalization Service* (Washington, DC: U.S. Government Printing Office, 1955): 14–15.

16. See Jeffrey Passel and D'Vera Cohn, *The Unauthorized Immigrant Population: National and State Trends, 2010* (Washington, DC: Pew Hispanic Center, Feb. 1, 2011).

17. See Richard Marosi, "New Border Foe: Boredom," *Los Angeles Times*, Apr. 21, 2011, A1.

18. See Teresa Watanabe, "Shortage of Skilled Workers Looms in U.S.," *Los Angeles Times*, Apr. 21, 2008, A1.

19. See Steven A. Camarota and Karen Jensenius, *Jobs Americans Won't Do? A Detailed Look at Immigrant Employment by Occupation* (Washington, DC: Center for Immigration Studies, Aug. 2009), especially table 1; American Immigration Law Foundation, "Mexican Immigrant Workers and the U.S. Economy: An Increasingly Vital Role," *Immigration Policy Focus* 1 (2) (Sept. 2002): 1–14; A.T. Mosisa, "The Role of Foreign-Born Workers in the U.S. Economy," *Monthly Labor Review* 125 (5) (2002): 3–14; Diane Lindquist "Undocumented Workers Toil in Many Fields," *San Diego Union-Tribune*, Sept. 4, 2006, A1; Gordon H. Hanson, "The Economic Logic of Illegal Immigration," *Council Special Report No. 26*, Washington, DC: Council on Foreign Relations, 2007. For an insightful case-study analysis of the replacement of domestic workers by the foreign-born in one key industry, see William Kandel and Emilio A. Parrado, "Restructuring the U.S. Meat Processing Industry and New Hispanic Migrant Destinations," *Population and Development Review* 31 (3) (Sept. 2005): 447–471.

20. See James DeFilippis, "On the Character and Organization of Unregulated Work in the Cities of the United States," *Urban Geography* 30 (1) (2009): 63–90.

21. See M. Tossi, "A Century of Change: The U.S. Labor Force, 1950–2050," *Monthly Labor Review* 125 (5) (2002): 15–28.

22. See Roberto Suro, *Remittance Senders and Receivers: Tracking the Transnational Channels* (Washington, DC: Pew Hispanic Center, Nov. 24, 2003); Migration and Remittances Unit,

World Bank, *Migration and Remittances Factbook*, 2008 (Washington, D.C.: The World Bank, 2008).

23. See Irene Bloemraad and Christine Trost, "It's a Family Affair: Intergenerational Mobilization in the Spring 2006 Protests," *American Behavioral Scientist* 57 (4) (Dec. 2008): 507–532; Josue David Cisneros, "(Re)Bordering the Civic Imaginary: Rhetoric, Hybridity, and Citizenship in *La Gran Marcha*," *Quarterly Journal of Speech* 97 (1) (Feb. 2011): 26–49.

24. See J. Esbenshade and B. Obzurt, "Local Immigration Regulation: A Problematic Trend in Public Policy," *Harvard Journal of Hispanic Policy* 20 (2008): 33–47; Kyle E. Walker and Helga Leitner, "The Variegated Landscape of Local Immigration Policies in the United States," *Urban Geography* 32 (2) (2011): 156–178; Monica W. Varsanyi, "Neoliberalism and Nativism: Local Anti-Immigrant Policy Activism and an Emerging Politics of Scale," *International Journal of Urban and Regional Research* 35 (2) (Mar. 2011): 295–311; Richard Fausset, "Alabama Enacts Strict Immigration Law," *Los Angeles Times*, June 10, 2011, A8.

25. See Walker and Leitner, "Variegated Landscape": 157; Nicholas Riccardi, "Utah's Right Has Its Own Way," *Los Angeles Times*, Mar. 20, 2011, A1; Andrew Seidman, "In Maryland, An Immigration Battle Redux," *Los Angeles Times*, July 22, 2011, A7.

26. See "Record Number of Illegal Immigrants Deported," *Los Angeles Times*, Aug. 13, 2010, A16; Miriam Jordan, "Deportations Hit Record Number," *Wall Street Journal*, Oct. 7, 2010, A6.

BIBLIOGRAPHY

Calavita, Kitty. *U.S. Immigration Law and the Control of Labor: 1820–1924*. London: Academic Press, 1984.

Calavita, Kitty. *Inside the State: The Bracero Program, Immigration, and the I.N.S.* New York: Routledge, 1992; repr., New Orleans: Quid Pro Quo Books, 2010.

Camarota, Steven A., and Karen Jensenius. *Jobs Americans Won't Do? A Detailed Look at Immigrant Employment by Occupation*. Washington, DC: Center for Immigration Studies, Aug. 2009.

Chang, Kornel. "Enforcing Transnational White Solidarity: Asian Migration and the Formation of the U.S.-Canadian Boundary." In *Nation and Migration: Past and Future*, edited by David G. Gutiérrez and Pierrette Hondagneu-Sotelo, 169–194. Baltimore: Johns Hopkins University Press, 2009.

Grant, Madison, and Charles Stewart Davison, eds. *The Founders of the Republic on Immigration, Naturalization, and Aliens*. New York: Scribner's, 1928.

Graybill, Andrew. *Policing the Great Plains: Rangers, Mounties, and the North American Frontier, 1875–1910*. Lincoln: University of Nebraska Press, 2007.

Hoerder, Dirk. *Cultures in Contact: World Migrations in the Second Millennium*. Durham: Duke University Press, 2002.

Honig, Bonnie. *Democracy and the Foreigner*. Princeton: Princeton University Press, 2001.

Morgan, Edmund S. *American Slavery, American Freedom*. New York: Norton, 2003.

Passel, Jeffrey S. *The Size and Characteristics of the Unauthorized Migrant Population in the U.S.: Estimates Based on the March 2005 Current Population Survey*. Washington, DC: Pew Hispanic Center, Mar. 7, 2006.

Passel, Jeffrey, and D'Vera Cohn. *The Unauthorized Immigrant Population: National and State Trends, 2010*. Washington, DC: Pew Hispanic Center, Feb. 1, 2011.

Price, Charles A. *The Great White Walls Are Built: Restrictive Immigration to North America and Australia*. Canberra: Australian National University Press, 1974.

Sadowski-Smith, Claudia. "Unskilled Labor Migration and the Illegality Spiral: Chinese, European, Mexican *Indocumentados* in the United States, 1882–2007." In *Nation and Migration: Past and Future*, edited by David G. Gutiérrez and Pierrette Hondagneu-Sotelo, 277–302. Baltimore: Johns Hopkins University Press, 2009.

Smith, Rogers M. *Civic Ideals: Conflicting Visions of Citizenship in U.S. History*. New Haven: Yale University Press, 1997.

Suro, Roberto. *Remittance Senders and Receivers: Tracking the Transnational Channels*. Washington, DC: Pew Hispanic Center, Nov. 24, 2003.

Torpey, John. "States and the Regulation of Migration in the Twentieth-Century North Atlantic World." In *The Wall Around the West: State Borders and Immigration Controls in North America and Europe*, edited by Peter Andreas and Timothy Snyder, 31–54. Lanham, MD: Rowman and Littlefield, 2000.

Zolberg, Aristide. "International Migration Policies in a Changing World System." In *Human Migration: Patterns and Policies*, edited by William McNeill and Ruth Adams, 241–286. Bloomington: Indiana University Press, 1978.

CHAPTER 8

·····································

INCLUSION, EXCLUSION, AND THE MAKING OF AMERICAN NATIONALITY

·····································

GARY GERSTLE

ANY examination of American nationality must contend with its contradictory character. On the one hand, this nationality harbors a civic creed promising all Americans equal rights irrespective of race, religion, sex, or national origin. On the other hand, certain religious and racial traditions within American nationality have defined the United States in exclusionary ways. Thus, while America proclaimed itself an open society, it also saw itself as a Protestant nation with a mission to save the world from Catholicism and other "false faiths"; and while it proclaimed that all men are created equal, it aspired, for much of its history, to be a white republic. Writing a history of American nationality requires, then, that one identify its inclusionary and exclusionary characteristics, what the balance between inclusion and exclusion has been during different periods of American history, and how and why that balance has changed over time.

The three nationalist traditions—the civic, the religious, the racial—have shaped American life. Laws governing immigration and citizenship—rules determining who has been allowed to enter America and to become a full member of American society and who has not—play an important part in this analysis, for they reveal a great deal about the kind of society America has aspired to be.

CIVIC NATIONALISM

·····································

America's civic nationalist principles can be found in two famous eighteenth-century phrases: "all men are created equal" and "we the people." These phrases expressed beliefs in the fundamental equality of all human beings; in every individual's right to life, liberty, and the pursuit of happiness; and in a democratic government that derives its legitimacy from the people's consent. These beliefs comprise a democratic universalism that can take root anywhere. But because they were enshrined in the American nation's two founding documents, the Declaration of Independence and the Constitution, they have marked something distinctive about the American people and their polity. In the 1940s, Gunnar Myrdal bundled these civic rights and principles together into a political faith that he called the "American creed." I prefer the more generic term "civic nationalism" that Michael Ignatieff and other students of the contemporary nation have used to denote these beliefs.[1]

American civic nationalism embodied the republican notion of popular sovereignty. The "people" would rule; they would determine the course to be taken by the governments—local, state, and federal—that had some role in their lives. America's civic nationalist tradition also promised a society free of discrimination—ethnic, religious, racial, or sexual. It offered America as a place where all individuals could pursue economic and cultural opportunity and secure their liberty and property. It called on America to open itself to foreigners willing to work hard, obey the law, and pledge allegiance to its democratic institutions. These potential immigrants were to be drawn not just from the ranks of the educated or privileged but, in the words of Emma Lazarus, from the world's "huddled masses yearning to breathe free."[2] America's civic nationalist tradition promised to set these downtrodden free and to allow them to pursue their economic dreams and to practice the faith and pursue the politics and fashion identities of their own choosing.

Choice—choosing one's national identity rather than having it imposed by a ruler or by heredity—was crucial to this civic nationalism. Prior to the American Revolution, rules of membership in nations had been dominated by Westphalian and mercantilist doctrines. Under these doctrines, states claimed complete and permanent sovereignty over their subjects, reserving the right to control their movement within state territory and their freedom to move beyond it. Because the strength of a state or monarchy was measured in numbers—the more people a sovereign could claim as subjects, the mightier the realm—European rulers were reluctant to permit their subjects to emigrate, unless the latter were paupers, criminals, or some other class of undesirables. Subjects who did move to another kingdom were still expected to give allegiance to their original state or monarch.

The British colonists in North America had begun to challenge this European state system in the mid-eighteenth century, in part for pragmatic reasons: the North American appetite for settlers from Europe had become insatiable. But the colonists made this materialist demand for labor into a political principle. Even prior to the 1770s, they had begun to develop rules for membership that were based on residence, consent, and voluntary loyalty rather than on birth, descent, and perpetual subjecthood. And when these colonists brought an independent United States into being, they committed themselves to two principles—freedom of movement into and out of the United States and ease of membership in the American polity—that were radical for the eighteenth-century world. The second principle, embodied in the country's first naturalization law (1790), gave every free European immigrant of "good character"—regardless of nationality, language, religion, or gender—the opportunity to become a citizen of the United States after residing in the United States only two years. This ease of affiliation made this naturalization law the most inclusive measure of its kind in the eighteenth-century world—a judgment that holds even if we take into account, as we must, the racial restriction for which this law has recently become so well known (a matter I will soon address). And even as subsequent Congresses made naturalization tougher to achieve, by mandating waiting periods stretching to five years and, at some points, longer, America continued to distinguish itself by the ease with which European immigrants could choose U.S. citizenship for themselves. Both the ease of joining the American polity and the ease of leaving it were part of the revolutionary settlement. So, too, was a willingness to accept into the polity religious groups who, in Europe, were excluded from membership. Thus, the United States extended full citizenship to Catholics a half-century before Great Britain and to Jews before the French revolutionaries did so. The freedom of movement guaranteed by the new nation in combination with the generous terms of civic membership made the United States a magnet for Europeans and established America's reputation early on for being a nation of immigrants.[3]

The Reconstruction Congresses that sat during and after the Civil War (1861–1871) further strengthened America's civic nationalist tradition not only by outlawing slavery but also by passing a broad anti-discrimination amendment. Section I of the Fourteenth Amendment (1868) declared that "no state shall deprive any person of life, liberty, or property, without due process of the law; nor deny to any person within its jurisdiction the equal protection of the laws." Over the next 150 years, these "due process" and "equal protection" clauses became the foremost weapons possessed by the federal government to battle discrimination against African Americans and other racial minorities, women, religious groups, and gays. These provisions worked to reinforce America's civic nationalist tradition.

A lesser known part of this Amendment's Section I did similar work: "All persons born or naturalized in the United States and subject to the jurisdiction thereof are citizens of the United States." These deceptively ordinary words actually constituted a ringing endorsement of the principle of equality first articulated in the Declaration of Independence. Anyone born on American soil automatically at birth became a citizen. That individual's race, ethnicity, religion, and sex were irrelevant; so, too, was the nationality (or "blood") of that person's parents. By the 1890s, the Supreme Court extended this birthright citizenship to the American-born children of Chinese and other East and South Asian immigrants who, by law, had been barred from becoming U.S. citizens. As part of the Civil War settlement, the United States had given itself the strongest system of birthright citizenship then extant anywhere in the world. It needs to be seen for what it was: a profound affirmation of America's civic nationalist tradition.[4]

RELIGIOUS NATIONALISM

At its origins, and for much of its history, the United States wanted to be a Protestant country. That meant not only that Protestants of all varieties would be able to worship free of interference from the state (or some state-endorsed religious establishment).

It meant as well that the country should do everything in its power to create a society in which Catholicism, and more specifically, papal influence, would have little or no import. This fear of Rome is difficult for twenty-first-century Americans to understand because it is no longer a motivating force in our politics or immigration policy. But, for most of American history, the Catholic Church's theology, liturgy, and rituals; its life-and-death struggle with European Protestants; its international size and power; and the control it was thought to exercise over rank-and-file Catholics alarmed American Protestants. Catholicism was depicted not only as the enemy of God but also as the enemy of republicanism. To Protestant Americans, the Church stood for monarchy, aristocracy, and other reactionary forces that America was seeking to escape. Where the pope "ruled," Protestants charged, "the people" most certainly did not. And, thus, Catholic influence had to be resisted, contained, and even eradicated.[5]

The intensity of anti-Catholicism did not surface in the constitutional debates of 1787; to the contrary, the framers put the country on the path to religious toleration by refusing to denigrate any religion by name or establish any faith as the country's official religion. The debates over ratification yielded a remarkable First Amendment to the Constitution, ratified in 1789, that prohibited Congress from passing any "law respecting an establishment of religion, or prohibiting the free exercise thereof." The naturalization law of 1790 further confirmed America's openness to religious diversity by putting no prohibition on the ability of immigrant Catholics, Jews, or members of another non-Protestant faith to become citizens of the United States. In law, America's civic nationalism was strong and its religious nationalism weak.[6]

But as evangelical Protestantism revived in early nineteenth-century America, anti-Catholicism resurged as well. The Catholic group that bore the brunt of American Protestant fury in the nineteenth century were the Irish who, when they arrived in the 1830s and 1840s, constituted the first mass immigration of Catholics to America. Fleeing an Ireland devastated by colonial rule and famine, these Irish immigrants were largely destitute; they had few skills, little access to good jobs, and not much familiarity with urban living. Many native Protestants viewed them as an urban underclass, cut off from "American" values and traditions, their assimilation to their new land blocked by what these Protestants took to be a fanatical and unholy devotion to the Catholic Church. America's first mass nativist movement, the Know-Nothings, arose in the 1840s and 1850s in reaction to the "Irish peril." The Know-Nothings stirred up anti-Irish sentiment and sparked vigilante attacks by Protestant gangs on Irish neighborhoods, Catholic schools, and even, in some cases, Catholic churches themselves. In their more "respectable" moments, the Know-Nothings organized politically to end Irish immigration, to remove the children of Irish-Catholic immigrants from parochial schools so that they could be educated in a proper Protestant environment, and to bar immigrants from holding public office and, in some cases, from voting.[7]

The politics of sectionalism and the outbreak of the Civil War sent Know-Nothing nativism into eclipse and also provided opportunities for Irish immigrants to demonstrate their loyalty to the Union, to rise in the social order, and to gain more respectability for their Catholic ways. Still, religiously motivated discrimination against Irish

Catholics persisted for another 100 years and expanded to other groups of Catholics—for example, Italians, Poles, French Canadians, and Mexicans. In 1928, the Republicans defeated the Democratic, Irish-Catholic nominee for President, Al Smith, by arousing anxiety about the threat a Catholic president would pose to the United States. And even in 1960, another Democratic hopeful and Irish Catholic, John F. Kennedy, had to appear before a group of Protestant ministers in Houston to prove to their satisfaction that his election would not make the Vatican the ruler of Washington.[8]

Recognizing the durability and depths of anti-Catholic hostility helps to make sense of the comprehensive infrastructure that American Catholics built to take care of their needs: parochial schools, universities, welfare agencies, fraternal organizations, and sports leagues were all part of this firmament. Catholic dedication to building a separate world reflected both the fact of their exclusion from many established institutions and their fear that the mainstream institutions that did admit them (such as public schools) would bring unbearable pressure upon them to sacrifice their faith.[9]

One can find similar kinds of anti-Catholic sentiments fueling America's territorial expansion in the nineteenth century. Americans conceived of their Manifest Destiny as a providential mission to expand their Protestant-republican nation to the farthest reaches of the North American continent. In the process, America would not only eliminate or corral pagan Indians but would also weaken Catholic presence and power in North America. These sorts of Protestant convictions provided an important justification for the war against Mexico in the 1840s (and for seizing half of Mexico's land) and later for the war against Spain in Cuba and Puerto Rico in 1898. Protestant Americans depicted Catholicism as a sinister force. On the one hand, it spread papal autocracy and crushed democracy. On the other hand, it rendered those who lived in Catholic lands weak and indolent, incapable either of distinguishing themselves in war (by demonstrating courage or valor) or in peace (through the habits of hard work, frugality, and inventiveness that Protestants had mobilized to turn the United States into an industrial juggernaut).[10]

Hard work, freedom, and republicanism were each depicted as part of America's core Protestant character; these "Protestant" characteristics had made the United States exceptional. America's continued welfare demanded that these qualities be cultivated and that Protestants maintain their position as the nation's core group. As the number of immigrants from Catholic, Christian Orthodox, and Jewish lands swelled in the late nineteenth century, more and more Protestants banded together under the banner of religious nationalism, demanding that "Anglo-Saxon" ascendancy—in the presidency, the Congress, the judiciary, the military, the foreign service, universities, corporations, and even in the immigration stream itself—be preserved.[11]

RACIAL NATIONALISM

Racial nationalism arose to justify the seventeenth- and eighteenth-century enslavement of African Americans in the southern states. This racial nationalism conceived of the country in racial terms, as a home for white people, which, in the eighteenth century, meant those of European origin and descent. Many of those who fashioned America's universalist and democratic political creed were also the architects of its racial nationalism—a paradox that has been one of the most fascinating and enduring in U.S. history.[12] Slave owners played key roles in the 1776 revolution against Britain and in drafting the 1789 Constitution, which both endorsed slavery and apportioned congressional delegates to ensure that slave owners would exercise disproportionate power in national affairs. The 1790 naturalization law described earlier as affirming American civic nationalism also created a racial test for citizenship—an immigrant had to be free and white in order to qualify for inclusion in the American nation—that would remain in force for more than 160 years (until 1952). For three-quarters of its history, in other words, America, by law, aspired to be a white republic.[13]

The North's victory over the slaveholding South in the Civil War (1861–1865) offered the United States an opportunity to uproot its racial nationalist tradition and reorganize the republic solely around its civic creed. Indeed, the abolition of slavery, the passage of the Fourteenth Amendment, and the wide-ranging efforts to empower freedmen and women in the years between 1863 and 1877 constituted what some have called a second American revolution—one committed, without racial qualification, to America's civic nationalist creed. But this revolution only partially succeeded. Propertied southern whites who had lost their political power during the Civil War regained it after 1877. Though these elites could not restore slavery, they did fashion a system of peonage that held rural blacks in economic semi-servitude and an ideology of Jim Crow that ensured African American segregation and subordination in politics and culture. White southerners stripped blacks of basic citizenship rights—to vote, hold elective offices, and sit on juries—while denying them access to any space, public or private, defined as white: schools, parks, restaurants, stores, theaters, churches, railroad cars, and bathrooms. Through this system of segregation, white Southerners revived America's tradition of racial nationalism for a new century and mocked black claims to be equal or full participants in the American nation.[14]

After 1877, racial nationalism also increasingly shaped American immigration law. Prior to the 1880s, America's liberal immigration policy constituted one of the fullest expressions of its civic nationalist creed. During this period, America welcomed virtually anyone, regardless of that person's national origin, who wished to make the United States his or her home. In the forty-year period from the 1880s to the 1920s, however, Congress and the Executive Branch replaced its open border policy with a "closed border" policy grounded largely in racial exclusions. Congress banned the immigration of Chinese laborers in 1882, and, as part of the Gentlemen's Agreement, President Theodore Roosevelt banned the immigration of Japanese laborers in 1907. While both actions were responses to regional anxieties—notably white westerners' worries that "yellow hordes" were taking over the Pacific Coast—they became national policies, endorsed and sustained by the federal government. Frankly racist justifications underlay such discriminatory practices: Chinese and Japanese were so different from Americans of European origin and were so primitive, restrictionists argued, they could never be civilized or acculturated. Opponents alleged that their biological constitution was such that they needed no rest and little food. They thus would outperform American workers on a sliver of an American workingman's wages and would drive the latter to ruin. These Asians were also alleged to know (or to care to know) nothing about democracy and citizenship and to be oblivious to the value of family life or moral probity. They were thought to be sexual predators (on white women) and the carriers of debilitating drug habits. They would contribute nothing to the American nation and had already harmed it by their presence. Fortunately, in the eyes of America's Asian immigrant opponents, no immigrant from East (and South) Asia could become a citizen, thanks to the 1790 law limiting naturalization to those who were free and white. The American nation had no place for these groups.[15]

In the 1920s, Congress extended its ban on immigration from East Asia to most of the world. And, for the first time, it struck at Europe and, in particular, at groups from southern and eastern Europe who were also thought to be racially inferior and thus damaging to America's "Anglo-Saxon" or "Nordic" stock. Congress had temporarily limited the immigration of "undesirable" Europeans in 1921. In 1924, it made those limitations permanent. Here is how Congressman Fred S. Purnell of Indiana described eastern and southern Europeans in 1924: "There is little or no similarity between the clear-thinking, self-governing stocks that sired the American people and this stream of irresponsible and broken wreckage that is pouring into the lifeblood of America the social and political diseases of the Old World." Purnell quoted approvingly the words of a Dr. Ward, who claimed that Americans had deceived themselves into believing that "we could change inferior beings into superior ones." According to Ward, Americans could not escape the laws of heredity: "We cannot make a heavy horse into a trotter by keeping him in a racing stable. We can not make a well-bred dog out of a mongrel by teaching him tricks." The acts that Ward dismissed as "tricks" included the learning by immigrants of the Gettysburg Address and the Declaration of Independence.[16]

Congressman J. Will Taylor of Tennessee, meanwhile, approvingly read to his colleagues an editorial piece from the *Boston Herald* warning that America was entering the same period of eugenical decline that had doomed Rome: "Rome had [mistaken] faith in the melting pot, as we have. It scorned the iron uncertainties of heredity, as we do. It lost its instinct for race preservation, as we have lost ours. It forgot that men must be selected and bred as sacredly as cows and pigs and sheep, as we have not learned." "Rome rapidly senilized and died," the editorial concluded, and so would America unless Congress took note of eugenical principles and passed the 1924 restriction legislation. The Immigration Restriction Act of 1924, also known as the Johson-Reed Act, passed both houses of Congress by overwhelming margins, drawing votes from congressman and senators from every region of the country, East and West, North and South, urban and rural. This law remained on the books until 1965, giving a decidedly racial cast to the American nation.[17]

This is not to suggest that no one opposed this law or generated alternative conceptions of nationhood at this time. In the first three decades of the twentieth century, sizeable and varied groups of Americans drawn from the ranks of liberal reformers, ethnic and racial minorities, and socialist radicals labored to invigorate the civic basis of American nationhood and to insist that equality and inclusion ought to remain the governing principles of their polity. Many Americans were drawn to Israel Zangwill's vision of America as a melting pot in which the races of many lands would be drawn together and forged into a single people. A much smaller group, but including individuals whose writings and politics would gain influence in subsequent decades—philosophers Horace Kallen and Alain Locke, literary critic Randolph Bourne, anthropologist Franz Boas, educator Rachel Davis-DuBois, and Indian reformer John Collier—pushed their thinking beyond inclusive programs of assimilation and began to argue that ethnic and racial pluralism would strengthen the egalitarian and democratic foundation of the American nation.[18]

Moreover, as nativist attacks on non-Protestant immigrants intensified, so did the resistance of these groups, manifest in the rapidly growing number of eastern and southern Europeans who became citizens and then mobilized politically, hoping to put into office politicians more sympathetic to their concerns. At stake was not just the ability to control public policy but also the ideological power to define the values for which America stood. A careful observer of the 1928 election would have noticed that a broad counter-mobilization against Protestant ascendancy and racial exclusivity was already in the works: voting returns revealed that Al Smith, while losing the election to Herbert Hoover, had carried the twelve largest cities in the United States.[19] But if the future belonged to the offspring of those immigrants who had mobilized in the 1920s and to a revivified civic nationalist tradition, the period from the 1880s to the 1920s was one in which racial and religious exclusion had triumphed. The racial and religious boundaries had narrowed in the early twentieth century. The country's urbanization and modernization at this time went hand in hand with the deepening of America's racial and religious nationalism.

EXCLUSION AND INCLUSION, 1870S–1990S

The forces working to narrow the American nation from the 1870s to the 1920s were global in scope. Strengthening nationhood had become politically imperative throughout the world. Strong nations were thought to require robust industrial economies and populations that were vigorous, productive, and disciplined. These nations were expected to project their power onto the world stage, by assembling strong armies and navies, and to flex their muscles through commerce, territorial expansion, and, if necessary, war. Even under the best of circumstances, nation building was not easy work. And many nations in the 1880s and 1890s seemed beset by deteriorating conditions: economic turmoil and depression, unemployment, class conflict, and regional and cultural resistance to projects of national consolidation. In these circumstances of economic and political uncertainty, and amidst the developing conviction that nation building was a zero-sum game—one nation's advance requiring another nation's retreat—nationalists everywhere sought assurance that their nations were destined to succeed. Many found this assurance in racialized discourses that spoke with conviction about the special qualities that inhered in their people. These discourses variously celebrated the superiority of "Anglo-Saxons," "English-speaking peoples," "Aryans," "Nordics," "Caucasians," whites, and the West. Many scholars lent their sanction to these discourses, making racial classification into a complex pseudo-science and urging politicians in various nations to pursue policies that would maximize their nation's stock of racial superiors and either minimize, segregate, or expel populations of racial inferiors. Immigration and naturalization restrictions, natalist programs for the racially advantaged, sterilization for the racially disadvantaged, bans on racial intermarriage, and segregation were all part of this policy brew, giving multiple expressions to this racial nationalist moment in world affairs. The prestige of racial science was such that its practitioners were able to take differences rooted in religion—the conflict between Protestants and Catholics and between Christians and Jews in America, for example—and render them racial. Thus, in 1924, congressmen stigmatized eastern and southern European Catholics, Jews, and Christian Orthodox not for their religious heterodoxy but for their racial inferiority. Racial science had alchemized religious divides into racial chasms.[20]

This era of racial nationalism reached its peak with the rise of Hitler in Germany and with the aggressive (and nearly successful) campaign to spread German power throughout Europe and, in the process, to rid the continent of its "racial inferiors," most notably Jews. Hitler's actions drew the world into a terrible world war. The unlikely alliance that massed against Germany ultimately dealt Hitler and his plans for an Aryan racial order a devastating defeat. Shock spread through the United States and other countries as the scale of Hitler's destruction of European Jewry became known. That this barbarism had occurred in Germany, whose culture was thought to sit at the pinnacle of Western Civilization, provoked a frank reckoning with the racial science that had enabled Hitler's rise. Meanwhile, Japan's dramatic strikes in 1941 and 1942 against every European and American imperial outpost in East and Southeast Asia punctured the myth of Western superiority. The colonial system that Europe had built across hundreds of years and legitimated with a variety of racial ideologies would never again be the same. In both Europe and Asia, World War II had dealt a serious blow to those who wanted to order the globe according to principles of racial superiority and inferiority.[21]

These were the circumstances in which civic nationalism in the United States regained its stature, its core beliefs conscripted with increasing force to fuel campaigns in America to topple both Protestant ascendancy and white supremacy. Gunnar Myrdal articulated his version of American civic nationalism, the American Creed, in 1944 when he published his landmark book, *An American Dilemma*. That same year, Thurgood Marshall, then an attorney for the NAACP Legal Defense Fund, articulated his own understanding of the need to revive American civic nationalism in a world torn apart by racism: "Distinctions based on color and ancestry are utterly inconsistent with our traditions and ideals. They are at variance with the principles for which we are now waging war. We cannot close our eyes to the fact that for centuries the Old World has been torn by racial and religious conflicts and has suffered the worst kind of anguish because of inequality of treatment for different groups."[22]

The revival of civic nationalism in America had actually begun in the 1920s and 1930s among southern and eastern Europeans and their descendants who were resisting the hardening of racial nationalism. Their movement widened in the 1930s in response to capitalist crisis. The labor movement that arose in those years was full of immigrants and their descendants—Irish, German, Italian, Jewish, Polish, Greek, Arab, French Canadian, Mexican, and others—united by their poverty and marginality and by their conviction that, as Americans, they deserved better. Marching under the banner of Americanism, working-class ethnics infused the first principles of the American republic—freedom, democracy, and opportunity—with insurgent and working-class meaning. Freedom now meant the right of a worker to speak his or her mind at work or to cast a ballot for a Democrat at the polling station without fear of reprisal from management. Democracy meant ending the regime of autocracy at the workplace and replacing it with one in which workers had a voice in the conditions of their labor. Opportunity only had meaning, trade unionists argued, if poor workers and their families had access to government-guaranteed forms of assistance, such as Social Security and unemployment insurance, that would cushion the effects of job loss, illness and death in the family, and old age.[23]

Ethnic workers made themselves heard not just in unions but in politics. Continuing the mobilization that had begun with the Al Smith campaign in the 1920s, immigrant Americans and their offspring cast their votes for another Democrat, Franklin Delano Roosevelt. They not only helped to carry him to victory in four elections but also helped to shift the balance of power in the United States from conservatism to liberalism and from a politics that glorified the free market to one that celebrated the role of government in regulating a capitalist system that, in their view, seemed unable to right itself. Rhetorically, this shift was couched in civic nationalist terms. As the ethnic workers glimpsed an opportunity to refashion America, they began to believe that America, finally, was opening itself to them. And their attachment to America deepened as a consequence.[24]

America's opening to ethnics manifested itself, too, in the growing celebration of America as a land of multiple peoples and cultures. New Dealers for the most part did not self-consciously promote religious pluralism or multiculturalism, nor did they describe their supporters as a "rainbow coalition" of different ethnic and racial groups. Indeed, in important ways, the New Deal reinvigorated older cultural and racial prejudices. The groups pouring into the Democratic Party were a diverse lot, however, and their very presence began to disrupt accepted ways of defining and representing the American nation.[25]

This became abundantly clear in World War II when the dominant and most honored image of the nation became that of the multiethnic platoon, with its Protestant, Irish, Polish, Italian, and Jewish soldiers fighting side by side to preserve American democracy and freedom.[26] At the same time, the phrase "Judeo-Christian" began to displace "Anglo-Saxon" and "Protestant" as a way to describe American civilization. No one did more to popularize this phrase than a Presbyterian minister, Everett R. Clinchy, who began to use it as a weapon against the totalitarian challenge that he believed America confronted. "Political party machines, led by Nazi Hitler, Communist Stalin, and Fascist Mussolini alike," Clinchy declared in 1938, "deny the sovereignty of God above all else, pour contempt on the spiritual values of the Judaeo-Christian tradition, and refuse to recognize those natural rights of freedom of conscience, freedom of church, press, of pulpit, and of religious organization work . . . Never before in history have Protestants, Catholics and Jews been as aware of each other's suffering and as willing to mobilize spiritual forces as American citizens." The Judeao-Christian tradition, he concluded, was the foundation of the "American Way of life."[27]

Following Clinchy's lead, an ecumenical group of clergymen distributed in 1942 a "Declaration of Fundamental Religious Beliefs Held in Common by Catholics, Protestants, and Jews." That same year, the National Conference of Christians and Jews successfully made Brotherhood Week, timed to coincide with Washington's birthday, into a nationwide event. Roosevelt himself chaired the event in 1943, declaring that Brotherhood Week "reminds us of the basic religious faith from which democracy has grown—that all men are children of one Father and brothers in the human family . . . [I]t is good to pledge renewed devotion to the fundamentals on which this country has been built." In 1944, Major General Frederick E. Uhl announced that "the way was open for Judaism, Protestantism and Catholicism to stand shoulder to shoulder before our swiftly expanding armed forces." By the end of the war, invocations to religious brotherhood and to the Judeo-Christian tradition as the American way had become ubiquitous. Religious nationalism, in the form of the Protestant ascendancy, had been knocked from its perch.[28]

The growing popularity of the notion that America was a Judeo-Christian civilization cannot be understood simply in terms of a Protestant elite magnanimously deciding to relinquish its privileged place. Rather, it must be understood as well in terms of the struggles of Catholic and Jewish immigrants and their children to declare civic nationalism—a creed that drew no distinctions on the basis of Protestant, Catholic, or Jew—to be the most honored of America's traditions. In this case, civic nationalism allowed immigrants who became Americans to become advocates for building a different America, all the while claiming that they were being true to America's fundamental promise. Civic nationalism generated among immigrants and their children both insistent demands for change and powerful cultural and political affiliations to their new home. It gave immigrants and their offspring reason to believe in the idea of America and to engage deeply in its democracy. Over time, it would accelerate their political and cultural integration.

The events of the 1930s and 1940s also challenged the color line and the legitimacy of America's racial nationalist tradition. Indeed, the challenges to that tradition, beginning in the late 1940s and continuing through the late 1960s, would be among the most serious in American history. In 1946, President Harry Truman desegregated the armed forces. In 1952, Congress repealed the 1790 naturalization law limiting citizenship to "free, white persons." In 1954, the Supreme Court reversed its "separate but equal"

1896 decision, now declaring that segregation was unconstitutional by the terms of the Fourteenth Amendment. And in 1964 and 1965, Congress, in response to a mass protest movement led by Martin Luther King, Jr., passed the most sweeping civil rights and voting rights legislation since Reconstruction. That same Congress also passed the Immigration Act of 1965, ending the racially based system of immigration restriction in place since the 1920s. After 1965, it became almost impossible for the American government to deny foreigners entry into America and access to citizenship on the basis of race. The result over the next forty years was an immigration wave unprecedented in its global origins and racial diversity. Finally, in 1967, the Supreme Court declared that a Virginia law forbidding marriage between a black woman and a white man was unconstitutional, bringing the entire edifice of state anti-miscegenation statutes crashing to the ground. In America, individuals in every state of the union would now be free to marry across the color line.[29]

The civil rights upheaval also challenged prevailing notions of cultural integration and incorporation. Through the "Black is Beautiful" movement in the 1960s, African Americans signaled that their political incorporation would not cost them their cultural pride or distinctiveness. Immigrant groups, both old and new, quickly adopted a similar stance in regard to their own ethnic cultures, thereby broadening and intensifying the effort to locate America's vitality in its ethnic and racial diversity. The breadth and strength of this movement, which took the name multiculturalism, would have been unimaginable to most immigrant and native-born Americans 100 years earlier.[30] And the diversity now upheld as an American ideal went beyond that embodied in the phrase "Judeo-Christian," which, in the context of the 1940s, referred principally to white Protestants, Catholics, and Jews.[31]

The rise of multiculturalism unleashed a prolonged period of conflict about its legitimacy. Many on the left embraced it only on the condition that it serve as a substitute ideology to American nationalism itself; minorities were encouraged to find authenticity, community, and goodness in their particular cultures—grounded in race, gender, and sexuality—and to reject mainstream American culture, including the civic nationalist tradition, as compromised by racism, imperialism, and sexism. Those on the right attacked multiculturalism for what they perceived to be its anti-Americanism and cultural relativism, both of which threatened to destroy the core ideals of the country's eighteenth-century political and cultural inheritance. Yet, by the 1990s, after two decades of culture wars, multiculturalism was no longer the property of the left or the right, but of a broad middle, which saw in it a superior creed for defining the meaning of America for the twenty-first century. In the eyes of this middle, and its tribunes, including Presidents Bill Clinton and George W. Bush, America ought to celebrate its cultural diversity while also calling on the country's diverse groups to embrace the principles of civic nationalism as their own.[32] Multiculturalism, from this point of view, offered a formula for making a celebration of diversity central to a program of national belonging.

American nationalism had moved a great distance across the second two-thirds of the twentieth century. That this country elected its first African American president in 2008, and that this president presided over a Supreme Court that does not even include a token Protestant in its ranks, reveals how much the traditions of racial and religious nationalism have weakened. But it would be a mistake to conclude that they are gone. The racial nationalist tradition, in particular, has roots so deep that the possibility of regeneration always remains; and, in the anti-Muslim sentiment that has become so pronounced in recent years, one can discern, too, the possibility of a religious nationalist revival.

AMERICA IN THE TWENTY-FIRST CENTURY

Nativism has shaped the early twenty-first century, evident in the increasing attacks on the immigrant presence in American society. Especially after 2005, many Americans have been claiming that "they" (the immigrants) are not like "us" (the native-born keepers of American traditions). "They" stand accused of subverting what "we" have built.[33] This anxiety takes two forms in particular: first, that America is in the process of becoming a "majority-minority" nation, with the white majority permanently displaced; and second, that America cannot survive the presence of Muslim immigrants in American society, since the latter are the carriers of a religion of "terror," "domination," and "oppression" (widespread denunciations of Shariah law are the latest manifestations of this anti-Islam orientation). These two manifestations of national fear found a common focus in the person of Barack Obama, the first minority president and the first, too, who is alleged to have a close affinity with Islam (Barack *Hussein* Obama); indeed, through much of his first term, some Americans believed that Obama was secretly a Muslim and that he had been indoctrinated into the Islamic faith during the years he spent as a boy in Indonesia. Obama is also only the third second-generation immigrant to become president of the United States, and he is the first to have an African father. The convergence of popular anxieties about race and religion on Obama helps to explain why his legitimacy as president during his first term was challenged more than virtually any other previous resident of the Oval Office.

In the anxiety about America becoming a "majority-minority" nation one can discern a hoary racial nationalist principle at work: namely, that "we" were meant to be a white or European nation. As America's non-European demographic future continues, ineluctably, to unfold, we can expect to see more declarations that the European or white character of America must be preserved; alternatively, we might see the racial nationalist tradition reinvent itself by declaring that the critical division in America is not between whites and non-whites but between blacks and non-blacks. In this second scenario, Asians and Latinos would be welcomed into a new American majority that construes its racial privilege in terms of being not black. America's color line underwent something of a similar shift when the descendants of eastern and southern European immigrants transitioned, in the 1930s and 1940s, from being racially suspect to being racially fit and, in the process, walled themselves off from other racially suspect groups whom they had left behind.[34] America may yet find a new way of defining and legitimating racial privilege for the twenty-first century.

Efforts to revive religious nationalism as a defining feature of America can be glimpsed, meanwhile, in popular anxiety about Islam. This new religious nationalism no longer defines itself as Protestant (though there are groups seeking to restore a Protestant Ascendancy) but as Western, and it claims to stand for the core principles of European humanism and American civic nationalism: celebration of life, freedom, individual rights, and the toleration of dissent. Islam, by contrast, is alleged to be a faith that denies its adherents freedom while celebrating war on all nonbelievers. In this version of religious nationalism, Protestants, Catholics, and Jews are called on to stand together to defend America and its Judeo-Christian tradition from Muslim assault.

The American fear of Islam today is reminiscent of America's fear of Catholicism 150 years ago. That America actually overcame its fear of the "Catholic menace"—though it took more than 100 years—offers hope that it can do so with regard to Islam as well. It is therefore possible that by 2050, we will be talking about America as an Abrahamic-Christian civilization, that phrase joining Muslims with Jews and Christians as joint stakeholders in the American nation. We are, at present, a long way from that formulation of American national identity.

Future configurations of American national identity will be shaped not just by cultural struggles but by economic circumstances as well. Economic distress and the crashing of the American dream of economic opportunity have darkened the country's mood toward immigrants. Richard Alba has made his hopeful scenario for blurring America's color lines—and, we might add, for dealing America's tradition of racial nationalism a final defeat—contingent upon an economy robust enough to generate ample economic opportunity for non-whites and whites alike.[35] He is right to do so. America's tradition of civic nationalism has always promised that good things would come to those willing to work hard and inventively. That promise must be honored in order for civic nationalism to regain its vigor and advance its integrative work.

NOTES

1. Gunnar Myrdal, *An American Dilemma: The Negro Problem and Modern Democracy*, 2 vols. (1944; New York, 1972), 1: esp. 3–4, 6; Michael Ignatieff, *Blood and Belonging: Journeys into the New Nationalism* (New York: Farrar, Straus, and Giroux, 1993), 5–6. For a fuller exploration of civic nationalist principles, see Gary Gerstle, *American Crucible: Race and Nation in the Twentieth Century* (Princeton, New Jersey: Princeton University Press, 2001), Introduction and Chapter 1; and Rogers M. Smith, *Civic Ideals: Conflicting Visions of Citizenship in U.S. History* (New Haven: Yale University Press, 1997).

2. Morris U. Schappes, ed., *Emma Lazarus: Selections from Her Poetry and Prose* (1947; New York: IWO Jewish-American Section, 1967), 48.

3. Aristide Zolberg, *A Nation by Design: Immigration Policy in the Fashioning of America* (Cambridge: Harvard University Press, 2006), 58–98; James H. Kettner, *The Development of American Citizenship, 1608–1870* (Chapel Hill: University of North Carolina Press, 1978);

Peter H. Shuck and Rogers M. Smith, *Citizenship Without Consent: Illegal Aliens in the American Polity* (New Haven: Yale University Press, 1985), chaps. 1–2; U.S. Congress, An Act to Establish an Uniform Rule of Naturalization, 1st Congress, 2d session, ch. 3 (Mar. 1, 1790), available at http://memory.loc.gov/cgi-bin/ampage?collId=llsl&fileName=001/llsl001.db&recNum=226.

4. U.S. Const., amends. 11–27, available at http://www.archives.gov/exhibits/charters/constitution_amendments_11-27.html; Eric Foner, *Reconstruction: America's Unfinished Revolution, 1863–1877* (New York: Harper & Row, 1988); Eric Foner, *The Story of American Freedom* (New York, 1988); Garrett Epps, The Citizenship Clause: A 'Legislative History,'" *American University Law Review* 60 (Dec. 2010): 331–391; Gerald L. Neuman, *Strangers to the Constitution: Immigrants, Borders, and Fundamental Law* (Princeton: Princeton University Press, 1996). See also *United States v. Wong Kim Ark*, 169 U.S. 649 (1898).

5. On the country's anti-Catholic origins and history, see John Higham, *Strangers in the Land: Patterns of American Nativism, 1860–1925* (New Brunswick: Rutgers University Press, 1955); David H. Bennett, *The Party of Fear: From Nativist Movements to the New Right in American History* (Chapel Hill: University of North Carolina Press, 1988), pt. I passim.

6. *An Act to Establish an Uniform Rule of Naturalization* (Mar. 26, 1790), 1 Stat 103–104. Various states, such as Massachusetts and South Carolina, did have laws establishing Protestantism as the official religion and barring non-Protestants from holding state office. See, for example, Johann N. Neem, *Creating a Nation of Joiners: Democracy and Civil Society in Early National Massachusetts* (Cambridge: Harvard University Press, 2008).

7. Oscar Handlin, *Boston's Immigrants, 1790–1865: A Study in Acculturation* (Cambridge: Harvard University Press, 1941); Bennett; *The Party of Fear*; Tyler G. Anbinder, *Nativism and Slavery: The Northern Know Nothings and the Politics of the 1850s* (New York: Oxford University Press, 1992); David R. Roediger, *The Wages of Whiteness: Race and the Making of the American Working Class* (London: Verso, 1999); Zolberg, *A Nation by Design*, chap. 5.

8. Bennett, *The Party of Fear*, 233–237, 319–321; Oscar Handlin, *Al Smith and His America* (Boston: Little, Brown, 1958).

9. David A. Gerber, *The Making of an American Pluralism* (Champaign: University of Illinois Press, 1989); John T. McGreevy, *Parish Boundaries: The Catholic Encounter with Race in the Twentieth-Century Urban North* (Chicago: University of Chicago Press, 1996); John T. McGreevy, *Catholicism and American Freedom: A History* (New York: W. W. Norton, 2003); Christopher J. Kaufmann, *Patriotism and Fraternalism in the Knights of Columbus: A History of the Fourth Degree* (New York: Crossroad, 2001); Paula Kane, *Separatism and Subculture: Boston Catholicism, 1900–1920* (Chapel Hill: University of North Carolina Press, 1994).

10. Reginald Horsman, *Race and Manifest Destiny: The Origins of American Racial Anglo-Saxonism* (Cambridge: Harvard University Press, 1981); Gerald Linderman, *The Mirror of War: American Society and the Spanish-American War* (Ann Arbor: University of Michigan Press, 1974), 114–173.

11. See, for example, Josiah Strong, *Our Country*, ed. Jurgen Herbst (1891; Cambridge: Harvard University Press, 1963).

12. For one of the most interesting explorations of this paradox, see Edmund Morgan, *American Slavery, American Freedom* (New York: W. W. Norton, 1975).

13. On the 1790 law, see Kettner, *The Development of American Citizenship*, and Matthew Jacobson, *Whiteness of a Different Color: European Americans and the Alchemy of Race* (Cambridge: Harvard University Press, 1998).

14. On the promise and failure of Reconstruction, see Eric Foner, *Reconstruction: America's Unfinished Revolution, 1863–1877* (New York: Harper & Row, 1988); Steven Hahn, *A Nation Under Our Feet: Black Political Struggles in the Rural South from Slavery to the Great Migration* (Cambridge: Belknap Press of Harvard University Press, 2003); Ira Berlin et al., *Slaves No More: Three Essays on Emancipation and the Civil War* (New York: Cambridge University Press, 1992). On the restoration of elite white power in the South and the implementation of Jim Crow, see C. Vann Woodward, *The Origins of the New South 1877–1913* (Baton Rouge: Louisiana State University Press, 1971); C. Vann Woodward, *The Strange Career of Jim Crow* (New York: Oxford University Press, 1955); Edward L. Ayers, *The Promise of the New South: Life after Reconstruction* (New York: Oxford University Press, 1992); David Blight, *Race and Reunion: The Civil War in American Memory* (Cambridge: Belknap Press of Harvard University Press, 2001).

15. On Chinese and Japanese exclusion, see Andrew Gyory, *Closing the Gate: Race, Politics, and the Chinese Exclusion Act* (Chapel Hill: University of North Carolina Press, 1998); Lucy Salyer, *Laws Harsh as Tigers: Chinese Immigrants and the Shaping of Modern Immigration Law* (Chapel Hill: University of North Carolina Press, 1995); Erika Lee, *At America's Gates: Chinese Immigration During the Exclusion Era, 1882–1943* (Chapel Hill: University of North Carolina Press, 2003); Yuji Ichioka, *The Issei: The World of the First Generation Japanese Immigrants, 1880–1924* (London: Collier Macmillan, 1988); Roger Daniels, *Not Like Us: Immigrants and Minorities in America, 1890–1924* (Chicago: Ivan R. Dee, 1997); Paul A. Kramer, "Empire against Exclusion in Early 20th Century Trans-Pacific History," *Nanzan Review of American Studies* 22 (2011): 13–32.

16. 68 *Congressional Record* H4389 (March 17, 1924). (statement of Rep. Purnell).

17. 68 *Congressional Record* H5872 (April 8, 1924) (statement of Rep. Taylor). On the 1924 law, see also Gerstle, *American Crucible*, chap. 3; Mae Ngai, *Impossible Subjects: Illegal Aliens and the Making of Modern America* (Princeton: Princeton University Press, 2004), chap. 1; Jacobson: *Whiteness of a Different Color*, chap. 7; Desmond King, *Making Americans: Immigration, Race, and the Origins of the Diverse Democracy* (Cambridge: Harvard University Press, 2000); John Higham, *Strangers in the Land*, chap. 11.

18. Gerstle, *American Crucible*, chaps. 2–3; Israel Zangwill, *The Melting-Pot: Drama in Four Acts* (1909; New York, The Macmillan Company, 1923); Gary Gerstle, "The Protean Character of American Liberalism," *American Historical Review* 99 (Oct. 1994): 1043–1073; Jeffrey C. Stewart, ed., *The Critical Temper of Alain Locke: A Selection of His Essays on Art and Culture* (New York: Garland Publishers, 1983); Horace Kallen, "Democracy vs. the Melting Pot," *The Nation* (1915): 190–194; Randolph Bourne, "Transnational America," in *The Radical Will: Selected Writings, 1911–1918*, ed. Olaf Hansen (New York: Urizen Books, 1977); George W. Stocking, Jr., *Race, Culture, and Evolution: Essays in the History of Anthropology* (New York: Free Press, 1968); Lawrence C. Kelly, *The Assault on Assimilation: John Collier and the Origins of Indian Reform Policy* (Albuquerque: University of New Mexico Press, 1983); Rachel Davis-DuBois, "Adventures in Intercultural Education" (Doctor of Education thesis, New York University, 1940).

19. Kristi Andersen, *The Creation of a Democratic Majority, 1928–1936* (Chicago: University of Chicago Press, 1979).

20. Marilyn Lake and Henry Reynolds, *Drawing the Global Colour Line: White Men's Countries and the International Challenge of Racial Equality* (New York: Cambridge University Press, 2008); Gary Gerstle, "Race and Nation in the United States, Cuba, and Mexico, 1880–1940," in Don H. Doyle and Marco A. Pamplona, eds., *Nationalism in the Americas* (Athens: University of Georgia, 2006), 272–304; Eric Hobsbawm, *Nations and Nationalism Since 1789: Programme, Myth, Reality* (New York: Cambridge University Press, 1990).

21. Lake and Reynolds, *Drawing the Global Colour Line*; Gerald Horne, *Race War: White Supremacy and the Japanese Attack on the British Empire* (New York: New York University Press, 2004); Gerstle, American Crucible, chaps. 5 and 6; Ashley Montagu, *Man's Most Dangerous Myth: The Fallacy of Race* (New York: Harper, 1942).

22. Quoted in Kevin M. Schultz, *Tri-Faith America: How Catholics and Jews Held Postwar America to Its Protestant Promise* (New York: Oxford University Press, 2011), 52; Myrdal, *An American Dilemma*.

23. Gary Gerstle, *Working-Class Americanism: The Politics of Labor in a Textile City, 1914–1960* (New York: Cambridge University Press, 1989); Lizabeth Cohen, *Making a New Deal: Industrial Workers in Chicago, 1919–1939* (New York: Cambridge University Press, 1990); George Sánchez, *Becoming Mexican American: Ethnicity, Culture, and Identity in Chicano Los Angeles, 1900–1945* (New York: Oxford University Press, 1993); David G. Gutiérrez, *Walls and Mirrors: Mexican Americans, Mexican Immigrants, and the Politics of Ethnicity* (Berkeley: University of California Press, 1995); Thomas Bell, *Out of This Furnace* (1941; Pittsburgh: University of Pittsburgh Press, 1976); Michael Denning, *The Cultural Front: The Laboring of American Culture in the Twentieth Century* (New York: Verso, 1998); James Barrett, "Americanization from the Bottom Up," *Journal of American History* 79 (December 1992): 996–1020.

24. Ibid.; Kristi Andersen, *The Creation of a Democratic Majority, 1928–1936* (Chicago: University of Chicago Press, 1979); Gary, Gerstle "Acquiescence or Transformation? Divergent Paths of Political Incorporation in America." In Jennifer Hochschild, Michael Jones-Correa, Claudine Gay, and Jennifer Chattopadhyay, eds., *Immigrant Political Incorporation: A Handbook* (New York: Oxford University Press, 2013). 306–322.

25. Jacobson, *Whiteness of a Different Color*; Denning, *The Cultural Front*; Stuart Svonkin, *Jews Against Prejudice: American Jews and the Fight for Civil Liberties* (New York: Columbia University Press, 1997); Kevin M. Schultz, "'Favoritism Cannot Be Tolerated': Challenging Protestantism in America's Public Schools and Promoting the Neutral State," *American Quarterly* 59 (Sept. 2007): 565–591; Gerstle, American Crucible, chaps. 4–5.

26. Denning, *The Cultural Front*; Gerstle, American Crucible, chap. 5.

27. Quoted in Schultz, *Tri-Faith America*, 58. See also Eric P. Kaufmann, *The Rise and Fall of Anglo-America* (Cambridge: Harvard University Press, 2004).

28. Quoted in Schultz, *Tri-Faith America*, 66 passim; William R. Hutchison, *Religious Pluralism in America: the Contentious History of a Founding Ideal* (New Haven: Yale University Press, 2003); Kaufmann, *Rise and Fall of Anglo-America*; Richard Alba, *Blurring the Color Line: The New Chance for a More Integrated America* (Cambridge: Harvard University Press, 2009); David A. Hollinger, *After Cloven Tongues of Fire: Protestant Liberalism in Modern American History* (Princeton: Princeton University Press, 2013).

29. Ngai, *Impossible Subjects*, chap. 7; Peggy Pascoe, *What Comes Naturally: Miscegenation Law and the Making of Race in America* (Cambridge: Harvard University Press, 2009); Gary Gerstle, "The Resilient Power of the States Across the Long Nineteenth Century:

An Inquiry into a Pattern of American Governance," eds. Desmond King and Lawrence Jacobs, *The Unsustainable American State* (New York: Oxford University Press, 2009), 61–87; David Reimers, *Still the Golden Door: The Third World Comes to America, 1943–1983* (New York: Columbia University Press, 1985); Hugh Davis Graham, *Collision Course: The Strange Convergence of Affirmative Action and Immigration Policy in America* (New York: Oxford University Press, 2002).

30. Gerstle, *American Crucible*, chap. 8.

31. Will Herberg, *Protestant, Catholic, Jew: An Essay in American Religious Sociology* (Garden City, NY: Anchor Books, 1960).

32. Gary Gerstle, "Minorities, Multiculturalism, and the Presidency of George W. Bush," in Julian Zelizer, ed., *The Presidency of George W. Bush: A First Historical Assessment* (Princeton: Princeton University Press, 2010), 252–281.

33. See, for example, Samuel P. Huntington, *Who Are We? The Challenges to America's National Identity* (New York: Simon and Schuster, 2004), and Patrick Buchanan, *State of Emergency: The Third World Invasion and Conquest of America* (New York: Thomas Sunne Books/St. Martin's Press, 2006).

34. Jacobson, *Whiteness of a Different Color*; David R. Roediger, *Working Toward Whiteness: How America's Immigrants Became White: The Strange Journey from Ellis Island to the Suburbs* (New York: Basic Books, 2005); Eric L. Goldstein, *The Price of Whiteness: Jews, Race, and American Identity* (Princeton: Princeton University Press, 2006); Gerstle, *American Crucible*, chaps. 4–5.

35. Richard Alba, *Blurring the Color Line*.

Bibliography

Alba, Richard. *Blurring the Color Line: The New Chance for a More Integrated America.* Cambridge: Harvard University Press, 2009.

Anbinder, Tyler G. *Nativism and Slavery: The Northern Know Nothings and the Politics of the 1850s.* New York: Oxford University Press, 1992.

Andersen, Kristi. *The Creation of a Democratic Majority, 1928–1936.* Chicago: University of Chicago Press, 1979.

Ayers, Edward L. *The Promise of the New South: Life after Reconstruction.* New York: Oxford University Press, 1992.

Barrett, James. "Americanization from the Bottom Up," *Journal of American History* 79 (December 1992): 996–1020.

Bell, Thomas. *Out of This Furnace.* 1941; Pittsburgh: University of Pittsburgh Press, 1976.

Bennett, David H. *The Party of Fear: From Nativist Movements to the New Right in American History.* Chapel Hill: University of North Carolina Press, 1988.

Berlin, Ira, et al. *Slaves No More: Three Essays on Emancipation and the Civil War.* New York: Cambridge University Press, 1992.

Blight, David. *Race and Reunion: The Civil War in American Memory.* Cambridge: Belknap Press of Harvard University Press, 2001.

Bourne, Randolph. "Transnational America." In *The Radical Will: Selected Writings, 1911–1918*, edited by Olaf Hansen. New York: Urizen Books, 1977.

Buchanan, Patrick. *State of Emergency: The Third World Invasion and Conquest of America.* New York: Thomas Sunne Books/St. Martin's Press, 2006.

Cohen, Lizabeth. *Making a New Deal: Industrial Workers in Chicago, 1919–1939.* New York: Cambridge University Press, 1990.

Daniels, Roger. *Not Like Us: Immigrants and Minorities in America, 1890–1924.* Chicago: Ivan R. Dee, 1997.

Davis-DuBois, Rachel. "Adventures in Intercultural Education." Doctor of Education thesis, New York University, 1940.

Denning, Michael. *The Cultural Front: The Laboring of American Culture in the Twentieth Century.* New York: Verso, 1998.

Epps, Garrett. "The Citizenship Clause: A 'Legislative History.'" *American University Law Review* 60 (Dec. 2010): 331–391.

Foner, Eric. *Reconstruction: America's Unfinished Revolution, 1863–1877.* New York: Harper & Row, 1988.

Foner, Eric. *The Story of American Freedom.* New York: W. W. Norton, 1998.

Gerber, David A. *The Making of an American Pluralism.* Champaign: University of Illinois Press, 1989.

Gerstle, Gary. *Working-Class Americanism: The Politics of Labor in a Textile City, 1914–1960.* New York: Cambridge University Press, 1989.

Gerstle, Gary. "The Protean Character of American Liberalism." *American Historical Review* 99 (Oct. 1994): 1043–1073.

Gerstle, Gary. *American Crucible: Race and Nation in the Twentieth Century.* Princeton: Princeton University Press, 2001.

Gerstle, Gary. "Race and Nation in the United States, Cuba, and Mexico, 1880–1940." In *Nationalism in the Americas,* edited by Don H. Doyle and Marco A. Pamplona, 272–304. Athens: University of Georgia, 2006.

Gerstle, Gary. "The Resilient Power of the States Across the Long Nineteenth Century: An Inquiry into a Pattern of American Governance." In *The Unsustainable American State,* edited by Desmond King and Lawrence Jacobs, 61–87. New York: Oxford University Press, 2009.

Gerstle, Gary. "Minorities, Multiculturalism, and the Presidency of George W. Bush." In *The Presidency of George W. Bush: A First Historical Assessment,* edited by Julian Zelizer, 252-81. Princeton: Princeton University Press, 2010.

Gerstle, Gary. "Acquiescence or Transformation? Divergent Paths of Political Incorporation in America." In *Immigrant Political Incorporation: A Handbook,* edited by Jennifer Hochschild, Michael Jones-Correa, Claudine Gay, and Jennifer Chattopadhyay, 306–322. New York: Oxford University Press, 2013.

Goldstein, Eric L. *The Price of Whiteness: Jews, Race, and American Identity.* Princeton: Princeton University Press, 2006.

Graham, Hugh Davis. *Collision Course: The Strange Convergence of Affirmative Action and Immigration Policy in America.* New York: Oxford University Press, 2002.

Gutiérrez, David G. *Walls and Mirrors: Mexican Americans, Mexican Immigrants, and the Politics of Ethnicity.* Berkeley: University of California Press, 1995.

Gyory, Andrew, *Closing the Gate: Race, Politics, and the Chinese Exclusion Act.* Chapel Hill: University of North Carolina Press, 1998.

Hahn, Steven. *A Nation Under Our Feet: Black Political Struggles in the Rural South from Slavery to the Great Migration.* Cambridge: Belknap Press of Harvard University Press, 2003.

Handlin, Oscar. *Boston's Immigrants, 1790–1865: A Study in Acculturation.* Cambridge: Harvard University Press, 1941.

Handlin, Oscar. *Al Smith and His America*. Boston: Little, Brown, 1958.

Herberg, Will. *Protestant, Catholic, Jew: An Essay in American Religious Sociology*. Garden City, NY: Anchor Books, 1960.

Higham, John. *Strangers in the Land: Patterns of American Nativism, 1860–1925*. New Brunswick: Rutgers University Press, 1955.

Hobsbawm, Eric. *Nations and Nationalism Since 1789: Programme, Myth, Reality*. New York: Cambridge University, 1990.

Hollinger, David A. *After Cloven Tongues of Fire: Protestant Liberalism in Modern American History*. Princeton: Princeton University Press, 2013.

Horne, Gerald. *Race War: White Supremacy and the Japanese Attack on the British Empire*. New York: New York University Press, 2004.

Horsman, Reginald. *Race and Manifest Destiny: The Origins of American Racial Anglo-Saxonism*. Cambridge: Harvard University Press, 1981.

Huntington, Samuel P. *Who Are We? The Challenges to America's National Identity*. New York: Simon and Schuster, 2004.

Hutchison, William R. *Religious Pluralism in America: The Contentious History of a Founding Ideal*. New Haven: Yale University Press, 2003.

Ichioka, Yuji, *The Issei: The World of the First Generation Japanese Immigrants*. London: Collier Macmillan, 1988.

Ignatieff, Michael. *Blood and Belonging: Journeys into the New Nationalism*. New York: Farrar, Straus, and Giroux, 1993.

Jacobson, Matthew. *Whiteness of a Different Color: European Americans and the Alchemy of Race*. Cambridge: Harvard University Press, 1998.

Kallen, Horace. "Democracy vs. the Melting Pot." *The Nation* (1915): 190–194.

Kane, Paula. *Separatism and Subculture: Boston Catholicism, 1900–1920*. Chapel Hill: University of North Carolina Press, 1994.

Kaufmann, Christopher J. *Patriotism and Fraternalism in the Knights of Columbus: A History of the Fourth Degree*. New York: Crossroad, 2001.

Kaufmann, Eric P. *The Rise and Fall of Anglo-America*. Cambridge: Harvard University Press, 2004.

Kelly, Lawrence C. *The Assault on Assimilation: John Collier and the Origins of Indian Reform Policy*. Albuquerque: University of New Mexico Press, 1983.

Kettner, James H. *The Development of American Citizenship, 1608–1870*. Chapel Hill: University of North Carolina Press, 1978.

King, Desmond. *Making Americans: Immigration, Race, and the Origins of the Diverse Democracy*. Cambridge: Harvard University Press, 2000.

King, Desmond S., and Rogers M. Smith. *Still a House Divided: Race and Politics in Obama's America*. Princeton: Princeton University Press, 2011.

Kramer, Paul A. "Empire against Exclusion in Early 20th Century Trans-Pacific History." *Nanzan Review of American Studies* 22 (2011): 13–32.

Lake, Marilyn, and Henry Reynolds. *Drawing the Global Colour Line: White Men's Countries and the International Challenge of Racial Equality*. New York: Cambridge University Press, 2008.

Lee, Erika. *At America's Gates: Chinese Immigration During the Exclusion Era, 1882–1943*. Chapel Hill: University of North Carolina Press, 2003.

Linderman, Gerald., *The Mirror of War: American Society and the Spanish-American War*. Ann Arbor: University of Michigan Press, 1974.

McGreevy, John T. *Parish Boundaries: The Catholic Encounter with Race in the Twentieth-Century Urban North.* Chicago: University of Chicago Press, 1996.

McGreevy, John T. *Catholicism and American Freedom: A History.* New York: W. W. Norton, 2003.

Montagu, Ashley. *Man's Most Dangerous Myth: The Fallacy of Race.* New York: Harper, 1942.

Morgan, Edmund. *American Slavery, American Freedom.* New York: W. W. Norton, 1975.

Myrdal, Gunnar. *An American Dilemma: The Negro Problem and Modern Democracy.* 2 vols. 1944; New York, 1972.

Neem, Johann N. *Creating a Nation of Joiners: Democracy and Civil Society in Early National Massachusetts.* Cambridge: Harvard University Press, 2008.

Neuman, Gerald L. *Strangers to the Constitution: Immigrants, Borders, and Fundamental Law.* Princeton: Princeton University Press, 1996.

Ngai, Mae. *Impossible Subjects: Illegal Aliens and the Making of Modern America.* Princeton: Princeton University Press, 2004.

Pascoe, Peggy. *What Comes Naturally: Miscegenation Law and the Making of Race in America.* New York: Oxford University Press, 2009.

Reimers, David. *Still the Golden Door: The Third World Comes to America, 1943–1983.* New York: Columbia University Press, 1985.

Roediger, David R. *The Wages of Whiteness: Race and the Making of the American Working Class.* London: Verso, 1999.

Roediger, David R. *Working Toward Whiteness: How America's Immigrants Became White: The Strange Journey from Ellis Island to the Suburbs.* New York: Basic Books, 2005.

Salyer, Lucy, *Laws Harsh as Tigers: Chinese Immigrants and the Shaping of Modern Immigration Law.* Chapel Hill: University of North Carolina Press, 1995.

Sánchez, George. *Becoming Mexican American: Ethnicity, Culture, and Identity in Chicano Los Angeles, 1900–1945.* New York: Oxford University Press, 1993.

Schappes, Morris U. ed., *Emma Lazarus: Selections from Her Poetry and Prose.* 1947; New York: IWO Jewish-American Section, 1967.

Schultz, Kevin M. "'Favoritism Cannot Be Tolerated': Challenging Protestantism in America's Public Schools and Promoting the Neutral State." *American Quarterly* 59 (Sept. 2007): 565–591.

Schultz, Kevin M. *Tri-Faith America: How Catholics and Jews Held Postwar America to Its Protestant Promise.* New York: Oxford University Press, 2011.

Shuck, Peter H., and Rogers M. Smith. *Citizenship Without Consent: Illegal Aliens in the American Polity.* New Haven: Yale University Press, 1985.

Smith, Rogers M. *Civic Ideals: Conflicting Visions of Citizenship in U.S. History.* New Haven: Yale University Press, 1997.

Stewart, Jeffrey C., ed. *The Critical Temper of Alain Locke: A Selection of His Essays on Art and Culture.* New York: Garland Publishers, 1983.

Stocking, George W. Jr. *Race, Culture, and Evolution: Essays in the History of Anthropology.* New York: Free Press, 1968.

Strong, Josiah. *Our Country.* Edited by Jurgen Herbst. 1891; Cambridge: Harvard University Press, 1963.

Svonkin, Stuart. *Jews Against Prejudice: American Jews and the Fight for Civil Liberties* New York: Columbia University Press, 1997.

Woodward, C. Vann. *The Strange Career of Jim Crow*. New York: Oxford University Press, 1955.

Woodward, C. Vann. *The Origins of the New South, 1877–1913* Baton Rouge: Louisiana State University Press, 1971.

Zangwill, Israel. *The Melting-Pot: Drama in Four Acts*. 1909; New York, The Macmillan Company, 1923.

Zolberg, Aristide. *A Nation by Design: Immigration Policy in the Fashioning of America*. Cambridge: Harvard University Press, 2006.

CHAPTER 9

....

RACE AND CITIZENSHIP

....

GREGORY T. CARTER

THE Naturalization Act of 1790, the United States' first law dictating who could achieve citizenship, stipulated that aliens must live in the country for 2 years, take an oath of support for the Constitution, possess a good character, and be a free white person. These criteria excluded indentured servants, slaves, free blacks, and American Indians. Women gained citizenship through their white fathers but, without property or the ability to vote, their status was secondary. This narrow conception of citizenship favored one segment of society. More important, it set a standard for future newcomers to attain or challenge.

The nation's first census took place the same year, with local marshals surveying heads of households in the 13 states and the districts of Kentucky, Maine, Vermont, and Tennessee. Five categories captured the population: free white males of 16 years and older, free white males younger than 16 years, free white females, all other free persons, and slaves. As with the naturalization law, these focused mainly on white males, with the others as outsiders in terms of citizenship. The survey resulted in a population of nearly 3.9 million: 3,140,000 free whites, 694,000 slaves, and 59,000 free nonwhite people. Eighty percent of the nation was white.[1] The founders imagined that the country would remain so, and their decisions established a status quo in regard to race and citizenship. Customs surrounding slavery, property, voting, and marriage had privileged white racial status before this point. Encounters between colonists and Indians, landowners and servants, and men and women of different racial groups demanded clarification regarding gender, race, and citizenship; more often than not, the resolutions privileged white males. Because of the founders' solipsism, whiteness, privilege, and citizenship bound to each other; white racial status was the fundamental requirement for citizenship, and nonwhiteness meant subordination. When minorities gained citizenship, it was easy to revoke or disregard, as African Americans in the pre–Civil War years, Japanese Americans facing internment, and Mexican Americans repatriated during the 1930s could attest.

This system relied on definitions of who was white—or, more important, who was not white—to determine who was worthy neither of citizenship nor of the privileges it bestowed. For the most part, these definitions became standards for other groups who would encounter the American system until the Immigration and Nationality Act eliminated racial barriers in 1952. But four forces complicated them: Racial mixture was already in progress, and hypodescent often failed to resolve the ambiguities it produced. Even when one drop of nonwhite blood was enough to exclude a mixed person, the boundaries between white and mixed were porous. Through social movements, minorities dissatisfied with ending up on the wrong side of the equation of citizenship with whiteness challenged their classification. They and their allies invoked the language of the founding documents, often deploying new meanings to extend equality. In addition, expansion presented questions of how to incorporate inhabitants of new territories, such as, American Indians, Mexicans Americans, and colonial subjects like Filipinos. Last, immigration brought nationalities outside Europe, calling on prerequisite cases to answer unforeseen questions of categorization, sometimes bestowing whiteness-as-citizenship on groups at which Americans may have scoffed previously.[2]

From the colonial period, our national, secular rhetoric has promised equality. At the same time, the authors of these words qualified their applicability, especially when considering race. But racial mixture, social movements, expansion, and immigration have wielded the ideal of inclusion against the realities of exclusion, expanding citizenship beyond the white supremacist definitions at the nation's foundation. This essay surveys the broad contours of inclusion in citizenship since then. The quartet of forces I list earlier have done this work in many arenas, but I will focus on the legal and legislative ones, where the meanings of race and citizenship changed on an official level, swaying local mores. For example, the redefinition of citizenship after the Civil War, however incomplete it may have been, made racial justice movements in the middle of the following century possible. Prominent cases and legislation both reflect and influence the understandings of these issues.

Of course, the meanings of race and citizenship have changed in leaps, sputters, and free-falls. I address this by presenting signature moments of national import, rather than introduce obscure ones, which require more contextualization. Similarly, the meanings have differed between, and within, locations. I offer several cases that contrast with the prominent racial situations of their times to illustrate how specialized situations test the meanings at large. Last, the meanings alter, depending on whom we are talking about. Whiteness-as-citizenship is at the center, but I present the black struggle to demonstrate how a group recovered from having been in the lowest level of society. The American Indian experience shows how loss of land coupled with genocide to remove them from citizenship. Similarly, Mexicans in the United States also were subjects of internal colonization, plus broken promises of equal citizenship. On the other hand, Asians have suffered being forever foreigners, clumped together and characterized as essentially alien. Altogether these experiences fit together in a narrative of how race had been the primary factor in determining citizenship.[3]

If the past featured more restriction, prejudice, and violence than the present, then the colonial period must have been the most restrictive of all. In reality, the discipline of racial boundaries was a process under construction during much of the seventeenth century. Race encompassed what later entered our parlance as ethnicity. Citizenship remained a local matter through the Revolutionary War. White supremacy had begun to take shape, but the institutional means to nurture it was still under development. Virginia served as the proving grounds where the meanings of race settled into the mode prominent in our history. How race, slavery, and exclusion coalesced in Virginia set the model for how race, citizenship, and privilege related nationwide. But even that proceeded ad hoc, in response to the complications that slavery, indentureship, and mixture presented that colony's ruling body. When the first Africans arrived in 1619, they were no lower than the white indentured servants they worked alongside. Desiring land and representation, Nathaniel Bacon initiated an uprising in 1676. The planter became the leader of an interracial movement of the poor, although he was a landowner himself. What started as a demand to remove Indians from the frontier became "a challenge to the very economic basis of the society: the chattel bond-labor form of master-servant relations."[4] To quell Bacon's Rebellion, the House of Burgesses conferred special meaning to white men, regardless of land ownership. At the same time, they firmed the connection between slavery and blackness. From then, shoring the boundary between white and nonwhite became a challenge they had to answer again and again, with mixture as the scourge of this endeavor. Virginia and Maryland instituted the first laws against interracial intimacy, establishing the illegitimacy of mixed offspring, dictating steep punishments (especially for white women and black men), and assigning slavery to their children. Still, interracial intimacy recurred, and they had to revise their laws to solve the challenges it presented. At first, children followed the status of their mothers. Eventually, having any black parentage at all determined slavery, and both servitude and blackness took their stations far below freedom and whiteness. Throughout this transition, white men received the lightest of punishments, and the laws worked to corral their property within their white kin. Other states followed the Old Dominion, and the rules for interracial intimacy became models for every other exclusion.[5]

By the time Thomas Jefferson wrote the Declaration of Independence, social norms in his home state allowed elite white men semiprivate liaisons with nonwhite women, excusing them from claiming the children as legitimate. His own father in-law fathered up to six children with his slave, Mary Hemings. Later, Jefferson did the same with his own, enslaved, half-sister in-law, Sally Hemings. However, he denied this publicly. To solve the questions of who could make claims in court, who could vote, and who could inherit property, Jefferson deemed blacks biologically inferior, and mixture as a threat to society. Yet, it was a central institution in Virginia, Louisiana, and South Carolina, where mixed offspring held intermediary, social positions. Their treatment predicted the exclusion of other racial groups after the government set the standard in 1790.

Soon after, territorial expansion started bringing more peoples to measure up to whiteness-as-citizenship, more often than not failing. With the Western bounty in mind, more Americans believed that the whole continent was theirs for the taking, a vessel to receive the way of life they had begun. Conquering Indians, taking their land, and excluding them from citizenship were central in this. From Thomas Jefferson to Andrew Jackson, seemingly benevolent policies toward American Indians veiled the desire for more territory. Presidents equipped agents with treaties to wrest land from Indians. If tribes rejected these, then they were unfit for democracy. Even if they did submit, the government used either the military to remove them, policies to disqualify their land ownership, or rationalizations that withheld citizenship from them. The Five Civilized Tribes (the Cherokee, Creek, Choctaw, Chicasaw, and Seminole nations) adopted white ways to protect their status in the Southeast. But American customs, plantation farming, and slave ownership were not enough to mark them as white citizens. Claiming sovereignty, as the Cherokee did, backfired, further distancing them from citizenship in locales that required land ownership. As outsiders on their own lands, they were easier targets for aggressive removal across the Mississippi, and then beyond. For the most part, American Indians did not hold U.S. citizenship until well into the twentieth century and, even with the Indian Citizenship Act of 1924, they did not have voting rights.[6]

The Southwest became another site for exclusion during the first half of the nineteenth century. In 1822, the newly independent Mexican government began inviting Americans to the state of Coajuila y Tejas. Led by Stephen F. Austin, these Texian entrepreneurs hoped to expand the South's agricultural prosperity, along with slavery. They formed unions with land-holding Tejanos, sometimes marrying into their families. At the same time, the Mexican government was centralizing under Antonio López de Santa Anna's 1835 constitution. The Texians and their allies revolted, forming the independent Republic of Texas. Almost immediately after their 1836 victory, they appealed to the U.S. government, wishing for annexation to become a slave state. It would take the Democratic, expansionist president James K. Polk to engage in war with Mexico. Some opposed this as treacherous, militaristic, and proslavery; others supported it as Manifest Destiny. But, rather than fully defeat the country, incorporating what Secretary of State James Buchanan called "an inferior, indolent, mongrel race," the United States took possession of the northern, less-populated portion. We wanted some of Mexico, not all of those Mexicans.[7]

Still, along with what would become the southwest quarter of the contiguous states, 7,000 families came with the United States' acquisition. An earlier draft of the Treaty of Guadalupe Hidalgo, which negotiated the surrender, promised to respect land grants the Mexican government had given. More importantly, it invited inhabitants to exchange their Mexican citizenship for American. "[They] shall be incorporated into the Union of the United States, and admitted as soon as possible," the original Article IX declared, "according to the principles of the Federal Constitution, to the enjoyment of all the rights of citizens of the United States."[8] However, the final draft removed the promise regarding land grants, making their holders vulnerable to dispossession, which Anglos practiced across the Southwest. The new Article IX also qualified the offer of American citizenship: "[They] shall be incorporated into the Union of the United States and be admitted at the proper time (to be judged of by the Congress of the United States) to the enjoyment of all the rights of citizens of the United States, according to the principles of the Constitution."[9] Technically they possessed whiteness-as-citizenship, but in reality they were far from it. Over a century later, Mexican American activists constructed a legal strategy that would work around this paradox.[10]

Slavery was the central issue around The Civil War, but some, like radical abolitionist, devout Christian, and famed orator Wendell Phillips, anticipated the post-war redefinition of citizenship, which he considered relevant to all minority groups in the United States. His peers in the New England Anti-Slavery Society had written into their constitution the goal of obtaining for racial minorities "equal civil and political rights and privileges with the whites."[11] Phillips declared in 1853, "Whether the varieties of the race began in one family or not, they are destined to meet in one family of people at last," providing destiny as the answer to scientists' monogenesis-polygenesis debate.[12] Rather than suggest any limitations, he predicted a future America that was fully integrated and mixed. The path of progress from Christianity to republicanism would complete the process, inevitably uniting the people into a diverse republic. He also addressed the inclusion of Chinese coming to California and the East Indians coming through Jamaica, Cuba, and Guiana. Phillips asked, "What if they were to apply for naturalization?"[13] He acknowledged that they were not white but he asserted that kinship in Christ, not color, would settle the question of their citizenship. If Chinese immigrants could learn Western ways, then they could be equal with all the other Americans. "If Fum Hoam can learn Christianity as well as silk-weaving and card-painting, he can substitute phonography for his alphabet of three thousand characters; and, after calling you brother for a generation or so, in good Yankee, he will marry your cousin, and then, how will you keep him out of Congress?"[14] To Phillips, this was utopia; to most, it was unthinkable.

The Supreme Court's decision in *Dred Scott v. Sandford* (1857) ruled that blacks could not be citizens, whether slave or free, disenfranchising many. In the majority opinion, Chief Justice Robert B. Taney wrote that just because one managed to settle in a free territory or pass through, that did not make one so—no more than one's wristwatch would be free. The justices' conclusions rested on the reasoning that the founders did not consider blacks as potential citizens, and that man was not created equal. So, while the *Dred Scott* decision addressed blacks and slavery in the short run, its rationale was relevant to any nonwhite group. If authorities could deem them outside the founders' intentions, then they could assign them to a class with no rights.[15]

Legal battles over the meanings of citizenship erupted throughout the Reconstruction era. These played out in distinctive ways in Louisiana, which had been a French and Spanish colony until 1803. With a population of whites, blacks, and Creoles of Color, these themes unfolded in ways both regionally specific and nationally applicable. Reconstruction had begun there when the Union assumed control of the state in 1863. Descendants of refugees from the Haitian Revolution, including free people of color who brought a conception of freedom bound with racial equality, joined the Republicans in establishing racial equality. Their identity, intrinsically mixed, black, white, and Indian, had discouraged them from embracing whiteness after the Louisiana Purchase. In 1868, these radical Creoles of Color influenced lawmaking, resulting in a state constitution that unified social and political rights into one rubric, public rights, which made an infraction of social rights as serious as any other. It stipulated, "All persons, without regard to race, color, or previous condition, born or naturalized in the United States, and subject to the jurisdiction thereof, and residents of this State for one year, are citizens of this State . . . They shall enjoy the same civil, political, and public rights and privileges, and be subject to the same pains and penalties."[16] The Creoles of Color's status in regard to both whiteness and blackness expanded the meanings of the civil rights struggles they undertook. They and their allies knew that limitations on any members of society set the way for widespread practices of white supremacy, so even after the state's 1879 constitution reversed the earlier convention's efforts, these radicals remained diligent regarding public rights for all.[17]

The same year, Congress adopted the Fourteenth Amendment, which redefined citizenship in momentous ways. The Civil Rights Act of 1866 already had granted citizenship to all born within the United States. The new amendment reinforced this, both reversing *Dred Scott* and shoring up the previous legislation against future attacks, whether from Congress or the Supreme Court. The Citizenship Clause also acknowledged that one possessed both state and national citizenship but stipulated that no state could interfere with privileges and immunities of the latter. The Due Process Clause required judicial fairness for all, especially when consequences would deprive someone of "life, liberty, or property." The Equal Protection clause also required fairness, specifically against prejudice. Altogether, the Amendment made national citizenship preeminent, with hopes of promoting equality. Reflecting the interests of radical Republican victors, it was supposed to help them drive the southern states to accept the new social order.

Later, in Louisiana, when a more conservative state legislature passed the Separate Car Act, the *Comité des Citoyens*, an interracial group of mostly Creoles of Color, deployed their sense of public rights to challenge racial segregation. In developing the test case, they ultimately retained Albion Tourgée, Civil War veteran, Reconstruction federal judge, and author, as lead counsel in their campaign, which concluded with the Supreme Court decision in *Plessy v. Ferguson*. Many assume that the Creoles of Color undertook this to protect their own, privileged status, forgetting that blacks and whites were among their ranks. Some have interpreted their work as relevant to the segregation of African Americans only. Others have cast it a lost cause, a legal folly but a moral victory. To the contrary, the effort was part of a utopian vision that they believed in, an attempt to transform society as a whole, not just address one issue. While many of these Creoles of Color appeared white, they knew that their mixture placed them lower than whiteness-as-citizenship. So they undertook this test case to challenge racial classification altogether. Their success would mean success for national citizenship in general.[18]

Tourgée suggested that the plaintiff be of white appearance, racially mixed and light-skinned, to challenge the law's unreliable system of racial classification. He dared the Supreme Court justices to see the Reconstruction Amendments as new, founding documents with principles that called for change: "This provision of section I of the Fourteenth Amendment *creates* a new citizenship of the United States embracing *new* rights, privileges, and immunities deliverable in a *new* manner, controlled by *new* authority, having a *new* scope and extent, depending on national authority for its existence and looking to national power for its preservation."[19] He invited them to transform the United States into a new, egalitarian nation that lived up to its most noble creeds.

However strongly Tourgée argued for a broad understanding of citizenship, the Court had already dismantled this construction via three previous decisions. In the *Slaughter-House Cases* (1873), they interpreted the Fourteenth Amendment narrowly, saying that equal protection was relevant only to the abolition of slavery, not the exploitation of a type of industry. They also weakened the potency of the Amendment by ruling that it only referred to rights given and taken on the federal level, not the state. *United States v. Cruikshank* (1876) further weakened national citizenship by saying that vigilante reprisals against black voters were individual crimes, not that of states, even when they clearly benefitted state politicians. This barred the federal government from wielding the Constitution to prosecute these offenses. Last, via its decision in the *Civil Rights Cases* (1883), the Supreme Court once again hobbled Congress by invalidating the Civil Rights Act of 1875, which intended to prohibit discrimination in public spaces, a goal reminiscent of the Creoles of Color's defense of public rights. These decisions were not as extreme as *Dred Scott*, but they had a similar effect, allowing states to dismantle black citizenship.[20]

Tourgée had used the trope of color-blindness since 1870, while holding a federal bench in North Carolina. Although he was receiving death threats from the Ku Klux Klan, he publicly announced that he would play no favorites administering the law, maintaining that "justice should be at least 'color-blind.'"[21] In the middle of the Klan uprising, he championed equality before the law in matters of jury selection, prosecution, and sentencing. In his Brief of Plaintiff in Error for *Plessy*, he repeated this trope, denouncing uses of law to make one class of people subject to another. Justice John Marshall Harlan adopted this saying in his sole dissent, and many associate the term with him. But, in the same document, Harlan protected the notion that whites would remain "the dominant race in this country . . . for all time."[22] While he could grasp black citizenship, equality was a different matter.

The Chinese fared even worse with Harlan, who called them both "a race so different from our own" and "incapable of assimilating with our people."[23] Politicians and labor leaders already had amplified animosity toward this group, resulting in the Chinese Exclusion Act (1882). This obviously racial legislation set the groundwork for every restrictive immigration policy for the coming decades. Harlan dissented in *United States v. Wong Kim Ark*, which did consider a United States–born Chinese a citizen under the Fourteenth Amendment. His contradictions (citizenship for blacks yet inferior to whites, colorblindness yet disdain for Chinese) made sense in a benevolent, yet white supremacist, vision of the United States.[24]

Racial prerequisite cases in state, territorial, and federal courts decided whether those applying for citizenship met the nation's naturalization requirements. These only began after Reconstruction, when immigration brought more newcomers from questionable locales, and ended in middle of the twentieth century, with the end of racial restrictions. Also before that point, state citizenship had more impact than national citizenship. Even though Congress extended eligibility to "aliens of African nativity and to persons of African descent" in 1870, not one litigant in prerequisite cases sued to be African American. In part, this was because the language emphasized descent from Africa;

anyone with an identity based anywhere else would find that illogical. More so, knowledge of American racial system made challenging the meaning of free white person, which neither made geographic specifications, nor carried associations with the African slave trade, more appealing. Even after emancipation, witnessing African Americans' lower status reinforced the preeminence of citizenship as white.[25]

Between 1871 and 1901, 11.7 million immigrants came to the United States, more than in the previous 230 years combined. Europeans made up 90 percent of these numbers. For the most part, these came from Northern and Western Europe, although in the 1890s, the number from Southern and Eastern Europe finally surpassed the other half. Even though the percentage of foreign born remained steady in every census from 1860 to 1920, hovering between 13.2 percent and 14.7 percent, the perception at the time was that immigrants were overtaking the country.[26] A weaker economy, easier transportation, mass communication, and political ideologies led to an era of reactionary nativism. Discrimination affected many immigrants, but in different ways. Unlike groups racially marked as nonwhite, the millions of Europeans faced few obstructions to their pursuit of success. Some have argued that they were not white on arrival, while others say they were. Some add that, either way, becoming white meant distancing themselves from blacks, a strategy that even fellow racial minorities practiced. Once here, European immigrants could enjoy plenty of opportunities, because they were closer to whiteness-as-citizenship. That left cultural assimilation as their principle obstacle. Robert E. Park and his followers studied this "process of interpenetration and fusion" and considered it one-directional, naturalizing the idea that minorities assimilated into the mainstream.[27] Once white immigrants had achieved that, their status was set. As with previous eras, whiteness-as-citizenship remained true at the end of the nineteenth century, and it would into the twentieth century.[28]

While progressive social scientists studied this process from the ivory tower, prerequisite cases approached the question of who could be white in a different arena. Judges repeatedly attempted to use standards that had never anticipated such exotic arrivals. Reflecting the comfort with overt racism at the time, judges easily decided against unattractive minorities, using three rationales: First, the intentions of the founding fathers was to limit naturalization to white persons, so the judges had a constitutional obligation to follow that stipulation. Then the framers of the Fourteenth Amendment may or may not have had particular nationalities in mind when they reformed national citizenship. Second, the common sense of regular Americans reflected the criteria for membership when divining congressional intent failed. Last, the latest in scientific knowledge held authority where the other two hampered the conclusions they hoped for. The judges were reasonable men and many would protest the label, racist, but they worked within specific contexts, using intellectual tools accessible to them. They took both the superiority of white men and the distinctiveness of other groups for granted. In the legal realm, the precedents they established impacted many groups, as well as anyone who resembled them, for decades to come.

The first of these cases, *In re Ah Yup*, deliberated whether a man from China qualified. Even before this 1878 decision, Chinese had been considered nonwhite. But

California Circuit Court judge Sawyer had to substantiate this position from scratch, and all three rationales supported him. He referred to debates around the 1870 amendment to see if those senators considered Chinese white. Charles Sumner had wanted to eliminate any mention of race or whiteness in the legislation, but others prevailed, specifically excluding Chinese from the white race. Considering the vernacular, Sawyer concluded, "As ordinarily used everywhere in the United States, one would scarcely fail to understand that the party employing the words 'white person' would intend a person of the Caucasian race."[29] No American would label Ah Yup, a member of a group already discriminated against, as white. Last, Sawyer cited schema from four racial scientists to corroborate the obvious. Linnaeus had named four racial groups by skin color; Blumenbach grouped Chinese with the Mongolian race rather than the Caucasian, which he called the most beautiful; Buffon agreed, with a few distinctions concerning hair, skin, and skull shape; and Cuvier reduced the number to three, with the Mongol, Caucasian, and Negro distinct from each other. All of these aged testimonies confirmed what Americans concluded on their own: Chinese were not white and should not be able to naturalize into citizenship.[30]

Judges were not always as thoughtful, exhaustive, and redundant as Sawyer. Most notorious for demonstrating the inconsistencies of racial prerequisite cases were the Supreme Court's decisions in *Ozawa v. United States* and *United States v. Bhagat Singh Thind*. The first, decided November 13, 1922, ruled that Takao Ozawa, a businessman who had submitted his petition for naturalization in 1915, was not white. He persisted in his case, not by challenging the classification but by arguing that Japanese were white. To support this, he presented his skin color, which was lighter than many. More significant, though, was his cultural argument. A U.S. Army veteran, Christian, and English speaker who sent his children to American schools, Ozawa understood whiteness to be more than physical appearance. These facets had worked before in racial identity cases, convincing courts that someone must be white if they act white. They especially resonated with progressive sociological arguments of the time, who praised acculturation. But conformity to white norms lost here against the Supreme Court's reliance on scientific evidence. Ozawa was "clearly of a race which is not Caucasian," and thus not white.[31]

Three months later, the same justices ruled on a similar case, considering common knowledge more trustworthy than scientific proof, which had supported them in *Ozawa*. Bhagat Singh Thind, also an Army veteran, had received U.S. citizenship once in Washington State and again in Oregon. The Immigration and Naturalization Service objected both times, moving the case up to the Supreme Court. Typical of prerequisite cases, this one would decide whether a particular ethnic group was white, this time "a high caste Hindu of full Indian blood, born at Amritsar, Punjab, India."[32] However, the justices had a second task, deciding whether a new law deemed previously naturalized Hindus ineligible. Thind's team built their argument around the leading scholarship, which classified northern Indians as Caucasians, the same racial group as whites. This would prevent the upset that Ozawa had experienced. However, this time the court elevated common sense above scientific evidence. As Justice Sutherland wrote in the decision, "What we now hold is that the words 'free white persons' are words of common speech, to be interpreted in accordance with the understanding of the common man, synonymous with the word 'Caucasian' only as that word is popularly understood."[33] Completing their second mission, the justices decreed that the Immigration Act of 1917, which had established the Asiatic Barred Zone, disqualified citizens of Indian descent who had gained the status via earlier legislation. The Immigration and Naturalization Service began revoking citizenship for 50 individuals who fell in this group, a small number but a harrowing principle.[34]

The Supreme Court's decision in *Weedin v. Chin Bow* (1927) showed another way to block racially undesirable segments. Chin Bow's grandfather, Chin Tong, was born in the United States and considered a citizen. His father, Chin Dun, was born in China and had never visited the United States until after his 10-year-old son, the respondent, was born. The Taft court ruled that children of American parents who never resided in the United States were not of American nationality, thus not eligible for entry. This principle drew on common law, just as *Wong Kim Ark* had, but unlike the English precedent, it set the limit to children, not grandchildren. Citizenship was not perpetually inheritable. This would not matter for white people, who could naturalize, but for aliens ineligible for citizenship, a father could forfeit his son's citizenship by never visiting the United States. These cases may look like narrow decisions, but they worked to solidify Asians in general as alien. So legislation against Chinese could lead to restrictions against Japanese, and then set a general standard for nonwhites. For example, dispossession of Mexicans made California's Alien Land Laws, which prohibited aliens ineligible for citizenship more sensible, later that made Japanese internment more acceptable.[35]

Minorities worked for racial equality throughout the nadir of American race relations around the turn of the century. For example, a coalition of blacks and whites founded the National Association for the Advancement of Colored People in 1909. Mexican Americans in Corpus Christi, Texas, founded the League of United Latin American Citizens in 1929. Native Americans followed 1924's Indian Citizenship Act and 1934's Indian Reorganization Act by strengthening intertribal voting blocs and writing tribal constitutions. The start of World War II energized efforts for equality, with the minority groups I have named earlier and many others hoping for Double Victory, over fascism abroad and racism at home. Were these calls to the nation to live up to its role as the champion of freedom? A phase when minorities rehabilitated their stations to better match that of whiteness-as-citizenship? A renaissance of Radical Reconstruction ideals? All three of these were true to a degree, but I want to emphasize the last: The Civil Rights movements of the mid-twentieth century used mass action to compel the federal government to revive citizenship in more expansive ways than the end of Reconstruction had left it. At the highest level of government, organizations urged legislation, carried legal campaigns, and rallied behind sympathetic administrations. On the grassroots level, they built the networks to register voters, boycotted, and endured violence. On both, the Fourteenth Amendment, the Fifteenth Amendment, and the Civil Rights Acts of 1866 and 1875 laid their intellectual and programmatic foundation.[36]

While the most prominent movement was the African American, Mexican Americans, Asian Americans, and Native Americans also used these strategies, sometimes following the blacks' model. Many present these as demonstrations by individual ethnic groups against specific grievances. However, these episodes from the 1940s through 1960s were about citizenship in general. Four cases especially show their relevance beyond the identities of those who precipitated them, as follow.

Korematsu v. United States (1944) dictated that the executive orders forcing Japanese Americans to internment camps were constitutional. Its impetus was one man evading internment, but the case really questioned whether individual rights of a citizen withstood national security, an issue relevant beyond that time. In the decision, Justice Hugo Black claimed that ruling against Fred Korematsu was not because of race, but because "we are at war with the Japanese Empire."[37] But this decision was overturned in 1983 when it became clear that the Solicitor General concealed testimony against the idea that Japanese in America were a threat. Two decades later, Fred Korematsu offered amicus briefs supporting the rights of citizens deprived of due process after the September 11 attacks.[38]

The plaintiff's lawyers in *Hernandez v. Texas* (1954) were addressing the lack of Mexican Americans on any jury in Jackson County, but they created a standard by which a group could levy a valid complaint on Constitutional grounds. The nine justices agreed that any group experiencing subordination deserved equal protection. In this case, it was Mexican Americans, but Earl Warren's response showed how the case addressed racism, not just discrimination. In other words, the assumptions that underpin a system of oppression, not just particular prejudicial practices, and not just the fact of biological differences we call race. This provided the basis for minorities beyond African Americans to argue Civil Rights cases.[39]

Decided just 3 weeks later, *Brown v. Board of Education* (1954) has received more attention than *Hernandez*. In affirming that separate was unequal, the *Brown* decision energized the following decades of the Civil Rights movement by indicating that in at least one branch of the federal government segregation was unacceptable. So, it was also a touchstone for other minority groups. The victory in *Brown* overturned *Plessy*, and its aim to reform public life resembled the mission of the Creoles of Colors' efforts. However, *Brown* addressed specific practices of racism, rather than the meanings of citizenship in general. While celebrated for decades to come, *Brown*'s achievements have been under attack since then; its opponents have been able to manipulate its weaknesses.[40]

Last, *Loving v. Virginia* (1967) deemed laws against interracial marriage unconstitutional, a satisfying conclusion to the story of one couple against a retrograde custom. Compared with integration, voting rights, and fair employment, interracial marriage seemed a minor topic. African Americans and other minorities were uneasy about it, censuring the prohibitions but also discouraging the practice. So the case involved a segment of society that had made unusual life choices. Its resolution date, beyond the usual Civil Rights timeline from 1955 to 1965, makes it seem tangential. But like *Korematsu*, *Hernandez*, and *Brown* it relied on the Equal Protection Clause; states could not antagonize a class of people. That connection to citizenship made *Loving* relevant to same-sex marriage four decades later.[41]

In reforming citizenship, the movements of the mid-twentieth century were successes. Washington made a commitment to voting rights. The integration of public facilities has become the norm. States interfere less with underrepresented groups. Overt statements of prejudice meet with quick censure. But the following decades featured an abandonment of race as a lens to analyze inequality, first by conservatives as a reaction to the changes of the 1960s, and then by liberals hoping to appeal to the middle. Since race refracts class, gender, sexuality, etc., that also diminished the effectiveness of the other analytic lenses as well. A generation later, whatever aptitude for discussing inequality along racial lines receded into denying that it was a problem, celebrating progress as a sign that it would soon disappear, or placing it behind other forms of inequality (for example, social class). But more often than not, a neoconservative tendency pinpointed culture as the source of inequality. Previously, the natural sciences explained it, but that would lead to biological essentialism now considered distasteful. Neoconservatives recognized individual talent not group disadvantage, dysfunctional values not institutional abandonment. The end result was that most Americans became unable to say what race or citizenship was. The former became mere physical appearance or identity politics; the latter became acculturation to popular culture. One step further, many understood racism as individual acts of meanness (e.g., "George Zimmerman shot Trayvon Martin"), not an organizing principle (e.g., "Black youth are suspect"). This vagary concealed how disparity has persisted in income, wealth accumulation, education, voting, and national security. As with the historic binding of whiteness, citizenship, and privilege, the bond remained true in the twenty-first century, as did its shadow, second-class citizenship based on race. Eduardo Bonilla-Silva, Michael Omi, and Howard Winant have helped explicate these distinctions. Tomás Almaguer, Ariela Gross, and Mark Elliott have done similar work for past eras and locales. But many topics remain rich for future research connecting the meanings of race and citizenship, including the early republic era, blood quantum, and war brides.[42]

Notes

1. U.S. Census Bureau, *1790 Census of Population and Housing.*
2. From here, it is easy to overlay white people in our contemporary sense with whiteness perpetual but that can be presumptuous. Rather than whiteness as physical appearance (which is unreliable) or whiteness as European descent (which the number of nationalities outgrew), I use the term whiteness-as-citizenship where I must describe whiteness as normative citizenship across time and place, and the state of having achieved it. Although the exact terms have always been in flux, this coinage represents the special status. It conveys the ongoing process for the subjects I speak of. Most important, it avoids the reification of whiteness; not all types who are now white would have been so throughout. Ian Haney López, *White by Law: The Legal Construction of Race*, Rev. and updated, 10th anniversary ed., Critical America (New York: New York University Press, 2006).
3. Paul R. Spickard, *Almost All Aliens: Immigration, Race, and Colonialism in American History and Identity* (New York: Routledge, 2007); Ronald T. Takaki, *Strangers from a*

Different Shore: A History of Asian Americans, Updated and rev. ed. (Boston: Little, Brown, 1998); Mia Tuan, *Forever Foreigners or Honorary Whites? The Asian Ethnic Experience Today* (New Brunswick, N.J.: Rutgers University Press, 1998).

4. Theodore Allen, *The Invention of the White Race*, The Haymarket Series (London and New York: Verso, 1994), 119.

5. A. Leon Jr. Higginbotham and Barbara K. Kopytoff, "Racial Purity and Interracial Sex in the Law of Colonial and Antebellum Virginia," *Georgetown Law Journal, 77*, 6 (1989); David R. Roediger, *How Race Survived Us History: From Settlement and Slavery to the Obama Phenomenon* (London and New York: Verso, 2010).

6. Reginald Horsman, *Race and Manifest Destiny: The Origins of American Racial Anglo-Saxonism* (Cambridge, Mass.: Harvard University Press, 1981); Mark Hirsch, "Thomas Jefferson, Founding Father of Indian Removal," *National Museum of the American Indian*, Summer 2009.

7. Neil Foley, *The White Scourge: Mexicans, Blacks, and Poor Whites in Texas Cotton Culture*, American Crossroads (Berkeley: University of California Press, 1997); David Montejano, *Anglos and Mexicans in the Making of Texas, 1836–1986*, 1st ed. (Austin: University of Texas Press, 1987); Thomas G. Paterson, *American Foreign Relations: A History*, 7th ed. (Boston, MASS.: Wadsworth Cengage Learning, 2010), 133.

8. Richard Griswold del Castillo, *The Treaty of Guadalupe Hidalgo: A Legacy of Conflict*, 1st ed. (Norman: University of Oklahoma Press, 1990), 179.

9. Ibid., 180.

10. Ariela Gross, "Texas Mexicans and the Politics of Whiteness," *Law and History Review 21*, 1 (2003).

11. Louis Ruchames, "Race, Marriage, and Abolition in Massachusetts," *Journal of Negro History 40*, 3 (1955): 33.

12. Wendell Phillips, "The United States of the United Races," *National Era*, September 15, 1853.

13. Ibid.

14. Ibid.

15. *Dred Scott v. Sandford*, 60 U.S. 393(1857).

16. Louisiana Constitution, Title I, Article II (1868).

17. Rebecca J. Scott, "Public Rights, Social Equality, and the Conceptual Roots of the Plessy Challenge," *Michigan Law Review* 106–105(2008); Shirley Elizabeth Thompson, *Exiles at Home: The Struggle to Become American in Creole New Orleans* (Cambridge, Mass.: Harvard University Press, 2009).

18. Thomas J. Davis, "More Than Segregation, Racial Identity: The Neglected Question in Plessy v. Ferguson," *Washington and Lee Race and Ethnicity Ancestry Law Journal 10*(2004); Mark Elliott, "Race, Color Blindness, and the Democratic Public: Albion W. Tourgée's Radical Principles in Plessy v. Ferguson," *The Journal of Southern History 67*, 2 (2001); Mark Golub, "Plessy as 'Passing': Judicial Responses to Ambiguously Raced Bodies in Plessy v. Ferguson," *Law & Society Review 39*, 3 (2005); Jules Lobel, *Success without Victory: Lost Legal Battles and the Long Road to Justice in America*, Critical America (New York: New York University Press, 2003); Charles A. Lofgren, *The Plessy Case: A Legal-Historical Interpretation* (New York: Oxford University Press, 1987).

19. Brief of Plaintiff in Error, *Plessy v. Ferguson*, 163 U.S. 537 (1896).

20. *The Slaughter-House Cases*, 83 U.S. 36(1873); *United States v. Cruikshank*, 92 U.S. 542(1876); *The Civil Rights Cases*, 109 U.S. 3(1883); Eric Foner, *Reconstruction: America's Unfinished*

Revolution, 1863–1877, 1st ed., The New American Nation Series (New York: Harper & Row, 1988).

21. Albion Winegar Tourgée, "Letter to Editor," *North Carolina Standard*, January 28, 1870.

22. *Plessy v. Ferguson, 163 U.S. 537(1896).*

23. Ibid; *United States v. Wong Kim Ark*, 169 U.S. 649 (1898).

24. Gabriel J. Chin, "The Plessy Myth: Justice Harlan and the Chinese Cases," *Iowa Law Review, 82*, 151 (1996).

25. Haney López, *White by Law: The Legal Construction of Race*.

26. Roger Daniels, "Immigration in the Gilded Age: Change or Continuity?," *OAH Magazine of History, Summer* (1999).

27. Robert Ezra Park and Ernest Watson Burgess, *Introduction to the Science of Sociology* (Chicago, Ill.: The University of Chicago Press, 1921), 736.

28. John Higham, *Strangers in the Land: Patterns of American Nativism, 1860–1925* (New Brunswick, N.J.: Rutgers University Press, 2002); Matthew Frye Jacobson, *Whiteness of a Different Color: European Immigrants and the Alchemy of Race* (Cambridge, Mass.: Harvard University Press, 1998); Peter Kolchin, "Whiteness Studies: The New History of Race in America," *Journal of American History 89*, 1 (2002); Michael Paul Rogin, *Blackface, White Noise: Jewish Immigrants in the Hollywood Melting Pot* (Berkeley: University of California Press, 1996).

29. *In Re Ah Yup*, 1 Fed. Cas. 223 (D. Cal. Cir. Ct. 1878).

30. Ibid.

31. *Takao Ozawa v. United States*, 260 U.S. 178(1922).

32. *United States v. Bhagat Singh Thind*, 261 U.S. 204(1923).

33. Ibid.

34. Ibid.

35. *United States v. Wong Kim Ark*; *Weedin v. Chin Bow*, 274 U.S. 657 (1927); Tomás Almaguer, *Racial Fault Lines: The Historical Origins of White Supremacy in California* (Berkeley: University of California Press, 1994).

36. Steven F. Lawson and Charles M. Payne, *Debating the Civil Rights Movement, 1945–1968*, 2nd ed., Debating Twentieth-Century America (Lanham: Rowman & Littlefield Publishers, 2006); Takaki, *Strangers from a Different Shore: A History of Asian Americans*.

37. *Korematsu v. United States*, 323 U.S. 214(1944).

38. Ibid; *Korematsu v. United States*, 584 F. Supp. 1406(1984).

39. *Hernandez v. Texas*, 347 U.S. 475 (1954); Neil Foley, "Over the Rainbow: Hernandez v. Texas, Brown v. Board, and Black v. Brown," *Chicano-Latino Law Review 25*, 139 (2005); Ian Haney López, "Hernandez v. Brown," *New York Times*, May 21, 2004.

40. *Brown v. Board of Education*, 347 U.S. 483(1954).

41. *Loving v. Virginia*, 388 U.S. 1(1967).

42. Eduardo Bonilla-Silva, *White Supremacy and Racism in the Post-Civil Rights Era* (Boulder, Colo.: L. Rienner, 2001); Eduardo Bonilla-Silva, *Racism without Racists: Color-Blind Racism and the Persistence of Racial Inequality in the United States*, 3rd ed. (Lanham: Rowman & Littlefield Publishers, 2010); John Hartigan, *What Can You Say? America's National Conversation on Race* (Stanford, Calif.: Stanford University Press, 2010); John L. Jackson, *Racial Paranoia: The Unintended Consequences of Political Correctness: The New Reality of Race in America* (New York: Basic Civitas, 2008); Michael Omi and Howard Winant, *Racial Formation in the United States: From the 1960s to the 1990s*, 2nd ed. (New York: Routledge, 1994).

BIBLIOGRAPHY

Allen, Theodore. *The Invention of the White Race, The Haymarket Series*. London and New York: Verso, 1994.

Almaguer, Tomás. *Racial Fault Lines: The Historical Origins of White Supremacy in California*. Berkeley: University of California Press, 1994.

Bonilla-Silva, Eduardo. *White Supremacy and Racism in the Post-Civil Rights Era*. Boulder, Colo.: L. Rienner, 2001.

Bonilla-Silva, Eduardo. *Racism without Racists: Color-Blind Racism and the Persistence of Racial Inequality in the United States*. 3rd ed. Lanham, Md.: Rowman & Littlefield Publishers, 2010.

Brown v. Board of Education, 347 U.S. 483 (1954).

Chin, Gabriel J. "The Plessy Myth: Justice Harlan and the Chinese Cases." *Iowa Law Review, 82*, 151 (1996): 151–182.

The Civil Rights Cases, 109 U.S. 3 (1883).

Daniels, Roger. "Immigration in the Gilded Age: Change or Continuity?" *OAH Magazine of History, Summer* (1999): 21–25.

Davis, Thomas J. "More Than Segregation, Racial Identity: The Neglected Question in Plessy v. Ferguson." *Washington and Lee Race and Ethnicity Ancestry Law Journal, 10* (2004): 1–41.

Dred Scott v. Sandford, 60 U.S. 393 (1857).

Elliott, Mark. "Race, Color Blindness, and the Democratic Public: Albion W. Tourgée's Radical Principles in Plessy v. Ferguson." *The Journal of Southern History, 67*, 2 (2001): 287–330.

Foley, Neil. *The White Scourge: Mexicans, Blacks, and Poor Whites in Texas Cotton Culture, American Crossroads*. Berkeley: University of California Press, 1997.

Foley, Neil. "Over the Rainbow: Hernandez v. Texas, Brown v. Board, and Black v. Brown." *Chicano-Latino Law Review, 25*, 139 (2005): 139–152.

Foner, Eric. *Reconstruction: America's Unfinished Revolution, 1863–1877*. 1st ed, The New American Nation Series. New York: Harper & Row, 1988.

Golub, Mark. "Plessy as 'Passing': Judicial Responses to Ambiguously Raced Bodies in Plessy v. Ferguson." *Law & Society Review, 39*, 3 (2005): 563–600.

Griswold del Castillo, Richard. *The Treaty of Guadalupe Hidalgo: A Legacy of Conflict*. 1st ed. Norman: University of Oklahoma Press, 1990.

Gross, Ariela. "Texas Mexicans and the Politics of Whiteness." *Law and History Review, 21*, 1 (2003): 195–206.

Haney López, Ian. "Hernandez v. Brown." *New York Times*, May 21, 2004, http://www.nytimes.com/2004/05/22/opinion/hernandez-v-brown.html.

Haney López, Ian. *White by Law: The Legal Construction of Race*. Rev. and updated, 10th anniversary ed, Critical America. New York: New York University Press, 2006.

Hartigan, John. *What Can You Say? America's National Conversation on Race*. Stanford, Calif.: Stanford University Press, 2010.

Hernandez v. Texas, 347 U.S. 475 (1954).

Higginbotham, A. Leon, Jr., and Barbara K. Kopytoff. "Racial Purity and Interracial Sex in the Law of Colonial and Antebellum Virginia." *Georgetown Law Journal, 77*, 6 (1989): 1967–2029.

Higham, John. *Strangers in the Land: Patterns of American Nativism, 1860–1925*. New Brunswick, N.J.: Rutgers University Press, 2002.

Hirsch, Mark. "Thomas Jefferson, Founding Father of Indian Removal." *National Museum of the American Indian*, Summer (2009): 54–58.

Horsman, Reginald. *Race and Manifest Destiny: The Origins of American Racial Anglo-Saxonism*. Cambridge, Mass.: Harvard University Press, 1981.

In Re Ah Yup, 1 Fed. Cas. 223 (D. Cal. Cir. Ct. 1878).

Jackson, John L. *Racial Paranoia: The Unintended Consequences of Political Correctness: The New Reality of Race in America*. New York: Basic Civitas, 2008.

Jacobson, Matthew Frye. *Whiteness of a Different Color: European Immigrants and the Alchemy of Race*. Cambridge, Mass.: Harvard University Press, 1998.

Kolchin, Peter. "Whiteness Studies: The New History of Race in America." *Journal of American History* 89, 1 (2002): 154–173.

Korematsu v. United States, 323 U.S. 214 (1944).

Korematsu v. United States, 584 F. Supp. 1406 (1984).

Lawson, Steven F., and Charles M. Payne. *Debating the Civil Rights Movement, 1945–1968*. 2nd ed, Debating Twentieth-Century America. Lanham, Md.: Rowman & Littlefield Publishers, 2006.

Lobel, Jules. *Success without Victory: Lost Legal Battles and the Long Road to Justice in America*, Critical America. New York: New York University Press, 2003.

Lofgren, Charles A. *The Plessy Case: A Legal-Historical Interpretation*. New York: Oxford University Press, 1987.

Loving v. Virginia, 388 U.S. 1 (1967).

Montejano, David. *Anglos and Mexicans in the Making of Texas, 1836–1986*. 1st ed. Austin: University of Texas Press, 1987.

Omi, Michael, and Howard Winant. *Racial Formation in the United States: From the 1960s to the 1990s*. 2nd ed. New York: Routledge, 1994.

Park, Robert Ezra, and Ernest Watson Burgess. *Introduction to the Science of Sociology*. Chicago, Ill.: The University of Chicago Press, 1921.

Paterson, Thomas G. *American Foreign Relations: A History*. 7th ed. Boston, Mass.: Wadsworth Cengage Learning, 2010.

Phillips, Wendell. "The United States of the United Races." *National Era*, September 15, 1853, 146.

Plessy v. Ferguson, 163 U.S. 537 (1896).

Roediger, David R. *How Race Survived US History: From Settlement and Slavery to the Obama Phenomenon*. London; New York: Verso, 2010.

Rogin, Michael Paul. *Blackface, White Noise: Jewish Immigrants in the Hollywood Melting Pot*. Berkeley: University of California Press, 1996.

Ruchames, Louis. "Race, Marriage, and Abolition in Massachusetts." *Journal of Negro History*, 40, 3 (1955): 250–273.

Scott, Rebecca J. "Public Rights, Social Equality, and the Conceptual Roots of the Plessy Challenge." *Michigan Law Review*, 106–105 (2008): 777–804.

The Slaughter-House Cases, 83 U.S. 36 (1873).

Spickard, Paul R. *Almost All Aliens: Immigration, Race, and Colonialism in American History and Identity*. New York: Routledge, 2007.

Takaki, Ronald T. *Strangers from a Different Shore: A History of Asian Americans*. Updated and rev. ed. Boston: Little, Brown, 1998.

Takao Ozawa v. United States, 260 U.S. 178 (1922).

Thompson, Shirley Elizabeth. *Exiles at Home: The Struggle to Become American in Creole New Orleans*. Cambridge, Mass.: Harvard University Press, 2009.

Tourgée, Albion Winegar. "Letter to Editor." *North Carolina Standard*, January 28, 1870, North Carolina Collection, University of North Carolina at Chapel Hill, Wilson Library.

Tuan, Mia. *Forever Foreigners or Honorary Whites? The Asian Ethnic Experience Today.* New Brunswick, N.J.: Rutgers University Press, 1998.

U.S. Census Bureau. *1790 Census of Population and Housing.*

United States v. Bhagat Singh Thind, 261 U.S. 204 (1923).

United States v. Cruikshank, 92 U.S. 542 (1876).

United States v. Wong Kim Ark, 169 U.S. 649 (1898).

Weedin v. Chin Bow, 274 U.S. 657 (1927).

CHAPTER 10

....

ASSIMILATION IN THE PAST AND PRESENT

....

RICHARD ALBA

Assimilation has been central to the U.S. experience of the incorporation of immigrants and their descendants, so much so that the idea remains at the core of present-day immigration discussions in the media and the social-science literature. Yet, assimilation as concept and theory remains clouded by various sorts of confusion, such as whether it requires assimilating immigrants and their children to jettison their ethnic culture and adopt that of the mainstream without alteration. Confusion about such key issues has spurred the rise in Canada and western Europe of an alternative term for assimilation, "integration," which is frequently defined by a contrast to assimilation, though the actual extent of the differences between the two ideas is itself unclear.

THE PARADIGMATIC EXPERIENCE

....

The historical defining moment of assimilation involves the large-scale entry into mainstream America of the descendants of Catholic and Jewish ethnics, primarily the second and third generations descended from Southern and Eastern European, along with Irish, immigrants. Assimilation to some degree affected these generations during the early part of the twentieth century, but their entry into the mainstream became a mass phenomenon during the quarter century following the end of World War II. In this period, too, the descendants of late nineteenth- and early twentieth-century Chinese and Japanese immigrants assimilated, demonstrating that the phenomenon has not been racially exclusive.[1] Nonetheless, given the small size of the East Asian groups in mid-twentieth-century America, the focus here will be on the much larger assimilation of the so-called white ethnics.

Little doubt exists about the outsider status of ethnic Catholics and Jews in the United States prior to the middle of the twentieth century.[2] The Jewish story of discrimination and social exclusion, especially the lack of acceptance in elite Protestant institutions such as Ivy League colleges,[3] is well known. But Catholic exclusion is at least as relevant to an analysis of the paradigmatic experience. For the Catholic groups were a largely working-class population whose second generation was not, on the whole, very successful in educational institutions (in contrast to eastern European Jews). They were also much more numerous than Jews, adding to the challenge of their integration into the mainstream. Moreover, anti-Catholicism was deeply embedded in the American identity, which historically had sharply distinguished itself from the hierarchical and authority-ridden structures of European societies, among which the Catholic Church figured prominently in the American Protestant imagination.

Catholics and Jews were the targets of sometimes ferocious prejudice and discrimination during the nineteenth and early twentieth centuries. For instance, in the nineteenth century, as scientific racism emerged, depictions of Irish Catholics as apes, thus subhuman and beastlike, became commonplace,[4] as illustrated by a famous Thomas Nast cartoon of a St. Patrick's Day "celebration" ("St. Patrick's Day, 1867—'The Day We Celebrate,'" Harper's Weekly, April 6, 1867). In the 1920s, as the drive to restrict immigration was moving toward a successful conclusion, the Ku Klux Klan resurrected itself, this time as much an anti-Catholic, anti-Jewish movement as an anti-black one. The Klan found many supporters among white Protestants in northern cities where immigrants had settled.[5] In 1928, when the Catholic Al Smith secured the Democratic nomination for president, white Protestants, supported by the preaching from many pulpits, mobilized to deny him the presidency; he lost the popular vote by a lopsided margin.

And yet just a few decades later, during the 1950s and 1960s, the animus against Catholics and Jews faded. They were socially ascendant and turning up with much greater frequency as the peers of Protestants—in school, at work, in neighborhoods, and, eventually, in family circles. The evidence is clear that by the 1970s, the young cohorts of Catholic groups like the southern Italians, who had until then lagged substantially behind the mainstream, were experiencing upward social mobility on a large scale; and they were intermarrying.[6] In addition, the exclusionary barriers against Jewish acceptance at elite colleges were removed, and for the first time, Jews joined their faculties in significant numbers.[7] Anti-Semitism fell into disrepute as the horrors of the Holocaust were revealed.

Today, the predominant explanation for this remarkable turnabout comes from race theory, in the form of the so-called "whiteness literature."[8] It begins with a correct observation: namely, that the boundary between the Protestant mainstream and Catholic and Jewish ethnics had racial aspects, that the ethno-religious minorities held a problematic, not fully white, racial status. One challenge for the ethnics was to achieve the status of full-fledged whites, which they succeeded in doing around mid-century. This happened partly because the skids were greased on their behalf by law and social policy and partly because of their own efforts to separate themselves from African Americans, thereby reinscribing the racial dividing line.[9]

The whiteness literature presumes that once the ethnics were accepted fully as whites, the distinctions and inequalities that separated them from native white Protestants more or less fell away. However, one has to ask from a sociological perspective: Why would that have happened? In the pre-1950 period, Protestant whites held important advantages over the newcomers but feared growing Catholic political power as well as the social and economic challenges posed by rapid Jewish mobility. Why would native white Protestants not defend their advantaged position? As Sherlock Homes famously said about the dog that didn't bark in the nighttime, that was a "curious incident."

This nonevent needs explanation because there were bases other than race for salient social distinctions among white groups, especially in religion but also in European national origin. This is not at all to say that Jewish and Catholic ethnics were at risk of suffering the outright and virtually total exclusion that African Americans still had to endure. But the United States, at least in regions where the white ethnics were numerous and their immigrant communities visible, could have evolved into a three-tier society, with the ethnics constituting an intermediate stratum. Indeed, in the early postwar period, these regions seemed to be heading in precisely this direction.[10]

In the Conan Doyle Sherlock Holmes mystery, "Silver Blaze," the solution comes from the recognition that the dog perceived the murderer (in fact, the dog's master) as non-threatening. We need a theory that, in a similar spirit, can account for the weakening of Protestant resistance to the mass entry of Catholics and Jews into the mainstream. Since in the usual case the competition among groups strengthens social distinctions, the solution here must involve a development that weakened the appearance of competition. A key element is therefore non-zero-sum mobility, which allowed the ethno-religious outsiders to gain socioeconomic parity with the native majority without threatening its members with a loss in status.[11]

The condition of non-zero-sum mobility is associated with the enormous expansion of opportunity that occurred during the several-decade period of prosperity that followed World War II. For instance, during the 1945–1970 period, the number of places at American colleges and universities expanded by a factor of five. Before the war, fewer than 10 percent of the college-age group continued its education beyond high school, but by 1970, nearly a third did. In addition, the occupational structure underwent changes in its middle and upper reaches that provided jobs appropriate for the educational attainments of the ascending ethnics.

The impact of non-zero-sum mobility in education is illustrated by the changes among second- and third-generation Italian Americans. During the first half of the twentieth century, the children of southern Italian immigrants had lagged behind in American schools.[12] They had high rates of truancy and frequently left school as soon as the law allowed in order to enter the labor market.[13] The obvious consequence was low educational attainment for the second generation and the channeling of them toward jobs where educational credentials were not important. This is where Nathan Glazer and Daniel Patrick Moynihan found them at mid-century in *Beyond the Melting Pot*.[14]

Yet, during the quarter century following the end of World War II, the Italians' educational attainment accelerated, and they caught up to native white Americans in such key respects as college attendance and graduation. An analysis of educational attainment by generation and birth cohort suggests that the critical shifts occurred across cohorts and thus reflect the historical evolution of the group's life chances.[15] For Italians born on American soil during the period of mass immigration, the gap in terms of college attendance that separated them from mainstream white Americans, typified by those of British ancestry, was very large: 2 to 1 and was even larger when it came to graduation from college. These gaps narrowed substantially for the cohort born during the late 1930s, a group whose education took place mainly after the war. For those born after 1950, the differences vanished and did not return.

Socioeconomic parity alone would not have been enough to effect the radical changes that occurred in the post-World War II period. Frequent and socially intimate contact across ethno-religious lines was also needed to reduce social distance and weaken stereotypes. One of the most consequential expressions of this social proximity is residential integration with the majority population, for this not only tends to engender equal-status contacts across boundaries but also gives members of a minority access to the spatially based resources and amenities that are normally under the control of the majority—good schools, safe streets, and so forth. Residential integration is probably most significant for minority children, who are able to attend better schools and to form interethnic friendships; as a result, many are able to gain the social skills (and confidence) necessary for success as adults in mainstream settings. In the middle of the twentieth century, this residential integration came about because of the creation of many new suburban communities where white families of diverse ethnic-religious origins could buy homes and commingle.[16]

A third condition enhanced the effectiveness of the other two: namely, a revision of the ideological or symbolic underpinnings of a social distinction to acknowledge that some members of the minority may have the same moral worth as members of the majority. Such a revision in the beliefs held by at least a portion of the majority (it is typical that an enlightened vanguard accepts moral parity well ahead of the majority's mass) makes the arrival of upwardly striving ethnic-minority members more acceptable than it would have previously been. The perceived moral worth of the ethnics was very much upgraded by World War II. The contributions that ethnics were making to the war effort were highlighted by wartime reporting and subsequently by postwar literature and cinema. The war and the two decades or so immediately following it could be said to represent the zenith of the melting pot ideal, at least for Americans of European origin. The ideal permeates popular novels about the war, such as Norman Mailer's *The Naked and the Dead*, many of them made into successful films. These novels and films served to interpret the war experience for a large segment of the American population.[17]

The post-World War II changes lowered the barriers to various forms of social intimacy across ethno-religious lines among whites and fostered a sharp rise in intermarriage, to the point, perhaps, that in many cases, as Robert Merton once put it, "the quadrisyllable, 'intermarriage,' is whittled down to a bisyllable, 'marriage.'"[18] Among the descendants of Italian immigrants, the intermarriage rate leaped to about 70 to 75 percent. These marriages often crossed religious lines as well as ethnic ones. As a consequence, Italian Americans, a heavily Catholic group in the immigrant generation, are now about evenly divided in the fourth generation between Catholic and non-Catholics.[19] Intermarriage has also become commonplace for Jews, a group that has made strenuous efforts to create an institutional infrastructure, including, for example, summer camps, to promote endogamy. According to recent survey research, Jews are now the religious group most likely to marry outside of their religion. According to the National Jewish Population Surveys, roughly half of recently married Jews have a partner who was not raised as a Jew.[20]

ASSIMILATION AS A HISTORICAL PHENOMENON

History provides lessons about the realities of assimilation and can disabuse us of some of the simplistic characterizations that serve more of a rhetorical purpose than an analytic one. One lesson concerns the decline in the salience and social significance of hierarchical social distinctions, such as Jew/Gentile and Italian/American, that is intrinsic to assimilation. These distinctions are equated today with the concept of a "social boundary."[21] Ever since Frederik Barth's groundbreaking studies, it has been recognized that ethno-racial groups are better defined by the existence of social boundaries separating them from others than by distinctive cultural traits.[22] Thus, the characteristics of, and changes undergone by, social boundaries are diagnostic for ethno-racial groups.

The boundary concept calls attention to the complex symbolic and social aspects that constitute a social distinction, including the ways a distinction may be institutionalized in a society (e.g., recognition of one group's holidays but not another's). The symbolic aspects often involve moral judgments on the more advantaged side of a boundary that allow individuals to justify their advantages on the grounds that "we are better than they are."

The boundary concept is especially useful in thinking about ethnic change and hence assimilation. Because of the inequality it organizes, a boundary is frequently a site of contestation, as each side seeks to shape the boundary in ways that meet its interests. But the contest is unequal since one side has superior resources and power. The members of the group on the more favored side have a strong incentive to maintain, if not reinforce, the boundary; and a good deal of sociological research indicates that under most circumstances, the inequalities anchored in a boundary are "durable," that is, strongly resistant to change.[23]

Assimilation can be conceptualized in terms of boundary-related changes, and a useful typology distinguishes among three types.[24] *Boundary crossing* corresponds to the classic version of individual-level assimilation: someone moves from one group to another, without any real change to the boundary itself. *Boundary blurring* implies that the social profile of a boundary has become less distinct: the clarity of the social distinction involved has become clouded, and individuals' location with respect to the boundary may appear ambiguous or indeterminate. The final process, *boundary shifting,* involves the relocation of a boundary so that populations once situated on one side are now included on the other: former outsiders are thereby transformed into insiders.

The distinctiveness of the mass assimilation of the postwar era is that it involved all three types. Boundary shifting was involved insofar as the racial boundary moved to unambiguously include the groups originating in southern and eastern Europe. Boundary blurring occurred insofar as ethno-religious distinctions among whites did not disappear, but their relevance in many social contexts faded. Individualistic boundary crossing had been taking place all along; its role did not contribute to the era's distinctiveness.

A second major lesson involves what could be called the "mainstream" (or, perhaps better, mainstreams) of the society. In a stratified society like the United States, where a majority group sits atop a hierarchical ethno-racial order, the mainstream can be viewed as encompassing those political, social, and cultural features that are valorized by members of the majority. An older conception of assimilation viewed it as a one-way process whereby the assimilating group adjusts to a stable mainstream society and culture.[25] However, the postwar era demonstrates that assimilation may involve substantial change to the mainstream itself.

That mainstream change is most evident in religion. Not only did the great majority of Catholics and Jews come to be seen as mainstream Americans, but also Catholicism and Judaism became "charter" religions, a shift first signaled in the famous postwar book by Will Herberg, *Protestant-Catholic-Jew*.[26] The American identity changed as a result: no longer was the United States a "Christian" (read: post-Reformation) nation; now it was a "Judeo-Christian" one, with Catholicism in the mix, too.

The religions as practiced certainly changed during the course of this incorporation into the mainstream. For instance, non-Orthodox forms of Judaism, including Reform Judaism with its muted religious services and commitments, found wide acceptance in the United States, and what had been a minor holiday in the Jewish calendar, Hanukkah, was elevated in status to provide Jewish children with an equivalent of Christmas; American Catholics have become known within their worldwide Church for combining a high level of religious observance with individualistic dissent from some Catholic teachings, such as those on birth control.[27] But, most important, Catholics and Jews did not convert en masse to Protestant forms of Christianity to become indistinguishable from the early-twentieth-century mainstream.

The implications of this mainstream incorporation can be observed in the increased occurrence of Jewish-Christian intermarriage. This intermarriage cannot be understood simply as a form of one-way assimilation, a boundary crossing of minority individuals into the religion of the dominant group. A third to a half of Jewish-Christian couples participate in Jewish congregations and raise their children as Jewish, while others join Christian churches or create a nondenominational family culture. An entire literature has arisen to counsel such intermarried couples. It appears that, for the most part, those who affiliate with Judaism do not locate themselves at the more devout end of the religious spectrum, and their family cultures typically include some Christian elements, such as Christmas celebrations.[28] No doubt, many of those who have adopted a

Christian religious identity also participate in some Jewish rituals, such as Passover *seders* at the in-laws, since these are, after all, family occasions as much as religious ones. In effect, the once sharp religious boundary has been blurred in the sense that rituals from both traditions are frequently practiced, and family life often straddles the boundary.

DEFINING AND THEORIZING ASSIMILATION

Bearing in mind the ways in which the historical reality of assimilation departs from some overly simple conceptions, Richard Alba and Victor Nee define assimilation as the "decline of an ethnic distinction and its corollary cultural and social differences. 'Decline' in this context means that a distinction attenuates in salience, that the occurrences for which it is relevant diminish in number and contract to fewer and fewer domains of social life. From the perspective of a minority, its members' ethnic origins become less and less relevant in relation to the members of another ethnic group (typically, but not necessarily, the majority group)."[29] This can happen for only a few individuals or on a large scale, up to that of the group itself. Assimilation, then, is not a binary phenomenon—an individual or group is assimilated or not—but a scalar one: there are degrees of assimilation. Assimilation then should not be equated with the disappearance of an ethno-racial group. It is also multidimensional; something can take place to a greater extent in some ways (e.g., linguistic) than in others (e.g., socioeconomic).

This conception, often dubbed "neo-assimilation," improves on previous ones in significant ways, in particular, the canonical conception delineated in the classic book by Milton Gordon.[30] For one thing, the older notion requires individuals to become members of the dominant group. Gordon's concept places its focus on shifts across a categorical boundary: it lends itself to an exclusive view of assimilation as boundary crossing. That would mean in the contemporary United States that non-whites must become whites. Such an idea is not workable in a contemporary multiracial society, where the possibility of assimilation on a large scale by members of non-white groups must be considered. Boundary crossing does occur everywhere, to be sure, but to limit our understanding of assimilation to this mechanism would mean closing our eyes to the ways that boundaries can change.

The neo-assimilation account envisions that assimilation can involve entry into a mainstream, as distinct from acceptance as a white American. This conceptual shift is associated with the recognition that assimilation can be promoted by changes that occur on both sides of an ethno-racial boundary, reducing their differences from each other and hence their distinctiveness. In principle, assimilation need not involve bilateral changes, but in the American context, it often has. Gordon's conception held that assimilation involved mainly one-way changes, whereby members of an ethnic minority accepted without change the culture of middle-class Anglo Americans (he did make an exception for religion). This one-way conception survives in the writings of Samuel

Huntington, who argued that new immigrants, especially from Latin America, need to accept America's Anglo-Protestant values.[31]

The distinction between one-way and two-way assimilation corresponds arguably to different social-psychological situations. One-way assimilation requires departure from one group and a discarding of signs of membership in it, linked to an attempt to enter into another, with all of the social and psychic burdens such a process entails—growing distance from peers, feelings of disloyalty, and anxieties about acceptance. The social psychology of this process was described as long ago as the 1940s by Irvin Child.[32] The two-way change scenario is conducive to boundary blurring: because changes are occurring on both sides, there is a degree of ambiguity about group membership, allowing minority-origin individuals at times to present themselves as similar to the majority. The social psychology of assimilation is quite different when boundaries are blurred. Then, assimilation is likely to be eased insofar as the individuals undergoing it do not sense a rupture between participation in mainstream institutions and familiar social and cultural practices and identities. Thus, they may not feel forced to choose between the mainstream and their group of origin. Moreover, individuals are likely to observe that other co-ethnics are in the same situation as themselves, and therefore they do not experience a sense of detachment from the group of origin. In the general case, assimilation of this type involves intermediate, or hyphenated, stages that allow individuals to see themselves, either simultaneously or sequentially, as members of an ethnic minority and of the mainstream.

The mechanisms bringing about contemporary assimilation operate at various levels—individual, familial, ethnic group, and institutional. They are unthinkable without the institutional changes that were initiated during the civil rights era, when the outlawing of discrimination increased its cost in nontrivial ways. Another legacy of that era is affirmative action, which, though contested, still influences the access of minority-group members to higher education as well as to many jobs.[33] Moreover, because the law fundamentally is expressed through normative ideas, legal change alters ideology. Today, few American whites can openly state racist views without meeting some form of censure.

In the contemporary institutional context, a principal mechanism of assimilation is simple enough: minority and immigrant-origin Americans seek to improve their social and material circumstances, and some assimilation often occurs as an unintended consequence of their efforts. The perception of opportunities motivates individuals to undertake changes that have assimilatory consequences, whether they are understood that way or not. And since, on average, opportunities are greater in the mainstream than they are in ethnic communities, individuals are also motivated to attempt to enter mainstream settings—in residence, in the labor market, and in other ways. It is useful to think of these opportunities in a broader way than the concept of upward socioeconomic mobility. For the second generation, improvement in social and material circumstances might translate into the ability to avoid an immigrant job (with its humiliations and incessant demands) or to own a home in a neighborhood suitable for raising one's family.[34]

AN ALTERNATIVE POINT OF
VIEW: SEGMENTED ASSIMILATION

Neo-, or mainstream-, assimilation theory is not the only theory about assimilation competing for attention in the intellectual marketplace. Another major effort is associated with the term "segmented assimilation" and was initially proposed by Alejandro Portes and Min Zhou.[35] They posit that assimilation can occur into different sectors, or "segments," of American society and therefore entails distinct trajectories by assimilating individuals and groups. One trajectory leads to the middle-class white mainstream; this is conventional or mainstream assimilation, consistent in their theory with the canonical concept of Milton Gordon. But another leads to incorporation into the racialized population at the bottom of U.S. society. According to Portes and Zhou, this "downward" trajectory may be followed by many in the second generation from the new immigrant groups, who are handicapped by their very humble starting points in U.S. society—that is, the low-class positions of their immigrant parents—and barred from entry to the white mainstream by their dark skin. On this route of assimilation, they are guided by the cultural models of poor, native-born African Americans and Latinos. Perceiving that they are likely to remain in their parents' status at the bottom of the occupational hierarchy and evaluating this prospect negatively because, unlike their parents, they have absorbed the standards of the American mainstream, they respond with oppositional stances and succumb to various temptations, such as dropping out of school and entering into deviant subcultures.

Portes and Zhou also envision a pluralist alternative to either "upward" (i.e., mainstream) or "downward" assimilation. That is, they argue that some individuals and groups are able to draw social and economic advantages by embedding much of their social life in an ethnic matrix (e.g., ethnic economic niches, ethnic communities). Under optimal circumstances, exemplified by the Cubans of Miami, immigrant-origin groups may even be able to equal within their ethnic communities and networks the socioeconomic opportunities that are afforded by the mainstream. In such cases, the pluralist route of incorporation would provide a truly viable alternative to assimilation as well as incentives for the second generation to preserve ethnic cultural and social attachments.

A key difference on the theoretical plane between neo- and segmented assimilation theories concerns the role of ethno-racial boundaries. In the segmented-assimilation conception of that role, ethno-racial boundaries are exogenous, that is, they are a prominent part of the societal social structure that affects the trajectory of incorporation of immigrant-origin groups and their members. According to this theory, because of racial boundaries, non-white groups face high hurdles, perhaps impossibly high ones, in attempting to enter the white mainstream. By contrast, the neo-assimilation theory considers that boundaries may be endogenous to assimilation processes, not just exogenous. In this conception, boundaries may change over time, eroded by large-scale assimilation of minority groups, as happened to the ethno-religious boundaries that excluded Catholics and Jews from the mainstream prior to the mid-twentieth century. This theory therefore envisions the possibility—but not the certainty—that present-day ethno-racial boundaries will be modified by the ongoing assimilation of many Asians, blacks, and Latinos. What this modification, should it occur, might mean—whether boundaries will become more contingent or, more unlikely, will fade more generally—is an unanswered question at this point.

THE EMPIRICAL EVIDENCE AND
THE ASSIMILATION DEBATE

The debate between these different theories dominates current discussions of the incorporation of contemporary immigrant groups. This debate takes place principally in terms of the position of the second generation in American society, although one should not ignore the assimilation that takes place during the lifetime of the immigrant generation.[36] Proponents of segmented assimilation see the second generation from many of the largest immigrant groups, such as the children of Mexican immigrants, as exposed to a high risk of downward assimilation, as evidenced by a failure to make significant socioeconomic progress beyond their immigrant parents.[37] Scholars operating from the perspective of neo-assimilation theory see the predominant direction of intergenerational change as toward the mainstream.[38]

The evidence cited on behalf of segmented-assimilation theory is generally couched in terms of the substantial gaps on many social-status indicators between the average white and numerous second-generation individuals whose parents came from the Caribbean and Latin America. In addition, scholars cite the higher risks to members of these groups of dropping out of school, living in poverty, experiencing unemployment, and being incarcerated.[39]

Without question, ethno-racial inequalities on major indicators such as educational attainment, occupational position, and earnings and income remain large and salient.[40] Thus, recent data indicate, for instance, that U.S.-born Mexican Americans have rates of high-school dropout that are at least twice as high as those of their non-Hispanic white peers and that their rates of college graduation fall behind mainstream norms by ratios of 1 to 2.5 or 1 to 3.[41] In a widely cited analysis, Edward Telles and Vilma Ortiz claim, moreover, that the educational progress of Mexican Americans stalls after the second generation.[42]

Research that finds support for mainstream assimilation generally begins by observing that, on average, the second generation of many groups takes large steps beyond the position of immigrant parents in both educational and labor-market terms. This intergenerational advance is so great that some scholars have concluded that there is a "second-generation advantage" that results from optimism about social mobility and the ability to selectively combine features of mainstream and ethnic cultures. Moreover, the second generation appears on average to be better off than the natives of the same racial population.[43]

Further, the identities and social relations of many in the second generation suggest an orientation toward the mainstream. A Pew Research Center study has found that six in ten second-generation Asians and Hispanics think of themselves as "a typical American," though many who say this also assert hyphenated identities.[44] Intermarriage rates are substantial, and interracial marriage appears to be in the process of being normalized. According to another analysis by the Pew Research Center, marriages that cross the major lines of race and Hispanic origin—as when Hispanics marry whites or blacks—are becoming much more common and now account for about one in seven marriages each year.[45] Most of these marriages unite the descendants of Asian or Latin American immigrants with white partners. Because of the increase in intermarriage, about a third of Americans say that they have a close relative of another race. Majorities of all groups are of the opinion that it is fine for a close family member to marry someone of another race.

Spreading intermarriage is giving rise to a growing population of youth who have grown up in racially mixed environments. While much is not known about the characteristics of this group, preliminary research suggests that those from families that mix whites and Asians or Hispanics feel themselves to be part of the mainstream society.[46] For example, the children of Mexican-white marriages feel less intensely Mexican, perceive less prejudice and discrimination, and are much more likely to marry non-Mexicans than are their counterparts from unmixed Mexican backgrounds.[47]

ASSIMILATION AND THE AMERICAN FUTURE

In reflecting on the future implications of this mixed picture, which seems to offer support to both mainstream and segmented assimilation theories, it is essential to also bear in mind some fundamental demographic and social-structural trends. Here, too, the picture is a mixed one.

Though assimilation is not synonymous with social mobility, there can be little doubt that assimilation depends on the perception of opportunities for the members of immigrant-origin groups to improve their lives. Such opportunities depend, in turn, on fundamental economic trends. In this respect, a critical fact is that recent years have been characterized globally by slow and uneven job growth, even before the Great Recession—which, in the United States, started in 2007–2008—and rising levels of economic inequality. The occupational structure appears to be undergoing some "hollowing out" of the middle since what growth occurs is concentrated at the top and the bottom of the job hierarchy.[48] These trends, should they continue, would not by themselves augur well for mainstream assimilation.

However, there is a countervailing demographic trend: namely, the opening up of many good jobs that will likely occur by 2035 as the massive and heavily white baby boom exits from the workforce. This will be accompanied by a rapid diversification of the working-age population because youthful birth cohorts that will be entering the ages of work and family formation are much more diverse than the baby boom ones. In fact, there will be many fewer whites entering the workforce than are leaving it. This demographic "changing of the guard" opens up the possibility of considerable non-zero-sum mobility, whereby the children of recent immigrants can ascend in the labor market without appearing to threaten the position of advantaged whites.[49]

Thus, the basic economic and demographic trends neither exclude assimilation into the mainstream for the second and third generations of contemporary immigrants nor guarantee it. It remains to be seen how much assimilation will occur. Regardless, it is reasonable to conclude that assimilation will remain a major part of the American story of immigrant-group incorporation.

NOTES

1. Richard Alba and Victor Nee, *Remaking the American Mainstream: Assimilation and Contemporary Immigration* (Cambridge: Harvard University Press, 2009), chap. 3.
2. Nancy Foner, *From Ellis Island to JFK: New York's Two Great Waves of Immigration* (New Haven: Yale University Press, 2000); Peter Schrag, *Not Fit for Our Society: Nativism and Immigration* (Berkeley: University of California Press, 2010).
3. Jerome Karabel, *The Chosen: The Hidden History of Admission and Exclusion at Harvard, Yale and Princeton* (New York: Houghton Mifflin, 2006).
4. Lewis P. Curtis, Jr., *Apes and Angels: The Irishman in Victorian Caricature*, rev. ed. (Washington: Smithsonian Institution Press, 1997).
5. Kenneth Jackson, *The Ku Klux Klan in the City, 1915–1930* (New York: Oxford University Press, 1967).
6. Alba and Nee, *Remaking the American Mainstream*, chap. 3.
7. Stephen Steinberg, *The Academic Melting Pot* (New York: McGraw-Hill, 1974).
8. Noel Ignatiev, *How the Irish Became White* (New York: Routledge, 1995); Matthew Frye Jacobson, *Whiteness of a Different Color: European Immigrants and the Alchemy of Race* (Cambridge: Harvard University Press, 1998); David Roediger, *Working Toward Whiteness: How America's Immigrants Became White: The Strange Journey from Ellis Island to the Suburbs* (New York: Basic Books, 2005).
9. Ira Katznelson, *When Affirmative Action Was White: An Untold History of Racial Inequality in Twentieth-Century America* (New York & London: W. W. Norton, 2005).
10. For example, Herbert Gans, *The Urban Villagers: Group and Class in the Life of Italian-Americans* (New York: The Free Press, 1962).
11. Richard Alba, *Blurring the Color Line: The New Chance for a More Integrated America* (Cambridge: Harvard University Press, 2009).
12. Joel Perlmann, *Ethnic Differences: Schooling and Social Structure Among the Irish, Italians, Jews & Blacks in an American City, 1880–1935* (Cambridge: Cambridge University Press, 1988).
13. Leonard Covello, *The Social Background of the Italo-American School Child* (Totowa, NJ: Rowman & Littlefield, 1972).

14. Nathan Glazer and Daniel Patrick Moynihan, *Beyond the Melting Pot: The Negroes, Puerto Ricans, Jews, Italians, and Irish of New York City* (Cambridge: MIT Press, 1963).
15. Richard Alba, "The Twilight of Ethnicity Among Americans of European Ancestry: The Case of Italians," *Ethnic and Racial Studies* 8 (Jan. 1985): 134–158.
16. Herbert Gans, *The Levittowners: Ways of Life and Politics in a New Suburban Community* (New York: Pantheon, 1967).
17. Gary Gerstle, *American Crucible: Race and Nation in the Twentieth Century* (Princeton: Princeton University Press, 2001).
18. Robert Merton, *Sociological Ambivalence & Other Essays* (New York; The Free Press), 221.
19. Alba, "The Twilight"; Richard Alba and Robert Orsi, "Passages of Piety: Generational Transitions and the Social and Religious Incorporation of Italian Americans," in *Immigration and Religion in America: Past and Present*, eds. Richard Alba, Albert Raboteau, and Josh DeWind (New York: New York University Press, 2008).
20. Sylvia Barack Fishman, *Double or Nothing: Jewish Families and Mixed Marriage* (Waltham, MA: Brandeis University Press, 2004), 6–7; Naomi Schaefer Riley, *'Til Faith Do Us Part: How Interfaith Marriage Is Transforming America* (New York: Oxford University Press, 2013).
21. Michèle Lamont and Virág Molnár, "The Study of Boundaries in the Social Sciences," *Annual Review of Sociology* 28 (2002): 167–195; Andreas Wimmer, *Ethnic Boundary Making: Institutions, Power, Networks* (New York: Oxford University Press, 2013).
22. Frederik Barth, *Ethnic Groups and Boundaries* (Boston: Little, Brown, 1969).
23. Charles Tilly, *Durable Inequality* (Berkeley: University of California Press, 1998); Wimmer, *Ethnic Boundary Making*.
24. Rainer Bauböck, "The Integration of Immigrants," Council of Europe (Strasbourg, 1994); Aristide Zolberg and Long Litt Woon, "Why Islam Is Like Spanish: Cultural Incorporation in Europe and the United States," *Politics & Society* 27 (1999): 5–38.
25. Milton Gordon, *Assimilation in American Life* (New York: Oxford University Press, 1964).
26. Will Herberg, *Protestant-Catholic-Jew* (New York: Anchor, 1960).
27. Andrew Greeley, *The Catholic Myth: The Behavior and Beliefs of American Catholics* (New York: Scribner's, 1990).
28. Fishman, *Double or Nothing*.
29. Alba and Nee, *Remaking the American Mainstream*, 11.
30. Gordon, *Assimilation in American Life*.
31. Samuel Huntington, *Who Are We? The Challenges to America's National Identity* (New York: Simon & Schuster, 2004).
32. Irvin Child, *Italian or American? The Second Generation in Conflict* (New Haven: Yale University Press, 1943).
33. John Skrentny, *The Minority-Rights Revolution* (Cambridge: Harvard University Press, 2002).
34. Philip Kasinitz, John Mollenkopf, Mary Waters, and Jennifer Holdaway, *Inheriting the City: The Children of Immigrants Come of Age* (New York and Cambridge: Russell Sage Foundation and Harvard University Press, 2009); Dowell Myers, *Immigrants and Boomers: Forging a New Social Contract for the Future of America* (New York: Russell Sage Foundation, 2007).
35. Alejandro Portes and Min Zhou, "The New Second Generation: Segmented Assimilation and Its Variants," *The Annals* 530 (1993): 74–96.

36. Dowell Myers and John Pitkin, "Assimilation Tomorrow: How America's Immigrants Will Integrate by 2030," report of the Center for American Progress (Nov. 2011).
37. Alejandro Portes and Rubén Rumbaut, *Legacies: The Story of the Immigrant Second Generation* (Berkeley: University of California Press, 2001).
38. Kasinitz et al., *Inheriting the City*.
39. Alejandro Portes, Patricia Fernández-Kelly, and William Haller, "Segmented Assimilation on the Ground: The New Second Generation in Early Adulthood," *Ethnic and Racial Studies* 28 (2005): 1000–1040.
40. Daniel Lichter, "Integration or Fragmentation? Racial Diversity and the American Future," *Demography* 50 (2013): 359–391.
41. Richard Alba and Jennifer Holdaway, eds., *The Children of Immigrants at School: A First Look at Integration in the United States and Western Europe* (New York: NYU Press, 2013).
42. Edward Telles and Vilma Ortiz, *Generations of Exclusion: Mexican Americans, Assimilation, and Race* (New York: Russell Sage Foundation, 2008).
43. Kasinitz et al., *Inheriting the City*.
44. Pew Research Center, "Second-Generation Americans: A Portrait of the Adult Children of Immigrants," report of Pew Research Center (Feb. 2013).
45. Wendy Wang, "The Rise of Intermarriage: Rates, Characteristics Vary by Race and Gender," report of Pew Research Center (Feb. 2012).
46. Sharon Lee and Frank Bean, *The Diversity Paradox: Immigration and the Color Line in the Twenty-First Century* (New York: Russell Sage Foundation, 2012).
47. Telles and Ortiz, *Generations of Exclusion*.
48. David Autor, "The Polarization of Job Opportunities in the U.S. Labor Market: Implications for Employment and Earnings," report of the Center for American Progress (Apr 2010).
49. Alba, *Blurring the Color Line*; Myers, *Immigrants and Boomers*.

Bibliography

Alba, Richard, and Victor Nee. *Remaking the American Mainstream: Assimilation and Contemporary Immigration.* Cambridge: Harvard University Press, 2009.

Foner, Nancy. *From Ellis Island to JFK: New York's Two Great Waves of Immigration.* New Haven: Yale University Press, 2000.

Gerstle, Gary. *American Crucible: Race and Nation in the Twentieth Century.* Princeton: Princeton University Press, 2001.

Gordon, Milton, *Assimilation in American Life.* New York: Oxford University Press, 1964.

Kasinitz, Philip, John Mollenkopf, Mary Waters, and Jennifer Holdaway. *Inheriting the City: The Children of Immigrants Come of Age.* New York and Cambridge: Russell Sage Foundation and Harvard University Press, 2009.

Lee, Sharon, and Frank Bean. *The Diversity Paradox: Immigration and the Color Line in the Twenty-First Century.* New York: Russell Sage Foundation, 2012.

Myers, Dowell. *Immigrants and Boomers: Forging a New Social Contract for the Future of America.* New York: Russell Sage Foundation, 2007.

Portes, Alejandro, and Rubén Rumbaut. *Legacies: The Story of the Immigrant Second Generation.* Berkeley: University of California Press, 2001.

Portes, Alejandro, and Min Zhou, "The New Second Generation: Segmented Assimilation and Its Variants," *The Annals* 530 (1993): 74–96.

CHAPTER 11

....

WHITENESS AND RACE

....

DAVID R. ROEDIGER

The price the white American paid for his ticket was to become white—:
and, in the main, nothing more than that, or, as he was to insist, nothing less. This incredibly limited not to say dimwitted ambition has choked
many a human being to death here: and this, I contend, is because the
white American has never accepted the real reasons for his journey.

—James Baldwin, "Introduction," *The Price of the Ticket: Collected*
Nonfiction 1948–1985 (1984)

ACADEMIC writing on race and whiteness by historians of immigration has a prehistory
and a continuing parallel track, more illustrious than its formal historiography. After
discussing that prehistory, the emergence, accomplishments, enduring quandaries,
and gaps in academic writings on immigration history and racial identity of Europeans
coming to the United States deserve attention. As academic writing has evolved over the
last two decades, a subfield called "critical whiteness" studies has taken shape with considerable emphasis on questions of immigration.[1]

Among current writers, Toni Morrison best exemplifies the activist-intellectuals of
color who have developed the prior and parallel tradition. In the 1993 special issue of
Time titled "The New Face of America," the articles and lavish advertisements vied with
each other in expressing exuberance over the thesis that new patterns of immigration,
intermarriage, and global business would quickly produce a United States that transcended race. It was left for Morrison to provide a short, ringing, and acerbic dissent.
In her contribution to the issue, "On the Backs of Blacks," Morrison soberly reflected
knowledge of how long immigration of groups regarded as racially suspect had been a
feature of U.S. history and of how often such immigration had reinforced, not undermined, a black-white color line. Morrison began with a reference to Stavros, the Greek
immigrant in Elia Kazan's film *America, America*. She recalled his journey in the film
from Ellis Island to shoeshining work in Grand Central Station. In the last scene of the
movie, as Morrison wrote, "Quickly, but as casually as an afterthought, a young black

man, also a shoe shiner, enters and tries to solicit a customer. He is run off the screen—
'Get out of here! We're doing business here!'—and silently disappears."[2]

As Morrison tartly continued: "This interloper into Stavros' workplace is crucial in the mix of signs that make up the movie's happy-ending immigrant story: a job, a straw hat, an infectious smile—and a scorned black." Thus an "act of racial contempt . . . transforms this charming Greek into an entitled white," and through it, his "future as an American is . . . assured." The story utterly deflated the more extravagant pretenses of this special issue of *Time* in which it appeared, but it was designed not to similarly deflate Kazan's film. Indeed, it was only through Morrison's championing of it, long before her *Time* essay, that I knew about the film, *America, America*. Far from predisposed to like Kazan's work, I came on her recommendation to see first his broad genius in showing the processes in which workers got jobs, and second the remarkable way that Stavros' dismissed competitor functioned in the final scene. That is, Morrison was far from chastising Kazan for introducing the African American character as "interloper" and "afterthought." Caught in—as a celebrated collection in which Morrison wrote the leading essay referred to it—a "house that race built," Kazan got the logic of that house right—suggesting that the black worker could be both a central presence and a walk-on in immigrant life.[3]

Morrison's evocation of Kazan's good and terrifying example of "playing in the dark" in *America, America* is most useful as a point of departure for this essay on immigrants, race, and whiteness. Morrison, as a historically minded novelist and as one of America's best essayists, began with the imagination of another artist. In large measure, such a choice of a place to start reflected the larger trajectory of thought about immigration and whiteness in U.S. intellectual history. The deepest reflections on this score had long come from creative writers, not from the immigration historians who generally regarded the immigrant as assimilating (or not) to an "American" identity rather than a white American one, a view Morrison's *Time* essay effectively skewers.[4]

Very often, fictional works carried deep meaning with exactly the same glancing quality that Morrison heard in Kazan. Thus, in Mike Gold's loosely autobiographical 1930 proletarian novel, *Jews Without Money*, the central character made his immigrant mother's terror on first arrival in the United States concrete by having her spend her first American night in a building "called the Nigger House" amid "groans and confusion on the floor of a crowded cellar for immigrants."[5] John Fante's protagonist in *Ask the Dust* (1939), a "filthy little Greaser," not exactly apologized for abusing his Latina partner by introducing his own "quivering . . . old wound" caused by hearing the epithet, "filthy little Greaser," applied to him as an Italian American.[6]

In novels set in workplaces, the intimate connections and professed disconnections of southern and eastern Europeans and African Americans were somewhat more fully elaborated. Thomas Bell's *Out of This Furnace* (1941), for example, introduced the possibility and difficulty of interracial working class solidarity through an appeal that the labor organizer Dobie made to an old man complaining of African Americans bringing dirt and decline to the Slavic area of Braddock, Pennsylvania: "I was just thinking it was once the Irish looking down on the Hunkies and now it's the Hunkies looking down on the niggers. . ... And for no better reason." At that point in the novel, such arguments provoked only shrugs.[7]

Fiction also offered early explorations of the process through which management understood that the immigrant's precarious hold on whiteness, and the attendant fears of other races and nationalities, could be used to divide workers. If William Attaway's brilliant *Blood on the Forge* (1941) was the most sophisticated example on this score, Upton Sinclair's neglected 1917 *King Coal* was probably the most voluble and didactic. In that novelization of the Colorado coal-mining wars that eventuated in the Ludlow Massacre, Sinclair told the story of the "race management" of immigrants through a young sociology student-cum-worker whose tendency to narrate as an ethnographer was both the strength and weakness of the book. According to the narrator: "The Americans and English and Scotch looked down upon the Welsh and Irish," who lorded it over "the Dagoes and Frenchies;" they, in turn denigrated "Polacks and Hunkies," who disdained "Greeks, Bulgarians, and 'Monty-negroes' [Montenegrins]." After another spate of eastern European distinctions came "Greasers, niggers, and, last and lowest, Japs."[8]

Morrison also emphasizes the precocious pushing at questions of race, whiteness, and immigration long before anything called "whiteness studies" influenced immigration history emphasizing work by intellectuals and activists of color. Frederick Douglass was perhaps the greatest early expert on these issues. Both finding great sympathy for immigrant oppression and worrying that immigrants would elbow African Americans off the lowest rungs of the job ladder, Douglass expressed empathy and anxiety when he warned that the Irish American "will find that in assuming our avocation he will also assume our degradation."[9] Attuned to possibilities of political alliance between abolitionists and the Irish (in both Ireland and the United States), Douglass wrote that when touring Ireland, he heard in the music "wailing notes" that he found resonant with the "wild notes" of African American slave music.[10] That sonic affinity, around a shared wail, would later feature in ongoing comparisons of African American music to that of several immigrant groups other than the Irish, including Jews and Slavs.[11]

Although there was every reason to point out that the degree and character of oppression suffered by European immigrants and blacks differed, the extent to which African American thinkers themselves insisted on comparing, as well as contrasting, the two experiences remains noteworthy. Thus, Du Bois—who certainly knew the differences between African American and new immigrant experiences regarding the likelihood of being the subject of the terror of lynching and of degrees of degradation within the criminal justice system as well as anyone—wrote of a "habit of killing" that victimized Hungarians and Italians as well as blacks and Indians in the early twentieth century.[12] Late in that century, Spike Lee's remarkable explorations of Italian American identity and race likewise insisted that understanding immigrant racism required glancing, telling references to affinities with the African American experience as well as distancing from it.[13]

Thus, a sense of sadness and bitterness ripened among black observers when immigrants often came to embrace a racial order conferring benefits on whites, although that bitterness coexisted with an appreciation of the logic and tragedy of that choice. In coauthoring Malcolm X's autobiography, Alex Haley captured the sadness in a near-concluding scene in which he and Malcolm saw a beautiful European immigrant family in an airport as the family was coming to the United States. They are, Malcolm acidly remarked, about to learn their first word of English: "nigger." Malcolm's one-liner was in fact not his alone but a bitter joke/observation circulating in African American tradition.[14]

Toni Morrison's version of the same joke added the dimension of tragedy and sympathy so present in Douglass. For her, "nigger" was the second word of English an immigrant learned, coming after the he or she learned to accept his or her submission to authority that made "okay" the first word learned.[15] The figure most systematic and profound in his inquiry into race and the "white" immigrant, novelist and essayist James Baldwin, similarly saw two sides to fitting into U.S. systems of white supremacy. Baldwin insisted that adopting a view of oneself as "white" was "absolutely a moral choice (for there are no white people)." Such a choice entailed for Baldwin a tragic, even "dimwitted," trading of rooted ethnic identities for a "lie" and for an overwrought, counterproductive "dream of safety" offered by whiteness. But he likewise acknowledged that a "vast amount of coercion" conditioned such a choice—that the U.S. economy and state acted as a whiteness "factory" during the period when new immigrants decided to pay what Baldwin called the "price of the ticket" by becoming white.[16]

Indeed, in the last twenty years, a period in which a substantial body of academic historical writing on whiteness, race, and immigration has appeared, the contributions of creative writers and of intellectuals of color, often activists, have remained central. Robert Lee's *Orientals*, for example, developed the idea that the Asian American worker became the "other" against which white male workers developed a sense of race, class, and gender analysis in the post-Civil War United States.[17] In legal studies, Ian Haney-Lopez's *White by Law* best analyzed the court cases on whiteness, immigration, and naturalization.[18] For the ways in which whiteness affected the history of Mexican Americans and in which Mexican American presences shaped whiteness, Latino historian Neil Foley offered the best monograph, the late Gloria Anzuldúa the best poetry, and the playwright and critic Cherríe Moraga the best memoir.[19]

Locating the origins of a critical white immigration history in ethnic studies, creative writing, and civil rights struggles need not minimize the ways in which academic immigration and ethnic history, to which this chapter now turns, embraced and furthered this area of inquiry. To an extent far greater than in labor history, for example, the *Journal of American Ethnic History* featured material on how immigrants encountered the racial order of the United States, and works on whiteness have won major prizes from the Immigration and Ethnic History Society. In part, this reflected the fact that some classic work in immigration history and on the history of nativism had developed important ideas and bases of knowledge that verged on the study of whiteness.[20] John Higham's idea of the new immigrants to the South as "in-between people" in the U.S. racial state is the best example here.[21] The support and advice of Rudolph Vecoli at University of

Minnesota's Immigration History Research Center also proved especially generative in exploring intersections of critical whiteness studies and immigration history.[22]

Noel Ignatiev's 1995 *How the Irish Became White* was the first influential book-length project by a historian studying the ways in which a group of European immigrants saw their whiteness questioned. Ignatiev also provocatively explored how those immigrants responded, by no means evenly or immediately, by moving to secure status and the relative advantage as whites.[23] One could push the origins of such research back a little further, to the wonderful historical sociology of black-Irish relations in Richard Williams' *Hierarchical Structures and Social Value* (1990), to the chapter on the Irish in my *The Wages of Whiteness* (1991), or even to Nora Faires and Nancy Faires Conklin's excellent earlier study of color, religion, and identity among Lebanese Americans in Birmingham, Alabama. However, Ignatiev's bold and highly cited book most decisively announced and invited the debates to come.[24]

Based on decades of Marxist study and factory-based activism as well as on dissertation work with the conservative Harvard immigration historian Stephan Thernstrom, Ignatiev's work benefited from new waves of immigration (including, at the time, new Irish immigrations) raising the issues of how and what newcomers learned about white supremacy in the United States.[25] The bold "Became White" in the title of Ignatiev's book reflected, like much of the early critical whiteness studies work, a profound debt to historical materialist scholarship that viewed race as anything but a natural category. In Ignatiev's case, and mine, the central influences were Theodore Allen, George Rawick, and W.E.B. Du Bois as historians, and James Baldwin as an essayist. Indeed, Baldwin's "On Being 'White' and Other Lies," originally appearing in the popular journal *Essence*, became a guiding star for early immigration histories of whiteness, insisting, as it did, that whiteness was a tragically learned behavior in the United States.[26]

If we date this body of work from the appearance of *How the Irish Became White*, academic historical writing on immigration history is barely two decades old—old enough, perhaps, to hazard the assessments of challenges exposed in the initial waves of scholarship, of the productivity of debates in the field, and of the most glaring gaps in the field that the balance of this essay offers, but not old enough for the occasionally dismissive critiques of the whole enterprise to have much persuasive power.[27] The new scholarship has produced a spate of useful studies of Italian Americans and whiteness,[28] an impressive grouping of books on Jewish Americans and whiteness,[29] important accounts of Arab immigrants and whiteness,[30] a similar concentration on the Irish,[31] a growing body of excellent work on whiteness in Mexican American history,[32] and solid general studies (above all, those of Matthew Jacobson) covering whiteness and immigration during most periods.[33]

However, whole nationalities and racialized groups are only beginning to be treated in published work. Happily, in the case of Finnish Americans in Peter Kivisto and Johanna Leinonen's new work and in Robert Zecker's work on race, whiteness, and the immigrant press in the Slovak American case, such work very much advances the state of the art, suggesting that the best is decidedly yet to come.[34] Just as important, the greatest contribution of the critical study of whiteness to immigration history is likely to come in sections of books devoted to broader topics, as, for example, in Jennifer Guglielmo's wonderful *Living the Revolution*, in Gabriela E. Arredondo's *Mexican Chicago*, in Russell Kazal's *Becoming Old Stock*, or in Linda Gordon's *The Great Arizona Orphan Abduction*.[35]

If we cannot know the success of critical whiteness studies in animating new histories of immigration quite yet, we can identify and assess some of the more and less productive debates raised by this subspeciality and some areas in which further research is certainly necessary. *How the Irish Became White* proved vulnerable to attack because of what was seen as a scant evidentiary base, in a book wanting to draw big and bold conclusions. To say that anti-radicalism conditioned critiques of Ignatiev is only to acknowledge what was sometimes directly expressed. Thus, Eric Arnesen fretted that the "political cult-like sensibility" of Ignatiev "should find a respectable place in university history departments." He regarded such acceptance as "a testament to the academy's perhaps overly generous and ecumenical culture (at least toward matters considered progressive)." Nathan Glazer's essay on Matthew Jacobson's work similarly found that Ignatiev's history (and my *Wages of Whiteness*) used history "like a club to beat 'whites' into an acknowledgement of what they had gained by the construction of whiteness."[36]

It is tempting to leave matters with the undeniable fact that wide political distances separate some immigration historians studying whiteness and their critics.[37] However, a more obdurate set of problems with evidence and tone would be left unexamined by doing so. Ignatiev's book is typical of many in that it concentrates on a city, Philadelphia, and then also grabs evidence from elsewhere. Similarly, Thomas Guglielmo's excellent *White on Arrival* focuses on Chicago and seizes evidence from elsewhere. My extended essays with James R. Barrett on the new immigrants, whiteness, and race similarly radiated out from Chicago and sometimes New York City. Thus, many foundational works have been curiously hybrid in their form. When works set out to treat the nation's history over long stretches of time, as in my *Working Toward Whiteness* or Karen Brodkin's *How Jews Became White Folks*, the gaps often seem as impressive as the grab bag of sources. A fair share of the evidence has come from literature, popular culture, anthropology, and, in my case, even psychology. With critical study of whiteness coming centrally out of two fields not necessarily known for their interdisciplinarity—immigration history and labor history—the American Studies- and Ethnic Studies-based interdisciplinary inflections of historical studies of whiteness were sometimes less than appreciated. Where intellectual, legal, and policy history of whiteness and immigration have been concerned, as in the fine work of Jacobson and Haney-Lopez, the evidentiary base across time is more even if not richer, but the social history predilections of immigration and especially labor history, are sometimes left unsatisfied by such contributions.[38]

A larger issue of narration remains. If social histories of labor and immigration have been most at home with close studies of daily life in a community, in studies of whiteness and immigration the telling but sometimes fleeting interracial interaction such as the one Morrison flagged is more often important than the daily ones. Even if much fuller documentation were possible, the story of immigrants' direct encounters with African Americans would have been episodic. That is, white workers succeeded in divorcing themselves from black neighbors, and racial discrimination in hiring and promotion left most factories (and many departments in integrated plants) segregated. In the antebellum years, migration was mostly to cities with relatively few black workers, who nonetheless defined the bottom rungs of existence where precarity regarding life, rights, and jobs was concerned. Decisive racial "dead-lines" were drawn around a neighborhood by an Irish gang, for example, and foot traffic was enough limited so that daily encounters did not occur, although the dead-line was itself a daily reality. Public transit, some jobs, some unions, and what Kevin Mumford has called "interzones" of vice took immigrants across the color line at times. However, that line also ensured that the conception of the nonwhite other was a product of irregular contact of, a desire to preserve advantage, and of an imagination constructed via popular culture and racial folklore.[39]

A second enduring and largely unremarked issue in writing of histories of whiteness and immigration concerns the tone and politics such histories reflect. As the Baldwin quote in the epigraph to this chapter suggests, there is ample room for the discussion of misery to enter such history. The miseries suffered by immigrants and the miseries they sometimes participated in inflicting on people of color are easily enough discussed, but not always so easily weighed against each other. More difficult still, especially for white writers, is broaching the subject of the ineffable miseries and losses of humanity attending immigrant workers' settling for being white as an identity—the miseries that Baldwin makes central. Eric Goldstein's wonderfully titled *The Price of Whiteness*, on Jewish Americans and race, is an exception in this regard. But generally, to stress the miseries of the European immigrant has verged uneasily on drawing an equal sign between those miseries and the ones visited on nonwhites. Indeed, Baldwin could be so brave in discussing European immigrant miseries, even in periods of upward mobility, because he so deftly disposed of any hint of overall commensurability in oppression. The "Irish middle passage," he wrote, was "foul as my own." But the Irish "became white when they got here and therefore began rising in the world, whereas I became black and began sinking."[40]

Among anti-racist scholars of immigration history and whiteness, there have been at least two contradictory pulls. These pulls have shaped in significant measure the most sustained, though no longer the most useful, debate in the field. The idea that immigrant groups "became white," on the one hand, shares not only the drama in the Baldwin writings that inspire such approaches but also the insistence that initial immigrant oppression was, in many, cases real and deep. It also shares Baldwin's emphasis on the fact that race is changing and made-up or, as Jacobson puts it, "fabricated."[41] On the other hand, the approach best typified by Thomas Guglielmo's *White on Arrival* stresses the stark difference from the outset in the plight of European immigrants and that of nonwhites. The first approach grows, for at least Ignatiev and myself, out of a broad New Left sensibility, formed in the context of the black freedom movement and Marxism. The second, and here again Guglielmo is the best example, likewise reflects anti-racist priorities, but those around the defense of affirmative action with the consequent necessity of drawing a sharp distinction between racial oppression and white ethnic experiences. Indeed, the results of a blurring of that distinction in rightward political motion are often on display in Matthew Jacobson's excellent account of the "white ethnic revival" in *Roots Too*. For better or worse, the supposedly salutary absence of "passion and politics—for which Arnesen hopes in a recent essay partly on the historiography of whiteness—is not much present in either approach, nor in his and Glazer's critiques.[42]

While politically distinct, the two strains in critical whiteness studies of immigrant history end up converging rather muddily when they encounter complex evidence from the past. So much is this the case that the usefulness of framing matters in terms of whether immigrants were always, or dramatically became, white is open now to serious question. Many commentators, however the drama is initially phrased by them, end up taking middle positions acknowledging that the truth is lodged perhaps somewhere between the two extreme alternatives. Thus, in my own early work, the Irish distinctly "became white," while later writings on immigrants from eastern and southern Europe mostly use Higham's and Orsi's term "in-between" to describe immigrant racial positions. An incredible array of terms and phrases suggesting such in-between-ness have proliferated: not-quite-white, not-yet-white, conditionally white, quasi-white, off-white, semi-racialized, whitening, becoming white, probationary whites, situationally white, whiteness on trial, aspiring whites, and so on. Such terms are variously used by most writers on immigration and racial identity, going back to the classic sociology of John Dollard, which once resorted to "our temporary Negroes" to describe immigrants to the South.[43] Changing racial status and identity are captured by such usages without equating European immigrant experiences to those of nonwhites.

If nothing else, such debates have encouraged us to specify what we mean by becoming white, being white, or being in-between. In doing so, it is apposite to call to mind that racial identity is both a matter of decision as well as of ascription. Placed into assigned identities both by the structures of power in the larger society and by specific groups and persons entering their lives, immigrants embraced such a categorization or contested it. For example, although he was white in terms of naturalization law, the great Greek American musician Johnny Otis, born John Veliotes, continually fit himself into black life, culture, struggle, and even looks, fostering fascinating possibilities and confusions.[44] In Arizona mines, perhaps the best-studied examples of various ways management used immigrants' race and nationality, Italian immigrants were ascribed at the least a situationally white status, but at times chose to speak Spanish rather than English and to fit themselves—around sports, religion, common treatment by bosses, and intermarriage—into Mexican American communities.[45] Thus, in thinking through how immigrants changed or remained the same regarding race, we need to consider not only how they were categorized but also what they did with how they were categorized.

The greatest contributions of *White on Arrival* probably lay not in sustaining the bold argument announced in its title but in sparking debate. That argument perhaps supposed overly much that the early twentieth century United States made firm distinctions between race and color, with Italians putatively on firm ground as white citizens because they so clearly qualified as white on the latter ground. (So much is this assumed to be the case that the Chicago race riot of 1919 becomes a "color riot" in *White on Arrival*.) In any case, some of the "on arrival" argument is given decisively back when Guglielmo holds that Italians had, at most, slight consciousness of themselves as white and seldom bothered to claim that identity until decades after their mass arrival. On this view, they participated energetically in restrictive covenant campaigns bent on allowing only Caucasians in their neighborhoods without a strong sense of themselves as white.[46] Guglielmo clearly made a signal contribution in complicating questions regarding the racial identity of immigrants by arguing, along with Robert Zecker, Catherine Eagan, and others, that racial knowledge in Europe mattered greatly in shaping how whiteness was understood in the United States. The "became white" storyline, so dramatic (and I think often correct in its outlines) as adopted from Baldwin, sometimes allowed for wrongly regarding the immigrant as a blank slate where racial knowledge was concerned, written on only by U.S. experiences and ideas. But Europe itself was a place of many-sided racial and national ordering, of anti-Semitism, of imperialism in Asia and Africa, of minstrel shows, and of anti-gypsy persecution.[47] The impact of such race-thinking before migration to the U.S. requires much further research.

As befits such a young area of inquiry, there are, in fact, many themes similarly needing further research in immigration history investigating whiteness and how newcomers learned U.S. racial hierarchies. These deserve mention in closing. Existing studies emphasize that such learning is deeply gendered, with immigrant men and women making different and unequal claims to knowledge of how race works in the United States. Certainly family and home have served as symbols to be defended against racial mixing. But the specific processes through which whiteness was nurtured and challenged in immigrant houses and neighborhoods is only beginning to be researched, with the recent books of Jennifer Guglielmo and Bronwen Walter suggesting the great possibilities for research on immigration, gender, and whiteness.[48] Likewise understudied—though here the works of Kazal on German Americans and of Goldstein on Jews are happy exceptions—is the role of religion in conditioning the nativist attacks on immigrants and how they responded to those attacks.[49] Not surprisingly, it was the immigrant groups least accepted as fully white and the time periods when they were most under scrutiny in terms of racial classification that have attracted the most attention from scholars. We mostly lack, for example, studies of Anglo-Saxon whiteness, except when those thought to possess that lineage fail to live up to their supposed racial excellence. Similarly among the "old stock" groups, the less-accepted Irish are more studied than the Germans, though Kazal's work is also exceptional in this regard. The whiteness of the various nationalities actively engaged in processes of settlement and dispossession of Indians is likewise too little explored.[50]

NOTES

1. On the emergence of critical whiteness studies, see David Roediger, "Critical Studies of Whiteness, USA: Origins and Arguments," *Theoria* (South Africa), 98 (Dec. 2001): 72–98. The epigraph at the beginning of this chapter is from James Baldwin, *The Price of the Ticket: Collected Nonfiction, 1948–1985* (New York: St. Martin's Press, 1985), xix–xx.
2. Toni Morrison, "On the Backs of Blacks," *Time*, Dec. 2, 1993 (special issue), 57. On this special issue of *Time*, see David R. Roediger, *Colored White: Transcending the Racial Past* (Berkeley: University of California Press. 2002), 2–5.

3. Morrison, "On the Backs of Blacks," 57; Toni Morrison, "Home," in *The House That Race Built*, ed. Wahneema Lubiano (New York: Random House, 1997), 3–12.

4. Toni Morrison, *Playing in the Dark. Whiteness and the Literary Imagination* (New York: Vintage, 1990); Morrison, "On the Backs of Blacks," 57.

5. Michael Gold, *Jews Without Money* (New York: International Publishers, 1930), 113.

6. John Fante, *Ask the Dust* (1939; Santa Barbara: Black Sparrow Press, 1980), 44–47.

7. Thomas Bell, *Out of This Furnace* (1941; Pittsburgh: University of Pittsburgh Press, 1976), 327–330.

8. Upton Sinclair, *King Coal: A Novel* (New York: Macmillan, 1917), 54. See also William Attaway, *Blood on the Forge* (1941; New York: Monthly Review Press, 1987), esp. 122–123. On race management and immigration generally, see Elizabeth Esch and David Roediger, "Race and the Management of Labor in U.S. History," *Historical Materialism*, 17 (2009): 3–43. And on race in Sinclair's industrial novels, see David R. Roediger and Elizabeth D. Esch, *The Production of Difference: Race and the Management of Labor in U.S. History* (New York: Oxford University Press, 2012).

9. Frederick Douglass, *The Life and Times of Frederick Douglass* (1892; New York: Cosimo, 2008), 214.

10. Frederick Douglass, *My Bondage and My Freedom* (New York City and Auburn, NY: Miller, Orton and Mulligan, 1855), 98; cf. Eric Lott, *Love and Theft: Blackface Minstrelsy and the American Working Class* (New York: Oxford University Press, 1993).

11. Attaway, *Blood on the Forge*, 130; Jeffrey Melnick, *A Right to Sing the Blues: African Americans, Jews, and American Popular Song* (Cambridge: Harvard University Press, 1999), esp. 174–180; David R. Roediger, *Working Toward Whiteness: How America's Immigrants Became White* (New York: Basic Books, 2005), 100–103.

12. For the quote and its context amid other bitter Du Bois allusions to the successful "training" of immigrants in white supremacy, see David R. Roediger, "Afterword: Du Bois, Race, and Italian Americans," in *Are Italians White? How Race Is Made in America*, eds. Jennifer Guglielmo and Salvatore Salerno (New York: Routledge, 2003), 261, 259–263.

13. John Gennari, "Giancarlo Giuseppe Alessandro Esposito: Life in the Borderlands," in *Are Italians White?*, esp. 239–245.

14. Malcolm X with Alex Haley, *The Autobiography of Malcolm X* (1965; New York: Grove Press, 1984), 399; for the circulation of the "first word' joke, see Roediger, *Working Toward Whiteness*, 103–104.

15. Morrison, in conversation with author. See also Derrick Bell, "Racial Libel as Ritual," *Village Voice*, Nov. 21, 1995, 53.

16. James Baldwin, "On Being 'White' . . . and Other Lies," *Essence*, Apr. 1984, 90, 92. For Baldwin's many and unsurpassed insights on whiteness, see Baldwin, *The Price of the Ticket*.

17. Robert Lee, *Orientals: Asian Americans in Popular Culture* (Philadelphia: Temple University Press, 1999).

18. Ian Haney-Lopez, *White by Law: The Legal Construction of Race* (New York: New York University Press, 1996).

19. Neil Foley, "Partly Colored or Other White: Mexican Americans and Their Problem with the Color Line," in *Beyond Black and White: Race, Ethnicity, and Gender in the U.S. South and Southwest*, eds. Stephanie Cole and Alison Parker (College Station: Texas A&M University Press, 2004), 123–144; Neil Foley, *The White Scourge: Mexicans, Blacks, and Poor Whites in Texas Cotton Culture* (Berkeley: University of California Press, 1997);

Gloria Anzuldua, *Borderlands/La Frontera: The New Mestiza* (San Francisco: Spinsters/ Aunt Lutte, 1987), esp. 134–135; Cherríe Moraga, "La Guera," in *This Bridge Called My Back: Writings by Radical Women of Color*, eds. Gloria Anzuldúa and Cherríe Moraga (New York: Kitchen Table Press, 1984), 27–34.

20. See "A Half-Jubilee: Twenty-Five Years of Multiracial Scholarship," *Journal of American Ethnic History*, 25 (Summer 2006): 43–52.

21. John Higham, *Strangers in the Land: Patterns of American Nativism, 1860–1925* (1955; New York: Atheneum, 1974), 169. See also Robert Orsi, "The Religious Boundaries of an In-between People: Street Feste and the Problem of the Dark-Skinned 'Other' in Italian Harlem, 1920–1990," *American Quarterly*, 44 (Sept. 1972): 335.

22. For his reflections, see Rudolph J. Vecoli, "Are Italian Americans Just White Folks?," in *Beyond the Godfather: Italian American Writers on the Real Italian American Experience*, eds. A. Kenneth Ciongoli and Jay Parini (Hanover, NH, University Press of New England, 1997), 311–322.

23. Noel Ignatiev, *How the Irish Became White* (New York: Routledge, 1995).

24. Richard E. Williams, *Hierarchical Structures and Social Values: The Creation of Black and Irish Identities in the United States* (Cambridge: Cambridge University Press, 1990); David R. Roediger, *The Wages of Whiteness: Race and the Making of the American Working Class* (London and New York: Verso Books, 1991), 133–163; Nora Faires and Nancy Faires Conklin, "'Colored' and Catholic: The Lebanese in Birmingham, Alabama," in *Crossing the Waters: Arabic-Speaking Immigrants to the United States before 1940*, ed. Eric Hooglund (Washington, DC: Smithsonian Institution Press, 1987), 69–84. See also Roediger, *Working Toward Whiteness*.

25. On Ignatiev particularly and Marxism generally in the founding of critical white studies, see David Roediger, "Accounting for the Wages of Whiteness: U.S. Marxism and the Critical History of Race," in *Wages of Whiteness and Racist Symbolic Capital*, eds. Wulf D. Hund, Jeremy Krikler, and David Roediger (Berlin: Lit Verlag, 2010), 16–17, 9–36. For an essay, and indeed a volume, directly inspired by this recent immigration and the opportunity it presents to ask new questions regarding the longer history of immigration, see James R. Barrett and David R. Roediger, "Making New Immigrants 'In-between': Irish Hosts and White Pan-Ethnicity, 1890–1930," in *Not Just Black and White: Historical and Contemporary Perspectives on Immigration, Race, and Ethnicity in the United States*, eds. Nancy Foner and George Fredrickson (New York: Russell Sage Foundation 2004), 167–196.

26. Theodore Allen, *The Invention of the White Race*, 2 vols. (New York: Verso, 1994); W.E.B. Du Bois, *Black Reconstruction in America, 1860–1880* (1935; New York: Free Press, 1998); Baldwin, "On Being 'White' . . . and Other Lies," 90, 92.

27. See especially Eric Arnesen, "Whiteness and the Historians' Imagination," *International Labor and Working Class History*, 60 (2001): 3–32.

28. See especially Guglielmo and Salerno, eds. *Are Italians White?*, and Thomas Guglielmo, *White on Arrival: Race, Color, and Power in Chicago, 1890–1945* (New York: Oxford University Press, 2003).

29. Karen Brodkin, *How Jews Became White Folks and What That Says About Race in America* (New Brunswick: Rutgers University Press, 1998); Michael Rogin, *Blackface, White Noise: Jewish Immigrants in the Hollywood Melting-Pot* (Berkeley: University of California Press, 1996); Eric L. Goldstein, *The Price of Whiteness: Jews, Race, and American Identity* (Princeton: Princeton University Press, 2006).

30. Faires and Faires Conklin, "'Colored' and Catholic," 69–84; Sarah Gualtieri, *Between Arab and White: Race and Ethnicity in the Early Syrian American Diaspora* (Berkeley: University of California Press, 2009); Alixa Neff, *Becoming American: The Early Arab Immigrant Experience* (Carbondale: Southern Illinois University Press, 1985).

31. Ignatiev, *How the Irish Became White*; Roediger, *Wages of Whiteness*, 133–163; Bronwen Walter, *Outsiders Inside: Whiteness, Place, and Irish Women* (New York: Routledge, 2000).

32. See note 19 above. See also Thomas Guglielmo, "Fighting for Caucasian Rights: Mexicans, Mexican Americans, and the Transnational Struggle for Civil Rights in World War II Texas," *Journal of American History* 92 (Mar. 2006): 1212–1237; Tomás Almaguer, *Racial Fault Lines: The Historical Origins of White Supremacy in California* (Berkeley: University of California Press, 1994); Laura Gómez, *Manifest Destinies: The Making of the Mexican American Race* (New York: New York University Press, 2007), esp. 81–116.

33. Matthew Jacobson, *Whiteness of a Different Color: European Immigrants and the Alchemy of Race* (Cambridge: Harvard University Press, 1998); James R. Barrett and David R. Roediger, "In-between Peoples: Race, Nationality and the 'New Immigrant' Working Class," *Journal of American Ethnic History*, 16 (Spring 1997): 3–44; Roediger, *Working Toward Whiteness*; Matthew Frye Jacobson, *Roots Too: White Ethnic Revival in Post-Civil Rights America* (Cambridge: Harvard University Press, 2006); Valerie Babb, *Whiteness Visible: The Meaning of Whiteness in American Literature and Culture* (New York: New York University Press, 1998).

34. Peter Kivisto and Johanna Leinonen, "Representing Race: Ongoing Uncertainties about Finnish-American Racial Identity," *Journal of American Ethnic History* 31 (2011): 11; Robert Zecker, *Race and America's Immigrant Press: How the Slovaks Were Taught to Think Like White People* (New York: Continuum, 2011). Likewise important is Peter G. Vellon, *A Great Conspiracy Against Our Race: Italian Immigrant Newspapers and the Construction of Whiteness in the Early 20th Century* (New York: NYU Press, 2014). For an elaboration on my views of the recent past and future possibilities of critical whiteness studies, see "Whiteness and Its Complications," *The Chronicle Review*, July 14, 2006, B-6 to B-8.

35. Jennifer Guglielmo, *Living the Revolution: Italian Women's Resistance and Radicalism in New York City, 1880–1945* (Chapel Hill: University of North Carolina Press, 2010), 81–89, 254–255; Gabriela E. Arredondo, *Mexican Chicago: Race, Identity and Nation, 1916–1939* (Urbana: University of Illinois Press, 2008), 58–82, 105–107; Russell A. Kazal, *Becoming Old Stock: The Paradox of German-American Identity* (Princeton: Princeton University Press, 2004), 109–129; Linda Gordon, *The Great Arizona Orphan Abduction* (Cambridge: Harvard University Press, 1999), 102–104, 183–184.

36. Eric Arnesen, "Passion and Politics: Race and the Writing of Working-Class History," *The Journal of the Historical Society* 6 (2006): 340, 342–343. Arnesen, "Whiteness and the Historians' Imagination," 13–16, more generally takes up the supposed lack of evidence that those in the mass antebellum Catholic migration were anything but unequivocally white, concentrating there more on my work than on Ignatiev's. See also Peter Kolchin, "Whiteness Studies: The New History of Race in America," *Journal of American History* 89 (June 2002), 164–168. For Glazer, see his "White Noise," *The New Republic* (Oct. 12, 1998), 54ff, where the critique is somewhat extended to include Jacobson.

37. See Kolchin, "Whiteness Studies," 166–167; Arnesen, "Passion and Politics," 329.

38. The most stern expressions of reservations regarding the multiple concerns of my work is found in Eric Arnesen, "A Whiter Shade of Pale," *New Republic*, June 24, 2002, 33–38. On psychoanalysis and critiques of studies of whiteness, see Roediger, "Accounting for the

Wages of Whiteness," 25–30; Brodkin, *How Jews Became White Folks*; Barrett and Roediger, "Making New Immigrants 'In-between,'" 167–196; Roediger, *Working Toward Whiteness*; Haney-Lopez, *White by Law*; Jacobson, *Whiteness of a Different Color*.

39. Kevin Mumford, *Interzones: Black/White Sex Districts in Chicago and New York In the Early Twentieth Century* (New York: Columbia University Press, 1997); Roediger, *Working Toward Whiteness*, esp. 167.

40. Goldstein, *Price of Whiteness*, 4–5; Baldwin, *Price of the Ticket*, xx. Perhaps the closest to Baldwin in accounting for immigrant racism and immigrant misery together is Rogin, *Blackface, White Noise*.

41. For Ignatiev on Baldwin, see "'Whiteness' and American Character: An Essay," *Konch*, 1 (1990): 136–139; Jacobson, *Whiteness of a Different Color*, ix.

42. Guglielmo, *White on Arrival*, viii and Thomas Guglielmo, "'No Color Barrier': Italians, Race, and Power in the United States," in *Are Italians White?*, 29–43; Jacobson, *Roots Too*, esp. 180–205. See also Arnesen, "Passion and Politics," 340–343; Glazer, "White Noise," 54; and Roediger, "Accounting for the Wages of Whiteness," 16–25.

43. Cf. Roediger, *Wages of Whiteness*, 133–163 and Barrett and Roediger, "Making New Immigrants 'In-between,'" 167–196; John Dollard, *Caste and Class in the Southern Town* (Garden City, NY: Doubleday Anchor, 1949), 93; Roediger, *Working Toward Whiteness*, 13.

44. On Otis, see George Lipsitz, *Midnight at the Barrelhouse: The Johnny Otis Story* (Minneapolis: University of Minnesota Press, 2010).

45. See, e.g., Philip J. Mellinger, *Race and Labor in Western Copper: The Fight for Equality, 1896–1916* (Tucson: University of Arizona Press, 1995), 160–161, 192–203; Katherine Benton-Cohen, *Racial Division and Labor War in the Arizona Borderlands* (Cambridge: Harvard University Press, 2009); Phylis Cancilla Martinelli, *Undermining Race: Ethnic Identities in Arizona Copper Camps* (Tucson: University of Arizona Press, 2009); Roediger, *Working Toward Whiteness*, 74, 85.

46. Guglielmo, *White on Arrival*, 6–13, 39–43.

47. Guglielmo, *White on Arrival*, 21–23; Zecker, *Race and America's Immigrant Press*; Catherine M. Eagan, "'White,' if 'Not Quite': Irish Whiteness in the Nineteenth-Century Irish-American Novel," *Eire-Ireland: A Journal of Irish Studies* 36.1–2 (Spring-Summer 2001): 66–81; Roediger, *Working Toward Whiteness*, 110–119.

48. Guglielmo, *Living the Revolution*; Walter, *Outsiders Inside*. See also Roediger, *Working Toward Whiteness*, 184–193 and Michael Miller Topp, "'It Is Providential That There Are Foreigners Here': Whiteness and Masculinity in the Making of an Italian American Syndicalist Identity," in *Are Italians White?*, 98–110.

49. Goldstein, *The Price of Whiteness*; Kazal, *Becoming Old Stock*, 36–38, 245–260.

50. Kazal, *Becoming Old Stock*; Ian Christian Hartman, "From Daniel Boone to the Beverly Hillbillies: Tales of a 'Fallen' Race, 1873–1968 (PhD dissertation, University of Illinois, 2011); Gerald Ronning, "Jackpine Savages: Discourses of Conquest in the 1916 Mesabi Iron Range Strike," *Labor History*, 44 (Aug. 2003): 359–382.

BIBLIOGRAPHY

Allen, Theodore. *The Invention of the White Race*. 2 vols. New York: Verso, 1994.
Almaguer, Tomás. *Racial Fault Lines: The Historical Origins of White Supremacy in California*. Berkeley: University of California Press, 1994.

Anzuldua, Gloria. *Borderlands/La Frontera: The New Mestiza*. San Francisco: Spinsters/Aunt Lutte, 1987.

Arredondo, Gabriela E. *Mexican Chicago: Race, Identity and Nation, 1916–1939*. Urbana: University of Illinois Press, 2008.

Attaway, William. *Blood on the Forge*. New York: Monthly Review Press, 1941; 1987.

Babb, Valerie. *Whiteness Visible: The Meaning of Whiteness in American Literature and Culture*. New York: New York University Press, 1998.

Baldwin, James. *The Price of the Ticket: Collected Nonfiction, 1948–1985*. New York: St. Martin's Press, 1985.

Barrett, James R., and David R. Roediger. "Making New Immigrants 'In-between': Irish Hosts and White Pan-Ethnicity, 1890–1930." In *Not Just Black and White: Historical and Contemporary Perspectives on Immigration, Race, and Ethnicity in the United States*, edited by Nancy Foner and George Fredrickson, 167–196. New York: Russell Sage Foundation 2004.

Bell, Thomas. *Out of This Furnace*. Pittsburgh: University of Pittsburgh Press, 1941; 1976.

Benton-Cohen, Katherine. *Racial Division and Labor War in the Arizona Borderlands*. Cambridge: Harvard University Press, 2009.

Brodkin, Karen. *How Jews Became White Folks and What That Says About Race in America*. New Brunswick: Rutgers University Press, 1998.

Dollard, John. *Caste and Class in the Southern Town*. Garden City, NY: Doubleday Anchor, 1949.

Douglass, Frederick. *The Life and Times of Frederick Douglass*. New York: Cosimo, 1982; 2008.

Du Bois, W.E.B. *Black Reconstruction in America, 1860–1880*. New York: Free Press, 1935; 1998.

Faires, Nora, and Nancy Faires Conklin. "'Colored' and Catholic: The Lebanese in Birmingham, Alabama." In *Crossing the Waters: Arabic-Speaking Immigrants to the United States before 1940*, edited by Eric Hooglund, 69–84. Washington, DC: Smithsonian Institution Press, 1987.

Fante, John. *Ask the Dust*. Santa Barbara: Black Sparrow Press, 1939; 1980.

Foley, Neil. *The White Scourge: Mexicans, Blacks, and Poor Whites in Texas Cotton Culture*. Berkeley: University of California Press, 1997.

Foley, Neil. "Partly Colored or Other White: Mexican Americans and Their Problem with the Color Line." In *Beyond Black and White: Race, Ethnicity, and Gender in the U.S. South and Southwest*, edited by Stephanie Cole and Alison Parker, 123–144. College Station: Texas A&M University Press, 2004.

Gennari, John. "Giancarlo Giuseppe Alessandro Eposito: Life in the Borderlands." In *Are Italians White? How Race Is Made in America*, edited by Jennifer Guglielmo and Salvatore Salerno, 239–245. New York: Routledge, 2003.

Gold, Michael. *Jews Without Money*. New York: International Publishers, 1930.

Goldstein, Eric L. *The Price of Whiteness: Jews, Race, and American Identity*. Princeton: Princeton University Press, 2006.

Gómez, Laura. *Manifest Destinies: The Making of the Mexican American Race*. New York: New York University Press, 2007.

Gordon, Linda. *The Great Arizona Orphan Abduction*. Cambridge: Harvard University Press, 1999.

Gualtieri, Sarah. *Between Arab and White: Race and Ethnicity in the Early Syrian American Diaspora*. Berkeley: University of California Press, 2009.

Guglielmo, Jennifer. *Living the Revolution: Italian Women's Resistance and Radicalism in New York City, 1880–1945*. Chapel Hill: University of North Carolina Press, 2010.

Guglielmo, Jennifer, and Salvatore Salerno, eds. *Are Italians White? How Race Is Made in America*. New York: Routledge, 2003.

Haney-Lopez, Ian. *White by Law: The Legal Construction of Race* (New York: New York University Press, 1996).

Higham, John. *Strangers in the Land: Patterns of American Nativism, 1860–1925.* New York: Atheneum, 1955; 1974.

Ignatiev, Noel. *How the Irish Became White.* New York: Routledge, 1995.

Jacobson, Matthew Frye. *Whiteness of a Different Color: European Immigrants and the Alchemy of Race.* Cambridge: Harvard University Press, 1998.

Jacobson, Matthew Frye. *Roots Too: White Ethnic Revival in Post-Civil Rights America.* Cambridge: Harvard University Press, 2006.

Kazal, Russell A. *Becoming Old Stock: The Paradox of German-American Identity.* Princeton: Princeton University Press, 2004.

Lee, Robert. *Orientals: Asian Americans in Popular Culture.* Philadelphia: Temple University Press, 1999.

Lipsitz, George. *Midnight at the Barrelhouse: The Johnny Otis Story.* Minneapolis: University of Minnesota Press, 2010.

Lott, Eric. *Love and Theft: Blackface Minstrelsy and the American Working Class.* New York: Oxford University Press, 1993.

Martinelli, Phylis Cancilla. *Undermining Race: Ethnic Identities in Arizona Copper Camps.* Tucson: University of Arizona Press, 2009.

Mellinger, Philip J. *Race and Labor in Western Copper: The Fight for Equality, 1896–1916.* Tucson: University of Arizona Press, 1995.

Melnick, Jeffrey. *A Right to Sing the Blues: African Americans, Jews, and American Popular Song.* Cambridge: Harvard University Press, 1999.

Moraga, Cherríe. "La Guera." In *This Bridge Called My Back: Writings by Radical Women of Color,* edited by Gloria Anzuldúa and Cherríe Moraga, 27–34. New York: Kitchen Table Press, 1984.

Morrison, Toni. *Playing in the Dark. Whiteness and the Literary Imagination.* New York: Vintage, 1990.

Morrison, Toni. "Home." In *The House That Race Built,* edited by Wahneema Lubiano, 3–12. New York: Random House, 1997.

Mumford, Kevin. *Interzones: Black/White Sex Districts in Chicago and New York In the Early Twentieth Century.* New York: Columbia University Press, 1997.

Neff, Alixa. *Becoming American: The Early Arab Immigrant Experience.* Carbondale: Southern Illinois University Press, 1985.

Roediger, David R. *The Wages of Whiteness: Race and the Making of the American Working Class.* London and New York: Verso Books, 1991.

Roediger, David R. *Colored White: Transcending the Racial Past.* Berkeley: University of California Press. 2002.

Roediger, David R. "Afterword: Du Bois, Race, and Italian Americans." In *Are Italians White? How Race Is Made in America,* edited by Jennifer Guglielmo and Salvatore Salerno, 261, 259–263. New York: Routledge, 2003.

Roediger, David R. *Working Toward Whiteness: How America's Immigrants Became White.* New York: Basic Books, 2005.

Roediger, David R. "Accounting for the Wages of Whiteness: U.S. Marxism and the Critical History of Race." In *Wages of Whiteness and Racist Symbolic Capital,* edited by Wulf D. Hund, Jeremy Krikler, and David Roediger, 16–17, 9–36. Berlin: Lit Verlag, 2010.

Roediger, David R., and Elizabeth D. Esch. *The Production of Difference: Race and the Management of Labor in U.S. History.* New York: Oxford University Press, 2012.

Rogin, Michael. *Blackface, White Noise. Jewish Immigrants in the Hollywood Melting-Pot.* Berkeley: University of California Press, 1996.

Sinclair, Upton. *King Coal: A Novel.* New York: Macmillan, 1917.

Vecoli, Rudolph J. "Are Italian Americans Just White Folks?" In *Beyond the Godfather: Italian American Writers on the Real Italian American Experience*, edited by A. Kenneth Ciongoli and Jay Parini, 311–322. Hanover, NH, University Press of New England, 1997.

Vellon, Peter G. *A Great Conspiracy Against Our Race: Italian Immigrant Newspapers and the Construction of Whiteness in the Early 20th Century.* New York: NYU Press, 2014.

Walter, Bronwen. *Outsiders Inside: Whiteness, Place, and Irish Women.* New York: Routledge, 2000.

Williams, Richard E. *Hierarchical Structures and Social Values: The Creation of Black and Irish Identities in the United States.* Cambridge: Cambridge University Press, 1990.

X, Malcolm, with Alex Haley. *The Autobiography of Malcolm X.* New York: Grove Press, 1965; 1984.

Zecker, Robert. *Race and America's Immigrant Press: How the Slovaks Were Taught to Think Like White People.* New York: Continuum, 2011.

....

CHAPTER 12

RACE AND U.S. PANETHNIC FORMATION

....

YEN LE ESPIRITU

PANETHNICITY refers to the development of bridging organizations and the general-ization of solidarity among heterogeneous subgroups that are racialized to be homo-geneous by outsiders.[1] As such, panethnic groups are not biologically differentiated groupings but are social, cultural and legal constructions. Whatever their basis of affin-ity, pan-movements involve shifts in levels of group identification from smaller bound-aries to larger-level affiliations. These developments cannot be explained adequately by the dominant theories in the field of U.S. immigration studies—theories of assimilation, amalgamation, "melting pot," or cultural pluralism. As an emergent phenomenon, pan-ethnicity focuses attention on ethnic change—on the "contingent, changeable, partial, inconstant, and ultimately social" nature of group boundaries and identities.[2]

Race has been a critical factor in the history of U.S. panethnic formation. While the formation of a consolidated white identity is self-motivated and linked to white privilege, panethnicity for people of color is a product of racial categorization and is intimately bound up with power relations. Contemporary research indicates that panethnic move-ments and organizations are thus self-conscious and often politicized responses to racial categorization, as groups with seemingly distinct histories and separate identities join forces around shared political and economic goals to protect and advance their collective interests. While institutional panethnicity has been extensively studied, far less attention has been paid to the ways in which individuals experience, understand, and respond to the panethnic label. The available evidence indicates that panethnic identity is generally a secondary identity that coexists, at times uncomfortably, with ethno-national identities.

WHITENESS AND PANETHNICITY
....

Since the 1980s, scholars have turned their attention to the social construction of white-ness, the process whereby the various European "nationalities" arriving in the United

States during the early twentieth century merged and gained access to race and class privilege as "whites." In a pioneering study of the legal origins of white racial identity, legal scholar Ian F. Haney-López reveals the arbitrary, inconsistent, and even contradictory criteria—skin color, national origin, culture, scientific evidence, and popular opinion—that state and federal courts used in "racial prerequisite cases" to determine who was "white" enough to become American, in compliance with the 1790 law that limited naturalization to "free white persons."[3] According to Haney-López, from 1878 to 1944, judges around the country willfully constructed whiteness by tying the opportunity and privileges of naturalized citizenship to racial criteria.[4] Haney-López concludes that law does more than legalize preexisting racial categories; it also defines racial identities and affirms "their relative privilege or disadvantage in U.S. society."[5]

The imprecisions and contradictions inherent in the legal establishment of racial boundaries, coupled with the legal entitlements and benefits accrued to whiteness, provided the impetus for various European "nationalities" to attempt to "become White."[6] Between the 1840s and the 1920s, "white ethnics"—immigrants from non-Anglo-Protestant Europe—were generally considered racially different from and inferior to those of Anglo Saxon descent.[7] By the 1920s, scientific racism had promoted the notion that "real Americans were white and that real whites came from northwest Europe."[8] Initially discriminated against in the United States, white ethnics fought to "become white" in large part by embracing U.S.-style racism against African Americans. According to David Roediger, white workers constructed a notion of "whiteness" and of white supremacy by disparaging black slaves as their inferiors. Along the same line, Noel Ignatiev reports that Irish immigrants evolved from an oppressed social class and earned the right to be considered "white" by aggressively aligning themselves with the Democratic Party and violently subjugating African Americans. To secure manual labor jobs for themselves, the Irish systematically forced African Americans out of the factories and into poverty and the ghetto, thereby solidifying the notion that "white man's work" was work from which African Americans were excluded.[9]

American Jews, whose religion excluded them from whiteness, did not become "white" until the 1950s. According to Karen Brodkin, in the post-World War II period, Jewish intellectuals were a driving force behind the "whitening" of American Jews, in part by emphasizing the quintessentially "American" characteristics of Jewish immigrant culture. As in the case of the Irish, the Jewish quest for whiteness was also cast in opposition to blackness, driving a wedge between Jews and African Americans. Brodkin argues that structurally, postwar policies like the GI Bill and FHA and VA mortgages effectively promoted the whiteness of southern and eastern Europeans, including Jews, because they were extended only to white GIs, even though they were billed as being open to all. These programs were thus de facto "affirmative action" for the male descendants of white European immigrants and undergirded their postwar upward mobility, allowing them, but not blacks, to "float on a rising economic tide."[10]

In the United States, then, the boundaries around whiteness have expanded over time to becoming more inclusive of white ethnic groups.[11] By the late twentieth century, for middle-class white Americans of European origin, their ethnicity was no longer something that influenced their lives and life chances unless they wanted it to. As Mary Waters explains, later-generation white ethnics had a choice to identify themselves with their ethnic ancestry or to identify themselves as "American," which, in U.S. racial discourse and practices, means "white." As discussed in the next section, unlike the lives of middle-class whites, the lives of nonwhite Americans have been and continue to be strongly circumscribed by their perceived race or national origin regardless of how much they may choose not to identify themselves in these terms.[12]

RACIAL PANETHNICITIES

Recognizing the value of whiteness, many immigrants from eastern and southern Europe actively petitioned the courts and popular opinion to be recognized as white. This self-initiated effort to become white differs markedly from the racial lumping and the systematic, legal, and official discrimination and violence experienced by groups of color in the United States. For the latter, panethnicity is largely a product of racial categorization—a racial classification system that ignores subgroup boundaries, lumping together diverse peoples of color in a single, expanded panethnic framework. Excessive categorization is fundamental to racism because it permits "whites to order a universe of unfamiliar peoples without confronting their diversity and individuality."[13] Even when those in subordinate positions do not initially regard themselves as being alike, "a sense of identity gradually emerges from a recognition of their common fate."[14]

For groups of color, racial lumping drives the formation of panethnic organizations and social practices. Unwilling or unable to listen to myriad voices representing particular sub-ethnic groups, government bureaucracies (and the larger society) often lump together diverse racial and ethnic minority groups into the four umbrella categories—blacks, Asian Americans, Hispanics/Latinos, and Native Americans—and treat them as single units in the allocation of economic and political resources.[15] In response to these state-offered incentives, members of the subgroups within each category begin to act collectively as panethnic groups to protect and advance their interests. In other words, panethnic mobilization is "partly a construction of the state."[16] The pervasive system of racial and ethnic classification in the United States creates incentives for ethnic groups to develop panethnic political and cultural projects:

> The data-gathering methods of the census and its use by government agencies in allocating resources, the mobilization techniques of political parties and lobbies, the organization of charities and nonprofit groups, the marketing techniques of the media—all these categorize and appeal to people as members of large ethno-racial groups, thereby fostering a sense of panethnic identity.[17]

Since the 1970s, panethnic organizations such as the National Council of La Raza, the Asian Pacific American Labor Alliance, and the National Urban Indian Development

Corporation have played an important role in securing rights and services, such as fair wages, safe working conditions, affordable housing, and economic opportunities, for their respective communities.[18] The case of Native Americans is unique because federal Indian policies pursue a two-pronged strategy. On the one hand, they recognize tribes as geopolitical units and the foci of various government programs and legislation, thus making tribal affiliation essential. On the other hand, the government insists that Indian-ness is the relevant ethnic distinction for political policy purposes, thus making pan-Indian organization necessary. In other words, the various levels of American Indian mobilization "are responses to a particular incentive structure largely determined by US Indian policies."[19]

When manifested in racial discrimination and violence, racial lumping necessarily leads to cross-group solidarity.[20] In the case of black Americans, the "one-drop rule," which was developed and violently enforced to protect slavery and to bolster Jim Crow segregation, allocates any person with any known African black ancestry to the stigmatized "black" category. By 1925, the one-drop rule was firmly established, adopted, and affirmed by not only white but also black America. The black pride movement of the 1960s and the harsh and uncompromising black-white model in American society greatly strengthened black unity, rousing black Americans to downplay color and class differences and to affirm blackness.[21] As Michael Dawson reports, a linked fate—a shared race and a shared history of racial discrimination—explains why African Americans, regardless of class divisions, have remained largely a politically cohesive group.[22] The virulence of anti-black racism also brought West Indian immigrants into the broader black umbrella, not only as members but also often as leaders of the "black" community, serving as power brokers for their largely African American constituencies.[23] Like African Americans, many Native Americans are racially mixed. The degree of racial mixture figures into government definitions of who is Indian and is certainly a recognized dimension of individual variation within Indian nations. But whites rarely make distinctions between different Indian groups, especially in urban areas; and, when distinctions are made, they are made on the basis of tribe, not race.[24]

For Asian Americans, anti-Asian violence often takes the form of "mistaken identity" hate crimes. The most notorious case of mistaken identity was the 1982 killing of Vincent Chin, a Chinese American who was beaten to death by two white men who allegedly mistook him for Japanese. Because the public seldom distinguishes among Asian American subgroups, anti-Asian violence concerns the entire group, crosscutting class, cultural, and generational divisions. Therefore, regardless of one's ethnic affiliation, anti-Asian violence requires counter-organization at the pan-Asian level.[25] The belief that all Asian Americans are potential victims propels Asian Americans to join together in self-defense to monitor, report, and protest anti-Asian violence. As an example, in the 1990s, when large numbers of Southeast Asian immigrants in Detroit began experiencing problems with racist violence, educational inequality, and poor housing, a small group of East and South Asian American activists created a successful youth leadership-training program organized around a pan-Asian identity and radical critiques of institutionalized racism. The group's success enabled it to move from panethnic to interethnic affiliation through an alliance with a Puerto Rican youth group also plagued by hate crimes, police brutality, and prosecutorial racism.[26]

Racial violence has also forged theretofore-unlikely alliances. Since September 11, 2001, South Asian Sikhs, with their long beards and turbans, are often mistaken for Muslims and have been the subject of occasional violent hate crimes.[27] In response to the conflation of Middle Eastern and South Asian-descended peoples, these two groups have begun to form political coalitions to combat hate crimes against their communities. Spickard describes the racial lumping that provided the impetus for the coalition: "It is tragic, but not accidental, that several of the people murdered or attacked in hate crimes just after September 11 were not Muslims, nor Arabs, nor Middle Eastern Americans at all, but rather Sikhs."[28]

Racial variation is greatest among and across Latino subgroups in the United States. As a result, Latinos "face the challenge of imagining themselves as a composite race that encompasses an assortment of diverse national origins, various cultural heritages, and disparate phenotypes."[29] Many Puerto Rican migrants are "black" by mainland definition and have experienced direct racism approaching the type suffered by non-Latino black Americans.[30] In contrast, most Cubans and South Americans, reflecting their middle-class backgrounds, look European and can blend into white America. Although Mexican Americans are racially diverse, most Americans consider them "brown" or "mestizo."[31] The class-color link tends to divide Latino subgroups, breeding intra-Latino racism and inequalities. Mexican American activists have advocated a version of Latino panethnicity that valorizes "brownness"; for "phenotypically distinctive Latinos," affirmation of brownness has become a way to assert an anti-racist racial solidarity while at the same time maintaining distance from blacks.[32] Some scholars have linked Latino reluctance to embrace a distinct panethnic identity with the insufficient strides for full citizenship that Latinos have made in American society.[33]

PANETHNICITY AND INTERNAL DIVERSITIES

Although racialization fuels panethnic mobilization, it does not automatically produce panethnic outcomes. That is, "even if the state imposes a racial structure on groups or if ethnic groups experience discrimination and racism, panethnicity does not always occur."[34] As the influx of new immigrants transforms the demographic composition of existing panethnic groups, group members face the challenge of bridging the class, ethnic, and generational chasms dividing the immigrants and the U.S.-born. Such internal diversities and a lack of shared histories in the United States can weaken the groups' abilities to speak with a unified political voice. This section focuses on the internal diversities and panethnic formations of Asian Americans and Latinos, two groups that continue to be transformed by new immigration.

Asian Americans

In the four decades since the emergence of the pan-Asian concept in the late 1960s, Asian American communities have changed in dramatic ways. No longer constrained by race-based exclusion laws and fueled by U.S. wars in Asia, Asian immigrants and refugees began arriving during the 1960s in much larger numbers than before. Many of the post-1965 arrivals have little direct experience with the Asian American movement and little reason to think of themselves as Asian American rather than as newcomers, low-wage workers, or members of different national and ethnic groups.[35] Moreover, recent immigration has further diversified Asian Americans along cultural, generational, economic, and political lines. In 2000, Japanese, Chinese, and Asian Indians consistently held more wealth at the top end than other Asian Americans, while non-Vietnamese Southeast Asians settled at the bottom end, making it difficult to forge pan-Asian identities and institutions.[36] Many Asian American studies scholars have critically pointed to the field's privileging of East Asians (the "old" Asian Americans) over South and Southeast Asians (the "new" Asian Americans)—a clear indictment of the suppression of diverse histories, epistemologies, and voices within the pan-Asian framework. For example, in an edited collection on South Asians in Asian America, Rajiv Shankar laments that South Asians "find themselves so unnoticed as an entity that they feel as if they are merely a crypto-group, often included but easily marginalized within the house of Asian America."[37]

Certainly, ethnic, generational, and class diversity pose new obstacles for pan-Asian mobilization. But to begin and stop the analysis here would be to engage in an "America-centric" approach to the question of the relation between race, ethnicity, nation, and migration. From this perspective, the analysis of pan-Asian ethnicity begins when the immigrants arrive on U.S. soil. Thus told, intra-Asian differences—along ethnic, class, and generational lines—become naturalized, unmediated by global politics and power. However, pan-Asian "racial formation" has been determined not exclusively by events in the United States but also by U.S. geopolitical interests in Asia and needs for different types and sources of labor—all of which have produced the particular ethnic, generational, and class configurations that have rendered the term "Asian American" problematic for the post-1965 community.[38]

Because of the multiple contexts of colonialism and its various extensions within the development of global capitalism, Asians in the United States have experienced different processes of racialization specific to each group's historical and material conditions. It is these historical and material conditions, rather than intrinsic intra-Asian differences, that explain the uneven formation of panethnicity among Asian Americans. In particular, different circumstances of exit—the product of different types of U.S. engagement in their respective countries—have shaped the size and timing of migration and the socio-economic status of different Asian groups and thus have profoundly affected the process of group formation and differentiation in the United States.[39] As an example, in an ethnographic study of an Asian panethnic community agency in northern California, Eileen Otis reports that national hierarchies with roots in U.S. colonial and neocolonial relations were reproduced in the distribution of staff positions in the agency, with individuals from more economically developed countries—that is, countries that were more closely tied to the United States—obtaining the coveted agency positions. With the exception of one staff member who came to the United States from Vietnam as a child, all of the staff members were from Asian "Tigers" or "developed" East Asian countries. Otis concludes that "it was no accident that those from countries with the strongest neocolonial ties to the U.S. obtained these positions, since individuals from countries like Hong Kong, Taiwan, and Thailand tend to have more opportunities to develop English language skills."[40]

Given their divergent migration histories and disparate economic backgrounds, Asian groups from different ends of the class spectrum—such as Filipino Americans and Vietnamese Americans—have few material reasons to come together under the pan-Asian umbrella. On the other hand, Asian Americans, due in part to occupational segregation and spatial concentration, have been relatively more successful than other panethnic groups at forging alliances.[41] Although great disparities exist within the Asian American grouping, overall, the major Asian American groups face relatively similar economic challenges. An analysis of fifty-five national Asian American organizations that were formed from 1970 to 1998 indicates that the occupational segregation of Asian Americans heightens panethnic consciousness, leading to the formation of pan-Asian institutions. More than one-quarter of these pan-Asian organizations shared the common goals of promoting civil, economic, and political rights for Asians in the United States as well as in their countries of origin.[42] Linda Vo's study of the Asian Business Association in San Diego provides an example. The city's Asian Americans joined the association because of shared professional interests and shared experiences of economic exclusion and employment discrimination.[43] In another example, Leland Saito reports that Japanese and Chinese Americans in Monterey Park, California, united to protest xenophobic attempts to remove Asian-language business signs.[44] Overall, these studies suggest that as Asian Americans find themselves without economic opportunities and fair treatment, they establish supportive pan-Asian alliances from which to strategize about their collective class interest.

Spatial concentration also facilitates the establishment of pan-Asian institutions. Since interests, competition, and conflict in the United States tend to be strongly regionalized, it follows that cooperation is more likely when sub-ethnic groups are concentrated in the same area. Asian Americans are far more concentrated geographically than the general U.S. population. In 2000, 65 percent of Asians lived in just five states: California, New York, Hawaii, Texas, and Illinois. Remarkably, 55 percent of all Asian Americans then lived in just six metropolitan areas: Los Angeles, New York, San Francisco, Honolulu, Washington DC-Baltimore, and Chicago. Finally, "all ten cities with the highest proportion of Asians were in the west and nine of them were in California."[45] These data indicate that although the Asian American population as a whole may seem relatively small on a national level, in many of the most dynamic states and metropolitan areas, Asian American numbers show that they constitute a vital part of that population. Asian residential enclaves are also likely to be made up of a blend of

Asian immigrants rather than based on a single national origin. Asian American spatial concentration, rough numerical equity, and relatively small numbers in these spaces have made it both possible and necessary for them to establish panethnic organizations to combat economic exclusion and discrimination.[46] There is also suggestive evidence of pan-Asian bloc voting in Asian-dense districts. For example, Vietnamese Americans in Orange County, California, consistently have voted for Japanese American and Korean American candidates who ran against white candidates at a level comparable to that which they gave to Vietnamese American candidates.[47]

Latinos

Since the 1980s, Latino activists of diverse origins have deployed the panethnic rubric to support a number of "Latino" issues such as bilingual education, immigration rights, and police reform. Although useful for building coalitions, the Latino category obscures and collapses the complex differences between and within the so-called Latino groups that have diverse historical experiences of oppression. As in the Asian American case, Latino subgroups, reflecting their diverse origins and experiences of incorporation into the U.S. structure, have diverse average class positions that have limited their potential for panethnic organization, especially between the largely white and middle-class Cubans and poor people of black, Indian, or mixed race from Puerto Rico, parts of Central America, and the Caribbean.[48] Moreover, the regional separation among the three major Latino groups—Mexican Americans in California and the Southwest, Puerto Ricans in New York and New Jersey, and Cubans in South Florida—has made it more difficult for them to organize panethnically.

Focusing on Latino subgroups in New York City, Ramón Grosfoguel proposes that we distinguish among Latinos who are "colonial/racial subjects," "colonial immigrants," and "immigrants" since these distinctions inform how dominant Euro-American groups react toward particular Latino subgroups. As colonial racialized subjects that have been incorporated into the U.S. empire, Puerto Ricans have historically been the targets of many racist representations in the Euro-American imaginary, which has greatly affected their standing among other Latinos. The racial stereotypes of Puerto Ricans, the oldest Latino group in New York City, affect the representations of all new Latino immigrants to the city, whether Colombians, Mexicans, Dominicans, Cubans, or Ecuadorians, causing the newcomers to resist the Latino rubric since such incorporation brings with it a stigmatized identity.[49]

According to Grosfoguel, "colonial immigrants" refer to those groups that come from countries that the United States dominates but never directly colonized. Given the relatively low standing of these countries in the international division of labor, immigrants from these countries endure similar forms of racial discrimination as those suffered by the "colonial/racial subjects."[50] Dominican immigrants constitute such a group. Coming from an economically depressed country and being racially mixed and limited-English speaking, Dominicans in New York City remained indistinguishable from Puerto

Ricans in the Euro-American social imaginary, no matter their efforts to distance themselves from Puerto Ricans. As a result, even though most Dominicans were from a higher-class background than Puerto Ricans, they eventually came to occupy the same economic niche as Puerto Ricans—at the bottom of the labor market in New York City.[51]

In Grosfoguel's formulation, the term "immigrants" refers to populations who, even when they may face some initial discrimination, are allowed eventual access to upward mobility.[52] The pre-1980s Cuban refugees were such a group. As part of its Cold War strategy, the U.S. government established the Cuban Refugee Program, which doled out more than $1 billion in federal assistance to fund the cost of education, welfare, hospitals, and other public services for Cubans who claimed to have fled communism. As a result, local officials came to associate Cuban identity with positive symbolic capital, which enabled Cubans to escape the negative symbolic capital of Puerto Rican racialization. However, during the 1980s, when the largely poor Cuban refugees from the "Mariel" flow arrived in New York, the Cuban Refugee Program had ended. Since the "marielitos" could not access state assistance and thus, in turn, were not protected from racial discrimination, they suffered a marginalization in the labor market similar to what Puerto Ricans and Dominicans and experienced.[53]

While new Latino immigrants to New York City initially distanced themselves from their socially distressed Puerto Rican neighbors, their repeated interactions with Puerto Ricans have facilitated the emergence of an overarching identity and the establishment of institutional panethnicity.[54] Living in small, often overcrowded spaces in working-class neighborhoods with large numbers of Puerto Ricans, Mexican and Dominican immigrants have benefited from the extended family and social networks of Puerto Ricans to help them find jobs and acquire information about city services; many ended up marrying Puerto Ricans.[55] As they interacted with each other in the daily-life settings of residence, neighborhood, and workplace, these Spanish-speaking residents developed an "experiential panethnicity." In Queens, for example, day-to-day interactions among various Latino groups eventually led to the institutionalization of panethnicity, in which community leaders created religious congregations, senior citizen centers, social service programs, cultural organizations, and political groups that served all Latinos.[56]

In Boston, Latino groups have managed to set aside their differences and unite around a series of panethnic issues broadly identified as "the needs of the community," which include affordable housing, AIDS, and high dropout rates for Latino high school students.[57] Similarly, evidence from one major point of overlap, Chicago, suggests that Mexican and Puerto Rican residents have managed at times to "transcend the boundaries of their individual ethnic groups and assert demands as a Latino population or group" in efforts to address shared problems such as improving schools and job opportunities for their respective communities.[58] Padilla concludes that a common sense of economic deprivation and political exclusion and an objectively similar class position were the essential factors for this panethnic cooperation. However, Latino panethnicity remains fragile and often frays in the context of economic uncertainty and increased competition for scarce resources. In Chicago, Puerto Rican residents have resented the

"Mexicanization" of their neighborhood and blamed the influx of Mexicans for their increasingly marginal position.[59] Such resentment prevents them from seeing their shared social location with Mexicans in Chicago's racialized political economy.

Most often, inter-Latino tension is subtle and frequently waged around issues of food, music, and other cultural traditions.[60] In San Francisco, for example, the dominance of Mexicans—and Mexican culture—undermined the fragile Latino coalition and marred efforts by community leaders since the 1960s to promote cross-group cultural events. Given the growing diversification of the city's Latino population, the dominance of Mexican salsa as a public symbol of Latinismo at Latino cultural festivals has led to "accusations of cultural cooptation on the part of some Mexicans and of cultural exclusion and domination on the part of some Central Americans."[61] In Chicago, Puerto Rican families use food and language to affirm the cultural integrity they feel is threatened by the forces of "Americanization" and "Mexicanization" that they and their children endure in schools, on television, and in their everyday lives.[62]

Finally, the media constitute one of the most important institutional sites for the forging of panethnic identities. Mainstream media outlets have a powerful interest in creating panethnic market segments to which they appeal and sell.[63] At the same time, ethnic media—radio stations, television programs, and newspapers and magazines—provide a vehicle for the expression of a shared cultural identity and the construction of panethnic projects and solidarity. As Itzigsohn reports, the Latino and Latina media "go way beyond simply creating a market segment and play an important role in promoting community institution building."[64] As an example, since its inception, *Latina* magazine, a bilingual women's magazine that was launched in 1996 for college-educated Latinas, has served as a medium through which latinidad has been constructed and reconfigured. Promoting an imagined panethnic Latino community, the magazine approaches standard topics such as celebrity portraits, love and romance, and entertainment-oriented stories with a strong investment in validating the latinidad of both the celebrities and magazine readers, celebrating the inclusion of Latinas in the U.S. entertainment industry and challenging the stereotypes of Latino men and women.[65]

INDIVIDUAL PANETHNICITY

As with institutional panethnicity, individual panethnicity emerges as a reaction to the forces of racial labeling and exclusion in American society. Upon entering the United States, immigrants discover that they are expected to be part of a broader panethnic group whose existence many did not know prior to arrival. As part of a larger process of incorporation into American society, many immigrants and their children gradually adopt the more inclusive panethnic identities. As an example, Itzigsohn and Dore-Cabral report that as Dominican immigrants integrate themselves into American life, they react to being labeled Hispanic or Latino by adopting this panethnic identity and constructing social, cultural, and political projects based on it. However, since Latinos are a multiracial group, individual experiences with racism diverge according to how each person looks in relation to the norms of whiteness.[66] Similarly, in a study on "pan-Asian ethnogenesis," Nazli Kibria finds that for second-generation Chinese and Korean Americans, the shared experience of being labeled *Asian* by others has driven them to adopt Asian American as a basis of affiliation and identity.[67] For immigrants from the Caribbean and Africa who find themselves labeled *black*, this process of racial ethnogenesis may be most complete given the rigid black-white distinction in the United States—a distinction that renders specific ethno-national affiliations invisible.[68]

As expected, U.S.-born, American-educated individuals appear to be much more receptive to panethnicity than their immigrant parents and foreign-born counterparts. This receptivity stems from their perceived common ground of culture and race and shared experiences of growing up in the United States as a racial other.[69] For second- and third-generation West Indians, their commitment to unite with the broader black community, including leading many of the early fights for black political representation in New York, stems from their recognition of the role of race as the central determinant of their life chances.[70] For second-generation Asians, the racialization of their ethnicity was an everyday and often taken-for-granted part of their lives.[71] At the same time, the increasing presence of South Asians has raised important questions about the boundary and content of Asian America. According to Bandana Purkayastha, although South Asians are officially categorized as Asian American, they are more often treated as black, Latino, or Muslim, but rarely as Asian American. In post-9/11 United States, the increasing use of religion as a marker of racial difference further contributes to this divergence, pushing South Asians toward privileging their ethno-national and South Asian identities rather than the broader pan-Asian one. Only the more consciously politicized South Asian Americans adopt the Asian American label alongside their South Asian and ethno-national identities.[72]

It was often in college that panethnicity became more than a label imposed from the outside but an identity to be actively embraced. The presence of panethnic student associations and ethnic studies programs and centers on college campuses is critical to the development of panethnic identity. According to Kibria, the Chinese and Japanese American college students whom she interviewed identified their joining of pan-Asian student organizations and enrolling in Asian American studies courses as watershed events in the development of their Asian American identity. Involvement in pan-Asian activities provided "an umbrella for socializing, self-exploration, and political activity" and "brought with it participation in pan-Asian friendship and social circles."[73] Purkayastha reports the same finding for South Asian Americans: being involved with pan-Asian organizations increases their awareness of the relevance of Asian Americanness to their multilayered identity.[74]

Intermarriage between ethnic subgroups is a good measure of panethnicity on the level of individuals. Just as intermarriage between major ethnic categories suggests the breaking down of social boundaries, so intermarriage within these categories can consolidate subgroups into one panethnic identity. There is evidence that intermarriage is occurring at substantial levels among Asian American subgroups and among Latino

subgroups. Analyses of 1980 and 1990 census data on marriage patterns in major metropolitan areas confirm that Asian American and Hispanic identities are "truly significant in the socially important process of mate selection."[75] Importantly, in most cases,
the tendency to marry panethnically is just as strong for the college-educated as for the
non-college-educated, suggesting that panethnicity has "far-reaching consequences for
personal preferences and identities."[76] The enduring strength of panethnic marital associations among U.S.-born Asian and Latino couples suggests that panethnicity should
remain strong and viable into the next generation, regardless of changes in immigration
levels and patterns. Cuban Americans seem to deviate from this pattern. A large survey
of high school children of Cuban immigrants in the Miami/Ft. Lauderdale area found
that the less acculturated students were more likely to adopt the Hispanic label while
the more acculturated ones preferred hyphenated American identities.[77] This finding
bespeaks the specificities of the Miami's Cuban case: the concentrated political and economic power of the city's acculturated Cubans enable them to disassociate from less
privileged Latino groups and to focus instead on their national identity.[78]

CHALLENGES AND POSSIBILITIES

In the United States, panethnicity is both a political response to the American racial
stratification and classification system and a form of assertive panethnic identity. In all,
researchers report the emergence of a dual identification pattern in which both panethnic and ethnic identities and affiliations coexist. Although panethnicity is likely to
increase in size and significance, it is not expected to supersede the specific ethnicities but to become part of a range of available ethnic options—an identity that can be
invoked or set aside in different situations for different cultural and political projects.
The boundaries between panethnicity and ethnicity are thus porous rather than rigidly
separate. This finding corroborates the current scholarship on ethnic identity, which
emphasizes "its multiple, fluctuating, and situational character."[79] This multitiered and
seemingly flexible pattern poses this challenge: how to affirm and define the broader
panethnic boundary that acknowledges a racialized similarity in the interests of shared
goals while at the same time maintaining and asserting the individuality of specific ethnic identities.

   The existing evidence suggests that panethnicity has been an efficacious but contested
category, encompassing not only cultural differences but also social, political, and economic inequalities. Although outsiders may have drawn the panethnic boundary, the
task of "bridging" belongs to the ethno-national groups. The panethnic group can be
exclusive, ignoring diverse viewpoints and subsuming nondominant groups, or it can be
inclusive, incorporating conflicting perspectives and empowering less established communities. Class, ethnic, and generational divisions can be obscured and perpetuated, or
they can be recognized and addressed. A study of second-generation Asian American
leaders at four public universities suggests that as the Asian population in the United

States has grown and diversified, the term "Asian American" itself has transformed and pluralized. The pluralization of the term's definition enables Asian Americans of diverse backgrounds to identify with the racial label by appropriating a variety of meanings to it. While the availability of these alternative meanings encourages some individuals to identify with "Asian American," it can also disengage others precisely because it can refer to any number of meanings.[80]

One issue that appears to tie seemingly diverse groups together, not only in the United States but also internationally, is U.S. (and also European) colonialism and imperialism around the world and the resultant racial hierarchies both abroad and at home. Although different Latino groups have vastly different immigration histories, socioeconomic profiles, and cultural traditions, their lives have all been greatly affected by U.S. foreign policy—an impetus for Latino migrants and nonmigrants uniting around the Latino concept.[81] In the same way, the disruptive and often-violent effects of American expansionism and militarism in the Asia Pacific region created a historical basis for solidarity among seemingly diverse and at-times hostile groups such as Japanese, Filipinos, Southeast Asians, Koreans, Pacific Islanders, multiracial Asians, and Asian adoptees.[82] Racism, U.S. colonialism, and Orientalism may also form the basis of larger and shifting coalitions. Today, working-class immigrants of diverse backgrounds coexist with African American and U.S.-born Latinos in urban communities across the country. This "social geography of race" has produced new social subjects and new coalitions. For example, young Laotian women in northern California have joined Chinese and Japanese Americans in panethnic struggles against anti-Asian racism and also against the "neighborhood race effects" of underfunded schools, polluted air and water, and low-wage jobs that they and their families share with their African American, Latino, Arab American, and poor white neighbors.[83] In the same way, recognizing their common histories of political fragmentation and disfranchisement, Japanese, Chinese, and Mexicans in the San Gabriel Valley of Los Angeles County formed political alliances to work together on the redistricting and reapportionment process in the Valley.[84]

The scholarship on U.S.-based panethnicity suggests that panethnic identity is associated with immigrants and their children, the product of migration to a new society. One direction for future research would be to examine whether panethnic identities, once formed in the diaspora, may be extended transnationally to migrant-sending societies via recurring individual contact between migrants and nonmigrants and the deliberate efforts of transnational media to foster panethnic identification in order to expand the appeal and consumption of their cultural products. A related area of research would be the examination of how diasporic communities have crafted transnational panethnic solutions to their shared history of economic, political, and cultural oppression. Finally, given our globalizing world and the resultant demographic changes, the construction of any panethnic identity is routed through relations and struggles with other communities of color. Today, working-class immigrants of diverse backgrounds coexist with African Americans and U.S.-born Latinos in urban communities across the country. What new social subjects and new coalitions have been produced by this "social geography of race"? In all, the examples cited in this chapter confirm the plural and ambivalent nature of panethnicity: it is a highly contested terrain on which different groups merge and clash over terms of inclusion and is also an effective site from which to forge crucial alliances with other groups both within and across the borders of the United States in their ongoing efforts to effect larger social transformation.

Notes

1. David Lopez and Yen Le Espiritu, "Panethnicity in the United States: A Theoretical Framework," *Ethnic and Racial Studies* 13 (1990): 198.
2. Ian Haney-López, *White by Law: The Legal Construction of Race* (New York: New York University Press, 1996), xiv.
3. Ibid.
4. Ibid., 2–3.
5. Ibid., 10.
6. Noel Ignatiev, *How the Irish Became White* (London and New York: Routledge, 1995).
7. Matthew Frye Jacobson, *Whiteness of a Different Color: European Immigrants and the Alchemy of Race* (Cambridge: Harvard University Press, 1998).
8. Karen Brodkin, *How Jews Became White Folks and What That Says About Race in America* (New Brunswick and London: Rutgers University Press, 1998), 28.
9. David Roediger, *The Wages of Whiteness: Race and the Making of the American Working Class* (London: Verso, 1999); Ignatiev, *How the Irish Became White*.
10. Brodkin, *How Jews Became White Folks*, 50–51.
11. Mary Waters, *Ethnic Options: Choosing Identities in America* (Berkeley: University of California Press, 1990); Monica McDermott and Frank L. Samson, "White Racial and Ethnic Identity in the United States," *Annual Review of Sociology* 31 (2005): 245–261; Ignatiev, *How the Irish Became White*.
12. Waters, *Ethnic Options*, 52, 157.
13. Robert Blauner, *Racial Oppression in America* (New York: Harper & Row, 1972), 113.
14. Tamotsu Shibutani and Kian M. Kwan, *Ethnic Stratification* (New York: MacMillan, 1965), 208.
15. Ira Lowry, "The Science and Politics of Ethnic Enumeration," in *Ethnicity and Public Policy*, ed. Winston A. Van Horne (Madison: University of Wisconsin System, 1982), 42–43.
16. Michael Jones-Correa, *Between Two Nations: The Political Predicament of Latinos in New York City* (Ithaca: Cornell University Press, 1998), 111.
17. Jose Itzigsohn, "The Formation of Latino and Latina Panethnicity Identity," in *Not Just Black and White: Immigration, Race, and Ethnicity, Then to Now*, eds. Nancy Foner and George Fredrickson (New York: Russell Sage Foundation Publications, 2004), 197.
18. Dina G. Okamoto, "Institutional Panethnicity: Boundary Formation in Asian American Organizing," *Social Forces* 85 (2006): 1.
19. Joane Nagel, "The Political Mobilization of Native Americans," *Social Science Journal* 19 (1982): 39.
20. Yen Le Espiritu, *Asian American Panethnicity: Bridging Institutions and Identities* (Philadelphia: Temple University Press, 1992).
21. Floyd James Davis, *Who Is Black? One Nation's Definition* (University Park: Penn State University Press, 1989).

22. Michael C. Dawson, *Behind the Mule: Race, Class and African American Politics* (Princeton: Princeton University Press, 1994).

23. Philip Kasinitz, *Caribbean New York: Black Immigrants and the Politics of Race* (Ithaca: Cornell University Press, 1992), 50–51, 54.

24. Stephen Cornell, *The Return of the Native: American Indian Political Resurgence* (New York: Oxford University Press, 1998), 132–138.

25. Espiritu, *Asian American Panethnicity*, chap. 6.

26. Yen Le Espiritu, Dorothy Fujita Rony, Nazli Kibria, and George Lipsitz, "The Role of Race and Its Articulations for Asian Pacific Americans," *Journal of Asian American Studies* 3 (2000): 132.

27. Lien Hoang, "Mistaken for Muslims, Sikhs Hit by Hate Crimes," NBCNews.com 8 March 2011, http://www.nbcnews.com/id/41962756/ns/us_news-crime_and_courts/t/mistaken-muslims-sikhs-hit-hate-crimes/#.U3jmRsaMBdo

28. Paul Spickard, "Whither the Asian American Coalition?" *Pacific Historical Review* 76 (2007): 602–603.

29. Silvio Torres-Saillant. "Inventing the Race: Latinos and the Ethnoracial Pentagon," *Latino Studies* 1 (2003): 123–151.

30. Clara E. Rodriguez, *Puerto Ricans: Born in the U.S.A.* (Boston: Unwin Hyman, 1989).

31. Lopez and Espiritu, "Panethnicity in the United States," 204.

32. Nancy Foner and George M. Fredrickson, "Introduction," in *Not Just Black and White: Immigration, Race, and Ethnicity, Then to Now*, eds. Nancy Foner and George Fredrickson (New York: Russell Sage Foundation Publications, 2004), 7.

33. Torres-Saillant, "Inventing the Race."

34. Okamoto, "Institutional Panethnicity," 2.

35. Espiritu et al., "The Role of Race," 131.

36. Paul Ong and Varisa Patraporn, "Asian Americans and Wealth," in *Wealth Accumulation and Communities of Color in the United States*, eds. Jessica Gordon Newbhard and Rhonda Williams (Ann Arbor: University of Michigan Press, 2006), 173–190.

37. Rajiv Shankar, "Foreword: South Asian Identity in Asian America," in *A Part, Yet Apart: South Asians in Asian America*, eds. Lavina Dhingra Shankar and Rajini Srikanth (Philadelphia: Temple University Press, 1998), x.

38. Yen Le Espiritu, "Asian American Panethnicity: Contemporary National and Transnational Possibilities," in *Not Just Black and White: Historical and Contemporary Perspectives on Immigration, Race, and Ethnicity in the United States*, eds. Nancy Foner and George Fredrickson (New York: Russell Sage Foundation, 2004), 223.

39. Espiritu, "Asian American Panethnicity: Contemporary National," 226–227.

40. Eileen Otis, "The Reach and Limits of Asian Panethnic Identity: The Dynamics of Gender, Race, and Class in a Community-Based Organization," *Qualitative Sociology* 24 (2001): 362.

41. Lopez and Espiritu, "Panethnicity in the United States."

42. Okamoto, "Institutional Panethnicity," 20.

43. Linda Trinh Vo, *Mobilizing an Asian American Community* (Philadelphia: Temple University Press, 2004).

44. Leland Saito, *Race and Politics: Asian Americans, Latinos, and Whites in a Los Angeles Suburb* (Urbana and Chicago: University of Illinois Press, 1998).

45. Amérádia, "Asian American Statistics," accessed December 11, 2011, http://www.ameredia.com/resources/demographics/asian_american.html.

46. Ronald Skeldon, "The Last Half Century of Chinese Overseas (1945–1994): Comparative Perspectives," *International Migration Review* 29 (1995): 576–579.
47. Christina Collet, "Bloc Voting, Polarization, and the Panethnic Hypothesis: The Case of Little Saigon," *Journal of Politics* 67 (2005): 907–933.
48. Lopez and Espiritu, "Panethnicity in the United States."
49. Ramón Grosfoguel, *Colonial Subjects: Puerto Ricans in a Global Perspective* (Berkeley: University of California Press, 2003), 144–145.
50. Grosfoguel, *Colonial Subjects*, 148.
51. Ibid., 167.
52. Ibid., 148–149.
53. Ibid., 169–171.
54. Robert Smith, *Mexican New York: Transnational Lives of New Immigrants* (Berkeley: University of California Press, 2005), 30–31.
55. Smith, *Mexican New York*, 34; Grosfoguel, *Colonial Subjects*.
56. Milagros Ricourt and Ruby Danta, *Hispanas de Queens: Latino Panethnicity in a New York City Neighborhood* (Ithaca: Cornell University Press, 2003), 10.
57. Carol Hardy-Fanta, *Latina Politics, Latino Politics: Gender, Culture, and Political Participation* (Philadelphia: Temple University Press, 1993).
58. Felix Padilla, *Latino Ethnic Consciousness: The Case of Mexican Americans and Puerto Ricans in Chicago* (Notre Dame, IN: University of Notre Dame Press, 1985), 163.
59. Gina Perez, *The Near Northwest Side Story: Migration, Displacement, & Puerto Rican Families* (Berkeley: University of California Press, 2004), 174.
60. Ibid., 176.
61. Laurie Kay Sommers, "Inventing Latinismo: The Creation of 'Hispanic' Panethnicity in the United States," *Journal of American Folklore* 104 (1991): 42.
62. Perez, *The Near Northwest Side Story*, 177.
63. America Rodriguez, *Making Latino News: Race, Language, Class* (Thousand Oaks: Sage, 1999).
64. Jose Itzigsohn, "The Formation of Latino and Latina Panethnic Identities," in *Not Just Black and White: Historical and Contemporary Perspectives on Immigration, Race, and Ethnicity in the United States*, eds. Nancy Foner and George Fredrickson (New York: Russell Sage Foundation, 2004), 210.
65. Katynka Zazueta Martínez, "Latina Magazine and the Invocation of a Panethnic Family: Latino Identity as It Is Informed by Celebrities and Papis Chulos," *The Communication Review* 7(2004): 155–174.
66. Jose Itzigsohn and Carlos Dore-Cabral, "Competing Identities? Race, Ethnicity and Panethnicity among Dominicans in the United States," *Sociological Forum* 15 (2000): 225–247.
67. Nazli Kibria, *Becoming Asian American: Second-Generation Chinese and Korean American Identities* (Baltimore: John Hopkins University Press, 2002).
68. Mary Waters, *Black Identities: West Indian Immigrant Dreams and American Realities* (Cambridge: Harvard University Press, 2001).
69. Suzanne Oboler, *Ethnic Labels, Latino Lives* (Minneapolis: University of Minnesota Press, 1992); Nilda Flores-Gonzalez, "The Racialization of Latinos: The Meaning of Latino Identity for the Second Generation," *Latino Studies Journal* 10 (1999): 3–31; Kibria, *Becoming Asian American*.
70. Kasinitz, *Caribbean New York*, 52.

71. Kibria, *Becoming Asian American*.
72. Bandana Purkayastha, *Negotiating Ethnicity: Second-Generation South Asian Americans Traverse a Transnational World* (New Brunswick: Rutgers University Press, 2005), 169–170.
73. Kibria, *Becoming Asian American*, 113.
74. Purkayastha, *Negotiating Ethnicity*, 171.
75. Michael J. Rosenfeld, "The Salience of Pan-National Hispanic and Asian Identities in U.S. Marriage Markets," *Demography* 38 (2001): 172.
76. Rosenfeld, "The Salience of Pan-National Hispanic and Asian Identities, 173.
77. Alejandro Portes and Dag MacLeod, "What Shall I Call Myself? Hispanic Identity Formation in the Second Generation," *Ethnic and Racial Studies* 19 (1996): 523–547.
78. Rodolfo Cortina, "Cubans in Miami: Ethnic Identification and Behavior," *Latino Studies Journal* 1 (1990): 60–73.
79. Kibria, *Becoming Asian American*, 102.
80. Jerry Z. Park, "Second-Generation Asian American Pan-ethnic Identity: Pluralized Meanings of a Racial Label," *Sociological Perspectives* 51 (2008): 557.
81. Jose Calderon, "'Hispanic' and 'Latino': The Viability of Categories for Panethnic Unity," *Latin American Perspectives* 19 (1992): 39.
82. Spickard, "Whither the Asian American Coalition?"
83. Espiritu et al., "The Role of Race;" Bindi Shah, "Making the 'American' Subject: Ethnicity, Gender, Culture and the Politics of Citizenship in the Lives of Second-Generation Laotian Girls" (PhD dissertation, University of California, Davis, 2002).
84. Saito, *Race and Politics*, 10.

BIBLIOGRAPHY

Blauner, Robert. *Racial Oppression in America*. New York: Harper & Row, 1972.
Brodkin, Karen. *How Jews Became White Folks and What That Says About Race in America*. New Brunswick and London: Rutgers University Press, 1998.
Cornell, Stephen. *The Return of the Native: American Indian Political Resurgence*. New York: Oxford University Press, 1988.
Davila, Arlene. *Latinos Inc., The Marketing and Making of a People*. Berkeley: University of California Press, 2001.
Davis, Floyd James. *Who Is Black? One Nation's Definition*. University Park: Penn State University Press, 1989.
Dawson, Michael C. *Behind the Mule: Race, Class and African American Politics*. Princeton: Princeton University Press, 1994.
Espiritu, Yen Le. *Asian American Panethnicity: Bridging Institutions and Identities*. Philadelphia: Temple University Press, 1992.
Espiritu, Yen Le. "Asian American Panethnicity: Contemporary National and Transnational Possibilities." In *Not Just Black and White: Historical and Contemporary Perspectives on Immigration, Race, and Ethnicity in the United States*, edited by Nancy Foner and George Fredrickson, 223. New York: Russell Sage Foundation, 2004.
Foner, Nancy, and George M. Fredrickson. "Introduction." In *Not Just Black and White: Immigration, Race, and Ethnicity, Then to Now*, edited by Nancy Foner and George Fredrickson, 7. New York: Russell Sage Foundation, 2002.

Grosfoguel, Ramón. *Colonial Subjects: Puerto Ricans in a Global Perspective.* Berkeley: University of California Press, 2003.

Haney-López, Ian. *White by Law: The Legal Construction of Race.* New York: New York University Press, 2006.

Hardy-Fanta, Carol. *Latina Politics, Latino Politics: Gender, Culture, and Political Participation.* Philadelphia: Temple University Press, 1993.

Ignatiev, Noel. *How the Irish Became White.* London and New York: Routledge, 1995.

Itzigsohn, Jose. "The Formation of Latino and Latina Panethnic Identities." In *Not Just Black and White: Historical and Contemporary Perspectives on Immigration, Race, and Ethnicity in the United States,* edited by Nancy Foner and George Fredrickson, 201. New York: Russell Sage Foundation, 2004.

Itzigsohn, Jose. "The Formation of Latino and Latina Panethnicity Identity." In *Not Just Black and White: Immigration, Race, and Ethnicity, Then to Now,* edited by Nancy Foner and George Fredrickson, 197. New York: Russell Sage Foundation Publications, 2004.

Jacobson, Matthew Frye. *Whiteness of a Different Color: European Immigrants and the Alchemy of Race.* Cambridge: Harvard University Press, 1998.

Jones-Correa, Michael. *Between Two Nations: The Political Predicament of Latinos in New York City.* Ithaca: Cornell University Press, 1998.

Kasinitz, Philip. *Caribbean New York: Black Immigrants and the Politics of Race.* Ithaca: Cornell University Press, 1992.

Kibria, Nazli. *Becoming Asian American: Second-Generation Chinese and Korean American Identities.* Baltimore: John Hopkins University Press, 2002.

Lowry, Ira. "The Science and Politics of Ethnic Enumeration." In *Ethnicity and Public Policy,* edited by Winston A. Van Horne, 42–43. Madison: University of Wisconsin System, 1982.

Oboler, Suzanne. *Ethnic Labels, Latino Lives.* Minneapolis: University of Minnesota Press, 1992.

Ong, Paul, and Varisa Patraporn. "Asian Americans and Wealth." In *Wealth Accumulation and Communities of Color in the United States,* edited by Jessica Gordon Newbhard and Rhonda Williams, 173–190. Ann Arbor: University of Michigan Press, 2006.

Paddila, Felix. *Latino Ethnic Consciousness: The Case of Mexican Americans and Puerto Ricans in Chicago.* Notre Dame, IN: University of Notre Dame Press, 1985.

Perez, Gina. *The Near Northwest Side Story: Migration, Displacement, & Puerto Rican Families.* Berkeley: University of California Press, 2004.

Purkayastha, Bandana. *Negotiating Ethnicity: Second-Generation South Asian Americans Traverse a Transnational World.* New Brunswick: Rutgers University Press, 2005.

Ricourt, Milagras, and Ruby Danta. *Hispanas de Queens: Latino Panethnicity in a New York City Neighborhood.* Ithaca: Cornell University Press, 2003.

Rodriguez, Clara E. *Puerto Ricans: Born in the U.S.A.* Boston: Unwin Hyman, 1989.

Rodriguez, America. *Making Latino News: Race, Language, Class.* Thousand Oaks: Sage, 1999.

Roediger, David. *The Wages of Whiteness: Race and the Making of the American Working Class.* London: Verso, 1999.

Saito, Leland. *Race and Politics: Asian Americans, Latinos, and Whites in a Los Angeles Suburb.* Urbana and Chicago: University of Illinois Press, 1998.

Shankar, Rajiv. "Foreword: South Asian Identity in Asian America." In *A Part, Yet Apart: South Asians in Asian America,* edited by Lavina Dhingra Shankar and Rajini Srikanth, x. Philadelphia: Temple University Press, 1998.

Shibutani, Tamotsu, and Kian M. Kwan. *Ethnic Stratification.* New York: MacMillan, 1965.

Smith, Robert. *Mexican New York: Transnational Lives of New Immigrants*. Berkeley: University of California Press, 2005.

Vo, Linda Trinh. *Mobilizing an Asian American Community*. Philadelphia: Temple University Press, 2004.

Waters, Mary. *Ethnic Options: Choosing Identities in America*. Berkeley: University of California Press, 1990.

Waters, Mary. *Black Identities: West Indian Immigrant Dreams and American Realities*. Cambridge: Harvard University Press, 2001.

CHAPTER 13

....

INTERMARRIAGE AND THE CREATION OF A NEW AMERICAN

....

ALLISON VARZALLY

SCHOLARS have studied immigrants' patterns of intermarriage to make larger claims about assimilation, cultural change, preservation and invention, the progress of civil rights movements, the nature and efficacy of colonial conquests, and ultimately the definition of who is an American. As the most intimate and arguably committed form of interracial or interethnic relationships, these marriages have tested and blurred existing ethno-racial categories and cultural boundaries as the transgressors defied familial and social conventions about the necessity of maintaining traditions and the integrity of established communities. Although all couples may confront the challenges of living and loving together, especially after adding children, those in mixed marriages have often faced more external opposition and attempted to bridge wider differences in values and expectations. Historians have thus interpreted persistent and lasting intermarriages between particular ethno-racial groups as a harbinger of more amiable ethno-racial relations, as part of a process of integrating and consolidating previously separate groups. Striking an optimistic note, some have wondered whether rising rates of intermarriage in recent years will erode ethno-racial divisions absolutely, generating a postracial society in which individuals no longer identify and differentiate themselves on the basis of ethnicity or race. Richard Rodriquez has eloquently described this view of the seemingly inevitable mixing and remixing of diverse Americans as a "browning" of the nation.[1]

However, others have quickly countered that not all interracial marriages are created equal. Asians and Latinos intermarry more regularly and their multiracial offspring more readily embrace the identity, "mixed race," than blacks, a distinction that may highlight a readier acceptance of newer immigrants from Asia and Latin America and the emergence of black/non-black rather than black/white as the most salient racial divide in the contemporary United States.[2] Distinctions in the gender and racial patterns of contemporary intermarriages, namely that black men and Asian ethnic women are, respectively, twice as likely to marry outside their ethno-racial group as black women and Asian ethnic men, or that white-Asian couples have the highest combined incomes and levels of education, also raise questions about social norms and opportunities.[3] Moreover, marriage to a person of another ethno-racial background does not always reduce prejudices or diminish a sense of difference; intermarriages can introduce and direct changes without collapsing the racial order. Certainly, intermarriage remains a uniquely revealing site for exploring questions about immigration and the creation of American cultures and ethno-racial hierarchies in the past and present. At every stage of U.S. history, the experiences of intermarried couples and the policies governing their unions have helped define membership, distribute political and economic privileges, and describe national identity.[4]

Among the earliest immigrants to the Americas, European colonizers—most notably the Spanish, French, and British—intermarried with indigenous peoples and African slaves, relationships that shaped the successes and character of their respective conquests. Historians of New France have depicted how French officials initially recommended the marriages of French traders and Indian women in the 17th century. Such liaisons would facilitate economic exchanges and grow the population. Without the integration and cooperation of Indians, the sparsely settled French colony could not expand the fur trade, protect its settlements, or assure military security. Indigenous peoples accepted miscegenation as a means of strengthening alliances and access to European goods. French officials imagined that French men would necessarily educate their Indian wives and contribute to the reproduction of "Frenchness" in the New World, an assumption that betrayed French cultural paternalism. However, in practice, the influence flowed in the opposite direction. Amerindians selected some merchandise, economic practices, and military tactics of the French, but eschewed French language, customs, and laws. French men appeared to "go savage," losing their French culture as they became members of their wives' families and communities.[5] Alarmed by such developments, French officials launched an ultimately futile effort in the second half of the 17th century to discourage intermarriages by importing French women from the metropole. Drawn from the lower ranks of French society, these so called *Filles du Roi*, did not suit the fancy of French men, perhaps because the women could not offer the advantages of their Indian rivals. Saliha Belmessous has argued that the failure of the policy of assimilation through intermarriage helped create a previously absent concept of race by the 18th century. French officials now criticized miscegenation and described differences between French settlers and Amerindians in racialized terms.[6] In formulating these ideas, Guillaume Aubert suggests that the colonizers drew upon and applied a metropolitan discourse about mixing intended to protect the racial purity of the French nobility to the French colonial population generally. Acceptance of intermarriage between French immigrants and Indians in New France, gave way to intolerance as French notions of ethnicity that were cultural became racial. Demographics and more inchoate racial views had also generated French-African marriages in the Caribbean and Louisiana in the early decades of the French presence there, but French authorities never advocated for such marriages and would more vehemently oppose them as slavery matured and such unions appeared to threaten the institution.[7]

Although the first Spanish immigrants to the Americas also intermarried with African and Indian peoples, such interactions were structured by their different intentions of conquest, specifically efforts to both convert Indian peoples into good Spaniards and depend on their labor. When these 16th-century settlement policies faltered, as the Indian population dropped precipitously due to disease and violence, colonial officials began to import African slaves to fill their needs. From the confluence of regular mixing among Spanish, Indian, and African peoples, greater competition over the gains of conquest emerged. An elaborate caste system developed that both named and organized the many racial types now populating New Spain by the second half of the 16th century. The classifications intended to confirm Spanish rule in the multiracial and multicultural society, by dividing the colonial population and creating a free wage-labor force. One could read the acknowledgment of the many racially mixed people, visually represented in the caste paintings consumed by Spanish colonial officials, the Catholic Clergy, naturalists, and others in the 18th century, as evidence of a greater racial tolerance. Yet, the use of such categories to determine cultural, political, and economic opportunities—access to land, eligibility for the priesthood and political offices, exemptions from tribute, certain protections, marriage rights—suggested otherwise. Among the discriminating principles embedded in the system were that reproduction among castes created new castes, the descendants of Spanish-Indian partners could steadily improve their status through marriages with Spaniards, and black blood corrupted more absolutely than native blood.[8] The leading role of Mestizos in Mexico's Revolutionary War, further highlights how racially mixed people suffered under the prevailing system.

Historians of British America reference the Spanish and French examples to highlight the emergence of a much narrower, binary racial system in their colonies. The legend and reality of the Pocahontas-Rolfe union stands out in large part because of its rarity. The marriage between the Englishman and Indian princess who surrendered her "savage ways" in favor of English customs, famously traveling to England where she received a warm welcome from the Queen, was celebrated as an alternative, desirable model of relations between English immigrants and American Indians through much of the 17th and 18th centuries. If only settlers would lay down their weapons and marry Indian women, peace and prosperity would prevail, English colonial and then later American leaders, including Thomas Jefferson, believed. This prescription depended on an incomplete understanding of the motives and context that had led Pocahontas to wed John Rolfe. Having lived with the English as a hostage, Pocahontas had discovered their resources and realized the value of an alliance between them and her Indian community. Following Algokian tradition, she orchestrated what proved to be a temporary détente by marrying and having children with Rolfe; she expressed affection for her husband, but appreciated his position as a member of an enemy people. The English appetite for land, expanding colonial population, and diminished fears of Indians, however, would limit the practical appeal of peace through Indian-English intermarriages and, thus, their numbers. The presumption of Anglo superiority also discouraged formal marriages, even though interracial sexual contacts happened frequently and produced significant numbers of mixed-race offspring.[9]

Scholars of slavery have explicated how intermarriages between African slaves and English immigrants—poor indentured servants whose working conditions and degree of freedom did not drastically differ from those of the first generation of black laborers—became impossible or at least highly suspect in a labor system increasingly defined by the separation of white freemen from black slaves. Miscegenation laws, which had no precedent in English common law or statute, debuted throughout the American South by the 1660s. The specifics of their language and patterns of enforcement exposed gender and class inequities, most conspicuously the authority of elite white men who alone might violate the color line and avoid social and legal punishment.[10]

The intermarriages among European immigrants in the 17th and 18th centuries, by contrast, figured prominently in the making of the new American and setting the conditions for independence, so insisted J. Hector St. John de Crèvecouer and other observers:

> He is either an European, or the descendant of an European, hence that strange mixture of blood, which you will find in no other country. I could point out to you a family whose grandfather was an Englishman, whose wife was Dutch, whose son married a French woman, and whose present four sons have now four wives of different nations. *He* is an American, who leaving behind him all his ancient prejudices and manners, receives new ones from the new mode of life he has embraced, the new government he obeys, and the new rank he holds.[11]

Of course his relatively cosmopolitan definition of American, excluded immigrants from Asia, Africa, and Latin America who fell into color categories Benjamin Franklin would label, "Black and Tawny." Class distinctions also circumscribed Crèvecouer's definition of American; he spoke dismissively of many poor whites on the frontier whom he hoped would become civilized or disappear. [12]

Citizens of the new American Republic would carry this selectively Eurocentric and white-centric understanding of national identity into Mexican territory in the early 19th century as they explored, traded, settled, and invited annexation. The first generation of Euro-American traders and trappers throughout what would become the American West often assimilated into the Indian tribes and Mexican communities they encountered. Historians estimate that approximately 15 percent of recorded marriages in California between 1822 and 1846 involved California women of means and well-traveled Anglo men connected through trade to diverse peoples and cultures. The migrants learned requisite languages, religions, and other cultural traditions and exhibited the "respectable" manners, material well-being, and fair skin that California women and their families desired. From the perspective of the Euro-American immigrants, such marriages offered political and economic access. From the perspective of Mexican and Indian families, such unions suggested a way of controlling a foreign threat and consolidating resources. Even after the U.S. conquest, California women married to Euro-American men continued to exercise dominant sway over cultural values, successfully transmitting the Spanish language and Mexican ideals of honor and kinship to their biethnic children.[13]

However, a later wave of immigrants, encouraged by the rhetoric of Manifest Destiny and the permissiveness of Mexico's immigration policies resisted integration. Their desire to claim and settle land rather than create commercial opportunities put them at odds with local populations.[14] Their deliberately protected separateness—they spoke English, remained American citizens, married one another, and railed against what they depicted as the corruption and incompetence of the Mexican government—provided the foundation for revolutionary action that precipitated the fateful U.S.-Mexican War. Fears about the legacies of intermarriage, namely the mixed character of the Mexican population of the Southwest, almost halted the momentum toward expansion. In 1848, insisting that "Ours, sirs is the Government of a white race," John Calhoun warned against repeating "the greatest misfortunes of Spanish America," which had permitted and been undone, he believed, by racial mixing.[15]

Despite Calhoun's cautions, the U.S. pushed forward and chose to manage "Mongrel Mexicans," by eschewing new intermarriages and slowly dispossessing them of property and political power. This process happened more quickly and completely in some locations of the American West. In San Francisco, Anglos readily established their control, overwhelming local Californios. Mexican women married to elite Anglo men did not suffer as dramatic a loss of status, but still felt their position diminished.[16] In New Mexico, where delayed statehood limited the political privileges (right to vote for president or run for governor) of even the most accomplished and affluent of Euro-Americans, intermarriages (approximately 6–11 percent of all marriages between 1890 and 1920) remained a common and respected means of accumulating land and wealth through the early 20th century.[17] Some of the territory's most prominent leaders were the children of or partners in marriages between Hispanics and Anglos, among them the territory's governor between 1897 and 1906, Miquel A. Otero. The acceptance of Anglo-Mexican marriages could coexist with and seem to fulfill a belief in Manifest Destiny that guided American imperialism. Euro-American men sometimes imagined themselves as the saviors of Mexican women, freeing them from the decadence and immorality that would have marked their lives with Mexican husbands. Some forecasted that the distinctiveness of Mexican blood could be erased and thus Anglo control secured through several generations of intermarriage. The promotion of these strategic, cross-cultural connections stood in sharp contrast to disapproval of intermarriages with the region's blacks and Indians.[18]

Meanwhile, in Southern Arizona, Euro-American-Mexican marriages continued through the 19th century and sustained the unrefined and erratic line between Mexican and "White American." The ascendance of race science, with its delineation of different racial types and assertions about the dangers of racial mixing in the 1910s and 1920s, however, had a chilling effect on marriages between Mexicans and Euro-Americans in Arizona and throughout the Southwest. More than 50 years after the signing of the Treaty of Guadalupe Hidalgo, the persistence of Mexicans as a separate cultural and racialized group dampened optimism about the possibility of amalgamation through intermarriage. The rising numbers of Anglo women in the region also reshaped marital opportunities. As important, Mexican Americans may no longer have seen intermarriage as a savvy political or economic decision after witnessing the acquisitive, aggressive behavior of Anglos. The decline contributed to heightened segregation and sharpened the distinction drawn between Mexicans and Whites. [19]

Incorporating the peoples and lands of Alta Mexico in the second half of the 19th century also rested upon discouraging the immigration of and intermarriages with Chinese, Japanese, and Filipino immigrants. As Peggy Pascoe depicted in her exhaustive history of miscegenation law, Western legislators elaborated antimiscegenation statutes to accommodate fears of intermarriage not only between whites and blacks, but whites and "Mongolians" (Chinese, Japanese, Koreans,) and eventually "Malays" (Filipinos). These prohibitions were intended to shore up the authority of white men and protect their property as much as to assure white racial purity. Although Asian immigrant men had not pursued white women with the hunger Westerners claimed, demographic imbalances, physical proximity, and the discovery of cultural commonalities did generate some intimacies and intermarriages. Filipinos proved more likely to find spouses outside their ethnic group than other Asian men because so few had married prior to their emigration and so few fretted about racial blending given the history of mixing in the Philippines. Moreover, as once subjects of the Spanish Empire and now nationals of an overseas territory of the United States, they had an understanding of American culture that made them more appealing to American-born and European-immigrant women. However, their very success with White working class and immigrant women became a leading complaint of White men who expressed their displeasure by attacking Filipinos and insisting upon their exclusion. Legislators soon obliged this nativism by passing the Tydings-McDuffie Act, which established the Philippines as a Commonwealth and reclassified Filipinos as aliens subject to a miniscule immigration quota.[20]

One strategy for obeying the law and still finding a wife was to marry a non-White woman. In the San Fernando Valley just north of Los Angeles and San Joaquin Valleys, vibrant communities of Mexican-Filipino families set down roots. The couples and sociologists who observed them noted how the Catholic faith and a familiarity, if not fluency in the Spanish language—legacies of a common colonial past—attracted these men and women. The partners also noted the appeal of their similar skin tones that allowed them to pass in public spaces without attracting undesirable attention.[21] Karen Leonard detailed the presence of Mexican-Punjabi communities in California's rural valleys during the 1910s and 1920s created through repeated intermarriages between young Mexican immigrant women and Punjabi immigrant men. The typically much younger Mexican wives would introduce their friends and relatives to the single, Punjabi acquaintances of their Punjabi husbands. In addition to complementary demographic imbalances and common agricultural labor, the spouses discovered similarities in material culture (language, food) and physical appearance that drew them together. Although their names and affection for their fathers and godfathers indicated the sway of Punjabi culture, the biethnic children learned more about and were encouraged to identify with their mother's traditions as evidenced in the languages they spoke, their

Catholicism, and choice of Mexican Americans as romantic partners. These leanings demonstrated not simply the strength of their mother's role in their education, but their father's deliberate choice not to stress their Punjabi heritage; the men reported having too little time given their work responsibilities and too little desire given their commitment to conventional Americanization. Even when particular minorities did not intermarry in a systematic, regular fashion that generated recognizable new communities, some chose to marry other non-Whites, not only because the law permitted those kinds of interracial relationships, but because they found unexpected cultural and economic commonalities.[22]

Although the intermarriages of Asian men in the American West suggested a creative, defiant, and sometimes dangerous solution to the desire for love and family in the absence of co-ethnic women, rising intermarriage rates between European ethnics in the middle third of the 20th century highlighted their consolidation and acceptance as White Americans. As new immigration from Europe, especially from Southern and Eastern nations, dropped sharply in the wake of the Johnson-Reed Act in 1924, and the sons and daughters of European immigrants met in the factories and mixed-ethnic neighborhoods of industrialized cities, and as Americanizing campaigns urged them to forget their ethnic heritage, drop the hyphens, and simply "melt" into America, they discovered connections and affections that defied the preferences of their parents. The experience of military service in units segregated from Asian and African Americans, but inclusive of various European ethics hurried this sense of solidarity. And, of course, the opportunities of suburbanization and higher education that the GI bill extended easily to European ethnics, but not their Asian American, Latin American, or African American peers also encouraged intermarriages and the equation of whiteness with European descent. In addition, European ethnics married because the law permitted them to do so. [23]

However, the importance of ethnicity did not disappear among the nation's Whites in the post-WWII period. Nor was its continued salience simply a reaction to the race-based activism and gains of African Americans through the 1960s and 1970s. Using New York City as a case study, Joshua Zeitz argued that Jewish, Italian, and Irish Americans still interpreted political, social, and cultural issues differently. Variations in how these White ethnics viewed authority, spirituality, and community contributed to the dissolution of Roosevelt's New Deal Coalition, with Catholics turning away from the Democratic Party and Jews shifting more decisively to the antiliberal New Left. Such observations invite the specific question of what role interethnic marriages among Jews, Italians, and Irish did or did not play in shaping political behavior and the general question of how ethnic differences survive, mutate, or dissipate within interethnic families. Ronald H. Bayor addresses this question in his investigation of the private forms of ethnicity that have persisted among Whites through the second half of the 20th century. He notes that even as the most visible, external expressions of ethnicity such as language or foods or festivals has faded, certain cultural patterns—deeper values, common reactions, and ways of thinking—have survived among Jewish, Italian, Irish, and other Euro-Americans despite their interethnic marriages. Psychologists who have noticed differences in the patterns of childrearing, mental illness, ideas toward disease, disease rates, and family values among White ethnics support this assertion.[24]

The persistent prohibition against marriages between Whites and Asian or African Americans appeared all the more egregious and incompatible with American principles as a maturing civil rights movement and heightened rhetoric about the necessity of practicing democracy in the Cold War era brought attention to discrimination in marriage. Freedom of marriage did not top the list of goals championed by most Civil Rights leaders who believed pursuing the cause could complicate or undermine more pressing concerns about equal opportunities in education, housing, and employment. Although Martin Luther King had once contemplated marrying a White woman, in 1958 he publicly sought to decouple the movement's efforts to create racial integration and interracial community from interracial marriage, assuring jittery Whites that "The Negro's primary aim is to be the White man's brother, not his brother in-law."[25] Despite his assertions, some individuals and organizations such as the NAACP came to recognize intermarriage as the ultimate expression of integration and to shed their early hesitance to challenge miscegenation laws. Their efforts would lead legislators and courts to replace or overturn antimiscegenation statutes, most definitively in the U.S. Supreme Court decision, *Loving v. Virginia* (1967). In that year, King would join Malcolm X in revising his stated position on intermarriage, observing that "the question of intermarriage is never raised in a society cured of the disease of racism."[26]

The *Loving v. Virginia* decision proved a powerful blow to inequality, even though it did not precipitate an immediate increase in interracial marriages. Within blossoming ethnic power movements, in fact, Black, Asian, and Chicano youths often denounced interracial marriages as a form of cultural genocide. Marrying within the group would assure the preservation and political force of traditions imperiled in the past by pressures to Americanize. For Asian ethnics who worried about rates of interracial marriage that outstripped other groups, they often accepted interethnic marriages as part of their invention of a panethnic, Asian community built upon common confrontations with discrimination. Although "Asian American" served strategic political interests, shared views and experiences also informed its creation. Immigrant parents noted a sense of being one race generated not only by the racial marks imposed on them, but the greater racial and ethnic diversity in the United States that illuminated similarities with other Asians. They typically advised their sons and daughters to marry within their ethnic group, but protested much less if their children married other Asians. Typically, second-generation Chinese, Korean, and Japanese Americans confessed feeling closer to and more interest in intermarrying with other East Asians, revealing socioeconomic and physical divisions among Asian Immigrants. Their preferences also indicated that, as East Asians growing up in the United States, they had similarly struggled to belong and manage the expectations of their parents, described as an emphasis on education, hard work, honesty, and family. More broadly, the making of Asian Americans reminds us that immigrant assimilations are multiple and may lead to integration into communities other than the white mainstream. The significance and survival of Asian American as an amalgamation, however, may dissipate as the fortunes of its ethnic components change in the United States or as Southeast Asians become more familiar.[27]

Complicating these debates about whether interracial marriage represented a pathway toward integration and equality or the surrender of political power through the collapse of cultural differences were interracial marriages that originated overseas and preceded immigration. As the United States became more diffusely involved in regions throughout the world during and after World War II, offering economic aid and intervening militarily, its civilians and soldiers came into intimate contact with other peoples. Wherever posted, American men developed sometimes fleeting, sometimes coerced, but sometimes consensual and lasting relationships with local women. Concerned that all such liaisons would cause tensions with local communities and leaders, the U.S. government at the request of the Armed Services, initially prohibited the immigration of war brides. Even after revising its policy toward soldier marriage through a series of bills passed between 1945 and 1952, Congress initially excluded Asian brides and refused the request of Black and White interracial couples, reflecting and reinforcing racial prejudices of the period. War brides gained a privileged immigration status marked by exemption from quotas, accelerated naturalization, complimentary housing and care before departure, and free transport to the United States. Their stories in part resemble those of other intermarried immigrants who struggled to build lives in a new country. Based upon personal narratives, American soldiers frequently celebrated their foreign wives' "feminine" and traditional qualities, presumably in contrast to the assertiveness of American women, but their wives countered such depictions, explaining their decision as an opportunity to thwart conventional gender roles and practice American freedoms. However, unlike other intermarried, immigrant women, war brides served as "a multifaceted prism through which Americans have sought to make meaning on a popular level of their relationships with other countries."[28] After World War II, Christina Klein and Susan Zeiger have observed, as the United States sought to win the loyalties of third-world peoples and justify its global reach, it conflated domestic and foreign relations and embraced war brides as evidence of the benevolence and success of its policies. In response to heightened Civil Rights activism and the search for peace between racial groups, these couples were also touted as an example of how diverse Americans could get along. Moreover, the heightened visibility of these war brides would practically encourage broader reforms, specifically an end to exclusionary policies toward Asian immigrants and the eventual substitution of preference categories for discriminatory, national quotas.[29] The elevation of family creation and reunification as a prevailing intention of immigration laws since 1965 gives new importance to marriages formed within and outside U.S. borders.

The reassuring and romanticized image of interracial war couples faded by the later Cold War as American doubts about the efficacy of U.S. overseas entanglements intensified. The transition began in Korea with the proliferation of prostitution districts explicitly sanctioned by the Korean government and tacitly endorsed by the U.S. military in the late 1950s and early 1960s. Although an estimated 11,000 Korean military wives would immigrate to the United States, most of whom had not worked in the sex trade, Americans paid little attention to these women, focusing instead upon lurid tales of Korean prostitutes. Americans would similarly interpret Vietnamese women as prostitutes or saboteurs whose relations with American men should be reviled, not revered. Such sentiments informed immigration policy; no longer would Vietnamese and other wives of American servicemen by the mid-1970s enjoy the special protections of the separate classification of war bride. Instead, they joined the general, undifferentiated pool of refugees.[30]

The history of war brides poses another crucial question for researchers of immigration. What is the significance of intermarriage completed *prior* to immigration, a sequence that challenges Milton M. Gordon's still influential theory of assimilation, which posits intermarriage as the culmination of a sequential series of adaptations.[31] Based upon U.S. Census data, Daniel Hidalgo and Carl Bankston concluded that marriage to American citizens and resident aliens became a main avenue of Southeast Asian migration between 1965 and 1975. Overwhelmingly women, these "marriage migrants" had become familiar with American culture and American men in the context of the Vietnam War, a familiarity that launched and accelerated their incorporation into American society. In contrast, Vietnamese refugees reaching the United States after 1975 proved less likely to marry non-Vietnamese. For both groups, the experience and memories of the war had a continuing, though declining effect on their connections with Americans as the century progressed. Considering the phenomenon of marriage migration by Asian women generally and currently, sociologists have contextualized popular stories about "mail-order brides" and foreign sex workers that connect migration and marriage to the abuse of poor, powerless women. To the contrary, they have noted that migration within or as a consequence of marriage can offer a unique path to social and economic mobility.[32]

More recently, the rising incidence of intermarriages and the election of Barrack Obama—son of a Kenyan immigrant and White American—have emphasized the complexities of migrations and racial mixing in a more globalized society as well as the prospects for new understandings of race and ethnicity. A more visible, and organized movement of mixed race Americans, who mounted a successful challenge to the U.S. Census' one-box rule and advocated for more fluid notions of identity in a multiracial nation, has also changed public perceptions and discourse. Yet, questions about belonging and place remain unsettled. Will intermarriages if frequent and numerous enough, ultimately render meaningless the very categories of ethno-racial difference that have changed over time, but continuously organized American immigrant experience? Will we settle on another system of classification?

The importance of these and other questions reinforce the value of continuing to study intermarriage and immigration in the past. Despite the turn toward the transnational in U.S. history, we still know too little about intermarriages that moved across multiple national borders and those created at the seams of or spaces betwixt nations. David A. Chang, Martha Hodes, and Ben H. Johnson offer exciting examples of this line of investigation. Defining borderlands as something other than the "region surrounding one border," Chang tells the story of Lakaakaa, a Concow American Indian, her Kanaka

Maoli husbands, and their children. He traces their paths back and forth across time, land, and water to illustrate the fluidity and multiethnic complexity of connected nodes in a global network.[33] Martha Hodes followed another couple (the Connollys) across racial and national borders to suggest not only the malleability, but the power of race. Eunice Connolly's poor, Irish-descent, New England family may have frowned upon her marriage to Smiley Connolly, a sea captain of African and European descent born in the Grand Cayman Island, believing she endangered her claims to White woman-hood by linking her fortunes to a man often designated and treated as Black despite his mixed-race heritage. However, her union and migration to the Carribbean, a region that described race in ternary terms and positioned the middle category of "colored" closer to White than Black, actually elevated her social status. There she enjoyed material com-forts and respectability that had eluded her in Massachusetts.[34] Exploring how the cos-mopolitan ideals of postrevolutionary, Mexican ideologue, José Vasconcelos, shaped the thinking of Texas members of the civil rights organization LULAC in the 1930s and 1940s, who were as ready to base their activism on an acknowledgment of their racial hybridity and collaborate with non-Whites as insistence of their whiteness and distinc-tion from other minorities, Ben H. Johnson's study exposes how interpretations of inter-marriage that originated outside the United States shaped local ideas and strategies.[35]

Historians are beginning to pay more attention, and should continue to do so, to immigrants arriving since 1965. Who are they marrying and not marrying? What ethno-racial and economic lines have they blurred or confirmed? Will new immigrants from Asia and Latin America repeat the patterns of European predecessors in creating larger categories of affiliation? What will these categories resemble? Will they assimilate as readily? Some researchers studying current immigration have already expressed their doubts, citing the persistent, relative socioeconomic disadvantages of Mexicans in par-ticular.[36] Others read intermarriage statistics for Hispanics more hopefully. The con-clusions of such research about the marriage patterns of recent immigrants, of course, could shape thinking about immigration reform in a nation whose citizens agree change is necessary, but cannot agree about the details of change. More theoretically, should we further interrogate the belief that intermarriage hurries integration or consolidation? How, when, and why are distinctions preserved and passed to new generations? For all the focus on intermarriages between defined racial groups, how has ethnicity fared especially among varied immigrants from Latin America who often resist the unity and utility of the labels, Latino or Hispanic? Can historians discover more about the pri-vate as much as the public meanings of intermarriage? This poses a particular challenge given the interiority of such relationships, but oral histories and memoirs may offer glimpses into lives that are often discussed from afar, but not understood from within. Lastly, if not exhaustively, our definitions of intermarriage have assumed heterosexual-ity, but how do more capacious and varied definitions of sexuality and gender invite studies of other kinds of intimate, lasting relationships? Ultimately, the marriages and families forged by immigrants that defied narrower descriptions of ethno-racial tradi-tions and community expose so much about the changing categories and hierarchies of belonging in American society.

NOTES

1. Richard Rodriquez, *Brown: the Last Discovery of America*, (New York: Viking, 2002): xi–xv.

2. Based upon data from the 2000 Census and in depth interviews of multiracial interviews, Jennifer Lee and Frank Bean, tested three different theories of contemporary racialization: the preservation of a White/non-White divide, which assigns Latinos and Asians to the Black side of a biracial system; the evolution of a triracial structure, common in Latin American and Caribbean countries, consisting of Whites, "honorary Whites" and Blacks; the emergence of a new color line that positions Latinos and Asians closer to White and reinforces the separateness of Blacks. The authors did not pay consistent attention to or differentiate between immigrants classified as black who originated in the Caribbean, Latin America, or Africa and, native-born, Black Americans. Jennifer Lee and Frank Bean, "Reinventing the Color Line: Immigration and America's New Racial/Ethnic Divide," *Social Forces* 86, no. 2 (December 2007): 561-568.

3. According to a study released by the Pew Research Center, among all American newlyweds between 2008 and 2010, 9% of Whites, 17% of Blacks, 26% of Hispanics, and 28% of Asians married outside their ethnoracial group. Nationally, 15% of all new marriages in 2010 crossed ethnic or racial lines. Residents of the American West were more likely to marry out than those of other regions. Wendy Wang, "The Rise of Intermarriage: Rates, Characteristics Vary by Race and Gender." Pew Research Center. Released Feb 16, 2012, accessed Feb 16, 2012.

4. David Hollinger, "Amalgamation and Hypodescent: The Question of Ethnoracial Mixture in the Story of the United States," *American Historical Review* 108, no. 5 (December 1, 2003): 1363–1389; Henry Yu, "Tiger Woods Is Not the End of History; or, Why Sex across the Color Line Won't Save Us All" *American Historical Review* 108, no. 5 (December 1, 2003): 1406–1414.

5. Guillaume Aubert, "'The Blood of France': Race and Purity of Blood in the French Atlantic World," *William and Mary Quarterly* 61, no. 3 (July 2004): 455.

6. Saliha Belmessous, "Assimilation and Racialism in Seventeenth and Eighteenth-Century French Colonial Policy," *American Historical Review* 110, no. 2 (April 2005): 322-329.

7. Aubert,. "The Blood of France," 342; Jennifer Spears, "Colonial Intimacies: Legislating Sex in French Louisiana," *The William and Mary Quarterly*, 60, no.1 (January 2003): 75-98.

8. Maria Elena Martinez, "The Language Genealogy, and Classification of 'Race,' in Colonial Mexico" in *Race and Classification: The Case of Mexican America*, edited by Ilona Katzew and Susan Deans-Smith (Palo Alto: Stanford University Press, 2009), 35–41; Ilona Katzew and Susan Deans-Smith, "Introduction: The Alchemy of Race in Mexican America," in *Race and Classification*, 1–24.

9. Camilla Townsend, *Pocahontas and the Powhatan Dilemma: An American Portrait*, (New York: Hill and Wang, 2004), 119; Peter Bardaglio, "'Shameful Matches': The Regulation of Interracial Sex and Marriage in the South Before 1900" in *Sex, Love, Race: Crossing Boundaries in North American History*, edited by Martha Hodes (New York: New York University Press, 1999), 112–140.

10. Bardaglio, "Shameful Matches," 113; Winthrop Jordan, *White Over Black: American Attitudes Toward the Negro, 1550-1812* (Chapel Hill: University of North Carolina, 1969); Martha Hodes, *White Women, Black Men: Illicit Sex in the Nineteenth Century South* (New Haven, CT: Yale University, Press, 1997).

11. J. Hector St. John de Crèvecouer, *Letters From an American Farmer* (Gloucester, MA: P. Smith, 1968);

12. Jared Sparks, ed. *The Works of Benjamin Franklin; Several Political and Historical Tracts Not Included in Any Former Edition and Many Letters Official and Private Not Hitherto Published with Notes* (Boston: Hillard, Gray & Co., 1840), 320.

13. Maria Raquel Casas, *Married to a Daughter of the Land: Spanish-Mexican Women and Interethnic Marriage in California, 1820-1880* (Reno, NV: University of Nevada, 2007): 8.

14. Deborah Moreno, "'Here the Society is United': 'Respectable' Anglos and Intercultural Marriage in Pre-Gold Rush California," *California History* 80, no. 1 (Spring 2001): 2–17.

15. John C. Calhoun and H. Lee Cheek. *John C. Calhoun: Selected Writings and Speeches.* (Washington, DC: Regency Pub, 2003).

16. Casas, *Married to a Daughter*, 108.

17. Percentages based upon Albuquerque, NM data; Pablo Mitchell, *Coyote Nation: Sexuality, Race and Conquest in Modernizing New Mexico, 1880-1920* (Chicago: University of Chicago Press, 2005), 109.

18. Ibid., 108; Anthony Mora, *Border Dilemmas: Racial and National Uncertainties in New Mexico, 1848-1912* (Durham, NC: Duke University Press, 2011), 136–138.

19. Bora, *Border Dilemmas,* 139. Katie Benton-Cohen, *Borderline Americans: Racial Division and Labor War in the Arizona Borderlands* (Cambridge, MA: Harvard University Press, 2009), 36–38, 160.

20. Peggy Pascoe, *What Comes Naturally: Miscegenation Law and the Making of Race in America* (New York: Oxford University Press, 2009); Linda España-Maram, *Creating Masculinity in Los Angeles's Little Manila: Working-Class Filipinos and Popular Culture, 1920s-1950s* (New York: Columbia University Press, 2006); Dorothy B. Fugita-Rony, *American Workers, Colonial Power: Philippine Seattle and the Transpacific West, 1919-1941*(Berkeley, CA: University of California Press, 2003).

21. Allison Varzally, *Making a Non-White America: Californians Coloring Outside Ethnic Lines* (Berkeley, CA: University of California Press, 2008): 103–107.

22. Karen Leonard, *Making Ethnic Choices: California's Punjabi Mexican Americans* (Philadelphia: Temple University Press, 1992), 115, 123–124; Varzally, *Making a Non-White America.*

23. Eli Lederhendler, *New York Jews and the Decline of Ethnicity, 1950-1970* (Syracuse, NY: Syracuse University Press, 2001); William Chafe, *The Unfinished Journey: America since World War II* (New York: Oxford University Press, 1986); Matthew Pratt Guterl, *The Color of Race in America, 1900-1940* (Cambridge, MA: Harvard University Press, 2001); Nell Irving Painter, *The History of White People,* (New York: Norton Press, 2010); Matthew Frye Jacobson, *Whiteness of a Different Color: European Immigrants and the Alchemy of Race,* (Cambridge, MA: Harvard University Press, 1998).

24. Lisa Neidert and Reynolds Farley, "Assimilation in the United States: An Analysis of Ethnic and Generation Differences in Status and Achievement." *American Sociological Review* 50, no. 6 (1985): 840–850.; Joshua Zeitz, *White Ethnic New York: Jews, Catholics, and the Shaping of Postwar Politics* (Chapel Hill, NC: University of North Carolina Press, 2007); Ronald H. Bayor, "Another Look at 'Whiteness:' The Persistence of Ethnicity in American Life," *Journal of American Ethnic History* 29, no. 1 (Fall 2009): 13–30.

25. Malcolm X quoted in Jonathan Zimerman, "Crossing Oceans, Crossing Colors: Black Peace Corps Volunteers and Interracial Love in Africa, 1961-1971," in *Sex, Love,*

Race: Crossing Boundaries in North American History, edited by Martha Hodes (New York: New York University Press, 1999), 516.

26. Malcolm X quoted in Zimmerman "Crossing Oceans, Crossing Colors," 524; Pascoe, *What Comes Naturally,* 247.

27. Nazil Kibria, "The Construction of 'Asian American:' Reflections on Intermarriage and Ethnic Identity Among Second-Generation Chinese and Korean Americans," *Ethnic and Racial Studies,* 20, no. 3 (1997): 523–544; Yen Le Espiritu, *Asian American Panethnicity: Bridging Institutions and Identities* (Philadelphia: Temple University Press, 1992); Larry Shinagawa, "Asian American Panethnicity and Intermarriage," *Amerasia Journal* 22, no. 2 (1996): 127–153.

28. Susan Zeiger, *Entangling Alliances: Foreign War Brides and American Soldiers in the Twentieth Century* (New York: New York University Press, 2010), 2.

29. Philip Wolgin and I. Bloemraad, "'Our Gratitude to Our Soldiers': Military Spouses, Family Re-Unification, and Postwar Immigration Reform." *Journal of Interdisciplinary History* 41, no. 1 (Summer 2010): 27–60; Christina Klein, *Cold War Orientalism: Asia in the Middlebrow Imagination, 1945-1961* (Berkeley, CA: University of California Press, 2003); Zeiger, *Entangling Alliances.*

30. Zeiger, *Entangling Alliances,* 203–235.

31. Milton M. Gordon, *Assimilation in American Life: The Role of Race, Religion and National Origins* (New York: Oxford University Press, 1964).

32. Daniel Hidalgo and Carl Bankston "Military Brides and Refugees: Vietnamese American Wives and Shifting Links to the Military, 1980-2000," *International Migration Review,* 46 (May 1, 2008): 167–185; Rajni Palriwala and Patricia Uberoi, eds. *Women and Migration in Asia,* (Los Angeles: Sage, 2008).

33. David A. Chang, "Borderlands in a World at Sea: Concow Indians, Native Hawaiians, and South Chinese in Indigenous, Global, and National Spaces," *Journal of American History* 98, no. 2 (September 2011): 384–403.

34. Martha Hodes, "The Mercurial Nature and Abiding Power of Race: A Transnational Family Story" *American Historical Review,* 108, no. 1 (Feb 1, 2003): 84–118.

35. Benjamin H. Johnson, "The Cosmic Race in Texas: Racial Fusion, White Supremacy, and Civil Rights Politics," *Journal of American History* 98, no. 2 (September 2011): 404–419.

36. Brian Duncan and Stephen J. Trejo, "Ethnic Identification, Intermarriage and Unmeasured Progress by Mexican Americans" in *Mexican Immigration to the United States,* edited by George Borjas (Chicago: University of Chicago Press, 2007).

BIBLIOGRAPHY

Casas, Maria Raquel. *Married to a Daughter of the Land: Spanish-Mexican Women and Interethnic Marriage in California, 1820-1880.* (Reno, NV: University of Nevada, 2007).

Chang, David. "Borderlands in a World at Sea: Concow Indians, Native Hawaiians, and South Chinese in Indigenous, Global, and National Spaces." *Journal of American History* 98, no. 2 (September 2011): 384–403.

Duval, Katherine. "Indian Intermarriage and Métissage in Colonial Louisiana." *William and Mary Quarterly* 65, no. 2 (April 2008): 267–304.

Gualtieri, Sarah M. A. *Between Arab and White: Race and Ethnicity in the Early Syrian American Diaspora.* (Berkeley: University of California Press, 2009).

Guyotte, Roland L. and Barbara Posades. "Interracial Marriages and Transnational Families: Chicago's Filipinos in the Aftermath of World War II." *Journal of American Ethnic History* 23, no. 2/3 (Winter/Spring 2006): 134–155.

Hodes, "The Mercurial Nature and Abiding Power of Race: A Transnational Family Story." *American Historical Review*, 108, no. 1 (Feb 1, 2003): 84–118.

Hollinger, David. "Amalgamation and Hypodescent: The Question of Ethnoracial Mixture in the Story of the United States," *American History Review* 108, no. 5 (December 1, 2003): 1363–1389.

Katzew, Ilona and Susan Deans-Smith., eds. *Race and Classification: The Case of Mexican America.* (Palo Alto: Stanford University Press, 2009).

Lee, Jennifer. *The Diversity Paradox: Immigration and the Color Line in Twenty-First Century America.* (New York: Russell Sage Foundation, 2010).

Lim, Julian. "Chinos and Paisanos: Chinese Mexican Relations in the Borderlands." *Pacific Historical Review.* 79, no. 1 (February 2010): 50–85.

Pacoe, Peggy. *What Comes Naturally: Miscegenation Law and the Making of Race in America.* (New York: Oxford University Press, 2009).

Sassler, Sharon. "Gender And Ethnic Differences in Marital Assimilation in the Early Twentieth Century." *International Migration Review* 39, 3. (Fall 2005): 608–636.

Varzally, Allison. *Making a Non-White America: Californians Coloring Outside Ethnic Lines, 1925-1955.* (Berkeley, CA: University of California Press, 2008).

Wiesner-Hanks, Merry. "Crossing Borders in Transnational Gender History." *Journal of Global History* 6, no. 3 (November 2011): 357–379.

Zeiger, Susan. *Entangling Alliances: Foreign War Brides and American Soldiers in the Twentieth Century.* (New York: New York University, Press, 2010).

....

CHAPTER 14

IMMIGRATION, MEDICAL REGULATION, AND EUGENICS

....

WENDY KLINE

U.S. history is rampant with stories of "medicalized nativism"—the fear of contamination from those born outside of the United States.[1] It still exists today; as medical historian Alan Kraut argues, "the double helix of health and fear remains encoded in American society and culture."[2] In the late nineteenth century, as fears of contamination latched onto eugenic anxieties about racial degeneration, the medical regulation of foreigners attempting to enter the United States became particularly intense. Ideas about contagion and degeneration characterized the medical regulation of immigrants around the turn of the twentieth century, and many of these ideas remain with us today.

THE IMMIGRANT MEDICAL EXAM ABROAD

In 1894, 13-year-old Mary Antin traveled with her mother and two siblings from Polotzk, Russia, to Boston, Massachusetts. As a promise to her uncle, she wrote a detailed account of her voyage, an activity that occupied her "for many hot summer hours." The letter would eventually end up in her published memoir, *The Promised Land*, a book which "established the genre of the immigrant autobiography."[3] Antin captures the dramatic experience of traveling to the New World from the viewpoint of an astonished young girl whose world had been turned upside down. Well before she entered the United States, she was subjected to countless medical inspections. In Berlin, for example, en route to Hamburg, her group was taken directly off of the train for this purpose:

> Here we had been taken to a lonely place where only that house was to be seen; our
> things were taken away, our friends separated from us; a man came to inspect us,
> as if to ascertain our full value; strange-looking people driving us about like dumb
> animals, helpless and unresisting; children we could not see crying in a way that

suggested terrible things; ourselves driven into a little room where a great kettle was boiling on a little stove; our clothes taken off, our bodies rubbed with a slippery substance that might be any bad thing; a shower of warm water let down on us without warning; again driven to another little room where we sit, wrapped in woolen blankets till large, coarse bags are brought in, their contents turned out, and we see only a cloud of steam, and hear the women's orders to dress ourselves,—"Quick! Quick!"[4]

Though Antin's talents as a young writer are remarkable, her experience en route to the "promised land" are typical of the late nineteenth century. Although Ellis Island remains in historical memory as "shorthand for the process of entry into the nation," the process actually began well before arrival on the nation's shores.[5] Many of those who sought entry into the United States around the time of Antin's journey never made it across the ocean. An 1891, federal immigration law required that immigrants receive a medical inspection prior to departure and again after arrival into the United States. The law required steamship companies to bear the responsibility of passengers' eligibility to enter the country. Hefty penalties ($100 fine plus return passage for each immigrant rejected) ensured cooperation much of the time.[6]

A cholera epidemic from Asia that reached the United States in the fall of 1892 further increased the fear that public health was under threat from abroad.[7] The United States rapidly passed a federal quarantine law that established a series of inspection stations along European and Asian points of departure. The law authorized the U.S. Public Health Service (PHS) to work in European ports to "monitor the prevalence of epidemic disease and to inspect and pass vessels wishing to embark for U.S. ports." Ten years later, similar agreements were made with China and Japan.[8] As Amy Fairchild argues, despite the lack of complete data, "the inspections abroad may have had a tremendous impact on the flow of immigration to the United States."[9] Rigorous medical inspections prevented many from leaving Europe or Asia.

ELLIS ISLAND AND MEDICAL INSPECTIONS IN THE UNITED STATES

Those who passed inspections abroad had to ready themselves for additional screening upon arrival in the United States. Beginning in 1892, approximately 70 percent of immigrants entering the United States passed through Ellis Island. When steamships entered the New York Harbor, state health officers did a preliminary scan for infectious diseases—namely, typhus, cholera, plague, smallpox, and yellow fever.[10] This was followed by U.S. Marine Hospital Service physicians who conducted brief, private medical exams in the individual cabins of first- and second-class passengers. Those traveling third-class or steerage, however, were placed on a barge headed for Ellis Island. Often, passengers were weak, exhausted, and malnourished. Many described the intense smells of sweat, disinfectants, and human waste that surrounded the barges, mingled with fear, anxiety, and apprehension of what was to come.[11]

Upon arrival on the island, immigrants, sometimes as many as 5,000 per day, entered through a series of gated passageways "resembling cattle pens."[12] Each received a tag, pinned on his or her clothing, with an identification number, and then proceeded up a flight of stairs with hand luggage to the main hall. The line inspection began at the top of the stairs, where a U.S. Marine Hospital Service physician analyzed prospective immigrants on their ascent. This allowed physician inspectors to assess the physical condition of each traveler under duress. They inspected hands, eyes, throats, postures, and scalps. Those deemed suspect of a mental or medical condition would receive a chalk mark on their right shoulder, indicating that they should be pulled from the line and inspected more closely.[13] As Amy Fairchild notes, this procedure occurred in full view of the others in line, generating anxiety and awareness of the standards used to determine whether one was worthy of entry into the United States. Though for most applicants, the medical examination lasted a matter of seconds, approximately 20 percent received a chalk mark and were turned off the line for further examination.[14]

Very few prospective immigrants were actually deported upon arrival, in part because of the rigorous inspections that took place prior to departure from abroad. During the peak years of immigration at Ellis Island, 1900–1914, an average of only 1 percent were deported each year.[15] Yet for many, this process was the most traumatic of the entire journey, frequently recounted by immigrants in their depictions of the experience.[16] For 25 million immigrants, as Amy Fairchild observes, "the moment of entry into the United States represented a profoundly consequential trial."[17] The 20 percent who were detained longer recounted the anxieties, fears, and humiliations of further inspection. Some recalled the embarrassment of having to remove their clothes in front of others, or the humiliation of daily delousing. Seventy years after his arrival from Ireland, Manny Steen recalled that the worst memory he had of Ellis Island was the physical exam. "The doctors were seated at a long table with a basin full of potassium chloride and you had to stand in front of them . . . and you had to reveal yourself . . . Right there in front of everyone!"[18] The very nature of the public exam reinforced to all participants and observers the increasing power of medical authority in America.

All prospective immigrants turned off the line were subjected to additional interrogation by a panel of three Immigration Service officers, regardless of whether they were medically certified upon further inspection. Here, questions focused not just on health and disease but also on occupation, family history, and finances. Immigration Service officers sought to determine the likelihood of an immigrant becoming a public charge. The intense interrogations by the officers, along with the medical exam, served as a reminder to immigrants that financial and physical health were essential to receiving the "golden ticket" of entry to the United States.

Historians have long debated the efficacy of a medical inspection system that relied on a brief visual overview of thousands of incoming immigrants. Even with new medical technology, such as the microscope (used to detect viruses), officers faced an impossible charge of effectively weeding out those "unfit" to enter the country. Indeed, during particularly heavy times, they were frequently instructed to pull fewer immigrants out of the inspection line, as they lacked the resources to detain and further question them. Some argue that this process served to reinforce a system of control and mechanization required to handle a new industrial labor force. Others turn to the importance of germ theory and the increasing power of medicine to determine the worthiness of perspective residents. Scientist Robert Koch had established the presence of microorganisms that spread disease, confirming for many the susceptibility of all Americans to foreign contagion and contamination. Any measure in place to prevent the spread of disease, however minute, seemed better than no measure at all.

PROGRESSIVISM AND EUGENICS

But more was at stake in the drama of medical inspection than the containment of disease. America at the turn of the century had become obsessed with a new ideal of progressivism that had the potential to invigorate the population by eliminating so-called weaknesses. The science of eugenics appealed to many as a modern approach to an age-old problem of decline. Generally speaking, progressivism represented a widespread and varied response to the multitude of changes brought by industrial capitalism and urban growth in the late nineteenth century. Making use of a new language of social efficiency and technical expertise, Progressive Era reformers approached social problems differently than their nineteenth-century forebears. In search of order to an increasing complex world, they called for a new social consciousness to strengthen American civilization. Within this context, the American eugenics movement emerged as a significant force that not only would shape immigration policy and sexual conduct during the Progressive Era but also would outlive its progressive roots to gain increasing authority in the 1930s, 1940s, and even later.

Like progressivism, eugenic ideology represented a complex combination of popular and scientific beliefs and interests that has confounded historians. As Diane Paul notes, "there is [currently] no consensus on what eugenics *is*." When the term was coined in 1883 by Francis Galton, a British statistician, he took the word from a Greek root meaning "good in birth." He defined eugenics as the science of improving human stock by giving "the more suitable races or strains of blood a better chance of prevailing speedily over the less suitable."[19] After studying prominent British families, he reasoned that most moral and mental traits, such as courage, intellect, and vigor, were passed on to offspring. Yet he also observed that the worthiest families produced the fewest children, and he believed that the results would be disastrous if something was not done. He proposed that "those highest in civic worth" should be encouraged to have more children (defined as "positive eugenics"), and those unworthy should be encouraged to have fewer or none ("negative eugenics").[20]

But in Progressive Era America, eugenic ideology appealed to reformers who represented a wide range of interests and politics and who applied their own varied definitions of eugenics. Social radicals such as Charlotte Perkins Gilman and Margaret Sanger embraced eugenics as a civilizing force that would further the rights of women as well as improve the race. Nativists such as Madison Grant (author of *The Passing of the Great Race*) viewed it as a justification for restraining the liberties of immigrants and the procreative powers of sexually promiscuous women. What these radicals and nativists had in common was a vision of the future in which reproductive decisions were made in the name of building a better race, though they may have disagreed on how to go about achieving this goal. Indeed, one of the strengths of the eugenics movement was its widespread popular appeal to a diverse audience, due in large part to its decidedly vague definition. It is important not to allow the words and actions of a few eugenic leaders to define the parameters of eugenic meaning in America. Instead, as Nancy Stepan suggests, "we need to recapture 'ordinary' eugenics and its social meanings." [21]

Eugenics gained authority and legitimacy in the early twentieth century, when the rediscovery of Gregor Mendel's laws of segregation and independent assortment led to the establishment of genetics. Working with peas in 1865, Mendel had found that hereditary material is transferred from parent to child. His contemporaries, however, were not impressed, and it was not until 1900 that scientists appreciated the significance of his findings.[22] Though eugenicists had been arguing for the importance of heredity in their quest for "race betterment" since the 1870s, they had lacked the scientific evidence to suggest how characteristics were transmitted to offspring. Mendel's laws established genetics as a serious science and lent legitimacy to the eugenic claim that social undesirables—including alcoholics, prostitutes, and even unwed mothers—would produce more of their kind by passing down their supposed genetic flaws to their children.[23] This assumption would have a profound effect on the medical inspection at Ellis Island, where pregnant women who arrived without a spouse in tow, for example, were frequently detained.

HENRY GODDARD, MENTAL TESTING, AND THE MORON

One American eugenicist in particular made significant use of this claim in his revision of feeblemindedness as a hereditary disorder. Henry Goddard, a psychologist and devout believer in the heritability of delinquent and immoral behavior, studied hundreds of cases of "feeblemindedness" at the Vineland Training School in New Jersey beginning in the 1900s. He was troubled by the lack of consensus over diagnosis and treatment of the feebleminded. Lacking a "common criteria," most medical superintendents at institutions for the feebleminded drew upon a wide range of approaches to understanding mental deficiency, ranging from physiological to sociological tests.[24] Goddard's interest in locating a standard system for diagnosing and classifying the wide range of mental deficiency he witnessed at the school led him to the psychological studies of French psychologist Alfred Binet. He found Binet's "Measuring Scale for Intelligence" effective in analyzing his own patients at Vineland and thus proposed that Binet's procedure be used to diagnose the feebleminded at all state institutions. His audience could not have been more receptive: the American Association for the Study of the Feeble Minded, comprised of institutional physicians and non-medical personnel, recognized the need for a standard diagnostic procedure and was quick to sponsor Goddard's proposal in 1910.[25]

What Goddard found so effective and original in Binet's method was that it introduced the concept of *mental normality*. Binet argued that psychologists and physicians had difficulty constructing a coherent cluster of categories to distinguish between the wide range in pathological appearance and behavior because they had nothing standard to measure them *against*. Without a language or a framework by which to understand what normal development was, there could be no hope of understanding the abnormal. So in 1908, the psychologist incorporated such a framework into his testing procedure by "establishing numerical norms for every level of a child's mental growth, based on samples of children's responses. By comparing an individual child's test results established for children of his age, one could determine the child's relative 'mental level.'"[26] It was thus *in opposition to normality* that mental deficiency came to be understood among physicians and psychologists. In the quest for categorizing and diagnosing the feebleminded, a new language and a structure for "normal" intellectual development emerged as a focal point.

Developed by psychologists and eugenicists, this language tapped into a burgeoning twentieth-century interest in the concept of normality and the centrality of intelligence to human progress. Though the western frontier of the United States was closing, progressivism emphasized a new natural resource that required not land but mental cultivation: intelligence. America would continue to expand through the "frontier of science." The key to progress, psychologists argued, was human intelligence. As JoAnne Brown argues, it was not labor or capital that "held real promise as the engine of civilization's advance in the new millennium; the mind, through science, would remake the world."[27]

Within this vision of progress, mental deficiency appeared as a factor that needed to be discarded, in the form of both the waste products of rapid urbanization and the remnants of rural backwardness. Physicians emphasized that feeblemindedness had increased as a result of "industrial and social stress" in cities as well as from a "marked deterioration in the quality of the [rural] population.[28] As normality became a "central organizing principle" of American society, those who displayed abnormal qualities suggesting an incapability of improvement received greater social stigma as potential threats to the advancement of civilization.[29] Concerns about the increasing flow of immigrants attempting to settle in the United States during this time heightened concern about their potential negative impact on American society.

Henry Goddard recognized the ability of this new language of progress and decay to capture public and professional support for the study of mental deficiency. His proposal to use a scale of mental measurement as a standard diagnostic procedure, like that of Alfred Binet, had widespread appeal in the United States. Between 1908, when Goddard first translated a version of the Binet scale and had it published in America, and 1930, over 9 million adults and children had been tested using this scale.[30] Standardized mental measurement, best exemplified in the intelligence quotient (or IQ), quickly gained legitimacy in the United States as a scientific procedure and cemented the authority of psychology as a serious science.

Binet's original scale of mental measurement had included two gradations of deficiency: the "idiot," who had a mental age of 2 years or younger, and the "imbecile," who had a mental age of 3 to 7 years. But Goddard was not satisfied that this scale adequately addressed the problem of mental deficiency. He believed that the greatest threat to civilization's advance lay with those who demonstrated a mental age of 8 to 12 years, a class that had not been given any particular name. In Goddard's opinion, this group, consisting of those closest to a "normal" mental age (13 or older), posed the greatest danger.

"We need a name for this high grade group for many reasons," Goddard argued in 1910 in front of the American Association for the Study of Feeblemindedness. "I presume no one in this audience, certainly none of the superintendents of institutions need to be reminded that the public is entirely ignorant of this particular group." By naming them, Goddard hoped to draw attention to their presence in the public school systems, where the Board of Education was "struggling to make *normal* people out of them" by keeping them in regular classes.[31]

But the board of education was making a grave error in treating them as normal, in Goddard's opinion. Even the highest grade of the feebleminded could never become normal, he argued; though they could *pass* for normal, making them the most likely culprits for spreading the defect to future generations. Rather than trying to disguise or ignore their disabilities, physicians and superintendents needed to underscore them. "One of the most helpful things that we can do," he declared, "would be to *distinctly mark out the limits of this class* and help the general public to understand that they are a special group and require special treatment."[32] In his study of deafness in American culture, Douglas Baynton suggests a similar effort to single out sign language in the Progressive Era as deviant. Because of this new emphasis on normality, reformers became increasingly intolerant of the "difference" that deafness or mental deficiency embodied.[33]

Goddard needed a word that would carry scientific legitimacy and arouse public concern, for, as Goddard stressed, physicians needed public assistance in hunting out the high-grades. Yet there was no word in the English language that adequately expressed the distinctiveness and urgency of their condition. Goddard therefore constructed his own term from the Greek word for foolish, "moronia," and the result was the diagnostic label of the "moron." "Fool or foolish in the English sense exactly describes this group of children," he announced. "The Century Dictionary defines a fool as one who is deficient in judgment, or sense, etc., which is distinctly the group we are working with [those of a mental age of 8 to 12]."[34] His use of the ancient language gave the term an almost timeless quality, which underscored what Goddard believed to be the permanence of the condition.

Goddard's interest in targeting those he believed to possess a mental age of 8 to 12 years old dated back to his graduate training with G. Stanley Hall at Clark University.

Hall, like his protégé, sought academic solutions to what he regarded as racial degeneracy and the decline of civilization. In particular, he addressed the "emasculating tendencies of higher civilization": as men evolved into higher beings, they became physically weaker and lost their virility, as evidenced by the emergence of neurasthenia.[35] Hall, like most scientists of the late nineteenth century, believed in the inheritance of acquired characteristics (to be overshadowed by Mendelian genetic theory by the early 1900s). As each generation advanced, Hall believed, it would pass on its acquired developments to the next generation, and thus civilization would continually evolve.

Central to this idea was recapitulation theory, which explained how children inherited their parents' acquired traits. As an individual developed, he or she would "follow the developmental path its forebears took." The more advanced the race, the longer development would take, and the highest stages of human development—advanced intelligence—occurred only within the white races. At the top of the evolutionary scale stood white civilized manhood, with white civilized womanhood just below.[36]

Hall thus proposed that while developing, young boys should be allowed to embrace primitive savagery as a natural and necessary phase that they would later outgrow. By "encouraging small boys to embrace their primitive passions instead of repressing them," as Hall argued, "educators could 'inoculate' boys with the primitive strength they would need to avoid developing neurasthenia."[37] The most difficult period of development, and by far the most dangerous, Hall posited, was during adolescence. Linking adolescence to recapitulation theory, he suggested that the growing independence of children 8 to 12 years old "corresponded to a lost primitive 'pigmoid' race."[38] Luckily, the more advanced races would outgrow this developmental phase, developing into civilized adults.

Goddard's choice of the moron to target those with a mental age of eight to twelve years—the age range that corresponded to a more "primitive race" in Hall's theories—was not a coincidence. Goddard came of age after the scientific discrediting of recapitulation theory and what was called "Lamarckism" or "soft heredity" (a theory of biological evolution holding that species evolve by the inheritance of traits acquired or modified through the use or disuse of body parts). Mendelian genetics, or "hard heredity," dismissed Lamarckism and its inclusion of environmental factors, claiming that traits were passed through genes and entirely independent from the external environment.[39] Goddard thus modernized his mentor's theories by applying them within a eugenic, hereditary framework. The moron represented those who could not develop beyond the primitive savagery of adolescence. He (or she), because of faulty genes resulting in low intelligence, remained trapped in this primitive phase of development.

Thus christened "morons," patients at Goddard's Vineland Training School and other feebleminded institutions across the country emerged in the 1910s as a distinct category of deficiency that posed a challenge to progressive culture. Yet the term itself was decidedly vague; claiming to represent those with a mental age of 8 to 12 years, it gave diagnosticians great leeway in determining who fit the category. By adding the "moron" class to the definition of feeblemindedness, Goddard effectively broadened the scope of mental deficiency to include a wider range of symptoms. This new category essentially blurred the distinction between what behavior was unmistakably "normal" and what was "pathological," allowing for new social "symptoms," such as unwed motherhood or prostitution, to permit a diagnosis of "feebleminded."

Goddard's central evidence for the dangerous and prolific nature of morons was set forth in his own popular work, *The Kallikak Family: A Study in the Heredity of Feeble-Mindedness*, published in 1912. In this study, he traced the ancestry of a young girl (called "Deborah") whom he considered a moron with "immoral tendencies" and found that her genetic flaw could be traced back to her great-great-great grandmother, a feebleminded tavern girl. From this one tavern girl, he claimed, had come 143 feebleminded descendants, including alcoholics, prostitutes, and criminals. While earlier pedigree studies, such as Richard Dugdale's *The Jukes* (1877) emphasized the importance of environmental influences on human development, the story of the Kallikak family emphasized heredity exclusively. Deborah's great-great-great grandfather, Martin, had married a prominent Quaker woman after his affair with the tavern girl, and from this union came hundreds of upstanding citizens. Deborah had had the misfortune of coming from Martin's first union, thus inheriting the defective gene, while her half-siblings profited from the strong genetic stock of both their parents. Goddard, never one to choose a name without significant meaning, invented "Kallikak" from the Greek words for good ("kallos") and bad ("kakos") to emphasize the inevitable destruction of worthy families through a moment of transgression.[40]

This radical redefinition of feeblemindedness, as an outward sign of a fundamental genetic flaw rather than of a slight mental impairment, had enormous implications, both for those already housed in institutions for the feebleminded and for those whose attitude, behavior, or appearance would target them for incarceration and sterilization in the future, including immigrants. The person labeled mentally deficient was no longer deemed an object of curiosity or sympathy but instead was perceived as a threat to the genetic health and stability of the race. According to this new definition, nothing in the environment—no amount of education, training, or nurturing—could alter the destructive potential stored within a feeble mind. And because "feeblemindedness" had never been a precise diagnostic term to begin with, it was easily manipulated into a catch-all term for any type of behavior considered inappropriate or threatening. By redefining the boundaries of mental disability to correlate with standards of social and sexual behavior, rather than with standardized levels of mental capability, the newly defined term of "feebleminded" also served to define what constituted *normal* behavior.

This transformation had an enormous impact on the medical regulation of immigrants in America. Fear that immigrants surreptitiously carried genetic deficiencies across the border resulted in a new series of mental health inspections. How would one detect a genetic deficiency, particularly that of a so-called "high-grade moron," who could pass as normal? The challenge of developing and testing a diagnostic procedure that would detect such a deficiency drew eugenic researchers to Ellis Island, where they were welcomed by Dr. Howard Knox, chief medical officer of Ellis Island from 1910 to 1916.[41] Knox himself developed mental fitness tests for immigrants, including wooden puzzles and cubes that challenged memory and problem-solving. He also invited Goddard to Ellis Island to see if he could help to identify the mentally (and thereby socially) deficient immigrants arriving on the island.

Between 1912 and 1913, Goddard conducted three highly controversial studies on Ellis Island immigrants, the results of which appeared in article form as "Mental Tests and the Immigrant" in the 1917 *Journal of Delinquency*. In May of 1912, he brought two female assistants to test immigrants using the Binet scale. One assistant hand selected immigrants whom she believed to be feebleminded (based on a visual assessment); the other then administered the test. Remarkably, Goddard found that the first nine immigrants handpicked as "defective" indeed tested as feebleminded. Later, he compared the rate of selection of his assistants versus those of the Public Health Service physicians and found that his assistants were correct in their assessment 80 percent of the time, while the PHS physicians had an accuracy rate of under 50 percent (based on forty-four immigrants). He used this evidence to suggest the importance of using experts trained to detect potential visual signs of mental defect.[42]

In 1913, Goddard spent seventy-five days administering tests to different immigrant groups to determine their average intelligence (the tests were given to thirty-five Jews, twenty-two Hungarians, fifty Italians, and forty-five Russians). His findings were profoundly disturbing to those who feared the influx of these immigrants: more than three-quarters of those tested received a score low enough to be diagnosed as "morons."[43] While immigrant advocates and many social scientists claimed that there was an inherent bias in such testing, anti-immigration proponents gladly took advantage of these statistics. Regardless of whether they indicated the innate intelligence of an entire ethnic group or were a sign that the "dregs" of each group were attempting to enter the United States didn't really matter—either way, it was a powerful argument to further immigration restriction and was used accordingly.

WHAT HAPPENED TO EUGENICS?

Few doubt the central role of eugenics in shaping U.S. immigration policy and regulation in the early twentieth century. While the restrictive policies and procedures at Ellis Island have received the most scholarly attention, similar restrictions took place on Angel Island on the West Coast and along the U.S.-Mexican border. The USPHS instituted quarantines, delousing, and fumigation along the border, affecting hundreds of immigrants daily and contributing to an anti-Mexican sentiment centered upon dirt and disease.[44]

There is less consensus over what happened to eugenics in the second half of the twentieth century, despite the fact that racism and nativism remain. Like many controversial historical topics in U.S. history, American eugenics has undergone a scholarly transformation over the past fifty years. Though the movement held enormous sway during the first half of the twentieth century, historians did not openly critique the movement until the 1960s. A new generation of scholars, influenced by the social upheavals of the decade, approached past events in American history with greater skepticism than their forebears. Just as biology textbooks were finally renouncing the legitimacy of eugenic principles, scholars began their attack on the insidious role of progressives bent on curbing the population of the so-called "unfit" in the early twentieth century. And for the first time, scholars linked the American eugenics movement to the Holocaust.

While the "Nazi connection" drew greater attention to the abuse of power in the U.S. eugenic movement, it also, unfortunately, distorted the local history. Linking American eugenics to genocide in Germany provided fodder for sensational histories and the occasional journalistic frenzy, but prevented most from integrating the story into mainstream social history. In other words, rather than ask why so many Americans embraced eugenic and hereditarian ideals in the first half of the twentieth century, many scholars vilified a small number of individual racists as responsible for generating an embarrassing mistake.

Despite this somewhat limiting approach to the history of eugenics, intellectual debates over the role of nature versus nurture in human development (or heredity versus environment) kept eugenics in the spotlight. If anything, such interest has only increased over the past few decades, as the human genome project and other technological developments have raised the bar of genetic engineering and its implications for society's future. Thus, trying to understand the history of the nature/nurture debate became of great interest to both intellectual and social historians.

This has become of even greater interest in the twenty-first century. "Is a New Eugenics Afoot?" asked historian and biologist Garland Allen in the October 2001 volume of *Science* magazine. Though he stressed to *Science* readers that the context of early twentieth-century eugenics was different from that of the twenty-first century, he warned that "we are poised at the threshold of a similar period in our own history and are adopting a similar mind frame as our predecessors."[45] The term "reprogenetics" first appeared around 1998 as a result of the Human Genome Project and the ethical issues surrounding genetic detection and germ-line engineering. "Reprogenetics," "new eugenics," "neo-eugenics," and even "new genetics" are increasingly employed to draw the implicit connection between current technology research and past abuses. For example, the Human Genome Project and Nazi history quickly became linked in discussions of public policy. Genetic mapping indicates for some the "brave new world" that seeks to "build a better race" at the expense of the weak and disempowered.

Others are not so sure eugenics ever went away. As Alison Bashford notes, historians have no trouble writing about eugenics' origins (the term was coined by Francis Galton in 1883), because they can. But where it ends, or changes, or disappears is subject to debate. "Where did eugenics go?" asked Bashford in 2010.[46] It depends on whom you ask. Some say it has just returned, some argue it never went away, and some suggest that recent debates on choice-based medical genetics have little to do with what happened in the early twentieth century. Regardless of the variation in interpretation, one thing is certain—these debates will not go away anytime soon.

NOTES

1. Alan M. Kraut, *Silent Travelers: Germs, Genes, and the "Immigrant Menace"* (Baltimore: Johns Hopkins University Press, 1994), 3.
2. Ibid., 9.
3. Mary Antin, *The Promised Land*, ed. and Introduction Werner Sollors (New York: Penguin Books, 1997), quoted in Ken Gewertz, "Revisiting 'the Promised Land,'" *Harvard University Gazette* (Mar. 6, 1997), http://news.harvard.edu/gazette/1997/03.06/RevisitingThePr.html.
4. Mary Antin, *The Promised Land* (Boston and New York: Houghton Mifflin Company, 1912), 146.
5. Amy L. Fairchild, *Science at the Borders: Immigrant Medical Inspection and the Shaping of the Modern Industrial Labor Force* (Baltimore: Johns Hopkins University Press, 2003), 1.
6. Fairchild, *Science at the Borders*, 58. Fairchild notes that there are no steamship company records available to quantify the impact of this procedure, but company brochures warned prospective immigrants of the consequences of the medical exam.
7. Kraut, *Silent Travelers*, 59.
8. Fairchild, *Science at the Borders*, 58.
9. Ibid., 59.
10. Kraut, *Silent Travelers*, 60.
11. Fairchild, *Science at the Borders*, 88.
12. Ibid., 88.
13. Kraut, *Silent Travelers*, 54–55.
14. Elizabeth Yew, "Medical Inspection of the Immigrant at Ellis Island, 1891–1924," *Bulletin of the New York Academy of Medicine* 56 (1980): 489.
15. Ibid., 492.
16. Kraut, *Silent Travelers*, 54.
17. Fairchild, *Science at the Borders*, 64.
18. Ibid.
19. Diane Paul, *Controlling Human Heredity* (Amherst: Humanity Books, 1999), 4; Dan Kevles, *In the Name of Eugenics: Genetics and the Uses of Human Heredity* (Boston: Harvard University Press, 1998), ix.
20. Paul, *Controlling Human Heredity*, 3–5.
21. Nancy Stepan, *The Hour of Eugenics: Race, Gender, and Nation in Latin America* (Ithaca: Cornell University Press, 1996), 6.
22. Paul, *Controlling Human Heredity*, 46.
23. See Kevles, *In the Name of Eugenics*, 41–56.
24. See Leila Zenderland, "The Debate Over Diagnosis: Henry Herbert Goddard and the Medical Acceptance of Intelligence Testing," in *Psychological Testing and American Society, 1880–1930*, ed. Michael M. Sokal (New Brunswick: Rutgers University Press, 1987), 46–74.
25. Ibid., 65.
26. Ibid., 62.
27. JoAnne Brown, *The Definition of a Profession: The Authority of Metaphor in the History of Intelligence Testing, 1890–1930* (Princeton: Princeton University Press, 1992), 41.
28. Walter E. Fernald, *The Burden of Feeble-Mindedness* (Boston: Massachusetts Society for Mental Hygiene, 1918), 6.
29. See Douglas Baynton, *Forbidden Signs: American Culture and the Campaign Against Sign Language* (Chicago: University of Chicago Press, 1996).

30. Brown, *The Definition of a Profession*, 39.
31. Goddard was also pointing out that "feeblemindedness" had been used inconsistently, sometimes referring to what he called "the entire range of mental defectives" and sometimes specifically referring to the highest grade. Henry H. Goddard, "Four Hundred Feeble-Minded Children Classified by the Binet Method," *Journal of Genetic Psychology* 17 (3) (1910): 445 (emphasis added).
32. Ibid. (emphasis added).
33. See Baynton, *Forbidden Signs*.
34. Goddard, "Four Hundred Feeble-Minded Children," 445.
35. Neurasthenia was a commonly diagnosed neurological disorder in the late nineteenth and early twentieth century that was characterized by fatigue and anxiety. See Gail Bederman, *Manliness and Civilization: A Cultural History of Gender and Race in the United States, 1880–1917* (Chicago: The University of Chicago Press, 1996), 88.
36. Ibid., 92.
37. Ibid., 97.
38. Ibid., 94.
39. Paul, *Controlling Human Heredity*, 40–49.
40. For a useful analysis of the significance of Goddard's Kallikak study, see James W. Trent, *Inventing the Feeble Mind: A History of Mental Retardation in the United States* (Berkeley: University of California Press, 1995), 163–65.
41. Kraut, *Silent Travelers*, 73.
42. Ibid., 74.
43. Ibid.
44. See Alexandra Minna Stern, *Eugenic Nation: Faults and Frontiers of Better Breeding in Modern America* (Berkeley: University of California Press, 2005), and Nayan Shah, *Contagious Divides: Epidemics and Race in San Francisco's Chinatown* (Berkeley, University of California Press, 2001).
45. Garland Allen, "Is a New Eugenics Afoot?" *Science* 294 (5540) (Oct. 5, 2001): 49–51.
46. Alison Bashford, "Where Did Eugenics Go?" in *The Oxford Handbook of the History of Eugenics*, eds. Alison Bashford and Philippa Levine (New York: Oxford University Press, 2010), 550.

BIBLIOGRAPHY

Antin, Mary. *The Promised Land*. Boston and New York: Houghton Mifflin Company, 1912.
Bashford, Alison. "Where Did Eugenics Go?" In *The Oxford Handbook of the History of Eugenics*, edited by Alison Bashford and Philippa Levine, 550. New York: Oxford University Press, 2010.
Baynton, Douglas. *Forbidden Signs: American Culture and the Campaign Against Sign Language*. Chicago: University of Chicago Press, 1996.
Bederman, Gail. *Manliness and Civilization: A Cultural History of Gender and Race in the United States, 1880–1917*. Chicago: The University of Chicago Press, 1996.
Brown, JoAnne. *The Definition of a Profession: The Authority of Metaphor in the History of Intelligence Testing, 1890–1930*. Princeton: Princeton University Press, 1992.
Daniels, Roger. *Coming to America: A History of Immigration and Ethnicity in American Life*. New York: Harper, 2002.

Deutsch, Nathaniel. *Inventing America's "Worst" Family: Eugenics, Islam, and the Fall and Rise of the Tribe of Ishmael*. Berkeley: University of California Press, 2009.

Dorr, Gregory Michael. *Segregation's Science: Eugenics and Society in Virginia*. Charlottesville: University of Virginia Press, 2008.

Dowbiggin, Ian Robert. *Keeping America Sane: Psychiatry and Eugenics in the United States and Canada, 1880–1940*. Ithaca: Cornell University Press, 1997.

Fairchild, Amy. *Science at the Borders: Immigrant Medical Inspection and the Shaping of the Modern Industrial Labor Force*. Baltimore: Johns Hopkins University Press, 2003.

Fernald, Walter E. *The Burden of Feeble-Mindedness*. Boston: Massachusetts Society for Mental Hygiene, 1918.

Haller, Mark H. *Eugenics: Hereditarian Attitudes in American Thought*. New Brunswick: Rutgers University Press, 1984.

Kevles, Daniel J. *In the Name of Eugenics: Genetics and the Uses of Human Heredity*. New York: Knopf, 1985.

Kline, Wendy. *Building a Better Race: Gender, Sexuality, and Eugenics from the Turn of the Century to the Baby Boom*. Berkeley: University of California Press, 2001.

Kluchin, Rebecca. *Fit to Be Tied: Sterilization and Reproductive Rights in America, 1950–1980*. Rutgers: Rutgers University Press, 2009.

Kraut, Alan. *Silent Travelers: Germs, Genes, and the "Immigrant Menace."* Baltimore: Johns Hopkins University Press, 1994.

Larson, Edward J. *Sex, Race, and Science: Eugenics in the Deep South*. Baltimore: Johns Hopkins University Press, 1995.

Paul, Diane. *Controlling Human Heredity*. Amherst: Humanity Books, 1999.

Rosen, Christine. *Preaching Eugenics: Religious Leaders and the American Eugenics Movement*. Oxford, New York: Oxford University Press, 2004.

Schoen, Johanna. *Choice and Coercion: Birth Control, Sterilization, and Abortion in Public Health and Welfare*. Chapel Hill: University of North Carolina Press, 2005.

Shah, Nayan. *Contagious Divides: Epidemics and Race in San Francisco's Chinatown*. Berkeley: University of California Press, 2001.

Stepan, Nancy. *The Hour of Eugenics: Race, Gender, and Nation in Latin America*. Ithaca: Cornell University Press, 1996.

Stern, Alexandra. *Eugenic Nation: Faults and Frontiers of Better Breeding in Modern America*. Berkeley: University of California Press, 2005.

Trent, James W. *Inventing the Feeble Mind: A History of Mental Retardation in the United States*. Berkeley: University of California Press, 1995.

Zenderland, Leila. "The Debate Over Diagnosis: Henry Herbert Goddard and the Medical Acceptance of Intelligence Testing." In *Psychological Testing and American Society, 1880–1930*, edited by Michael M. Sokal, 46–74, New Brunswick: Rutgers University Press, 1987.

CHAPTER 15

....

THE WORLD OF THE
IMMIGRANT WORKER

....

JAMES R. BARRETT

THE British labor historian E. P. Thompson called *The Making of the English Working Class* a kind of collective biography of England's laborers and their development into a politically conscious social class. Born in the welter of early industrialization, Thompson argued, the English working class reached its maturity in the 1830s with the emergence of large-scale unions and the Chartist struggles for the franchise. This process was not strictly economic or political in nature. A distinct working-class culture also emerged, and it was through the transmission of this culture that class was understood and reproduced across the generations.[1]

Long after Thompson's book appeared in the mid 1960s, it continued to inspire American social historians who took it as a kind of model, and for a while it seemed to work.[2] But as American social historians worked to apply Thompson's modexl of British working-class formation, they encountered a vital difference separating the stories of these two societies. Successive waves of migration over 200 years vastly complicated the process of class formation in the nation. The lessons that were learned, the organizations and ideas that emerged, the leaders who rose over the course of one generation in England were reinvented over and over again with each generation of immigrant workers who entered the United States. In encountering urban–industrial society, sometimes for the first time, each immigrant group brought its own culture, language, and institutions, vying with one another over the model that would best fit their experiences and needs in the new world. In this situation, the formation of working-class cultures was often segmented on the basis of ethnocultural identity with characteristic labor institutions—unions, fraternal and educational groups, and even radical political parties organized along ethnic lines.[3]

In the United States, this "making" occurred over and over again in one community of migrant people after another. The resulting working-class cultures and movements were always in danger of fragmentation along lines of race, religion, ethnicity, gender and skill.[4] The challenge facing working-class organizers in the United States was how best to bridge these divisions in order to build a strong movement based on diverse peoples. Immigration lies at the heart of this narrative.

In early industrialization, a generation of young Yankee farm women constituted America's first factory proletariat in New England's textile towns. In cities and smaller industrial communities, they mixed with British, Ulster Irish, and native-born skilled workers and a population of laboring poor, including free and enslaved blacks, to constitute the American working-class population.[5] By the 1830s, a labor movement and a class culture and politics, not unlike Thompson's, had emerged—trade unions, cooperatives, "working men's" institutes, political parties, newspapers, and a small class of intellectuals who espoused a new view of political economy reflecting the experiences and interests of working-class people. By the middle of the nineteenth century, this first generation of American industrial workers had "learned the rules of the game."[6] They demanded not only better wages but also shorter hours, universal free education, and other reforms aimed at making the United States a more egalitarian society.

Within a decade of America's first labor movement in the 1830s, however, its cities were increasingly overwhelmed by a new tide of immigrants, German artisans and Irish peasants above all, who transformed the face of America's working-class population. In the 1840s, nativist movements swept the society and promising local labor movements were torn apart along ethnic and religious lines. In Philadelphia, Catholic and Protestant handloom weavers who had helped to create the city's vibrant General Trades Union and waged a successful general strike now turned on one another in streets and workplaces over which version of the Bible was the proper one for Philadelphia's school children.[7]

Herbert Gutman conceptualized this process as one of interaction between these successive waves of migrants and the evolving fabric of an urban industrial society. Each generation of immigrant workers faced these tensions anew, and each generation of labor activists sought to face the problem by either excluding immigrants entirely or by developing strategies to bring their constituents together across these lines. The process was even more complex than Gutman suggested because it was racially fraught, as people of color migrated to American industrial cities from Asia, the American South, and Mexico, raising the prospect of racial conflict. It is a mistake to consider European immigrants in isolation from these migrants of color who faced many of the same challenges. Throughout most of the twentieth century and in many cases earlier, immigrant workers toiled alongside blacks and Latinos, fashioning their own identities and institutional and cultural lives in the midst of this ethnic and racial diversity, while retaining some sense of their distinct cultures.

Between the 1880s and the mid-1920s, more than 25 million "new immigrants" arrived in the United States, increasingly from eastern and southeastern Europe. They joined the earlier generation, largely from northwestern Europe, and a smaller population from Asia, mostly Chinese. At about the same time that this huge wave began to diminish, during World War I and in the following decade, internal migration brought millions of African American and Mexican workers and their families to industrial communities. These migrations produced the modern American working-class population. With some notable exceptions, the new immigrants became increasingly segregated in terms of both ethnicity and class in the course of their settling into industrial cities.[8]

The interaction of diverse ethnic groups and the effort to integrate women and racial minorities created a multiethnic American working-class culture and the nation's powerful industrial union movement in the era between the Great Depression and the postwar era. After the immigration reforms of 1965, a new immigrant working class has emerged amidst the catastrophic decline of the labor movement, but the dynamic tension over the integration of immigrant workers has continued.

While immigration historians have traditionally focused on particular communities of European immigrants and their children in the era up to World War II, recent studies of these immigrant workers' experiences have stressed their *relational* quality, that is, an interethnic approach. Studies of the labor migration since the revision of immigration laws in 1965 likewise stress comparisons and contrasts between the various groups involved. If it were ever possible to write of American ethnic working-class communities in splendid isolation from one another, it certainly is not now.

Varieties of Immigrant Working-Class Community

Immigrant workers created their communities in a diverse range of industrial spaces: metropolitan neighborhoods, small industrial cities, and coal mining and steel mill towns. Few lived in "ethnic ghettos"; their communities instead tended to be physically integrated but culturally segregated. They built their distinct ethnic cultures and institutions within larger urban spaces that were quite diverse, where they often came into contact with workers from other ethnic groups at work and in the community. Yet they retained their connections to distinctive ethnic communities and cultures.[9] Thus, for all the diversity of many industrial cities, immigrant working-class neighborhoods often displayed a peculiarly closed, communal quality. As the composition of workforces changed, competition for jobs and confrontations between strikers and strikebreakers often pitted one ethnic group against another. The West Side Irish dock neighborhoods in Manhattan were classic cases, but Chicago, Boston, Philadelphia, and other cities were also riddled with "dead lines"—imaginary boundaries, enforced by neighborhood gangs and aimed at keeping ethnically distinct communities separated from one another.

Two of the most impressive examples of ethnocultural working-class cultures of the late nineteenth and early twentieth centuries were those created by German workers in Chicago and other cities and the one that emerged amidst the massive influx of Russian and East European Jews, notably on the Lower East Side of Manhattan.

Chicago's late nineteenth-century radical labor movement was a patchwork of ethnic organizations, ranging from the mainline trade unions (occupied mostly by the more skilled English speakers) to the Knights of Labor assemblies (followed particularly by the immigrant Irish who often mixed their labor reform and union activity with radical Irish nationalism) to the socialist and anarchist unions and working-class cultures created especially by German and Bohemian immigrants. Theirs was a more cerebral world than we might envision for a nineteenth-century laboring community, one where worker–intellectuals might quote Goethe or Shakespeare as readily as Marx. Such remarkable characters as the Haymarket anarchists August Spies and Michael Fischer, along with many others who will never make it onto the pages of history books, were self-taught free thinkers "exceedingly well read in philosophy, history, literature, and political economy," according to labor historian James Green. Working all day, usually at manual labor, they spent their evenings reading and debating the issues of the day. Such radical subcultures were a way of life for thousands of immigrant workers.[10]

The obsession of the era's businessmen with the danger posed by such radicals helps to explain tragedies like the events at Haymarket (1886) and other violence against immigrant workers. In the aftermath of the Haymarket riot, city fathers raided the offices of unions and political organizations, shutting down workers' newspapers and indicting key radical leaders in a trial that resulted in the execution of some and imprisonment of others. It was the first of several "Red Scares" in which authorities tended to associate the radical threat with immigrant workers and their organizations. Such tendencies reemerged in the World War I era and the early 1920s and again in the decade following World War II, which we associate with the term "McCarthyism."[11]

On the Lower East Side at the turn of the century, an impressive array of economic, cultural, philanthropic, and intellectual institutions knitted Jewish immigrant workers into a rich radical subculture—Yiddish theatre, literature, journalism, and art. The Socialist *Daily Forward* edited by Abraham Cahan, one of the community's foremost intellectuals, became the voice of a transnational Yiddish working class drawn from Russia and nations throughout Eastern Europe, though challenged in the interwar years by a lively Communist daily, *Freiheit*. The Workmen's Circle organized study groups and social events, while the Hebrew Trades organized Yiddish unions.[12]

More than in most immigrant communities, Jewish women played a vital part in labor and socialist activities. They not only organized "new unions" along industrial lines, led giant strikes in garment manufacturing, and fostered the cross-class alliances embodied in the Women's Trade Union League (1903–1950), but, as members of the Socialist and later the Communist Party, they also pioneered much of early American feminism.[13]

What happened with such a flourish on the Lower East Side occurred to a lesser extent in immigrant communities throughout the country. However, many immigrant workers and their families lived not in cities but in relatively small factory, mill, and mine towns. Ethnic enclaves with fairly elaborate institutional and organizational forms could certainly form in such places. The steel river mill towns up and down the Monongahela and Allegheny rivers, for example, contained a range of ethnic groups—Poles, Slovaks, Russians, Ukranians, Ruthenians, each organized around its ethnic parish, each with its own fraternal/beneficial and cultural groups. The topographies of these river mill towns reflected their social structures, with the black and the most recent immigrant laborers down along the river "flats" closest to the mills, Irish and British skilled workers occupying the slopes of the hill along with some lower level management, and the mill superintendents and town professionals up near the top of the hill, farthest from the mill.[14]

The copper mining and smelting town of Butte, Montana, offers a particularly striking case of a cohesive ethnic enclave and its transformation with successive waves of immigrant workers. Throughout the late nineteenth and early twentieth centuries, the miners came overwhelmingly from Ireland, especially the small copper mining region around Cork. They created a vibrant local culture based on their parishes and fraternal and nationalist organizations. The miners, the town's Irish born patriarch Marcus Daly, and its small business and professional class shared Butte's Irish cultural institutions, and Daly's Anaconda Corporation hired through parish networks, often posting job notices in Gaelic. Daley knew the leaders of the Butte Miners Union intimately, paid his miners relatively good wages, and enjoyed tranquil labor relations for a generation. Butte's most serious social division was not along class lines but between this solid core of settled, organized, church-going families and a peripheral group of transient, single young men who frequented Butte's wide-open saloons, brothels, and casinos. The Butte Miners Union became a bulwark of defensive ethnic working-class culture, and Butte became an Irish preserve in the far west.[15]

But all of this changed in the decade before World War I, as it did in other industries and regions. A corporate merger movement, new production technologies and management methods, and the unprecedented flood of immigrants from a much broader geographic spectrum into American factories, mills, and mines produced a new and more contentious era in industrial relations. Standard Oil's Amalgamated Copper Company bought out Daly, scrapped his paternalistic management system, introduced new technology and a speed up, and assembled a "disposable workforce" of truly remarkable diversity—not only Finns and Slavs of all sorts, but also Syrians, Afghans, and Egyptians—38 ethnic groups in all. Such diversity was characteristic of one industry after another in the early twentieth century.[16] Men and women from more than 40 nationality groups labored in Chicago's meat packing plants, dozens of nationalities toiled underground in the anthracite and bituminous coal industries, and a similar array produced the nation's steel. Ethnic conflict was not unusual, but the most striking result of all this was the level of solidarity and militancy diverse groups of immigrants achieved in the face of seemingly insurmountable odds. The World War I era was a moment of great labor mobilization not despite but, rather, because of the legions of "new immigrants" in American industry.

In Chicago, where the Stockyards Labor Council's organizers set out to build an inter-ethnic, interracial organization, 10,000 Polish and Lithuanian laborers poured into the unions in one month. The new movement embraced not only the most recent, unskilled immigrants, but also thousands of black migrants. In steel, a similar movement allied with local church and fraternal groups to penetrate the mill towns' immigrant cultures, employing multilingual organizers and flyers printed in numerous languages. Here again, the new immigrants responded with great enthusiasm. In the anthracite and bituminous coalfields, Italians, Poles, Hungarians, Slovaks, Belgians, and others—a bewildering array of ethnic groups—were drawn together with the help of bilingual organizers and radicals in each of the communities. In Butte, a new Metal Mine Workers' Union sparked to life when 165 miners were burned alive in a mine accident in 1918. Composed of all the new ethnic groups as well as younger, more radical Irish immigrants, the new union replaced the old Butte Miners' Union and led a revolt.[17]

Such interethnic organizing occurred in industrial outposts throughout the United States during these years; without an interethnic approach, activists recognized, there would be no labor organization at all. Likewise, traditional studies focused on particular ethnic communities make it difficult for historians to understand how such multiethnic and multiracial movements emerged. Studying class experiences and the emergence of the new movements requires an interethnic approach.

In smaller, ethnically diverse mine and mill towns, it became difficult to maintain the integrity of distinct ethnic cultures over time. The result was the gradual emergence of broader identities based on social class, religion, and race. We often envision cities as the bastions of working-class cosmopolitanism, but remote mining camps and other outposts of "frontier capitalism" in Canada, the United States, and other rapidly developing societies might be better places to see the social and cultural effects of global migration. In coal and metal mining, for example, employers drew their labor forces from a staggering range of peoples. New immigrants embraced a pan-Slavic "Mill Hunky" identity in the steel valley areas of Ohio and western Pennsylvania.[18] A broader American Catholic identity gradually and unevenly subsumed a variety of ethnic groups in the interwar and World War II era.[19] And much of the scholarship on "whiteness" reveals the emergence of white racial identity among immigrant workers who had never thought in these terms.[20] But there is little doubt that experience of social class also formed the basis of such broader identities, particularly with the emergence of a militant industrial union movement in the 1930s and 1940s, which embraced a broad spectrum of working-class people across ethnic, racial, skill, and gender lines.

We still know little about what might be called *hybrid* ethnic working-class cultures. In the earlier generation of nineteenth-century immigrants, German-speaking Marxists created an ethnically expansive movement.[21] Swedish, Danish, and Norwegian labor and socialist activists built an interethnic "Scandinavian" movement based on ethnic building trades unions and socialist language federations.[22] A combination of native discrimination and proletarianization produced even closer interethnic identification and relations among some "new immigrants" from various backgrounds drawn together in often rather brutal industrial environments. Slavic immigrant steelworkers in Harrisburg, Pennsylvania, for example, shared not only common industrial grievances but also the middle class and native workers' scorn for "Hunkies." By the postwar era, Slavic steelworkers in the Pittsburgh region embraced the label with pride: "Yes, I am a Mill Hunky."[23] Rudolph Vecoli noted a similar process among Finnish, Croatian, and other iron ore miners in northern Minnesota who came to be called and also came to see themselves as "Iron Rangers." While the immigrants were extremely diverse and recognized distinctions among themselves, the fact that they were so often lumped together began to shape their own consciousness.[24] Donna Gabaccia and Fraser Ottanelli delineate what they term a "Latin melting pot" phenomenon in which Italian immigrants and Spanish-speaking workers created hybrid radical working-class subcultures in a variety of settings around Europe and North and South America.

Perhaps the most striking U.S. case of interethnic radical culture developed in Tampa's Ybor City where Cubans, Spaniards, and recent Sicilian immigrants created a rich culture of opposition, a radical industrial union, and important cultural and economic institutions embracing women workers, despite the strength of *machismo* in Latin culture.[25] But Ybor City was not unique. Such interethnic cultures thrived in cities throughout North and South America. The anarchist and anarchosyndicalist labor movements of these regions were based in large part on the interaction of immigrants from Italian, Spanish, and other backgrounds.[26] Among both Italians and Germans, political repression in the old country and the decision of political militants to follow the migrants abroad both facilitated such internationalization of labor radicalism.[27]

This process may have advanced further and more quickly in smaller industrial communities where it was more difficult to sustain the sort of elaborate ethnically segmented local cultures characteristic of large cities. In coal mining towns and smaller manufacturing cities, recent immigrants interacted with those from other backgrounds in the factory or down in the mine, where the workforces were necessarily diverse and all nationalities shared common tasks and dangers.[28] In Illinois mining towns, Belgian and Italian anarchists joined with other activists in forging such a vibrant movement that small communities like Spring Valley, Illinois, joined metropolises like New York and Chicago on the itineraries of international radical figures such as Emma Goldman and Luigi Gagliano.[29]

Textile mill towns in the South were quite homogeneous with native-born whites normally tending looms and a small number of blacks in auxiliary and maintenance positions. Early twentieth-century textile mill towns in New England and Pennsylvania, however, were remarkable mixtures of people. Immigrant mass strikes rocked these towns throughout the second and third decades of the twentieth century. One center of such activity was Lawrence, Massachusetts, where an earlier generation of British and Irish workers had largely given way to Poles, Lithuanians, Italians, and Russian and East European Jews.[30] The jumble of ethnic, national, and international solidarities displayed in such strikes begins to suggest the remarkable complexity of immigrant workers' mentalities. This is conveyed in David Montgomery's observation that these immigrant strikers could often be seen arranged by ethnic group, marching behind the American flag, and singing the *Internationale*.[31]

With labor at a premium and the cost of living skyrocketing, immigrant workers revolted during the World War I years with strikes exploding in one open-shop industry after another—meat packing, garment manufacturing, coal mining, and, of course, steel in the great strike of 1919. Many of these multiethnic movements were crushed in Open Shop movements after World War I, but they signaled the arrival of a new generation of labor activists and a new set of strategies that set the stage for the interethnic and interracial industrial union movements of the 1930s and 1940s. We have just begun to write the ethnic history of such organizing.[32]

THE WORLD OF WORK

An immigrant worker often found his or her job through networks—a recommendation from one's family, friends, neighbors, or priest. Yet such networks excluded as well as integrated newcomers. In early twentieth-century New York the Irish county societies often provided such an introduction in particular industries. As a result, workers from certain parts of Ireland ended up doing certain kinds of work. Kerry men were found among paper handlers, those from Donegal in the city's construction excavations and tunnel work, those from Clare on the lower West Side docks. Irish domestics provided leads for sisters and nieces for work as maids or cooks. The county societies persisted long after the heyday of Irish immigration not only for of their dances and outings, but also because they were excellent places to find work.[33] Political and neighborhood connections also allowed the Irish to get jobs on the police and fire department and other government work. Even Irish "greenhorns" had access to parish and political networks. It went without saying, however, that where the Irish were in a position to "put in a good word," newer migrants were at a distinct disadvantage.[34]

Such networking within ethnic communities often led to work niches where one ethnic group tended to dominate an industry, at least in the short run. This was true of Russian and Eastern European Jews in New York's garment manufacturing industry, once the preserve of Irish and German women. As early as 1897, about 60 percent of the New York's Jewish labor force worked in the apparel field where 75 percent of the workers in the industry were Jews. Italians undercut the Jewish rates considerably, especially in women's clothing, entering the industry in large numbers from the turn of the century on. By 1905 perhaps 35 percent of workers in the women's clothing industry were Italian, mostly women. The Jewish workers' main response was to organize interethnically, an effort leading to growth of the International Ladies Garment Workers' Union in New York and to the Amalgamated Clothing Workers' of America in Chicago.[35] Due in part to high levels of education, Jewish immigrants were moving out of these niches and into government jobs, teaching, and the professions as early as the interwar years.[36]

Meanwhile, Italian men undercut Irish laborers in unskilled construction work and on the docks. By 1910 almost one-fourth of Italian men in New York worked as building laborers and represented one out of every five of the city's construction workers. Conflicts ensued between ethnic groups competing in the labor market, but the Italians pushed the Irish not so much out, but up. The Irish moved into skilled or foremen positions from the end of the nineteenth century on. By 1910, an estimated 72 percent of Irish construction workers were in skilled jobs and many were becoming small contractors.[37] As late as World War II, 80 percent of New York's Italians were still in blue-collar jobs, though they moved gradually into more skilled positions with many of the rest owning small businesses. By the late twentieth century, with the advent of the newest immigrants, many had moved into management and the professions.[38]

In general, the lower the skill level, the more brutal and arbitrary the employment system—even in those cases where ethnic and neighborhood connections counted. In the Chicago stockyards, thousands of Polish, Lithuanians, black migrants, and others lined up in front of the various slaughterhouses. It helped to know someone, but otherwise, the foreman simply picked those who appeared to have the strongest arms and backs.[39]

On Manhattan's West Side, Irish longshoremen needed to be close to their work for the morning "shape-up" in a volatile casual labor market. The functioning of this market, carefully cultivated by the shippers, virtually guaranteed ethnic competition over jobs. New York harbor on the eve of World War I had about three longshoremen for every job. Twenty-five hundred men might be hired on a typical day, but 5000 or more would shape-up. Whatever conflict might have risen from cultural tensions, employers' habit of introducing outsiders to lower wages or break up labor organizations reinforced a suspicion of strangers and enhanced animosities among ethnic groups.[40] Italian and black workers gradually made their way onto the waterfront, sometimes as strikebreakers, but where they could, as in Manhattan, the Irish preserved the best jobs for themselves. Employers' habit of introducing blacks and recent immigrants as strikebreakers heightened tensions between the Irish and later migrants.[41]

Earlier immigrants could be mentors to the newcomers or bosses. The Irish, who moved up only gradually from laboring to skilled jobs, were most apt to manage newer immigrants on construction sites or in factory, mine, or mill, on New York's docks, or in Chicago's slaughterhouses. Others became small contractors.[42]

Labor historians have often stressed the importance of "preindustrial" work cultures immigrants brought with them from the old world, but these were often brutally suppressed. Foremen at the Ford Highland Park assembly plant might not be able to converse with their immigrant charges, but they learned at least one phrase in Polish, Italian, and other languages—"Hurry up!" Polish workers writing home often employed animal metaphors to convey their work and their treatment.[43] Bosses had their own lessons to teach immigrant workers, and one of these had to do with who held power in the workplace.

Something like the ethnic niches carved out by Irish, Jewish, and Italian immigrants in the early twentieth century reemerged at its end in the newest immigration to New York, as Chinese, Mexicans, Puerto Ricans, Dominicans, and other recent groups settled into the city's remaining garment industry and other light manufacturing and service jobs. While the labor market and the nation's economy have changed enormously, along with the ethnic composition of its working-class population, some aspects of immigrants' employment situations have changed little from the twentieth century. Many of these ethnic niches are characterized by low wages and dismal working conditions, as they were in the early twentieth century.[44]

In the most recent generation of immigration, the Mexican field hand or service worker has become a kind of symbol for immigrant workers, but even the common assumption that most Asian immigrant groups are moving quickly into the professional middle class and the suburbs is somewhat misleading. Large numbers of East and South Asian immigrants have arrived with education and resources and soon established small business or entered the professions. Some managed to skip the city entirely and move directly to the suburbs. But millions of Chinese, Southeast Asian, Korean, and Filipino immigrants work in factories or service jobs, while thousands of South Asian, Middle Eastern, and African immigrants drive taxis or work in small shops or restaurants.[45] In New York City, as late as 1990, one-third of Chinese immigrants worked in low-wage restaurant jobs, while 18,000 toiled in the city's thicket of 450 small garment shops. The result, according to a labor market study in the early 1990s, was that Chinese workers earned only 57 percent of their counterparts in industries with lower concentrations of Chinese.[46]

Nor have the most recent immigrants tended to displace African Americans from the better-paid manufacturing and other blue collar jobs. In general, it seems, they have gone in one of two directions—into the professions, technical positions, or small businesses where there is little competition with blacks, or into low-wage domestic, service and manufacturing jobs that African Americans have largely abandoned.[47]

The mixed employment situation facing recent labor migrants at the end of the twentieth century was summed up by a Chinese immigrant: "New York offers many fortunes but unequal opportunities for newcomers. Not everyone can make it here. It is like a happy melting pot for some, a pressure cooker for many others, and still a dumpster for the unfortunate."[48]

AMERICANIZATION FROM THE BOTTOM UP

Changes in the way we look at immigration history have brought us back rather forcefully to an older theme—acculturation. Some immigration historians and sociologists even seem prepared to resurrect the old "melting pot" image in an effort to grasp the process by which European immigrants became American workers. But the older "straight line" notions neglect obvious ways in which ethnicity persisted as a vital form of identity, while more subtle notions of have become so diffuse and ill defined that the term is no longer very useful in explaining working-class ethnicity.[49]

The current research on this process of "becoming American" stresses the gradual integration of immigrant workers into broader social and political movements, and their own agency in creating a new multiethnic society and culture in the United States in the course of the twentieth century.[50] As Gary Gerstle notes, the new work on "Americanization," much of it written by labor historians, emphasizes the immigrants' own roles in creating "many Americanisms." "Thus," Gerstle concludes, "Americanization lost the clear linearity it has possessed in earlier accounts and became a chaotic, pluralistic site of postmodern invention." In the 1980s and early 1990s, there was a continuing emphasis on particularism and racism, especially in the new immigration fields of Latino/Latina and Asian American history.[51] The big change among social historians has been this turn toward the interethnic, the process of acculturation, and the creation of a society characterized by diversity and hybrid cultures, politics, and social movements.

A number of influences have produced this shift in perspective. Urban historians, in placing immigrant communities into the broader political economy of industrial cities, have described the creation of multiethnic neighborhoods and noted considerable social contact across ethnic lines, even as these cities became increasingly segregated in terms of race.[52] Likewise, the systematic application of gender as a category of analysis and an analytical tool to explore immigrant workers within and between ethnic enclaves has also tended to situate particular ethnic gender and sexual subcultures within a broader context.[53]

Studies of racial identity have examined the process by which many European immigrants entered American society in marginal racial categories and then gradually achieved an ascribed status as "whites." More importantly, perhaps, historians are just beginning to analyze the immigrants' own values and attitudes regarding race. These undoubtedly drew on old world prejudices and notions of difference, but they were increasingly influenced by mainstream U.S. racial ideology and practice. Too often for European immigrants, developing an identity as "American" was linked to a process by which they also came to identify as "white." The most important influence of "whiteness studies" in immigration history has been the investigation of racist values, language, and repertories of behavior, that is, the reproduction of racism among immigrant people and the implications of all this for African American, Latina/Latino, and Asian migrants who were excluded from that broader identity. The relationship between Americanization and racism among European immigrant workers has emerged as a major theme in recent work on race, politics, and culture in the twentieth century.[54]

The questions and categories that have done most to turn scholars toward what Vecoli termed an "interethnic" approach have often derived from working-class history. At work and in the community, Vecoli argued, we need far more attention to "patterns of attraction and repulsion, integration and segregation, cooperation and conflict, as they operated in various spheres."[55] An earlier generation of scholarship on Americanization stressed various elite efforts to acculturate immigrants—employer, government, and settlement house programs, with the more recent work tending to stress the coercive dimensions of these efforts.[56] Labor historians' initiatives rise in part from their traditional concerns with working, living, and political experiences *shared* by workers from a variety of ethnic backgrounds and with efforts to understand the process of working-class formation in the midst of great ethnic and racial diversity. The contention, one that requires a good deal more research, is that much of the gradual acculturation immigrant workers experienced likely occurred more through informal contacts at the workplace or in the community than through any sort of formal, top-down process.

Labor historians have tended to focus on social movements, including unions and political organizations, which were often interethnic in their composition and perspective and seem to have played a role in "Americanization" either through informal contacts and experience in organizing campaigns, strikes, and protests, or through formal educational programs. There were several elements to labor's version of Americanism. Not surprisingly, activists frequently emphasized basic civil liberties, particularly free speech, and encouraged immigrants to speak up and defend their rights. Such ideals were hardly abstract. In coal company, steel mill, and many other open shop industrial communities, organizing often began with a struggle for free speech, with immigrants learning the values of these freedoms in the midst of organizing activities, strikes, and demonstrations.

Organizers might also struggle to instill a measure of ethnic tolerance (what today we might call "multiculturalism"), if only because successful organizing demanded such tolerance in the context of great ethnic diversity. Besides teaching immigrants inter-ethnic solidarity, unions did more than any civics lesson to impart the principles and methods of democratic government by relating them to practical matters: wages, hours, and working conditions. For many immigrant workers, introduction to the American political and economic system came not through night-school classes but through translated discussion and debate at union meetings, informal conversations at work, or labor movement publications printed in various languages. And the union's version of Americanism was likely to be different from the one conveyed in employer programs, emphasizing the free expression of one's opinions and the importance of solidarity with fellow workers to demand one's rights.[57]

Labor activists frequently invested their material demands with the power of democratic rhetoric by speaking of an "American standard of living," by which they meant higher wages, shorter working hours, and decent working conditions. Such appeals could be used to *exclude* some, as in the case of the working-class agitation against Chinese immigrants, but they could also facilitate integration of newcomers, imparting the basic values of the movement while establishing its legitimacy in the eyes of the public at large. During World War I, this notion of an American standard provided unions with a patriotic image and immigrant workers with the prospect of an ideal American life for themselves and their children.[58]

Labor's own version of Americanism reflected the era's patriotic discourse. During the Great Steel Strike (1919), the organizers' *Strike Bulletin* asked, "Why are Strikers Called 'Foreigners'?" and answered in four different languages: "The papers say you foreign workers ought to be 'Americanized.' What does that mean? It means—or ought to mean—to make Americans of you, to teach you American ideals....The right of workmen in America to belong to labor unions and to bargain with their employers . . . is an **AMERICAN** right and the strike is an **AMERICAN** method, recognized as constitutional and legal. . . .If you believe in **FREEDOM**, you have **AMERICANISM** in your heart, wherever you were born and whatever language you speak. You will make good Americans if you are willing to **FIGHT** for freedom by **PEACEABLE, LEGAL** methods."[59] "The steelworkers' meetings," head organizer William Z. Foster concluded, "were schools in practical Americanization."[60]

The argument is not that social class was more important than ethnicity in immigrants' identity. Rather, working-class settings and experiences can help us understand how immigrant workers came to terms with their new environments and, in turn, how ethnic diversity shaped the process of class formation in the industrial United States. If we assume any particular trajectory for this process, or make too many assumptions about immigrant workers on the basis of their shared wage earning status, we tend to oversimplify an experience that immigration historians have already demonstrated is vastly complex and contingent on numerous factors related to ethnic difference. The extremely high volume of return migration, the strength and persistence of ethnic institutions in working-class communities, and the language and behavior of immigrant workers themselves all suggest the continuing significance of ethnic identity throughout the early twentieth century and beyond.[61] But as the second generation of the various ethnic communities mixed with African American and Mexican migrants in the interwar years, the fusion of these cultures produced an interethnic popular culture at the very center of American life.[62]

UNIONIZATION AND THE NEW IMMIGRANT WORKING CLASS

The full demographic effect of the dramatic revision of immigration law in 1965, blunted in the late sixties by economic problems in the United States, did not immediately produce a huge wave of immigrant labor. By the late 1970s and for most of the following three decades, however, boom conditions, the demand for low wage labor as a result of the globalization of markets, and the gradual disintegration of the American labor movement created considerable demand for immigrant labor. The effects can be seen most clearly in California, but such effects are not restricted to the West coast, as immigrants have spread to small industrial centers throughout the United States, including the South. Between 1970 and 2000, California's labor force doubled, but its already large Latino component grew by 500 percent, and its Asian American component, by 800 percent. By 1990 one-third of the LA population was composed of immigrants. The figure for the United States overall was about 8 percent. Interestingly, this great wave of immigration still did not equal proportionally the one in the early twentieth century. The proportion of immigrants in the United States was about twice as high as that in 1990, while about half of New York City's population was foreign born in 1910. While a disproportionate number of Asian immigrants entered high skilled technical and professional positions, most Mexicans and Central Americans settled into low-wage service and light manufacturing jobs. By the 1990s, about two-thirds of Latino/as were laborers or factory and service workers.[63] In this sense, the most recent Latino immigrants have occupied a position in the labor market roughly comparable to the Eastern European immigrants of the early twentieth century.[64]

The arrival of these newest immigrants has paralleled a dramatic decline in the labor movement, particularly since the early 1980s. It has been produced by aggressive employer tactics, hostile government policy and legislation, low-wage global competition, and uninspired union leadership, but the labor movement remains a site of organization and protest, as it was for earlier generations of immigrants. The immigrant proportion of the working-class population has expanded at a rate nearly comparable to the last great wave of immigration at the turn of the nineteenth and in the early twentieth century.[65]

There is a fit, of course, between the decline of unions and changes in the nation's occupational structure from a manufacturing to a service and information based economy. The newer immigrants are concentrated in difficult-to-organize sectors with low union rates and this assured that most would not be union members.

Yet many immigrants, and particularly Latino/a workers, have embraced the union message. Like so many immigrants before them, they often viewed labor organization as both an avenue of upward social mobility and a means of socialization and acculturation, as part of the process of becoming American. The most successful campaigns share a number of strategies in common with earlier immigrant organizing. They often employ radicals from within or outside the community, mobilize solidarity movements through existing community institutions, especially religious congregations, and rely on mass actions by rank and file workers. As in earlier movements, the most receptive have tended not to be the most recent but, rather, those who have either settled in and "learned the rules of the game" or those who arrived in the United States with either trade union or ideological commitments, as in the case of some immigrants from El Salvador and Guatemala.[66] Some of these movements among both Latino and Asian workers on both coasts have established worker centers that provide not only employment information and translation services, but also language classes and legal advice for undocumented immigrants.[67]

One factor that has changed in terms of immigrant workers' prospects for organization was the labor movement's attitude toward them. Historically, unions had exhibited their own nativism and supported immigration restriction. Craft unions, exclusive by nature, long advocated immigration restriction and many of the AFL's constituent unions refused to organize immigrants, women, and racial minorities. Throughout most of the late nineteenth and twentieth centuries, the AFL and later the AFL-CIO defined immigrants not only as outsiders to "American Labor," but also as a threat to it. As a result, labor supported quotas, literacy tests, and other barriers. A variety of other movements, including labor reform and even radical organizations, defined the notion of "Labor" narrowly, excluding many immigrants from its embrace. The Knights of Labor, a remarkably open group by the standards of the time, organized the unskilled, immigrants, women, and African American workers, but they refused Chinese. The strong right wing of the Socialist Party of America tended to support immigration restriction and largely ignore the plight of African Americans in part because many of these radicals subscribed to reigning racial analyses that placed both blacks and most recent immigrants much lower on the racial scale than the native-born and older immigrant groups like the British and Germans. Labor agitation against Asian and particularly Chinese immigrant laborers, often led by Irish immigrants, was particularly severe throughout the late nineteenth century, and continued in Seattle, San Francisco, and other cities with large Chinese population well into the twentieth century.[68]

Having been anti-immigrant for more than a century, organized labor's position on immigration policy has been transformed in the early twenty-first century. This dramatic shift in policy has been both a cause and effect of the transformation of its membership base through the successful organization of immigrant workers. The AFL-CIO now supports amnesty programs and a system that would gradually legalize the status of millions of undocumented immigrants, while it actively defends the rights of immigrant workers

As David Roediger notes, the very term "American labor," assumed for so long to be synonymous with the white male working-class, has gone through a profound change in the period since the 1960s. In terms of the unionized portion of the labor force, this shift as well as changes in the nation's occupational structure, particularly the decline in manufacturing and the rise of service work, created a very different labor movement.[69]

As late as the 1980s, half of the U.S. labor force and more than half of its unionized component consisted of white males, more than a third of them in manufacturing and most of the rest in traditional male jobs in construction and transportation. White males now represent only a third of the unionized work force. The immigrant share has roughly doubled with Latinos and Latinas predominating, while the heart of the union movement has shifted from manufacturing and construction to service and public sector jobs. The black proportion of union labor has remained fairly consistent over the past 30 years, ranging from 13 percent to about 15 percent. Thus, the new labor movement is increasingly immigrant and female.[70]

In the case of Mexican immigrants, organizers could tap into a long tradition of unionism and political activism, not only in California and the Southwest, but also in Chicago and other parts of the industrial heartland. From the CIO organizing in field and factory in the 1930s and 1940s through the United Farm Workers Movement of the 1960s and 1970s, Mexican activists saw labor organization as part of a broader campaign for the civil rights of immigrants and their children. As in earlier organizing campaigns and strikes among immigrant workers, community networks and solidarity provided great cohesion for these movements.[71] As the "new unions" of the early twentieth century had served as vehicles of defense and assimilation for Eastern European and Italian immigrants, so the CIO unions served this purpose for Mexican and black migrants in the 1930 and 1940s.[72]

As it did in the industrial union movements of the Depression era and World War II, participation of immigrant workers has strengthened the labor movement in a number of ways. The movement's most successful organizing drives have tended to come in the hotel and restaurant and service industries with heavy concentrations of immigrant workers who have been very receptive to the unions' call. At the local level, organizing campaigns and strikes by immigrant workers have led to alliances with community groups, particularly religious congregations—a development that had greatly facilitated organization of immigrant workers in earlier eras. The transnational character of these workers' lives and contacts have facilitated international solidarity movements, as in the anti-sweatshop and solidarity campaigns in strikes and lockouts. In this way, they have helped to globalize the perspective and strategies of American labor at a moment when the globalization of capital has required such methods.[73]

But if the new immigrant working class is revitalizing the labor movement, we should not expect the product to mirror the movement built by the last great wave of European immigrants and black and Mexican migrants in the 1930s and 1940s. Much of the activity below the surface of the recent immigrant rights movement is based in religious congregations, particularly Catholic parishes, which were first built by European and are now revitalized by Latino immigrants, but also Evangelical and Pentecostal communities of the largest cities. This movement was most visible in the huge demonstrations across the nation in March and May of 2006, when millions of immigrant workers and their families marched to protest legislative and physical attacks on immigrants, and in smaller demonstrations since then. Because the most recent labor migration seems to have touched virtually every corner of the United States, the movement extended to the South (where recent Central American immigrants have been instrumental in union-building) as well as to the industrial heartland and the largest cities on the coasts. While Spanish-speaking immigrants were the largest and most visible component of this movement, African, East and South Asian, Eastern European, Irish, and other groups have also taken part. Immigrants' rights marches in Chicago and New York are likely to include not only Mariachi bands, but also Korean drummers, African dancers, and Irish pipes. The flags of nations around the world fly alongside the Stars and Stripes.[74]

The immigrants' rights marches focused mainly on legislative issues and were rooted in the community and churches as much as in unions, but they also harkened back to labor traditions. It was not a coincidence that immigrant workers chose for the date of their mobilizations May First, a holiday commemorating labor's rights and labor's strength in cities and towns throughout the world, but one that was born among immigrant workers in the industrial heartland of the United States.[75] And while the marches were mainly covered as festive occasions, newspapers noted that in certain service and manufacturing industries with large immigrant workforces all work ceased. In pressing for their political and civil rights, Mexican and other immigrant workers had launched something that the United States has not seen in generations—a 1-day general strike. The 2006 demonstrations recalled the history of the holiday and the labor movements surrounding it, even as the marchers' complexions changed and they raised their banners around new issues confronting American workers.

NOTES

*   I would like to thank the late Mark Leff for his comments.
1. E. P. Thompson, *The Making of the English Working Class* (New York: Pantheon Books, 1963).
2. On Thompson's influence on U.S. labor historians, see David Brody, "The New Labor History and the Old," *Labor History* 20 (1979): 111–126; Alan Dawley, "The Peculiarities of the Americans," *Radical History Review* 19 (Winter 1979): 33–59.

3. James R. Barrett, "Unity and Fragmentation: Class, Race, and Ethnicity on Chicago's South Side, 1900–1922," *Journal of Social History*, 18 (1984): 37–56; James R. Barrett, "Americanization from the Bottom, Up: Immigration and the Remaking of the Working Class in the United States, 1880–1930," *Journal of American History* 79 (December 1992): 1009–1011; Richard Jules Oestreicher, *Solidarity and Fragmentation: Working People and Class Consciousness in Detroit, 1875–1900* (Urbana, IL: University of Illinois Press, 1986).

4. Herbert Gutman, "Work, Culture, and Society in Industrializing America," in *Work, Culture, and Society in America: Essays in American Working-Class and Social History*, ed. Herbert G. Gutman (New York: Knopf, 1976); Barrett, "Americanization from the Bottom, Up."

5. Thomas Dublin, *Women at Work: The Transformation of Work and Community in Lowell, Massachusetts, 1826–1860* (New York: Columbia University Press, 1979); Alan Dawley, *Class and Community: The Industrial Revolution in Lynn* (Cambridge, MA: Harvard University Press, 1976); David Montgomery, "The Working Classes of the Pre-Industrial City," *Labor History*, 19: 1 (Winter 1968): 3–22.

6. Dublin, *Women at Work*; Dawley, *Class and Community*; Bruce Laurie, *Artisans into Workers: Labor in Nineteenth-Century America* (New York: Hill and Wang, 1989); Bruce Laurie, *Working People of Philadelphia, 1800–1850* (Philadelphia: Temple University Press, 1980); Edward Pessen, *Most Uncommon Jacksonians; The Radical Leaders of the Early Labor Movement* (Albany, New York: State University of New York Press, 1967; Sean Wilentz, *Chants Democratic: New York City and the Rise of the American Working Class, 1788–1850* (New York: Oxford University Press, 2004). On "rules of the game," see E. J. Hobsbawm, "Custom, Wages, and Workload in the Nineteenth Century," in *Laboring Men: Studies in the History of Labor*, ed. Hobsbawm, (New York: Doubleday, 1967), 405–436.

7. See David Montgomery, "The Shuttle and the Cross: Weavers and Artisans in the Kensington Riots of 1844," *Journal of Social History* 5 (Summer 1972): 411–466 on the Philadelphia riots, and on nativism more generally, Peter Schrag, *Not Fit for Our Society: Nativism and Immigration* (Berkeley, CA: University of California Press, 2010).

8. Roger Daniels, *Coming to America: A History of Immigration and Ethnicity in American Life* (New York: Harper Perennial, 1990), 121–126; Rudolph Vecoli, "Ethnicity and Immigration," *Encyclopedia of the United States in the Twentieth Century*, eds. Stanley Kutler, et al. (New York: Charles Scribner's Sons, 1996), 162–168.

9. Thomas J. Philpott, *The Slum and the Ghetto: Immigrants, Neighborhood Deterioration and Middle-Class Reform, Chicago, 1880–1930* (New York: Oxford University Press, 1978), 141–144; Kathleen Neils Conzen, "Immigrants, Immigrant Neighborhoods, and Ethnic Identity: Historical Issues," *Journal of American History* 66: 3 (December 1979), 603–615; James R. Barrett, *Work and Community in the Jungle: Chicago's Packing House Workers, 1894–1922* (Urbana, IL: University of Illinois Press, 1987), 78–81; Dominic Pacyga, "The Ethnic Neighborhood: The Myth of Stability and the Reality of Change," in *Ethnic Chicago: A Multicultural Portrait*, eds. Melvin G. Holli and Peter d'A. Jones, (Grand Rapids, MI: Wm. B. Eerdmans Publishing Co., 1995), 604–617.

10. James R. Green, *Death in the Haymarket: A Story of Chicago, the First Labor Movement, and the Bombing that Divided Gilded Age America* (New York: Pantheon Books, 2006), quote, 139; *German Workers in Chicago: A Documentary History of Working Class Culture from 1850 to World War I*, eds. Hartmut Keil and John B. Jentz with the assistance of Klaus Ensslen (Urbana, IL: University of Illinois Press, 1988); *German Workers in*

Industrial Chicago, 1850–1910: A Comparative Perspective, eds. Hartmut Keil and John B. Jentz (DeKalb, IL: Northern Illinois University Press, 1983); Stanley Nadel, *Little Germany: Ethnicity, Religion, and Class in New York City, 1845–80* (Urbana, IL: University of Illinois Press, 1990); Dorothee Schneider, *Trade Unions and Community: The German Working Class in New York City, 1870–1900* (Urbana, IL: University of Illinois Press, 1994); Oestreicher, *Solidarity and Fragmentation*.

11. John Higham, *Strangers in the Land: Patterns of American Nativism, 1860–1925*, (New York: Atheneum, 1963) 222–233; Robert K. Murray. *The Red Scare: A Study in National Hysteria, 1919–1920* (Minneapolis: University of Minnesota Press, 1955); William Preston, *Aliens and Dissenters: Federal Suppression of Radicals, 1903–1933* (Cambridge: Harvard U. Press, 1963); Arthur J. Sabin, *Red Scare in Court: New York Versus the International Workers Order* (Philadelphia: University of Pennsylvania Press, 1993).

12. Hutchins Hapgood, *The Spirit of the Ghetto: Studies of the Jewish Quarter of New York* (New York: Funk and Wagnalls, 1902); Irving Howe, "Jewish Labor, Jewish Socialism," in *World of Our Fathers* (New York: Random House, 1976); Tony Michels, *A Fire in their Hearts: Yiddish Socialists in New York* (Cambridge, MA: Harvard University Press, 2005); Moses Rischin, *The Promised City: New York's Jews, 1870–1914* (Cambridge, MA: Harvard University Press, 1962).

13. Susan Glenn, *Daughters of the Shtetl: Life and Labor in the Immigrant Generation* (Ithaca, NY: Cornell University Press, 1990); Annelise Orleck, *Common Sense and a Little Fire: Women and Working-Class Politics in the United States, 1900–1965* (Chapel Hill: University of North Carolina Press 1995); Sydney Stahl Weinberg, *The World of Our Mothers: The Lives of Jewish Immigrant Women* (Chapel Hill, NC: University of North Carolina Press, 1988); Meredith Tax, *The Rising of the Women: Feminist Solidarity and Class Conflict, 1880–1917* (Urbana, IL: University of Illinois Press, 2001).

14. Margaret F. Byington, *Homestead: The Households of a Mill Town*, with a new introduction by Samuel P. Hays (1910, reprint: Pittsburgh: University Center for International Studies, 1974), 17–21.

15. David Emmons, *Butte's Irish: Class and Community in an American Mining Town, 1875–1925* (Urbana, IL: University of Illinois Press, 1989), 2–254.

16. Emmons, *Butte's Irish*, 255–291.

17. Barrett, *Work and Community in the Jungle*; David Brody, *Steelworkers in America: The Non-Union Era* (New York: Harper and Row, 1960); James R. Barrett, *William Z. Foster and the Tragedy of American Radicalism* (Urbana, IL: University of Illinois Press, 1999), 71–101; Victor Greene, *The Slavic Community on Strike* (Notre Dame, IN: Notre Dame University Press, 1968); John H.M. Laslett, *Colliers Across the Sea: a Comparative Study of Class Formation in Scotland and American Midwest, 1830–1924* (Urbana, IL: University of Illinois Press, 2000); Emmons, *Butte's Irish*, 364–386; Caroline Waldron (Merithew), "The Great Spirit of Solidarity: The Illinois Valley Mining Communities and the Formation of Interethnic Consciousness, 1889–1917," Unpublished Ph.D. dissertation, University of Illinois at Urbana-Champaign, 2000; Thomas Mackaman, "The Foreign Element: New Immigrants and American Industry, 1914–1924," Unpublished Ph.D. dissertation, University of Illinois at Urbana-Champaign, 2009.

18. Ewa Morawska, *For Bread and Butter: Life Worlds of East Central Europeans in Johnstown, Pennsylvania, 1890–1940* (New York: Cambridge University Press, 1985), 108–110, 157–181; Karel Bicha, "Hunkies: Stereotyping the Slavic Immigrants, 1880–1920," *Journal of American Ethnic History* 2 (Spring 1982): 16–38; James R. Barrett and David R. Roediger,

"Inbetween Peoples: Race, Nationality, and the 'New Immigrant' Working Class," *Journal of American Ethnic History* 16 (May 1997): 28–30; Rudolph Vecoli, "An Inter-Ethnic Perspective on American Immigration History," *Mid-America* 75 (April–July 1993): 223–235.

19. Timothy J. Meagher, *Inventing Irish America: Generation, Class, and Ethnic Identity in a New England City, 1880–1928* (Notre Dame, IN: Notre Dame University Press, 2001); James R. Barrett, *The Irish Way: Becoming American in the Multi-Ethnic City*, (New York: Penguin Press, 2012).

20. David R. Roediger, *The Wages of Whiteness: Race and the Making of the American Working Class* (London: Verso, 1991); Michale Rogin, *Blackface, White Noise: Jewish Immigrants in the Hollywood Melting Pot* (Berkeley, CA: University of California Press, 1996); Barrett and Roediger, "Inbetween Peoples," 3–44; David R. Roediger, *Toward the Abolition of Whiteness* (London: Verso, 1995): 181–194; Dana Frank, "White Working Class Women and the Race Question," *International Labor and Working Class History* 54 (Fall 1998): 80–102; David R. Roediger, *Working Toward Whiteness: How America's Immigrants Became White; The Strange Journey from Ellis Island to the Suburbs* (New York: Basic Books, 2005).

21. Schneider, *Trade Unions and Community*; Nadel, *Little Germany*.

22. Per Nordhal, "Henry Bengston and Swedish-American Socialism in Chicago," and Anita R. Olson, "A Scandinavian Melting Pot in Chicago," in *Swedish-American Life in Chicago: Cultural and Urban Aspects of an Immigrant People, 1850–1930*, eds. Philip J. Anderson and Dag Blanck (Urbana, IL: University of Illinois Press, 1992).

23. Morawska, *For Bread and Butter*, 108–110, 157–181; Bicha, "Hunkies"; Barrett and Roediger, "Inbetween Peoples," 28–30.

24. Vecoli, "An Inter-Ethnic Perspective on American Immigration History." See also Thomas Bell's proletarian novel, *Out of this Furnace* (Boston: Little, Brown and Co., 1941).

25. Donna R. Gabaccia and Fraser Ottanelli, "Diaspora or International Proletariat? Italian Labor, Labor Migration, and the Making of Multiethnic Worker States, 1815–1939," *Diaspora* 6 (Spring 1997): 61–84; Gary R. Mormino and George E. Pozzetta, *The Immigrant World of Ybor City: Italians and Their Latin Neighbors in Tampa Florida, 1885–1985* (Urbana, IL: University of Illinois Press, 1987); Hewitt, "The Virile Voice of Labor."; Nancy A. Hewitt, *Southern Discomfort: Women's Activism in Tampa, Florida, 1880s–1920s* (Urbana, IL: University of Illinois Press, 2001).

26. Donna R. Gabaccia, "Internationalism and Italian Labor Migration, 1870–1914," *International Labor and Working Class History* 45 (Spring 1994): 63–79.

27. Franco Ramella, "Between Village and Job Abroad: Italian Migrants in France and Switzerland," in *Roots of the Transplanted, Volume 2: Plebian Culture, Class, and Politics in the Life of Labor Migrants*, eds. Dirk Hoerder, Horst Rossler, and Inge Blank (Boulder: East European Monographs; New York: Distributed by Columbia University Press, 1994), 276–279; Dirk Hoerder, "The German Immigrant Worker's Views of America in the 1880s" in *In the Shadow of the Statue of Liberty: Immigrants, Workers, and Citizens in the American Republic*, ed. Marianne Debouzy (Urbana, IL: University of Illinois Press, 1992), 5–22.

28. See for example, Waldron (Merithew), "The Great Spirit of Solidarity"; Caroline Waldron and James R. Barrett, "'We Are All Brothers in the Face of Starvation': Forging an Interethnic Working-Class Consciousness in the 1894 Bituminous Coal Strike," *Mid-America*, 83 (Summer 2001): 121–154; Ronald Creagh, "Socialism in America: French Speaking Coal Miners in the Late Nineteenth Century," in *In the Shadow of the Statue of Liberty*, ed. Debouzy, 143–156. See also, Mildred Allen Beik, *The Miners of Windber: The*

Struggles of New Immigrants for Unionization (University Park, PA: Penn State University Press, 1996).

29. Waldron (Merithew), " 'The Great Spirit of Solidarity.' "

30. On the homogeneous southern mill towns, see Jacquelyn Dowd Hall, James LeLoudis, Robert Korstad, *Like a Family: The Making of a Southern Cotton Mill World* (Chapel Hill, NC: University of North Carolina Press, 1987) and on Lawrence, Bruce Watson, *Bread and Roses: Mills, Migrants, and the Struggle for the American Dream* (New York: Viking, 2005).

31. David Montgomery, "Immigrants, Industrial Unions, and Social Reconstruction in the United States, 1916–1923," *Labour/Le Travail*, Vol. 13 (Spring 1984): 101–114; David Montgomery, "Racism, Immigrants, and Political Reform," *Journal of American History*, Vol. 87: 4 (March 2001): 1253–1274.

32. Mackaman, "The Foreign Element."

33. John T. Ridge, "Irish County Societies in New York, 1880–1914," in *The New York Irish*, eds. Ronald H. Bayor and Timothy J. Meagher (Baltimore: Johns Hopkins University Press, 1996), 280, 297; Kerby A. Miller, *Emigrants and Exiles: Ireland and the Irish Exodus to North America* (New York: Oxford University Press, 1985), 500.

34. Roediger, *Working toward Whiteness*, 74–76.

35. Nancy Foner, *From Ellis Island to JFK: New York's Two Great Waves of Immigration* (New Haven, CT: Yale University Press, 2000), 79–82.

36. Foner, *From Ellis Island to JFK*, 231–235; Ruth Jacknow Markowitz, *My Daughter, the Teacher: Jewish Teachers in the New York City Schools* (New Brunswick, NJ: Rutgers University Press, 1993)

37. Foner, *From Ellis Island to JFK*, 81–82; John R. McGivigan and Thomas J. Robertson, "The Irish American Worker in Transition, 1877–1914," in *The New York Irish*, 311–312; Suzanne Model, "The Ethnic Niche and the Structure of Opportunity: Immigrants and Minorities in New York City," in *The Underclass Debate*, ed. Michael Katz, (Princeton: Princeton University Press, 1993), 181–182, 172.

38. Roger Waldinger, *Still the Promised City? African-Americans and New Immigrants in Postindustrial New York* (Cambridge, MA: Harvard University Press, 1996), 102–105; Foner, *From Ellis Island to JFK*,

39. Barrett, *Work and Community in the Jungle*, 28–30.

40. Bruce Nelson, Divided We Stand: American Workers and the Struggle for Black Equality (Princeton: Princeton University Press, 2001), xx–xxviii; Calvin Winslow, "Introduction," in *Waterfront Workers: New Perspectives on Race and Class*, ed. Calvin Winslow (Urbana, IL: University of Illinois Press, 1998), 7; Eric Arnesen, "Biracial Waterfront Unionism in the Age of Segregation," in *Waterfront Workers*, ed., Winslow, 22–23; Calvin Winslow, "Men of the Lumber Camps Come to Town': New York Longshoremen in the Strike of 1907," in *Waterfront Workers*, 68–69, 83–84, 86–87, fn 90; Calvin Winslow, "On the Waterfront: Black, Italian, and Irish Longshoremen in the New York Harbor Strike of 1919," in *Protest and Survival: Essays for E. P. Thompson*, eds. John Rule and Robert Malcolmson (London: Merlin Press, 1993), 389–390.

41. Foner, *From Ellis Island to JFK*, 81–82; Nelson, *Divided We Stand*, xli; Howard Kimeldorf, *Battling for American Labor: Wobblies, Craft Workers, and the Making of the Union Movement* (Berkeley, CA: University of California Press, 1999), 24–26; Peter Cole, *Wobblies on the Waterfront: Interracial Unionism in Progressive-Era Philadelphia* (Urbana, IL: University of Illinois Press, 2007), 24–26; Charles Barnes, *The Longshoremen*

(New York: Survey Associates, 1915), 5–7. See also Lorenzo J. Greene and Carter G. Woodson, *The Negro Wage Earner* (New York: Russell and Russell, 1930), 113, 133.

42. John Bodnar, *Immigration and Industrialization: Ethnicity in an American Mill Town, 1870–1940* (Pittsburgh: University of Pittsburgh Press, 1977), 6–7, 9, 57, 71–72.

43. Adam Walaszek, "'For in America Poles Are Like Cattle': Polish Peasant Immigrants and Work in America," in *In the Shadow of the Statue of Liberty*, ed. Debouzy, 83–94; Stephen Meyer, *The Five Dollar Day: Social Control in the Ford Motor Company, 1908–1921* (Albany: State University of New York Press, 1981), 56; "Negro Laborers on the Subway," *New York Times*, September 1, 1901, SM14; "Almost a Riot in Brooklyn," *New York Times*, November 5, 1891, 10; "Success Story of an Italian Boy," *Chicago Tribune*, December 1, 1907, 1; Bodnar, *Immigration and Industrialization*, 6–7, 9, 57, 71–72. See also, Roediger, *Working toward Whiteness*, 74–75, David Montgomery, The Fall of the House of Labor: The Workplace, the State, and American Labor Activism, 1865–1925 (NewYork: Cambridge University Press, 1987)., 92–93.

44. Foner, *From Ellis Island to JFK*, 89–107.

45. Nicole Therese Ranganath, "Wedding Women to Tradition: The Politics of Marriage in the Indian Diaspora, 1947–2002," Unpublished Ph.D, dissertation, University of Illinois at Urbana-Champaign, 2003; Youn-Jin Kim, "From Immigrants to Ethnics: The Life-Worlds of Korean Immigrants in Chicago," Unpublished Ph.D. dissertation, University of Illinois at Urbana-Champaign, 1991.

46. Roger Waldinger, *Still the Promised City?* 123–124; Foner, *From Ellis Island to JFK*, 94–95.

47. Roger Waldinger and Michael I. Lichter, *How the Other Half Works: Immigration and the Social Organization of Labor* (Berkeley, CA: University of California Press, 2003), 206–213, 218–233; Waldinger, *Still the Promised City?* 57–93.

48. Quoted in Min Zhou, "Chinese: Divergent Destinies in Immigrant New York" in *New Immigrants in New York*, second edition, ed. Nancy Foner (New York: Columbia University Press, 2001), 141.

49. Ewa Morawska, "In Defense of the Assimilation Model," *Journal of American Ethnic History* 13 (Winter 1994): 76–87; Elliott Barkan, "Race, Religion, and Nationality—A Model of Ethnicity from Contact to Assimilation," *Journal of American Ethnic History* 14 (Winter 1995): 38–75. For examples of "straight line" notions of assimilation, see Herbert Gans, "Symbolic Ethnicity: The Future of Ethnic Groups and Culture in America," *Ethnic and Racial Studies* 2:1 (January 1979): 1–20; Richard Alba, *Ethnic Identity: the Transformation of White America* (New Haven, CT: Yale University Press, 1990).

50. Russell Kazal, "Revisiting Assimilation: The Rise, Fall, and Reappraisal of a Concept in American Ethnic History," *American Historical Review* 100(April 1995): 437–471; Gary Gerstle, "Liberty, Coercion, and the Making of Americans," *Journal of American History* 84 (September 1997): 524–558; John Higham, "Integrating America: The Problem of Assimilation in the Nineteenth Century," *Journal of American Ethnic History*, vol 1: 21 (Fall 1981): 7–25; Elliott A. Barkan, "Race, Nationality, and Religion in American Society"; Oliver Zunz, "American History and the Changing Meaning of Assimilation," *Journal of American Ethnic History* Vol. 4, No. 2 (Spring 1985): 53–72.

51. Gerstle, "Liberty, Coercion," 527; *The Invention of Ethnicity*, ed. Werner Sollors (New York: Oxford University Press, 1989).

52. Conzen, "Immigrants, Immigrant Neighborhoods and Ethnic Identity," 603–615; Olivier Zunz, *The Changing Face of Inequality: Urbanization, Industrial Development, and Immigrants in Detroit, 1880–1920* (Chicago: University of Chicago Press, 1982).

53. Joan Scott, "Gender: A Useful Category of Historical Analysis," *American Historical Review* 91(December 1986): 1053–1085. For the historiography of immigrant women, see Donna R. Gabaccia, *From the Other Side: Women, Gender, and Immigrant Life in the United States, 1820–1990* (Bloomington, IN: Indiana University Pres, 1994); Suzanne Sinke, "A Historiography of Immigrant Women in the Nineteenth and Twentieth Centuries," *Ethnic Forum* 9 (1–2) 1989: 122–145; and for useful applications of gender as an analytical category in immigrant history, Nancy Hewitt, "The Voice of Virile Labor: Labor Militancy, Community Solidarity, and Gender Identity among Tampa's Latin Workers," in *Work Engendered: Toward a New Understanding of Men, Women, and Work*, ed. Ava Baron (Ithaca: Cornell University Press, 1991) and Glenn, *Daughters of the Shtetl*. Issues of sexuality in relation to ethno-cultural values in immigrant communities remain largely unexplored. See George Chauncey's discussion of the relationship between gay and ethnic working-class subcultures in *Gay New York: Gender, Urban Culture, and the Making of the Gay Male World, 1890–1940* (New York: Basic Books, 1994); Timothy Gilfoyle, *City of Eros: New York City, Prostitution, and the Commercialization of Sex, 1790–1920* (New York: W. W. Norton, 1992); and Kevin J. Mumford, *Interzones: Black/White Sex Districts in Chicago and New York in the Early Twentieth Century* (New York: Columbia University Press, 1997).

54. George Sanchez, "Race, Nation, and Culture in Recent Immigration History" in *Journal of American Ethnic History* 18 (Summer) 1999, 69; Roediger, *The Wages of Whiteness*; Rogin, *Blackface, White Noise*; Barrett and Roediger, "Inbetween Peoples"; Roediger, *Toward the Abolition of Whiteness*, 181–194; Mathew Frye Jacobsen, *Whiteness of a Different Color: European Immigrants and the Alchemy of Race* (Cambridge, MA: Harvard University Press, 1998); David R. Roediger and James R. Barrett, "Irish Hosts and White Pan-Ethnicity, Or, Who Made the 'New Immigrants' Inbetween?" in *Not Just Black and White: Immigration and Race, Then and Now*, eds. Nancy Foner and George Frederickson (New York: Russell Sage Foundation Press, 2004). For a gendered reading of this process, see Frank, "White Working-Class Women and the Race Question," 80–102; Thomas Holt, "Explaining Racism in American History," in *Imagined Histories: American Historians Interpret the Past*, eds. Anthony Molho and Gordon Wood (Princeton: Princeton University Press, 1998), 107–119.

55. Vecoli, "An Inter-Ethnic Perspective on American Immigration History," quotes, 17.

56. Higham, *Strangers in the Land*, 234–263; Stephen Meyer, III, "Adapting the Immigrant to the Line: Americanization in the Ford Motor Company, 1914–1921," *Journal of Social History* 14 (1980): 67–82; Rivka Shpak Lissak, *Pluralism and Progressives: Hull House and the New Immigrants, 1890–1919* (Chicago: University of Chicago Press, 1989); John F. McClymer, "The Americanization Movement and the Education of the Foreign-Born Adult, 1914–1925," in *American Education and the European Immigrant, 1840–1940*, ed. Bernard J. Weiss (Urbana, IL: University of Illinois Press, 1982), 96–116.

57. James R. Barrett, "Americanization from the Bottom, Up." See also, William M. Leiserson, *Adjusting Immigrant and Industry* (New York: Harper, 1924), 234–245; Neil Betten, "Polish-American Steelworkers: Americanization through Industry and Labor," *Polish American Studies* 33 (Autumn 1976): 31–42; David J. Saposs, "The Problem of Making Permanent Trade Unionists out of the Recently Organized Immigrant Workers," 1919, folder 5, box 21, David J. Saposs Papers, Wisconsin State Historical Society, Madison, WI. For a parallel process at work among immigrant hotel workers speaking seventeen different languages in present day Minneapolis, see Peter Rachleff, "A Union of Immigrants Wins the

Minneapolis Hotel Strike," *Labor Notes*, 257 (August 2000): 1,14. The Service Employees International Union employed comparable successful strategies in a Chicago area janitors' strike by a union comprised most heavily of Polish, Hispanic, and Asian immigrants.

58. Lawrence Glickman, "Inventing 'The American Standard of Living': Gender, Race and Working-Class Identity, 1880–1920", *Labor History* 34 (1993): 221–235; Peter Shergold, *Working-Class Life: The American Standard in Comparative Perspective, 1899–1913* (Pittsburgh: University of Pittsburgh Press, 1982); Barrett, *Work and Community in the Jungle*, 142–146; Mary McDowell, "The Struggle for an American Standard of Living," in *Mary McDowell and Municipal Housing: A Symposium*, ed. Caroline Hill (Chicago: Miller Publishing Company, 1938), 62–66, esp. 66; Barrett, "Americanization from the Bottom, Up," 1009–1011.

59. *Iron and Steelworkers Bulletin*, No. 5,1, Mary Heaton Vorse Papers, box 120, Archives of Labor and Urban Affairs, Reuther Library, Wayne State University, Detroit, MI.

60. William Z. Foster, *The Great Steel Strike and Its Lessons* (New York: B. W. Huebsch, Inc, 1920), 204.

61. Mark Wyman, *Round Trip to America: The Immigrants Return to Europe, 1880–1930* (Ithaca: Cornell University Press, 1993); Adam Walaszek, *Reemigracja ze Stanow Zjednoczonych do Polski po I Wojniej Swiatowej, 1919–1924* (Cracow, 1983), (English abstract); Dirk Hoerder, "Immigration and the Working Class: the Remigration Factor," *International Labor and Working Class History* 21 (1087): 28–41; and Ewa Morawksa, "Return Migrations: Theoretical and Research Agenda" in *A Century of European Migration, 1830–1930*, eds. Rudolph J. Vecoli and Suzanne Sinke (Urbana, IL: University of Illinois Press, 1991), 277–292. See also David Montgomery, *The Fall of the House of Labor*, 74; Donna Gabaccia, "The 'Yellow Peril' and the 'Chinese of Europe:' Global Perspectives on Race and Labor, 1815–1930," *in Migration, Migration History, History: Old Paradigms and New Perspectives*, eds. Jan Lucassen and Leo Lucassen (New York: Peter Lang, 1997), 185.

62. Barrett, "Americanization from the Bottom, Up"; Ronald Edsforth, "Made in the USA: Mass Culture and the Americanization of Working-Class Ethnics in the Coolidge Era," ed. John Earl Haynes (Washington, D.C.: Library of Congress, 1998), 244–273; Michael Denning, *The Cultural Front: The Laboring of American Culture in the Twentieth-Century* (London: Verso, 1996).

63. Roger Waldinger and Mehdi Bozorgmehr, "The Making of a Multicultural Metropolis" in *Ethnic Los Angeles*, eds. Roger Waldinger and Mehdi Bozorgmehr (New York: Russell Sage Foundation, 1996), 8–14; David Lopez and Cynthia Feliciano, "Who Does What? California's Emerging Plural Labor Force," in *Organizing Immigrants: The Challenge for Unions in Contemporary California*, ed. Ruth Milkman (Ithaca: LIR Press, 2000), 32, 35–36.

64. Roger Waldinger and Mehdi Bozorgmehr, "The Making of a Multicultural Metropolis," 20.

65. Dan Clawson and Mary Ann Clawson, "What Has Happened to the U.S. Labor Movement: Union Decline and Renewal," *American Journal of Sociology* 25 (1995): 95–119.

66. Leon Fink, *The Maya of Morganton: Work and Community in the Nuevo New South* (Chapel Hill, NC: University of North Carolina Press, 2003); Roger Waldinger and Claudia Der-Martirosian, "Immigrant Workers and American Labor: Challenge . . . or Disaster?" in *Organizing Immigrants*, ed. Milkman, 49–80.

67. Dan Clawson, *The Next Upsurge: Labor and the New Social Movements* (Ithaca, NY: Cornell University Press, 2005), 99–118; Waldinger and Der-Martirosian, "Immigrant Workers and

American Labor: Challenge"; Rachel Sherman and Kim Voss, "'Organize or Die': Labor's New Tactics and Immigrant Workers," in *Organizing Immigrants,* ed. Milkman, 81–108.

68. Robert Asher, "Union Nativism and the Immigrant Response," *Labor History* 23:3 (Summer 1982): 325–348; Julie Greene, *Pure and Simple Politics: The American Federation of Labor and Political Activism, 1881–1917* (New York: Cambridge University Press, 1998), Gwendolyn Mink, *Old Labor and New Immigrants in American Political Development: Union, Party and State, 1875–1920* (Ithaca, New York: Cornell University Press, 1986); Mark Pittenger, *American Socialists and Evolutionary Thought, 1870–1920* (Madison, WI: University of Wisconsin Press, 1993); Alexander Saxton, *Indispensable Enemy: Labor and the Anti-Chinese Movement in California* (Berkeley, CA: University of California Press, 1971); Dana Frank, *Purchasing Power: Consumer Organizing, Gender and the Seattle Labor Movement, 1919–1929* (New York: Cambridge University Press, 1994).

69. David Roediger "What if Labor Were Not White and Male? Re-centering Working-Class History and Reconstructing Debate on the Unions and Race," *International Labor and Working-Class History,* 51, (1997): 72–95.

70. John Schmitt and Chris Warner, *The Changing Face of Labor, 1983–2008* (Washington, D.C.: Center for Economic and Policy Research, 2009).

71. Zaragosa Vargas, *Labor Rights Are Civil Rights: Mexican American Workers in Twentieth-Century America* (Princeton, N.J.: Princeton University Press, 2005); Vicki L. Ruíz, *Cannery Women, Cannery Lives: Mexican Women, Unionization, and the California Food Processing Industry, 1930–1950* (Albuquerque: University of New Mexico Press, 1987); Vicki L. Ruiz, *From Out of the Shadows: Mexican Women in Twentieth-Century America* (New York: Oxford University Press, 1998), 72–98, 122–128, 132–136. 99–111, 147–150; David G. Gutierrez, *Walls and Mirrors: Mexican Americans, Mexican Immigrants, and the Politics of Ethnicity* (Berkeley, CA: University of California Press, 1995), 103–110, 147–149, 170–171, 179–206.

72. George Sanchez, *Becoming Mexican American: Ethnicity, Culture, and Identity in Chicano Los Angeles, 1900–1945* (New York: Oxford University Press, 1993), 249.

73. Clawson, *The Next Upsurge.*

74. *Chicago Tribune,* March 11, 2006, 1; March 26, 2006, 3; May 2, 2006, 1, 6, 13; May 2, 2008, 2,3; *Los Angeles Times,* May 2, 2006, A1, A18, B1, B13; May 3, 2006, B1; May 2, 2008, B1; *New York Times* May 2, 2006, A1, A18, A24;

75. Donna T. Haverty-Stacke, *America's Forgotten Holiday: May Day and Nationalism, 1867–1960* (New York: New York University Press, 2009).

BIBLIOGRAPHY

Barrett, James R. *Work and Community in the Jungle: Chicago's Packing House Workers, 1894–1922* (Urbana, IL: University of Illinois Press, 1987).

Barrett, James R., "Americanization from the Bottom, Up: Immigration and the Remaking of the Working Class in the United States, 1880–1930," *Journal of American History* 79 (December 1992), 996–1020.

Barrett, James R., *The Irish Way: Becoming American in the Multi-Ethnic City,* (New York: Penguin Press, 2012).

Bodnar, John, *Immigration and Industrialization: Ethnicity in an American Mill Town, 1870–1940* (Pittsburgh: University of Pittsburgh Press, 1977).

Brody, David, *Steelworkers in America: The Non-Union Era* (New York: Harper and Row, 1960).

Emmons, David, *Butte's Irish: Class and Community in an American Mining Town, 1875–1925* (Urbana, IL: University of Illinois Press, 1989).

Fink, Leon, *The Maya of Morganton: Work and Community in the Nuevo New South* (Chapel Hill, NC: University of North Carolina Press, 2003).

Foner, Nancy, *From Ellis Island to JFK: New York's Two Great Waves of Immigration* (New Haven, CT: Yale University Press, 2000).

Glenn, Susan, *Daughters of the Shtetl: Life and Labor in the Immigrant Generation* (Ithaca, NY: Cornell University Press, 1990).

Herbert G. Gutman, *Work, Culture, and Society in America: Essays in American Working-Class and Social History* (New York: Knopf, 1976).

Michels, Tony, *A Fire in their Hearts: Yiddish Socialists in New York* (Cambridge, MA: Harvard University Press, 2005).

Mink, Gwendolyn, *Old Labor and New Immigrants in American Political Development: Union, Party and State, 1875–1920* (Ithaca, New York: Cornell University Press, 1986).

Montgomery, David. *The Fall of the House of Labor: The Workplace, the State, and American Labor Activism, 1865–1925* (New York: Cambridge University Press, 1987).

Nelson, Bruce, *Divided We Stand: American Workers and the Struggle for Black Equality* (Princeton: Princeton University Press, 2001).

Roediger, David R., *The Wages of Whiteness: Race and the Making of the American Working Class* (London: Verso, 1991).

Roediger, David R., *Working Toward Whiteness: How America's Immigrants Became White: The Strange Journey from Ellis Island to the Suburbs* (New York: Basic Books, 2005).

Ruíz, Vicki L., *From Out of the Shadows: Mexican Women in Twentieth-Century America* (New York: Oxford University Press, 1998).

Sanchez, George, *Becoming Mexican American: Ethnicity, Culture, and Identity in Chicano Los Angeles, 1900–1945* (New York: Oxford University Press, 1993).

Saxton, Alexander, *Indispensable Enemy: Labor and Anti-Chinese Movement in California* (Berkeley, CA: University of California Press, 1971).

Vargas, Zaragosa, *Labor Rights are Civil Rights: Mexican American Workers in Twentieth-Century America* (Princeton, N.J.: Princeton University Press, 2005).

Waldinger, Roger, *How the Other Half Works: Immigration and the Social Organization of Labor* (Berkeley, CA: University of California Press, 2003).

Waldron, Caroline (Merithew), "The Great Spirit of Solidarity: The Illinois Valley Mining Communities and the Formation of Interethnic Consciousness, 1889–1917" (Unpublished Ph.D. dissertation, University of Illinois at Urbana-Champaign, 2000).

CHAPTER 16

....

NEIGHBORHOODS, IMMIGRANTS, AND ETHNIC AMERICANS

....

AMANDA I. SELIGMAN

IN order to understand urban environments, Americans often mentally divide up cities into smaller, more readily understandable units. Depending on where they are and how much they know about local history, people may refer to such areas as neighborhoods, parishes, or subdivisions. Parish boundaries are defined by the Roman Catholic church, which has apportioned the entire world up into administrative units. *Subdivision* is a real-estate term, referencing the development of multiple plats of land by one or a few homebuilders in a relatively short period of time. The term *neighborhood* is more widespread and generic, reflecting a sensibility that an area is both internally cohesive and distinctively bounded from other portions of the city. Because neighborhoods are unofficial and subject to definition by each urbanite, their boundaries are often contested, both literally and figuratively.

Members of the same ethnic group often clustered within particular residential neighborhoods in American cities. In smaller cities, bounded neighborhoods sometimes sheltered members of only one ethnic group, fostering both community cohesion and isolation from other groups. More often, especially in larger American cities, neighborhood life brought members of different ethnic communities into contact with one another. Those contacts were sometimes hostile or even violent, reinforcing a sense of interethnic difference and urban territoriality. But living in proximity to members of different groups also familiarized immigrant Americans and their children with ethnic strangers, fostering amicable relations, including friendships and intermarriage made possible in multiethnic contexts. Whatever sense of interethnic camaraderie was built within shared neighborhood boundaries, however, stopped at racial lines. In the twentieth century, as southern blacks migrated to northern cities, they crossed and recrossed a series of bounded neighborhood lines avidly defended by white ethnic residents who feared that violations of racial boundaries would undermine neighborhood cohesion and lead to decreased property values and undesirable interracial sexual contact.

The experience of the effects of neighborhood boundaries varied not only with ethnicity and class, but also with gender, age, generation, size of the ethnic group in the city, and the size of the city itself. In New York City's Italian Harlem, for example, historian Robert Orsi found that neighborhood boundaries particularly constrained women, who organized and around whom was organized the *domus*, the home, while men enjoyed a wider latitude in the neighborhood's streets.[1] By contrast, argued historian Thomas Jablonsky, in Chicago's Back of the Yards neighborhood, although immigrant parents lived and worked entirely within the neighborhood's boundaries, their children stepped out into the wider city via the city's park system.[2] Neighborhood boundaries must always be understood with a certain fluidity, with an eye to how inhabitants and visitors established their meanings. They were never absolutely fixed, and people experienced them differently depending on their personal circumstances. The relationships between ethnic Americans and urban neighborhoods have been probed by historians, but not explored in any systematic fashion. The purpose of this essay, therefore, is not to lay out a theory of how ethnic and neighborhood boundaries interact. Rather, this essay offers a preliminary sketch of the parameters that should be considered in future studies.

ESTABLISHMENT AND DISCERNMENT OF NEIGHBORHOOD BOUNDARIES

When European migrants first established cities in North America, the urban environment was compact enough that a healthy person could readily traverse a city's entire breadth on foot in a relatively short period.[3] Because the "walking city" could be easily discerned in its entirety, residents felt little need to distinguish subareas with different names. With the growth of cities over the eighteenth and nineteenth centuries, as well as the development of mechanized travel such as the railroad, streetcar, and the automobile, urbanites' cognitive maps of their environs changed. They might live in one district, work in a second, travel to a third for recreation, read about a fourth, and never see a fifth. In order to distinguish these areas from one another, city dwellers named them. The Bowery, for example, emerged in nineteenth-century New York City as an entertainment district.[4] Insofar as such areas were residential in character, they constituted neighborhoods, reflecting the idea that people who shared a common urban space lived also as neighbors in relationship to one another. Some neighborhoods were most easily recognized by their centers, with only loosely delineated edges, but as the propensity for dividing up cities proliferated, observers also defined neighborhood boundaries. A neighborhood is usually a walkable area, arising from how residents going about their daily business, using the space to procure food and other necessities, socialize and commute locally to work. Once residents step into a bus, streetcar, automobile, or train, they were probably headed for a different neighborhood.

American cities are in a legal sense creatures of their state governments, which issue their charters and define their rights. But geographic divisions within cities are multiple, with different categories and names offered by different actors and scholarly observers. City governments, for example, often divided municipalities up into numbered, political wards in order to allocate representation and services across the voting population. Such divisions, routinely gerrymandered for a variety of administrative and partisan ends, did not necessarily account for whether residents found the political boundaries meaningful. Real estate developers and dealers have also assigned neighborhood identifiers to the locations where they are active. In contrast to politicians, their goals have been to distinguish desirable from undesirable areas and to sell urban property, whether subdivisions they constructed themselves or housing already long in existence.

Finally, in the early twentieth century, University of Chicago sociologist Robert Park famously argued that the city was "a mosaic of little worlds which touch but do not interpenetrate."[5] Park, his colleagues, and their students in the Chicago School of Sociology postulated that the city consisted of "natural areas," defined by physical features, in which the social characteristics of an area were constant despite the movement of different population groups in and out of local residences. They examined, for example, whether rates of suicide or juvenile delinquency were constant over time within neighborhood limits. In order to facilitate the collection of quantifiable, longitudinal data for their studies, sociologists at the University of Chicago sent graduate students out across Chicago to identify, name, and discover the boundaries of all the "community areas" that made up the city.[6] Although offering only imperfect results—including some "neighborhoods" with names and boundaries that residents did not recognize—the community areas enjoyed great traction in Chicago and were adopted by city government for some planning purposes. Responding to pressure from scholars and charitable agencies in other cities who wanted similar tools for measuring social change, the U.S. Census Bureau in 1940 for the first time published information about numbered census tracts designated for 64 American cities, a process that was finally completed for all U.S. counties in 2000.[7]

Despite such official and private efforts to describe how cities are divided into distinctive neighborhoods, residents of urban places use their own conceptual categories to describe the centers and boundaries of the areas they inhabit. Often the definition of such neighborhoods was based on the extent of settlement in an area by people who shared an ethnic affiliation; the neighborhood, in short, was the area within which members of a particular immigrant group and their descendants lived in proximity to each other. The name of the most populous or visible group in the area sometimes became synonymous with the place itself. In contrast to the fixed boundaries delineated for the Chicago School's sociological model of "neighborhood succession," such ethnic toponomy meant that neighborhood names were subject to change with the mobility of the population. For example, New York City's Little Italy, readily identifiable for roughly a century in lower Manhattan, shrank as the Chinatown area to its west expanded.[8] Even in neighborhoods that were ethnically heterogeneous—common in large cities—the most visible group's name defined the area, giving rise to the impression of greater ethnic homogeneity than actually existed.

Religious institutions frequently served to define urbanites' experiences of neighborhood. Many city residents often walked from their homes to their houses of worship, for practical and religious reasons. Jewish law, for example, helps account for the propensity of Orthodox Jews to live within walking distance of their synagogues. On the Sabbath, Jews are forbidden to engage in productive work, to ride or drive, and to carry objects from one "domain" to another, or within any public "domain." This restriction precludes carrying infants and pushing strollers or wheelchairs, making participation in worship difficult for the elderly and mothers of small children. To solve this dilemma, a number of urban Jewish communities and congregations have worked with municipal officials to define an *eruv*. This is a space that, according to Jewish law, creates a symbolic private "domain" within which Jews can undertake acts of carrying on the Sabbath. The perimeter typically consists of fences, buildings, railway lines, and roads, which, if not fully contiguous, are "completed" by erecting poles and wires to close any gaps. The *eruv* then functions as one symbolic representation of the community's limits, creating a describable residential area for observant Jews.[9]

The Roman Catholic church similarly helped to define adherents' local urban experiences through the definition of parish boundaries, within which Catholics were expected to worship and attend parochial school. In the mid twentieth century, American Catholic officials struggled over whether worshippers should be served by ethnically or geographically based parishes. The presence of multiple Catholic church structures within a small area of a city is a sign of a neighborhood that was multiethnic and was served by national parishes until the Roman Catholic church shifted toward geographic parishes. In both cases, however, parish boundaries were clearly delineated and functioned to define the limits of parishioners' neighborhoods. Members of other religious groups did not have the edges of their neighborhoods defined for them but still felt the psychological pull of the houses of worship at the center of their residential districts. Until automobiles made travel for worship relatively convenient and inexpensive, adherents of religions with only small numbers of fellow congregants tried to live within reasonable commuting distance of the few religious institutions that served their needs.

Urban residents also use features of the physical environment to conceptualize the centers and edges of their neighborhoods. Commercial streets, for example, served nearby residents who preferred not to travel far to purchase food and dry goods, as well as co-ethnics who moved elsewhere but preserved the tastes of their upbringing. Stores catering to the tastes of immigrant groups for certain spices, foods, and commercial goods from their native countries gave the area a particular ethnic flavor at their centers. Segments of transportation infrastructure—such as alleys, train tracks, and viaducts—demarcated the edges of some neighborhoods. Public spaces such as parks belonged to residents of one neighborhood or another, sometimes serving as centers, sometimes as boundaries. Architecture also provides clues to the local definition of neighborhood. Although not necessarily authentically Chinese, for example, the presence of green tiled roofs accented with red paint and recessed balconies signals an American Chinatown with Chinese food for outsiders and goods and services for insiders.[10] In cities whose neighborhoods had once stood on the suburban periphery and then been swallowed up by the growing urban center, a farmhouse or old inn or tavern might suggest that the observer has entered an area with a distinctive identity. Street names, whether official or honorary, sometimes also hint at a neighborhood's population's ethnic history.

Urban residents occasionally reinforced the official or unofficial boundaries of their neighborhoods with public speech and action. In the later parts of the twentieth century, property owners in aging districts, for example, sometimes sought recognition as a "historic district" in order to capture tax credits for preservation of their buildings. Business owners and real estate dealers, seeking to capitalize on the popularity of a certain church or to distance the area where they worked from what they regarded as undesirable elements of the local population, sometimes took it upon themselves to designate particular places with new monikers, which sometimes caught on among new residents. For example, in the 1970s, leaders in the Edgewater area of Chicago successfully fought to secede from the Uptown community area of which it was a part. The activists' goal was to get the area's tony housing stock recognized as quite distant from the illegal drug activity and crime that plagued the portion of the area associated with southern whites, Native Americans, and other recent migrants.[11] The religious procession was common on feast days in Catholic communities. The routes that parishioners marched on such occasions roughly traced out the parish boundaries, demonstrating for insiders and outsiders alike what they thought their neighborhood boundaries were. Historians such as Jordan Stanger-Ross and Joseph P. Sciorra have used procession routes to map parishioners' changing cognitive neighborhood maps.[12] Tens or even hundreds of thousands of people turned out to observe these parades and incidentally reify local religious neighborhood boundaries. Other forms of neighborhood boundary policing are less easily captured by the historical record but functioned nonetheless. School children recognized strangers to the neighborhood and let them know when they had crossed boundaries. Youth with artistic talents used graffiti to signal, among other topics, their sense of local territoriality. Gangs of young men sometimes simply warned strangers off—with words or fists—when they transgressed neighborhood boundaries.

NEIGHBORHOOD EXPERIENCES

Immigrants from Europe often found their way to particular urban enclaves through chain migrations. Relying on letters from friends and family, newspapers, travel guides, and the testimony of returned acquaintances, immigrants determined which locations were promising locales for beginning life in America. They particularly prized areas inhabited by familiar people whose social networks would help them to obtain work. In some cases, in smaller cities and industrial suburbs, migrants settled in rare but truly homogeneous areas. A few blocks on which every resident shared the same mother tongue could constitute a truly homogeneous neighborhood. But even when immigrants formed ethnically identified neighborhoods, they were not completely isolated. For example, in order to emphasize the high degree of segregation in the Polish Hill District in Pittsburgh, John Bodnar, Roger Simon, and Michael P. Weber write of sections and streets that were 80 to 90 percent homogeneous.[13] More commonly, in larger cities, by contrast, even as migrants clustered near acquaintances from home, they mingled on a daily basis among neighbors with unfamiliar origins. The *Hull-House Maps and Papers* study of the environs surrounding the premier Chicago settlement house in 1895 identified a few blocks monopolized by Bohemian and Italian occupants but also depicted a neighborhood whose housing stock was deeply integrated.[14] Although Hull-House's residents organized activities that catered in an ethnically selective fashion to the distinct national groups that resided in the area, the immigrants and their children who occupied Chicago's Near West Side at the turn of the twentieth century shared the streets.

Urban neighborhoods served both to insulate members of different ethnic groups from one another and to bring them into contact. While ethnically homogeneous neighborhoods were rare, the numerical dominance of one group in an area could create a sense that members controlled the neighborhood. In ethnically mixed neighborhoods, residents with diverse ancestries mingled with results that varied from riot to romance. The extent to which such neighborhoods functioned as communities is a distinct question, with the answer resting in the size of the area and the strength of local institutions. Neighborhoods as conceptualized both by insiders and outsiders ranged so much in size, from several hundred households to more than a hundred thousand residents, with the degree of residential mobility also varying, that no simple correspondence between neighborhood and community life can be safely assumed. Consequently, neighbors sometimes knew each other by name and sight and sometimes did not. They functioned as neighbors because they occupied and traversed the same pocket of urban space, not because they were necessarily intimately familiar with one another.

Immigrants who arrived in the United States with relatively few resources but urban destinations tended to settle in neighborhoods inhabited by other immigrants, some from their home regions and some from elsewhere in Europe. The housing stock in initial settlements tended to be low quality and densely populated. Families crowded into small apartments to sleep and eat, often sharing quarters with other families. Some migrants planned to stay in the United States only a short time and made little connection with their local neighborhood; but others viewed themselves as permanently resettled and invested their monies and their emotions in their new environs. While women's lives largely centered on labor based within the home and they built social networks within and in close proximity to the buildings where they lived, such housing conditions impelled men and children out into local streets, where they came into frequent contact with their neighbors. The emotional range of such contacts ran the gamut of human possibility, from hatred to love to studied indifference. Immigrants and their children who prospered sufficiently to move out of crowded neighborhoods to areas of secondary urban settlement that forced street level contact less urgently nonetheless continued to gather in public spaces, making and remaking the neighborhood experience for one another.

The constant usage of neighborhood streets and other public spaces fostered innumerable interactions among residents. Although many contacts were functional or positive, as residents went about their daily business or sought to nurture community, at times they were tinged with tensions. Neighborhood denizens sometimes challenged strangers on the street over their right to be there, reflecting sporadic turf wars that defined ownership of neighborhood public spaces. In Roman Catholic areas, testing classically took the form of the question, "What parish are you from?" Rooted in a sense that local residency legitimized one's presence in a locale, this sort of exchange established whether the questioner and auditor were neighbors. An unsatisfactory response could prompt a hostile interchange that could escalate from verbal exchanges to physical violence. Boys and men, sometimes organized into gangs, chased away or beat interlopers—or were repelled themselves—illustrating who held the power to control the uses of local streets. Privately organized efforts to defend members against such hostility might aggravate neighborhood violence. Such conflict could also occur between established residents of the same neighborhood, in a struggle for local power, as a manifestation of local disputes over ethnic or gang primacy in an area or as a result of an ongoing conflict over access to neighborhood resources such as parks. Broader urban ethnic conflict, whether sporadic or sustained, also sometimes had neighborhood-based manifestations, as rioters sought out targets where they lived in noticeable concentrations. In October 1871, for example, white Los Angeles residents retaliated against the shooting death of a white man during an intraethnic Chinese gang fight by attacking the Chinatown neighborhood, burning and looting buildings and lynching residents.[15] However, with the notable exception of interracial rioting in response to attempted racial integration of housing, discussed later, most interethnic mob violence in American history has not been treated by historians as embodying neighborhood-based disputes. Neighborhoods, instead, function in most historical studies as backdrops of action for tensions based in work, class, and ethnicity itself, rather than place.

Some occupants of neighborhood public spaces were not in fact residents of the area but came into it for other purposes, such as to work or to spend leisure time. These activities, too, could provoke local conflict, when strangers entered guarded neighborhood spaces. One of the appeals of some working-class immigrant districts was their proximity to a range of employment opportunities. The availability of multiple worksites benefitted residents who changed employers frequently and who sent all possible family members into the labor force. When jobs were readily available, non-residents might be welcomed into a neighborhood, to work and perhaps to spend their money in local saloons. But in recessionary times, residents could try to protect "their" jobs by hindering strangers' ability to traverse neighborhood spaces in their search for employment. These processes could also work in reverse. Instead of provoking territoriality, a neighborhood dweller's sense of the scope of the city to which he or she had access could also grow with travels throughout urban space. A successful and peaceful visit to an unfamiliar portion of a city could introduce someone to new places where they might want to live, loosening an urbanite's bond with his neighborhood of residence.

In a similar fashion, urban politics also had the dual capacity to ground participants in the neighborhood or to broaden them out beyond the local to the citywide context. In cities with ward or territorial based representation, the tie between the successful politician and the local neighborhood was fundamental. Distributing the perquisites of office to the local political base who elected them ensured that aldermen and city councilors were returned to office. By contrast, politicians who aspired to higher office built coalitions that took them beyond their neighborhood of origin without breaking local ethnic ties. Political parties also balanced their citywide tickets ethnically to fight the perception that any single group or place held sway.

Ethnic urban neighborhoods fostered sexual and romantic relationships among neighbors, of both the same and different national origins. As young people moved around the streets of their neighborhoods, they inevitably met and became attached to romantic partners. In tightly knit, ethnically homogeneous neighborhoods, parents often succeeded in maintaining control over their daughters' romantic liaisons. Robert Orsi's *The Madonna of 115th Street*, for example, explains that, "Individuals were warned that to violate the blood bonding of the *domus* meant disaster."[16] Girls must grow up to marry, but only other Italians were acceptable within the community. In the post-World War II period, Jordan Stanger-Ross found among Philadelphia's Italians a similar and persistent inclination to marry locally and within the ethnic group, even as late as 1990.[17] By contrast, heterogeneous neighborhoods also facilitated the creation of new familial bonds across ethnic lines between members of different groups who lived in close proximity to one another. The most famous artistic representation of such relationships and their local consequences is the 1957 Broadway musical *West Side Story*'s interpretation of Shakespeare's *Romeo and Juliet*, in which Tony (Polish) and Maria (Puerto Rican) fall in love, leading to a fatal gang war between Tony's Jets and the Sharks of Maria's brother Bernardo. In less disastrous cases, cross-ethnic romances resulted in the creation of families with mixed or reduced ethnic identities in the next generation. Homosocial friendships formed in the neighborhood context had a similar effect of bridging ethnic boundaries. George Chauncey's *Gay New York* suggests that the varying familial migration patterns and cultural norms of Italians and Jews in the city accounted for the differences in reported homosexual activity in adjacent areas of the Lower East Side in the early twentieth century.[18]

Especially in the middle and late twentieth century, residents of urban neighborhoods sometimes created community-based organizations in order to bind neighbors to one another and to deal with the range of problems they perceived in their environs. The founding of such organizations, whose members typically specified their geographic boundaries in writing, had the effect of defining particular residents in and out of the neighborhood. The community organization that has received perhaps the most sustained scholarly attention is the Back of the Yards Neighborhood Council (BYNC), which was based in the ethnically diverse residential area adjacent to Chicago's South Side stockyards. The BYNC, founded in 1939, was the first major group organized by

Saul Alinsky, widely considered the father of community organizing in the United States.[19] But a host of organizations, ranging in scale from a city block to areas that encompassed 100,000 residents and networks of local organizations such as ACORN (Association of Community Organizations for Reform Now), proliferated across the country in the twentieth century.[20] As intensely local organizations, they tended to work on issues of immediate concern to area residents, such as beautification or improvement of local services. Some organizations, as they brought neighbors together to work on common problems, successfully encouraged cooperation among neighbors of diverse ethnic origins. In some cases, however, the common problem engaged members perceived was the incursion into the neighborhood of undesirable residents, often African Americans. In such cases, then community organizations expressed and exacerbated rather than ameliorated intergroup antagonisms.

RACIAL TRANSITION

Whatever permeability characterized white neighborhood boundaries when they were occupied by diverse groups of European immigrants and their descendants disappeared in the twentieth century in response to the first and second waves of the Great Migration of African Americans from the South to the urban North and West. The moderate moments and levels of mutual tolerance sometimes found in relationships among ethnic Americans in a shared geographic area only rarely extended to interracial neighborhoods. When African Americans sought housing on blocks and in neighborhoods that whites and ethnic Americans regarded as theirs, they usually encountered a combination of the following three responses: (1) visible expressions of racial hostility, including mobbing and attacks on private property, (2) the activation of community-based organizations that sought legal means of protecting the neighborhood's racial homogeneity, and (3) the departure of whites from the residential area. These responses tend to be referred to in popular parlance and scholarship by the shorthand term "white flight," but in my view this phrase glosses over the extent to which whites tried to keep their neighborhoods racially homogeneous before they abandoned them.[21]

During and after each of the world wars, large numbers of black Southerners escaped Jim Crow and sought new work opportunities and greater personal freedom in northern and western urban centers. Like earlier groups of European immigrants' chain migrations, African Americans followed their kin to urban centers, using letters and newspapers to guide their settlement patterns. Typically, migrants initially sought housing in areas that were already occupied by other African Americans, usually areas of older housing. Although prior to World War I the relatively small number of blacks in large cities like New York and Chicago lived clustered together in heterogeneous areas, the increased black population prompted whites to conceptualize racially defined neighborhood boundaries beyond which they did not welcome blacks except in transit to work. A range of behaviors, from cold shoulders to verbal and physical expressions of

NEIGHBORHOODS, IMMIGRANTS, AND ETHNIC AMERICANS   295

hostility, kept black migrants informed of where whites tolerated their presence. The protection of such neighborhood boundaries meant that the residential options available to African Americans were increasingly deteriorated and crowded with newcomers, yet still costly. So blacks with some financial means available to them tested the fixity of the boundaries in their search for better housing conditions. In cities whose residential areas were already built up, the desire for improved housing inevitably meant looking in neighborhoods occupied by nonblacks, often older ethnic residential areas. In most cities, new private housing developed in the twentieth century was marketed exclusively to white buyers. Once an area was opened to black settlement by a leading edge of residents who could purchase homes, African Americans of less wealth tended to follow, effectively "turning" a neighborhood from white to black occupancy.[22]

For much of the twentieth century, white homeowners and tenants were so hostile to the prospect of African American neighbors that they would not live in racially integrated neighborhoods. Their reasons—sometimes expressed publicly, sometimes left ineffable—included both personal racist feelings and also the logic of the racialized housing market. On the emotional side, whites' resistance to blacks stemmed from a familiar racist catalog: fears of equitable interracial sexual contact; expectations of a decline in public school standards in an interracial context; experiences of criminal activity that whites generalized beyond perpetrators to all African Americans; hostility over competition for jobs; and broad cultural stereotyping. On the economic front, white property owners understood themselves to have made a substantial financial investment in their homes, a sentiment reinforced in the middle of the twentieth century by the rise of the notion of the "American dream" of homeownership and the federal government's protection of mortgage payments from taxation. Precisely because of white racism, the housing market was divided into two audiences of white and black buyers. The operation of the "dual housing market" meant that once African Americans started occupying property in a white neighborhood, whites could no longer hope to sell to other white buyers. Instead, they had to sell either to real estate middlemen or African Americans. Although the shortage of housing in the African American market meant that blacks paid a premium to buy property, whites took losses on their investments as they sold quickly. This general process was widely recognized and publicized at mid-century, fueling a perception that the presence of African Americans in a neighborhood degraded its financial value and exacerbated already poor interracial relations.

Thomas J. Sugrue's landmark study of Detroit elaborated on sociologist Gerald Suttles' conceptualization of "defended neighborhoods" to distinguish how white residents in some neighborhoods offered only token resistance to African American in-migration from those where their hostility was sustained.[23] Some forms of neighborhood defense rested primarily of interactions with existing neighbors. In the first half of the twentieth century, property owners often formed racial restrictive covenants with nearby property owners or wrote racial restrictions into their deeds, making it a breach of contract to sell or rent a home to an African American. In 1948, in the case of *Shelley v. Kraemer*, the U.S. Supreme Court ruled legal enforcement of such deeds and restrictions to be unconstitutional. For decades after the *Shelley* ruling, however, property owners controlled to whom they offered their houses for sale and arranged for sales only to people whom they considered appropriate for the neighborhood, such as people they already knew or members of the same ethnic group. In Italian South Philadelphia, for example, parents frequently sold their homes to their children for a nominal payment.[24] Such transactions both provided for the financial stability of the next generation and preserved the racial and even ethnic makeup of the neighborhood. In other neighborhoods with less kin-based social cohesion, residents organized campaigns to discourage their neighbors from selling their property, distributing "This House Not for Sale" placards to display in windows. Different white ethnic groups responded to the black in-migration they feared differently. Jews, for example, who could sell their synagogues to in-migrant congregations, moved away relatively easily. By contrast, in *Urban Exodus* Gerald Gamm argues that Catholics, whose churches inscribed their relationship to their faith and neighborhood and whose dioceses owned their religious physical plant, dug their heels in and resisted blacks more directly.[25] The results in either case ended up being the same: segregated, all-black neighborhoods throughout the north and south.[26]

In many areas, whites responded to the perceived breaching of neighborhood boundaries, or the arrival of a black family on a new block within the neighborhood, with public expressions of their hostility. The first few black residents on a white block might find their homes surrounded by an angry mob or the target of bricks thrown through windows or Molotov cocktails on their porches. The extent of violence in Chicago in the 1950s was such that historian Arnold Hirsch labeled the period "an era of hidden violence."[27] Whites also deployed neighborhood-based organizations to deter would-be black neighbors. The classic expression of these lawful approaches to neighborhood defense is Lorraine Hansberry's play *A Raisin in the Sun*, in which a representative of the local homeowners' association offers to buy the Younger family's newly purchased house back from them. Starting in the late 1960s and early 1970s, white residents of a few areas, such as Chicago's Austin and Milwaukee's Sherman Park, tried to find ways to encourage whites to remain in interracial neighborhoods. There were few such efforts, however, and they were rarely successful. For the most part, whether they defended or left a neighborhood undefended, whites eventually moved out of areas where blacks took up occupancy.

The process of racial transition from white to black meant that neighborhood boundaries were repeatedly hardened, dissolved, and recreated. Social scientists of the Chicago School used the term "neighborhood succession," a metaphor borrowed from ecology, to describe this process. In some cases, the perceived neighborhood boundaries were the same before and after racial transition was complete. In Chicago, for example, the strength of the scholarly "community area" definition of neighborhoods, reinforced by the city government's adoption of sociologists' base map, was such that the neighborhood's names and boundaries stayed fairly constant despite the population change. The new residents did of course sometimes make use of new referents, such as calling a strip of streets beginning with the letter K "K-Town." In other cases, however, neighborhoods were redefined around the new populations. Jesse Hoffnung-Garskof suggests that while whites in New York City's Washington Heights "often saw the arrival of people of color as a shifting of neighborhood boundaries, Puerto Rican and black residents argued that the boundaries were the same and that they had crossed them."[28] Whether new residents of an urban area use the same name and boundaries to refer to it or discover new ways to delimit their spaces, the notion of breaking down a city into conceptually manageable neighborhood spaces persisted.

THE LATE TWENTIETH CENTURY

The latter decades of the twentieth century introduced greater concentrations of migrants from beyond Europe to the mix of urban ethnic neighborhoods. Although immigrants from Asia, Central and South America, and the Middle East had been present in American cities in small numbers since the nineteenth century, changing immigration laws and international demographic and political pressures gave these groups greater prominence in the late twentieth century. Dearborn, Michigan, for example, developed a large concentration of Middle Eastern immigrants, particularly but not exclusively from Lebanon. Readers of this essay may have noticed that much of the scholarship on the degree of ethnic segregation and conflict dates from the 1970s, when historians influenced by the moral lessons of the African American Civil Rights Movement sought to interpret its significance for other American groups. How scholars explain neighborhood boundaries and ethnic patterns in the context of twenty-first century over immigration is shifting. In the new period, Rachel Buff, for example, attentive to the heightened conflict over sharing the perquisites of citizenship with new immigrants, coined the term "denizenship" to describe how migrants occupy urban spaces.[29] Residents of ethnic neighborhoods continue to experience both interpersonal and ethnic conflict and cooperation within local boundaries as they explore how they fit into the larger urban landscape. For example, ongoing, low-level hostility between African American residents and Korean American grocery store owners was revealed in the wake of the civil disorders in Los Angeles in 1992, which were overtly a response to the acquittal of white police officers tried for assaulting Rodney King.[30] By contrast, in roughly the same period, ethnographer Roger Sanjek found extensive interethnic and interracial collaboration in civic projects in the Elmhurst-Corona section of Queens, New York.[31] Racial lines, however, show permeability only in one direction. Although many middle-class African Americans have made their way into otherwise ethnically integrated neighborhoods and suburbs, majority black neighborhoods in old central cities remain places where few non-blacks seek homes.

The late twentieth century experience of gentrification added a new component to the contestation of urban neighborhoods. As residential diversity gained a new cultural cachet in the post–Civil Rights movement era, a certain slice of the middle and upper middle classes sought out urban neighborhoods characterized by active street life and a population with international flair. Gentrifiers included young, upwardly mobile whites seeking affordable housing; childless gay couples who anticipated a more tolerant response than heterosexual, family oriented suburbs would offer them; and highly educated, professional African Americans. The presence of well-to-do residents whose investments in their homes raised both their own property values and the tax levies of their established but less wealthy neighbors generated a variety of local tensions over the character and control of neighborhood resources. Because many gentrifiers ostensibly hoped to maintain the diversity of their neighborhoods rather than simply displace existing residents, class and cultural conflicts played out in new ways. In Washington, D.C.'s Mount Pleasant neighborhood, for example, residents dismayed by the public urination of Latino men who socialized on the area's streets did not respond by having the police simply evict the offenders. Instead, they wrote a grant proposal to support public toilets.[32] Scholars have also noticed the increasing propensity of migrants eventually to settle in suburban areas, whose spatial features offer different opportunities for interethnic contact than afforded by dense urban neighborhoods.[33]

In summary, then, fixing the relationship between ethnic and neighborhood boundaries is a problem as complex as establishing the meaning and boundaries of any one neighborhood, which varied within a place and from person to person. For some urban dwellers, the neighborhood was the home place, requiring defense against strangers and providing the opportunity to locate a mate. For others, the local neighborhood was only a way station onto the larger city. Designation of neighborhoods and their boundaries is an enduring way by which Americans infuse meaning into the urban landscape, but their significance rests with each person who apprehends them.

NOTES

1. Robert A. Orsi, *The Madonna of 115th Street: Faith and Community in Italian Harlem, 1880–1950*, 3rd edition (New Haven & London: Yale University Press, 2010; originally published 1985), chapters 4 and 5.

2. Thomas J. Jablonsky, *Pride in the Jungle: Community and Everyday Life in Back of the Yards Chicago* (Baltimore and London: The Johns Hopkins University Press, 1993), chapter 6.

3. For the classic descriptions of the walking city, see Sam Bass Warner, Jr., *Streetcar Suburbs: The Process of Growth in Boston (1870–1900)*, 2nd Edition (Cambridge, MA, and London: Harvard University Press, 1978; originally published 1962), 15–21; and Kenneth T. Jackson, *Crabgrass Frontier: The Suburbanization of the United States* (New York and Oxford: Oxford University Press, 1985), 20–44 and 313–314.

4. Kenneth T. Jackson, "Bowery," *The Encyclopedia of New York City*, 2nd edition, ed. Kenneth T. Jackson (New Haven & London: Yale University Press, 2010), 148.

5. Robert E. Park, "The City: Suggestions for the Investigation of Human Behavior in the Urban Environment," in, *The City, with an Introduction by Morris Janowitz*, ed. Robert E. Park, Ernest W. Burgess, and Roderick D. McKenzie (Chicago and London: University of Chicago Press, 1974; originally published 1925), 40.

6. For example, see Chicago Fact Book Consortium, *Local Community Fact Book, Chicago Metropolitan Area, 1980, Based on the 1970 and 1980 Censuses* (Chicago: Chicago Review Press, 1984). On the community areas, see Sudhir Venkatesh, "Chicago's Pragmatic

Planners: American Sociology and the Myth of Community," *Social Science History* 25:2 (Summer 2001): 275–317.

7. Joseph J. Salvo, "Census Tracts," *Encyclopedia of the U.S. Census*, 2nd ed. Margo Anderson Constance, Citro, and Joseph Salvo, eds., (Washington, D.C.: CQ Press, 2011), 82–84.

8. Mary Elizabeth Brown, "Little Italy," *Encyclopedia of New York City*, 2nd ed. Kenneth T. Jackson, ed. (New Haven & London: Yale University Press, 2010), 758.

9. I would like to thank Lisa Silverman for her assistance with this paragraph.

10. David Chuenyan Lai, "The Visual Character of Chinatowns," in *Understanding Ordinary Landscapes*, ed. Paul Groth and Todd W. Bressi, 81–84 (New Haven and London: Yale University Press, 1997).

11. Amanda Seligman, "Edgewater," *The Encyclopedia of Chicago*, edited by Janice L. Reiff, Ann Durkin Keating, and James R. Grossman (Chicago: Chicago Historical Society, 2005), [http://www.encyclopedia.chicagohistory.org/pages/413.html].

12. Jordan Stanger-Ross, *Staying Italian: Urban Change and Ethnic Life in Postwar Toronto and Philadelphia*. (Chicago: The University of Chicago Press, 2009), 67–89; Joseph Sciorra, "'We Go Where the Italians Live': Religious Processions as Ethnic and Territorial Markers in a Multi-ethnic Brooklyn Neighborhood," in *Gods of the City*, ed. Robert A. Orsi, 310–340 (Bloomington and Indianapolis: Indiana University Press, 1999).

13. John Bodnar, Roger Simon, and Michael P. Weber, *Lives of their Own: Blacks, Italians, and Poles in Pittsburgh, 1900–1960* (Urbana: University of Illinois Press, 1982), 209.

14. The map referenced here is excerpted at "Hull House Maps Its Neighborhood," *The Encyclopedia of Chicago* [http://www.encyclopedia.chicagohistory.org/pages/410008.html]. The full study is *Hull-House Maps and Papers, a Presentation of Nationalities and Wages in a Congested District of Chicago, Together with Comments and Essays on Problems Growing out of the Social Conditions, by Residents of Hull-House, a Social Settlement at 235 South Halsted Street, Chicago, Ill.* (New York, Boston: T. Y. Crowell &Co., [1895]).

15. Paul A. Gilje, *Rioting in America* (Bloomington and Indianapolis: Indiana University Press, 1996), 127.

16. Orsi, 82.

17. Stanger-Ross, 102–103.

18. George Chauncey, *Gay New York: Gender, Urban Culture, and the Making of the Gay Male World, 1890–1940* (New York: Basic Books, 1994), 72–73.

19. The major works on Back of the Yards and the BNYC are Jablonsky, *Pride in the Jungle*, and Robert A. Slayton, *Back of the Yards: The Making of a Local Democracy* (Chicago and London: The University of Chicago Press, 1986).

20. For an overview of the breadth of community organizing activity in the US, see Patricia Mooney Melvin, ed. *American Community Organizations: A Historical Dictionary* (New York: Greenwood Press, 1986).

21. For a fuller expression of this argument, see Amanda I. Seligman, *Block by Block: Neighborhoods and Public Policy on Chicago's West Side* (Chicago: University of Chicago Press, 2005).

22. In general on white hostility to black neighbors, see Stephen Grant Meyer, *As Long as They Don't Move Next Door: Segregation and Racial Conflict in American Neighborhoods* (Lanham, MD and Oxford: Rowman & Littlefield, 2000). For a synthetic account of discrimination against African Americans in the North, see Thomas J. Sugrue, *Sweet Land of Liberty: The Forgotten Struggle for Civil Rights in the North* (New York: Random House, 2008).

23. Thomas J. Sugrue, *The Origins of the Urban Crisis: Race and Inequality in Postwar Detroit* (Princeton: Princeton University Press, 1996), 235–246.
24. Stanger-Ross, 46–51.
25. Gerald H. Gamm, *Urban Exodus: Why the Jews Left Boston and the Catholics Stayed* (Cambridge, MA: Harvard University Press, 1999).
26. For examples in Atlanta, see Ronald H. Bayor, *Race and the Shaping of Twentieth-Century Atlanta* (Chapel Hill: University of North Carolina Press, 1996) and Kevin M. Kruse, *White Flight: Atlanta and the Making of Modern Conservatism* (Princeton and Oxford: Princeton University Press, 2005).
27. Arnold R. Hirsch, *Making the Second Ghetto: Race and Housing in Chicago, 1940–1960* (Chicago: University of Chicago Press, 1998; originally published Cambridge: Cambridge University Press, 1983), chapter 2.
28. Jesse Hoffnung-Garskof, *A Tale of Two Cities: Santo Domingo and New York after 1950* (Princeton and Oxford: Princeton University Press, 2008), 100.
29. Rachel Buff, *Immigration and the Political Economy of Home: West Indian Brooklyn and American Indian Minneapolis, 1945–1992* (Berkeley: University of California Press, 2001).
30. On Korean Americans in this context, see Sumi K. Cho, "Korean Americans vs. African Americans, Conflict and Construction," 196–211, and Elaine H. Kim, "Home is Where the *Han* Is: A Korean American Perspective on the Los Angeles Upheavals," 215–235, both in *Reading Rodney King, Reading Urban Uprising*, ed. Robert Gooding-Williams (New York & London: Routledge, 1993).
31. Roger Sanjek, *The Future of Us All: Race and Neighborhood Politics in New York City* (Ithaca and London: Cornell University Press, 1998), especially part IV.
32. Gabriella Gahlia Modan, *Turf Wars: Discourse, Diversity, and the Politics of Place* (Malden, MA: Blackwell Publishing, 2007), chapter 4, "The Politics of Filth," pp. 137–169.
33. S. Mitra Kalita, *Suburban Sahibs: Three Immigrant Families and Their Passage from India to America* (New Brunswick, N.J.: Rutgers University Press, 2003); Chia Youyee Vang, *Hmong America: Reconstructing Community in Diaspora* (Urbana, Chicago, and Springfield: University of Illinois Press, 2010), 59.

BIBLIOGRAPHY

Barton, Josef J. *Peasants and Strangers: Italians, Rumanians, and Slovaks in an American City, 1890–1950* (Cambridge, MA: Harvard University Press, 1975).

Bayor, Ronald H. *Neighbors in Conflict: The Irish, Germans, Jews, and Italians of New York City, 1929–1941* (Baltimore and London: The Johns Hopkins University Press, 1978).

Gabaccia, Donna R. *From Sicily to Elizabeth Street: Housing and Social Change among Italian Immigrants, 1880–1930* (Albany: State University of New York Press, 1984).

Gamm, Gerald H. *Urban Exodus: Why the Jews Left Boston and the Catholics Stayed* (Cambridge, MA: Harvard University Press, 1999).

Hirsch, Arnold R. *Making the Second Ghetto: Race and Housing in Chicago, 1940–1960* (Chicago: The University of Chicago Press, 1998; originally published Cambridge: Cambridge University Press, 1983).

Howell, Ocean. *Making the Mission: Planning and Ethnicity in San Francisco* (Chicago: University of Chicago Press, 2015).

Jablonsky, Thomas J. *Pride in the Jungle: Community and Everyday Life in Back of the Yards Chicago* (Baltimore and London: The Johns Hopkins University Press, 1993).

Looker, Benjamin. *A Nation of Neighborhoods: Imagining Cities, Communities, and Democracy in Postwar America*. Chicago: University of Chicago Press, 2015.

Looker, Benjamin. "Microcosms of Democracy: Imagining the City Neighborhood in World War II-Era America." *Journal of Social History* 44, no. 2 (Winter 2010): 351–378.

Looker, Benjamin. "Visions of Autonomy: The New Left and the Neighborhood Government Movement of the 1970s." *Journal of Urban History* 38 (3) (May 2012): 577–559.

McGreevy, John T. *Parish Boundaries: The Catholic Encounter with Race in the Twentieth-Century Urban North* (Chicago: University of Chicago Press, 1996).

McMahon, Eileen M. *What Parish Are You From? A Chicago Irish Community and Race Relations* (Lexington, KY: University Press of Kentucky, 1995)

Mooney Melvin, Patricia. "Changing Contexts: Neighborhood Definition and Urban Organization." *American Quarterly* 37, no. 3 (1985): 357-367.

Orsi, Robert A. *The Madonna of 115th Street: Faith and Community in Italian Harlem, 1880–1950*, 3rd edition (New Haven & London: Yale University Press, 2010; originally published 1985).

Rieder, Jonathan. *Canarsie: The Jews and Italians of Brooklyn against Liberalism* (Cambridge, MA: Harvard University Press, 1985).

Rotella, Carlo. *The World Is Always Coming to an End: Pulling Together and Apart in a Chicago Neighborhood* (Chicago: University of Chicago Press, 2019).

Sanjek, Roger. *The Future of Us All: Race and Neighborhood Politics in New York City* (Ithaca and London: Cornell University Press, 1998).

Seligman, Amanda I. "Neighborhoods." In *Encyclopedia of Milwaukee*, edited by Margo Anderson and Amanda I. Seligman, https://emke.uwm.edu/entry/neighborhoods/.

Stanger-Ross, Jordan. *Staying Italian: Urban Change and Ethnic Life in Postwar Toronto and Philadelphia* (Chicago: The University of Chicago Press, 2009).

Sugrue, Thomas J. *The Origins of the Urban Crisis: Race and Inequality in Postwar Detroit* (Princeton: Princeton University Press, 1996).

Talen, Emily. *Neighborhood* (New York: Oxford University Press, 2018

Wilson, William Julius, and Taub, Richard P., *There Goes the Neighborhood: Racial, Ethnic, and Class Tensions in Four Chicago Neighborhoods and their Meaning for America* (New York: Knopf, 2006).

Yans-McGlaughlin, Virginia. *Family and Community: Italian Immigrants in Buffalo, 1880–1930* (Ithaca: Cornell University Press, 1977).

CHAPTER 17

MACHINE BOSSES, REFORMERS, AND THE POLITICS OF ETHNIC AND MINORITY INCORPORATION

STEVEN P. ERIE AND VLADIMIR KOGAN

POLITICAL machines, the bosses who controlled them, and the reformers who fought against them have been a mainstay of America's ethnic history. A comparison between urban politics in the nineteenth, twentieth, and early twenty-first century provides a way to understand American ethnic politics. Does the incorporation of immigrants and minorities in the early twenty-first century follow the same political dynamics as in earlier periods of American history? Or, have the processes and character of ethnic political incorporation fundamentally changed over time? Answering both of these questions requires a reconsideration of the pivotal role played by urban political leaders and institutions in shaping the political emergence and suppression of various immigrant and ethnic groups throughout American political history. Although many scholarly accounts identify big-city party bosses as ethnic integrators—fashioning and rewarding multiethnic "rainbow coalitions"—and paint political reformers as defenders of native-born Protestants, the political record points to a much more nuanced and complicated pattern of racial and ethnic politics.

New York City and Chicago, two well-studied cities with strong machine and ethnic political traditions, provide good exemplars. In the nineteenth century, New York politician William Tweed (commonly known as Boss Tweed) built Tammany Hall—the executive committee of New York City's Democratic Party and a known hotbed of political corruption—through the political mobilization and incorporation of Irish Americans. In Tweed's wake, the Irish firmly controlled Tammany Hall and much of city politics until the 1930s, only partially incorporating later-arriving immigrant groups. In the twentieth century, New York's famed reform mayor, Fiorello La Guardia (1934–1945), defeated Irish-controlled Tammany Hall, in part by appealing to and including

Jews, Italian Americans, and, to a much lesser extent, African Americans in his political coalition.

In Chicago, legendary Chicago Mayor Richard J. Daley (1955–1976) established the city's powerful Democratic machine while providing few accommodations to the city's African American community. These are among the leading examples of nineteenth and twentieth century boss and reform rule. In the early twenty-first century, urban politics continues to parallel many of these dynamics, with New York's Afro-Caribbean community confronting challenges of leadership development and political inclusion in the face of rear-guard resistance from the remnants of the once-powerful borough party organizations.

BOSS TWEED, TAMMANY HALL, AND THE IRISH

William M. Tweed was an early leader of Tammany Hall, the legendary political machine that played a major role in New York City politics from the mid-nineteenth century to the 1960s. Tammany Hall controlled Democratic Party nominations and patronage in Manhattan from the Civil War until the election of reform mayor Fiorello La Guardia in 1933. Despite a brief resurgence in the 1950s, Tammany collapsed in the 1960s.

Tweed, of Scotch Irish ancestry, had become head of Tammany Hall in 1863 and consolidated control over city government by early 1869. The reign of the so-called, "Tweed Ring," with the boss's political allies appointed to key public offices, was short lived. In 1871, Tweed was arrested and later convicted of stealing an estimated $25 million to $45 million—between $1 billion and $2 billion in 2010 dollars—or even more from New York City's treasury through fraud and corruption.

The initial research on Boss Tweed's legacy and, more generally, nineteenth-century Tammany Hall, was firmly rooted in the early twentieth-century muckraking tradition and focused on the techniques and epic scale of the Tweed Ring's graft and corruption. By the 1960s, however, a more positive scholarly view of Tweed and Tammany Hall began to emerge. Seymour J. Mandelbaum's *Boss Tweed's New York*[1] invoked communications and organization theory to show how Tweed organized and centralized a political marketplace, exchanging patronage jobs for the political support and votes of newly enfranchised immigrant voters.

The new paradigm placed Boss Tweed and urban political machines at the center of efforts to incorporate the first generation of European immigrants, particularly the Irish, into American democracy. Between 1846 and 1855, 1.4 million Irish immigrants escaping the potato famine came to the United States. Though nearly all were rural cottars and laborers, more than 90 percent of the migrants would settle in cities. The immigrants were field laborers, not farmers, in a single-crop economy that had failed. Because of the transatlantic packet boat routes, most of the immigrants landed in the eastern port cities of New York, Boston, and Philadelphia and were too poor to move inland. The Irish diaspora dramatically altered the complexion of these northern cities. By 1850, there were 133,730 Irish-born inhabitants of New York City, 26 percent of the total population.[2]

The Irish migration soon took political form. The machine represented the dominant urban political institution of the late nineteenth century. Assisted by early party leaders such as Boss Tweed, the Irish became arguably its leading architects. By 1890, Irish bosses ran most of the big-city Democratic machines constructed in the post-Civil War era. Party organizations such as Tammany Hall organized and linked the "input" and "output" dimensions of the local political system. On the input side, precinct captains mobilized the electorate. Local bosses controlled party caucuses and conventions and thus nominations to local offices. By controlling voters and officeholders, the machine could control the output side of politics—patronage jobs, contracts, franchises, and services. The machine maintained itself in power by skillfully deploying these resources. Bosses purchased voter support with individual economic inducements such as offers of public jobs or services.

Advancing a cultural theory, Daniel Patrick Moynihan,[3] a senator from the state of New York (1977–2001), argued that urban machines like Tammany Hall were transplants of village life in Ireland. Other scholars such as Martin Shefter[4] focused on the role of entrepreneurial political leaders. Party bosses like Tweed built centralized machines by successfully resolving the organization's maintenance needs—creating a winning supply of votes, rewarding and disciplining the party's henchmen, controlling public officials, and securing adequate party financing and patronage.

Boss Tweed's prodigious efforts at incorporating and rewarding poor Irish immigrants are well documented. First, he cranked up Tammany's naturalization mill. During his short tenure, the city's electorate nearly doubled in size, from 71,000 to 135,000 voters. Under "Honest John" Kelly, Tweed's successor, Tammany's citizenship factory continued to churn out now-eligible voters. By Kelly's death in 1886, Tammany had naturalized nearly 80 percent of the city's Irish, German, and other "old" (western European) immigrants. These new citizens swelled the ranks of machine voters and helped consolidate Tammany's hold over the party and the city.

During this formative stage of machine building, Tammany and other big-city Democratic Party organizations did more than mobilize immigrant voters. They also substantially increased public spending in order to reward these supporters. Boss Tweed, for example, embarked on a program in the late 1860s of massive deficit financing in part to enlarge the city payroll. A contemporary observer estimated that there were 12,000 to 15,000 members of Tweed's "Shiny Hat Brigade," the holders of newly created municipal sinecures. Under Tweed, the city's debt nearly tripled, rising from $36 million in 1868 to $136 million at the end of 1870. By 1868, Tweed controlled state as well as city government. He broadened his appeal to immigrant and working-class voters, such as the Irish, through state subsidies to Catholic schools and to religious charities.

As Tammany Hall and the other big-city Democratic machines consolidated power, they began to turn their back on the "rainbow" approach to coalition building and public spending. To reduce the threat of middle-class and business tax revolt, post-Tweed Tammany Hall, now firmly under Irish control, fashioned alliances with the business community. What ensued was a late nineteenth-century era of municipal retrenchment as per capita public spending and debt fell. The machine's monopoly status and more conservative fiscal policies did not bode well for later arriving immigrants. An entrenched Tammany Hall would no longer quickly turn out newly minted voters. Between 1886 and 1897, under boss Richard Croker, the city's electorate grew at one-half the rate it had under his predecessor "Honest John" Kelly (1872–1886)—33 percent as opposed to 68 percent.[5]

The paradigm of big-city bosses and machines as ethnic integrators best fits the case of the nineteenth-century Irish immigrants. For the Irish, there were Old World roots to their political skills. In Ireland, the late eighteenth-century and early nineteenth-century struggle to repeal the Penal Laws, which had reduced Irish Catholics to penury and powerlessness, brought the Irish group solidarity and experience with mass political organization. The Irish would also benefit politically from the spread of the national educational system in the early nineteenth century. The proportion of the population who spoke English rose from an estimated 50 percent in 1800 to 95 percent in 1851. Yet the development of the American party system also shaped the character of Irish American political participation. The Irish affected by the famine arrived in the late 1840s and early 1850s as the parties were entering their modern or mobilization phase. Urban Irish immigrants benefited from the fierce competition among urban Democratic Party factions in their electoral contests with Whigs and Republicans.

New Immigrants and the Rise of La Guardia's Reform Coalition

During the last two decades of the nineteenth century, growing economic and political hardships in parts of Europe transformed the ethnic composition of migrants arriving in American cities. While earlier waves of immigration were dominated by Irish and German families, newcomers came increasingly from southern and eastern Europe during this period. In 1890, Jews—from Russia and Poland—and Italians represented one in twenty New York residents; over the next four decades, the figure would rise to 36 percent of the total, or more than one in three New Yorkers.

Although the immigrants generally supported Democrats and voted for Tammany Hall candidates, Italians and Jews were clearly the machine's junior partners. These groups received far more limited public benefits than Irish supporters and, partly as a result, maintained weaker ties to the party organization. This arrangement represented a deliberate, and in many ways rational, decision on the part of Tammany bosses. Among Italians, for example, the growing population counts greatly overestimated the group's electoral importance due to very low naturalization rates among Italian immigrants.

A large number of Italian immigrants were temporary workers who eventually moved back to Europe.

Unlike its energetic efforts to incorporate Irish and German immigrants, the now-entrenched Manhattan machine had few incentives to invest resources in helping Italian immigrants attain citizenship and thus become eligible voters. Although Italians won some low-level positions within the organization, Italian voters received substantially fewer benefits in exchange for their support compared to the machine's core constituency, the Irish.

By contrast, Jews posed a considerably greater threat to the continued electoral dominance of the Tammany machine and thus won substantially greater recognition. Overall, Jewish voters were more numerous compared to their Italian counterparts and were also far less reliably Democratic, creating a swing bloc large enough to potentially help unseat the machine in a strong anti-Tammany year. During the tenure of powerful boss Charles Francis Murphy (1902–1924), Tammany diligently courted Jewish voters. Boss Murphy assiduously rooted out anti-Semitism within the party while Tammany-linked politicians in the state legislature provided strong symbolic support for the Jewish community through the introduction of legislation outlawing discrimination.[6] However, in their effort to attracting Jewish voters, neither Boss Murphy nor his successors attempted to redistribute political resources away from the Irish. Although the machine helped many Jews find well-paying government jobs, these were primarily new positions created through the dramatic expansion of the city's public school system during this period rather than a reallocation of spots previously filled by Irish workers.

This two-tiered coalition—Irish at the core with Jews and Italians enjoying the residual benefits—helped preserve the electoral dominance of the Tammany machine through the 1920s. However, by the early 1930s, the local Democratic Party faced serious challenges to its continued rule. First, highly publicized scandals triggered a series of investigations that exposed deep corruption within the organization, stirring anti-Tammany sentiment. The Great Depression also strained city finances, triggering deep retrenchment in the city budget. In an effort to protect Irish positions, city leaders concentrated the cuts on the public schools, hitting Jews particularly hard. Finally, national presidential campaigns that featured Franklin Delano Roosevelt and Al Smith, the first Catholic to run for president, led to substantial mobilization and participation among new immigrants, Italians in particular. These new voters did not have the same ties to the local Democratic machine, nor did they enjoy access to the substantial benefits that depended on Tammany's continued electoral success.

Collectively, scandal, retrenchment, and record turnout dramatically weakened the machine's electoral foundation and deprived it of key resources needed to sustain its political operation. In 1933, Tammany-supported Mayor John Patrick O'Brien—first elected to the job a year earlier after corruption scandals had forced out another machine-backed incumbent—was defeated by former Congressman Fiorello Henry La Guardia in a three-way race. Although La Guardia was a nominal Republican, he came from the shrinking progressive wing of the party and was a strong supporter of

Roosevelt's New Deal. La Guardia rose to prominence in 1917 when he defeated another Tammany candidate and won a congressional seat long controlled by the party machine.

His personal background and political history made La Guardia a particularly effective candidate to woo Jewish and Italian voters. Born to Italian immigrant parents, La Guardia was half-Jewish and could speak Yiddish. During his time in Congress, La Guardia made himself a strong advocate for immigrants, opposing efforts to enact new barriers to naturalization and immigration. He had also opposed Prohibition and for many years worked with grassroots groups to naturalize Italian immigrants and register them to vote.[7] Unlike Tammany Hall, which saw organized labor as a threat to its power and heavily cracked down on unions, La Guardia was friendly with both unions and New York's Socialist Party, two groups with close ties to the Jewish community. Perhaps most critical to the 1933 election, La Guardia also had strong supporters in the native-born reform community that had long sought to eliminate corruption and bring about changes in local government that would weaken the Democratic machine.

La Guardia's success—and, in particular, the role of new immigrants in his electoral coalition—presents an important challenge to the conventional scholarly wisdom about the machine-reform dynamic. Both Edward C. Banfield and James Q. Wilson's classic text on urban politics, *City Politics*,[8] and Richard Hofstadter's historical account in *The Age of Reform*[9] stress the sharp ethnic and racial divide that defined the battle lines between machine bosses and reformers. Both of these accounts emphasized the importance of immigrants in providing electoral support for the machines and identified the native born—especially white-collar professionals and Protestants—as the political base of the reformers. Although perhaps an adequate description of La Guardia's first election, the conventional model does a poor job of explaining the patterns of electoral support that led to La Guardia's two subsequent terms and the pivotal role of new immigrants in supporting the reform slate during these elections. In his successful 1933 mayoral campaign, La Guardia ran on a combined Republican-City Fusion Party ticket. The ticket was ethnically balanced, with Italian and Jewish candidates nominated for prominent offices. La Guardia won a substantial number of votes from these two groups and also from other Republicans and reform voters.

Once in office, La Guardia worked quickly to dismantle the apparatus of the Tammany machine and to create new opportunities for his supporters. The mayor greatly expanded the reach of civil service reforms, eliminating thousands of politically appointed positions and replacing them with jobs filled on the basis on merit and competitive exams. His administration also changed the formal qualifications required for many city jobs, increasing the weight given to formal schooling and imposing educational requirements for many city jobs. Both sets of reforms benefited La Guardia supporters, especially well-educated Jews who received much greater access to city jobs previously reserved for Tammany Hall's Irish supporters. In addition, La Guardia appointed both Jews and Italians to powerful positions in city government. La Guardia's outspoken opposition to Nazism, amid rising tensions in Europe, further strengthened his stature in the Jewish community.

Overall, La Guardia's reforms proved to be resoundingly successful in forging a new electoral coalition that attracted substantial support from Jews and Italians, two groups that had been neglected by the Democratic machine. In 1937, La Guardia became the first reform mayor in the city's history to be re-elected for a second term, winning more than 60 percent of the vote in heavily Italian precincts and almost 70 percent in Jewish districts. Four years later, La Guardia was re-elected once again. In the third contest, he again secured strong support from Jews, winning more than 70 percent of the vote in Jewish precincts. His support among Italians, however, declined somewhat due to both greater efforts by Democrats to win back the Italian vote and La Guardia's criticism of Mussolini and support for Roosevelt's interventionist foreign policy. La Guardia won a minority of the Irish and German vote in 1937, and his support among these pro-Tammany voters slipped even further in 1941.[10]

In both of the latter two elections, La Guardia also won overwhelmingly among African American voters. This sustained support is perhaps surprising, given the limited gains that blacks had made during the La Guardia administration. Blacks were hit particularly hard by the Great Depression, which only worsened their already-poor living conditions and further intensified grievances in the face of continued discrimination in both housing and employment. In 1935, false rumors that police had killed a black child accused of shoplifting sparked a riot in heavily black Harlem. In the aftermath, La Guardia appointed a biracial commission to investigate the causes of the riot. When the commission released a report highly critical of city government, however, the mayor buried the report and largely ignored its findings and recommendations.

There is little doubt that La Guardia sympathized with the struggles of New York blacks and invested more effort than his predecessors did in bringing needed economic development to black neighborhoods. Particularly after the riot, La Guardia appointed African Americans to several prominent public positions and opened new relief bureaus in Harlem. However, progress for the black community under La Guardia was uneven. In 1943, the mayor's support for a new housing project that planned to exclude African American residents helped contribute to another round of racial rioting in Harlem.

Indeed, the experience of African Americans during this period highlights La Guardia's mixed legacy in bringing about greater minority political incorporation in New York. Groups at the core of the La Guardia reform coalition—in particular, Jews and Italians—won access to greater public benefits under the mayor's watch. Blacks, however, remained much more on the periphery, replicating the two-tiered electoral coalition that had been the hallmark of the Tammany machine. Some of reforms pushed through by La Guardia would later hamper future incorporation efforts by emerging minorities. For example, strong civil service protections that insulated bureaucrats from political control would eventually come to represent a key barrier to reversing a culture of racism and discrimination. Excessive educational requirements kept many qualified blacks from attaining public employment. Decades later, strict height requirements for firefighting jobs put in place to limit the reach of patronage politics would also keep Puerto Rican immigrants and their family members from securing city firefighting jobs.[11]

Richard J. Daley, the Chicago Machine, and African Americans

Richard J. Daley, who served both as Chicago's long-serving mayor and Democratic Party chieftain from the mid-1950s to his death in 1976, was arguably the most powerful twentieth-century urban boss. Despite the fact that he ruled the city with an iron hand and extended his influence deeply into state and national politics, Richard J. Daley and his son Richard M. Daley, Chicago's mayor from 1989 to 2011, would be among the last of a dying breed of big-city bosses.

The post-World War II era marked the decline and demise of nearly all of the old-style urban party organizations. The machine's traditional supply of patronage jobs and social services dwindled. The flight of industry and the white middle class to the suburbs cut sharply into the tax base of the older northern cities. The introduction of merit systems in the 1940s and 1950s cut further into the machine's patronage stock. In the 1960s, new urban political actors—public sector unions and minorities—mounted a frontal assault on the remnants of the patronage system using collective bargaining agreements and court-ordered affirmative action. The machine's control over social services weakened in the face of competition from the federal government and labor unions. The New Deal's legacy of social insurance and welfare programs lay beyond the bosses' apparent reach.

Perhaps the most serious challenge to boss rule was the rapidly changing character of the big-city electorate. Wartime and postwar prosperity benefited white ethnics, the machine's traditional supporters, many of whom had moved to the suburbs. Those who remained in the city demanded low taxes, homeowner rather than social services, and the preservation of white neighborhoods and property values. The postwar machines also faced the challenge of accommodating a third wave of poor migrants to the cities. Southern blacks flocked to northern cities like Chicago in the largest domestic migration in history. They were later joined by Hispanics migrating from Mexico, Puerto Rico, and Latin America. In Chicago, African Americans and Hispanics constituted a majority of the population in 1980, up from one-quarter in 1960. The new migrants demanded the machine's traditional benefits—patronage and welfare services—at a time when the bosses were less able to supply them. Nevertheless, the Daley machine would show remarkable ingenuity and resiliency in the face of declining resources and shifts in the big-city electorate.

Chicago's African American community appeared well positioned to make claims on the Daley machine. Richard A. Keiser[12] argues that by 1950, African Americans had achieved more political empowerment in Chicago than any other city. The city's robust inter- and intra-party electoral competitiveness in the early twentieth century created strong incentives for competitors to woo the African American vote. Even though the black vote was small in this era, when it was mobilized, it could make a difference in competitive elections.

At first, the Chicago Democratic machine avidly courted the minority vote. Congressman William Dawson, the only black in Daley's inner circle, controlled Chicago's massive South Side ghetto. Blacks on the South Side and on the racially changing West Side supplied the margin of victory in three of Mayor Daley's six victorious campaigns. In the 1955 election, Daley defeated his Republican opponent by 127,000 votes, receiving a 125,000-vote plurality in heavily black machine-run wards. In 1963, when white homeowners staged a major revolt against the Daley machine because of a 100 percent increase in property taxes since 1955, Daley narrowly defeated his Polish American Republican challenger only because of a massive black vote in machine-controlled wards.

Despite their electoral fealty, African Americans received few material rewards from the Daley organization. Rather than giving Congressman Dawson significant power or patronage, Daley rewarded him with control of vice and gambling in the South Side ghetto. Blacks comprised 40 percent of Chicago's population in 1970, but only 20 percent of the municipal workforce, largely in menial positions. Untangling the complex relationship between the Daley machine and the black community, William Grimshaw[13] documented the creation of several distinct party regimes. Daley carefully chose which black politicians to elevate within the party hierarchy, particularly Catholics and public employees to better ensure their loyalty. The poorer "black belt" wards on the South Side fared worse than the "plantation wards" on the West Side.

When Martin Luther King Jr. arrived in Chicago in 1966 to lead dramatic marches into all-white neighborhoods as part of an open-housing campaign, he was greeted by handpicked African American leaders with strong allegiances to the Daley machine. The resulting "summit accord" between King and the mayor, in which the protest marches would stop while city leaders would press for fair housing, was never seriously implemented under the Daley administration. In 1968, after King's assassination, Daley issued his infamous "shoot to kill" order to police during the ensuing ghetto riots.

The Daley organization judiciously used welfare-state programs to control the minority vote and siphon off discontent at minimal cost to the city treasury and tax-conscious white homeowners. Public housing and Aid to Families with Dependent Children (AFDC) represented major New Deal programs used to placate black constituents. Migrating blacks confronted an acute housing shortage in Chicago as the machine collaborated with real-estate brokers to confine blacks to the crowded ghetto. Daley secured federal money to build low-income housing projects, and these public housing projects not only soothed the fears of white ethnics, but they also concentrated the black vote and made it more controllable. Although the machine exerted little control over AFDC eligibility, it assisted black claimants in securing welfare benefits and claimed credit for increasing benefits. Under machine auspices, the AFDC participation rate for black families in Chicago rose from 18 percent in

1969 to 32 percent in 1979. The machine also commandeered Great Society programs to build support in the black community, particularly among the middle class. Federal antipoverty programs created sizable employment opportunities for managers and service providers.[14]

Using federal programs to influence the black vote, the Daley machine by the late 1960s had developed a new formula for electoral success: mobilize the white ethnic vote, particularly in wards undergoing racial transition. Appealing to white ethnics, Daley froze the property tax rate; prioritized homeowner and neighborhood services such as street repair, tree trimming, and garbage collection; and supported the preservation of white neighborhoods and schools. In contrast, the large African American vote, so crucial in 1963, was no longer needed for victory. In fact, the black vote now loomed as a risk, particularly if black independents could capture it and challenge machine hegemony. The machine worked at diluting the now-superfluous minority vote. Wards on the South Side were racially gerrymandered. When black sublieutenant William Dawson died in 1970, the machine groomed no replacement.

After Daley died in 1976, the machine's winning formula seemed to unravel. In 1983, black mayoral candidate Harold Washington fashioned a rainbow coalition of blacks, Hispanics, and white liberals to narrowly defeat Republican candidate Bernard Epton. The city's white ethnics, the machine's traditional mainstays, voted heavily for Epton. Washington's razor-thin victory depended on a massive mobilization of black voters. In 1979, only 35 percent of eligible blacks had voted; in 1983, an unprecedented 73 percent of black voters went to the polls. Yet Washington's victory and the prospects for an enduring rainbow coalition proved to be short-lived. In 1987, Washington died while still in office, creating a succession problem. In 1989, Richard M. Daley, the legendary boss's son, defeated Washington's appointed successor and rebuilt the machine with white ethnic, Hispanic, and business support. Once again, African Americans were left largely on the outside looking in.

AFRO-CARIBBEANS IN TWENTY-FIRST-CENTURY NEW YORK CITY

By the second half of the twentieth century, the weakening of the Democratic Party machines in both Chicago and New York created new—if temporary—opportunities for minority empowerment. In both cities, emerging African American leaders took advantage of the openings to increase representation and participation for the black community. In the 1980s and early 1990s, fragmentation among Democratic ranks helped lead to the election of the first black mayors in both cities, Harold Washington in Chicago (1983–1987) and David Dinkins in New York (1990–1993), although both headed weak administrations and served only one term each. In contrast to Chicago, however, African American leaders in New York succeeded in institutionalizing some of their newfound influence following Dinkins' re-election loss to Republican Rudy Giuliani. Black officials rose up through the ranks to secure top leadership roles in the various Democratic Party organizations in the outer boroughs.

Contrary to theoretical predictions that black mobilization would come primarily through the creation of successful "rainbow coalitions," uniting blacks with Latinos and other underrepresented minorities, the growing influence of African American leaders in New York did not translate into a new minority-led alliance. Indeed, near the end of the twentieth century, strong political coalitions between blacks and other minority groups failed to materialize, with conflict and tension marking both black Asian and black Latino relations.[15]

Dramatic growth in Afro-Caribbean migration under America's post-1965 immigration regime—with a large share of the newcomers from English-speaking Caribbean areas settling in New York City—created serious divisions even within the black community. By the year 2000, more than 500,000 Afro-Caribbeans were living in New York City, compared to just under 1.5 million African Americans.[16] Rather than helping to incorporate the new immigrants into the political process to enlarge the size of the black voting bloc, however, African Americans within the established Democratic Party organizations have fought to preserve their own influence against attacks from emerging Caribbean political challengers.

Growing conflict between black-led Democratic Party organizations and the new wave of Caribbean immigrants belied the central role historically played by Caribbean leaders in the party. During the 1940s and 1950s, New Yorkers of Caribbean decent represented some of the most powerful black faces in the Democratic Party. When Saint Lucian-born Hulan Jack was elected as the borough president of Manhattan in 1954, he became the highest-ranking black elected official in the country. By the late 1960s, however, Caribbeans were replaced by a new generation of African American activists who took on leadership roles in Democratic organizations in Brooklyn, Queens, and the Bronx, home to ethnically segregated neighborhoods where a substantial share of New York's black population lived.[17]

Black Democratic Party leaders have been slow to embrace the growing ranks of Afro-Caribbeans who have arrived in the post-1965 wave of immigration, even though most have settled in many of the same historically black neighborhoods in the outer boroughs. Although African Americans and Caribbean immigrants share many of the same political priorities, including concerns about continued discrimination and police abuse, and have both supported Democrats in national elections, the two groups have failed to form a unified political front.

During the 1980s, Caribbean political organizations—led by generally more conservative leaders than the overall immigrant population—broke ranks with other black groups in several high-profile contests. In the mid-1980s, a group of 150 prominent Caribbean leaders supported the re-election of Mayor Ed Koch—a conservative Democrat who had alienated many in the African American community—in the hope of increasing their access to the mayor, who was expected to win another term.

Black leaders also resented Caribbean support won by other local white candidates who were facing strong insurgent challenges from African American opponents. In 1984, for example, leaders of the African American community attempted to unseat Brooklyn state senator Marty Markowitz by backing a strong challenger to him for the Democratic nomination. Although representing an increasingly black district, Markowitz successfully retained his seat by vigorously courting the Afro-Caribbean vote.[18]

In addition, leaders within the Democratic borough organizations have done little to speed the political incorporation of ethnic Caribbeans. Despite very low levels of naturalization, particularly among more recent arrivals, and even lower rates of voter registration and participation, the dominant Democratic Party has not organized a campaign to encourage immigrants to become citizens or voters. According to political science scholar Reuel Rogers, the party's approach has been marked by "benign neglect":

> Although hundreds of thousands of Afro-Caribbeans have been migrating to New York since the 1960s, the city's parties have played almost no proactive role in encouraging their political participation. New York's Democratic Party has been more inclined to ignore Afro-Caribbean newcomers, even in the face of their growing numbers, expanding residential enclaves, and obvious potential for electoral influence, in boroughs such as Brooklyn and Queens. Party elites mostly have turned a blind eye to the immigrants, and sometimes even blocked their entry into the political system.[19]

In the face of political mobilization within the Afro-Caribbean community, party leaders have followed two strategies. First, they have used their influence to support incumbents who faced Caribbean challengers. For example, the election of Una Clarke to the City Council in 1991, becoming the first Caribbean-born person to be elected to New York's City Council, was initially challenged in court by the party-supported candidate. When such efforts have proved unsuccessful, party leaders have followed the Chicago and Tammany model by selectively incorporating handpicked Caribbean leaders into the party organization, without addressing the needs or representational aspirations of the broader immigrant community.

REASSESSING BOSSES AND REFORMERS AS ETHNIC INTEGRATORS

Throughout American political history, municipal governments and their elected leaders have played a central role in incorporating newcomers into the political process. In the nineteenth century, political bosses and their machines assisted many immigrants, primarily Irish and German, in laying down roots and provided them access to jobs and critical social services. Although many machines were marked by patronage and corruption, it is important to recognize that political parties during this period served a critical redistributive function, channeling a significant share of governmental resources to needy urban populations.

Over the long term, however, political bosses did not prove to be unwavering allies of immigrants and minority groups. Although party organizations reached out to new groups when they faced competition from political opponents, by the twentieth century, entrenched machines largely neglected more recent waves of immigrants and, at times, discouraged participation from new voters who threatened to destabilize their electoral hegemony. In some cities during this period, it was political reformers, long considered opponents of immigrant interests, who reached out to groups marginalized by the political machine. In New York, reform mayor Fiorello La Guardia helped open local government to Italian and Jewish immigrants. In later years, another reformist leader, Mayor John Lindsay (1966–1973), similarly created new opportunities in the city for African Americans.

Indeed, the historical record suggests that the level of electoral competition—rather than the identity or partisanship of political incumbents—has had the most important impact on the extent of political empowerment of immigrant and minority groups. Political parties have reached out to and mobilized excluded groups when they have faced strong the likelihood of losing elections to their political opponents. Under these conditions, party leaders have courted potentially pivotal and unattached voters to strengthen their electoral base. By contrast, entrenched parties—facing only weak opponents and a consistent record of election victories with large margins—have been free to pursue a more narrow distribution of public benefits, rewarding their core supporters. New groups that arrived after the formation of the governing coalition, like Jews and Italians under the Tammany machine, did not share equally in the fruits of victory.

Outside of major immigration destinations in the North, which have been the focus of the case studies examined in this chapter, the politics of race and nationality tended to follow a different historical trajectory. In smaller suburban cities, like those in the Southwest, strong party organizations did not emerge. Instead, reformers won early political victories and used their control of local government to adopt electoral institutions—off-year elections, at-large districts, council-manager forms of government—that effectively depressed participation among minority groups and lower-income, poorly educated voters.[20] In this region, reformers did indeed fit the conventional wisdom academic accounts of native leaders' opposition to minority incorporation, although they appeared to be motivated primarily by the logic of electoral survival rather than a deeply rooted Anglo-Saxon Protestant "ethos."

Although individual political leaders, such as specific political bosses and reformers, made important personal contributions to the history of ethnic and immigrant politics in America, their most important and long-lasting impact may have been in the design of political institutions. In many cases, these institutions survived the administrations of individual leaders and continued to shape the pattern of political participation long afterward. In the Southwest, for example, reform institutions like at-large elections proved effective in diluting the voices of geographically concentrated minority populations, especially Latinos, for many decades. These groups did not attain recognition or representation until the Voting Rights Act led to the establishment of district (ward) elections. In many cities, the adoption of civil service reforms have greatly limited political discretion in public employment, with mixed effects on historically underrepresented minority groups.

While urban government has attracted much of the attention from scholars interested in understanding the politics of ethnic and minority incorporation, it is important to note that many issues critical to determining the nature of access and political participation have historically fallen under the purview of higher levels of government. The path to incorporation for newcomers has been shaped most critically by laws regulating immigration, naturalization, and voting, which in most cases have fallen outside of direct local government control. During the late nineteenth century, for example, state legislatures throughout the country eliminated voting by noncitizens, a common practice in many states during the previous era, and adopted literacy tests that disproportionately hurt immigrant voters. Such developments greatly limited the voices of immigrants and also created opportunities for political entrepreneurs like Boss Tweed who were intent on building new political coalitions by helping naturalize potential political allies. In the 1970s, by contrast, the federal Voting Rights Act proved pivotal in providing new legal tools to groups previously excluded from local government.

Broader issues of immigrant and minority access and political participation that were so salient in the nineteenth and twentieth centuries continue to attract substantial attention, particularly among scholars of election law. Current political debates about what some see as the discriminatory impact of laws that require voters to present photo identification, voter registration requirements, and efforts to limit public services for undocumented immigrants tap into the same political undercurrents and grievances that animated the conflicts between newcomers and their more established neighbors in earlier periods of American history. Although today's immigrants come primarily from Latin America and Asia, the experiences of northern, southern, and eastern Europeans can help inform our understanding of the struggles facing these groups and identify the political barriers and empowerment strategies needed to ensure their full participation in the American political process.

It is also likely that immigration from developing countries—a growing phenomenon in global gateway cities but one that is also increasingly present in other American regions that have not historically attracted a large numbers of foreigners—will challenge existing client-patron political relationships and lead to realignment of traditional political alliances. Some scholars have predicted that the growing number of Latino and Hispanic migrants, both from Mexico and other parts of Latin America, will not follow the traditional paths of political, economic, and social integration and assimilation that have characterized the experience of European immigrants in the nineteenth and twentieth centuries.[21]

Emerging scholarship that examines the political dynamics among new immigrant communities suggests that these predictions will prove to be too pessimistic. Given the reality that many new immigrants continue to settle in areas with large populations of native minorities—in many major cities, Latino centers have developed in historically Africa American neighborhoods—it is likely, however, that new immigrant flows will lead to rivalry and political conflict among ethnic communities. These changes may also create conditions ripe for the emergence of new ethnic political bosses who can successfully mobilize newcomers and build lasting organizations grounded in their own co-ethnic bases of political support. It remains to be seen whether these leaders will adopt the same political strategies of patronage politics and machine rule that marked the era of the Irish boss, or whether the ethnic bosses of the twenty-first century will create new political models based on the unique social and cultural institutions of these communities.

NOTES

1. Seymour J. Mandelbaum, *Boss Tweed's New York* (New York: John Wiley & Sons, 1965).
2. Steven P. Erie, *Rainbow's End: Irish-Americans and the Dilemmas of Urban Machine Politics, 1840–1985* (Berkeley: University of California Press, 1988), 25–26.
3. Daniel Patrick Moynihan, "The Irish," in *Beyond the Melting Pot*, eds. Nathan Glazer and Daniel Patrick Moynihan (Cambridge: MIT Press, 1964), 217–287.
4. Martin Shefter, "The Emergence of the Political Machine: An Alternative View," in *Theoretical Perspectives on Urban Politics*, eds. Willis D. Hawley et al, (Englewood Cliffs, NJ: Prentice-Hall, 1976), 14–44.
5. Erie, *Rainbow's End*, 53.
6. Chris McNickle, *To Be Mayor of New York: Ethnic Politics in the City* (New York: Columbia University Press, 1993).
7. Ronald H. Bayor, *Fiorello LaGuardia: Ethnicity and Reform* (Arlington Heights, IL: Harland Davidson, Inc., 1993).
8. Edward C. Banfield and James Q. Wilson, *City Politics* (Cambridge: Harvard University Press, 1963).
9. Richard Hofstadter, *The Age of Reform* (New York: Random House, 1995).
10. Bayor, *Fiorello La Guardia*, 143–144, 158–159.
11. Roger David Waldinger, *Still the Promised City? African-Americans and New Immigrants in Postindustrial New York* (Cambridge: Harvard University Press, 1996), chap. 7.
12. Richard A. Keiser, *Subordination or Empowerment? African-American Leadership and the Struggle for Urban Political Power* (New York: Oxford University Press, 1977).
13. William Grimshaw, *Bitter Fruit: Black Politics and the Chicago Machine, 1931–1991* (Chicago: University of Chicago Press, 1995).
14. Erie, *Rainbow's End*, 166–169.
15. Claire Jean Kim, *Bitter Fruit: The Politics of Black-Korean Conflict in New York City* (New Haven: Yale University Press, 2003); Michael Jones-Correa, *Between Two Nations: The Political Predicament of Latinos in New York City* (Ithaca: Cornell University Press, 1998).

16. Reuel R. Rogers, *Afro-Caribbean Immigrants and the Politics of Incorporation: Ethnicity, Exception, or Exit* (New York: Cambridge University Press, 2005), 44.

17. Philip Kasinitz, *Caribbean New York: Black Immigrants and the Politics of Race* (Ithaca: Cornell University Press, 1992).

18. Ibid., 228–230.

19. Rogers, *Afro-Caribbean Immigrants and the Politics of Incorporation*, 83.

20. Amy Bridges, *Morning Glories: Municipal Reform in the Southwest* (Princeton: Princeton University Press, 1997).

21. Samuel P. Huntington, *Who Are We: The Challenges to America's National Identity* (New York: Simon & Schuster, 2004).

Bibliography

Ackerman, Kenneth D. *Boss Tweed: The Rise and Fall of the Corrupt Pol Who Conceived the Soul of Modern New York*. New York: Carroll & Graf, 2005.

Banfield, Edward C., and James Q. Wilson *City Politics*. Cambridge: Harvard University Press, 1963.

Bayor, Ronald H. *Fiorello La Guardia: Ethnicity and Reform*. Arlington Heights, IL: Harland Davidson, Inc., 1993.

Biles, Roger. *Richard J. Daley: Politics, Race, and the Governing of Chicago*. DeKalb: Northern Illinois University Press, 1995.

Bridges, Amy. *Morning Glories: Municipal Reform in the Southwest*. Princeton: Princeton University Press, 1997.

Browning, Rufus P., Dale Rodgers Marshall, and David H. Tabb. *Protest is Not Enough*. Berkeley: University of California Press, 1984.

Cohen, Adam, and Elizabeth Taylor. *American Pharaoh: Mayor Richard J. Daley—His Battle for Chicago and the Nation*. Boston: Little, Brown, 2000.

Erie, Steven P. *Rainbow's End: Irish-Americans and the Dilemmas of Urban Machine Politics, 1840–1985*. Berkeley: University of California Press, 1988.

Grimshaw, William. *Bitter Fruit: Black Politics and the Chicago Machine, 1931–1991*. Chicago: University of Chicago Press, 1995.

Henderson, Thomas M. *Tammany Hall and the New Immigrants*. New York: Arno Press, 1976.

Hofstadter, Richard. *The Age of Reform*. New York: Random House, 1955.

Huntington, Samuel P. *Who Are We: The Challenges to America's National Identity*. New York: Simon & Schuster, 2004.

Jones-Correa, Michael. *Between Two Nations: The Political Predicament of Latinos in New York City*. Ithaca: Cornell University Press, 1998.

Kasinitz, Philip. *Caribbean New York: Black Immigrants and the Politics of Race*. Ithaca: Cornell University Press, 1992.

Keiser, Richard A. *Subordination or Empowerment? African-American Leadership and the Struggle for Urban Political Power*. New York: Oxford University Press, 1997.

Kim, Claire Jean. *Bitter Fruit: The Politics of Black-Korean Conflict in New York City*. New Haven: Yale University Press, 2003.

Mandelbaum, Seymour J. *Boss Tweed's New York*. New York: John Wiley & Sons, 1965.

McNickle, Chris. *To Be Mayor of New York: Ethnic Politics in the City*. New York: Columbia University Press, 1993.

Moynihan, Daniel Patrick. "The Irish." In *Beyond the Melting Pot*, edited by Nathan Glazer and Daniel Patrick Moynihan, 217–287. Cambridge: MIT Press, 1964.

Myers, Gustavus. *The History of Tammany Hall*. New York: Boni and Liveright, 1917.

Pinderhughes, Dianne M. *Race and Ethnicity in Chicago Politics: A Reexamination of Pluralist Theory*. Urbana: University of Illinois Press, 1987.

Rogers, Reuel R. *Afro-Caribbean Immigrants and the Politics of Incorporation: Ethnicity, Exception, or Exit*. New York: Cambridge University Press, 2005.

Royko, Mike. *Boss: Richard J. Daley of Chicago*. New York: Signet, 1971.

Shefter, Martin. "The Emergence of the Political Machine: An Alternative View." In *Theoretical Perspectives on Urban Politics*, edited by Willis D. Hawley et al., 14–44. Englewood Cliffs, NJ: Prentice-Hall.

Waldinger, Roger David. *Still the Promised City? African-Americans and New Immigrants in Postindustrial New York*. Cambridge: Harvard University Press, 1996.

CHAPTER 18

....

IMMIGRATION, ETHNICITY, RACE, AND ORGANIZED CRIME[1]

....

WILL COOLEY

ON January 20, 2011, more than 800 law enforcement agents began predawn raids that netted nearly 125 suspected organized crime figures. U.S. officials claimed the sweep, which targeted syndicates in New York, New Jersey and Rhode Island, was the largest mob roundup in FBI [Federal Bureau of Investigation] history. U.S. Attorney General Eric Holder declared that those apprehended were "among the most dangerous criminals in our country" and that the Mafia remained a major threat "to the economic well-being of this country."[2] The arrests captured headlines across the nation and confirmed that ethnicity continued to shape organized crime syndicates, especially within the Italian American Mafia. Yet framing this episode historically, the massive FBI bust revealed more about the misconceptions of the ethnic coherence of organized crime by law enforcement, popular historians, and academicians promulgating the "ethnic succession" model.

Scholars have generally used the theory of ethnic succession to explain the shifting dominance of the informal economy by immigrant newcomers. This narrative does not attach firm boundaries to crime dominance but contends that Irish immigrants governed the streets and rackets beginning in the late nineteenth century, with Jews gaining through Prohibition and Italians rising to prominence before and during the Depression. In the 1960s, rights revolutions inspired Latinos and African Americans to rise up and challenge white sway over profitable rackets in their neighborhoods. In the late twentieth century, changes in immigration laws and the fall of Communism bolstered Eastern European and Asian syndicates.

According to ethnic succession proponents, push-and-pull factors explain the ethnic turnover in gangland. Poverty and discrimination pressed immigrants into organized crime as a route to social and economic mobility. Once these groups became acculturated, they became securely "American" and had no use for illegitimate economy. The sons of mobsters garnered formal educations on leafy college campuses, not on mean streets. Another explanation posits that organized crime syndicates weaken over time through turnover and the complacency that comes with success and are pushed out by newer, hungrier, and fiercer ethnic groups no longer willing to abide outsiders dominating illicit activities in their communities. Despite an occasional challenge to the ethnic succession model, scholars have emphasized cycles of immigration, ethnic bonds, and the pursuit of upward mobility to explain the changing cast of ethnic groups seizing authority over vice markets.

This essay analyzes how immigration and ethnicity shaped delinquent youth groups (gangs) and adult organized crime syndicates (mobs). It recognizes the role of ethnicity in these associations, as gangs and mobs used ethnic ties to create trust in undertakings outside the protections of law and arbitration. Yet when it comes to change over time, historians lean far too heavily on the ethnic succession theory. To fully understand the people and processes in the underworld, scholars need to take into account the reality of interethnic cooperation, the continuing relevance of class, and the advantages of whiteness. Once scholars strip organized crime of its ethnic and racial teleology, they can put organized crime at the center of historical investigation, and expose the persistence of the interconnections of corruption, politics, and capitalism.

YOUTH GANGS

Youth gangs have long been part of the American urban scene. Gangs flourished in immigrant neighborhoods suffering from a lack of adequate police protection and government services. Enclaves developed their own rhythms, but in general the immigrant population was transient, not well acculturated, and disconnected from mainstream society. Existing social controls were weak and stressed by large numbers of unattached young men. Many immigrants arrived with a warranted suspicion or outright hostility to the state and were met by discrimination. For these immigrants, black markets served as the means to meeting collective and individual needs, and some viewed crime as a necessary alternative to poverty.

Identifiable street gangs appeared in American cities soon after the Revolutionary War. They were not necessarily criminally inclined but were seemingly predisposed to stake out and defend "turf" in burgeoning cities. As Irish immigrants came ashore, territorial conflicts took on a decidedly ethnoreligious cast. In Philadelphia, hate-filled rumbles occurred with such regularity that they took on semiformal features, including cheering spectators and set war zones. Yet alliances and geographies were in constant flux, defying easy categorization. Gangs could incorporate ethnic others while still maintaining original ethnic identities and articulating conflict in ethnic terms. For many young males, navigating the urban scene taught acute lessons on the consequences of not being in the right places, with the right people, at the right times. Identity lessons came hard; bruises and scars reminded them that they lived in a world of some-one else's making.

As the market revolution took hold in the mid-1800s, gangs evolved from merely bludgeoning each other to more sophisticated operations. Small neighborhood bands branched out and absorbed other gangs, organizing into broad factions. Clever, brazen gang leaders recognized that their skills were in demand in political and economic gray areas. Employers and unions locked in violent struggles in hypercompetitive and inef-fectually regulated marketplaces made use of their muscle for slugging duty, while gangs served political machines as "repeaters" (young men hired to vote using false identities) and intimidators. In return, grateful politicians sheltered gangs from law enforcement. Gangs and urban politics were a match made of necessity in the rude republic, and the gang sometimes provided an ambitious young man with the know-how to rise in poli-tics. In Philadelphia, William McMullen emerged from the Killers street gang to alder-man, political boss, and wise old man of city politics. Future mayor Richard J. Daley's stint in the euphemistically named Hamburg Athletic Club in Chicago taught the aspir-ing politician the importance of brute-force organization.[3] Entrepreneurial young men turned crime into commerce by violently manipulating the blood sport called *democ-racy,* exploiting the illicit demands of consumers, and taking advantage of the contradic-tions in the modern market economy.

Urban gangs began as socialization agents for marginalized youths, and as a result gang members usually shared the same basic profile. They were primarily—but not exclusively—male and predominantly from poor and working-class backgrounds. They joined for material gain, a sense of power and prestige, protection, and excitement. Most were only in a gang for a short term, often regarding membership as their best chance to secure money and avoid a hungry belly. Others were sick of getting their lunch money stolen and found that the harassment stopped within a brotherhood. There was safety in numbers, and while flying the right colors made them less anxious about their surround-ings, gang membership actually inflated the probability of being a victim of violence, in part because gang life eventually required engaging in combat. The rough-and-tumble environment created strong pressures to join, but gang membership was far from the inevitability postulated by Herbert Asbury and Frederick Thrasher, as the majority of urban, poor adolescents avoided gang life. But even those who stayed clear understood that gangs and turf battles were a quotidian reality in many neighborhoods.[4]

As gangs adapted to meet the demands of expanding commercial and political mar-kets, they still remained rooted in ethnic, working-class neighborhoods. The gang ethos merged ethnic pride with localized power. On the one hand, youth gangs protected their enclaves from outsiders. Jewish gang members, for instance, rose in stature by chasing out extortionists and attacking anti-Semitic street toughs who assaulted and robbed street peddlers and pulled the beards of the devout. Yet once gangs became established, they regularly became the new extortionists. Many formed "protection" rackets target-ing area licit and illicit businesses. Neighbors may have breathed a sigh of relief when Max "Kid Twist" Zwerbach publicly resolved in the first decade of the twentieth cen-tury that no "mick" or "wop" would rule over the Jewish Lower East Side. Once his gang consolidated power, however, they brutally extorted Jewish businesses and ensured that frightened voters would reliably reelect the Tammany ticket.[5] Residents were left to wonder if they were better off with the devil they knew.

Economic and racial realities played an even bigger part in gang activities in the post-World War II era. Concerns over a pandemic of juvenile delinquency were overblown, but market forces gradually changed the character of gangs, notably among nonwhites. European Americans assimilated into white neighborhoods, where adults tempered gang activities through employment, recreational alternatives, and social pressures. Simultaneously, black and Latino adolescents encountered a declining jobs base, intensified residential segregation, and socioeconomic isolation. Increasing numbers did not graduate out of gangs, but rather began to see it as their means to earn a living. By the late 1960s, expansive and ambitious "supergangs" emerged, providing unconventional role models for youngsters who saw fewer masculine alternatives in straight careers.

Into this combustible mix stepped the drug trade. A new round of laws in the 1970s enshrined severe penalties for adult peddlers, thus shifting this activity to job-starved youths. The acts transformed scores of gangs from social groups into narcotics-selling operations. Street gangs did not accept the drug culture uncritically, and many discouraged members from using narcotics because it made them unreliable comrades. As a Philadelphia gang member succinctly stated, "You can't nod and gang-war at the same time."[6] Certain gangs even acted as antidrug vigilantes, running drug dealers out of their neighborhoods.

At the same time, many gangs could not resist the drug trade's ample profits, altering gang behaviors and culture. In some gangs, traditional activities such as hanging out, sports, and even rumbles were replaced by the daily grind of drug dealing. "When I think about that shit—fighting and fucking people over and running from the police—it was crazy," a member of a New York City drug crew working during the crack epidemic recalled. "It was just kid stuff."[7] Similarly, a Mexican American gang member in San Antonio indicated the businesslike orientation of his group. "If you ain't making money . . . bringing something to the boys that's profitable for everyone, then we don't need you."[8] While there is little doubt that youth gangs became more focused outlaw capitalism, scholars differ widely on when this transformation occurred and to what extent members were active in narcotics trafficking. All agree that ethnicity remained a significant factor in gang life, though, especially as the war on drugs targeted minority males. Indeed, the more advanced narco-gangs owed much of their organizational strength to the pressures of prison culture. As black and Latino inner-city communities became increasingly marginalized, certain teenagers viewed gangs as one of the few ways of making it in America. Unfortunately, most street-level dealers found that the logic of late capitalism extended to drug markets, as the lion's share of profits flowed up to gang leaders. Over time, the drug trade became entrenched in certain ghettoized areas as the most available aspect of the modern economy. Local denizens resigned to this reality grudgingly understood that gang members, who were often relatives and acquaintances, had their life-chances narrowed significantly by race, class, and geography.

The drug trade further strained relations between youth gangs and their communities. Gangs throughout the twentieth century paradoxically functioned as ethnic support groups and extorters, defenders of neighborhoods and exploiters of neighbors, dualities that have puzzled scholars trying to make sense of gang life. Gangs were usually defined by ethnicity and almost always by place, but young men and other local residents often had the most to fear from gang members of their own ethnic group. Gangs exerted potent power through an earned reputation for ultraviolence and the aggressive intimidation of witnesses. Locals were seldom willing to cooperate with authorities investigating gang-related crimes; hence, many went unsolved. Gang violence created a "culture of terror" in communities silenced by fear. For example, many black and Latino gangs formed as defense units against marauding whites and racist police forces. In the 1960s, significant numbers of these gang members immersed themselves in political ideologies. Economic deprivation and government repression generally precluded full political realization, and by the 1970s, many of these gangs took advantage of breaks in the informal economy—especially the drug trade—and forfeited community support. Loose confederations such as the Bloods and Crips in Los Angeles merged a predilection for mayhem with the determination to control large swaths of turf. Rather than fostering ethnic and racial solidarity, gangs throughout American history reserved harsh violence for members of rival gangs from their own ethnoracial background. In the case of African American gangs in the 1970s and 80s, this intraracial carnage blunted the racial solidarities desired by political activists. Although academicians regularly stress the sense of identity, brotherhood, and pride gangs instilled in youths, neighbors remained less sanguine.

Gangs to Gangsters

The gangster, Herbert Asbury argued, began his career as a member of a juvenile gang and then "naturally graduated" into mob ranks.[9] Although youth gang members who pursued crime as an adult career were a small minority, most mobsters started as gang members. In the 1910s and 1920s, the capable alumni of the Five Points gangs in Manhattan such as Owney Madden, Johnny Torrio, and Frank Nitti turned lessons learned in petty ventures into thriving rackets. In some cases, young men were actively groomed by adult gangsters. Researchers have found notably tight relationships between Chinese organized crime figures and youth gangs, as ritualized recruitment drew gifted future gangsters into an "apprenticeship."[10] The vast majority of youth gang members graduated out of gangs, but others were ushered into adulthood with crime as a career.

Success in organized crime necessitated a degree of collaboration with government officials, law enforcement, and legitimate businesses. Here again, ethnic and neighborhood ties came in handy. Gangsters involved in formidable crime cliques maintained relations with friends and relatives in conventional occupations. Like machine politicians, mobsters believed the system worked best when it benefited people through favors and relationships. Scholars generally recognize the correlations among ethnicity, syndicated crime, and machine politics, yet the specific workings of these associations are understudied. The frequent assertion that organized crime was an alien, immigrant conspiracy bubbling beneath the surface of American life obscured the more significant links between the underworld and respectable society.

The criminal response to the American experiment with alcohol prohibition reflected the attempts to bring order to chaotic illicit markets through collaborations that crossed ethnic boundaries. In 1919, the "drys" finally triumphed in their long campaign to rid the nation of the legal sale of alcohol. Not surprisingly, the young men who had cut their teeth in vice and labor racketeering—ventures that required territorial conquests, accounting knowledge, pragmatic use of violence, and political payoffs—were ready and eager to distribute booze to a thirsty public. Mob boss Joseph Bonanno called Prohibition the "golden goose," an opportunity "too good to be true."[11] Prohibition quickly turned into an enforcement nightmare, and in city after city, juries nullified liquor laws by refusing to convict even those whose guilt appeared beyond question. City police forces, responding to general sentiment in urban America, joined the free-for-all by becoming willing accomplices. The profits were tremendous, and gangsters often felt they had little to hide. "I give the public what the public wants," Al Capone declared. "I never had to send out high pressure salesmen. Why, I could never meet the demand."[12] Waxey Gordon, born to poor tenement family on Lower East Side, started as a pickpocket before moving into the more lucrative trades of bookmaking, narcotics and strikebreaking. Gordon was late to tap the potential in illicit alcohol, but in the late 1920s he and his partners muscled into breweries in New Jersey that by 1931 returned profits at the rate of $2,277,000 per year. According to *Time* magazine, Gordon was fond of limousines, kept an ornate apartment with three master bedrooms, and spent $4200 for leather-bound volumes of Scott, Dickens, and Thackeray.[13] Although the peevish magazine tried to mock his ostentatious striving, the blurred lines of legitimacy allowed many gangsters to move out of ethnic ghettos and mingle with Jazz Age bohemians.

Prohibition also advanced the "organization" of "organized crime." Young hoodlums got crash-course schooling in production, management, money-laundering, tax evasion, and bribery. In many cities, organized crime resembled business with regular payrolls, capital investments, manufacturing and distribution centers, and retail outlets. Bootleggers formed alliances across cities and regions, and peace conferences attended by a *Who's Who* of the underworld granted territory and arbitrated disputes. Although gang violence exploded during the Prohibition era, syndicates went to great lengths to resolve conflicts in the absence of legal channels. Local and regional "commission" meetings used Roberts Rules of Order, set prices, and adjudicated disputes. In Philadelphia, bootleggers erected their own criminal court system. Vice markets generally remained unruly, violent, and subject to local pressures, but as Prohibition faded, gangsters flush with cash branched out into legitimate and illicit businesses.[14]

While nearly all historians agree that Prohibition gave rise to modern organized crime, the era also marks the end of the historical consensus on the role of ethnicity, the level of organization, and the power of syndicates. Young men seized the opportunity for upward mobility provided by Prohibition. These mobsters also realized that the experiment would come to an end and looked to centralize other vice rackets under their rule. Proponents of the ethnic succession model view rationalization during Prohibition and its aftermath as the beginnings of modern organized crime—led and directed by Italians. Many gangsters definitely considered ethnic ties vital to maintaining their unlawful undertakings. Organized crime required containing violence to avoid attracting the attention of the public and police, maintaining solidarity in the face of prosecution, and corrupting officials through secretive relationships. Studies of Italian crime families by Mark Haller and Annelise Anderson show that that ethnicity remained an organizing principle for criminal operations throughout the twentieth century.[15]

Due to the importance of ethnicity in ensuring a modicum of trust in the perilous business of organized crime, many scholars argue that the informal economy was strictly and lethally ordered along ethnic lines. In general, these historians see the twentieth century as the triumph of the Italian American Mafia. Italians, they contend, were more successful at building hierarchal quasi-governments because of their tight family structures and their cultural values of loyalty and obedience. Moreover, Italians were supposedly better disciplined than their Irish and Jewish rivals and more disposed to use ferocious violence to manage territory and resolve disagreements. In the eyes of one popular historian, the Italian ascendancy was quite simply a matter of "blood and power," as Irish syndicates in Boston and Chicago and Jewish mobs in Detroit and Philadelphia were either killed off or reduced to hired hands for the Mafia.[16] Jews had been the most prominent players during the early years of Prohibition, yet by the 1930s Italian muscle ruled. According to Selwyn Raab, even the notorious mobster Meyer Lansky was downgraded to a "junior partner" who "took orders and never gave them." "The Jews don't fuck with the Italians," Mafioso James Fratianno boasted. "They learned that a long time ago."[17]

The dramatic story of an Italian ascendency is compelling, and government officials, the media, and Hollywood have all advanced it. The iconic *Godfather* films and *Sopranos* television series depicted organized crime masterminded by a potent Italian Mafia. Skeptics, however, note that many criminal centralization efforts not only failed, but the ethnic cooperation that marked the Prohibition years continued. While, as Peter Reuter notes, "the Mafia's unique stability and its notoriety cannot be denied,"[18] the notion that organized crime was dictated by a businesslike entity made up of Italian mobsters is not borne out by the evidence. For starters, the conception of Italians as trigger-happy assassins while Jews were merely "mob accountants" is largely a myth (and partly driven by crude ethnic stereotypes). In New York City, Alan Block illustrates that both groups were willing practitioners of bloodshed, but there is no evidence that this carnage was brought about by ethnic rivalry. In fact, Block finds a high degree of interethnic cooperation.[19] When Lucky Luciano tried to centralize the prostitution racket, his top lieutenants were Jews, and he worked closely with Lansky and Bugsy Siegel in several endeavors. The lethal Brooklyn organization known popularly as "Murder Inc." incorporated a mélange of different ethnicities. While historians subscribing to the ethnic succession model often point to the murder of Dutch Schultz as signaling the end of

Jewish power, his death came not at the hands of Italians but of two Jewish assassins, Charles Workman and Mendy Weiss, working at the behest of Louis Buchalter. The fall of prominent Jewish gangsters Buchalter, Jacob Shapiro, and Schultz came because of intense government prosecutions, not Italian might. Likewise, Jewish gangsters such as Siegel and Lansky were never mere underlings of the Italian Mafia; rather they continued to operate on their own volition well after Prohibition ended. Cross-ethnic partnerships persisted in the New York area—such as the complex motor fuel tax-evasion schemes involving collaborations between Soviet Jewish émigrés and La Cosa Nostra families in the 1980s—even if some reluctant gangsters had to be enticed to set aside their ethnic parochialism through the promise of big scores.[20]

Indeed, organized crime syndicates in other cities displayed even more interethnic cooperation than the Big Apple. The postwar, five-family Mafia structure in New York City stressing kin and Italian ethnicity was not replicated in Boston, Chicago, or Detroit, though historians and government officials strove to convince the public that Italian jurisdiction extended throughout the country. The national meetings called to rationalize bootlegging during Prohibition, events that many historians point to as the beginnings of Italian hegemony, actually included numerous non-Italians. Among those in attendance at the famed Atlantic City convention in 1928, for instance, were Frank Erickson, Larry Fay, Owney Madden, George Remus, and Solly Weissman, comprising a veritable league of nations in the underworld. Chicago's ethnically diverse Outfit included men such as Murray Humphreys (Welsh), Gus Alex (Greek), and Frank Schweihs (German). In government testimony, James Fratianno claimed that the Los Angeles Mafia had to murder Mickey Cohen because he "was Jewish and he did not belong to the La Cosa Nostra." Later in his statement, though, Fratianno listed a series of Jews and other non-Italians deeply involved in the inner workings of organized crime, including Sidney Korshak, who Fratianno asserted "practically runs the Mafia industry."[21] Fratianno also tried but failed to get involved with the mob's supreme accomplishment of the twentieth century, Las Vegas. Here again, the investors comprised a blend of ethnicities, including Thomas McGinty from Cleveland, Isadore "Kid Cann" Blumenfeld from Minneapolis, and Peter Licavoli of Detroit. The belief that only Italians could be "made" was probably important to Italian mobsters such as Fratianno for reasons of loyalty and honor, but in practice sophisticated gangsters pushed ethnic "codes" aside in the pursuit of lucre. As Albert Fried demonstrates, nearly every urban syndicate was ethnically integrated, as gangsters "embraced the principle of a rational sense of community" and "enlightened self-interest" rather than hewing to excessive clannishness.[22] In sum, the ethnic succession of hegemony over the rackets did not take place.

The perception that white-ethnics moved out of organized crime through upward mobility also requires further inquiry. Scholars regularly assert that younger white-ethnics do not view organized crime as an attractive life, and the newer generation lacks the "stomach" for street-level operations. Indeed, Francis Ianni's in-depth study of an Italian crime family noted that only a small fraction of males followed their fathers into illegitimate business. According to Ianni, legitimacy was always the family's goal, and thus he posits organized crime for white-ethnics as a "way station on the road to ultimately respectable roles in American society."[23] To be sure, prominent examples of this process abound. Waxey Gordon sent his son to Duke University, while the sons of Meyer Lansky and Tommy Lucchese matriculated at West Point.

Yet when scholars put organized crime at the center of the historical narrative and recognize the interplay between legitimate and illegitimate enterprise, ethnicity loses some of its salience. Not all white ethnics waltzed off to the suburbs (and proponents of ethnic succession have failed to explain why suburbanization would dilute organized crime rather than spreading it into new territories). As the opening vignette of this essay demonstrates, many Italian Americans remain ensconced in the informal economy. Similarly, Irish mobs such as the Winter Hill Gang in Boston and the Westies in New York City remained formidable long after the Hibernian presence in organized crime supposedly faded. In this respect, the realities of working-class life and constricted opportunities overwhelm the increasing acceptance of white ethnics by the Anglo-Protestant establishment. Viewing organized crime as, in Daniel Bell's words, a "queer ladder" that would gradually be discarded by ethnic groups plays to the methodological bias that organized crime is alien and aberrant to the American norm.[24] On the contrary, corruption was crucial to the creation of business empires. Howard Abadinsky's textbook on organized crime smartly includes as discussion of John Jacob Astor, Cornelius Vanderbilt, Jay Gould, Leland Stanford, and John D. Rockefeller as organized crime figures, demonstrating that systematic illegality was as American as apple pie.[25] Likewise, for many working-class men and women engaged in organized crime, the illegal activity comprised their steady job.

Although the drug trade had a particularly odious reputation, its increasing role in organized crime during the late twentieth century did not quell the links between crime and corruption. Blue-chip American banks such as American Express, BankAtlantic, and Wachovia were implicated in laundering immense sums of drug money, paying fines while preposterously denying they were aware of the provenance of small-denomination currency transfers to offshore accounts. Gradually, law enforcement ascertained that the drug trafficking did not emanate from disadvantaged communities; rather, it was facilitated by powerful elites in the country's loftiest economic and social perches.[26] In contrast to bootleggers of the Prohibition era who became public figures, major American drug dealers have maintained low profiles, pushed underground by negative public opinion toward narcotics. Yet it would be naïve to think that drug money has not corrupted the political process.

Indeed, the associations among organized crime, ethnicity, and corrupt government officials have remained strong even as the classic urban machines sputtered out. In the latter half of the twentieth century, the proliferation of the illegal narcotics trade enhanced the transnational flavor of these linkages, deeply damaging the stability of Latin American and Caribbean governments. Jamaican posses, for example, arrived on the American scene in the early 1980s. They originated as enforcers working for rival political factions on an island where, as one ghetto dweller noted, elections meant everything "because we know that if our party loses, we will starve."[27] Once set loose, posses became hard to direct, and drug profits broke the cord that had bound them to their political patrons. Posse members understood well that any distinctions between politicians and "Johnny-Too-Bad" gangsters were a mirage. Posse leader Delroy Edwards admitted his involvement in criminal operations but reminded anyone who would listen that then-Prime Minister Edward Seaga "is the biggest gangster of them all."[28]

Edwards, mythologized as the first man to deal "crack" cocaine on the streets of Brooklyn, made connections with Columbian suppliers to expand his operations from New York to Texas and places in-between.[29] While organized crime operations never took the form of structured, bureaucratic, nationwide syndicates as charged by federal government commissions, entrepreneurial gangsters like Edwards were always receptive to new schemes and business partnerships. The ability to spread out into new territories separated syndicated operations from neighborhood crooks.

This expansion did not come easy, however. It required taking the risk of moving beyond ethnic ties into joint ventures with other power brokers and often using severe but rational violence. Although some of these far-flung mobs had formal initiation rules steeped in ethnic lore, most syndicates were informal, flexible, and short lived and thus better equipped to meet shifting consumer demands and find opportunities for corruption ploys. Organized crime worked best, it seems, when innovators took advantage of moralistic laws preventing a product or service in demand (drugs, prostitution, loan sharking, gambling) and engaged ethically challenged businesspeople and public officials (stock fraud, toxic waste disposal, money laundering). Syndicates were useful in these situations, because these "friends" provided social capital and could dispense credible threats. As Henry Hill noted, he valued his association to the Lucchese crime family even though it never paid him a dime. Rather, it afforded "wiseguys" like Hill "protection from other guys looking to rip them off. That's what it's all about. That's what the FBI can never understand—that what [crime syndicates] offer is protection for the kinds of guys who can't go to the cops."[30] Solitary operators had little chance in the underworld, and being "connected" brought a level of orderliness to outlaw capitalists unable to rely on the justice system to protect property rights and settle disputes.

In the late twentieth century, experts repeatedly predicted the inevitable slow death of white-ethnic organized crime. Yet while law enforcement spent countless hours and spiraling sums of money trying to defeat criminal syndicates, cunning men and women continued to exploit black market opportunities. This was particularly true for the hard-pressed American working class as decent employment disappeared in the post-industrial economy. Contrary to the charges of moralists and neoliberals, these "hustlers" were not trapped in cycles of poverty or lacking work ethic, but they understood that insignificant jobs translated to poverty and stigmatization. The potential rewards of the underground economy were simply too good to pass up. In addition, while the day-to-day work of organized crime was ridden by anxiety, it also required personal initiative, ingenuity, and offered chances for autonomy, a sharp contrast to many of the menial "careers" available otherwise. While the effects of racism, deindustrialization, and capital flight have certainly come down hardest on nonwhites, racial biases embedded in the criminal justice system also obscured white working-class participation in criminal ventures. For instance, though African Americans and Latinos were much more likely to be arrested and punished by the state for involvement in drug dealing, stud-ies showed that whites and nonwhites sold drugs at similar rates.[31] The premise of eth-nic succession, besides ignoring interethnic collaboration, discounted the significance and persistence of class within the white population. This oversight was evident as law enforcement made it a habit to spike the football after successful prosecutions. In 1987, then-U.S. Attorney Rudy Giuliani boasted that "there's not going to be a Mafia in five to ten years" after the Pizza Connection heroin-smuggling verdicts, in part because the recruits for the Mafia were now in "high school, colleges, law school, medical schools, in record numbers, and [the Mafia is] a thing of the past." Decades later, after another mass roundup of Italian American mobsters, a chastened FBI admitted that arresting and convicting mob bosses "several times over has not eradicated the problem."[32] Contrary to Giuliani's narrative, many white-ethnics had not advanced into the middle class.

WHITENESS AND ORGANIZED CRIME

The interethnic cooperation that marked much of the twentieth century had a decid-edly pale hue, a fact rarely acknowledged or examined by scholars, the media, and law enforcement. Although the urban zones where organized crime flourished were often black-and-tan affairs that permitted a high degree of racial mixing, when it came to business white criminals maintained a fairly distinct color line, leaving nonwhite gang-sters exposed to law enforcement, excluded from money-spinning schemes, and with-out fundamental political contacts. Organized crime functioned through a series of partnerships rather than a monolithic, corporate structure. Why, then, did these part-nerships rarely extend to nonwhites? Was organized crime another structure where "whiteness" was made and solidified? Gangsters, and many organized crime studies, appear to have a race problem.

With some notable exceptions, historians have not paid much attention to non-white, especially black, organized crime. Part of this stems from the belief that African Americans, for a host of reasons, were simply incapable of organizing crime. As early as 1901, the pioneering sociologist Frances Kellor declared black crime was the "out-growth of impulse rather than of well laid plans and complicated schemings."[33] Later in the century, writers continued to insist that blacks just did not possess the characteris-tics to organize large-scale syndicates. "Some Negroes have not shown the hard working peasant attitude that made some of the other groups more successful," organized crime authority Ralph Salerno claimed in 1969. "As Negroes did not or were not able to start their own stores and small businesses, so they did not organize their crime but engaged in amateur robbery and casual violence."[34] In these enduring formulations, innate racial characteristics made blacks unable to perform the intricate tasks involved in network-ing crime. Besides some notable examples, scholars have not effectively challenged the stereotype of aimless black crime, and it is a resilient popular culture and media trope. In Barry Levinson's 1950s-era drama *Liberty Heights*, savvy but snakebitten Jewish gangsters in Baltimore lose control of numbers betting to a buffoonish black hoodlum named Little Melvin, who promptly mishandles operations and is forced to cede it back. The depiction did little justice to African American gambling ventures in the actual Charm City, where Little Willie Adams adroitly parlayed proceeds from the numbers racket to become a real estate developer, venture capitalist, political power broker, and philanthropist.[35]

Skeptics also depicted black urban life as too chaotic to develop of durable, self-perpetuating criminal concerns, arguing that blacks lacked the necessary family ties. Building on the work of E. Franklin Frazier and Daniel Patrick Moynihan, they posited that the characteristics of black life made them more individualistic criminals, in contrast to the strong family-based organizations of white-ethnics. While the social disorganization of the inner city supplied eager recruits to street gangs, they maintained this turmoil hindered the development of lasting criminal consortiums. Thus, black criminals tended toward reckless, violent crime that alienated the community, limited links to corrupt law enforcement, and brought negative media attention. In contrast, white crime "families" engendered community tolerance by supplying desired goods and services while keeping drugs and prostitution out of their own neighborhoods.

Critics also argued that the violence perpetrated by nonwhite criminals was fundamentally different than that performed by whites. Unlike the rational violence neatly restrained by European American syndicates, one scholar claimed that nonwhite gang mayhem was defined by "mindless brutality and nihilism."[36] Another researcher actually credited the Italian Mafia for reducing street crime through local quasi-governance, but as the Mafia receded from urban neighborhoods in the 1960s, it left "these areas to the anarchy and violence that result as the new barbarian warlords vie for the mantle of power."[37] During Senate hearings on Asian organized crime in 1991, Senator William Roth of Delaware suggested that while there were clear similarities between La Cosa Nostra and Asian syndicates, the "one difference . . . is violence. The Asian groups are much more inclined to use violence than the LCN, particularly outside of their own group." FBI specialists confirmed Roth's insinuation, stating that Asian mobs included a "hair trigger element" and engaged in "a lot of overt violence . . . as opposed to the La Cosa Nostra."[38] The testimony was an alarming whitewashing of Mafia violence and demonstrated that law enforcement experts had joined some historians and Hollywood in promulgating the legend of the white-ethnic mobster as a "man of honor": a humble, principled businessman who looked out for his family, kept his neighborhood safe, and reserved violence for those who were also involved in crime. According to ethnic-succession proponents, the loss of street control by these honorable men had ultimately contributed to the urban crisis. As Fast Eddie Felsen remarked in Martin Scorsese's *The Color of Money*, "This used to be a nice, average bad neighborhood. Now look at it."[39]

Similarly, because these authorities mistakenly conceived of white-ethnic organized crime as an ideal type—highly structured, hierarchical, and efficient—other collectives paled in comparison. Criminologists charged that most black and Latino drug operations did not really achieve the standard definition of "organized crime" because they operated on a diffuse basis, with members reporting that the seller kept most of the profits rather than "kicking up" to leaders. As one San Diego gang member stated, "The gang don't organize anything."[40] Yet this arrangement echoes the operations of Italian American Mafia families. These groups operated not as strict business hierarchies but rather as shadow governments that supplied members with protection and a set of rules. Associates received no salaries and were expected to earn on their own. The structure provided a degree of predictability and honesty in the informal economy, but syndicates operated more as clubs than as firms. As one long-time member of Philadelphia's Bruno organization noted, "The Family don't run anything."[41] Differences in operational methods and mores existed across ethnocultural lines, but these differentiations need to be contextualized and not merely ascribed to racial dissimilarities. Although critics chalked up nonwhite crime syndicate shortcomings to race, the limitations of these gangsters were mainly due to the inability to make connections with politicians, public officials, and law enforcement, associations usually foreclosed by racism. In the spectrum of gangs and organized crime, not all ethnic groups were afforded the same opportunities to engage in the highest levels of corruption and illicit enterprise.

In addition, while advocates of the ethnic succession model frequently identified blacks and Asians as "new" ethnics taking over from white-ethnic syndicates, these groups had extensive lineages in organized crime. Historians believe that Chinese Tongs originated in California in the 1860s. They were even more systematic than most white mobs, dealing in opium, gambling, extortion, and political patronage in urban Chinatowns. Occasionally, Tong rivalries burst forth in spectacular "wars" in cities such as Cleveland, New York, and San Francisco, but they usually filled quieter functions as de facto politicians, law enforcement, and banks for communities facing suspicion and outright persecution. The New York City Tongs have existed in the same basic locations for well over a century, demonstrating remarkable stability and resilience. As the federal government relaxed immigration restrictions in the second half of the twentieth century, Chinese mobs grew in strength, preying on vulnerable immigrants. A 1990 study of Manhattan's Chinatown estimated that 81 percent of restaurants and 66 percent of other businesses paid tribute to extortionists.[42]

Likewise, African Americans were hardly "new" immigrants in the 1960s. Black gangs were among the first in New York, though Luc Sante notes an "odd silence" from the historical record on their activities.[43] By the early 1900s, African Americans established thriving organized crime operations in numerous cities, mainly based around gambling ventures. "Policy," as it was often called in the black community, provided thousands of jobs for employment-starved African Americans. The daily numbers game built on the dreams of men and women who wagered their nickels and dimes looking for a big break also made a select few "kings" (and the occasional "queen") extremely wealthy. Policy operators were usually the moneyed individuals in black ghettoes and burnished their reputations and businesses by supplying startup funds for small businesses, providing loans, and donating to churches and civil rights groups. Indeed, Negro League Baseball probably would not have existed without the goodwill of policy kings and the necessity of laundering gambling proceeds.[44]

Contrary to accepted wisdom, blacks did not lack the "cohesive kinship system" necessary to organize crime—in fact, many black syndicates had tight family ties. In greater Chicago, the Kelly Brothers and Jones Brothers emerged as the preeminent policy operators. In New York, Frank Lucas deliberately brought relatives from North Carolina to assist him in breaking the Mafia's grip over heroin sales in the late 1960s. Similarly, the disciplined narcotics trafficking operation run by the Chambers Brothers in Detroit recruited dealers from their tiny hometown of Marianna, Arkansas. When indictments came down in 1988, eleven of the twenty-two defendants were connected to Marianna. Black street gangs regularly cultivated a familial ethos; the notorious Garland Jeffers of Gary, Indiana, dubbed his operation "The Family." Upset that the entrenched white mob used blacks only as menial drug pushers, The Family integrated management through force, leaving twenty-two dead in 1972.[45]

Yet as the Jeffers' anecdote suggests, blacks were not invited to eat at the white table. Organized crime usually functioned through networks that commonly crossed ethnic lines. Syndicates provided rough governance to make operations run smoothly, but members were not necessarily beholden to "bosses." Individual entrepreneurship, not hierarchy, determined the success of business. Yet nonwhites were virtually excluded from these arrangements. Why?

This question has not been sufficiently addressed. Revisionist scholars argue that "race neutral" discussions of gangs and organized crime are absurd.[46] Race—not spatial factors and the assimilation process—determined many gangland functions. The benefits of making and enforcing whiteness started at the youth gang level and continued into adult mobs. European American youth gangs facilitated assimilation through associations with political machines and other powerful organizations, while membership in black youth gangs reinforced cultural separation. Tellingly, some white gangs actually traced their origins, as well as their community support, to neighborhood defense against the "invasions" of nonwhites.

At the adult level, the color line became even more apparent. White organized crime figures repeatedly declined opportunities to collaborate with nonwhites, driving these entrepreneurs into circumscribed ghettos. When business proved profitable even within these boundaries, white gangsters launched hostile takeover bids. While white mobs initially encountered mixed success in these incursions, by 1951 the black magazine *Color* lamented that the "war on numbers racket kings" led to white command over formerly black operations in Chicago, New York, Pittsburgh, and Cleveland.[47] As Nicholas Gage concluded in 1967, "the mafia is *not* an Equal Opportunity Employer."[48]

The lack of partnerships kept nonwhites in secondary positions in organized crime. Most importantly, it kept them from building the affiliations with politicians and law enforcement crucial to the success of crime ventures. Indeed, many of the white conquests of black crime operations were spearheaded by corrupt law enforcement officials. "In the ghettos," a Congress of Racial Equality officer stated in 1967, "contempt for the police is partly rooted in the knowledge that some of them are serving the white racketeers who are bleeding the community."[49] White takeovers, often with the complicity of corrupt government officials, further scarred disadvantaged communities and deepened distrust in the justice system. To a degree, the black gang violence that burst forth in the late twentieth century resulted from the power vacuums and frustrations created through the destruction of established black crime networks in the 1940s and 1950s. As blacks gained a share of political power in American cities, some African American gangs tried to make connections to nascent black political machines. These efforts, though, were usually destabilized by punitive state and federal drug laws, antagonistic urban police forces, chaotic drug markets, and splits within black communities.[50]

Despite these examples, scholars should not reduce the complicated racial landscapes in gangs and organized crime to "white versus nonwhite." Race-making was a complicated process, and white-ethnic rivalries percolated. As Irving Spergel finds, the Italian stickball teams that became youth gangs to keep blacks and Puerto Ricans out of their neighborhoods in post-World War II New York also fought the encroachment of Irish interlopers.[51] Interethnic alliances among whites that soured could take on a tribal edge as violence proliferated. With the exception of labor racketeering, the old saw of "gangsters only kill each other" mostly held true, and the vast majority of violence in the underworld was intraethnic and personal. Regardless of race, a mobster typically had the most to fear from his closest friends. Yet in a larger sense, the advantages of whiteness that shaped American politics, economics, and geographies were also present in the underworld. Even gangsters knew that whiteness had its privileges.

CONCLUSION

In the face of methodological challenges, historians have produced high-quality material on gangs and organized crime. Most of these works ably situate organized crime within other social and economic contexts, thereby revealing how crime interrelates with politics, social mobility, labor relations, and capitalism. Although organized criminals functioned on the margins, their practices often parodied bourgeois life. Gangsters often made affiliations through the social capital of neighborhood-, class- and race-based connections. The violence and corruption that marked the underworld materialized via cracks in the façade of respectable society. Scholars ably demonstrate that gangs provided ethnic youths with a surrogate family, affording a sense of pride, place, and identity, and that adult crime syndicates also used ethnic solidarities to manage aspects of the informal economy.

Yet scholars should be wary of pushing the ethnic angle of gangs and organized crime too far. Many popular works and government reports fall into this trap, insisting that gangs and mobs were rigid, hierarchal organizations with ethnicity serving as the glue. These studies are primarily top-down examinations that are inadequately devised, poorly sourced, and rely on innuendo and hearsay. Mobs, above all the Italian Mafia, emerge from these accounts as master-puppeteers, conspiratorial shadow empires behind almost every significant unlawful activity from political assassination to rising garbage bills. Most of these works implicitly view the ethnic succession of organized crime from white-ethnic to nonwhite as an aspect of urban declension. Occasionally, they openly wax nostalgic for the orderly, rules-based organized crime of white ethnics by contrasting those regimes to the supposedly wild, irrational crime of blacks and other minorities. As such, they fail to adequately understand and historicize factors such as the long histories of organized crime by nonwhite minorities and the policies of exclusion that kept them out of power circles. Societal, technological, and policy changes—notably deindustrialization, the war on drugs, and the increasing availability of handguns—also often escape careful consideration. In addition, by mythologizing La Cosa Nostra as a "national machine" that was the gangland equivalent of General Motors, criminal undertakings by other ethnic and racial groups appear misleadingly disorganized. Differences in how ethnic and racial groups approached organized crime surely exist, but these variations should be balanced with aspects such as racism and macroeconomic shifts.

Inventive, entrepreneurial outlaw capitalists have long entered the fertile territory of the American informal economy for personal gain. In a similar (but decidedly less violent) vein, innovative, energetic historians will find the field of gangs and organized crime ripe for study. More studies outside of New York and Chicago are sorely needed, as well as those that explore the transnational aspects of immigrant gangs and vice markets, especially the rise of Latin American cartels. Historians certainly could complicate the law enforcement obsession with arresting gang leaders and syndicate "bosses" to stem corruption, a tactic that has long proven ineffective and possibly escalated violence. Detractors have long tarred labor unions as infested by racketeers, but few detailed examinations of the interplay of gangsters, employers, unionists and the state exist. Further comparative research on white-collar crime and traditional organized crime would be useful, as these endeavors share many of the same characteristics but stem from different ethnic and socioeconomic milieus and inspire contrasting reactions from government officials and the public. The effects of technology, capital mobility, and societal changes such as women's roles in gangs and organized crime are also understudied. These and other aspects need to be placed in wider social and cultural contexts to avoid the depiction of gangs and organized crime as anomalies. In doing so, historians will likely reveal as much about the mainstream as the margins.

NOTES

1. The author thanks Eric Schneider, Bryan Nicholson, Brian Hoffman, and Ronald Bayor for their comments and suggestions.
2. William K. Rashbaum, "Nearly 125 Are Arrested in Sweeping Mob Roundup," *New York Times*, January 21, 2011, A21.
3. David R. Johnson, "Crime Patterns in Philadelphia, 1840–70," in Allen F. Davis and Mark H. Haller, eds., *The Peoples of Philadelphia: A History of Ethnic Groups and Lower-Class Life, 1790–1940* (Philadelphia, PA: Temple University Press, 1973, 104–107; Adam Cohen and Elizabeth Taylor, *American Pharaoh: Mayor Richard J. Daley: His Battle for Chicago and the Nation* (Boston, MA: Little, Brown, 2000), 27–30.
4. Herbert Asbury, *The Gangs of New York: An Informal History of the Underworld* (Alfred A. Knopf, 1927), xvi; Frederic Thrasher, *The Gang: A Study of 1,313 Gangs in Chicago*

(Chicago, IL: University of Chicago Press, 1927), 65, 173; Michael Lalli, Leonard D. Savitz, Lawrence Rosen, *City Life and Delinquency: Victimization, Fear of Crime, and Gang Membership* (Washington, DC: U.S. Department of Justice, 1977), 51–55; Mercer L. Sullivan, *"Getting Paid": Youth Crime and Work in the City* (Ithaca, NY: Cornell University Press, 1989), 110–111; Martin Sanchez Jankowski, *Islands in the Street: Gangs and American Urban Society* (Berkeley, CA: University of California Press, 1991), 40–41.

5. Albert Fried, *The Rise and Fall of the Jewish Gangster in America, Revised Edition* (New York, NY: Columbia University Press, 1993), 30.

6. *Time*, "Return of the Gang," July 23, 1973, 32.

7. Terry Williams, *The Cocaine Kids: The Inside Story of a Teenage Drug Ring* (New York, NY: Addison-Wesley, 1989), 60.

8. Avelardo Valdez, "Toward a Typology of Contemporary Mexican American Youth Gangs," in Louis Kontos, David Brotherton, and Luis Barrios, eds., *Gangs and Society: Alternative Perspectives* (New York, NY: Columbia University Press, 2003), 24–25.

9. Herbert Asbury, *The Gangs of New York: An Informal History of the Underworld* (Alfred A. Knopf, 1927), xv.

10. Ko-lin Chin, *Chinatown Gangs: Extortion, Enterprise, and Ethnicity* (New York, NY: Oxford University Press, 1996), vii–viii.

11. Joseph Bonanno, *A Man of Honor: The Autobiography of Joseph Bonanno* (New York, NY: Simon and Schuster, 1983), 65.

12. Daniel Okrent, *Last Call: The Rise and Fall of Prohibition* (New York, NY: Scribner, 2010), 274.

13. *Time*, "End of Wexler," December 11, 1933, 13; Jenna Weissman Joselit, *Our Gang: Jewish Crime and the New York Jewish Community, 1900–1940* (Bloomington, IN: Indiana University Press, 1983), 94–96.

14. Mark H. Haller, "Urban Crime and Criminal Justice: The Chicago Case," *Journal of American History* 57:3 (December 1970), 623; Okrent, *Last Call*, 272–275.

15. Annelise Graebner Anderson, *The Business of Organized Crime: A Cosa Nostra Family* (Stanford, CA: Hoover Institution Press, 1979); Mark H. Haller, *Life Under Bruno: The Economics of an Organized Crime Family* (Conshohocken, PA: Pennsylvania Crime Commission, 1991).

16. Stephen Fox, *Blood and Power: Organized Crime in Twentieth-Century America* (New York, NY: William Morrow & Company, 1989).

17. Selwyn Raab, *Five Families: The Rise, Decline, and Resurgence of America's Most Powerful Mafia Empires* (New York, NY: St. Martin's Press, 2005), 86–87.

18. Peter Reuter, *Disorganized Crime: The Economics of the Visible Hand* (Cambridge, MA: MIT Press, 1983), 159–160.

19. Alan Block, *East Side-West Side: Organizing Crime in New York, 1930–1950* (New Brunswick, NJ: Transaction Books, 1983), 130–131, 139, 148.

20. Joseph D. Pistone with Richard Woodley, *Donnie Brasco: My Undercover Life in the Mafia* (New York, NY: New American Library, 1987), 261; James O. Finckenauer and Elin J. Waring, *Russian Mafia in America: Immigration, Culture and Crime* (Boston, MA: Northeastern University Press, 1998), 153.

21. President's Commission on Organized Crime, *Organized Crime and Money Laundering* (Washington, DC: Government Printing Office, 1984), 46.

22. Fried, *The Rise and Fall of the Jewish Gangster in America*, 122.

23. Francis A.J. Ianni, *A Family Business: Kinship and Social Control in Organized Crime* (New York, NY: Russell Sage Foundation, 1972), 76, 88, 193.

24. *Daniel Bell*, "Crime as an American Way of Life: A *Queer Ladder* of Social Mobility," in *The End of Ideology* (Glencoe, IL: The Free Press, 1960), 116–117.

25. Howard Abadinsky, *Organized Crime* 4th Ed. (Chicago, IL: Nelson-Hall Publishers, 1994), 59–71.

26. Ralph Blumenthal, *Last Days of the Sicilians* (New York, NY: Times Books, 1988), 104–108, 317; Robert Mazur, "Follow the Dirty Money," *New York Times*, September 13, 2010, A31.

27. Laurie Gunst, *Born Fi' Dead: A Journey through the Jamaican Posse Underworld* (New York, NY: Henry Holt and Co., 1995), 66.

28. Gunst, *Born Fi' Dead*, 150.

29. Leonard Buder, "Jury Convicts Man as Chief of Drug Ring," *New York Times*, July 26, 1989, B1.

30. Nicholas Pileggi, *Wiseguy: Life in a Mafia Family* (New York, NY: Simon and Schuster, 1985), 56–57.

31. Michelle Alexander, *The New Jim Crow: Mass Incarceration in the Age of Colorblindness* (New York, NY: The New Press, 2010), 97, 123–125, 131.

32. Michael Oreskes, "Giuliani Says Trials Weaken the Mob," *New York Times*, March 3, 1987, B3; Rashbaum, "Nearly 125 Are Arrested in Sweeping Mob Roundup," A21.

33. Frances Kellor, "The Criminal Negro," *The Arena* 25:3 (March, 1901), 314.

34. Ralph Salerno and John S. Tompkins, *The Crime Confederation: Cosa Nostra and Allied Operations in Organized Crime* (Garden City, NY: Doubleday & Company, 1969), 381.

35. *Liberty Heights*, Directed by Barry Levinson (Los Angeles, CA: Warner Brothers, 1999); Antero Pietila, *Not in my Neighborhood: How Bigotry Shaped a Great American City* (Chicago, IL: Ivan R. Dee, 2010), 116–123.

36. William Kleinknecht, *The New Ethnic Mobs: The Changing Face of Organized Crime in America* (New York, NY: The Free Press, 1996), 209.

37. James M. O'Kane, *The Crooked Ladder: Gangsters, Ethnicity, and the American Dream* (New Brunswick, NJ: Transaction Publishers, 1992), 98–99.

38. U.S. Senate, *Asian Organized Crime, Hearing before the Permanent Subcommittee on Investigations of the Committee on Governmental Affairs* (Washington, DC, 1992), 19.

39. *The Color of Money*, Directed by Martin Scorsese (Los Angeles, CA: Touchstone Pictures, 1986).

40. Scott Decker, Tim Bynum, and Deborah Weisel, "A Tale of Two Cities: Gangs as Organized Crime Groups," *Justice Quarterly* 15:3 (September 1998), 412–413.

41. Haller, *Life Under Bruno*, 1.

42. U.S. Senate, *Asian Organized Crime*, 14.

43. Luc Sante, *Low Life: Lures and Snares of Old New York* (New York, NY: Farrar, Straus, Giroux, 1991), 234–235.

44. Shane White, Stephen Garton, Stephen Robertson, and Graham White, *Playing the Numbers: Gambling in Harlem Between the Wars* (Cambridge, MA: Harvard University Press, 2010), 213–217.

45. William M. Adler, *Land of Opportunity: One Family's Quest for the American Dream in the Age of Crack* (New York, NY: Atlantic Monthly Press, 1995); 217, 302; Sudhir Alladi Venkatesh and Steven D. Levitt, "'Are We a Family or a Business?' History and Disjuncture in the Urban American Street Gang," *Theory and Society* 29:4 (August, 2000), 428; *Time*, "The Godfather in Gary," November 13, 1972, 258.

46. Christopher Adamson, "Defensive Localism in White and Black: A Comparative History of European-American and African-American Youth Gangs," *Ethnic and Racial Studies*

23:2 (March 2000), 272–298; John H. Hagedorn, "Race Not Space: A Revisionist History of Gangs in Chicago," *The Journal of African American History* 91 (Spring, 2006), 194–208.

47. *Color*, "War on Numbers Racket Kings," June, 1951, 32–35.

48. Nicholas Gage, "Bias in the Mafia: Negroes are Barred from 'Executive' Posts in Organized Rackets," *Wall Street Journal*, October 26, 1967, 1, 23.

49. Gage, "Bias in the Mafia," 1.

50. Walter B. Miller, "Youth Gangs in the Urban Crisis Era," in *Delinquency, Crime and Society*, James F. Short, ed. (Chicago, IL: University of Chicago Press, 1976), 110; Andrew V. Papachristos, *A.D., After the Disciples: The Neighborhood Impact of Federal Gang Prosecution* (Peotone, IL: National Gang Crime Research Center, 2001), 41–45.

51. Irving Spergel, *Racketville, Slumtown, Haulburg: An Exploratory Study of Delinquent Subcultures* (Chicago, IL: University of Chicago Press, 1964), 64–65.

BIBLIOGRAPHY

Albini, Joseph L. *The American Mafia: Genesis of a Legend* (New York, NY: Appleton-Century-Crofts, 1971).

Anderson, Annelise Graebner. *The Business of Organized Crime: A Cosa Nostra Family* (Stanford, CA: Hoover Institution Press, 1979).

Bernstein, Lee. *The Greatest Menace: Organized Crime in Cold War America* (Boston, MA: University of Massachusetts Press, 2002).

Block, Alan. *East Side-West Side: Organizing Crime in New York, 1930–1950* (New Brunswick, NJ: Transaction Books, 1983).

Chin, Ko-lin. *Chinatown Gangs: Extortion, Enterprise, and Ethnicity* (New York, NY: Oxford University Press, 1996).

Diamond, Andrew. *Mean Streets: Chicago Youths and the Everyday Struggle for Empowerment in the Multiracial City, 1908–1969* (Berkeley, CA: University of California Press, 2009).

Finckenauer, James O., and Waring, Elin J. *Russian Mafia in America: Immigration, Culture and Crime* (Boston, MA: Northeastern University Press, 1998).

Fried, Albert. *The Rise and Fall of the Jewish Gangster in America, Revised Edition* (New York, NY: Columbia University Press, 1993).

Gunst, Laurie. *Born Fi' Dead: A Journey through the Jamaican Posse Underworld* (New York, NY: Henry Holt and Co., 1995).

Moore, Joan W. *Homeboys: Gangs, Drugs and Prison in the Barrios of Los Angeles* (Philadelphia, PA: Temple University Press, 1978).

Reuter, Peter. *Disorganized Crime: The Economics of the Visible Hand* (Cambridge, MA: MIT Press, 1983).

Schneider, Eric C. *Vampires, Dragons, and Egyptian Kings: Youth Gangs in Postwar New York* (Princeton, NJ: Princeton University Press, 1999).

Venkatesh, Sudhir. *Gang Leader for a Day: A Rogue Sociologist Takes to the Streets* (New York, NY: Penguin Press, 2008).

White, Shane, et al. *Playing the Numbers: Gambling in Harlem Between the Wars* (Cambridge, MA: Harvard University Press, 2010).

Witwer, David. *Shadow of the Racketeer: Scandal in Organized Labor* (Urbana, IL: University of Illinois Press, 2009).

CHAPTER 19

....

THE MYTH OF ETHNIC SUCCESS

Old Wine in New Bottles

....

STEPHEN STEINBERG

In his 1967 book on *The Social Background of the Italo-American School Child*, Leonard Covello quotes an Italian peasant as saying, "If our children don't go to school, no harm results. But if the sheep don't eat, they will die. The school can wait but not our sheep."[1] In *The Ethnic Myth*, published in 1981, I used this as the epigraph for my chapter on "Education and Social Mobility: The Myth of Jewish Intellectualism and Catholic Anti-Intellectualism" because I thought it epitomized the way that culture can only be understood when placed in historical and social context.[2] This Italian peasant was not disparaging education per se but was responding to the circumstances and exigencies of his life, and quite literally so: "If the sheep don't eat, they will die."

Fast forward a generation to 1990. A student of Italian descent tells my class that when he was growing up, "All I ever heard was, 'It's either education or the pick and shovel.'" This nugget of folk wisdom epitomize the sea change in cultural attitudes as Italians leapfrogged, first from an agricultural to an urban economy and then from an industrial to a postindustrial economy. For my student's generation, the "pick and shovel" was an iconic representation of a bygone era, and education had become a cultural imperative. This was another reminder that "culture," despite appearances to the contrary, is never fixed in time but always adapts to the changing circumstances and exigencies of peoples' lives. Indeed, this should be the guiding theoretical principle for making sense of whatever empirical regularities exist between ethnicity and social class attainment.

The *fact* of ethnic success—the empirical correlation between ethnicity and social class—is widely observed and easily documented. But there is also a *theory* of ethnic success that traces these empirical outcomes to ethnic factors. And since ethnicity is conceived of as a cultural phenomenon, consisting of distinctive values and codes of behavior, it is readily assumed that culture is the fulcrum of "ethnic success." The danger here is of reifying culture—of failing to take into account its foundation in material and social class factors. To assert "class" is not to deny "culture," but rather to explore its backward linkages to the constellation of historical and material factors that engendered and sustained those cultural factors in the first place.

This was the logic and strategy I deployed in *The Ethnic Myth*. In a chapter entitled "The Myth of Ethnic Success: The Jewish Horatio Story," I argued that Jewish immigrants escaped poverty sooner than other immigrants because they arrived with previous industrial experience and a higher rate of literacy. A key question is whether these two factors—previous industrial experience and a high rate of literacy—should be regarded as mutually reflecting economic and material conditions or whether, as is often assumed, the high rate of Jewish literacy stemmed from a distinctly religious imperative that valorizes study of the Talmud and education in general. In *The Transformation of the Jews*, Calvin Goldscheider and Alan Zuckerman dispute this latter claim. They show that literacy among European Jews varied widely by region, reflecting economic conditions. As they write: "Patterns of education among the Jews of Paris, Berlin, Vienna, and Budapest differed dramatically from those of Warsaw, Lodz, Vilna, and the medium-sized cities and towns that housed most of the Jews of Poland, Rumania, and half those of Hungary." They go on to argue:

> The intensity of modernization combined with the size, structure, and organizational strength of the Jewish community to determine educational patterns among the Jews. *There is no evidence that differential Jewish values on education among these communities account for these differences.*[3]

Of paramount significance is that Jewish immigrants arrived in the United States with occupational skills that provided the foundation for intergenerational mobility. In the Pale of Settlement, the western provinces in czarist Russia where Jews were required to live, Jews fulfilled their legendary role in commerce and trade, and this experience fit perfectly in America's burgeoning industrial economy.[4] They also developed skills in an astonishing array of crafts, as was documented in an 1897 Russian census that was brought to light by an economist, Israel Rubinow, in a 1907 report for the U.S. Bureau of Labor, "The Economic Condition of Jews in Russia."[5] The census showed that in the Pale, 32 percent were engaged in commerce, most often as traders in agricultural products such as grain, cattle, hides, and furs. Another 38 percent were employed in manufacturing or as artisans. Jews were dominant in clothing manufacture and the clothing trades, skills that they transferred to New York's burgeoning garment industry, providing immigrants with work and the Jewish community with a crucial economic anchor.

Studies by the 1911 Immigration Commission showed that Jews were first in a large number of crafts, including hat and cap makers, furriers, tailors, bookbinders, watchmakers, cigar-packers, and tinsmiths. Many others were jewelers, painters, dressmakers, photographers, locksmiths, bakers, butchers, metal workers, and workers in the building trades.[6] Not only were these skills in demand in cities where Jews settled, but they also formed the basis for small businesses, which in turn served as a springboard of mobility for future generations. Historian Selma Berrol had it right in her 1976 article in the *American Jewish Historical Quarterly*:

> [M]ost New York Jews did not make the leap from poverty into the middle class by going to college. Rather, widespread utilization of secondary and higher education *followed* improvements in economic status and was as much a result as a cause of upward mobility.[7]

In other words, mobility was not a rags-to-riches story, but rather an intergenerational phenomenon whereby immigrants first secured an occupational and economic foothold. Only then were their children and grandchildren positioned to use schools as a springboard of mobility.[8]

A problem with most mobility studies is that they are based on comparisons between independent generational cohorts. The data may well indicate a pattern whereby the children of immigrants leapfrog over their parents, but the statistical pattern obscures the actual process whereby "rags" morphed into "riches." With this in mind, I dispatched an older student who spoke Yiddish to locate elderly Jewish men in nursing homes in New York City as well as South Florida. Her marching orders were simple: interrogate these subjects about their occupational experiences prior to and after immigrating to the United States and the occupations of their sons and grandsons. These "occupational genealogies," extending across three generations, point up the pivotal role played by the occupational skills that immigrant Jews brought with them from Eastern Europe.[9]

For example, in Russia, one subject collected cow hides from farmers, tanned them, and in a classic middleman role, sold them to shoemakers and shoe manufacturers in urban centers. In New York, he started up a business tanning hides for bag manufacturers. After his three sons came into the business, they began manufacturing leather bags, wallets, and luggage. Together, they had seven sons: four doctors and three lawyers.

Another subject was a small grocer in Bessarabia, Romania. After the Cossacks destroyed his store, Petersen emigrated with his five young sons and a daughter. With the help of a loan from a landsmanshaft organization, he opened a grocery store, which prospered. Together with his five sons, he opened a larger store, and eventually they built a chain of thirty-two stores. The next generation of males all became professionals: seven doctors, three lawyers, and a psychologist.

I plead guilty here of highlighting two cases that serve my argument. However, a consistent pattern emerged from the interviews: Jewish immigrants parlayed skills they brought over from Europe into small entrepreneurial business. In most cases, their sons did *not* go to college but entered the family business, often expanding it into a more lucrative enterprise. Typically, it was the grandchildren of these immigrant entrepreneurs who made the leap to college and, with astonishing regularity, entered the professions, usually as doctors or lawyers. As I like to add, tongue in cheek, the misfit became a professor.

To state that the Jewish success story was largely a matter of historical timing should not detract from the individual dimension—the ingenuity and dogged enterprise of immigrants who developed successful businesses that improved the living standards of their families, including access to good schools in what the Chicago sociologists termed "the area of second settlement." Pluck mattered, but so did luck. Not only did Jews arrive with the right skills at the right time, but, just at the point when they consolidated their class position, there was a vast expansion of higher education that opened up opportunities for their children. Today, a far less favorable set of institutional forces are in place, which may well augur the demise of the legendary Jewish success story.

THE MODEL MINORITY MYTH: ASIAN AMERICANS AS PROXY JEWS

As Toni Morrison has famously written, immigrants *become* American by joining the chorus singing praise to the American Dream.[10] They do so in their literature and drama and, alas, in their knowledge production as well. As part of their baptism as Americans, each ascendant ethnic group delegates one of its best and brightest to earn a PhD and, beginning with the dissertation, to tell their collective story of triumph over adversity. In addition to hard work, fortitude, and perseverance—all individual traits—these fledgling scholars give the success story a social scientific twist, citing ethnic values and solidarities as the driving force of ethnic mobility.

Nathan Glazer cast the ideological mold for this genre. His first book, *American Judaism*, based on his dissertation at Columbia, offered an inspirational narrative of crisis and redemption.[11] In his later work, Glazer spun the Jewish success myth: Jews succeeded, he argued, because of a reverence for learning, an entrepreneurial spirit, industry, fortitude, sobriety, and other such cultural virtues.[12] His fatal error was that he gave short shrift to premigration factors—previous industrial experience and higher rates of literacy—that gave Jewish immigrants a decisive head start and put them on a trajectory of intergenerational mobility. By lumping Jews together with the other "huddled masses," the props were in place for what Thomas Sowell has called "the classic American success story—from rags to riches against all opposition."[13]

Ironically, in an autobiographical essay, Glazer does not romanticize "the Jewish passion for education" in the least. As he wrote:

> In education, once again I think we were placed with that very large group, not written about much in memoirs and histories, in which the passion for education was muted. That meant we would get more education than our Italian neighbors, but we were not expected to go to college.

And he added:

> I am enough of a sociologist to know that the fact that I was not put under any pressure to work or contribute to family expenses was simply that I was the youngest [of five children].[14]

Another fortuitous circumstance was that the City College of New York was tuition-free when he enrolled as a freshman in 1940. Yet in his role as a sociologist, Glazer propagated the idea that Jews succeeded through education.

What Glazer did for Jews in propagating a success myth, Richard Gambino did for Italians, Andrew Greeley for Irish, Richard Novak for Slavs, and Betty Lee Sung for Chinese.[15] And this genre of success stories continues among the progeny of the post-1965 immigrants who enter sociology and are eager to tell the story of their group's triumph over adversity. This might be called "the sociology of self-congratulation." Of course, a modicum of collective braggadocio might be forgiven, given the struggles these groups endured, except that self-congratulation has an insidious flip side when applied to the racial "other." In celebrating "our" cultural virtues and advancing a theory about how "we" made it, there is the sinister implication that "they" lacked "our" cultural virtues with respect to family, work, and education. The "model minority" is cast as the antithesis to the "problem minority."[16]

However, the model minority myth is unique in that it was not woven by ethnic insiders but rather, as Thomas Nakayama has asserted, "is a discursive practice by non-Asian Americans."[17] A precursor of this discourse appeared in a 1957 article in the *New York Times* by William McIntyre under the caption: "Chinatown Offers Us a Lesson."[18] McIntyre marveled that in New York City's Chinatown, there was virtually no juvenile delinquency. The reason? "Growing up in such an insulated and emotionally snug family life, the child develops characteristics that seem peculiarly 'Chinese'—reservoirs of patience, unflagging capacity for work and dislike for physical violence." Not only that but, according to McIntyre, "as universal as brown eyes among the Chinese is the desire for education." McIntyre's veneration for the Chinese extends even to his claim that "Chinese families are early to bed (10 P.M.) and early to rise (7:30 A.M.)."[19] Alas, what we see here is the invention of a model minority, one that combines Confucianism and Calvinism into an invincible amalgam.

It was not until January 1966 that the model minority myth entered scholarly discourse. This came with an article by sociologist William Petersen entitled "Success Story, Japanese-American Style," published in no less a public venue than *The New York Times Magazine*. The timing could not have been more perfect in terms of its racial subtext. The civil rights movement had attained its legislative objectives with the passing of the 1964 and 1965 Civil Rights Acts, and the movement was making a strategic shift from "liberty" to "equality" as black leaders called for "compensatory programs" to open up channels of opportunity for blacks in jobs and education. What better time to invoke the "Success Story, Japanese-American Style."[20]

Indeed, the rhetorical frame for Petersen's article consisted of an invidious comparison between Japanese and blacks. According to Petersen, centuries of racial oppression have permanently impaired the black psyche—so much so that "when new opportunities, even equal opportunities, are opened up, the minority's reaction to them is likely to be negative—either self-defeating apathy or a hatred so all-consuming as to be self-destructive. For all the well-meaning programs and countless scholarly studies now focused on the Negro, we barely know how to repair the damage that the slave traders started."[21]

According to Petersen, what was unique about the Japanese is that they over-came oppression without governmental intervention or preferential treatment. As he wrote:

> Barely more than 20 years after the end of the wartime camps, this is a minority that has risen above even prejudiced criticism. By any criterion of good citizenship that we choose, the Japanese Americans are better than any other group in our society, including native-born whites. They have established this remarkable record, moreover, by their own almost totally unaided effort. Every attempt to hamper their progress resulted only in enhancing the determination to succeed. Even in a country whose patron saint is the Horatio Alger hero, there is no parallel to this success story.[22]

Here Petersen has crafted the perfect victim: one who "revolts against revolt" and resurrects himself or herself through sheer determination, buttressed by those quintessential solidarities of family and ethnic group, as well as through education, which he dubs as "the key to success."

With some rhetorical dressing, Petersen had refurbished Glazer's theory of Jewish success. Furthermore, Petersen's rendition of the Japanese success story played into a distinctively Jewish agenda. As early as 1964, Norman Podhoretz, editor of *Commentary*, was on record in rejecting the "radical" direction that the civil rights movement had taken when Roy Wilkins and other civil rights leaders advocated compensatory programs that would give "special treatment" to blacks as a remedy for past oppression.[23] After publication of his piece in the *New York Times*, Petersen would go on to become *Commentary*'s point man on affirmative action. On the one hand, he lampooned Robert O'Neil's 1975 book, *Discriminating Against Discrimination*, which defended preferential admissions in the 1974 *DeFunis* case.[24] On the other hand, he showered praise on Glazer's 1976 book, *Affirmative Discrimination*, which was the first book-length polemic against affirmative action in which Glazer compared affirmative action to the Nuremberg Laws.[25]

In 1981, Petersen was again in the pages of *Commentary*, heaping praise on Sowell's *Ethnic America*.[26] With a rhetorical sleight of hand, Sowell used the success of Asian Americans to argue that blacks cannot blame "race" for their problems. If blacks lag behind other races, it is because of cultural aberrations rooted in slavery itself. The hidden political agenda behind the model minority myth was never to exalt Asian Americans but rather to weave a success story that would undercut black demands for the kinds of compensatory programs that evolved into affirmative action policy. Not only that, but in the escalating conflict over affirmative action policy, Asian Americans were cast as proxy Jews, thus allowing Jewish opponents of affirmative action to invoke the myth of "success through education" without seeming to argue out of naked self-interest.

After its 1966 debut in the *New York Times Magazine*, another article appeared in *U.S. News and World Report* that shifted the focus from Japanese to Chinese: "Success Story of One Minority Group in U.S." Aside from "a tight network of family and clan loyalties," Chinese are exalted for their "strict discipline," leading children "to attend school faithfully, work hard at their studies—and stay out of trouble." Followed by the invidious comparison to blacks: "What you find, back of this remarkable group of Americans, is a story of adversity and prejudice that would shock those now complaining about the hardships endured by today's Negroes." Finally, the perverse subtext bubbles to the surface: "At a time when it is being proposed that hundreds of billions be spent to uplift Negroes and other minorities, the nation's 300,000 Chinese Americans are moving ahead on their own with no help from anyone else."[27]

Five years passed before the model minority appeared in another major publication. In June 1971, *Newsweek* published an article under the furtive title, "Success Story: Outwhiting the Whites."[28] However, it was not until the 1980s, in the context of a fierce national debate over affirmative action, that the Asian American success story appeared in a slew of the nation's mass circulation magazines.[29] To wit:

- *Newsweek*, "Asian Americans: 'A Model Minority,'" Dec. 6, 1982.
- *Newsweek on Campus*, "The Drive to Excel," cover story, April 1984.
- *Newsweek*, "A Formula for Success," Apr. 1984.
- *U.S. News & World Report*, "Asian-Americans: Are They Making the Grade?" Apr. 1984.
- *The New Republic*, "The Triumph of Asian Americans: America's Greatest Success Story," July 1985.
- *Psychology Today*, "The Oriental Express," July 1986.
- *Fortune*, "America's Super Minority," Nov. 1986.
- *Newsweek,* "A `Superminority' Tops Out," May 1987.
- *Time*, "The New Whiz Kids," Aug. 1987.

David Bell's article in *The New Republic* (noted above) is especially noteworthy. Written with academic sobriety, Bell concedes that some of Jewish and Asian American success is due to selective migration of highly educated immigrants. Nevertheless, he joins the chorus by making invidious comparisons to blacks:

> Rather than searching for a solution to their problems through the political process, Jewish, Chinese, and Japanese immigrants developed self-sufficiency by relying on community organizations. The combination of their skills, their desire for education, and the gradual disappearance of discrimination led inexorably to economic success.[30]

Ironically, Bell's rebuke of blacks for relying on "the political process" is reminiscent of Booker T. Washington's 1895 speech at the Atlanta Exposition in which he admonished blacks to avoid politics and "artificial forcing."[31] In 1895 "artificial forcing" pertained to laws guaranteeing civil rights, including the right to vote. In 1985, "artificial forcing" pertained to affirmative action, which drove a wedge into the wall of occupational segregation.

A number of Asian American scholars recognized the political agenda that lurked behind the exaltation of Asian Americans and objected to specious comparisons between Asian Americans and blacks. The first scholar to do so was Kiyoshi Ikeda, in a 1971 review of Petersen's book, *Japanese Americans: Oppression and Success.* Ikeda rejected Petersen's contention that Japanese suffered worse oppression than African Americans. As Ikeda wrote: "The histories of oppression simply are not parallel or similar in level and type. From the inception of immigration, the Japanese in America always had the support of firm, cross-national agreements and legal protections to insure that they could develop and maintain ethnic institutions in a hostile environment." Ikeda said flat out: "The Japanese-Americans are not a self-made people."[32]

According to sociologists Arthur Sakamoto and Keng-Loong Yap, by the late 1980s, the model minority myth (MMM) emerged as "a key theme in studies of Asian Americans. It is mentioned in virtually every academic book ever written for an Asian American Studies audience."[33] A common objection was that this upbeat narrative of success eclipsed the fact that many Asian American immigrants were poor and confronted barriers of racism. These scholars also objected to the politics behind MMM, especially the invocation of the Asian model minority to undercut support for affirmative action and other programs targeted for African Americans. Sakamoto and Yap could not be more emphatic on this point:

> According to the MMM, the "model minority" image has been used essentially as propaganda by politically conservative commentators to emphasize the openness of American society and to argue against government programs such as affirmative action and welfare that disproportionately help racial and ethnic minorities.[34]

In yet another exposé of the surreptitious politics of MMM, Theodore Hsien Wang and Frank H. Wu write:

> One of the increasingly prominent fallacies in the attacks on affirmative action is that Asian-Americans are somehow the example that defeats the rationale for race-conscious remedial programs. House Speaker Newt Gingrich and California governor Pete Wilson are two of the many political leaders who point to Asian-Americans and their supposed success in American society to assert that affirmative action is not needed.[35]

In a section titled "Asian-Americans as Pawns in the Debate," Wang and Wu condemn the deployment of the MMM "for Machiavellian political purposes," adding that these divisive politics only feed racial backlash, deflecting attention away from the struggles of Asian Americans against discrimination.

Despite adamant repudiation by Asian American scholars, in 1990, *Commentary* published yet another article on "America's 'Model Minority.'" Louis Winnick, a new contributor, acknowledges that Asian American scholars have spoken out against the "hyperbolic excesses" of the model minority construct, principally by calling attention to the struggles of poor and working-class Asian Americans who are far from a success story. But Winnick dismisses this with the observation that "all mass migrations are accompanied by hardship and privation," and returns to the familiar refrain, now explicitly coupling Asian Americans with Jews:

> The achievements of both Jews and Asians are largely the consequence of a common ensemble of cultural values . . . They include an unswerving devotion to family, extended as well as nuclear; the high premiums paid and sacrifices endured for educational advance; the disproportionately low rates of crime and welfare dependency; a well-developed propensity, through thrift and self-denial, toward capital accumulation—that is, the willingness to defer gratification for future goals; a strong bent toward self-employment that seems to wane among the assimilated generations.[36]

Part of the reason for the persistence of the model minority myth is that it resonates with the dominant American myth of America as a land of opportunity. Without doubt, many Asians also buy into this feel-good narrative.[37] However, it would be a mistake to take this exaltation of Asian Americans at face value.[38] Rather, it is because the model minority myth serves a unique ideological function in relation to the great unresolved issue in American history: the legacy of slavery and the ongoing policy debates over restitution for past wrongs. The MMM is invoked to make the specious claim that the problem is not oppression, and if only people have the right cultural stuff, they can make that momentous leap from pariah to paragon.

In 1999 Claire Jean Kim, a political scientist, aptly described the politics behind the myth: "The renaissance of the model minority myth in the early 1980s coincided with the start of a vigorous conservative campaign to turn the clock back on civil rights, affirmative action, redistricting, and social welfare programs . . . Once again, the model minority myth has conscripted Asian Americans into the conservative war to protect (or, in this case, reprieve) White privileges from Black encroachment."[39]

The ultimate hypocrisy is that the infamy of the Japanese internment has been invoked to gloss over another infamy—slavery and its vestiges in the present.

THE MYTH OF "ACTING WHITE"

"Acting white" is the latest in a lineage of victim-blaming neologisms. In the 1950s, the problems of black schoolchildren were blamed on "cultural deprivation." In the 1960s and 1970s, a putative "culture of poverty" was to blame. In the 1980s and 1990s, "underclass" became a buzzword. Then came the appropriation and debasement of Marx's conception of "capital," which was meant to apply to entire systems of domination and exploitation and instead was reduced to an individual trait to be measured on a scale of gradation. In the first iteration, blacks were said to have a deficit of "human capital," then "cultural capital," and, most recently, "social capital." All of these discourses have one thing in common: they deflect attention away from the institutions that engender and sustain racial oppression, and they locate the sources of disadvantage among blacks themselves. Each incarnation of this cultural blaming-of-the-victim has been deconstructed and discredited by critics, but, as with the legendary hydra, each severed head grows back as two.[40]

"Acting white" entered the discourse with a 1986 paper by John Ogbu and Signithia Fordham under the title "Black Students' School Success: Coping with the Burden of 'Acting White.'" Invoking resistance theory, they argued that black students sabotaged their own education by spurning the behavior associated with academic success: speaking standard English, spending long hours doing homework, striving for high grades, enrolling in advance placement courses, and aspiring to college. According to Ogbu and Fordham, instead of striving to do well academically, black youth do the opposite: they defiantly refuse to learn. Still worse, they ridicule and harass high-achieving black students. In effect, they reject "the code of the schools" for "the code of the streets."[41]

What is astounding—and itself begs for analysis—is the rapidity with which the "acting-white" theorem was thrust to the center of both scholarly and popular discourses and has currency even today.[42] In 2004, President Obama invoked the terminology in his keynote address to the Democratic National Convention:

> Go into any inner city neighborhood, and folks will tell you that government alone can't teach kids to learn. They know that parents have to parent, that children can't achieve unless we raise their expectations and turn off the television sets and eradicate the slander that says a black youth with a book is acting white. No, people don't expect government to solve all their problems.[43]

Poof! If only black youth would turn off their television sets and cease regarding schooling as an act of racial betrayal, we could reduce the racial gap in academic outcomes. The political implications are clearly stated: government alone can't teach kids to learn and people don't expect government to solve all of their problems. What better example of the political use of the acting-white discourse! With a rhetorical sleight of hand, responsibility is shifted away from the powerful institutions of government that could make a difference and placed on the shoulders of ordinary people who are virtually powerless against these societal forces.

Critics have challenged the "acting-white" thesis in terms of its factual accuracy, as well as its implications for social policy. The most extensive empirical study was published in the *American Sociological Review* in 2005: "It's Not 'a Black Thing': Understanding the Burden of Acting White and Other Dilemmas of High Achievement," by Karolyn Tyson, William Darity Jr., and Domini R. Castellino. This was a rigorous study of eight public secondary schools in North Carolina based on intensive interviews with eighty-five students, forty of whom were black.[44] Tyson et al. found that most students, black and white alike, expressed a desire to do well academically. Relatively few black students enrolled in AP courses, but this was not because these students feared peer reaction, but rather because they felt they could not hack the courses academically. Those black students (mostly female) who did enroll in AP courses, expressed angst over the fact that there were so few blacks. In other words, the surface reality sustained the perception of AP courses as "white."

Even more telling, high-achieving students, *regardless of race*, were often tagged as "nerds" or "geeks." Or they were seen as "snooty" or "high and mighty," reflecting the fact that most of the students enrolled in AP courses came from affluent families. In other words, to the extent that "acting white" existed at all, it was more rooted in notions of class and gender than in race per se.[45]

Corroborating evidence for this position is found in Paul Willis's classic study of white youth in a working-class town in England. Willis observed that these "lads"— remember, they are all white—developed a male counter-school culture in which they regarded education as "a waste of time" and "for sissies," not "real men." Instead, they valorized physicality, chauvinism, and machismo. The striking parallels with Fordham's findings in her study of Capital High suggests that "acting white" has little or nothing to do with race per se, but is fundamentally a matter of poverty and joblessness.

In an afterword written for the second edition of *Learning to Labor*, Willis wrote the following with the United States in mind:

> [F]ar from being "ignorant," "anachronistic," "pathological," and in need of eradication, such cultural responses may in certain important respects, be *in advance* of the understanding of the liberal agencies. "The lads'" culture, for instance, is involved in making its own realistic bets about its best chances in a class society and about how best to approach an impoverished future in manual work. Meanwhile, their advisors are tying themselves up in humanistic, developmental knots which bear very little relation to the actual labouring future of their pupils. This suggests just how far liberal, humanistic, generally "left" illusions can be from the reality of the oppressed and the real possibilities facing them. *Learning to Labour* helped to block the escape hatch of "cultural deprivation" and to reevaluate liberal aims in education.[46]

Willis throws down the gauntlet to the liberal project on education and its failure to link education to larger systems of domination and inequality. Indeed, we have to ask whether the liberal faith in education as "a great equalizer" amounts to a convenient escape from confronting the societal forces that stunt the lives of the children who inhabit our classrooms. To be sure, schools must do what they can to offset the effects of poverty and racism, but it behooves us to confront these cold realities instead of raising false hopes that schools can remedy the very deep divisions of race and class that rend American society.[47]

No better refutation of the "acting-white" theorem exists than in the early work of John Ogbu himself. In his first book, *Minority Education and Caste*, published in 1978, Ogbu conducted a comparative study of six nations that had caste-like minorities: the

United States, Great Britain, New Zealand, India, Japan, and Israel. By "caste-like minorities," Ogbu meant that they bore the stigma of caste: they were branded as outcasts from birth and confronted pervasive discrimination in all societal institutions, especially in the realm of work. Ogbu observed that in all six societies, minorities exhibited patterns of "educational retardation," and in the aftermath of the civil rights movement in the United States and anti-colonialist revolts in the Third World, all six societies launched a series of liberal reforms aimed at remedying educational retardation among minority youth. Generally speaking, these projects failed to significantly alter the racial gaps in academic outcomes. Ogbu concluded on a revelatory note: "The lower school performance of blacks is not itself the central problem but an expression of a more fundamental one, namely caste barriers and the ideologies that support them. . ... *The elimination of caste barriers is the only lasting solution to the problem of academic retardation.*"[48]

This was a bold pronouncement that impugns school reformers for addressing symptoms rather than root causes. According to Ogbu, their efforts are destined for failure for two reasons.

> First, blacks still perceive and respond to their schooling, both consciously and unconsciously, in terms of how they see their chances in the future to use and benefit from education like their white peers; second, the cognitive and other school- and job-related attributes blacks develop continue to be those adaptive to their social and occupational roles rather than those demanded by the positions occupied by the dominant whites and stressed by their education.[49]

This is not an argument against school reform but rather against the chimera of invoking the mantra of "education" as a magical solution for the deep and persistent inequalities of race and class.[50] It is either a leap of faith or willful delusion to think that we can live in a society where more than half of black children are born into poverty, pluck them out of ghettos that are the refuge for our nation's racial pariahs, funnel these students into schools with droves of others like themselves, and expect teachers to redress conditions that ultimately reflect the patent failures of American democracy.[51]

Nor is the problem simply that we don rose-tinted glasses and see education as a panacea. It is worse than that. The false promise of education is a subterfuge, deployed to camouflage the fact that the United States does not have the political will to link education reform to a larger project of class transformation and reparations for centuries of racial oppression. Until these inequalities are eradicated, black children will continue to bear the burden not of *acting white* but rather of *being black*.

ACKNOWLEDGEMENTS

This paper had its inception at a working conference on the model minority myth sponsored by the Asian/Pacific/American Institute at New York University (Mar. 14, 2008).

I am grateful to Jack Tchen for organizing this event and to the participants for their feedback. Thanks also to Ron Bayor for his helpful comments to an earlier draft of this paper.

NOTES

1. Quoted in Leonard Covello, *The Social Background of the Italo-American School Child* (Totowa, NJ: Rowman & Littlefield, 1967), 256. Covello's book was originally a doctoral dissertation at New York University in 1944 and was based on research in both Italy and New York City.
2. Stephen Steinberg, *The Ethnic Myth*, 3rd ed. (Boston: Beacon Press, 2001), 128–150.
3. Calvin Goldscheider and Alan S. Zuckerman, *The Transformation of the Jews* (Chicago: University of Chicago Press, 1984), 106 (emphasis added). In the case of the renowned yeshivot and Torah academies in Lithuania, Goldscheider and Zuckerman state that "the great Jewish learning associated with Lithuanian Jewry was a product of the absence of alternative opportunities in jobs and education for men. Where opportunities for work and education emerged, there was less emphasis on extended study in Talmud academies. With few jobs and opportunities, the values placed on traditional study for men were reinforced" (107). On the other hand, in Poland in 1925, three-fourths of Jewish girls of school age, but only 30 percent of the boys, attended school. Goldscheider and Zuckerman attribute this disparity to "the high levels of poverty among Polish Jews" and "the relative availability of work for Jewish boys" (106).

    Nor can it be assumed that literacy in Yiddish language and culture was a factor in the Jewish success story. In a 1969 paper, Miriam Slater, an anthropologist, argued that the style and content of traditional Jewish scholarship were fundamentally at odds with the requirements of modern secular education and, if anything, would have operated as a deterrent to educational achievement in the United States. She concluded that "it was a striving for material success, not a passion for learning, that spurred Jews up the educational ladder." Slater, "My Son the Doctor: Aspects of Mobility Among American Jews," *American Sociological Review* 34 (June 1969): 359–373.
4. In his study of Russian Jewish immigrants in Providence, Rhode Island, Joel Perlmann found that "a very considerable number of East European Jewish immigrants made their way into the American economy through commercial pursuits rather than as members of the working class as that term is usually understood." Joel Perlmann, "Beyond New York: The Occupations of Russian Jewish Immigrants in Providence, R. I. and in Other Small Jewish Communities, 1900–1915," *Journal of American Jewish History*, 72 (3) (Mar. 1983): 309–332. For a detailed account of the transfer of skills from Europe to America and the role that these continuities played in intergeneration mobility, see Ewa Morawska, *Insecure Prosperity: Small-Town Jews in Industrial America, 1890–1940* (Princeton: Princeton University Press, 1996).
5. Israel Rubinow, "The Economic Condition of Jews in Russia," *Bulletin of the Bureau of Labor*, no. 72 (Washington, DC: Government Printing Office, 1907): 487–583. A far more detailed account, relying on a wider array of sources, is provided by Goldscheider and Zuckerman in *The Transformation of the Jews*, ibid., chap. 4.
6. U.S. Immigration Commission, *Immigrants in Industries*, vol. VIII (Washington, DC, 1911), and Gerald Rosenblum, *Immigrant Workers* (New York: Basic Books, 1973), 70–81.

7. Selma C. Berrol, "Education and Economic Mobility: The Jewish Experience in New York City, 1880–1920," *American Jewish Historical Quarterly* (Mar. 1976): 271.

8. The importance of intergenerational mobility is emphasized in a special issue of *The Future of Children*, "Opportunity in America" (vol. 16 (2) (Fall 2006)), www.futureofchildren.org. In the same volume, see Robert Haveman and Timothy Smeeding, "The Role of Higher Education in Social Mobility"; Jens Ludwig and Susan Mayer, "'Culture' and the Intergenerational Transmission of Poverty: The Prevention Paradox"; and Emily Beller and Michael Hout, "Intergenerational Social Mobility: The United States in Comparative Perspective."

9. Louise Farkas, "Occupational Genealogies of Jews in Eastern Europe and America, 1880–1924" (master's thesis, Queens College, 1982); Stephen Steinberg, "The Rise of the Jewish Professional," *Ethnic and Racial Studies*, 9 (4) (Oct. 1986): 502–513.

10. Toni Morrison, "On the Backs of Blacks," *Time*, Dec. 2, 1993 (article reprinted in *Arguing Immigration*, ed. Nicolaus Mills (New York: Touchtone, 1994), 97–100).

11. Nathan Glazer, *American Judaism* (Chicago: University of Chicago Press, 1957).

12. Nathan Glazer, "The American Jew and the Attainment of Middle Class Rank: Some Trends and Explanations," in *The Jews*, ed. Marshall Sklare (New York: Free Press, 1958), 143; Nathan Glazer and Daniel Patrick Moynihan, *Beyond the Melting Pot* (Cambridge: MIT Press, 1963 and 1970), 155–159.

13. Thomas Sowell, *Ethnic America* (New York: Basic Books, 1981), 98.

14. Nathan Glazer, "From Socialism to Sociology," in *Authors of Their Own Lives: Intellectual Autobiographies of Twenty American Sociologists*, ed. Bennett M. Berger (Berkeley: University of California Press, 1992), 192–193.

15. Richard Gambino, *Blood of My Blood: The Dilemma of the Italian-Americas* (Garden City, NY: Anchor Press, 1975); Andrew Greeley, "The Ethnic Miracle," *Public Interest* (Fall 1976): 20–36; Richard Novak, *The Rise of the Unmeltable Ethnics* (New York: Macmillan, 1972); Betty Lee Sung, *The Story of the Chinese in America* (New York: Collier, 1975). Note that all of these works were published during the "ethnic revival" of the early 1970s.

16. Phillip Lee, "The 'Asian' Category in MCAS Achievement Gap Tracking: Time for a Change," *Asian American Policy Review* (2011), available with login ID at http://isites.harvard.edu/icb/icb.do?keyword=k74751&pageid=icb.page412509.

17. Thomas K. Nakayama, "§Model Minority' and the Media: Discourse on Asian America" *Journal of Communication Inquiry* (1988), available at http://jci.sagepub.com/content/12/1/65.extract.

18. William A. McIntyre, "Chinatown Offers Us a Lesson," *New York Times*, Oct. 6, 1957, reprinted in *The Virgin Islands Daily News*, Dec. 11, 1058, available at http://news.google.com/newspapers?nid=757&dat=19581211&id=kHdaAAAAIBAJ&sjid=PocDAAAAIBAJ&pg=6497,3240779.

19. Ibid., 54.

20. William Petersen, "Success Story: Japanese-American Style," *New York Times Magazine*, Jan. 9, 1966, 20–43.

21. Ibid., 21.

22. Ibid., 21.

23. "Liberalism and the Negro: A Round-Table Discussion," *Commentary* 37 (Mar. 1964): 25–42.

24. DeFunis v. Odegaard, 416 U.S.312 (1974).

25. William Petersen, Review of Robert M. O'Neil, *Discrimination Against Discrimination: Preferential Admissions and the DeFunis Case, Commentary* (June

1976): 88; and Review of Nathan Glazer, *Affirmative Discrimination: Ethnic Inequality and Public Policy, Commentary* (May 1976), 78–80. For Glazer's prominent role in forging anti-affirmative action discourse, see Stephen Steinberg, "Nathan Glazer and the Assassination of Affirmative Action," *New Politics*, 9 (3) (Summer 2003), available at http://nova.wpunj.edu/newpolitics/issue35/Steinberg35.htm.

26. William Petersen, review of *Ethnic America*, by Thomas Sowell, *Commentary* (Oct. 1981), 76–78.

27. "Success Story of One Minority Group in U.S.," *U.S. News and World Report*, Dec. 26, 1966, available at http://www.dartmouth.edu/~hist32/Hist33/US%20News%20&%20World%20Report.pdf.

28. "Success Story: Outwhiting the Whites," *Newsweek*, June 21, 1971, 24–25.

29. Thomas K. Nakayama, "Model Minority' and the Media: Discourse on Asian America," Journal of Communication Inquiry (1988), available at http://jci.sagepub.com/content/12/1/65.extract.

30. David A. Bell, "The Triumph of Asian-Americans," *The New Republic*, July 15 & 22, 1985, 29.

31. The full text of that statement reads: "The wisest among my race understand that the agitation of questions of social equality is the extremist folly, and that progress in the enjoyment of all the privileges that will come to us must be the result of severe and constant struggle rather than of artificial forcing." Booker T. Washington, "1895 Atlanta Compromise Speech," Sept. 18, 1895, available at http://historymatters.gmu.edu/d/39/.

32. Kiyoshi Ikeda, "A Different 'Dilemma,'" review of *Japanese Americans: Oppression and Success, Social Forces*, vol. 51, by William Petersen (June 1973), 498–499.

33. Arthur Sakamoto and Keng-Loong Yap, "The Myth of the Model Minority Myth," All Academic Research (paper presented at the annual meeting of the American Sociological Association, Montreal Convention Center, Montreal, Quebec, Canada, Aug 11, 2006), available at http://citation.allacademic.com//meta/p_mla_apa_research_citation/0/9/6/0/1/pages96013/p96013-1.php.

34. Ibid., 2.

35. Theodore Hsien Wang and Frank H. Wu, "Beyond the Model Minority Myth," in *The Affirmative Action Debate*, ed. George E. Curry (Cambridge: Perseus Books, 1996), 191–207.

36. Louis Winnick, "America's 'Model Minority,'" *Commentary* (Aug. 1990): 24.

37. One survey at a large university found that Asian American students perceived themselves as more prepared, motivated, and more likely to succeed than whites, and that perception was shared by whites as well. Paul Wong, Chienping Faith Lai, Richard Nagasawa, and Tieming Lin, "Asian Americans as a Model Minority: Self-Perceptions and Perceptions by Other Racial Groups," *Sociological Perspectives*, 41 (1) (1998): 95–118.

38. For a recent account of anti-Asian bigotry, see Rosalind S. Chou and Joe R. Feagin, *The Myth of the Model Minority: Asian Americans Facing Racism* (Boulder: Paradigm Publishers, 2008).

39. Claire Jean Kim, "The Racial Triangulation of African Americans," *Politics and Society*, 27 (205) (1999): 120. Note, too, that even though Asian Americans stand to gain disproportionately from cutbacks to affirmative action in higher education, solid majorities have voted against anti-affirmative action ballot initiatives. In 2001, 61 percent of Asian Americans voted against Proposition 209 in California, and in 2006, 75 percent voted against Proposition 2 in Michigan. See "Asian Americans for Affirmative

Action," *The Nation*, Jan. 8, 2007, available at http://www.thenation.com/blog/asian-americans-affirmative-action.

40. For a recent work that mythologizes ethnic success, see Amy Chua and Jed Rosenfeld, *The Triple Package* (New York: Penguin Press, 2014), and my critique, "Tiger Couple Gets It Wrong on Immigrant Success," *Boston Review*, Mar. 11, 2014, available at http://bostonreview.net/books-ideas/stephen-steinberg-chua-rubenfeld-triple-package.

41. Signithia Fordham and John Ogbu, "Black Students' School Success: Coping with the Burden of 'Acting White'" *The Urban Review*, 18 (3) (Sept. 1986): 176–206. In a subsequent study of a high school that was more than 99 percent black, Fordham made the acting-white thesis the centerpiece of her analysis. She contended that these students had cultivated a "black identity" in opposition to the stigmatizing and dehumanizing stereotypes associated with white racism, and school success amounted to a liquefaction of their black selves. Signithia Fordham, *Blacked Out: Dilemmas of Race, Identity, and Success at Capital High* (Chicago: University of Chicago Press, 1996), 283.

42. Two professors of education described the "acting-white" postulate as providing "one of the dominant theories used to explain the black-white achievement gap." Erin McNamara Horvat and Kristine S. Lewis, "Reassessing the 'Burden of 'Acting White': The Importance of Peer Groups in Managing Academic Success," *Sociology of Education* 76 (4) (Oct. 2003), 265.

43. Barack Obama, 2004 Democratic National Convention Keynote Address, July 27, 2004, http://obamaspeeches.com/002-Keynote-Address-at-the-2004-Democratic-National-Convention-Obama-Speech.htm.

44. Karolyn Tyson, William Darity Jr., and Domini R. Castellino, "It's Not 'a Black Thing': Understanding the Burden of Acting White and Other Dilemmas of High Achievement" *American Sociological Review* 70 (4) (Aug. 2005): 582–605, available at http://www.tc.columbia.edu/students/see/events/Darity_et_al_Understanding_Burden_Acting_White.pdf.

45. No doubt, Capital High, the school that Signithia Fordham studied in Washington, DC, had a different youth culture than the eight schools studied in North Carolina, but this suggests that "acting white" might be more characteristic of inner-city schools in the urban North. Fordham, *Blacked Out*.

46. Paul Willis, *Learning to Labor: How Working Class Kids Get Working Class Jobs*, 2nd ed. (New York: Columbia University Press; Morningside edition, 1981), 205 (emphasis in original).

47. Samuel Bowles and Herbert Gintis, *Schooling in Capitalist America*, 2nd ed. (1976; Chicago: Haymarket Books, 2011); Henry J. Perkinson, *The Imperfect Panacea: American Faith in Education*, 4th ed. (New York: McGraw-Hill, 1995); David F. Labaree, "The Winning Ways of a Losing Strategy: Educationalizing Social Problems in the United States" 58 (4) *Educational Theory* (2008): 447–460.

48. John Ogbu, *Minority Education and Caste* (New York: Academic Press, 1978), 357 (emphasis in original).

49. Ibid., 359. Note the resonances with Leonard Covello's account in *The Social Background of the Italo-American School Child*.

50. Gordon Lafer makes this argument with respect to job training programs in *The Job Training Charade* (Ithaca: Cornell University Press, 2004).

51. Also see Richard Rothstein, *Class and Schools* (New York: Teachers College Press, 2004).

BIBLIOGRAPHY

Berrol, Selma C., "Education and Economic Mobility: The Jewish Experience in New York City, 1880–1920," *American Jewish Historical Quarterly* (March 1976), 257–271.

Bowles, Samuel and Herbert Gintis, *Schooling in Capitalist America*, Orig. pub. 1976, 2nd ed. (Chicago: Haymarket Books, 2011).

Fordham, Signithia and John Ogbu, "Black Students' School Success: Coping with the Burden of 'Acting White,'" *The Urban Review*, 18:3 (September 1986), 176–206.

Fordham, Signithia, *Blacked Out, Dilemmas of Race, Identity, and Success at Capital High* (Chicago: University of Chicago Press, 1996).

Glazer, Nathan, "The American Jew and the Attainment of Middle Class Rank: Some Trends and Explanations," in *The Jews*, ed., Marshall Sklare. (New York: Free Press, 1958).

Goldscheider, Calvin and Alan S. Zuckerman, *The Transformation of the Jews* (Chicago: University of Chicago Press, 1984).

Greeley, Andrew, "The Ethnic Miracle," *Public Interest* (Fall 1976), 20–36

Labaree, David F., *Someone Has to Fail: The Zero-Sum Game of Public Schooling* (Boston: Harvard University Press, 2011).

Lafer, Gordon, *The Job Training Charade* (Ithaca, NY: Cornell University Press, 2004).

Liebow, Eliot, *Tally's Corner* (Boston: Little, Brown, 1967).

Morawska, Ewa, *Insecure Prosperity: Small-Town Jews in Industrial America, 1890–1940* (Princeton: Princeton University Press, 1996).

Perlmann, Joel, "Beyond New York: The Occupations of Russian Jewish Immigrants in Providence, R. I. and in Other Small Jewish Communities, 1900–1915," *Journal of American Jewish History*, 72:3 (March 1983).

Petersen, William, "Success Story: Japanese-American Style," *New York Times Magazine*, 6 (January 9, 1966), 20–43.

Rothstein, Richard, *Class and Schools* (New York: Teachers College Press, 2004).

Slater, Miriam, "My Son the Doctor: Aspects of Mobility Among American Jews," *American Sociological Review*, 34 (June 1969), 359–373.

Steinberg, Stephen, *The Ethnic Myth*, 3rd ed. (Boston: Beacon Press, 2001).

Steinberg, Stephen, Nathan Glazer and the Assassination of Affirmative Action, *New Politics*, 9:3 (Summer 2003). Available at http://nova.wpunj.edu/newpolitics/issue35/Steinberg35.htm.

Steinberg, Stephen, "Poor Reason: Culture still doesn't explain poverty," *Boston Review online* (January 3, 2011). Available at http://bostonreview.net/BR36.1/steinberg.php.

Steinberg, Stephen, "The Rise of the Jewish Professional," *Ethnic and Racial Studies*,9:4 (October 1986): 502–513.

Tyson, Karolyn, William Darity, Jr. and Domini R. Castellino, "It's Not 'a Black Thing': Understanding the Burden of Acting White and Other Dilemmas of High Achievement," *American Sociological Review*, 70 (August 2005), 582–605. Available at http://www.tc.columbia.edu/students/see/events/Darity_et_al_Understanding_Burden_Acting_White.pdf.

Willis, Paul, *Learning to Labor* (New York: Columbia University Press, 1977).

CHAPTER 20

....

IMMIGRATION AND ETHNIC DIVERSITY IN THE SOUTH, 1980–2010

....

MARY E. ODEM

SINCE the 1980s the Southeast has become a major new immigrant destination in the United States. Largely bypassed in the last great wave of immigration to this country (1890–1920), the region is now home to millions of immigrants from Latin America, Asia, Africa, and the Caribbean. In towns, cities, and suburbs throughout the Southeast, one finds Vietnamese noodle shops, Mexican panaderías, Korean barbecue, and Colombian bakeries. Baptist and Methodist churches share the religious landscape with Hindu temples, Vietnamese Catholic churches, Buddhist shrines, Latino evangelical congregations, and Catholic parishes that honor Our Lady of Guadalupe. Mexican and Guatemalans work alongside African Americans in poultry and meatpacking plants in the rural South, and Vietnamese, Korean, and Chinese entrepreneurs have established ethnic retail districts in metropolitan Atlanta and Washington DC. Affluent formerly white suburbs now include residents from South Asia, China, and Japan. Garden apartment complexes and mobile home parks are home to people from rural villages in Mexico and the Guatemala highlands, and urban neighborhoods in Mexico City, Lima, and San Salvador.

Mass immigration has triggered an unprecedented series of changes in the social, economic, and cultural life of the region, and inaugurated a new era in southern history. A region historically defined by a black/white racial divide has become a multi-ethnic, multiracial society over the course of just two decades. This essay examines some of the key areas of research in the growing body of scholarly literature on new immigrant populations and their impact on rural, urban, and suburban areas of the South. Scholars from numerous disciplines—history, geography, sociology, anthropology, and cultural studies—have contributed to this scholarship, using a range of different methodologies and approaches. Because of the newness of the topic, much of the literature is in the form of articles and chapters in edited volumes. A few monographs on immigration in the contemporary South have been published recently and no doubt more are in the works.

Latin American and Asian immigration has received the most attention from scholars to date and thus will be the main focus of this chapter. African and Caribbean immigration to the Southeast, which has also grown rapidly since the 1980s, remains an important subject for future research.[1] The first part of the essay addresses why the Southeast became a new immigrant destination in the late twentieth century and examines the backgrounds of immigrant populations who have settled there. It then turns to a discussion of some of the most fruitful areas of current research: economic incorporation and the transformation of southern workplaces; immigrant settlement and changing ethnic and racial dynamics in the suburban South; and racial formation of Latino and Asian immigrants. The essay concludes by addressing significant areas for further research. For purposes of this essay, the South is defined as those states that share a history of slavery, secession, and the legal institution of racial segregation and its undoing by the Civil Rights movement. Because of my interest in new immigration states, Texas and Florida are omitted from this group, because they have a longer and different history of immigration. The remaining 10 states—Georgia, North Carolina, South Carolina, Virginia, Tennessee, Alabama, Mississippi, Arkansas, Louisiana, and Kentucky—had only small populations of immigrants prior to the 1970s.

These southern states did not attract immigrants in large numbers until the late twentieth century largely because of the slower pace of industrial development and the presence of a large number of poor blacks and whites who provided a steady pool of low-wage labor. During the last great wave of immigration to the United States at the turn of the twentieth century, small groups of immigrant workers from Europe and China settled in the region, but the vast majority headed to urban areas in the Northeast, Midwest, and West to become part of the industrial work force, and to areas of expanding commercial agriculture such as the Southwest to work as farm laborers.

In the last decades of the twentieth century, however, economic restructuring and growth and new refugee and immigration policies have drawn Asian and Latin American immigrants to the South in ever-increasing numbers, turning the region into the most rapidly growing immigrant destination in the country. Economic globalization has contributed to the transformation of the southern economy, leading to the decline of some industrial sectors and expanding economic investment in others. Global competition has caused plant closings and layoffs in the steel, textiles, and apparel industries as production has shifted to lower-cost areas in Southeast Asia, China, and the Philippines. At the same time, domestic and foreign corporations have been drawn to the South because of the relatively low taxes, cheap nonunion labor, and significant government subsidies provided to attract investment. Foreign automobile companies (Mercedes, Honda, Hyundai) have built factories in Alabama, North Carolina, South Carolina and Tennessee.[2]

Southern cities, such as Atlanta, Birmingham, Greensboro, and Charlotte have become important locations for commercial banking and financial industries, high-tech research and manufacturing, and bio-medical research. Many of the country's largest corporations now have their headquarters in the Southeast, including Wal-Mart, Home Depot, Bank of America, and Federal Express. Rapid population growth accompanied business expansion in southern cities, creating high demand in the construction and service industries and consequently a need for low-wage labor. In addition, poultry-, pork-, and seafood-processing plants have opened throughout the rural South. The poultry-processing industry in particular has flourished in the region; nearly half of all poultry processing in the country is now concentrated in Georgia, Alabama, Arkansas, and North Carolina. Vigorous economic growth made the Southeast a strong magnet for foreign-born workers at all skill levels, from agricultural laborers and construction workers to physicians, computer programmers, and engineers.

Changes in U.S. immigration and refugee policies also contributed to the rise in Asian and Latin American immigration to the Southeast. The landmark Hart-Cellar Act of 1965, which abolished the discriminatory national origins quotas, created numerical limits that applied equally to all countries and raised significantly the annual number of immigrant admissions. The act made family reunification the cornerstone of U.S. immigration policy and established visa categories for workers in occupations with insufficient labor supply. These changes not only led to a significant increase in Asian immigration to the United States overall, but also helped to direct many of those immigrants to the South. A serious shortage of doctors and nurses especially in rural areas and inner cities in the country attracted a growing number of foreign-trained healthcare professionals. Doctors and nurses from the Philippines, India, Pakistan, and other Asian countries increasingly filled positions in hospitals and clinics in the rural South as well as in southern cities. By 1990, Asian Indians made up the largest share of foreign-born physicians in the country and Filipinos the largest share of foreign-born nurses. Medical professionals were only part of the high-skilled labor flow to the U.S. South. Foreign-born engineers, computer experts, bio-medical researchers, business executives, academics, and highly trained technicians settled in metropolitan Atlanta, northern Virginia, Charlotte, and Research Triangle Park, North Carolina.[3]

Southeast Asians (Vietnamese, Cambodians, and Laotians) first came to the Southeast in large numbers as part of the federal government's refugee resettlement efforts following the fall of the U.S.-backed South Vietnamese government in 1975. The original refugees were predominantly military personnel, former government officials, and wealthy business owners. They were followed by a second, much larger wave of refugees in the late 1970s and 1980s, who were far less affluent—farmers, laborers, fishermen, small business owners and their families. Most had fled the country with few belongings and spent months, sometimes years, in crowded refugee camps before settling in the United States. The federal government followed a policy of dispersing Southeast Asian refugees throughout the country in an effort to lessen the impact on receiving communities.[4] Numerous southern cities and towns became settlement areas for Vietnamese, Laotian, and Cambodian immigrants. After their initial settlement, many Vietnamese decided to move to places where they could live near relatives and larger ethnic communities. New Orleans, Atlanta, and northern Virginia became main southern destinations for Vietnamese immigrants in this secondary migration.

A different set of immigration policies directed the flow of Latin American immigration to the Southeast. The passage of the Immigration Reform and Control Act (IRCA) of 1986, contributed to a major shift in the destinations of Mexican and Central American migrants from traditional destinations in Texas and California to new locations in the United States.[5] IRCA's key features included stronger border controls, new sanctions on employers who hired undocumented immigrants, and the legalization of immigrants who could demonstrate that they had resided and worked in the United States for at least five years. Under IRCA, approximately 3 million immigrants gained permanent legal residence. Of these, 2.3 million were Mexicans; the remaining 700,000 included immigrants from El Salvador, Guatemala, the Philippines, Colombia, Haiti and several other countries.[6] Free to move about the country, increasing numbers of newly legalized immigrants left the crowded job and housing markets in California and the Southwest to pursue better opportunities elsewhere. With its booming economy and lower cost of living, the Southeast became a favored destination for many Latino immigrants, initially from Texas and California and later directly from Mexico, Central America, and South America.

Together, economic restructuring and growth and new immigration and refugee policies produced a rapid and dramatic rise in Asian and Latin American immigration populations in the Southeast. The impact of immigration has been felt in both the rural and urban South. Although the majority of Latino and Asian immigrants have settled in the South's metropolitan areas—Atlanta, Raleigh-Durham-Chapel Hill, Charlotte, Greenville, Birmingham, and Nashville—significant numbers of both professional and low-wage immigrants have moved to small towns and rural areas throughout the Southeast.

Great diversity in terms of national origin and language, socioeconomic status, ethnicity, and legal status characterize Asian and Latino populations in the South. The largest national groups among Asians are Vietnamese, Indian, Chinese, and Korean. Immigrants and refugees from numerous other Asian countries, including the Philippines, Cambodia, Thailand, Indonesia, and Laos, have joined them. Among Latin American immigrants, the largest national group by far is Mexican, but there are significant numbers of Guatemalans, Salvadorans, Hondurans, Dominicans, Colombians, and Venezuelans. The Latino immigrant population is further divided along lines of race and ethnicity and includes whites of European descent, *mestizos* (mixed race, usually of Spanish and Indian descent), Afro-Caribbeans, and indigenous peoples from Guatemala and Mexico.

There are significant differences in socioeconomic and occupational status within Asian and Latino populations in the South. Southeast Asians who arrived as refugees worked in low-wage jobs, and a large number were on public welfare. Over time, many Vietnamese have acquired the resources to establish small businesses such as restaurants, jewelry shops, appliance and automotive repair shops, and nail and hair salons. South Asians, Japanese, Koreans, and Chinese (from Taiwan and the mainland) commonly arrived with the educational credentials to seek jobs in professional, scientific, and technical fields. These groups, especially Chinese and Korean immigrants, have been active as well in establishing businesses in major southern cities.

There is an expanding group of Latino professionals in the Southeast, many of whom serve the Latino population as lawyers, accountants, dentists, and doctors. Other Latinos are small entrepreneurs—owners of contracting and landscaping companies, retail shops, restaurants, cleaning and child-care businesses, and taxi companies. The largest number of Latino immigrants in the South work as laborers in agriculture, food processing, manufacturing, service, and construction—low-wage jobs previously occupied by poor whites and African Americans. Mexicans and Central Americans are concentrated in the low-wage sector, whereas South Americans and Caribbeans, who tend to have higher educational levels, are more likely to work in higher-status occupations.

Differences in legal status also characterize Asian and Latino immigrant populations. They include refugees, naturalized citizens, legal residents, temporary workers, and undocumented immigrants. As in the rest of the country, a significant portion of Latino immigrants in the South is undocumented. A report by the Urban Institute estimated that in 2000, between 40 and 49 percent of all immigrants in the states of North Carolina, Georgia, and Arkansas were undocumented, and between 30 and 39 percent in South Carolina, Mississippi, Alabama, and Tennessee.[7] The increase in unauthorized immigration in the South reflects national trends. As of 2005, 11 million undocumented immigrants resided in the United States, and they constituted fully one-third of all immigrants in the country. Of the undocumented, 78 percent are from Mexico and other Latin American nations.[8]

ECONOMIC INCORPORATION AND THE TRANSFORMATION OF SOUTHERN WORKPLACES

The incorporation of immigrants into southern industries and the social and economic consequences of this development has been the subject of a number of studies. Most have focused on Latino immigrants in the low-wage economy, whereas a few have addressed immigrant entrepreneurs. Since the 1980s immigrant labor has fueled the economic growth and competitiveness of key southern industries—agriculture, construction, landscaping, food-processing, forestry, janitorial services, hospitality, carpet and furniture production. Reliance on immigrant labor, both documented and undocumented, is now a structural feature of the southern economy that has had and will continue to have significant social, economic, and political consequences for the region.

The use of immigrant labor has boosted corporate profits and reduced costs for consumers, but has also generated fears of job displacement and wage cuts on the part of native-born workers, both black and white. Policy experts disagree sharply about the impact of new immigrant workers on the low-wage labor force, with some arguing that they drive down the wages of native-born workers and others contending that they fill jobs that no one else wants. The expansion of urban and rural economies in the late twentieth century South no doubt created many new jobs that the native-born labor force could not fill. At the same time, as in the previous eras of high immigration, U.S. employers have used the ready supply of immigrant labor to speed up production, suppress wages, fragment the labor force, and undermine worker protests.

The widespread use of immigrant labor in the South is part of the neoliberal reorganization of the economy and labor market. In the highly competitive global economy, U.S. corporations have cut labor costs by creating a more "flexible" workforce through strategies of part-time work, outsourcing, subcontracting, and the recruitment of foreign-born workers. For workers in the United States, *flexibility* has meant the erosion of benefits, job security, safe working conditions, and collective bargaining rights. A number of scholars (Griffith, Fink, Stuesse, Marrow) have examined the reorganization of the poultry processing industry in the rural South. Poultry corporations began large-scale hiring of immigrant workers (both documented and undocumented) during a period of rapid expansion between 1980 and 2000, when American consumption of chicken doubled. Native-born and foreign-born workers alike have suffered from the harsh conditions in meat and poultry plants, including production speed-ups, disregard for health and safety standards, and pervasive violation of minimum wage laws.[9]

Griffith's research shows that prior to the arrival of Mexican workers in the late 1980s, African-Americans dominated the labor force of the poultry processing and meat-packing industries in North Carolina. In a hazardous industry with a high turnover of employees, black workers typically had moved in and out of jobs in response to family needs, to recover from workplace injuries, and to take a break from the rigors of work in the plants. The arrival of Mexican workers made it harder for them to return to jobs after a temporary absence. The growing supply of immigrant workers and managers' stated preference for Mexican over African-American workers has exacerbated racial tensions between the two groups.[10]

Angela Stuesse has examined the impact of economic restructuring on labor relations and collective organizing in the poultry industry in rural Mississippi, where immigrants from Mexico, Guatemala, and South America now work alongside African Americans. The use of labor contractors to hire foreign-born workers has enabled poultry plants to evade government regulations, lower wages, and neglect health and safety standards. African Americans have tended to blame immigrants for the deteriorating work conditions in the plants, whereas immigrants have interpreted the resistance of black workers (production slowdowns and long breaks) as evidence of laziness or lack of education. The ethnic and racial divisions have hampered the efforts of local labor activists to organize poultry workers in defense of their rights.[11]

Similar tensions exist among native-born and immigrant workers in rural industries in eastern North Carolina. Using ethnographic research and interviews, Helen Marrow compares how Latinos are faring in one North Carolina county that is predominantly white and characteristic of the new rural South, with an expanding economy based primarily on food-processing, and in another county that is predominantly black and typical of the old rural South with a stagnant economy based on tobacco agriculture and textile production. The racialized class structure in the rural South, she argues, has placed Latino newcomers in more competitive, and thus more conflict-ridden situations with African Americans than whites in southern workplaces.[12]

In contrast to other scholars who have emphasized the exploitation and harsh conditions for immigrant workers in the food-processing industries, Marrow argues that the newer rural industries like poultry processing have provided opportunities for Latino immigrants to establish a living and achieve moderate socioeconomic mobility at a time when such opportunities are stagnating in traditional immigrant gateways. The prospects for economic security and advancement were more limited for immigrants working in manufacturing and textiles. Her findings challenge standard depictions of the rural South as a place of economic stagnation and hostility to outsiders. Although not a path to the middle class, food-processing jobs, Marrow contends, are providing immigrants and their children an opportunity to achieve economic security as part of the rural working class. Importantly, they are not becoming part of a jobless, excluded underclass comparable to what scholars have observed in the central cities of traditional immigrant gateways.[13]

The arrival of Latino immigrant workers also has impacted industries with a predominantly white workforce like the carpet industry of northwest Georgia. A center of textile production for most of the twentieth century, Dalton, Georgia, and the surrounding southern Appalachian region has become a global center for the mass production of wall-to-wall carpeting. Until the 1970s, industries in the region relied primarily on the labor of low-income whites. Even after the civil rights revolution of the 1960s, a system of corporate paternalism preserved mill jobs for white workers and excluded blacks at the price of a strict anti-union workplace.[14]

In the 1980s and 1990s, however, according to research by Zúñiga and Hernández-León, carpet industrialists broke with paternalism and white privilege in the workplace by recruiting and hiring Mexican laborers on a mass scale. As Griffith found with the poultry industry, the influx of immigrants solved employers' problems of high turnover and labor shortages and weakened the ability of native workers to negotiate for better wages and conditions. Not surprisingly, the arrival of Mexicans in southern Appalachia has created tensions with native whites who perceive immigrants as a source of competition and displacement. Newly formed anti-immigrant organizations and established hate groups like the Ku Klux Klan have grown in size and influence in the South since the 1990s as a result of mounting white resentment toward Latino immigrants.[15]

The incorporation of Latin American and Asian immigrants into the southern workforce has generated not only conflict but also new forms of racial and ethnic collaboration.[16] Labor organizers, civic leaders, and social justice activists have sought to mediate racial conflicts and forge new multiethnic coalitions. Leon Fink's richly detailed study of worker protest in the poultry industry in Morganton, North Carolina shows how indigenous people from Guatemala joined with Mexican and American workers in a 1995 strike and subsequent union building campaign supported by organizers from the Laborer's International Union of North America (LIUNA).[17] African American labor leaders in Mississippi also have worked with Latino advocates in the Mississippi Immigrant Rights Alliance (MIRA) and the Mississippi Poultry Workers' Center to organize poultry workers from different backgrounds and strengthen their voice in the industry. MIRA, a statewide coalition of immigrant, labor, and civil rights advocates, works with progressive elected officials to promote fair treatment of immigrants in Mississippi.[18]

In another sign of racial and ethnic collaboration, established civil rights groups in the South have expanded their political agendas to address the discrimination and exploitation of immigrants. The Southern Poverty Law Center (SPLC) of Montgomery, Alabama, a biracial civil rights organization founded in 1971, has documented and protested the harsh, discriminatory treatment of Latino workers by employers and nativist groups in the South. In 2004, the SPLC created the Immigrant Justice Project and published the exposé *Close to Slavery*, which details widespread abuses of immigrant labor in the federal H-2 programs that supply "guest workers" for the agricultural, forestry, and other industries. A number of black and white labor leaders and civil rights activists have publicly supported Latino-led initiatives for immigrant rights, such as the campaign for drivers' licenses for undocumented immigrants in Georgia and the mass marches in defense of immigrants' rights that took place across the South in April 2006.[19]

In one of the few studies of the economic incorporation of ethnic entrepreneurs, Bankston and Zhou examine the entrance of Vietnamese refugees into the fishing industry in southern Louisiana and other Gulf Coast communities. With little education, but advanced fishing skills, many Vietnamese were drawn to this industry and worked initially as laborers for seafood-processing companies and then as self-employed fishermen once they acquired enough capital to buy a boat, which they typically accomplished by pooling resources with family and community members. According to Bankston and Zhou, fishing is the industry that has offered the greatest possibility for self-employment for the Vietnamese who settled in southern Louisiana and other coastal communities.[20]

Their entrance into the competitive fishing industry led to conflicts with local white fishermen who complained about Vietnamese fishing and boat handling techniques that clashed with established practices and sometimes with state and federal regulations. Local fishermen also resented the large catches of the Vietnamese who more often worked collaboratively and for longer hours than was customary for locals. Voluntary agencies worked with the Coast Guard to teach the Vietnamese about the regulations and customs of commercial fishing in the area, but tensions sometimes erupted into violence. Some white fishermen made death threats, cut fishing nets, and burned boats of Vietnamese competitors. Vietnamese responded by forming the Vietnamese Fishermen Association of America to represent their interests. Over time, many of those connected to the seafood industry have come to terms with the Vietnamese presence. Numerous seafood companies have, in fact, profited from wholesaling and retailing of shrimp and fish caught by Vietnamese fishermen. Still, resentment lingers among some white fishermen, who continue to view the Vietnamese as illegitimate competitors.

To date, there has been little scholarly investigation of the economic and social impact of highly skilled immigrant workers in southern corporations, hospitals, research centers, and businesses. A compelling memoir by Indian physician, Abraham Verghese, about his experiences as a doctor to HIV-AIDS patients in rural Tennessee highlights some of the issues that scholarship on this subject could explore. Born in Ethiopia to South Indian parents, Verghese completed his medical training in India, and then left for the United States in 1980 for postgraduate training. He was part of the wave of foreign-born medical professionals and students who responded to the shortage of interns, residents, and doctors in the United States. Verghese writes about the hierarchy that governed the placement of medical students and physicians. Foreign-born interns, residents, and doctors were channeled into positions least desired by native-born Americans, in understaffed, underfunded big city hospitals and small hospitals in isolated, economically depressed rural areas.[21]

Verghese followed the latter path and did his internship and residency in a small hospital in East Tennessee in the foothills of the Appalachian Mountains, and after further training in infectious diseases in Boston, he returned as a staff physician and with an appointment as assistant professor at East Tennessee State University. He joined other foreign physicians from India, Korea, Pakistan, and the Philippines who staffed the small community hospitals in the region of southwest Virginia, east Tennessee, and Kentucky. Verghese explains how Indian doctors and medical students created an informal national employment network that provided guidance to newcomers about hospitals that welcomed foreign graduates and where they could receive good training in particular fields. He writes movingly of his interactions with his southern patients and co-workers and of the strong attachment he developed for the people and places in Appalachia.[22] By opening a window into the lives of Asian Indian physicians in the rural South, Verghese's memoir suggests questions for research about highly skilled immigrants in the U.S. South.

Did foreign-born professionals in other fields—engineering, science, computers, and business—encounter similar occupational hierarchies? Did they create ethnically based occupational networks to provide information and guidance to fellow immigrants? Were there significant differences in career opportunities and social interactions for immigrant professionals who settled in large metropolitan areas compared to rural areas? How did the southern context and the historic black/white racial divide shape their interactions with supervisors, co-workers, and clients?

IMMIGRANT SETTLEMENT
IN THE SUBURBAN SOUTH

Asian and Latin American immigration has transformed the racial and ethnic dynamics in southern neighborhoods as well as southern workplaces. Several scholars have begun to examine the impact of immigrant settlement on residential patterns in southern metropolitan areas. In keeping with national trends, immigrants to the urban South have been bypassing the inner city and moving directly to suburban locations, a development that marks a significant departure from the historical pattern of immigrant settlement in central city neighborhoods. In the early twentieth century many immigrant groups formed ethnic enclaves in American cities, where residence, religious institutions, and businesses were concentrated. In the immigrant destinations of New York, Chicago, San Francisco, Detroit, and Boston, these neighborhoods were initially European in origin.

Later in the century, new waves of immigrants from the Caribbean, Latin America, and Asia often settled in the same neighborhoods that Germans, Italians, Eastern European Jewish, and Polish immigrants had once occupied. Inner city ethnic enclaves offered advantages and disadvantages. They provided new immigrants social and economic support and cultural familiarity as they adapted to American society, yet these areas were overcrowded, with poor quality housing and services, and underfunded schools. As immigrants or their children and grandchildren advanced economically and socially, they left urban ethnic enclaves for higher quality neighborhoods in the suburbs where they became more integrated socially, economically, and geographically with the majority group. Suburbanization was a distinct phase in the assimilation process.

Although immigrants continue to populate central cities, since the 1980s an increasing number have been migrating directly to suburban locations. Deindustrialization, economic neglect and decline of inner cities, and the growth of suburbs as employment as well as residential centers have all contributed to the shift toward suburban settlement. Audrey Singer's study of the new geography of immigration in the United States shows that, by 2000, more immigrants in metropolitan areas lived in suburbs than central cities and that rates of immigration growth for suburbs exceeded those for cities.[23] Immigrant suburban settlement is part of a nationwide phenomenon but is particularly pronounced in metropolitan areas in the South and elsewhere that experienced dramatic growth in the post-World War II period. In metropolitan Atlanta, for example, nearly 96 percent of foreign-born residents lived in suburban locations in 2000.

The trend of suburban settlement creates a new context for the social, economic, and political incorporation of immigrants and raises important questions for researchers. Are immigrant groups creating ethnic enclaves in the suburbs as they did in the inner cities? Or has suburban settlement facilitated social and economic integration with the majority group as it did in the past? Current research indicates that immigrant groups in southern suburbs are not forming dense ethnic enclaves. Instead, households, places of worship, and shops and businesses are often separated geographically, and members of a particular ethnic group are more residentially dispersed from one another than in past eras of immigration. Several studies suggest, however, that socioeconomic status affects the level of ethnic concentration and dispersal in southern metropolitan areas. Especially for high-skilled, high-income immigrants, there is less pressure to cluster in ethnic neighborhoods upon arrival because they face fewer economic and social barriers than in the past. Residential dispersal in southern suburbs is common among South Asian, Chinese, and Korean immigrants, and has increased among Vietnamese and Vietnamese Americans as their socioeconomic status has improved. A few studies have shown a greater tendency for Latino immigrants (who are predominantly working class) to cluster in specific neighborhoods, but even Latino residential patterns are more dispersed than in previous periods.

Immigrant settlement in southern suburbs has been shaped by the region's history of racial segregation and inequality and at the same time is transforming historic patterns. Studies of immigrant settlement in metropolitan Atlanta and Washington, DC show that immigrants arriving in the 1980s and 1990s settled in majority-white suburbs where jobs and economic growth were concentrated and avoided majority-black neighborhoods, which were marked by high rates of poverty and stagnant economic growth. In Atlanta, Vietnamese, Korean, Chinese, and Latino immigrants moved into suburban neighborhoods north of the city center in Dekalb, Cobb, and Gwinnet Counties, which were developed in the 1960s and 1970s to accommodate middle-class white families. A main attraction for immigrants in both Atlanta and northern Virginia has been the availability of affordable housing, especially multifamily apartment complexes and subdivisions with modest single-family homes. The growing populations of diverse groups of immigrants, plus a steady increase of African-American residents have transformed formerly all-white suburbs in both Atlanta and Washington, DC into multi-ethnic, multiracial neighborhoods. At the same time, racial residential segregation has continued. In Atlanta, with the growth of outer-ring suburbs in the 1980s and 1990s, affluent and middle-income white residents have continued to move farther outward to new subdivisions with larger homes and more racially homogenous populations, whereas poor AfricanAmericans constitute the overwhelming majority of residents in underserved central city neighborhoods.[24]

Smith and Furuseth's research on Charlotte finds that Latino immigrants have formed several distinct residential clusters in aging, middle-ring suburbs that were built in the post-World War II era. In the 1980s, these neighborhoods lost white residents who sought housing in further out suburbs or in the gentrifying city center and they gained not only more immigrants, but also more African American residents and became more solidly working class in character. One of the Latino residential clusters shows stable incomes, an increase in home ownership, and a number of Latino-owned and oriented businesses that have helped to reverse economic decline in the area. In contrast, another neighborhood where Latinos have settled is economically distressed with poor housing and support services and a rising crime rate. Their work calls on researchers to pay attention to differences in suburban neighborhoods in terms of socioeconomic status of residents and the quality of housing and social services, all of which have consequences for how immigrant residents and their children will fare in the United States. Movement into the suburbs clearly can no longer be equated with socioeconomic mobility and integration with the mainstream.[25]

Scholars have also raised questions about the impact of suburban settlement and residential dispersal on the formation of ethnic bonds and identity. Considering that urban ethnic enclaves were central to the creation of ethnic community for earlier groups of immigrants, has dispersed suburban settlement meant weaker ethnic ties? Several scholars have found that immigrants have created and maintained ethnic ties in the suburban South through the development of ethnic commercial districts. Joseph Wood finds that among the Vietnamese in northern Virginia, "residences, churches, cemetery plots and other distinctive ethnic markers are by and large dispersed and rarely noticeable."[26] Where the Vietnamese have created a distinct ethnic presence is in their retail districts, where Vietnamese restaurants, shops, and small businesses are concentrated. Koreans have created similar commercial districts in Annandale, Virginia, where one-third of all Korean businesses in metropolitan Washington, DC are concentrated. According to Frank Cha, "The strip malls and shopping plazas that comprise much of the downtown area feature a plethora of signs featuring Korean characters, storefront windows displaying Korean made goods, and building facades influenced by Korean architecture."[27] Ethnic commercial districts serve multiple material and symbolic purposes. They provide economic opportunities for small entrepreneurs and a place to shop for ethnic goods and service; they also bolster a sense of ethnic community among geographically dispersed ethnic groups.

Both Asian and Latino entrepreneurs have created bustling commercial and retail districts in metropolitan Atlanta. The largest concentration of ethnic commerce is along Buford Highway where there are numerous ethnic and multi-ethnic shopping plazas such as Chinatown Square (1988), Asian Square Mall (1993), and Plaza Fiesta (2000).[28] The largest entrepreneurial groups in the Buford Highway area are Chinese, Korean, Vietnamese, and Latino, mostly Mexican. Due to their earlier arrival in Atlanta and greater resources upon arrival, the Asian entrepreneurs, especially the Chinese and Koreans, own a greater share of the businesses and property along Buford Highway, even though they constitute a small percentage of the ethnic population that now lives in the area. But the number of Vietnamese and Latino-owned businesses has grown dramatically since the 1980s. Many Latino entrepreneurs have rented space in Plaza Fiesta, an indoor mall with restaurants, bakeries, and clothing and jewelry stores. Plaza Fiesta frequently hosts weekend events such as dance and music performances and has become a central gathering place for Latinos and Latino immigrants throughout the metropolitan areas.

Religious institutions have also served to organize ethnic communities in dispersed suburban locations. Ethnic Catholic parishes and Protestant churches, Hindu and Buddhist temples, and mosques now mark southern suburban landscapes and provide central gathering locations for immigrants where they can share in the practice of familiar rituals and celebrations.

New media technologies (cell phones, e-mail, the Internet) have come to play a central role in forging and sustaining ethnic ties across geographical distance, but so far this subject has not been addressed in studies of immigration to the South. The Internet is perhaps the most powerful new means of linking immigrant and ethnic groups across space. Many ethnic organizations and groups, whether they are related to business, sports, culture or politics, have created websites, listservs, and blogs that link people around common ethnic identities and interests. Facebook and social media, which are especially popular among ethnic youth, are other venues for creating ethnic identities and networks. New forms of forging ethnic community and identity require new methods of scholarly investigation. To understand ethnicity in the late twentieth and early twenty-first centuries, scholars of immigration need to experiment with qualitative and quantitative methods for analyzing websites, blogs, facebook, and twitter. The Internet may be the location for ethnic enclaves of the twenty-first century.

RACIAL FORMATION OF NEW IMMIGRANTS IN THE SOUTH

How immigrants became incorporated into the racial hierarchy of the United States has been a central concern for historians of immigration, especially in the field of whiteness studies. David Roediger and other scholars have argued that Irish and later southern and eastern European immigrants were initially perceived as "racially inbetween" people in the black/white binary that structured American society in the nineteenth and the first half of the twentieth centuries.[29] Over time, as they came to understand and accept the racial hierarchy in the United States, immigrants and their children sought and eventually gained acceptance as white Americans. Becoming white was intrinsic to the process of Americanization.

The pressure to embrace whiteness was perhaps nowhere more pronounced than in the Jim Crow South. According to David Goldfield, the historic pattern for European immigrants in the South was "the suppression of ethnic identity" in favor of white racial solidarity. "The relatively low numbers of immigrants and the abiding racial divide promised an ethnic meltdown to a degree much greater than in larger northern cities," he writes.[30] Even the small population of Chinese immigrants in Mississippi managed a shift to white or "near white" status over the course of one generation, according to James Loewen. The price of this shift was adherence to white norms and values and disassociation from African Americans.[31]

Those interested in the racial formation of immigrants in the South of the late twentieth and early twenty-first centuries have to consider the altered racial terrain of the post-Civil Rights era. Civil rights legislation dismantled the system of legalized racial segregation and the political disfranchisement of African Americans and set the stage for the growth of the black middle class and black political leadership in the South. The sources of racial and economic inequality, however, were not dismantled in the wake of the Civil Rights movement, and although legally sanctioned segregation ended, white abandonment of cities and public schools ensured that de facto segregation would expand. Thus, one finds in the contemporary South both black economic success and high black poverty, both significant signs of racial integration and the isolation and neglect of black inner city neighborhoods.

Scholars are just beginning to examine the racial incorporation of immigrants in the post-Civil Rights South. So far most of these studies have focused on Latino immigrants from Mexico, Central America, and South America. In the first edited collection on this topic, *Being Brown in Dixie* (2011), sociologists Cameron Lippard and Charles Gallagher argue that Latin American immigration has created a new "ethnoracial" order in the South based on skin color, ethnicity, and nativity in which "being 'brown' matters as much as being 'black' or 'white.'"[32] The new racial system, which continues to denigrate blackness and privilege whiteness has a third racial category between blacks and whites that Latinos occupy. Articles in the edited volume examine racial discrimination that Latinos face in housing, education, employment, and the criminal justice system in the South. These forms of institutional discrimination, according to Lippard and Gallagher, contribute to the construction of Latinos as a distinct and subordinate racial group. Mexicans, Cubans, and other Latino groups, they argue, are lumped into the same racial/ethnic category despite differences in national origins, phenotype, and socioeconomic status. Although the South's new ethnoracial order is still in the process of formation, the authors predict that immigrant and native-born Latinos will continue to occupy a separate racial status between whites and blacks.

Their work engages an ongoing debate about how Latinos as the new largest racial/ethnic minority are influencing the traditional black/white color line in the United States. Some scholars argue that Latinos are being subsumed into expanded categories of black or white depending on skin tone, with dark-skinned Latinos considered black and lighter-skinned Latinos considered white.[33] Others argue that Latinos are forging a new, middle race category between black and white.[34] A third view posits the emergence of a black-nonblack racial binary in the United States, in which Latino immigrant groups distance themselves from blackness and are eventually integrated into a broadened category of nonblacks.[35] Most of the studies of racialization and Latinos are based on research conducted in regions of the country with more established Latino populations. Clearly, more research is needed about Latinos and Latino immigrants in the South to understand the changing racial dynamics in this region of the country. Scholars should take into account both different local contexts and the diversity of Latino groups as they analyze the racialization of immigrants in the South.

A recent study by Helen Marrow provides insight into the process of racialization in the rural South. Her work focuses on rural counties in North Carolina where Latin Americans migrated to work in poultry-processing plants and textile factories. Most migrated from Mexico with smaller numbers from Central America and South America. Marrow argues the rural southern context has fundamentally shaped immigrants' encounter with race. The racialized class structure of the rural South pits immigrants against African Americans more often than whites in workplaces and schools. The competition at the low end of the rural labor market, in particular, has heightened tensions and conflicts between immigrants and blacks. Latinos interviewed by Marrow reported better relations with white southerners and more discrimination from black southerners. These perceptions, along with immigrants' own anti-black stereotypes and whites' preferences for immigrants over African Americans in workplaces and neighborhoods, has led to racial distancing from blacks on the part of Latino immigrants.[36] The emerging racial dynamics, Marrow argues, suggest that Latin American newcomers are being incorporated into rural southern society as "nonblacks," on the more privileged side of "an emerging black-nonblack color line."[37]

Although Marrow examines racial formation at the level of individual interactions in the rural South, Irene Browne and Mary Odem examine the role of the state, specifically, anti-immigrant laws and statutes, in the racial construction of Latino immigrants in the metropolitan South. They analyze anti-immigrant rhetoric and exclusionary policies in metropolitan Atlanta, which rose sharply in the early twenty-first century due to declining economic conditions and heightened national preoccupation with terrorism and "illegal immigration" following the attacks of September 11, 2001. Public outcry about "illegals" stealing jobs, burdening taxpayers, and increasing crime rates led local and state officials in Atlanta and Georgia to pass an array of laws and ordinances that restrict or deny Latino immigrants' access to health care, housing, employment, social services and higher education and subject them to a high level of surveillance by law-enforcement authorities.[38]

The dominant figure in the political discourse about immigration is the "illegal Mexican," typically imagined as a worker in construction, lawn maintenance, or other manual occupation. This representation not only collapses the real differences in nationality, culture, class, legal status, and racial identification that characterize the Latin American population in Atlanta, but also constructs Latinos as a foreign race that poses a danger to American society and is not suitable for full membership in the nation. The laws and policies that have emerged out of the anti-immigrant backlash fuse legal status and national origin with race, and institutionalize the boundaries separating Latino immigrants from "real" Americans.

According to the authors, being "Black" no longer automatically locates one at the bottom of the racial order. An association with blackness can sometimes benefit immigrants, especially in a metropolitan area like Atlanta that has a large black middle-class and prominent African American politicians, professionals, and business leaders. Dominican immigrants in Atlanta have found it advantageous to be able to pass as Black in certain circumstances, for this identity signals citizenship and belonging. In contrast, an association with Latinos signals "illegality" and "foreignness."[39]

By no means has the historic construction of black Americans as racial "others" disappeared, as Ajantha Subramanian makes clear in one of the few studies so far to explore the racial construction of Asian immigrants in the contemporary South. Based on interviews with Asian Indian professionals in North Carolina, Subramanian argues that affluent Indians have attempted to define themselves in cultural terms that avoid any reference to race. South Asians began migrating to the Research Triangle Park area in the 1970s and 1980s to work as doctors, engineers, scientists, and academics. Their wealth has "ensured their segregation from other nonwhite populations and their entry into previously white-dominated social spaces of the university, the corporation, the research institution, and the gated community."[40] In the past, during the period of Asian exclusion, elite Indians responded to the American racial hierarchy by claiming an Aryan, or white identity. With the American embrace of multiculturalism in the post-Civil Rights era, this strategy is no longer necessary. Asian Indians interviewed by Subramanian embraced their cultural distinctiveness, emphasizing, especially, Hindu customs and traditions. However, they did not conceive of Indian identity and culture in terms of race and disassociated themselves from minority racial groups in the United States. As one Indian businessman remarked: "We are not even considered minorities because we are economically well off. By extension, we don't think of ourselves as minorities."[41]

More research is needed on other immigrant groups and other southern contexts for a fuller understanding of the racial incorporation of Asian and Latino immigrants in the late- twentieth- and early twenty-first-century South. The diversity of immigrant groups, the greater acceptance of multiculturalism, and the growth of black political and economic influence in the post-Civil Rights era have altered the racial terrain and the previous path of assimilation into whiteness followed by European immigrants. The differences in socioeconomic status, nationality, ethnicity, and legal status mean that Asian and Latino immigrants will enter and transform the South's racial system in multiple and complex ways. As Subramanian suggests, instead of whiteness, high status immigrants may embrace ethnic and cultural distinctiveness and, at the same time, negate or deny racial difference. Marrow urges us to look at how particular local contexts shape processes of racial formation. She found racial distancing between working-class immigrants and blacks in the rural South, but race relations and identities may develop quite differently in urban areas like Atlanta that have a significant middle- and upper-class African American population and a more diverse Latin American population. Does an association with blackness benefit immigrants in certain contexts, as Browne and Odem's study suggests? Comparative studies of different local contexts and different immigrant groups will help to illuminate the ways in which socioeconomic status, national origins, and geographical context interact to shape the racialization process. How immigrants of African descent are integrated into the South's racial system is a question of particular relevance, given the social, political, and historical significance of African Americans in the region. Have they been incorporated as "black" or have differences of national origin and social class been more salient in their experiences? To date, there are few published studies of this topic in the South, but future research on Afro-Caribbean and sub-Saharan African immigrants will no doubt add significantly to our understanding of racialization in the contemporary South.[42]

In addition to race and class, legal status has become a powerful mark of difference and inequality in the South, with particular ramifications for Latino newcomers. According to Browne and Odem, state laws and policies and anti-immigrant rhetoric have fused legal status, national origin, and race in the construction of Latin American immigrants as foreign, unwanted outsiders. Additional research is needed about the impact of local immigration policies to evaluate just how pervasive and entrenched this racial classification of Latinos is. The responses of different groups of immigrants to the anti-immigrant backlash is another topic worthy of study. To what extent have Latin American immigrants sought to distance themselves from the maligned category of "illegal Mexican"; to what extent have they perceived common experiences and struggles with other Latino immigrants? Addressing these questions will help to illuminate the complex ways that the mass immigration of the late twentieth century has altered the racial order of the contemporary South.

NOTES

1. John R. Logan, "Who Are the Other African Americans? Contemporary African and Caribbean Immigrants in the United States," in *The Other African Americans: Contemporary African and Caribbean Immigrants in the United States*, Eds. Yoku Shaw-Taylor and Steven A. Tuch. Roman & Littlefield Publishers: Lanham, MD, 2007: 49–67.

2. Raymond A. Mohl, "Globalization, Latinization and the *Nuevo* New South," *Journal of American Ethnic History* 22 (Summer 2003): 31–66.

3. David Reimers, "Asian Immigrants in the South," in *Globalization and the American South*, Eds. James C. Cobb and William Stueck. Athens: University of Georgia Press, 2005: 100–135.

4. Min Zhou and Carl L. Bankston. *Growing up American: How Vietnamese Children Adapt to Life in the United States*. New York: Russell Sage, 1998, chs. 2–3.

5. Douglas S. Massey, Jorge Durand, and Nolan J. Malone, *Beyond Smoke and Mirrors: Mexican Immigration in an Era of Economic Integration*. New York: Russell Sage, 2003. For a discussion of IRCA's implications for the Southeast, see Mohl, "Globalization, Latinization, and the Nuevo New South."

6. Roger Daniels, *Guarding the Golden Door: American Immigration Policy and Immigrants Since 1882*. New York: Hill and Wang, 2004, 219–259; Massey, Durand, and Malone, *Beyond Smoke and Mirrors*, 24–51, 105–141; Jorge Durand, Douglas S. Massey, and Emilio A. Parrado, "The New Era of Mexican Migration to the United States," *Journal of American History* 86 (September 1999): 518–536.

7. Jeffrey S. Passel, Randolph Capps, and Michael E. Fix, "Undocumented Immigrants: Facts and Figures," Washington, D.C.: The Urban Institute, 2004, [www.urban.org/url.cfm?ID=1000587]; Jeffrey S. Passel, "Unauthorized Migrants: Numbers and Characteristics," Washington, D.C.: Pew Hispanic Center, 2005, [http://pewhispanic.org/files/reports/46.pdf].

8. Jeffery S. Passel, "Size and Characteristics of the Unauthorized Population in the U.S." Washington, D.C.: Pew Hispanic Center, 2006, [http://pewhispanic.org/reports/report.php?ReportID=61].

9. Steve Striffler, *Chicken: The Dangerous Transformation of America's Favorite Food*, New Haven, Conn.: Yale University Press, 2005.

10. David Griffith, "Rural Industry and Mexican Immigration and Settlement in North Carolina," in *New Destinations: Mexican Immigration in the United States*, Eds. Víctor Zúñiga and Rubén Hernández-León. NewYork: Russell Sage Foundation, 2005: 50–75.

11. Angela C. Stuesse, "Race, Migration, and Labor Control: Neoliberal Challenges to Organizing Mississippi's Poultry Workers," in *Latino Immigration and the Transformation of the U.S. South*, Eds. Mary E. Odem & Elaine Lacy. Athens, GA: University of Georgia Press, 2009.

12. Helen Marrow, *New Destination Dreaming: Immigration, Race, and Legal Status in the Rural American South*. Stanford, CA: Stanford University Press, 2011.

13. Ibid.

14. Rubén Hernández-León and Victor Zúñiga, "Appalachia Meets Aztlan: Mexican Immigration and Intergroup Relations in Dalton, Georgia," in *New Destinations*, Eds. Zúñiga and Hernández-León, 244–274.

15. Ibid.

16. Barbara Ellen Smith, "Across Races and Nations: Social Justice Organizing in the Transnational South," in *Latinos in the New South: Transformations of Place*, Eds. Heather

As. Smith and Owen J. Furuseth. Aldershot, England and Burlington, VT: Ashgate, 2006, 235-256.

17. Leon Fink, *The Maya of Morganton*. Chapel Hill: University of North Carolina Press, 2003.

18. Stuesse, "Race, Migration, and Labor Control."

19. Mary Bauer, *Close to Slavery: Guestworker Programs in the United States*. Montgomery, AL: Southern Poverty Law Center, 2007, [http://www.splcenter.org/pdf/static/SPLCguestworker.pdf]; Ellen Griffith Spears, "Civil Rights, Immigration, and the Prospects for Social Justice Collaboration," in *The American South in a Global World*, Eds. James L. Peacock, Harry L. Watson, and Carrie R. Matthews. Chapel Hill: University of North Carolina Press, 2005, 235–246.

20. Carl L. Bankston, III and Min Zhou, "Go Fish: the Louisiana Vietnamese and Ethnic Entrepreneurship in an Extractive Industry," *National Journal of Sociology* 10, no. 1 1996: 1–18.

21. Abraham Verghese, *My Own Country: A Doctor's Story*. NewYork: Simon and Schuster, 1994.

22. Ibid.

23. Audrey Singer, "The Rise of New Immigrant Gateways," Washington, DC: Brookings Institution, 2004.

24. Mary E. Odem, "Unsettled in the Suburbs: Latino Immigration and Ethnic Diversity in Metro Atlanta," in *Twenty-First Century Gateways: Immigrant Incorporation in Suburban America*, Eds. Audrey Singer, Caroline Brettell, and Susan Hardwick.Washington, DC: Brookings Institution Press, 2008: 105–136; Marie Price and Audrey Singer, "Edge Gateways: Immigrants, Suburbs and the Politics of Reception in Metropolitan Washington," in *Twenty-First Century Gateways*, Eds. Singer, Brettell, and Hardwick, 137–170.

25. Smith, Heather A. Smith and Owen J. Furuseth. "The 'Nuevo South': Latino Placemaking in the Middle-Ring Suburbs of Charlotte" in *Twenty-First Century Gateways*, Eds. Singer, Brettell, and Hardwick, 281–307.

26. Joseph Wood, "Vietnamese American Place Making in Northern Virginia," *Geographical Review* 87, no. 1 (January 1997): 58–72.

27. Frank Cha, "Remapping the 38th Parallel in the Global South: Korean Immigration in Southern Spaces," *The Global South* 3, no. 2 (Fall 2009): 34–35.

28. Susan M. Walcott, "Overlapping Ethnicities and Negotiated Spaces: Atlanta's Buford Highway," *Journal of Cultural Geography* 20, no. 1 (Fall/Winter 2002): 51–75.

29. David R. Roediger, *Working Toward Whiteness: How America's Immigrants Became White*. New York: Basic Books, 2005.

30. David Goldfield, "Unmelting the Ethnic South: Changing Boundaries of Race and Ethnicity in the Modern South," in *The American South in the Twentieth Century*, Eds. Craig S. Pascoe, Karen Trahan Leathem, and Andy Ambrose. Athens: University of Georgia Press, 2005: 26.

31. James W. Loewen, *The Mississippi Chinese: Between Black and White*. Prospect Heights, Il: Waveland Press, 1988 (1971).

32. Cameron E. Lippard and Charles A. Gallagher, *Being Brown in Dixie: Race, Ethnicity, and Latino Immigration in the New South*. Boulder & London: First Forum Press, 2011: 314.

33. Joe Feagin and Jorge Cobas, "Latinos/as and White Racial Frame: The Procrustean Bed of Assimilation," *Sociological Inquiry* 78(2008): 39–53.

34. Reanne Frank, Ilana Redstone Akresh, and Bo Lu, "Latino Immigrants and the U.S. Racial Order," *American Sociological Review* 75, no. 3 (2010): 378–401.
35. George A. Yancey, *Who is White? Latinos, Asians, and the New Black/Nonblack Divide.* Boulder, CO: Lynne Rienner, 2003.
36. Marrow, *New Destination Dreaming*, chs. 4–5.
37. Ibid., 238.
38. Irene Browne and Mary E. Odem, " 'Juan Crow' in the *Nuevo* South: Racialization of Guatemalan and Dominican Immigrants in the Atlanta Metro Area," *DuBois Review* 9 no. 2 (Fall 2012): 321–337.
39. Ibid.
40. Ajantha Subramanian, "North Carolina's Indians: Erasing Race to Make a Citizen," in *The American South in a Global World*, Eds. James L. Peacock, Harry L. Watson and Carrie R. Matthews. Chapel Hill: University of North Carolina Press: 192–201.
41. Ibid., 194–195.
42. Marilyn Halter and Violet Showers Johnson, Eds. *African and American: West Africans in Post-Civil Rights America.* New York: NYU Press, 2014.

Bibliography

Bankston III, Carl L. and Min Zhou. "De Facto Congregationalism and Socioeconomic Mobility in Laotian and Vietnamese Immigrant Communities: A Study of Religious Institutions and Economic Change." *Review of Religious Research* 41 (June 2000): 453–470.

Browne, Irene and Mary Odem. "'Juan Crow' in the *Nuevo* South: Racialization of Guatemalan and Dominican Immigrants in the Atlanta Metro Area." *DuBois Review: Social Science Research on Race* 9, no. 2(Fall 2012): 321–337.

Cha, Frank. "Remapping the 38th Parallel in the Global South: Korean Immigration in Southern Spaces." *The Global South* 3, no. 2 (Fall 2009): 32–49.

Feagin, J. R. and J. A. Cobas. "Latinos/as and White Racial Frame: The Procrustean Bed of Assimilation." *Sociological Inquiry* 78(2008): 39–53.

Fink, Leon. *The Maya of Morganton.* Chapel Hill: University of North Carolina Press, 2003.

Gill, Hannah. *The Latino Migration Experience in North Carolina.* Chapel Hill: University of North Carolina Press, 2010.

Griffith, David. "Rural Industry and Mexican Immigration and Settlement in North Carolina," in *New Destinations: Mexican Immigration in the United States*, Eds.Víctor Zúñiga and Rubén Hernández-León. New York.: Russell Sage Foundation, 2005: 50–75.

Joshi, Khyati Y. and Jigna Desai, Eds. *Asian Americans in Dixie: Race and Migration in the South.* Chicago: University of IL Press, 2013. A welcome new collection, this book was published after the writing of this essay and therefore not addressed in the essay.

Leong, Karen J. et al., "Resilient History and the Rebuilding of a Community: The Vietnamese American Community in New Orleans East." *Journal of American History* 94, no. 3 (2007): 770–779.

Lippard, Cameron D. and Charles A. Gallagher. *Being Brown in Dixie: Race, Ethnicity, and Latino Immigration in the New South.* Boulder & London: First Forum Press, 2011.

Marrow, Helen B. *New Destination Dreaming: Immigration, Race, and Legal Status in the Rural American South.* Stanford, CA: Stanford University Press, 2011.

Mohl, Raymond. "Globalization, Latinization, and the Nuevo New South," *Journal of American Ethnic History* 22(4): 31–66.

Odem, Mary E. "Unsettled in the Suburbs: Latino Immigration and Ethnic Diversity in Metro Atlanta," in *Twenty-First Century Gateways: Immigrant Incorporation in Suburban America*, Eds. Audrey Singer, Caroline Brettell, and Susan Hardwick. Washington, DC: Brookings Institution Press, 2008: 105–136.

Odem, Mary E. and Elaine Lacy, Eds. *Latino Immigration and the Transformation of the U.S. South*. Athens, GA: University of Georgia Press, 2009.

Smith, Heather A. and Owen J. Furuseth, Eds. *Latinos in the New South: Transformations of Place*. Aldershot, England and Burlington, VT: Ashgate, 2006.

Smith, Heather A. and Owen J. Furuseth. "The 'Nuevo South': Latino Placemaking in the Middle-Ring Suburbs of Charlotte," in *Twenty-First Century Gateways: Immigrant Incorporation in Suburban America*, Eds. Audrey Singer, Caroline Brettell, and Susan Hardwick. Washington, DC: Brookings Institution Press, 2008: 281–307.

Subramanian, Ajantha. "North Carolina's Indians: Erasing Race to Make a Citizen," in *The American South in a Global World*, Eds. James L. Peacock, Harry L. Watson and Carrie R. Matthews. Chapel Hill: University of North Carolina Press, 2005: 192–201.

Verghese, Abraham. *My Own Country: A Doctor's Story*. New York: Simon and Schuster, 1994.

Winders, Jamie. "Nashville's New 'Sonido': Latino Migration and the Changing Politics of Race," in *New Faces in New Places: The Changing Geography of American Immigration*, Ed. Douglas S. Massey. New York: Russell Sage, 2008: 249–273.

Wood, Joseph "Vietnamese American Place Making in Northern Virginia." *Geographical Review* 87, no. 1 (January 1997): 58–72.

Zhao, Jianli. *Strangers in the City: The Atlanta Chinese, Their Community, and Stories of their Lives*. New York and London: Routledge, 2002.

Zhou, Min and Carl L. Bankston. *Growing up American: How Vietnamese Children Adapt to Life in the United States*. New York: Russell Sage, 1998.

Zúñiga, Víctor and Rubén Hernández-León, Eds. *New Destinations: Mexican Immigration in the United States*. New York: Russell Sage Foundation, 2005.

CHAPTER 21

ALLEGIANCE, DUAL CITIZENSHIP, AND THE ETHNIC INFLUENCE ON U.S. FOREIGN POLICY

DAVID BRUNDAGE

IMMIGRANTS and their descendants have been making efforts to influence U.S. foreign policy since the earliest days of the republic. The effectiveness of such efforts has varied considerably from group to group and the ethnic influence has been stronger in some historical periods than in others. Moreover, despite the 1975 assertion of Nathan Glazer and Daniel P. Moynihan that "the immigration process is the single most important determinant of American foreign policy," the influence of ethnic groups has been largely overshadowed by that of business lobbies and of relatively insulated coteries of foreign policy professionals. Nonetheless, the efforts of various descent groups in the foreign policy arena have been a significant, if clearly subordinate, force in shaping America's relationship with the wider world.[1]

Yet there has been relatively little historical research on the topic and the work that does exist is uneven in both coverage and quality. Historians of American foreign relations have generally found the topic to be a poor fit with the main approaches in their field. While many have sought to illuminate connections between domestic forces on the one hand and foreign policy on the other (sometimes so effectively that, in the words of Walter LaFeber, "the distinction between domestic and foreign affairs virtually disappeared"), their focus has been mainly on business or agricultural interests, not on ethnic groups. Meanwhile, historians of immigration and ethnicity have been more concerned with the abiding problem of assimilation and with topics such as work, family, gender, and, more recently, processes of racialization than with ethnic activism on foreign policy issues. In fact, for immigration historians, who had been central participants in forging the "new social history" of the 1960s and 1970s, the whole subject of foreign affairs long seemed stale and old-fashioned.[2]

All of this is now changing rapidly, spurred on by the transnational turn in the writing of American history, a remarkable resurgence of the field of diplomatic history (now more broadly conceived as the study of "the United States in the world" and more attuned to social and cultural approaches than ever before), and the growing interest of scholars in both contemporary and historical manifestations of diasporic identities, cultural hybridity, and the phenomenon that some have labeled "long-distance nationalism." It is thus now possible to sketch the main outlines of a history of the ethnic influence on U.S. foreign policy, drawing on a growing and increasingly sophisticated body of work. This history can be divided roughly into four phases. Between the nation's founding and the early twentieth century, ethnic political activism was largely dominated by Irish immigrants and their descendants, many of whom remained in close contact with nationalist movements in their homeland and used a variety of strategies to influence American foreign policy in a direction that favored such movements. Irish Americans were not the only nineteenth-century ethnic group making efforts to influence U.S. foreign policy, but the diversity of ethnic activists (and, more significantly, the diversity of their aims) exploded in the second phase of this history, the years before and after World War I. The third phase, the era of the Cold War, saw greater unanimity, as activists representing Eastern Europeans, Jewish Americans, Cuban Americans, and others worked for policies that generally reinforced a hard-line U.S. stance toward the Soviet Union. A splintering of this consensus has accompanied the end of the Cold War and the emergence of the United States as the sole global superpower, while some new developments, especially the phenomenon of dual citizenship, have also marked the shifting terrain of ethnic politics in the fourth phase of this history.[3]

DIVIDED LOYALTIES?

American ethnic groups that have worked to support the interests of real or symbolic homelands have long been vulnerable to the charge of divided loyalties. This charge initially arose in the era of World War I, when widespread opposition to America's entry into the war among some immigrant groups (Germans and Irish in particular) led prominent political figures, including both Woodrow Wilson and Theodore Roosevelt, to condemn what they dubbed the "hyphenate," the immigrant with allegedly dual or divided loyalties. This way of perceiving immigrant allegiance had serious implications, shaping not only the federal government's harassment of German and Irish Americans during World War I, but, more profoundly and in combination with powerful currents of anti-Asian racism, the internment of 120,000 Japanese Americans (two-thirds of them U.S. citizens) during World War II. The government's treatment of Muslim and Middle Eastern Americans in the years following the September 11, 2001, attacks reflected similar fears about their loyalties, along with a strong element of racial and, in this case, religious prejudice.[4]

Such a perspective was not limited to politicians, but was also central to the work of the first historians to systematically examine ethnic activism in the foreign policy arena. Louis L. Gerson, for example, who published the first full scholarly survey of the topic in 1964, took a title that echoed the language of Wilson and Roosevelt themselves and sought not just to document the various lobbying activities of American ethnic groups, but also to demonstrate their utter inappropriateness. The "once hyphenated, always hyphenated" phenomenon, which Gerson believed was growing in strength, constituted a serious threat to national unity and fundamentally distorted American foreign policy. This was a view widely shared among scholars in the 1950s and early 1960s and seriously undercut the contribution their research might otherwise have made.[5]

Although traces of this perspective can still be found in the work of both conservative and liberal critics of multiculturalism, most scholars now hold that the longtime American belief in what Maldwyn Jones called "the old Ciceronian dilemma, namely that the multiple loyalties of citizens were a threat to political unity," is completely unfounded. Even Tony Smith, a political scientist who has argued vigorously that the ethnic influence on U.S. foreign policy is greater than generally appreciated and that its negative effects significantly outweigh any of its potential benefits, is at pains to distinguish his position from earlier views, carefully referring to "conflicted," rather than "divided," immigrant loyalties, for example, to "avoid impugning the patriotism of those who have a strong sense of ethnic identity." Thomas Ambrosio speaks for the current consensus in labeling the fear of divided immigrant loyalties a "bogeyman."[6]

Another political scientist, however, has taken this revisionism one step further. Far from representing just another form of interest group lobbying, Yossi Shain contends, ethnic efforts to influence U.S. foreign policy need to be seen as expressions of a new kind of diasporic politics profoundly reshaping the contemporary world. Arguing that the efforts of U.S.-based diasporas on behalf of their homelands have constituted an important vehicle with which previously disenfranchised groups have won a voice in American life, Shain also maintains that when they champion causes such as democracy, human rights, or religious tolerance, these diasporas can play an important role in reshaping the political culture of their homelands themselves. Shain's conclusion on this point is far too optimistic but his deeply transnational approach, emphasizing the potential reverberations of U.S. ethnic political activism abroad, is on the mark. The long (if episodic) activism of Irish nationalists in the United States, for example, had profound effects on the history of Ireland itself, though, as the case of Irish American support for the IRA during the Northern Irish conflict suggests, these effects were not always as salutary as Shain believes.[7]

An assumption running through much of the scholarship on this topic, that presidents, secretaries of state, and other foreign policy "insiders" have been individuals without any discernable ethnic loyalties *themselves*, is also open to question. Until very recent times, of course, these insiders have been overwhelmingly drawn from descendants of those that Charlotte Erikson memorably called "invisible immigrants": the British. Yet only the diplomatic historian Alexander DeConde has probed the implications of this fact, arguing that Anglo Americans have been far and away the most influential ethnic group in the shaping of U.S. foreign policy and that they have invariably shaped it in a pro-British direction. The implications of this perspective are significant: when Woodrow Wilson (Scots and Scots-Irish in background, whose mother had been born in England) led America into war on Britain's side, was he any less a "hyphenate" than the German and Irish Americans he denounced? Still, the precise ways in which Anglo Americans' ethnic or national loyalties (as opposed to their class or racial identities or their general orientation toward the interests of business) influenced their policymaking is a question that remains badly in need of further exploration.[8]

THE NINETEENTH CENTURY

Whatever the significance of the Anglo American influence, it remains true that other groups began to push their way into foreign policy debates over the course of the nineteenth century. The Irish were the pioneers, but Germans, Poles, and Hungarians all gradually added their voices as well. By the time of the 1848 revolutions in Europe, political activists claiming to speak for such groups often worked not only to support their specific national homelands, but also to further what they saw more expansively as *international* causes, such as republicanism or democracy. And in the global rush for empire that began in the 1870s, some activists brought a new kind of politics of anti-imperialism to the fore, opposing not only British, Russian, and Austro-Hungarian imperial projects, but also, by century's end, that of the United States as well.

Irish American activism actually began even before the nineteenth century, surfacing in the first major debate in the history of U.S. foreign relations, the fight over the Jay Treaty with Britain in 1795. Irish republican émigrés in Philadelphia and New York, many of them in flight from Britain's increasingly harsh repression of the radical Society of United Irishmen back in Ireland, played an important role in this debate, providing vocal support for the Jeffersonian opposition to the treaty and thus triggering a Federalist backlash in the form of Adams's Alien and Sedition laws later in the decade. Though it is sometimes assumed that an unthinking Anglophobia was the sole motivation for Irish hostility to the treaty, recent research makes clear that the Irish émigrés were driven as much by their support for the French Revolution and "the rights of man" as by their opposition to British rule in Ireland. The legacy of these commitments can be tracked into the early nineteenth century, surfacing in the enthusiastic backing that many Irish Americans gave to the U.S. cause in the War of 1812.[9]

Somewhat better known is the Fenian Brotherhood, the transatlantic and oathbound society committed to winning Irish independence from Britain by force of arms, which drew thousands of young Irish American men to its ranks during and after the American Civil War. The Fenians built especially strong support among those who had fled the Irish famine, many of whom, as Kerby Miller demonstrated, saw themselves as "exiles" rather than voluntary emigrants and became enthusiastic recruits to the Fenians' brand of "physical force" nationalism. Armed Fenian incursions across the border into Canada in 1866 and 1870, often regarded as hopelessly futile and romantic gestures, are better seen as strategic (albeit unsuccessful) efforts to weaken the British Empire, build international support for Irish independence, and perhaps even drag the United States into a war with Britain. This last objective was not as unrealistic as it might sound, given the way that the sympathy of British political and economic elites for the Confederacy had reinvigorated an already long tradition of popular Anglophobia in the United States. Though obviously not an "ethnic lobby" as we would understand the term today, the Fenians can be seen as using filibustering and force to try to influence U.S. foreign policy.[10]

The Fenian movement declined after 1870, but organized Irish American political activity continued along more traditional lines, with Irish politicians and newspaper editors agitating against a variety of U.S. diplomatic agreements with Britain, ranging from fishery accords to Northwestern boundary settlements. The goal of driving a wedge between the United States and Britain underlined their efforts to influence American policy over such seemingly disparate international events as the Venezuelan boundary dispute (1895) and the South African War (1899–1902). Yet just as the Irish republican émigrés of the 1790s were motivated by more than kneejerk Anglophobia, so these later efforts at least sometimes reflected a broader political current within late nineteenth-century Irish American nationalism: that of anti-imperialism. Recent research, in addition to stressing the involvement of Irish American workers in a wide variety of social reform movements in the late nineteenth century, has revealed a deep strain of anti-imperialist feeling among some Irish American nationalists, one best expressed in the weekly "Colonization Column" of Patrick Ford's widely-read newspaper, *The Irish World and American Industrial Liberator*. This sentiment led significant numbers of Irish Americans to oppose not only British imperialism in the South African War— ignoring, however, the Boers' own brutal treatment of black Africans—but also the rise of *American* imperialism in the Caribbean and especially the Philippines, which some began calling "America's Ireland."[11]

There is a temptation to see this activism on the part of the American Irish as an atypical case, the exception rather than the rule in the nineteenth century. But other immigrants and nationalist émigrés were also intermittently active in trying to influence U.S. policy toward their homelands. Failed Polish insurrections in 1830, 1848, and 1863, for example, launched successive waves of exiles toward the United States, where some of them worked to win the support of the American government for Polish independence—unsuccessfully, it should be noted, since every president from Jackson to Lincoln viewed the question as a purely internal affair of the Russian Empire. Similarly, Hungarian followers of Lajos Kossuth, who arrived in America following the defeat of their revolution against the Hapsburg monarchy in 1849, rallied to their leader during his dramatic American tour of 1851–1852, part of an unsuccessful bid to win U.S. diplomatic and military assistance for a new revolt. Likewise, German '48ers, while best known for their critical impact on the labor and antislavery movements in America, also continued to make efforts on behalf of political democracy in the German states. More generally, a distinct strain of immigrant activism can be discerned in the American responses to the 1848 revolutions, and, in the anti-imperialist movement at the close of the nineteenth century, both Polish and Jewish immigrant nationalists can be found making arguments similar to that of the Irish. Though more research is needed on all of these groups, these examples make it clear that Irish America was not the only nine-teenth-century ethnic group making efforts to influence U.S. foreign policy.[12]

THE ERA OF WORLD WAR I AND AFTER

The coming of World War I has attracted some of the richest scholarship on ethnicity and foreign policy, not surprisingly since as the major European powers were edging toward war, the United States was experiencing its greatest surge of immigration to date. In the decade and a half before the outbreak of fighting, over 13 million people arrived in the United States and the foreign-born as a percentage of the total U.S. population reached its all-time high. More to the point, many of the immigrants were coming from countries directly involved in the hostilities. In fact, nearly a third of the American pop-ulation *as a whole* was connected in one way or another to the war, with thirteen percent of the population born in countries actively involved in hostilities and another seven-teen percent having one or more parent born in a belligerent country. But ethnic groups responded in strikingly different ways: while many Germans, Scandinavians (oppos-ing alliance with the Russian empire), and Irish (opposing alliance with the British) rallied for American neutrality, British, Italian, Russian, Polish, Armenian, southern Slavic, and Czech Americans all tended to favor U.S. intervention. The ethnic divide was equally apparent after the war, with some hailing Wilson for his role in bringing about the sovereignty of Poland, Czechoslovakia, and Yugoslavia, while Irish American orga-nizations bitterly criticized his unwillingness to extend the right of self-determination to Ireland, which was in the midst of a bloody War of Independence even as the Paris Peace Conference was opening its proceedings. Building on the predispositions of vari-ous ethnic groups, some governments and nationalist leaders in Europe actively worked to mobilize their kinfolk in the United States to pressure Congress or the Wilson admin-istration for various ends. Little wonder then that this was the era when the notion of the "hyphenate" as a major factor in American diplomacy first emerged.[13]

Activists representing the large German and Irish communities predictably took cen-ter stage. With the outbreak of war in 1914, the National German-American Alliance, which had been founded in 1901 to further German cultural and political influence in the United States and which now claimed more than 2 million members, threw itself into an effort to defend the homeland, joining with other German American organiza-tions in massive campaigns for an embargo on the export of war supplies to Britain and to prevent U.S. entry into the war. Joined by virtually the entire German American press, the Alliance nonetheless fell victim to the concerted attack on its work, which surfaced in Wilson's 1916 presidential campaign and gathered tremendous momentum after the United States entered the war in 1917. By the spring of 1918, the Alliance had dissolved and German American assimilation had accelerated dramatically under the force of anti-German propaganda and government harassment.[14]

Irish American activists also worked actively for U.S. neutrality and later to shape postwar American foreign policy in favor of Irish independence. In the years between 1916 and 1923, Irish nationalism became a true mass movement in the United States. The Friends of Irish Freedom (FOIF), founded in 1916, claimed nearly 300,000 members by 1919 and the American Association for the Recognition of the Irish Republic (AARIR), founded in 1919 by Eamon de Valera, the president-in-exile of the proclaimed Irish Republic, was even more significant. By 1921 the organization had 700,000 members and had raised over $10 million for the republican cause in Ireland. This activity was an almost textbook example of diaspora nationalism, the phenomenon of mass nationalist enthusiasm among a people living outside the borders of their envisioned nation state. Still, lines of tension could be discerned within the movement. While both the FOIF and the AARIR were led by the now sizeable Irish American middle class, for example, Irish American workers also spoke out on questions of war and Irish independence. Their views, however, were more likely to be expressed in the proclamations of central labor bodies like the Chicago Federation of Labor or, more dramatically, in labor actions like the 1920 boycott of British ships initiated by Irish American longshoremen, in cooperation with an Irish American feminist organization called the American Women Pickets for the Enforcement of America's War Aims.[15]

But what, in the end, was the effect of all of this activity on Wilson's actual policies? Certainly the fact that many of the campaigners claimed to speak for ethnic communities with numerous birthright or naturalized citizens—and of voting age—meant that their voices could not be entirely ignored. Walter Lippmann believed (and his view has been echoed in some recent historical work) that Wilson's proposal for a League of Nations represented, at least in part, an effort to satisfy the Democratic Party's various competing ethnic constituencies. Since a return to the traditional balance of power in Europe after the war would inevitably favor some immigrant homelands over others, this argument goes, Wilson and his advisors sought to reorganize European politics through multilateral institutions in a way that would harmonize competing American *domestic* interests. This essentially ethnic interpretation of Wilson's postwar peace policy, however, goes too far. Other influences, in particular the views of a number of liberal and liberal-left intellectuals, were probably more important in shaping the president's thinking on multilateralism, though it bears noting that some of these intellectuals (Jane Addams, Morris Hillquit, James H. Maurer, and Oswald Garrison Villard for instance) were highly visible supporters of Irish independence with links to Irish nationalist organizations. In this period, as in some others, the ranks of those who could legitimately be considered Irish nationalists went far beyond the ranks of those who were ethnically Irish American.[16]

Meanwhile among the smaller ethnic groups there were relatively clear winners and losers. Allied efforts to win the wartime backing of American Jews (who were repelled by the alliance with Czarist Russia and whose support for Zionism was beginning to grow in these years), for example, shaped not only Wilson's verbal endorsement of

Zionist goals, but also the British government's promise (a deliberately ambiguous one, to be sure) in its 1917 Balfour Declaration to establish a "national home" for Jews in Palestine. On the other hand, Armenian Americans who worked to obtain U.S. support for the short-lived Armenian Republic of 1918–1920 ended up with little to show for their efforts. Though the American Committee for the Independence of Armenia (1918–1927) also received some verbal support from Wilson, it experienced near total failure in its work to influence U.S. foreign policy, the result of a set of factors that included Allied vacillation, Wilson's own indecisiveness, tensions between Armenian nationalists and the Protestant missionaries who sometimes supported them, and the isolationism that increasingly characterized American politics as a whole in the 1920s.[17]

How much weight should be given to the ethnic role in shaping this isolationism is itself an open question. Tony Smith has argued that even as Fascism, Nazism, and German and Japanese military expansionism grew ominously in the interwar years, ethnic activism in the foreign policy arena functioned as "a drag on American involvement in world affairs." Research on specific groups, however, does not bear this out. Jewish Americans, for example, who had been divided over U.S. entry into World War I, responded with alarm to the rise of Nazism. In March 1933, just 2 months after Hitler assumed the German chancellorship, the American Jewish Committee, the American Jewish Congress, and B'nai B'rith were holding large anti-Nazi rallies, while other Jewish organizations spearheaded a highly publicized boycott of German goods and Jewish leaders lobbied the U.S. government (with little success) to open the gates to those fleeing the Nazis' anti-Semitic campaigns. As Roosevelt gradually intensified his criticism of Nazi atrocities, Jewish Americans increased their support for the Democratic Party and, with the outbreak of war, gave wholehearted support to the Allied cause.[18]

Research on political activism within the large German and Italian American communities in these years complicates the picture somewhat. German Americans shifted in large numbers to the Republican Party in the 1918 and 1920 elections, which may well have bolstered that party's isolationist leanings. But this "politics of revenge," as Frederick Luebke called it, was visibly fading as early as 1922. Moreover, the rapid retreat from a German cultural identity during World War I prevented Hitler from mobilizing large numbers of German Americans to his cause during the 1930s: the pro-Nazi German American Bund was both small in size (with less than 7000 members at its peak) and made up predominantly of new (post-World War I) German immigrants, not German Americans with deep roots in the United States.[19]

The situation among Italian Americans was somewhat different. Many of them took pride in what they saw as Mussolini's achievements after taking power in 1922 and Mussolini made systematic, and at least sometimes effective, efforts to mobilize Italians in the United States for political purposes, establishing the *Direzione Generale degli Italiani all'Estero* to organize Italian communities abroad and replacing the term "emigrant" with that of "citizen" in the Fascist lexicon. Vigorously contested by Italian American leftists and anti-Fascists in many places, Italian American support for the Fascist regime nonetheless remained an important feature of American life up until the very eve of the war. Still, the relatively low rates of naturalization and political participation among Italian Americans and the scarcity of influential Italian American politicians—with the notable exception of the New York congressman and mayor, Fiorello La Guardia, who was anything but an isolationist—sharply limited their impact on foreign policy.[20]

A much more striking example of such lack of political influence was the case of the Japanese in the United States. Even more than Mussolini, the Japanese government regarded the emigrants as a diaspora to be mobilized for the larger good of the Empire. On the other hand, concentrated overwhelmingly in the far western states and racialized by law and social practice as nonwhite (first-generation Issei were thus classified as "aliens ineligible for citizenship"), Japanese immigrants were in no position to exert any significant political influence on American policy makers. Their transnational orientation mainly took the form of remittances and, in some cases, sending their children to Japan to be educated. The traditional view of American isolationism, it should be noted, has itself come under revision lately, with recent work highlighting the role of business and other nongovernmental actors in vastly expanding America's international presence in the 1920s and 1930s and emphasizing that the increasing U.S. domination of Central America and the Caribbean, in particular, was anything but "isolationist." Still, the unwillingness of the American government to confront the growing dangers posed by German and Japanese military expansion was real enough and remains an important feature of these decades. The role of ethnic group activism in fostering this unwillingness, however, was negligible.[21]

THE COLD WAR

With the advent of the Cold War, the political activities of a number of descent groups dovetailed with and reinforced U.S. foreign policy in its confrontation with the Soviet Union. Though naturally not every group fits this pattern, the efforts of Eastern European, Jewish, and Cuban Americans support what some scholars have seen as a kind of Cold War ethnic "internationalism." The Cold War has become one of the most dynamic areas of research in the field of diplomatic history, partly because of the opening up of new archives in the former Soviet Union, but much of the new work has been focused on the Third World, where "hot" is a better descriptor than "cold" for the myriad conflicts of the years from 1945 to the early 1990s. By contrast, much research on the foreign policy activism of domestic ethnic groups has continued to focus mainly on Europeans, especially Eastern Europeans, not surprisingly given that Poles, Hungarians, Czechs, and other Eastern European groups were becoming increasingly active in American political life generally by the middle of the twentieth century and that the situation of their homelands and other nations within the Soviet sphere of influence was so central to popular understandings of the stakes of the Cold War.[22]

Eastern European activists were somewhat atypical in that they coordinated much of their political work through a multinational umbrella organization, the Assembly of Captive European Nations (ACEN), founded in 1954, which lobbied heavily for a hard-line stance vis-à-vis the Soviet Union. Still, as with ethnic activism in the World War I era, the impact of their efforts is difficult to assess. Certainly, a number of factors limited ACEN's influence, including the relative insulation of the foreign policy establishment, the executive branch's domination of foreign affairs, the persistence of Anglo American cultural dominance in policy circles, and the lingering prejudice against Southern and Eastern Europeans in American life generally. Foreign policy during the Cold War remained the preserve of what one scholar has called a "small, cohesive club of academics, diplomats, financiers, lawyers and politicians that ascended to power during World War II." Another obstacle to effectively measuring the influence of ACEN (and that of particular national lobbies like the Polish American Congress) is the fact that their objectives so closely resembled those that American policy makers would have probably pursued anyway. Still, it seems likely that the pressure exerted by such groups did serve to lower the possibility of any sort of rapprochement with the Soviet Union.[23]

The question of ethnic group efficacy, however, while important, does not exhaust the range of salient issues in the study of Eastern European Cold War-era activism. Recent research by Anna D. Jaroszyńska-Kirchmann, for example, has tracked displaced persons and refugees from a devastated Poland through various postwar European refugee camps and finally into what she calls a worldwide "Polish political diaspora," determined to support the emerging fight against communism. One of the most interesting aspects of this history is the complex relationship that developed between this new diaspora and the by now well-established Polish American community in the United States. Differentiated by class background (the new émigrés were much more middle class than the earlier migrants, who were overwhelmingly from peasant and working-class backgrounds) as well as by length of time in America and by political views, the relationship between the postwar diaspora and Polish Americans was one marked as much by misunderstanding and conflict as by cooperation. This is an approach that could well be fruitfully applied to other groups of Eastern Europeans in Cold War America.[24]

Like Poles and Slavs, Eastern European Jews had also experienced a great deal of prejudice in the early decades of their settlement in the United States and though anti-Semitism was in decline after World War II, Jews remained a small group, less than three percent of the total U.S. population. Yet from the founding of Israel through the close U.S.–Israeli alliance of today, Jewish American activists built and maintained what eventually became the most influential ethnic lobby in the United States. This began in the early postwar years, when, facing a difficult 1948 reelection fight and attuned to the high levels of political participation among Jewish Americans, Truman provided diplomatic recognition to Israel eleven minutes after the existence of the new state was declared. There was, to be sure, a strong element of political calculation on Truman's part, but it is also true that the powerful role that understandings of the Holocaust played in American politics and culture in the postwar years provided a good deal of moral legitimacy and urgency to pro-Israel activism.[25]

Cold War considerations also came into play, as the new state—despite the socialist beliefs of some of its founders—moved decisively from potential neutrality into the U.S. camp, enabling Israel's American supporters to trumpet its role as a counterweight to Soviet influence in the Middle East. The pro-Israel lobby, however, only really came into its own with the founding of the American Israel Public Affairs Committee (AIPAC) in 1951. AIPAC's leaders disassociated their organization from the traditionally liberal domestic political orientation of many American Jews, enabling the organization to develop close ties to Congressional Republicans as well as Democrats and to exert influence on administrations as politically diverse as those of Lyndon Johnson and Ronald Reagan. The 1967 Arab–Israeli War galvanized wider American public support for Israel, but the unity of Jewish Americans behind Israel subsequently came under strain as a result of Israel's invasion of Lebanon, the Jonathan Pollard spy case, the growing influence of Orthodox and ultra-Orthodox Judaism in Israel, and the first Palestinian Intifada. The American Israel lobby, however, has for the most part weathered these strains. Tremendous controversy greeted the central argument of John Mearsheimer and Stephen Walt's 2007 study of *The Israel Lobby and U.S. Foreign Policy* that AIPAC's effectiveness had served to "jeopardize U.S. national security." But few have taken issue with the conclusion of political scientists David M. Paul and Rachel Anderson Paul, based on a broad and carefully constructed comparative analysis, that the Israeli American lobby is the single most influential ethnic lobby on the current scene.[26]

The anti-Castro Cuban American lobby is another one whose influence has outlasted its Cold War origins. The involvement of Cuban émigrés in the politics of their homeland actually has a very long history, stretching back to the 1880s and 1890s, when José Martí agitated for Cuban independence from a base in New York City, drawing significant support among working-class Cuban immigrants there and in several Florida communities, especially Tampa and neighboring Ybor City. Nonetheless, it was only with the Cuban Revolution and the several waves of migration that followed—scholars have identified four such waves between 1959 and the early twenty-first century, each distinctive in its socioeconomic features—that a strong Cuban American voice in shaping U.S. policy emerged. The fact that Cuban Americans are an even a smaller group than American Jews (at 1.3 million, just half a percent of the population in 2000) makes it difficult to explain their apparently outsized influence.[27]

The sheer intensity of Cuban American political views certainly has to be part of the explanation. Like the nineteenth-century Irish and the postwar Poles, many of the Cubans who began arriving in the United States in 1959 regarded themselves as exiles rather than as immigrants. Nonetheless, as Cuban America has grown and become more diverse in generational, socioeconomic, and racial terms, scholars have given more attention to the ideological diversity of the community, a feature not always apparent to outsiders. In her study of Cuban exiles and Cuban Americans in south Florida from 1959 to the mid-1990s, for example, María Cristina García examines forms of political activity ranging from membership in paramilitary groups to support for the influential hard-line anti-Castro Cuban American National Foundation (CANF), whose intensive lobbying of Congress has been extremely effective, to support for groups like the Cuban Committee for Democracy that favor dialogue with the Cuban government.

Cuban American political views were never monolithic, a theme developed even further in Susan Eva Eckstein's study of the array of differences (including political differences) between the 1959 "exiles" and the "new Cubans" who arrived in the United States a generation later. Still, the concentration of Cuban Americans in the critical swing state of Florida, along with high levels of naturalization and voting participation, have given the hard-line position an enormous amount of influence, especially—but not only—within the Republican Party.[28]

The protests from Cuban Americans that accompanied Nelson Mandela's 1990 visit to Miami (after he had acknowledged his admiration for Castro in a U.S. television interview) and the subsequent African American boycott of the Miami tourist industry (after the city rescinded its welcome to the South African anti-apartheid leader) highlight a theme that could use more scholarly attention: the conflicts that have occasionally erupted between different descent groups over questions of foreign policy. Yossi Shain is surely correct in arguing that, as a consequence of slavery and the slave trade, the ways in which African Americans have related to Africa are "fundamentally different from the ways other ethnic groups—descendants of immigrants who chose America or came as refugees—relate to their countries of origin or symbolic homelands." Specifically, key U.S.-based leaders and movements have more often identified broadly with the African people and the African diaspora, particularly in the Caribbean—or, more broadly still, with what Penny Von Eschen calls an "internationalist anticolonial discourse"—than with any particular African nation state or nationalist movement. African Americans have a long history of foreign policy activism, with World War I–era figures as diverse as W.E.B. Du Bois and Marcus Garvey staking out strong positions on international issues ranging from Belgian atrocities in the Congo to the American military occupation of Haiti. Du Bois's famous statement that "the problem of the twentieth century is the problem of the color line" was, of course, international at its very core: he referred explicitly to "the relation of the darker to the lighter races of men in Asia and Africa, in America and the islands of the sea." Such views gained more and more adherents among African Americans over the course of the century. Widespread anger at Italy's 1935 invasion of Ethiopia, for example, sparked conflict between African Americans and some Italian Americans but also led to the further growth of an international orientation among many African Americans, reflected in the founding of the Council on African Affairs in 1937.[29]

But it was in the era of the Cold War that African American foreign policy activism produced its greatest results. Linking the goals of domestic racial equality with that of decolonization, African American leaders pressed the cause of anti-colonialism in Washington, achieving a key objective with the establishment of a bureau of African affairs in the U.S. State Department in 1958. Though some of them, notably the NAACP's Walter Francis White and Roy Wilkins, couched their advocacy in the rhetoric of liberal anti-communism, African American activism came into direct conflict with established U.S. foreign policy on a number of issues, notably that of South Africa, even after the Cold War–era marginalization of left-wing figures like Du Bois and Paul Robeson. While policy makers continued to view South Africa as a major bulwark against Soviet influence in the region, African American activists began intensifying their efforts to isolate the nation in the 1960s, winning a major victory with the U.S. adoption of economic sanctions against that nation—over Ronald Reagan's veto—in 1986. The result of legislative pressure exerted by the Congressional Black Caucus combined with mass demonstrations and civil disobedience on a scale not seen since the 1960s, this victory marked what Shain calls "one of the most effective diasporic efforts to alter world politics in recent years."[30]

AFTER THE COLD WAR

In the years since the fall of the Soviet Union, ethnic group activism in the foreign policy arena has come into its own. The increasing salience, from the perspective of some descent groups, of what are at least partly international issues such as trade, labor rights, immigration policy, and environmental protection, combined with the end of the Cold War and the emergence of violent nationalist conflict involving the homelands of some American ethnic groups (particularly those from the former Yugoslavia), rapidly led to a situation in which such groups were likely to see lobbying and other forms of exercising influence as increasingly important, even necessary. And the international situation that existed during the 1990s, in which the United States lacked a clearly defined enemy, appeared for a time to provide greater leeway for ethnic activism. On the other hand, the attacks of 9/11 and the subsequent U.S. declaration of a "war on terror" undoubtedly weakened the ability of many ethnic groups to influence foreign policy, though there has been little research on this last point.[31]

Over the course of the 1990s, both "old" and "new" groups moved to the fore. Irish Americans concerned with the conflict in Northern Ireland, who, since the mid-1970s, had been bitterly divided between moderates on the one hand and republican supporters of Sinn Féin and the IRA on the other, now solidified behind the Sinn Féin–backed peace process and successfully brought pressure to bear on the Clinton administration to further that process, in the face of considerable resistance from the Conservative government that held power in Britain until 1997. Meanwhile, the first Intifada, the Gulf War, and the emergence of an Israeli-Palestinian peace process, along with an urge to counter the effectiveness of pro-Israel lobbying, stimulated the emergence of an Arab American voice on foreign policy issues, building on the work of organizations like the American-Arab Anti-Discrimination Committee and the Arab American Institute, both founded in the 1980s with a mainly domestic focus. The Arab American ability to influence U.S. policy in the Middle East, however, has been sharply limited by the very deep ethnic, religious, and political divisions within what is, after all, a pan-ethnic community (consisting of Christians and Muslims, Lebanese and Palestinians, etc.) and, even more significantly, by the reverberations of 9/11, which focused the attention of Arab American organizations away from foreign policy and toward the now more pressing domestic issues of discrimination and racial profiling.[32]

Like Arab Americans, Asian Americans are also a pan-ethnic group, and one that faces numerous obstacles in achieving a unified political voice on either international or domestic matters. Moreover, the legacy of anti-Asian racism has meant that even relatively modest efforts on foreign policy have been, as Paul Watanabe notes, "more discouraged than encouraged, more derided than applauded." Nonetheless, research by Yen Le Espiritu and others has highlighted the ways in which the differences among Chinese, Filipino, Korean, Indian, and Vietnamese Americans have been gradually overcome as such groups have "become aware of common problems and goals that transcended parochial interests and historical antagonisms." The principal umbrella organization, the National Council of Asian Pacific Americans, while dealing mainly with domestic affairs, has also taken up issues with international dimensions, such as immigration reform and fair treatment for Filipino and Hmong veterans (of World War II and the Vietnam conflict, respectively). Though the foreign policy efforts of most of the more specifically national organizations (such as the Japanese American Citizens League and the Korean American Coalition) have been sporadic, Indian Americans have been an increasingly significant force in shaping U.S. policy toward South Asia and the Indian government has also made efforts to politically mobilize a population that it appears to see in classic diasporic terms.[33]

While Cuban Americans have been the most politically active Latino group to date, there are good reasons to believe that Mexican Americans, the fastest growing population group, will play an increasingly important role in foreign policy. Although there are obstacles to their achieving this, including the relatively young and heavily working-class composition of the Mexican American population, there are also international issues, especially relating to trade, immigration, and border control, that are of pressing importance to this community. Moreover, the emergence of a vibrant immigrant rights movement, with particular strength among Mexican Americans, in the first decade of the twenty-first century may well be a harbinger of things to come. As David Gutiérrez and other scholars have shown, the Mexican population of the Southwest has long been politically divided by class and immigration status. Nonetheless, in the 1970s and 1980s, organizations such as the League of United Latin American Citizens, the Mexican American Legal Defense and Education Fund, the American G.I. Forum, and the National Council of La Raza, in coordination with the small but highly effective Congressional Hispanic Caucus, managed to prevent the enactment of the most extreme proposals for immigration restriction being debated in Congress, and these groups won a major victory with the inclusion of an amnesty program in the 1986 Immigration Reform and Control Act for those who could document their residency in the country since 1982.[34]

The Mexican government, which played a role in shaping this outcome as well, has been associated with an even more significant development: the increasing global acceptance, or at least tolerance, of dual citizenship. In the late 1990s, along with a host of other countries in Latin America and the Caribbean, Mexico passed a new nationality law that recognized the dual citizenship of its U.S. residents, revoking previous laws that stripped Mexican citizenship from those who became naturalized citizens of another country. On the "receiving" side of this new equation, by the end of the twentieth century, France,

Britain, and Canada all permitted immigrants who naturalized to retain their original citizenship and even the United States, which had long demanded the complete renunciation of previous citizenship as a condition of naturalization—a reflection of the deep fears about divided loyalties with which this essay began—had liberalized its policies along similar lines, though here the liberalization has been shaped more by court decisions than by legislation. Scholars have proposed a number of explanations for this global phenomenon, which first began to emerge in the 1980s and accelerated dramatically in the following two decades. These include increasing levels of migration, a lessening of nation states' historic concerns about international conflicts over the diplomatic protection of their citizens, growing support for women's equality (which has resulted in recognition of the rights of mothers—not just fathers, as in the past—to pass their nationality on to their offspring), and the growing perception on the part of political elites in immigrant-sending nations that maintaining transnational ties with their countrymen abroad might generate both economic and political benefits.[35]

There is a great deal that remains unclear about this important phenomenon. Even the number of actual dual citizens in the United States (or anywhere else) is unknown, although it is certainly increasing. By the late 1990s, according to one study, more than a half a million children born in the United States each year had at least one additional nationality, and worldwide there were "tens of millions" of people who were citizens of one state but who were also "subject to the call of another state of which they are also citizens." The long-term consequences for both sending and receiving nations also remain uncertain. While Peter Spiro has argued that policy liberalization in the United States reflects a drastic devaluation of the very meaning of citizenship (replacing its traditional implications of shared sacrifice and identity with a much more limited and instrumental significance), most scholars to date believe that such concerns are overstated.[36]

It is also difficult to predict what this development will mean for ethnic political activity and U.S. foreign policy. While it might seem likely to further facilitate a transnational identity among at least some migrants, allowing them (now as U.S. citizens) to effectively work for homelands and homeland causes that they hold even more dearly than in the past, research on the recent political activities of Dominicans and Mexicans in the United States does not seem to bear this out: though both groups are now permitted to take part in homeland elections, a very small percentage of the eligible populations have chosen to do so. This would seem to suggest that, as Peter Kivisto has put it, "in becoming naturalized citizens, immigrants have opted to hang their political loyalties on the receiving country's peg rather than on the homeland peg." Before one resuscitates the old fear of the "hyphenate," it is also worth considering Reed Ueda's sensible point that immigrants may be more likely "to embrace the national identity of their host country if they have the security of not losing the benefits of citizenship in their country of origin."[37]

The global reach of the recent dual citizenship phenomenon prompts a final observation by way of conclusion. Though increasingly sophisticated and helpful in many ways, much of the research on this topic remains mired in a version of American exceptionalism, an assumption that, as one scholar has put it, "the extent to which ethnic minorities are able to shape foreign policy is a uniquely American phenomenon." It is not clear that this was ever true: in Britain and France, in particular, the nineteenth- and twentieth-century polities included numerous groups of newcomers (Italian, Jewish, and central European nationalists, exiled '48ers, anti-Nazi and anticommunist émigrés, etc.) who worked to influence the foreign policies of their adopted countries. It is even less true in our own era, when some 217 million people worldwide live outside the countries of their birth and when groups as diverse as Slovenians in Australia and Tamils in Norway have struggled to achieve political objectives for homelands sometimes literally on the other side of the world. A more fully comparative approach to this important topic is one that should be on the agenda.[38]

NOTES

1. Nathan Glazer and Daniel P. Moynihan, "Introduction," in *Ethnicity: Theory and Experience*, ed. Nathan Glazer and Daniel P. Moynihan (Cambridge, MA: Harvard University Press, 1975), 23–24.

2. Walter LaFeber, "Liberty and Power: U.S. Diplomatic History, 1750–1945," in *The New American History*, ed. Eric Foner (revised and expanded edition; Philadelphia: Temple University Press, 1997), 378. For two insightful surveys of the field of immigration and ethnic history in the 1990s—neither of which mentions the topic of ethnic influences on foreign policy—see Rudolph J. Vecoli, "From *The Uprooted* to *The Transplanted*: The Writing of American Immigration History, 1951–1989," in *From "Melting Pot" to Multiculturalism: The Evolution of Ethnic Relations in the United States and Canada*, ed. Valeria Gennaro Lerda (Rome: Bulzoni Editore, 1990), 25–53; and James P. Shenton and Kevin Kenny, "Ethnicity and Immigration," in *The New American History*, 353–373. For immigration historians' enduring interest in the problem of assimilation, see Russell A. Kazal, "Revisiting Assimilation: The Rise, Fall, and Reappraisal of a Concept in American Ethnic History," *American Historical Review* 100, 2 (April 1995): 437–471. For a recent work that brings the fields of immigration and diplomatic history into fruitful dialogue, emphasizing particularly the influence of foreign affairs on migration and immigration policy, see Donna R. Gabaccia, *Foreign Relations: American Immigration in Global Perspective* (Princeton, NJ: Princeton University Press, 2012).

3. For the transnational turn in American history, see many of the essays in *American History Now*, ed. Eric Foner and Lisa McGirr (Philadelphia: Temple University Press, 2011), but especially Erez Manela, "The United States in the World," 201–220, and Mae M. Ngai, "Immigration and Ethnic History," 358–375. For an insightful overview of contemporary research on diaspora, hybridity, transnationalism, and the like, see Stéphane Dufoix, *Diasporas* (Berkeley: University of California Press, 2008). For "long-distance nationalism," see Benedict Anderson, *The Spectre of Comparison: Nationalism, Southeast Asia, and the World* (London: Verso, 1998), 58–74.

4. For an overview of this issue, see Mona Harrington, "Loyalties: Dual and Divided," in *Encyclopedia of American Ethnic Groups*, ed. Stephan Thernstrom (Cambridge, MA: The Belknap Press of Harvard University Press, 1980), 676–686. For World War I-era efforts to "swat the hyphen," see John Higham's still valuable work, *Strangers in the Land: Patterns of American Nativism, 1860–1925* (1955; New Brunswick, NJ: Rutgers University Press, 2002),

194–222. The most influential interpretation of the decision to intern Japanese Americans remains Roger Daniels, *Concentration Camps USA: Japanese Americans and World War II* (New York: Holt, Rinehart and Winston, 1971), 42–73. For the impact of post-9/11 developments on Middle Eastern and Muslim Americans, placed in a historical framework that includes both the treatment of German Americans during World War I and Japanese American internment, see Anny Bakalian and Mehdi Bozorgmehr, *Backlash 9/11: Middle Eastern and Muslim Americans Respond* (Berkeley: University of California, Press, 2009), especially 32–65. See also Gary Gerstle, "The Immigrant as Threat to American Security: A Historical Perspective," in *From Arrival to Incorporation: Migrants to the U.S. in the Global Era*, ed. Elliott R. Barkan, Hasia Diner, and Alan M. Kraut (New York: New York Press, 2008), 217–245.

5. Louis L. Gerson, *The Hyphenate in Recent American Politics and Diplomacy* (Lawrence: University of Kansas Press, 1964), vii, 234–235. See also Gerson, *Woodrow Wilson and the Rebirth of Poland, 1914–1920: A Study in the Influence on American Policy of Minority Groups of Foreign Origin* (New Haven: Yale University Press, 1954). Lawrence H. Fuchs was nearly alone among scholars in these years in offering a generally positive assessment of ethnic involvement in foreign affairs. See Fuchs, "Minority Groups and Foreign Policy." *Political Science Quarterly* 74, no. 2 (June 1959): 161–175.

6. Maldwyn A. Jones, *The Old World Ties of American Ethnic Groups* (London: H.K. Lewis, 1976), 5; Tony Smith, *Foreign Attachments: The Power of Ethnic Groups in the Making of American Foreign Policy* (Cambridge, MA: Harvard University Press, 2000), 1–4, 24, 47; Thomas Ambrosio, "Ethnic Identity Groups and U.S. Foreign Policy," in *Ethnic Identity Groups and U.S. Foreign Policy*, ed. Thomas Ambrosio (Westport, CT: Praeger, 2002), 3. For examples of conservative and liberal critiques of multiculturalism, see Samuel P. Huntington, *Who Are We? The Challenges to America's National Identity* (New York: Simon & Schuster, 2004) and Arthur M. Schlesinger, *The Disuniting of America* (New York: Norton, 1992).

7. Yossi Shain, *Marketing the American Creed Abroad: Diasporas in the U.S. and Their Homelands* (Cambridge, UK: Cambridge University Press, 1999), x, xii-xv, 8; David Brundage, *Irish Nationalists in America: The Politics of Exile, 1798–1998* (New York: Oxford University Press, 2016).

8. Charlotte Erickson, *Invisible Immigrants: The Adaptation of English and Scottish Immigrants in Nineteenth-Century America* (Coral Gables, FL: University of Miami Press, 1972); Alexander DeConde, *Ethnicity, Race, and American Foreign Policy: A History* (Boston: Northeastern University Press, 1992), x.

9. Marianne Elliott, *Wolfe Tone: Prophet of Irish Independence* (New Haven, CT: Yale University Press, 1989), 262–263, 270–271; Michael Durey, *Transatlantic Radicals and the Early American Republic* (Lawrence: University Press of Kansas, 1997), 236–240; David A. Wilson, *United Irishmen, United States: Immigrant Radicals in the Early Republic* (Ithaca, NY: Cornell University Press, 1998), 40–42, 56; Maurice J. Bric, *Ireland, Philadelphia and the Re-invention of America, 1760–1800* (Dublin: Four Courts, 2008), 243–249; Joanne B. Freeman, "Explaining the Unexplainable: The Cultural Context of the Sedition Act," in *The Democratic Experiment: New Directions in American Political History*, ed. Meg Jacobs, William J. Novak, and Julian E. Zelizer (Princeton, NJ: Princeton University Press, 2003), 20–49; Alan Taylor, *The Civil War of 1812: American Citizens, British Subjects, Irish Rebels, and Indian Allies* (New York: Knopf, 2010), 9–10, 81–88, 327–329.

10. Kerby A. Miller, *Emigrants and Exiles: Ireland and the Irish Exodus to North America* (New York: Oxford University Press, 1985), 335–344; Christian G. Samito, *Becoming American Under Fire: Irish Americans, African Americans, and the Politics of Citizenship During the Civil War Era* (Ithaca, NY: Cornell University Press, 2009), 120–125, 172–193. For a good sampling of some of the most interesting recent transnational research on the Fenians, see *The Black Hand of Republicanism: Fenianism in Modern Ireland*, ed. Fearghal McGarry and James Richard Redmond McConnel (Dublin: Irish Academic Press, 2009).

11. Eric Foner, *Politics and Ideology in the Age of The Civil War* (New York: Oxford University Press, 1980), 150–200; David Brundage, *The Making of Western Labor Radicalism: Denver's Organized Workers, 1878–1905* (Urbana: University of Illinois Press, 1994), 25–52; Matthew Frye Jacobson, *Special Sorrows: The Diasporic Imagination of Irish, Polish, and Jewish Immigrants in the United States* (1995; Berkeley: University of California Press, 2002); Niamh C. Lynch, "'Live Ireland, Perish the Empire': Irish Nationalist Anti-Imperialism, c. 1840–1900" (PhD diss., Boston College, 2006); Bruce Nelson, "'From the Cabins of Connemara to the Kraals of Kaffirland': Irish Nationalists, the British Empire, and the 'Boer Fight for Freedom,'" in *The Irish in the Atlantic World*, ed. David T. Gleeson (Columbia: University of South Carolina Press, 2010), 154–175.

12. Florian Stasik, *Polish Political Émigrés in the United States of America, 1831–1864* (Boulder, CO: East European Monographs, 2002); John H. Komlos, *Louis Kossuth in America, 1851–1852* (Buffalo, NY: East European Institute, 1973); Donald S. Spencer, *Louis Kossuth and Young America: A Study of Sectionalism and Foreign Policy, 1848–1852* (Columbia: University of Missouri Press, 1977); Bruce C. Levine, *The Spirit of 1848: German Immigrants, Labor Conflict, and the Coming of the Civil War* (Urbana: University of Illinois Press, 1992); Timothy Mason Roberts, *Distant Revolutions: 1848 and the Challenge to American Exceptionalism* (Charlottesville: University of Virginia Press, 2009); Jacobson, *Special Sorrows*, 200–216.

13. For good overviews, see DeConde, *Ethnicity, Race and American Foreign Policy*, 81–98, and Smith, *Foreign Attachments*, 50–54.

14. Frederick C. Luebke, *Bonds of Loyalty: German Americans and World War I* (De Kalb: Northern Illinois University Press, 1974); Russell A. Kazal, *Becoming Old Stock: The Paradox of German-American Identity* (Princeton, NJ: Princeton University Press, 2004).

15. Alan J. Ward, *Ireland and Anglo-American Relations, 1899–1921* (London: Weidenfeld & Nicolson, 1969); F. J. Carroll, *American Opinion and the Irish Question, 1910–1923* (New York: St. Martin's, 1978); John P. Buckley, *The New York Irish, Their View of American Foreign Policy, 1914–1921* (New York: Arno, 1976); Joseph E. Cuddy, *Irish-America and National Isolationism, 1914–1920* (New York: Arno, 1976); Michael Doorley, *Irish-American Diaspora Nationalism: The Friends of Irish Freedom, 1916–1935* (Dublin: Four Courts, 2005); Elizabeth McKillen, *Chicago Labor and the Quest for a Democratic Diplomacy, 1914–1924* (Ithaca, NY: Cornell University Press, 1995); David Brundage, "American Labour and the Irish Question, 1916–1923," *Saothar: Journal of the Irish Labour History Society* 24 (1999): 59–66; Joe Doyle, "Striking for Ireland on the New York Docks," in *The New York Irish*, ed. Ronald H. Bayor and Timothy J. Meagher (Baltimore: Johns Hopkins University Press, 1996), 357–373.

16. Joseph P. O'Grady, ed., *The Immigrants' Influence on Wilson's Peace Policies* (Lexington: University of Kentucky Press, 1967); Melvin Small, *Democracy and Diplomacy: The Impact of Domestic Politics on U.S. Foreign Policy, 1789–1994* (Baltimore: Johns Hopkins University Press, 1996); 43; Robert W. Tucker, "Immigration and Foreign Policy: General

Considerations," in *Immigration and U.S. Foreign Policy*, ed. Robert W., Tucker, Charles B. Keely, and Linda Wrigley (Boulder, CO: Westview, 1990), 1–14; Smith, *Foreign Attachments*, 51–52; Thomas J. Knock, *To End All Wars: Woodrow Wilson and the Quest for a New World Order* (New York: Oxford University Press, 1992); Brundage, *Irish Nationalists in America*.

17. Jonathan Schneer, *The Balfour Declaration: The Origins of the Arab-Israeli Conflict* (London: Bloomsbury, 2010), 154–159; Gregory L. Aftandilian, *Armenia, Vision of a Republic: The Independence Lobby in America, 1918-1927* (Boston: Charles River Books, 1981). See also Richard G. Hovannisian, *The Republic of Armenia*. 4 vols. (Berkeley: University of California Press, 1971–1996).

18. Smith, *Foreign Attachments*, 47, 54; Aaron Berman, *Nazism, the Jews, and American Zionism, 1933–1948* (Detroit: Wayne State University Press, 1990), 38; Roger Daniels, *Coming to America: A History of Immigration and Ethnicity in American Life* (1990; 2nd ed., New York: Perennial, 2002), 296–302; DeConde, *Ethnicity, Race and American Foreign Policy*, 105, 109, 115. For the fullest treatment of these issues, see Richard Breitman and Allan J. Lichtman, *FDR and the Jews* (Cambridge, MA: The Belknap Press of Harvard University Press, 2013).

19. Luebke, *Bonds of Loyalty*, 223–231; Kazal, *Becoming Old Stock*; Sander A. Diamond, *The Nazi Movement in the United States, 1924–1941* (Ithaca, NY: Cornell University Press, 1974); Philip Jenkins, *Hoods and Shirts: The Extreme Right in Pennsylvania, 1925–1950* (Chapel Hill: University of North Carolina Press, 1997).

20. John P. Diggins, *Mussolini and Fascism: The View from America* (Princeton, N.J.: Princeton University Press, 1972); Gaetano Salvemini, *Italian Fascist Activities in the United States*, ed. Philip V. Cannistraro (New York: Center for Migration Studies, 1977); Philip V. Cannistraro, *Blackshirts in Little Italy: Italian Americans and Fascism, 1921–1929* (West Lafayette, IN: Bordighera, 1999). For La Guardia, see Ronald H. Bayor, *Fiorello La Guardia: Ethnicity and Reform* (Arlington Heights, IL: Harlan Davidson, 1993).

21. Yuji Ichioka, *The Issei: The World of the First Generation Japanese Immigrants, 1885-1924* (New York: Free Press, 1988), 2; Eiichiro Azuma, *Between Two Empires: Race, History, and Transnationalism in Japanese America* (New York: Oxford University Press, 2005); Azuma, "Dancing with the Rising Sun: Strategic Alliances between Japanese Immigrants and Their 'Home' Government," in *The Transnational Politics of Asian Americans*, ed. Christian Collet and Pei-te Lien (Philadelphia: Temple University Press, 2009), 25–37. For recent work that challenges the traditional view of isolationism in interwar period, see Victoria De Grazia, *Irresistible Empire: America's Advance Through Twentieth-Century Europe* (Cambridge, MA: Belknap Press of Harvard University Press, 2005) and Thomas F. O'Brien, *Making the Americas: The United States and Latin America from the Age of Revolutions to the Era of Globalization* (Albuquerque: University of New Mexico Press, 2007), 97–155.

22. Smith, *Foreign Attachments*, 54. For a good example of the recent Third World focus in Cold War studies, see Odd Arne Westad, *The Global Cold War: Third World Interventions and the Making of Our Times* (Cambridge: Cambridge University Press, 2005).

23. Stephen A. Garrett, "Eastern European Ethnic Groups and American Foreign Policy," *Political Science Quarterly* 93, no. 2 (Summer 1978): 301–323; Michael Clough, "Grass-Roots Policymaking: Say Good-Bye to the 'Wise Men,'" *Foreign Affairs* 73, no. 1 (January–February 1994): 2–3; Ambrosio, "Ethnic Identity Groups and U.S. Foreign Policy," 6. See also Z. A. Kruszewski, "The Polish American Congress, East-West Issues, and the

Formulation of American Foreign Policy," in *Ethnic Groups and U.S. Foreign Policy*, ed. Mohammed E. Ahrari (New York: Greenwood, 1987), 83–100.

24. Anna D. Jaroszynska-Kirchmann, *The Exile Mission: The Polish Political Diaspora and Polish Americans, 1939–1956* (Athens: Ohio University Press, 2004). See also John J. Bukowczyk, *And My Children Did Not Know Me: A History of the Polish-Americans* (Bloomington: Indiana University Press, 1987), 85–104.

25. John Snetsinger, *Truman, the Jewish Vote, and the Creation of Israel* (Stanford, CA: Hoover Institution Press, 1974); Michael Joseph Cohen, *Truman and Israel* (Berkeley: University of California Press, 1990); Hasia R. Diner, *We Remember with Reverence and Love: American Jews and the Myth of Silence After the Holocaust, 1945–1962* (New York: New York University Press, 2009), 311–320.

26. Herbert Druks, *The Uncertain Friendship: The U.S. and Israel from Roosevelt to Kennedy* (Westport, CT: Greenwood, 2001); Steven T. Rosenthal, *Irreconcilable Differences: The Waning of the American Jewish Love Affair with Israel* (Hanover, NH: University Press of New England, 2001); Gabriel Sheffer, "Loyalty and Criticism in the Relations between World Jewry and Israel," *Israel Studies* 17 (Summer 2012): 77–85; John J. Mearsheimer and Stephen M. Walt, *The Israel Lobby and U.S. Foreign Policy* (New York: Farrar, Straus and Giroux, 2007), 8; David M. Paul and Rachel Anderson Paul, *Ethnic Lobbies and US Foreign Policy* (Boulder, CO: Lynne Rienner, 2009), 27–28, 136–141.

27. Gerald Eugene Poyo, *"With All, and for the Good of All": The Emergence of Popular Nationalism in the Cuban Communities of the United States, 1848–1898* (Durham, NC: Duke University Press, 1989); Louis A. Pérez, *Cuba and the United States: Ties of Singular Intimacy* (1990; 3rd ed., Athens: University of Georgia Press, 2003), 77–81.

28. Richard R. Fagen, Richard A. Brody, and Thomas J. O'Leary, *Cubans in Exile: Disaffection and Revolution* (Stanford, CA: Stanford University Press, 1968); María Cristina García, *Havana USA: Cuban Exiles and Cuban Americans in South Florida, 1959–1994* (Berkeley: University of California Press, 1996), 7–8. 120–168; Susan Eva Eckstein, *The Immigrant Divide: How Cuban Americans Changed the US and Their Homeland* (New York: Routledge, 2009), 88–126.

29. Shain, *Marketing the American Creed Abroad*, 35–36; Robert G. Weisbord, *Ebony Kinship: Africa, Africans, and the Afro-American* (Westport, CT: Greenwood, 1973), 89–114; Penny M. Von Eschen, *Race against Empire: Black Americans and Anticolonialism, 1937–1957* (Ithaca, NY: Cornell University Press, 1997), 1–2, 7–21; DeConde, *Ethnicity, Race and American Foreign Policy*, 105–108; Brenda Gayle Plummer, "The Afro-American Response to the Occupation of Haiti, 1915–1934," *Phylon* 43, 2 (Spring 1982): 125–143. For the conflict over Mandela's comments, see García, *Havana USA*, 212.

30. Shain, *Marketing the American Creed Abroad*, 84. For a sampling of recent work on this topic, see *The African American Voice in U.S. Foreign Policy Since World War II*, ed. Michael L. Krenn (New York: Garland, 1998), Mary L. Dudziak, *Cold War Civil Rights: Race and the Image of American Democracy* (Princeton, NJ: Princeton University Press, 2000), and Francis Njubi Nesbitt, *Race for Sanctions: African Americans against Apartheid, 1946–1994* (Bloomington: Indiana University Press, 2004).

31. For the growth of ethnic activism with the end of the Cold War, see especially Smith, *Foreign Attachments*, 64–76. For the potential impact of the "war on terror," see Robert M. Entman, *Projections of Power: Framing News, Public Opinion, and U.S. Foreign Policy* (Chicago: University of Chicago Press, 2003).

32. Andrew J. Wilson, *Irish America and the Ulster Conflict, 1968–1995* (Washington, DC: Catholic University of America Press, 1995); Conor O'Clery, *The Greening of the White House: The Inside Story of How America Tried to Bring Peace to Ireland* (Dublin: Gill & Macmillan, 1996); Shain, *Marketing the American Creed Abroad*, 92–131; Paul and Paul. *Ethnic Lobbies and US Foreign Policy*, 50–53.

33. Paul Y. Watanabe, "Asian-Americans and U.S.-Asia Relations," in *Ethnic Identity Groups and U.S. Foreign Policy*, 135–136; Yen Le Espiritu, *Asian American Panethnicity: Bridging Institutions and Identities* (Philadelphia: Temple University Press, 1992), 30; Paul and Paul. *Ethnic Lobbies and US Foreign Policy*, 37–41; Kim Geron, et al., "Asian Pacific Americans' Social Movements and Interest Groups," *PS: Political Science & Politics* 34 (2001): 619–624; Jason A. Kirk, "Indian-Americans and the U.S.–India Nuclear Agreement: Consolidation of an Ethnic Lobby?" *Foreign Policy Analysis* 4 (July 2008): 275–300.

34. David G. Gutiérrez, *Walls and Mirrors: Mexican Americans, Mexican Immigrants, and the Politics of Ethnicity* (Berkeley: University of California Press, 1995); Juan Gómez-Quiñones, *Chicano Politics: Reality and Promise, 1940–1990* (Albuquerque: University of New Mexico Press, 1990).

35. For a sampling of important work in this burgeoning field, see Michael Jones-Correa, "Under Two Flags: Dual Nationality in Latin America and Its Consequences for Naturalization in the United States," *International Migration Review* 35 (2001): 997–1029, and *Dual Citizenship in Global Perspective: From Unitary to Multiple Citizenship*, ed. Thomas Faist and Peter Kivisto (New York: Palgrave Macmillan, 2007). For a good summary of the main factors shaping the growing acceptance of dual citizenship, see Miriam Feldblum, "Managing Membership: New Trends in Citizenship and Nationality Policy," in *From Migrants to Citizens: Membership in a Changing World*, ed. T. Alexander Aleinikoff and Douglas B. Klusmeyer (Washington, DC: Carnegie Endowment for International Peace, 2000), 475–499.

36. T. Alexander Aleinikoff and Douglas B. Klusmeyer, "Plural Nationality: Facing the Future in a Migratory World," in *Citizenship Today: Global Perspectives and Practices*, ed. T. Alexander Aleinikoff and Douglas B. Klusmeyer (Washington, DC: Carnegie Endowment for International Peace, 2001), 63, 79; Peter J. Spiro, *Beyond Citizenship: American Identity After Globalization* (New York: Oxford University Press, 2008).

37. José Itzigsohn, "Migration and Transnational Citizenship in Latin America: The Cases of Mexico and the Dominican Republic," in *Dual Citizenship in Global Perspective*. 113–134; Peter Kivisto, "Conclusion: The Boundaries of Citizenship in a Transnational Age," in *Dual Citizenship in Global Perspective*, 283; Reed Ueda, "Immigration in Global Historical Perspective," in *The New Americans: A Guide to Immigration Since 1965*, ed. Mary C. Waters, Reed Ueda, and Helen B. Marrow (Cambridge, MA: Harvard University Press, 2007), 22.

38. John Snetsinger, "Race and Ethnicity," in *Encyclopedia of American Foreign Policy*, ed. Richard Dean Burns, Alexander DeConde, and Fredrik Logevall, 2nd ed. (New York: Scribner's, 2002) 3: 290. Dufoix, *Diasporas* 93; Zlatko Skrbis, *Long-Distance Nationalism: Diasporas, Homelands and Identities* (Aldershot, UK: Ashgate, 1999); Øivind Fuglerud, *Life on the Outside: The Tamil Diaspora and Long-Distance Nationalism* (London: Pluto, 1999).

Bibliography

Ahrari, Mohammed E., ed. *Ethnic Groups and U.S. Foreign Policy*. New York: Greenwood, 1987.

Ambrosio, Thomas, ed. *Ethnic Identity Groups and U.S. Foreign Policy*. Westport, CT: Praeger, 2002.

Brundage, David. *Irish Nationalists in America: The Politics of Exile, 1798–1998*. New York: Oxford University Press, 2016.

Cannistraro, Philip V. *Blackshirts in Little Italy: Italian Americans and Fascism, 1921–1929*. West Lafayette, IN: Bordighera, 1999.

Collet, Christian, and Pei-te Lien, eds. *The Transnational Politics of Asian Americans*. Philadelphia: Temple University Press, 2009.

DeConde, Alexander. *Ethnicity, Race, and American Foreign Policy: A History*. Boston: Northeastern University Press, 1992.

Dufoix, Stéphane. *Diasporas*. Berkeley: University of California Press, 2008.

Eckstein, Susan Eva. *The Immigrant Divide: How Cuban Americans Changed the US and Their Homeland*. New York: Routledge, 2009.

Espiritu, Yen Le. *Asian American Panethnicity: Bridging Institutions and Identities*. Philadelphia: Temple University Press, 1992.

Faist, Thomas, and Peter Kivisto, eds. *Dual Citizenship in Global Perspective: From Unitary to Multiple Citizenship*. New York: Palgrave Macmillan, 2007.

Gabaccia, Donna R. *Foreign Relations: American Immigration in Global Perspective*. Princeton, NJ: Princeton University Press, 2012.

García, María Cristina. *Havana USA: Cuban Exiles and Cuban Americans in South Florida, 1959–1994*. Berkeley: University of California Press, 1996.

Gerson, Louis L. *The Hyphenate in Recent American Politics and Diplomacy*. Lawrence: University of Kansas Press, 1964.

Gutiérrez, David G. *Walls and Mirrors: Mexican Americans, Mexican Immigrants, and the Politics of Ethnicity*. Berkeley: University of California Press, 1995.

Jacobson, Matthew Frye. *Special Sorrows: The Diasporic Imagination of Irish, Polish, and Jewish Immigrants in the United States*. 1995; Berkeley: University of California Press, 2002.

Jaroszynska-Kirchmann, Anna D. *The Exile Mission: The Polish Political Diaspora and Polish Americans, 1939–1956*. Athens: Ohio University Press, 2004.

Jones-Correa, Michael. *Between Two Nations: The Political Predicament of Latinos in New York City*. Ithaca: Cornell University Press, 1998.

Jones, Maldwyn A. *The Old World Ties of American Ethnic Groups*. London: H.K. Lewis, 1976.

Kazal, Russell A. *Becoming Old Stock: The Paradox of German-American Identity*. Princeton, NJ: Princeton University Press, 2004.

Krenn, Michael L., ed. *The African American Voice in U.S. Foreign Policy Since World War II*. New York: Garland Pub, 1998.

Miller, Kerby A. *Emigrants and Exiles: Ireland and the Irish Exodus to North America*. New York: Oxford University Press, 1985.

Nesbitt, Francis Njubi. *Race for Sanctions: African Americans against Apartheid, 1946–1994*. Bloomington: Indiana University Press, 2004.

O'Grady, Joseph P., ed. *The Immigrants' Influence on Wilson's Peace Policies*. Lexington: University of Kentucky Press, 1967.

Paul, David M., and Rachel Anderson Paul. *Ethnic Lobbies and US Foreign Policy*. Boulder, CO: Lynne Rienner, 2009.

Rosenthal, Steven T. *Irreconcilable Differences: The Waning of the American Jewish Love Affair with Israel.* Hanover, NH: University Press of New England, 2001.

Said, Abdul Aziz, ed. *Ethnicity and U.S. Foreign Policy.* New York: Praeger, 1977.

Shain, Yossi. *Marketing the American Creed Abroad: Diasporas in the U.S. and Their Homelands.* Cambridge, UK: Cambridge University Press, 1999.

Smith, Tony. *Foreign Attachments: The Power of Ethnic Groups in the Making of American Foreign Policy.* Cambridge, MA: Harvard University Press, 2000.

Von Eschen, Penny M. *Race against Empire: Black Americans and Anticolonialism, 1937–1957.* Ithaca, NY: Cornell University Press, 1997.

CHAPTER 22

···

HISTORIANS AND SOCIOLOGISTS DEBATE TRANSNATIONALISM

···

PETER KIVISTO

DURING the early 1930s, approximately 25,000 Finns from Finland and North America migrated to Karelia, a region of the Soviet Union that abuts the eastern border of Finland and is home to an ethnic population whose language is related to Finnish. The Finns' labor was actively cultivated by Soviet officials who were intent on developing Karelia's lumber industry and knew that this could not happen without a growing supply of workers, at least a segment of which should possess relevant skills. In the case of the 6000 Americans and 2000 Canadians—both immigrants and their second generation offspring—who made the journey, the organization responsible for recruitment and organizing the move was known as Soviet Karelian Technical Assistance, run by two Finnish American communists who worked closely with the ranking Finn in the Kremlin hierarchy.

These migrants held leftist political views, but membership in the Communist Party was not a prerequisite for acceptance. However, in addition to being healthy and exhibiting a willingness to work in difficult circumstances, applicants were required to provide a reference from an official of a communist-affiliated organization. Not surprisingly, conservative Church Finns were not targeted by recruiters. But neither were non-Finnish political leftists. There was much talk and published commentary within the North American Finnish community about "Karelian fever," the excitement exhibited by those attracted to the prospect of assisting in the building of the Labor Republic. For many commentators, this collective enthusiasm indicated that ideological factors contributed significantly to the decision to emigrate. At the same time, the ethnic character of the move led others to stress the role of a shared culture in shaping the decision. Without discounting either of these as partial accounts of the motivating causes, the evidence to date suggests that these two factors played a less substantial role than did the quest for economic security and opportunity. In short, those caught up in Karelian fever were first and foremost labor migrants in search of a better life. Or, in other words, their motives for departing North America as the Great Depression took hold were the same as their reason for settling in locales such as Michigan, Minnesota, and Ontario in the first place.

This is borne out by the fact that once they discovered how undeveloped and oppressive conditions were in Karelia, Finns made known their disenchantment and within a few years at least 1500 North Americans had exited the Soviet Union.[1] Others would do so later—those who wisely had not given up their passports. It is unknown exactly how many followed, but some estimates put the figure as high as 40 percent.[2] For those who remained, dark times were to follow as Soviet officials redefined a group once seen as invited workers as bourgeois nationalist enemies of the state. Beginning in 1934, an explicit campaign to challenge "Finnish nationalism" was launched, part of which demanded that immigrants acquire Soviet citizenship and assimilate into Russian culture. When the authorities deemed many Finns to be recalcitrant, freedom of movement—always in short supply—was curtailed. A purge began in earnest, which included widespread arrests, deportations to far-flung prison camps, and executions— the exact numbers of which are still a matter of considerable uncertainty, though there is general consensus that Finns were proportionally a highly victimized group during the Stalinist purges.[3]

These Finnish leftists were engaged in transnational practices before the term came into fashion. This example points to the need to explore both here and there, which in a case involving Canada, Finland, the Soviet Union, and the United States, makes it necessary to recognize the complex matrix of border crossing social space that frames both the patterns of mobility and the structures of immobility evident in all those events from the original movement out of Finland to North America, through the period of Karelian fever, and including the aftermath.

WHAT WE TALK ABOUT WHEN WE TALK ABOUT TRANSNATIONALISM

Moving from A to B, whether that involves moving across town, across the country, or crossing the borders of nation states, makes necessary entering into a sustained process of navigation and negotiation as one comes to terms with the new "here." At the same time, coming to terms with what is now "there" also involves navigation and negotiation, this time with a former way of life and with people who remain (at least for the time being) behind.[4] In the end, the outcomes of the duality of navigating and negotiating with here and there varies considerably, based on a range of factors such as what Amartya Sen would call the capabilities of the movers; the socioeconomic, political, and cultural realities of both here and there; the responses to movers by those who stayed and by those who claim the new here as their own, including, of course, the role of state actors; and the nature and range of the power differentials that structure patterns of social interaction. To add yet another layer of complexity to the picture, it is generally not certain precisely when or if the end—the termination—of the process occurs.

Since the early 1990s, efforts have been made to create various theoretical models or conceptual grids that are intended to capture how immigrants interact over time with and relate to various actors and institutions in both the receiving and the sending country, and in some instances to co-ethnics elsewhere as well. These efforts have been framed under the rubric "transnationalism," a term that was introduced into immigration studies in the early 1990s.[5] The relative newness of the term can be seen by the fact that when Silvia Pedraza-Bailey drew her conceptual map of immigration research in 1990, she discussed indications of interest in "the impact of emigration on sending societies" in order to provide analyses of the "total process of migration."[6] She referred to this as one of her map's "blue highways," by which she meant one of the back roads. She noted in passing that in efforts to conceptualize this total process, one scholar, Roger Rouse, had "proposed that we reconceptualize it as a 'transnational migrant circuit.' "[7]

The First Phase: Defining Transnational Migration

A major road construction project commenced the same year that Pedraza-Bailey's presented her map in the form of a conference organized by Nina Glick Schiller, Linda Basch, and Cristina Szanton Blanc and co-sponsored by the New York Academy of Sciences, the Wenner-Gren Foundation, and the Institute for the Study of Man. The publication of the conference proceedings 2 years later marked a watershed event in the subsequent evolution of the concept.[8]

The term "transnationalism" was used earlier in somewhat different contexts, only one of which addressed the topic of immigration: Randolph Bourne's essay on "transnational America." However, what Bourne had in mind was quite different from this new formulation, for his concern was with the role that immigrants might play in revitalizing a national culture that he feared had grown anemic.[9] During the 1920s, the term "transnational economy" was used by some economists as essentially a synonym for international economy, while five decades later political scientists Robert Keohane and Joseph Nye used the idea of transnational relations to stress the growth of the international interdependency of nations.[10] In short, what Glick Schiller and her colleagues had in mind was a novel concept that was in fundamental ways unconnected to these earlier uses of the term.

Transnational immigration was depicted as a new phenomenon that had arisen during the latter part of the twentieth century, a type of migration that served to distinguish it from earlier migrations. In particular, the proponents of this new concept contended that immigrants who settled in the United States during the Great Migration that began around 1880 were *not* transnational migrants. Rather, they were immigrants who left their homelands with the full expectation of making a clean break from their respective nations of origin, which was in turn reinforced by the receiving society's assimilative demands. In contrast, contemporary immigrants were depicted as evidencing a desire to establish new social relations in the receiving country while simultaneously maintaining ties to the country of origin. As such, rather than describing them as immigrants, Glick Schiller and her colleagues suggested that they should be seen as transmigrants.[11] If immigrants are people for whom mobility is seen as a singular event in a life course characterized primarily by permanent settlement, first there and later here, transmigrants are prepared to be permanently mobile. In their early formulation, no distinctions were made among the groups of the Great Migration. Thus, the circular migration characteristic of Italians versus the tendency of Jews to leave the old world behind was ignored.

Transnational migration is located in the larger context of what Saskia Sassen has described as the "global footlooseness of corporate capital."[12] Just as capitalism, with the rise of a transnational capitalist class, is less and less bound by the constraints of nation-states, so too are transmigrants. In other words, transnationalism from above is countered by transnationalism from below. Critical of what they see as the economic reductionism of Wallerstein's world systems theory, Basch, Glick Schiller, and Szanton Blanc nonetheless make clear that transnational migration is itself the product of global capitalism.[13] At the same time, the fluidity of transmigrant identities is seen as a form of resistance to "the global political and economic situations that engulf them. . . ."[14]

In accounting for the causal factors contributing to the shift from immigration in the past to transmigration at present, two were considered to be of primary importance: changes in communications and transportation technologies. In terms of the former, the letter from the Great Migration was replaced by telephone calls, e-mail and, more recently, Skype, while for the latter, the steamship was replaced by jet airliners. Thus, in contrast to what was described as the progressive attenuation of contact with the place of origin for immigrants in the past, today's migrants are in a position to take advantage of technological advances that make possible the perpetuation of a variety of networks—economic, political, religious, cultural, and kinship—across the boundaries of nation-states. This in turn signals the emergence of an alternative to assimilation—and cultural pluralism—for transnationalism was in this initial formulation construed as a new mode of incorporation, one that was thought likely to become the predominant mode, an assessment reiterated somewhat later by Stephen Castles when he wrote, "It is possible that transnational affiliations and consciousness will become the predominant form of migrant belonging in the future."[15]

Integrally linked to this sense that transnationalism was a novel form of inclusion was its advocates' embrace of the postnationalist idea that nation-states were becoming less consequential and capable of enforcing a singular ideal of national identity in the face of challenges to received notions of citizenship—seen for example in challenges to the Hague Convention's aversion to multiple citizenship—and in the emergence of an international human rights regime. The dramatic increase in dual citizenship is testimony to changes currently underway.[16]

All of this was based on very little empirical research. Rather than developing a research agenda that sought to determine whether transnational social fields exist and if so how durable they might be, the starting point tended to be based on the assumption that transnationalism was a pervasive and robust feature of contemporary migration. That being said, Glick Schiller and colleagues can be credited with launching what has become a rapidly evolving and perhaps not surprisingly often inchoate field, one that initially appeared to offer more than it could deliver, but nonetheless set the stage for thinking seriously about both how to frame the field of immigration studies and what transnationalism as a phenomenon might actually amount to. Journals were created such as *Identities, Diaspora: A Journal of Transnational Studies*, and *Global Networks* and research centers were established, the most prominent being the Oxford University Transnational Communities Programme. And the number of conferences, articles, and books focusing on themes concerning transnationalism proliferated. By the turn of the century, transnationalism had clearly arrived.

The Corrections

It was within the social sciences—anthropology and sociology in particular—that efforts to theorize transnationalism were rooted. Those historians who were prepared to engage this developing discourse were often inclined to be scholars who felt "an unease with nationalism and the nation-state"[17] or sought to repudiate "the tyranny of the national,"[18] but they also tended to have "limited tolerance for grand theories of global change."[19] Moreover, historians (and historical sociologists such as Nancy Foner, Peter Kivisto, and Ewa Morawska) were inclined to want to build on a scholarly tradition rather than embracing the approach of Glick Schiller and others that sought to affect a rupture with it in order to clear the path for articulating a novel paradigm.

Jon Gjerde succinctly captured the former position in his state of the field essay appropriately titled "New Growth on Old Vines." He contended, for example, that the "ethnic Turnerians" were transnationalists *avant la lettre* and recalled that Frank Thistlethwaite urged immigration historians to forge an approach that overcame the "salt water curtain."[20] While he found that a transnational perspective could have the salutary effect of expanding the horizon of immigration research to include the sending country as well as the receiving one, he nonetheless also thought that the old questions concerning the integration of immigrants and their offspring into the fabric of the receiving society persist.[21]

Alejandro Portes, a figure committed to building on the sociological tradition rather than repudiating it, agreed with Gjerde about the continuing need to consider the matter of immigrant incorporation. At the same time, he arrived at the view that transnationalism was a phenomenon that needed to be factored into the equation. Portes and colleagues called for the articulation of a middle-range theory of transnationalism, one that was more amenable to quantitative analysis than the initial version.[22] Rather than investigating transnational *social fields*, he pressed for exploring transnational *practices* such as travel back and forth to the homeland, remittances, and political, economic, and sociocultural engagements that involve cross border connections. Focusing

on the present, he, along with Luis Guarnizo and William Haller, sought to complement the ethnographic studies that constituted the bulk of research up to that point
with survey research based on data collected as part of the Comparative Immigrant
Entrepreneurship Project.

The study examined three immigrant groups in the United States that cannot be seen
as representative of the immigrant population writ large: Colombians, Dominicans,
and Salvadorans. But the findings are instructive insofar as they revealed that most
immigrants are not engaged in transnational practices, particularly if they are defined
in a manner that stresses ongoing routine activities rather than more sporadic involve-
ments. This was true of both political engagements[23] and transnational entrepreneurship, where the percentage of those involved in such activities regularly was in the single
digits.[24] This is not to suggest that transnationalism is necessarily of minor significance,
for Portes and his associates concluded that the impact of such practices on both those
who remained behind in the homeland and immigrants not directly involved in transnational activities might be substantial. Moreover, in contrast to the idea that transnationalism was a new mode of incorporation antithetical to assimilation, they posed the
possibility that the two might be capable of coexisting.[25]

This rethinking of the relationship between assimilation and transnationalism was
but an instance of a more general process of taking stock—of reconsidering and revising
what we talk about when we talk about transnationalism. Ewa Morawska considered
this author's attempt to represent "immigrant transnationalism as a form of ethnic-path
assimilation" to be "the first such attempt in the field."[26] If so, others quickly and quite
independently arrived at a similar conclusion. Peggy Levitt, Josh DeWind, and Steven
Vertovec, three of the more prominent proponents of transnationalism, concluded that
host society incorporation and transnationalism can occur simultaneously,[27] a position
that Glick Schiller would come to embrace, as well.[28]

The second major revision of the earliest articulation of migrant transnationalism
concerned the presumed novelty of the phenomenon. Critics were quick to point out
that the past/present distinction central to the earliest articulation of transnationalism
was empirically flawed, as one could find abundant evidence to indicate that transnationalism was a common feature of the last migratory wave.[29] This point was readily
conceded by transnationalism's proponents, though often with the proviso that developments in "transportation and communication technologies have made it possible
for immigrants to maintain more frequent, immediate and closer contact with their
home societies, and, in a real sense, have changed the very nature of transnational connections."[30] Those concerned that this argument skirted the border of technological
determination pointed out that the existence of a particular technological construct
does not determine if, how, when, and why it is used; rather uses are socially defined.[31]
In addition, there was insufficient attention paid to the digital divide. Nevertheless,
opened up was the prospect of past/present comparisons based on a shared assumption that transnationalism is not a qualitatively new phenomenon.[32] Finally, especially
in the wake of 9/11 and the resurgence of evidence for the continued potency of nation-
states—which still quite clearly sought to maintain a monopoly on the deployment of

violence—transnational theorists began to move beyond the postnational perspective by conceding that states remain significant features of transnational social fields.[33]

These revisions were often made with qualifiers. Moreover, although the concept became more deeply embedded in immigration studies, a widely agreed upon definition did not emerge. The term is relatively delimited in the hands of some, while it is quite elastic in the case of others. Portes can be seen as an example of the former, while Levitt and Glick Schiller are exponents of an expansive notion of transnationalism. This is reflected in their distinction between transnational being and belonging. Whereas they define being as consisting of "actual social relations and practices that individuals engage in," belonging "refers to practices that signal or enact an identity which demonstrates a conscious connection to a particular group." They cite as examples wearing a crucifix or Star of David, stressing that such actions are "symbolic but concrete visible actions."[34]

Why Levitt and Glick Schiller would want to disavow the idea that wearing such markers of religious identity are not symbolic acts is not on the surface obvious, but one reason may have to do with their desire to distance themselves from the possibility of developing a concept that could be seen as paralleling the one advanced by Herbert Gans in his classic essay on symbolic ethnicity, which predicted a progressive erosion of the ethnic factor in shaping the identities of the third and subsequent generations of European-origin immigrants. Symbolic ethnicity referred to a desire to feel ethnic without necessary behavioral consequences.[35] Levitt, for instance, has questioned those who consider transnationalism to be a first-generation phenomenon, destined to largely disappear as the children of immigrants come of age.[36] This is an example of the persistence of the assumption that transnationalism exists is fairly robust ways and that it is not likely to disappear. To the extent that this is an apt characterization of an underlying assumption shaping a considerable amount of transnational research, it suggests that the agenda calls for capturing instances of transnationalism, but not instances where it is not there, is not particularly robust, or may be in decline.

This is but one indication that transnationalism is embedded in immigration studies, but that despite the revisions to its original formulation it remains a contested concept. But, I would suggest, this needs to be qualified insofar as we distinguish transnationalism as a perspective from transnationalism as a phenomenon. As I will argue below, the former is more widely embraced, though not entirely unproblematically, while the latter is the primary locus of ongoing debate, and will likely be so in the future.

TRANSNATIONALISM AS A PERSPECTIVE

Historians and social scientists widely accept the idea that transnationalism is a perspective that has the potential to complement research that is framed by the parameters of the nation-state. As such, transnationalism is often depicted as an optic or a lens that affords researchers the ability to explore topics from a different angle of vision than when operating within the boundaries of the nation. Sven Beckert, one of the six participants in an *"AHR* Conversation on Transnational History," echoed this position by describing transnational history as a "way of seeing" that he thought was capable of addressing a wide range of topics from a variety of methodological approaches. He went on to suggest that while nation-states should remain of central importance, the virtue of transnational research is that it "pays attention to networks, processes, beliefs, and institutions that transcend these politically defined spaces."[37]

Some of the participants in the conversation expressed some skepticism about transnationalism. C. A. Bayly, for instance, thought that the term "transnationalism" was essentially a synonym for international history—but a synonym that is unduly restrictive.[38] Matthew Connelly contended that, "Transnational history has become a brand, to the point that some invoke the term and talk the talk when doing very conventional kinds of scholarship."[39] Despite such reservations, participants pointed to exemplary examples of scholarship framed in a transnational perspective, such as Paul Gilroy's *The Black Atlantic*.[40] Patricia Seed's assessment appeared reflective of the group as a whole when she concluded that transnational history was of value insofar as it supplemented—rather than attempted to supplant—more traditional local, regional, or state-level histories.[41] A curious feature of the conversation was that none of the participants was an immigration historian, but this general assessment was reiterated in another venue by one such historian, Donna Gabaccia, who while describing her first two books as written in a transnational mode, asserted that transnationalism could be readily grafted onto the existing paradigm of immigration history.[42]

A body of scholarship has emerged that reveals the virtues of a transnational approach. In terms of examining cross-border networks of immigrants who maintain an ongoing connection between here and there, two ethnographic works stand out as models. The first is Peggy Levitt's *The Transnational Villagers*, an account of the forging of kinship ties as well as religious and political networks that link the Dominican immigrants residing in Jamaica Plain, Boston to Miraflores, their village of origin.[43] The second is Robert Courtney Smith's *Mexican New York*, a 15-year study of a New York–based hometown association that has over time raised money and supervised numerous public improvements in a town Smith calls Ticuani, including paving and lighting the town square, building a primary and a secondary school, renovating a church damaged by an earthquake, and constructing a potable water system. Given the length of Smith's involvement with his subjects, he is able to offer a detailed and nuanced account of transnational practices while hinting at the potential limits to the connection over time and across generations (e.g., the second generation is not inclined to become involved in the hometown association).[44]

Two other studies of note advance our understanding of the admittedly underdeveloped field of emigration: Mark I. Choate's *Emigrant Nation* and David Fitzgerald's *A Nation of Emigrants*.[45] Both are state-centered works, with Choate's examining the varied ways—cultural, political, and social—that the Italian state sought to facilitate the construction of a transnational nationalism that linked the expatriate communities around the globe to the homeland, including locales such as the Americas where voluntary labor migrants had settled and in Italy's efforts at colonial expansion in North Africa. His particular focus is on the activities of the Italian government after the passage of the 1901 Law of Emigration, which signaled a shift that treated "emigration as an international expansion instead of an internal hemorrhage."[46] Fitzgerald undertakes a comparable analysis of the efforts of the Mexican state from the early twentieth century to the present to address the fact that one in ten of its citizens had moved north of the border. He traces the shift away from policies that sought to control or contain emigration to those that were designed to manage and maintain influence over their émigré population. In both instances, as Choate and Fitzgerald insightfully indicate, the actions of the two respective states were complemented by the activities of the Catholic church in both sending and receiving countries.

These and other empirical studies reveal the significance of expanding the frame of reference of traditional immigration research. Or, in short, they highlight the rationale for employing a transnational lens. But are they shaped by transnational theory? While some, such as the historians who took part in the *AHR* conversation, appear prepared to accept a perspective that is not a theory, others have sought to locate the perspective in terms of a theoretical framework. In doing so, two interrelated propositions have been developed. The first concerns the promotion of what has been described as a social field approach. The second is corrective in nature, seeking to redefine society in a manner that does not equate it with the nation-state, which is rooted in a critique of what has been defined as methodological nationalism.

While other transnational theorists have spoken about transnational social spaces or social formations, Levitt and Glick Schiller have preferred to use the idea of "social field," a term generally associated with Pierre Bourdieu, who viewed it as the structured space within which certain social relations play out, predicated on the types and combinations of capital responsible for defining the field. While fields contain a variety of institutions, Bourdieu tended not to stress them as much as he stressed the field as a site of struggle in contexts always characterized by differentials of power and access to resources. Struggles are expressions of agency on the part of actors, but rather than being conceived simply in terms of individual choices, such choices are structured by what he describes as "objective relations between positions."[47] Building on this perspective, Levitt and Glick Schiller contend that a social field is "a set of multiple interlocking networks of social relationships through which ideas, practices, and resources are unequally exchanged, organized, and transformed."[48]

A transnational social field is simply one in which those networks cut across two or more national borders. As such, it constitutes an analytic framework for raising and attempting to answer a variety of empirical question about any particular research site, such as the nature of the field's objective positions, the size, density, scope, and function of any particular network, the number of networks at play, the resources potentially available, the institutional character of the field, and the level of actor embeddedness in it.

If there is an impediment to thinking in terms of transnational social fields, it is presumed to be the deleterious consequences of what has been dubbed "methodological nationalism." According to Andreas Wimmer and Nina Glick Schiller, there are three interrelated forms that methodological nationalism takes. The first, they contend, is evident when theorists of modernity ignore the fact that modern societies have arisen in the context of national communities. Nations and nationalism are, in other words, invisible. The second is the result of taking for granted nationalism in its various manifestations, thereby naturalizing the nation-state. Rather than being invisible, nations and nationalism become part of the familiar furniture of the intellectual mindset, and thus are viewed uncritically.[49] Though the term "methodological nationalism" has been patterned after the term "methodological individualism," it is different insofar as it is concerned with an unreflective acceptance of empirical circumstances rather than, as with methodological individualism with what Johann Arnason describes as "a controllable choice of premises."[50] I would simply add two points. First, the broad stroke criticism of theorists from the classic era of Durkheim and Weber through the era of Parsonian thought up to the present with figures such as Bourdieu, Habermas, and Luhmann is made possible by a reading that is at best injudicious. Second, the issue is not in actuality a methodological one, but rather one of vision or focus.

This is precisely what is involved in Wimmer and Glick Schiller's third form, which they characterize as territorial limitation, by which they mean "the territorialization of social science imaginary and the reduction of the analytical focus to the boundaries of the nation-state." The result is a perspective that demarcated the boundaries of the empirical world to be considered as those of the nation-state, which became a "container society."[51] Moving beyond a position in immigration studies that circumscribed the empirical framework to the borders of immigrant-receiving countries is uncontroversial, but it leaves unanswered the question about how best to locate nation-states within a transnational framework. Matthew Frye Jacobson graphically depicted the nation state in an era of transnational approaches as "the gum from the sidewalk that we can never quite scrape from our shoes."[52] One gets the sense that some proponents of transnationalism, particularly those who do not make a clear distinction between is and ought, or between scholarship and partisanship, really do want to scrape the nation-state away. However, near the end of their article, Wimmer and Glick Schiller offer a cautionary comment by observing that the continuing significance of nation-states and nationalism makes it essential to factor this reality into transnational theory and research.[53]

At present, transnationalism in immigration studies remains a perspective in search of a theory. Efforts have been made to move beyond the very general idea of viewing social relations outside of the confines of nation-states via the consideration of transnational social fields, but they remain chiefly at the level of constructing typologies of varied forms of transnationalism predicated on considerations of a range of factors from the global to the local (the most highly developed example being that of Morawska.[54] However, as Wimmer and Glick Schiller rightly understood the situation, while it is important to wrestle with the complexity and the sheer magnitude created by transnationalism's more expansive perspective, the goal is to create a theoretical framework that "necessarily limits the range of possible interpretations, as well as the empirical domains that can be meaningfully interpreted. To understand means to reduce complexity."[55] As such, a satisfactory theory of transnationalism remains very definitely a work in progress.

TRANSNATIONALISM AS PHENOMENON

Evidence of transnationalism past and present abounds. Few would dispute this fact. How that evidence is sifted and interpreted—particularly in light of the current lack of a coherent theoretical model to frame empirical research—becomes the source of contention. The real questions become: how significant a phenomenon is transnationalism and how durable over time is it likely to be? Proponents such as Glick Schiller, Levitt, Portes, and others contend that it is a singularly significant feature of contemporary immigration and they tend to think that it will persist as the second generation comes of age. Skeptics question one or both of these assessments, none so insistently as Roger Waldinger, beginning with an article coauthored with David Fitzgerald, "Transnationalism in Question."[56]

Part of Waldinger's unease with the phenomenon of transnationalism as presented by its key spokespersons parallels the criticisms discussed earlier. In addition, he calls into question whether the term itself is a misnomer, suggesting that a more apt term might be "bi-localism,"[57] which is akin to Elliott Barkan's brief on behalf of the idea of "trans-localism" as a counterpart to transnationalism that entails "moderate and periodic, somewhat causal and uneven" homeland connections.[58] Second, Waldinger contends that contemporary immigrants are overwhelmingly characterized by ethnic particularism, whereas fairly large numbers of immigrants during the Great Migration viewed themselves as "workers of the world"—as did the Finns who departed from the center of the capitalist metropole to Karelia after the cessation of that migration.[59] Third, he concludes that transnational connections are not only quite limited, but also fragile. In terms of their limited nature, he notes that only a small minority of migrants engage in a high degree of transnational relations.[60] In terms of fragility, he points to hometown associations, which have elicited considerable interest in the literature, portraying them as being characteristically subject to internal conflicts, which undermines their long-term sustainability.[61] Finally, Waldinger contends that transnationalism is not a theory, but rather ought to be viewed as a process, and in this regard he sees it as akin to assimilation.[62]

However, Waldinger is not simply a critic. Rather, he has developed an argument that is designed to offer an alternative way of thinking about migration than the commonly held approaches toward both transnationalism and assimilation. In his estimation, proponents of both transnationalism and assimilation share a common shortcoming, which is that they offer explanations of the social processes they seek to understand without considering the political. Despite lip service to the continuing salience of the state in the revisions of transnationalism, he contends that the state has not really been taken seriously; furthermore, inattentiveness to the state has been a consistent feature of the influential approach to assimilation promoted by Richard Alba and Victor Nee.[63]

Borders matter and states are the arbiters of who has a legitimate right to cross their borders either to exit or enter and who does not, and in the case of the receiving society, in determining who will and who will not be given the opportunity to become a member of the national community, while the citizenry expresses its views about the expectations it has for newcomers to prove themselves as worthy and loyal members of the polity. Succinctly put, "States seek to bound the societies they enclose: they strive to regulate membership in the national collectivity as well as movement across territorial borders, often using illiberal means to fulfill liberal ends."[64] Taking issue with the portrayal of the global economy as borderless when it comes to would-be migrants seeking to improve their lives, he points to the fact that states are willing to go to extraordinary lengths to control their borders in the interest of preventing unwanted migrants from "crashing the gates."[65] The contemporary immigration policies of the United States, like those of every other liberal democracy, are exclusionary—seeking to preserve the binary divide between insiders and outsiders.[66]

This leads to his understanding of the role of the state vis-à-vis those on the inside. The overarching state interest remains the same: to maintain control over a population. In the case of those residing within the boundaries of the nation, the state seeks to "cage" that population, "constraining social ties beyond the territorial divide, while reorienting activities toward the interior."[67] Viewing migration as first and foremost a political phenomenon, states strive to transform foreigners into nationals. Unlike assimilation, which stresses the decline of the ethnic factor and the entry of newcomers over time into the societal mainstream, Waldinger describes the transformation as a form of "political resocialization."[68] Assimilation entails the emergence of new patterns of relatedness between newcomers and established residents in which the former are brought into the orbit of the latter's social world, in some instances on more-or-less equal terms and in other instances in segmented fashion. Being transformed into a national of the receiving society involves acquiring an identity that makes people insiders, a process that simultaneously distinguishes them from outsiders, including citizens of their former homeland. This happens regardless of whether the newcomers end up in the societal mainstream or on the margins.[69]

The internal and external aspects of national identity need not necessarily operate according to the same ideological script. Waldinger thinks that at present the US is becoming increasingly inclusive internally, while remaining externally exclusive. This was not always so, for historically the nation was exclusive both internally and externally, the former being seen most obviously in the extended effort to exclude African Americans from full societal membership, first during slavery and then during the Jim Crow era. Internal exclusivity shaped perceptions of national identity, defined in terms of race (white), ethnic origin (Anglo-Saxon), and religion (Protestant). This led to demands for newcomers to assimilate by shedding their pasts and transforming themselves into WASP clones. That the cultural elites of earlier periods of American history were confident about their capacity to so transform immigrants, for an extended period from the founding of the republic up to the beginning of the twentieth century, when a more pessimistic view of the incorporative capacity of the nation took hold, the nation's immigration laws were inclusive in terms of religion and national origin.[70] Waldinger does not spend time addressing shifts in immigration laws, because his central point is simply that once national identity took shape, so too did the distinction between citizens and aliens.

While this particular binary has not changed over time, the internal change that has transpired over the course of the past century has resulted in a pluralistic rendering of national identity in which ethnic groups have come to be seen as a legitimate part of the political and cultural landscape. At the same time, Waldinger concurs with David Hollinger's post–ethnic America thesis, which stresses the options people have in regard to ethnic attachments, ranging from distancing to embracing.[71] The result is that the nation has witnessed a shift from internal exclusivity in the past to inclusivity, but one in which the significance of individualism tends to preclude the possibility of the hardening of ethnic group affiliations and allegiances. Put another way, ethnic pluralism has been recognized at the same time that its salience has declined, particularly vis-à-vis national identity. The result is liberal nationalism, which ought to be viewed as "the exclusionary doctrine best suited to the normal, multicultural American of the early twenty-first century, and therefore the view most likely to be internalized by the new and candidate Americans of our times."[72]

Transnationalism's Future

It is a safe bet to predict that a transnational perspective will inform immigration research in significant ways in the future, and it will be employed without controversy. The idea of seeing the whole picture—of viewing migration both in terms of emigration and immigration—opens up new avenues of scholarship the benefits of which we are only now beginning to see. That being said, such an expanded scope of inquiry presents challenges, not the least of which are the costs involved in the need to pay attention to "there" to the same extent that immigration studies has traditionally paid attention to "here." Such challenges are not so much conceptual as they are practical and operational.

But what about transnationalism as a phenomenon? Waldinger's position can be read, not as he suggests as an alternative to the general perspective of the key proponents of transnationalism, but rather as a complementary or revised version. He is quite correct that despite claims to take seriously the role of the state, to date those he is critical of have failed to do so. And it is equally true that his parallel claim about the sole emphasis on the social at the expense of any consideration of the political within the long history of thinking about assimilation, from Park to Alba, is on target. The state plays a singularly consequential role in determining migratory flows, including whether or not there is an ability to move back and forth with relative ease. As such, its actions will determine if and for how long transnationalism is a viable option.

In Waldinger's discussions, he, at least implicitly, describes the current situation in terms of states and citizens mutually reinforcing any particular stance on potential newcomers. However, the reality is more complex since states do not always act without internal tensions and conflicts and the opinions of citizens are often divided. Perhaps a starting point for a more empirically adequate perspective might derive from John Higham, who while viewing the nation-state as an entity that "will remain for a long time the strongest political structure in the world," nevertheless considered it to be "under siege" with "the abounding trust it once enjoyed eroding," the net result being that though strong it is "less capable of dominating the subgroups within their boundaries."[73] This viewpoint offers a corrective to Waldinger's account insofar as it grants a level of agency to ordinary people—both citizens and immigrants—who have the capacity to question the legitimacy of the state and can therefore potentially undermine, subvert, or resist its ability to "cage."

Waldinger correctly contends that transnationalism ought to be conceived as a *"normally* recurring phenomenon" that is episodic rather than a permanent characteristic of contemporary immigrants.[74] While no one example can suffice to make a compelling argument on this score, the radical Finns who moved first to North America and then to Karelia and then for some back to Finland and/or North America exhibited a desire to transcend the nation in the interest of international worker solidarity, and thus they are prime candidates to be designated transmigrants. Indeed, their propensity to move across international borders persisted over a span of more than three decades. But it came to an end.

Notes

1. Irina Takala, "From the Frying Pan into the Fire," *Finnish Studies* 8 (2004): 120.
2. Reino Kero, *Neuvosto-Karjalaa: Pohjois-Amerikan Suomalaiset Tekniikan Tuojina 1930-luvun Neuvosto-Karjalaasa* (Helsinki: Societas Historica Finlandiae, 1983), 230.
3. Michael Gelb, "'Karelian Fever': The Finnish Immigrant Community during Stalin's Purges," *Europe-Asia Studies* 45 (1993): 1091–1116.
4. Roger Waldinger, "Between 'Here' and 'There': Immigrant Cross-border Activities and Loyalties," *International Migration Review* 42 (2008): 3–29.
5. Peggy Levitt and B. Nadya Jaworsky, "Transnational Migration Studies: Past Developments and Future Trends," *Annual Review of Sociology* 33 (2007): 129–156; Peter Kivisto and Thomas Faist, *Beyond a Border: The Causes and Consequences of Contemporary Immigration* (Thousand Oaks, CA: Pine Forge/Sage, 2010), 127–159.
6. Silvia Pedraza-Bailey, "Immigration Research: A Conceptual Map," *Social Science History* 14 (1990): 55–56.
7. Ibid., 59.
8. Nina Glick Schiller, Linda Basch, and Cristina Szanton Blanc, eds., *Toward a Transnational Perspective on Migration* (New York: New York Academy of Sciences, 1992); see also Linda Basch, Nina Glick Schiller, and Cristina Szanton Blanc, ed., *Nations Unbound: Transnational Projects, Postcolonial Predicaments, and Deterritorialized Nation-States* (Basel, Switzerland: Gordon and Breach, 1994; Nina Glick Schiller, Linda Basch, and Cristina Szanton Blanc, "From Immigrant to Transmigrant: Theorizing Transnational Migration," *Anthropological Quarterly* 68 (1995): 48–63; and Nina Glick Schiller, "The Situation of Transnational Studies," *Identities* 4 (1997): 155–166.
9. Randolph Bourne, "Trans-national America," *The Atlantic Monthly* (July, 1916: 86–97).
10. Robert O. Keohane and Joseph S. Nye, *Power and Interdependence: World Politics in Transition* (Boston: Little Brown, 1977).
11. Glick Schiller, et al., *Toward a Transnational Perspective*, 1 and Glick Schiller, "The Situation of Transnational Studies," 158.

12. Saskia Sassen, *Losing Control? Sovereignty in an Age of Globalization* (New York: Columbia University Press, 1996), 6.

13. Basch, et al., *Nations Unbound*, 30–34.

14. Glick Schiller, et al., *Toward a Transnational Perspective*, 11.

15. Stephen Castles, "Migration and Community Formation under Conditions of Globalization," *International Migration Review* 36 (2002): 1158.

16. David Jacobson, *Rights across Borders: Immigration and the Decline of Citizenship* (Baltimore: The Johns Hopkins University Press, 1996); Yasmin Soysal, *Limits of Citizenship: Migrants and Postnational Membership in Europe* (Chicago: University of Chicago Press, 1994); Kivisto and Faist, *Beyond a Border,"* 234–245.

17. Michael McGreer, "The Price of the 'New Transnational History,'" *The American Historical Review* 96 (1991): 1066; see also David Thelen, "The Nation and Beyond: Transnational Perspectives on United States History," *The Journal of American History* 86 (1999): 965–975.

18. Donna R. Gabaccia, "Is Everywhere Nowhere? Nomads, Nations, and the Immigrant Paradigm of United States History," *The American Historical Review* 86 (1999): 1115, quoting Gérard Noiriel.

19. Ibid., 1123.

20. Jon Gjerde, "New Growth on Old Vines: The State of the Field: The Social History of Immigration to and Ethnicity in the United States," *Journal of American Ethnic History* 18 (1999): 44 and 47.

21. Ibid., 53–55.

22. Alejandro Portes, Luis Eduardo Guarnizo, and Patricia Landolt, "The Study of Transnationalism: Pitfalls and Promise of an Emergent Research Field," *Ethnic and Racial Studies* 22 (1999): 217–237.

23. Luis Eduardo Guarnizo, Alejandro Portes, and William Haller, "Assimilation and Transnationalism: Determinants of Transnational Political Action among Contemporary Migrants," *American Journal of Sociology* 108 (2003): 1211–1248.

24. Alejandro Portes, Luis Eduardo Guarnizo, and William Haller, "Transnational Entrepreneurs: An Alternative Form of Immigrant Economic Adaptation," *American Sociological Review* 67 (2002): 293.

25. Ibid., 295.

26. Ewa Morawska, "Disciplinary Agendas and Analytic Strategies of Research on Immigrant Transnationalism: Challenges of Interdisciplinary Knowledge," *International Migration Review* 37 (2003): 621; see Peter Kivisto, "Theorizing Transnational Immigration: A Critical Review of Current Efforts," *Ethnic and Racial Studies* 24 (2001): 549–577.

27. Peggy Levitt, Josh DeWind, and Steven Vertovec, "International Perspectives on Transnational Migration: An Introduction," *International Migration Review* 37 (2003): 567–571; see also Steven Vertovec, "Migrant Transnationalism and Modes of Transformation," *International Migration Review* 38 (2004): 970–1001.

28. Peggy Levitt and Nina Glick Schiller, "Conceptualizing Simultaneity: A Transnational Social Field Perspective on Society," *International Migration Review* 38 (2004): 1002.

29. Nancy Foner, "What's New about Transnationalism? New York Immigrants Today and at the Turn of the Century," *Diaspora* 6 (1997): 355–376; Ewa Morawska, "Immigrants, Transnationalism, and Ethnicization: A Comparison of This Great Wave and the Last," in *E Pluribus Unum? Contemporary and Historical Perspectives on Immigrant Incorporation*, eds. Gary Gerstle and John Mollenkopf, 175–212. New York: Russell Sage Foundation, 2001.

30. Nancy Foner, *In a New Land: A Comparative View of Immigration* (New York: New York University Press, 2005).
31. Peter Kivisto, "Social Spaces, Transnational Immigrant Communities, and the Politics of Incorporation," *Ethnicities* 3 (2003): 15–16.
32. Pyong Gap Min, "A Comparison of Post-1965 and Turn-of-the-Century Immigrants in Intergenerational Mobility and Cultural Transmission," *Journal of American Ethnic History* 18 (1999): 65–94.
33. Levitt, et al., "International Perspectives on Transnational Migration," 567.
34. Levitt and Glick Schiller, "Conceptualizing Simultaneity," 1010.
35. Herbert Gans, "Symbolic Ethnicity: The Future of Ethnic Groups and Cultures in America," *Ethnic and Racial Studies* 2 (1979): 1–20.
36. Peggy Levitt, "Roots and Routes: Understanding the Lives of the Second Generation Transnationally," *Journal of Ethnic and Migration Studies* 35 (2009): 1225–1242.
37. C.A. Bayly, Sven Beckert, Matthew Connelly, Isabel Hofmeyr, Wendy Kozol, and Patricia Seed, "*AHR* Conversation on Transnational History," *The American Historical Review* 111 (2006): 1459.
38. Ibid., 1442.
39. Ibid., 1447.
40. Paul Gilroy, *The Black Atlantic: Modernity and Double Consciousness* (London: Verso, 1993).
41. Bayly, et al., "*AHR* Conversation on Transnational History," 1463.
42. Gabaccia, "Is Everywhere Nowhere? 1117.
43. Peggy Levitt, *The Transnational Villagers* (Berkeley: University of California Press, 2001).
44. Robert Courtney Smith, *Mexican New York: Transnational Lives of New Immigrants* (Berkeley: University of California Press, 2006).
45. Mark I. Choate, *Emigrant Nation: The Making of Italy Abroad* (Cambridge: Harvard University Press, 2008); David Fitzgerald, *A Nation of Emigrants: How Mexico Manages Its Migration* (Berkeley: University of California Press, 2009).
46. Choate, *Emigrant Nation*, 50.
47. Pierre Bourdieu and Loïc Wacquant, *An Invitation to Reflexive Sociology* (Chicago: University of Chicago Press, 1992), 97.
48. Levitt and Glick Schiller, "Conceptualizing Simultaneity," 1009.
49. Andreas Wimmer and Nina Glick Schiller, "Methodological Nationalism and Beyond: Nation-State Building, Migration, and the Social Sciences," *Global Networks* 2 (2002): 302–308.
50. Johann P. Arnason, "An Interview with Johann P. Arnason: Critical Theory, Modernity, Civilizations, and Democracy" (interviewed by Paul Blokker and Gerard Delanty), *European Journal of Social Theory* 14 (2011): 125.
51. Wimmer and Glick Schiller, "Methodological Nationalism and Beyond," 307.
52. Matthew Frye Jacobson, "More 'Trans-', Less 'National,'" *Journal of American Ethnic History* 25 (2006): 74.
53. Wimmer and Glick Schiller, "Methodological Nationalism and Beyond," 326.
54. Ewa Morawska, *A Sociology of Immigration: (Re)Making Multifaceted America* (Hampshire: Palgrave Macmillan, 2009), 155–178.
55. Wimmer and Glick Schiller, "Methodological Nationalism and Beyond," 326.
56. Roger Waldinger and David Fitzgerald, "Transnationalism in Question," *American Journal of Sociology* 109 (2004): 1177–1195.
57. Ibid., 1182.

58. Elliott R. Barkan, "America in the Hand, Homeland in the Heart: Transnational and Translocal Immigrant Experiences in the American West," *Western Historical Quarterly* 35 (2004): 340.

59. Roger Waldinger, "Immigrant Transnationalism," *Sociopedia.isa* (2011). Available at [www.sagepub.net/isa/resources/pdf/ImmigrantTransnationalism.pdf]: 4.

60. Thomas Soehl and Roger Waldinger, "Making the Connection: Latino Immigrants and Their Cross-border Ties," *Ethnic and Racial Studies* 33 (2010): 1489–1510.

61. Roger Waldinger, Eric Popkin, and Hector Aquiles Magana, "Conflict and Contestation in the Cross-border Community: Hometown Associations Reassessed," *Ethnic and Racial Studies* 31 (2008): 843–870; for a contrasting assessment, see Alejandro Portes, Cristina Escobar, and Renelinda Arana, "Bridging the Gap: Transnational and Ethnic Organizations in the Political Incorporation of Immigrants in the United States," *Ethnic and Racial Studies* 31 (2008): 1056–1090.

62. Waldinger and Fitzgerald, "Transnationalism in Question," 1179; see also Roger Waldinger, "The Bounded Community: Turning Foreigners into Americans in Twenty-first Century Los Angeles," *Ethnic and Racial Studies* 30 (2007): 343.

63. Richard Alba and Victor Nee, *Remaking the American Mainstream: Assimilation and Contemporary Immigration* (Cambridge: Harvard University Press, 2003).

64. Waldinger, "The Bounded Community," 343.

65. Ibid., 346.

66. Roger Waldinger, "Immigrant 'Transnationalism' and the Presence of the Past," in *From Arrival to Incorporation*, eds. Elliott R. Barkan, Hasia Diner, and Alan M. Kraut, 267–285. New York: New York University Press, 2008.

67. Roger Waldinger, "Between 'Here' and 'There,'" 2008: 9.

68. Waldinger, "The Bounded Community," 2007: 347.

69. Ibid., 344.

70. Aristide Zolberg, *A Nation by Design: Immigration Policy in the Fashioning of America* (New York and Cambridge: Russell Sage Foundation and Harvard University Press, 2006).

71. David Hollinger, *Post-ethnic America: Beyond Multiculturalism* (New York: Basic Books, 1995).

72. Waldinger, "The Bounded Community," 2007: 347.

73. John Higham, "The Future of American History," *The Journal of American History* 80 (1994): 1289.

74. Waldinger, "Between 'Here' and 'There,'" 8. See also Roger Waldinger, *The Cross-Border Connection: Immigrants, Emigrants, and Their Homelands* (Cambridge: Harvard University Press, 2015) and Nancy L. Green, *The Limits of Transnationalism* (Chicago: University of Chicago Press, 2019).

Bibliography

Basch, Linda, Nina Glick Schiller, and Cristina Szanton Blanc, eds. *Nations Unbound: Transnational Projects, Postcolonial Predicaments, and Deterritorialized Nation-States* (Basel, Switzerland: Gordon and Breach, 1994).

Foner, Nancy. "What's New about Transnationalism? New York Immigrants Today and at the Turn of the Century." *Diaspora* 6 (1997), 355–376.

Glick Schiller, Nina, Linda Basch, and Cristina Szanton Blanc, eds. *Towards a Transnational Perspective on Migration* (New York: New York Academy of Sciences, 1992).

Green, Nancy L. *The Limits of Transnationalism* (Chicago: University of Chicago Press, 2019).

Guarnizo, Luis Eduardo, Alejandro Portes, and William Haller. "Assimilation and Transnationalism: Determinants of Transnational Political Action among Contemporary Migrants." *American Journal of Sociology* 108, 6 (2003), 1211–1248.

Kivisto, Peter. "Theorizing Transnational Immigration: A Critical Review of Current Efforts." *Ethnic and Racial Studies* 24, 4 (2001), 549–577.

Levitt, Peggy and Nina Glick Schiller. "Conceptualizing Simultaneity: A Transnational Social Field Perspective on Society." *International Migration Review* 38, 3 (2004), 1002–1039.

Levitt, Peggy and B. Nadya Jaworsky. "Transnational Migration Studies: Past Developments and Future Trends." *Annual Review of Sociology* 33 (2007), 129–156.

Morawska, Ewa. "Immigrants, Transnationalism, and Ethnicization: A Comparison of This Great Wave and the Last." in *E Pluribus Unum? Contemporary and Historical Perspectives on Immigrant Incorporation*. eds. Gary Gestle and John Mollenkopf (New York: Russell Sage Foundation, 2001), 175–212.

Morawska, Ewa. *A Sociology of Immigration: (Re)Making Multifaceted America*. (Hampshire, UK: Palgrave Macmillan, 2009).

Portes, Alejandro, Luis Eduardo Guarnizo, and Patricia Landolt. "The Study of Transnationalism: Pitfalls and Promise of an Emergent Research Field." *Ethnic and Racial Studies* 22, 2 (1999), 217–237.

Portes, Alejandro, William Haller, and Luis Eduardo Guarnizo. "Transnational Entrepreneurs: An Alternative form of Immigrant Economic Adaptation." *American Sociological Review* 67, 2 (2002), 278–298.

Vertovec, Steven. "Migrant Transnationalism and Modes of Transformation." *International Migration Review* 38, 3 (2004), 970–1001.

Waldinger, Roger. "Immigrant 'Transnationalism' and the Presence of the Past," in *From Arrival to Incorporation*, eds. Elliott R. Barkan, Hasia Diner, and Alan M. Kraut (New York: New York University Press, 2008), 267–285.

Waldinger, Roger. "Immigrant Transnationalism." *Sociopedia.isa*. (2011). Available at www.sagepub.net/isa/resources/pdf/ImmigrantTransnationalism.pdf. Accessed on December 14, 2011.

Waldinger, Roger, *The Cross-Border Connection: Immigrants, Emigrants, and Their Homelands* (Cambridge: Harvard University Press, 2015).

Waldinger, Roger and David Fitzgerald. "Transnationalism in Question." *American Journal of Sociology* 109, 5 (2004), 1177–1195.

Wimmer, Andreas and Nina Glick Schiller. "Methodological Nationalism and Beyond: Nation-State Building, Migration, and the Social Sciences." *Global Networks* 2, 4 (2002), 301–334.

CHAPTER 23

....

WRITTEN FORMS OF COMMUNICATION FROM IMMIGRANT LETTERS TO INSTANT MESSAGING

....

SUZANNE M. SINKE

"IMMIGRANT letter"—the words already connote a relationship across borders, a vision of "America," and a key source for the study of mobile people. As scholarship shifted from a focus on "immigrants" to those who cross borders (often more than once), so, too, did the study of "immigrant letters" move to intertwine with other studies of personal writings. In addition, scholars embraced technological changes, so that their sources included much more than messages written on paper, sealed in envelopes, and sent through postal systems. To these traditional letters, scholars added electronic media, from e-mail to instant messaging. In the late twentieth century and beyond this complicated the collection process just as migrants shifted their expectations for frequency and form of contact across borders. What remains is the importance of letters and their recent counterparts in communications as a source for various types of inquiry about migration and about the connections migration creates and sustains across borders.

What constitutes an "immigrant letter" either in the past or today? How did technological developments intertwine with national and international communication networks and education systems to make writing and sending letters across borders not just possible, but likely? How did the study of immigrant letters develop? What are some of the ways scholars use letters in studying migration? And, finally, what do the communication developments of the late twentieth century and beyond suggest for the study of communications across borders? These questions guide this essay. Though correspondence and other communications across borders formed a central part of the source material for scholarship about immigration in the twentieth century, their role in the twenty-first century remains less secure.

DEFINITIONS

Around 1860 Berthold Woltze of Berlin painted a classic image titled a *Letter from America* [*Ein Brief aus Amerika*]. In it, an elderly woman sits at a table, a letter unfolded and ready to read at arms length from her bespectacled face. Over her left shoulder an older man looks on, as does a young woman. One might envision this as a family where the parents and perhaps a younger sister together read the news that came from the son/brother off in the United States. The young woman's blushing cheeks and bright eyes demonstrate sparks of interest, perhaps even a desire to migrate herself. "Dearest parents and sister," one might expect to hear. The image fits the classic definition of an immigrant letter on many levels: a letter written from a person in America to relatives at home; a letter read by several people (and hence not exactly private in the sense of one recipient); a letter that both confirmed the writer's status and made recommendations about the possible migration of others. Along these lines—take as a definition of "immigrant letter" the correspondence of one person who migrated across the national border into the United States with the intention of settlement or extended sojourn, written to someone in another country. Already the definition finds detractors, for where is the option for the correspondence to other migrants, perhaps a brother and sister, in the United States but in different states? If they correspond the letter no longer crosses a border, but their thoughts may well be crossing back to comparisons of their one-time home. And what then do we call the letters of the parents back to the son? In the rare cases where correspondence in two directions exists, they all may fall under the "immigrant letters" heading—though just as likely an archivist cataloged them in another way, for example under "emigrant letters" or more broadly: "family papers." And how would one categorize the letters of someone who returned to a homeland? Authors use different definitions of "immigrant letters." Broadly conceived the category could include all correspondence back and forth, to and from a person involved in international migration to the United States at some point in his or her life. More narrowly, it would only include the migrant's writings while in the United States to a homeland.

Publication constitutes another stumbling block for definitions. Do letters written specifically for a newspaper count? What if a newspaper editor changed them substantially? What if we do not know? In reasonably literate areas of emigration published letters made their way into local newspapers. Local authorities might even try to recruit a potential migrant to become a correspondent. At other times, editors would gain permission to print a letter newly arrived from America. If the editor wanted to discourage emigration, the chosen letter might demonstrate that, or vice versa. Whether the letters of migrants to ethnic newspapers in the United States should fall into the general definition remains open as well. They can share many characteristics with those crossing national borders, and in some cases the U.S. newspapers also went back to homelands for others to read. One could posit that the trend in correspondence went from more letters open to multiple readers in the colonial era toward more private exchange moving into the twentieth century. Yet the spread of ethnic publications and literacy meant more people writing to publications. In the early twenty-first century, social networking of various kinds in digital media indicates a shift to include more publically visible communications again. In the electronic age, the definition of "letter" is crucial.

For many parts of Europe in the nineteenth and into the twentieth century, a letter was often like the Woltze image, read simultaneously by a family group. The salutations sometimes made that clear: Dear father, brother and sisters. Perhaps each person had a turn, so each could savor the touch of the paper, see the familiar script, feel the presence of the individual through the words that one might read silently while internally conjuring the voice of the writer. It could be treasured—or not. In the latter case, what would the chances be that someone preserved it for future generations? In the case of a major German nineteenth-century letter collection, the editors undertook systematic comparisons of statistical data on migrants in general compared with the letter writers specifically. The writers tended to be more affluent, somewhat better educated, and more often male than the U.S. migrant population from their homeland in general. Moreover, it was the families of more wealth and stability (landed) who saved these letters across time.[1] Whether content influenced saving remains even harder to gauge.

To study correspondence requires decisions about what to include. If a letter mentions a photo, a piece of cloth, a bank note, a newspaper article, they constitute some part of the exchange. The study of remittances, so central to economic histories of migration, requires a clear accounting of these items. Yet on the level of correspondence, where do they fit? Scholars who seek to be systematic in their evaluation of letters must define what constitutes a letter. Consider: what if multiple writers enclose separate sheets in one envelope; what if one person pens most of a letter, but a different person adds a postscript; or what if a single author writes several segments across a space of time on one sheet, complete with different dates for each, and then sends it as one unit. Such decisions hinge on what people seek to uncover. To the degree that digitization offers larger scales of analysis, these become crucial decisions.

If issues of sharing and publication cause concern for the nineteenth and early twentieth centuries, issues of venue plague definitions of the later twentieth century even more. How should one characterize the cassette tapes or video tapes sent back to family members? They too used the postal system to bring messages across borders. The line to cover communications blurs even more as regular telephone connections, first with land lines, and then with cell phones and computer technology made talking across the distance much more than a poetic turn of phrase—one that some nineteenth century writers liked to invoke at times. And then phones shifted to include written messages as well when texting and miniature electronic keyboards became more commonplace.

Moreover, the shift to e-mail and other computer-assisted communications both broadened the meaning of mail significantly and created massive challenges for the archivists of the recent past. For scholars studying the correspondence of migrants, the distinctions of synchronous or asynchronous format may be as important as those of which venue a correspondent chooses. Even if one limits the definitions of letter to written words, social networking spaces from ethnic website discussion boards to Facebook offer a variety of virtual writing options that may cross borders. In an electronic world, knowing where the writer of a message resides may not be obvious. As generations mature for whom correspondence on paper seems antiquated, the collection of electronic ephemera becomes crucial for future historians.

Written and Sent

On another level, studying immigrant letters requires delving into how education, transportation, and communications functioned. Letters, and later other forms of communication as well, relied on societal infrastructure. The ability to buy supplies like paper and ink or the knowledge of how to produce them; the ability to write or the knowledge of someone who could and would write for you; the presence of an ongoing connection such as a postal or telecommunications agreement—all of these formed basic requirements for immigrant letters. Assuming that people wanted to keep in contact after migration—and this is not something to assume for everyone—then the options varied across time. At any chronological juncture some had greater access than others in terms of personal ability, opportunity, and resources. Briefly, that history goes something like this.

Throughout the colonial era, most Europe-descended people could not write, but there were a few, and some would serve as scribes for those who could not. Even fewer people of non-European backgrounds possessed basic literacy. In addition to literacy, people needed the tools of the trade: pen and paper, luxury goods for the early colonial era. The same trade routes that brought goods back and forth across the Atlantic carried messages, sometimes in the form of letters. Letters had to make their way to port cities and onto ships bound in the right direction. Writers hoped for a trusted agent or returnee to carry the letter. Barring that, mail went from hand to hand among those who engaged in trade. If the letter made it across the ocean, it might land in a port and await someone to call for it or take it further. Often letters went astray somewhere in the process. For the early colonial era, writers could not anticipate much more than one letter exchange a year on a transatlantic route, and sending multiple versions of the same letter with different ships helped ensure that at least one might arrive.

As trade and population grew, so did the regularity of shipping, so that by the mid-1700s a packet service connected a number of North American ports with contacts across the Atlantic. Production of paper and ink (needed for printers) increased, meaning easier availability of necessary items for potential letter writers. Larger populations included greater numbers of literate individuals: more men than women, more affluent than poor, more city residents than rural dwellers. Those who migrated may have been slightly more literate than their contemporaries, in part because access to knowledge was crucial in making decisions of this sort. Most people, however, remained illiterate. Outside the European descended population, literacy remained low through the colonial era.

After independence, Africans coming as slaves constituted the largest migrant population until the official end of the international slave trade. This group faced barriers to education that would have allowed literacy. In the rare cases where literate Africans found themselves caught in the slave trade, other constraints made correspondence practically impossible. In the nineteenth century, the proportion of migration from various parts of Northern and Western Europe increased. Primary education made inroads in these regions, as it did in North America. Even more important in terms of immigrant letters, the United States developed an infrastructure to handle communications. Some historians called this an Information Revolution, with obvious parallels to late twentieth-century developments. The U.S. postal system grew in size and importance, meaning migrants as well as those born in the country turned to post offices to organize the transfer of information. The presence of a post office embodied not just the state, but linkages that could span borders.[2] Migration tended to develop in tandem with infrastructure both in various parts of the world as well as internally within the United States.

More specialized shipping, making it easier and more comfortable to cross the Atlantic, combined with regular schedules of shipping mail. Letters still went astray at times, but correspondents anticipated they usually would arrive. Not every person whose name appears in the signature line of a migrant's letter could write, as we know from descriptions of those who acted as scribes and collections where multiple sets of handwriting for the same name make that obvious. But the ability to write increased the chances and frequency of correspondence substantially.

By the mid-nineteenth century, the introduction of steamships increased the speed of knowledge transfer. Moreover, trade across the Pacific and along the coast of the Americas increased. Migrants followed these paths as well, particularly after the discovery of gold in California in 1848. And wherever migrants went, letters followed. Even more frequently as shipping migrants increased in importance, letters became a key source of migration. Money from the United States, and then prepaid tickets crossed the borders as shipping and railroad lines found a market among previous arrivals for their services. Thus letters fueled the nineteenth century migration on at least two crucial levels. First, as "America letters" they often demonstrated the advantages of the United States, creating the interest in migrating. Second, they frequently provided the means for migration through direct financial support. As industrialization spread the web of railroads, so too did the sources of migration to the United States expand. Letters made the comparisons obvious—where was it easier to get land, a position with better wages, or a spouse. At a time of decision-making for those facing similar circumstances, the person who got the prepaid ticket and the offer of a place to stay and help getting started had greater chances of actually making the move than did someone without them. The government interest in promoting internal unity and trade led to agreements about rates for sending items, and to more standard postage stamps, a process that then expanded to include international letters. The streamlining of postal payment helped ensure people would not miss letters based on inability to pay. Staying in touch cost less. The letters of migrants embodied the personal connections that communications across borders fostered. References to keeping a letter close to one's heart or caressing the paper served as rhetorical devices, but also as an indication that people used the physical presence of a letter as a reminder of the person absent.

Familiarity spurred migration, as people joined family members, neighbors, and fellow religious believers. The public nature of "America letters," sometimes published in newspapers, shared among family to friends, helps explain the development of chains of migration from one specific town or region to another specific area sometimes thousands of miles away. The same strands made it clear when potential migrants might be better served staying where they were, and at times they suggested moving elsewhere. Though religion and state-building sometimes sparked the desire for literacy, migration became a contributing force as well. People sought to read and write to friends and family at a distance, and they used the letters they received as models to a much greater extent than any correspondence manuals.

The twentieth century saw not just improvements in roads, railroads, and steamships used for transportation, but the addition of air travel later in the century. Telephones and then computers joined other communications. For most migrants, however, paper and pen epistles sent via the post remained the primary form of staying in touch with others through much of the twentieth century. Letters from the United States still had some meaning, though by late in the century they could travel more quickly, and expectations of how often one might write could escalate as a result. If some in the early colonial era anticipated a letter exchange once a year, by the late twentieth century as migration rates to the United States rose again people might expect letters to go back and forth a couple of times a month if not weekly, and via computer at the end of the century the scale shrank to days and even hours. Postal time constituted a key component of visions of time generally, from shipping season to weekly packet to instant message.

The late twentieth-century communications revolution resonated somewhat more heavily with the affluent and educated people who made up a significant minority of this era's migration. These skilled migrants included many who fueled the revolution directly, foreign-born individuals who peopled the graduate schools and technological development sectors of U.S. companies. To be tech-savvy and earning a good income meant options for international communications, though in which form depended in part on whether there was a digital divide between the locations in contact. Yet writing back to those one left behind also took place among the manual labor sector. Among Mexican migrants in one study community, for example, extensive correspondence took place despite several possible alternative modes of communications.[3]

Literacy made this possible. Basic education became more common in some areas where migration began to swell, while almost universal literacy existed in other places. More importantly, the spread of English as the lingua franca of much of the world made information about the United States available to more people. It remained the prerogative of migrants to decide if and how often to write, but the ability to write increased. As globalization spread trade and information linkages, migration to the United States also diversified, aided by the loosening of nationality restrictions. Older migration circuits to Asia and Latin America resumed or grew and new ones developed, including to Africa. Circulating people equated with circulating letters for most of these.

One major caveat to this neat and somewhat teleological story: in every era, the tides of technology and literacy did not reach all areas equally. So even in the late twentieth century there could be migrants trying to contact those in an area without reliable postal connections, telephone service, or other communications options that people in the United States took for granted. And political developments such as war and dictatorship could severely limit or eliminate connections, at least for a time. World War I and World War II both interrupted the lines of communication in severe ways. Not only did postal ties diminish to a third party trickle, but censorship, a weapon of governments, fell on private correspondence as it did on public utterance and publication. At other times, self-censorship, either not writing or limiting what one writes, might be the best choice to avoid endangering either writer or recipient. The history of the letters of migrants is thus partly one of technology, of education, and of state power.

Immigrant Letters as Sources

Sociologists of the Chicago School discovered the personal correspondence of international migrants as a source just after the turn of the twentieth century, using this as one avenue for exploring the social problems they associated with immigrants. William Thomas and Florian Znaniecki included letters as one part of their multivolume work on the *Polish Peasant in Europe and America*. Thereafter, as interest among historians on social topics grew during the 1920s and beyond, some of the first historians of immigration, including Marcus Lee Hansen, George Stephenson, and Theodore Blegen, began publishing letters by migrants, offering these as windows into the immigrant experience. Finding a history of a white but non-English population within the United States featured importantly in this endeavor. The historians provided limited information on the authors, and generally took the letters at face value. In some cases the letters had appeared initially in an ethnic newspaper. Some were by leading members of ethnic communities. In this, letter collections could both illuminate migrant experience and help create a particular ethnic American history. [4]

Social history, rising to prominence through the 1960s, provided the impetus for much greater attention to migrants as part of a general interest in history from the bottom up. Finding, preserving, and publishing letters of migrants became a part of this endeavor. Most of the surviving letters that originated in the United States from migrants existed closer to their original addressed destinations outside the United States. Researchers in other countries, sometimes in cooperation with those in the United States, undertook campaigns to collect these. At first the collections tended to target Northern and Western Europe: Norway, the Netherlands, Britain, Germany, and Finland. [5] Finding the real audience for these collections remained a bit unclear, for the general interest in migration of the late twentieth century meant public appeal that warranted less scholarly styles for at least some of the results.

The BABS-Gotha German letter project exemplifies this trend. Perhaps more than most, the scholars associated with this project tried to make the letters they found accessible to audiences on a variety of levels. By transcribing, translating, and annotating information found in the letters with further genealogical information about the authors, then comparing the letter writers to migrants in various statistical databases, the BABS group provided a model. For a more general German audience, they produced a paperback with some selected sections from letters, liberally interspersed with pictures and other illustrations from the period. For an English audience, they produced a larger set of letter collections with extensive commentary including information on the language, literary style, and orthography; annotations explaining places and events mentioned in the letters; and additional biographical information on the authors. The editors also published in both German and English a collection of Civil War letters. Meanwhile, the collection moved and expanded with another collection drive, this time with a focus on the former East German states.[6]

In these collections, letters took the macroeconomic forces of wages and labor demand and translated them into the micro-scale of an individual finding a job and making more money than in a homeland. Letters took the macroeconomic forces of massive industrialization in one area demanding many workers and showed the human scale of families divided. Letters took the macro-demographic forces of more marriageable men than women, too many workers or too few, and put them in specific calls to come or messages to wait. Apart from the refugees of political or religious persecution or those escaping an agricultural disaster such as the potato famine, most migrants to the United States followed the economic cycles that characterized so many migrant letters. What was the cost of land, of housing, of foodstuffs, of other items and services the writers and readers expected to need? What could one anticipate for a yield on farmland; earn in wages; buy with what earned? The ubiquity of such pieces of information in nineteenth and early twentieth-century letters illustrated their function.

> Will has earned from fifteen to twenty pounds this spring, we expect him every day. I shall have that money to buy cattle . . . if I go down the river a little way I can get cattle at £2 or £2.5s. a head. This is a good place for selling butter; the butter at Faner was quite yellow at the beginning of the summer, but the butter here is much more yellow. The price of corn and flour will rise here presently. A barrel of flour now costs £1.5s, of your money and the potatoes are 2s.0d. This is the best place I have ever seen for men to obtain work . . . .[7]

This letter, transcribed and translated from Welsh, probably also underwent standardization in terms of the punctuation and spelling. The editor did not comment on this process, but at least the place name, "near Fortwinibego," indicated some possible irregularities. Compare the exacting (if still printed) version from an Irish migrant's letter:

> Rent is 300 Dollars p^r year flower 6 Dollars p^r hundred butter 37 ½ Cents by the pound beef 10.c beacon 20c potatoes 1 Dollar p^r Bushell and Every thing Else in proportion as the Crops mist in this Country Laste year and produse buying up for the army this warr is not a popular warr here . . . .[8]

Transcription, in contrast to translation, more often came closer to the original, though in this case the editors provided copious notes to explain obscure phrases or unclear terms.

Some scholars took up the challenge of seeing alternatives to the United States, comparing letters from Brazil, for example.[9] As the number of collections increased featuring migration to other countries, especially countries of major migrations, comparisons became possible in a different way. The imperative to collect letters continued through the late century, and expanded as new groups, especially those part of the post-World War II migrations, began to seek sources for their own histories. What did scholars expect to learn from the letters? Research goals (and to a degree funding options) drove the kinds of collection projects, the types of additional information they solicited, and the presentation formats they choose for distribution.

Who could use a collection depended on many factors. When Larry Seims provided both the original Spanish and an English translation of the letters he published by Mexican undocumented migrants, his choice meant no opportunity to check elements of the original handwriting.[10] Having the translation meant including half as many letters as in a translation-only collection. The absence of biographical data other than that in the letters left much room for speculation on whether the writers always wrote accurately (and in fact a couple of the letter exchanges indicated people were withholding pertinent information or even stretching the truth). Pseudonyms or incomplete names closed off the opportunity for further biographical data. Each decision about what to include and what to exclude, predicated on real restrictions of time, money, and access, in addition to choices based on assumed uses meant closing off certain kinds of analysis. Letters, it turned out, served as sources for many kinds of history and a wide range of other kinds of study.

Types of Analysis

Since the 1990s, the disciplines interested in the correspondence of international migrants expanded, as did the types of analysis in which they engaged. Of the many that now engage correspondence and communications more broadly by migrants, a few of the more noteworthy categories include language, rhetoric, literature, linguistics, education, communications, sociology, and social anthropology, in addition to history. They differ substantially, including in the format of data needed to carry out studies. Within history, scholars also engage in a wide variety of approaches. If some still use the letters for a poignant example to a pattern found mainly in other sources, others take letters as their main font of information. Here, too, the range of inquiry is broad.

Basic epistolary elements form one of the categories of study. Early twentieth-century researchers Thomas and Znaniecki identified what they called "bowing letters," in which peasants would follow formulaic models. These opened with a religious salutation, followed by references to the health of receivers and senders, and then greetings or "bows" to each relative. In some cases, the bows could be quite clearly implied: "Dear Parents: I send you my lowest bow, as to a father and mother, and I greet you and my brothers with these words: 'Praised be Jesus Christus'...."[11] According to the authors this pattern served to maintain connections to family across the distance. Though many of the writers lacked extensive education, they could tie to families through ritualized phrases. As a model, several parts of this pattern resonated with later collections, to the point that editors of collected volumes in later years often omitted the formulaic greetings, health and family references, and sometimes the final salutations. If scholars primarily sought information of the new land and adjustment, then eliminating the repetition meant a tighter focus and more space for additional letters.

The exclusions could go much further, with long passages from different letter writers becoming the story of a migrant group.[12] What contributed to this was the repetition of other kinds of information, whether wages and working conditions in a city, repeated perceptions of something as "American," discussions of community events or national news.[13] All could reach a point of diminishing returns, where scholars would find one letter or passage could stand for many. These tended to serve more popular audiences, for other scholars could not utilize the letters as effectively for their own research. Still, through the late twentieth century and beyond, scholars who translated and edited collections of letters also commented on the contents.[14] In the case of the Bochum–Gotha collection, this included analyses such as positing several models of assimilation seen in letters.

As other scholars of intellectual developments in language, sometimes labeled discourse, turned their attention to letters of previous centuries, few looked to the letters of migrants specifically, but their insights offered possible lenses through which to view these sources. Examining the formulaic took various forms, from tracing the development, use and contents of letter manuals as a window on language development to charting the expression of emotion. This linguistic interest, combined with a quantitative bent in some scholarship set the stage for content analysis of migrant letters. On a simple scale, this could mean demonstrating a general difference in ages of correspondents and number of illnesses and deaths reported in letters going back and forth between the quite literally "old" and the "new" worlds, as Herbert Brinks did in a Dutch American collection that housed correspondence in both directions.[15] The fruits of content analysis also moved scholars beyond collections, into monographs such as Kerby Miller's *Emigrants and Exiles*. Miller posited the strength of a motif of exile in letters of Irish migrants, in part to blame conditions beyond one's control for high emigration rates and to hide the shift in class relations taking place within Ireland.[16]

A more ambitious attempt at analyzing Irish letters a decade later became a model for other scholars, though the focus was outside the United States. David Fitzpatrick, in *Oceans of Consolation*, combined collection and analysis, in this case for the letters of Irish migrants to Australia. Fitzpatrick, echoing many earlier studies, found common elements included ritualized introductory phrases, references to correspondence and then health, and a final (slightly less consistent) form of farewell. Fitzpatrick went on to analyze themes that arose commonly in these letters, using a basic form of content analysis to chart the frequency in his collection. Fitzpatrick's hefty volume encompassed both extensive letter collections (without elisions), and a book-length section on the prominent themes: reciprocity, negotiation, and reflections among them.[17] Exile was not among the most common in this case.

Few historians tried to be as systematic in terms of content analysis. But those in other fields did. The digitization of one collection allowed German linguist Stephan Elspass to examine language patterns such as the degree of formality, grammar, vocabulary, spelling, as well as the primary and secondary functions of these letters. Among historians a slightly different avenue of study developed with David Gerber, who suggested the "epistolary ethics" of familiar letters—those sent to close friends or family members in a previous homeland in order to maintain relationships. In particular he added to previous areas of study such as comments on reciprocity, conveyance, privacy, and processes or writing, to include the emotional states of those sending and receiving letters. Others, such as Sonia Cancian, connected his scholarship to that on emotions generally, examining the expressions of emotions in letters for those in different types of relationships from courtship and marriage to parent–child associations. Finding both the similarities and differences of expressions of emotion in the letters of migrants compared to a more elite U.S. standard formed the work of others. For example, Sinke found few expressions of love in letters arranging marriages of Dutch or German migrants of the late nineteenth century.[18] To the degree that historians follow trends in the field generally, attention to emotions fits with the cultural turn of the 1990s and beyond.

FUTURE DIRECTIONS

Far easier is it to read the past than to predict the future. A few trends in studying communications of mobile people, however, do show promise. First, though historians tend to shy away from quantification, the possibilities of studying bodies of migrant correspondence through computerized databases grows apace. Online sources can provide options for transcription and translation, whether under academic supervision or in an open source marketplace. The Immigration History Research Center at the University of Minnesota, for example, published on its website a collection of immigrant letters from its collection, as well as links to other migrant letter collections. Visual image of the letter, transcription, English translation in searchable format: this level of preparation requires time, skills, and money. In turn bringing text into machine-readable form opens it to content analysis of a systematic sort and on a much broader scale, benefitting studies of rhetoric, ideas, linguistics, and any other number of fields. Moreover, the translation options should facilitate comparisons across groups.

The migrant groups of the late twentieth century already people the pages of recent historical studies, just as they have dominated the work of other fields of social science. Historical scholarship on communications of these groups may include more traditional letters, such as Larry Seims' collection of originals and translations of correspondence between Mexican and Central American migrants without documents from the late twentieth century.[19]

As sound cassettes, video recordings, computer e-mail, and then texting came to supplement and then replace other written communication, historians faced the challenges of (1) locating materials about communications crossing borders, (2) adjusting or reinventing methods of study given these new media, and (3) archiving materials for the future, part of a much broader challenge to make sure ephemeral media do not disappear entirely, or get lost in formats too antiquated for future researchers to access. Historians have a particular role in encouraging migrants to save messages from different media. Interdisciplinary study and cooperation affords historians the opportunity to demonstrate how much "new" patterns actually replicate those of the past, a message many scholars of late-twentieth century and twenty-first century migrants need to hear. At the same time, historians can selectively incorporate research based on techniques pioneered in other fields, such as virtual ethnography for discussion boards, or geographic information systems mapping capabilities for connecting locations and scale of communications.

Migrants continue to communicate with those left behind and others of their background. Speed clearly differentiates the newer technology from the days of paper and pen. Sound recording and video imaging began making their way into migrant correspondence in the late twentieth century. As digital connections improved, the interactive written session emerged. And as migrants turn to different forms of communication, the expectations also change. Some of the standard practices may disappear, while others develop. The older forms of "bowing" may not be there, but newer elements such as the assurance of connection or affection may take up a more important role.

Studying communications across borders in the digital age already required rethinking older skills, and in the wake of increased nativism after the September 11 attacks, the attention to contacts across borders between both groups and individuals grew. The challenge of chronicling and evaluating messages on social media whether by a young man reacting in an ethnic chat room to an Islamic religious pronouncement or a girl writing to distant relatives and embedding a video of how she plays the violin, remains. Historians should play an important role in identifying the commonalities as well as the innovations inherent in this transnational and digital age.

NOTES

1. Wolfgang Helbich and Walter D. Kamphoefner, "How Representative are Emigrant Letters? An Exploration of the German Case," in *Letters Across Borders: The Epistolary Practices of International Migrants*, eds. Bruce S. Elliott, David A. Gerber, and Suzanne M. Sinke (New York: Palgrave Macmillan, 2006), pp. 29–55.
2. Richard R. John, *Spreading the News: The American Postal System from Franklin to Morse* (Cambridge: Harvard University Press, 1995) and David M. Henkin, *The Postal Age: The Emergence of Modern Communications in Nineteenth-Century* America (Chicago: University of Chicago Press, 2006).

3. Miguel Angel Vargas, "Epistolary Communication between Migrant Workers and their Families," in *Letters Across Borders: The Epistolary Practices of International Migrants*, eds. Bruce S. Elliott, David A. Gerber, and Suzanne M. Sinke (New York: Palgrave, 2006), pp. 124–138.

4. William I. Thomas and Florian Znaniecki, *The Polish Peasant in Europe and America*, 5 volumes, vols. 1 and 2 (Chicago: University of Chicago Press, 1918); Theodore Blegen, ed. *Land of their choice: The Immigrants Write Home* (Minneapolis: University of Minnesota Press, 1955); Theodore C. Blegen, *Frontier Parsonage: The Letters of Olaus Fredrik Duos, Norwegian Pastor in Wisconsin, 1855–1858*, (1947) and *Norwegian Migration to America: The American Transition*, (1940) both from the Norwegian-American Historical Association in Northfield, MN; George M. Stephenson, "When America was the Land of Canaan," *Minnesota History Magazine* 10, 3 (1929): 237–260.

5. For example see Charlotte Erickson, *Invisible Immigrants: The Adaptation of English and Scottish Immigrants in Nineteenth Century America* (Coral Gables: University of Miami Press, 1972).

6. Walter D. Kamphoefner and Wolfgang Helbich, eds. *Germans in the Civil War: The Letters They Wrote Home* (Chapel Hill: University of North Carolina Press, 2006); Walter D. Kamphoefner, Wolfgang Helbich, and Ulrike Sommer, eds. *News from the Land of Freedom: German Immigrants Write Home* (Ithaca: Cornell University Press, 1991).

7. Letter from John and Margred Owen to Griffith Owen, Baraboo, Wisconsin to Vaner near Dolgelley, Old Britain, May 27, 1847 trans. from Welsh and reprinted in "Documents," *Wisconsin Magazine of History*, 13, 4 (June 1930), p. 411.

8. William Heazelton, Pittsburgh, Pennsylvania to John Greeves, Bernagh, County Tyrone, 29 May 1814, reproduced in Kerby A. Miller, Arnold Schrier, Bruce D. Boling, and David N. Doyle, *Irish Immigrants in the Land of Canaan* (New York: Oxford University Press, 2003), p. 622.

9. Josephine Wtulich, ed. and trans., *Writing Home: Immigrants in Brazil and the United States, 1890–1891* (New York: Columbia University Press, 1986).

10. Larry Siems, ed. *Between the Lines: Letters Between Undocumented Mexican and Central American Immigrants and Their Families and Friends* (Tucson: University of Arizona Press, 1992).

11. Letter from Konstanty Butkowki to Parents, South Chicago to Poland, December 6, 1901, translated, edited and excerpted in William I. Thomas and Florian Znaniecki, *The Polish Peasant in Europe and America*, vol. 1 (New York: Alfred A. Knopf, 1927), p. 782.

12. Niels Peter Stilling and Anne Lisbeth Olsen, *A New Life: Danish emigration to North America as described by the emigrants themselves in letters 1842–1946* (Aalborg: Danish Society for Emigration History, 1994).

13. Max Paul Friedman, "Beyond 'Voting with their Feet': Toward a Conceptual History of 'America' in European Migrant Sending Communities, 1860s to 1914," *Journal of Social History*, 40, 3 (Spring 2007): 557–575.

14. See for example, Herbert J. Brinks, ed., *Dutch American Voices: Letters from the United States, 1850–1930* (Ithaca: Cornell University Press, 1995).

15. Herbert J. Brinks, "Impressions of the 'Old' World, 1848–1940," *European Contributions to American Studies* 20 (1991): 34–47.

16. Kerby A. Miller, *Emigrants and Exiles: Ireland and the Irish Exodus to North America* (New York: Oxford University Press, 1985).

17. David Fitzpatrick, *Oceans of Consolation: Personal Accounts of Irish Migration to Australia,* (Ithaca: Cornell University Press, 1994).

18. Stephan Elspaß, *Sprachgeschichte von unten. Untersuchungen zum geschriebenen Alltagsdeutsch im 19. Jahrhundert* (Tübingen: Niemeyer 2005); David A. Gerber, "Epistolary Ethics: Personal Correspondence and the Culture of Emigration in the Nineteenth Century," *Journal of American Ethnic History* 19, 4 (Summer 2000): 3–23; Sonia Cancian, *Families, Lovers, and their Letters* (Winnipeg: University of Manitoba Press, 2010); Suzanne M. Sinke, *Dutch Immigrant Women in the United States, 1880–1920,* (Urbana: University of Illinois Press, 2002), 19–20; Suzanne M. Sinke, "Marriage through the Mail: North American Correspondence Marriage from early Print to the Web," in *Letters across Borders,* (New York: Palgrave Macmillan, 2006), pp. 75–94.

19. Larry Siems, ed. *Between the Lines: Letters Between Undocumented Mexican and Central American Immigrants and Their Families and Friends* (Tucson: University of Arizona Press, 1992).

Bibliography

Chartier, Roger, Alain Boureau, and Cécile Dauphin, eds. *Correspondence: Models of Letter-Writing from the Middle Ages to the Nineteenth Century.* Princeton: Princeton University Press, 1997 [1991 French edition].

Constable, Nicole. *Romance on a Global Stage: Pen Pals, Virtual Ethnography & "Mail Order" Marriages.* Berkeley: University of California Press, 2003.

Decker, William Merrill. *Epistolary Practices: Letter Writing in America Before Telecommunications.* Chapel Hill: University of North Carolina Press, 1998.

Dierks, Konstantin. *In my power: Letter writing and communication in Early America.* Philadelphia: University of Pennsylvania Press, 2009.

Elliott, Bruce S., David A. Gerber, and Suzanne M. Sinke, eds. *Letters Across Borders: The Epistolary Practices of International Migrants.* New York: Palgrave Macmillan, 2006.

Gerber, David A. *Authors of Their Lives: The Personal Correspondence of British Immigrants to North America in the Nineteenth Century.* New York: New York University Press, 2006.

Henkin, David M. *The Postal Age: The Emergence of Modern Communications in Nineteenth-Century America.* Chicago: University of Chicago Press, 2006.

Immigration History Research Center, Digitizing Immigrant Letters, http://ihrc.umn.edu/research/dil/index.html. Accessed February 2, 2012.

Kamphoefner, Walter D., and Wolfgang Helbich, eds. *Germans in the Civil War: The Letters They Wrote Home.* Chapel Hill: University of North Carolina Press, 2006.

Mahler, Sarah J. "Transnational Relationships: The Struggle to Communicate Across Borders," *Identities: Global Studies in Culture and Power* 7, 4 (2001), 583–619.

Stanley, Liz. "To the Letter: Thomas and Znaniecki's The Polish Peasant and Writing a Life, Sociologically," *Life Writing* 7, 2 (August 2010), 139–151.

CHAPTER 24

ETHNICITY, RACE, AND RELIGION BEYOND PROTESTANT, CATHOLIC, AND JEWISH WHITES

R. STEPHEN WARNER

WILL HERBERG'S *Protestant–Catholic–Jew* was the most widely cited and influential interpretation of American religion at the end of the 1950s. Herberg claimed that post-World War II American society had become organized into three self-identified and peacefully coexisting religious "melting pots," which among them included nearly every white person in the country. "By and large, to be an American today means to be either a Protestant, a Catholic, or a Jew."[1] In the background was a lengthy process through which each of these three groups had both shaped and assimilated to their shared religion at the same time that each group came to regard the religion of the other two as equally legitimate expressions of the spiritual side of the "American Way of Life." Herberg's basic theory helps us understand the role of religion in the lives of migrants and minorities in the United States in the twenty-first century.

A HALF CENTURY OF RELIGIOUS CHANGE

Yet in only twenty years after its publication, Herberg's portrait was roundly dismissed as hopelessly partial and increasingly dated. As religious historian Martin Marty wrote in his introduction to a 1983 reissue of the book, Herberg "failed to anticipate almost every important turn" in American religion from the 1960s on.[2] He overlooked the prophetic role that Black Church leaders played in the civil rights movement. He did not anticipate that evangelicalism would successfully challenge the hegemony of mainline Protestantism nor that, partly in response to politicized evangelicalism, millions of Americans would opt entirely out of religious identification by the end of the century. In terms especially important for our present purposes, Herberg could not imagine that a new wave of immigration would require both recognizing Islam, Hinduism, and Buddhism as American religions and coming to grips with a far larger nonwhite population. By the 1980s, it had become unacceptable to confine a thesis about American religion to Protestant, Catholic, and Jewish white people.

Nonetheless, it is our thesis that Herberg's underlying insight—that religious difference is the intergroup difference most acceptable in American civic culture and that religious organization is the most promising avenue for incorporation of cultural minorities in the wider society—remains valid. Using Herberg's analysis as an inspiration, but not a template, we will survey the nexus of religious and racial-ethnic identities in the United States today and attempt to understand their dynamics.

In both his blind spots and his insights, Herberg was a product of his time. Not only did other prominent 1950s social critics fail to see that the racial and gender status quo was about to be shaken up, but also the three-way scheme of religious identification was not Herberg's alone. He was at pains to say that his three-prong system was simply "the prevailing view of contemporary America."[3] Perhaps his favorite anecdote, one for which, tellingly, he provided no citation, was the story of an encounter between a sergeant and a recruit in World War II. When the inductee gave "none of the above" as his answer to the question about which of the three religious communities he belonged to, the sergeant "exclaimed in exasperation, 'Well, if you're not Catholic, or Protestant, or Hebrew, what in blazes *are* you?'" For his 1950s readership, Herberg evidently didn't need to point out that World War II and Korean War dog tags included religion as one of only a few bits of vital information that a medic or chaplain would need to know in an emergency: name, serial number, blood type, most recent tetanus shot, and religious preference, which was indexed by the letters P (Protestant), C (Catholic), and H (Hebrew), with a blank space for no preference. Those were the only options that the culture of the time knew of. Perhaps the nonconformist was Greek Orthodox. But even in the 1940s, before Herberg presented his thesis, America was not simply a "Christian nation."

HERBERG'S INSIGHT: RELIGION AS ALLOWABLE DIFFERENCE IN THE UNITED STATES

The heart of Herberg's theory was his profound insight that religion in America serves as a refuge for cultural particularity. Here is his now-famous proposition about immigrants and their religions:

> Of the immigrant who came to this country it was expected that, sooner or later, either in his own person or through his children, he would give up virtually

everything he had brought with him from the "old country"—his language, his nationality, his manner of life—and would adopt the ways of his new home. Within broad limits, however, his becoming an American did not involve his abandoning the old religion in favor of some native American substitute. Quite the contrary, not only was he expected to retain his old religion, as he was not expected to retain his old language or nationality, but such was the shape of America that it was largely in and through his religion that he, or rather his children and grandchildren, found an identifiable place in American life.[4]

Herberg's idea—that it is especially in and through their religions that immigrants find an identifiable place in American life—informs much of the growing literature on the religious affiliations and communities of new (i.e., post-1965) immigrants.[5] The 2009 report of the Social Science Research Council on religion and the new immigration states that "the importance of religion for the incorporation of immigrants and their children into American society was a truism" for students of late-nineteenth and twentieth century immigration, even if, until recently, religion had escaped the attention of those who study post-1965 immigration. But new research shows that "religion has not lost any of its power to shape the incorporation of immigrants."[6]

Raymond Brady Williams, one of the pioneers of research on post-1965 immigrant religion, gave the idea his own particular formulation when he applied it to the case of immigrants from India and Pakistan:

> In the United States, religion is the social category with clearest meaning and acceptance in the host society, so the emphasis on religious affiliation and identity is one of the strategies that allows the immigrant to maintain self-identity while simultaneously acquiring community acceptance.[7]

The Hindu, Muslim, and other immigrants whose religious institutions in the United States were studied by Williams received earlier attention in the post-1965 immigration and religion literature than did many other groups (especially Mexicans and Filipinos). Nonwhite and mostly non-Christian, Indians and Pakistanis stood out in the United States. Coming from the world's most religiously diverse and actively religious region, they were used to standing out. Disproportionately well-educated, many of them professional, and most of them fluent in English, they were approachable by U.S. researchers. Those researchers, in turn, became accustomed to hearing from them that they greatly appreciated the religious freedom they experienced in America and consequently were "more religious in the U.S. than they had been in their home countries."[8]

Almost as if they had read Herberg, who took the experience of Jews in America as paradigmatic for his theory—"nothing is more characteristically American than the historical experience of American Jewry"[9]—some Hindu and Muslim leaders cited the example of Jews as a model for their own aspirations to maintain their non-Christian traditions as religious minorities in the United States For example, in her comprehensive account of Hinduism in America, Indian American sociologist Prema Kurien writes:

Hindu community leaders have long sought to emulate the model of Jewish Americans ... as a highly successful group that is integrated into mainstream American society while maintaining its religious and cultural distinctiveness, close community ties, and connections with the home country, [in other words] a group that has been able to "fit in" while remaining different.[10]

Availing themselves of the special status of religion in the United States, even as they did not share the dominant religious identity, Jews are widely perceived among new immigrants as a successful model of how to remain persistently different from the majority while becoming fully integrated in the society.

ADAPTATION OF RELIGIOUS INSTITUTIONS TO THE AMERICAN CONTEXT

Herberg's 50-year-old insight stands as a viable generalization (if not an infallible rule): post-1965 immigrants still find their religion to be a powerful aid in promoting their incorporation into American society. But they must adapt their institutions to new realities. For example, just as eastern European Jews left the isolated *shtetl* for crowded neighborhoods in New York and, later, Conservative synagogues in the suburbs, so also Hindu temples and Islamic centers look very different in America than in the countries of immigrant origin. Many American Hindu temples enshrine a range of Hindu deities that would not be found together on the same premises in India. Many American mosques are populated by people who would not be found together in the same prayer space in a Muslim country. Such adaptations are due to the need to create a critical mass of devotees in a late modern society characterized by both its pattern of dispersed settlement of diverse populations and its friendliness to religion in general.

Herberg knew that adaptation and incorporation did not take place overnight. Let us look again at the last clause of what I earlier called "Herberg's now-famous proposition" about immigrants' religion: "[I]t was largely in and through his religion that he, *or rather his children and grandchildren*, found an identifiable place in American life."[11] Gender-exclusive language aside, Herberg was pointing to the fact that religious incorporation was a multigenerational process. Generational succession is perhaps the most urgent occasion for the many adaptations that religious institutions must undertake if they are to maintain viability in the United States.

To understand the process of generational succession, Herberg drew especially from the writings of Marcus Lee Hansen and Oscar Handlin, which in turn were largely based on the trajectories of nineteenth-century immigrants. Following what he called "Hansen's Law"—"what the son wishes to forget, the grandson wishes to remember"[12]—Herberg saw old-country culture "transmuting" into religion over three generations. The immigrant first generation wants to bring to America as much old-country life as possible. The second generation wants to fit in to the new country and thereby has to distance itself from old-country ways. By contrast, the third generation, secure in being American, wants to reconnect with its roots. But because so much was forgotten by the alienated second generation, what was left for the roots-hungry third generation to remember was only the Americanized version of the immigrants' religion.

As in the past, immigrant religion in America is still subject to change over generations. But the specific three-generation process that Herberg perceived can no longer, if indeed it ever was, be taken as a general model. Intergenerational transition at the start of the twenty-first century takes many different forms. For one thing, English-language acculturation in the second generation happens faster. But widespread support for "multiculturalism" also means that there is less coercive pressure toward Americanization. Moreover, because the post-1965 immigrant flow had not (as of the time of this writing in 2012) been subject to the drastic curtailment imposed in the 1920s, lines between immigrant generations are often less clear-cut than in the past.

An example of Herberg's "transmutation" was the progressive broadening of the identities of immigrant Catholics. Those who came from Sicily first became Italian, those from Poznan became Poles, and those from Bavaria, Germans. Not without struggle, their offspring were eventually incorporated into an Irish-dominated Catholic church where homilies were preached in English and the mass celebrated in Latin.

By the 1990s, post-1965 American Islam could be seen doing something similar, where the vernacular Arabic and Urdu of the immigrant generation was replaced in the lives of their children by English in everyday social interaction and in the Friday sermon (*khutbah*) in the mosque, where the prayer was led in Qur'anic Arabic. (Although not as thoroughly as Irish clergy dominated the Catholic church, Pakistanis are overrepresented among mosque leaders.)

But the ethnicity-to-religion transmutation is quicker for post-1965 Muslims. Partly because so many Muslim immigrants to the United States are highly educated when they arrive and because they pass educational advantages and aspirations on to their children, the post-1965 second generation of Muslim immigrants has been well represented in American universities for decades. In the Muslim Students Association, second-generation Muslim immigrants meet Muslims from a wide variety of cultures with whom they share not their parents' native languages but their parents' religion, and they often enthusiastically embrace their "religious" over their "cultural" identities.[13] In effect, they foreshorten the Herberg-Hansen intergenerational religious revival by a whole generation.

By contrast, second-generation Hindus, arguably following another aspect of the American Jewish experience, have been seen as growing into an all-India panethnic group. Even more than the Muslim second generation, they typically pursue higher education. Having grown up in white American suburbs where their parents practice their religion mostly at home, many encounter critical masses of co-ethnic and co-religionist peers for the first time at events organized by the Hindu Students Council on their university campuses. But the ethnicity the emerging group has in common is based less in language—Indian immigrants stem from a staggering variety of language backgrounds—than in Indian nationality and broadly Hindu identity. Those who embrace their Hindu roots as a socially significant identity have less reason to reach beyond the diverse Indian American community, and, influenced by a Hindu national-ist program articulated by influential organizations and intellectuals, they often system-atically conflate their Hindu and Indian identities.[14] So Hinduism in America is much more an ethnic religion than is Islam.

Like second-generation Muslims, second-generation Korean Protestants privilege religion over ethnicity, publicly embracing their "Christian" identities over against their Korean identities, even as they gravitate toward exclusively Korean American Christian gatherings.[15] But second-generation Mexican Catholics, like second-generation Hindus, are drawn to a deep mix of their religious and cultural heritages, in part because of the nearness of the border, the frequency of crossings, and the continued flow of immi-grants. This pattern of ethnicized religion has been theorized by Catholic theologians as "inculturation" and by specifically Latino theologians as *mestizaje*.[16]

Yet the religious-cultural mix that second-generation Indian Hindus and Mexican Catholics embrace is not a simple case of cultural survival. They are adaptations. Because of the internal diversity of both sending countries, the ethnic Hinduism of Indian Americans and the *mestizaje* Catholicism of Hispanic Catholics are broader and less attached to specific old-country locales than the cultures the various streams of immi-grants brought with them. For example, the Bhagavad Gita is increasingly a unifying scripture among lay Hindus, and the Virgin of Guadalupe has become a pan-Hispanic religious icon. Immigrant religion is indeed changed in the American context, but not necessarily at the expense of ethnic identification.

RESEARCH ON POST-1965 IMMIGRATION AND RELIGION

Raymond Williams' report that Indian and Pakistani immigrants claimed to be "more religious in the U.S. than they had been in their home countries" served as something of a guiding premise among pioneer researchers who were encouraged (by me, among others) to seek out and study post-1965 immigrant religion. In default of census data (questions about religion are not permitted in the census of households) and in view of the limitations of sample surveys (immigrant religious minorities are typically too small to show up in standard samples of the whole population), most studies of immigrant religion before the 2000s were qualitative case studies of specific communities.

Thus, from the late 1980s onward, there emerged a large body of literature on, to men-tion only a few examples, Korean and Chinese Protestant congregations and student associations, Hispanic Catholic parishes, Hindu temples and other gatherings, Muslim communities, and religious centers for Thai, Sri Lankan, and Chinese Buddhists.[17] Yet this sort of research entailed "sampling on the dependent variable," looking for immigrant religion in places where immigrants have gathered religiously. Such sampling bias does not invalidate the findings of these excellent studies on which this chapter draws heavily, but it does mean that the often-heard claims of high levels of religious activity have to be understood as applying, first of all, to the religiously active people who make them.

Beginning roughly in 2000, data from well-funded, large-scale surveys especially targeting immigrants and religious and ethnic minorities—but not drawing their samples solely from the ranks of the religiously active—became available. For example, the "New Immigrant Survey" (NIS) reports religion and national origin information on 6,381 cases drawn from a sample of all individuals who were granted legal permanent residency in 2003. The NIS therefore excludes undocumented immigrants, a significant bias, but the interviews were conducted in the language of the respondent's own choosing, giving their answers more face validity. The "American Religious Identification Survey" (ARIS) is based on random-digit-dialed telephone interviews (in English and Spanish) with a huge sample (N = 54,461) of native and immigrant populations in 2008. ARIS repeats questions asked in 1990 and 2001, allowing assessment of change over time. The Pew Forum's "U.S. Religious Landscape" study, conducted in 2007, also surveyed very large numbers (35,000 telephone interviews), permitting accurate estimates of small religious minorities (e.g., Muslims, Hindus, and Buddhists, each of which constitutes a bit more or less than 1 percent of the U.S. population) but asking more religion questions than the ARIS. The "National Survey of American Life" is a nationally representative study of African Americans, black Caribbeans, and non-Hispanic whites based on 6,082 face-to-face interviews conducted in 2001–2003. All of the foregoing surveys are based on interviews with individuals, but in 2012, the Pew Forum released "Faith on the Move," a comprehensive compilation of census and other official data on the religious affiliations of international migrants by 231 countries of origin and destinations around the world. The work of Phillip Connor, who was primary researcher for "Faith on the Move," stands out for its cross-national comparative perspective.[18]

The findings of these surveys differ in many details. Nonetheless, drawing on these and other sources, it is possible to address more precisely many issues of immigrant religious affiliation and participation. For example, based on the NIS, Akresh refutes the generalization that immigrants are more religious in the United States than they were at home.[19] As a good deal of previous research, as well as common sense, would lead us to expect, migration itself is disruptive of such discretionary behavior as going to church. Yet the NIS data also show something equally important for our purposes: the longer an immigrant resides in the United States, the more religiously active he or she becomes. In other words, religious participation of immigrants in the United States rebounds after the shock of the move. Connor's cross-national data show that the religious observance of immigrants to other countries does not rebound in the same way. Thus, the United States is experienced as uniquely friendly to immigrant religion. This is a bit of confirmation for Herberg's notion that becoming American goes hand in hand with becoming religious. We will return to this observation.

Three other facts about new immigrants documented in these and other surveys (which have been clear to thoughtful observers long before the quantitative data emerged) are important for our topic. Most post-1965 immigrants are, in terms of

U.S. racial classifications, nonwhite. The great majority are Christian. And they hail disproportionately from religiously active parts of the world. These observations bear on our expansive recasting of Herberg's thesis.

The racial composition of post-1965 immigrants: In the 1950s, the Protestants, Catholics and Jews that Herberg focused on were whites of relatively recent (i.e., 1880–1920) European origin. By contrast, the typical post-1965 immigrant is a person of color from Latin America, the Caribbean, Asia, the Middle East, or Africa. (Only one in six hails from Europe or Canada.) Implications of these facts for our topic will be developed later.

The religions of post-1965 immigrants: What is less widely reported is that most (somewhere between two-thirds and three-fourths) of post-1965 immigrants are Christian. Thus, widespread notions to the contrary notwithstanding, the most immediate religious effect of the new immigration is not the de-Christianization of American society but the de-Europeanization of American Christianity.[20] It was not the case, for example, that by 2000 there were more Muslims in the United States than Jews or Presbyterians, although Muslims will surely overtake both groups later in the twenty-first century. After Christian, by far the second largest religious identity in the United States is "none," both among immigrants (10 percent) and the population at large (16 percent).

Yet immigrant Christians are themselves about two-thirds Catholic, so another impact of the new immigration on religious demography is to maintain the Catholic share of the population while deepening the Protestant decline. By the second decade of the twenty-first century, Protestants will likely constitute a minority of Americas. Already in the 1950s, Herberg sensed that Protestants perceived themselves to be a minority, because in the face of the increasing acceptance of Catholics and Jews, they could not take their former dominance for granted. Fifty years later, the attitude of American Protestants toward their imminent actual minority status ranged from multicultural enthusiasm to outspoken embitterment.

Nonetheless, the post-1965 immigration of non-Christians did significantly diversify American religious demography beyond the Protestant-Catholic-Jewish triad. Muslims, Hindus, and Buddhists (along with Sikhs, Jains, and others) became visible both demographically (in numbers of adherents) and institutionally (in their mosques and temples). With the exception of some early twentieth-century convert organizations, Hinduism in America is almost entirely attributable to post-1965 immigration from India (and Indian communities in Africa and the Caribbean). In that sense, Hinduism in America qualifies as a religion primarily of co-ethnic immigrants, even more than Judaism did at the turn of the last century.

By contrast, about a third of American Buddhists are white converts; many of the others stem from often mutually incomprehensible sectarian and linguistic traditions that have followed different trajectories for two millennia. In most accounts, Buddhism is experienced by its millions of American adherents as profoundly meaningful on a personal basis, but it does not lend itself to group solidarity on a wide scale. Notwithstanding the fact that many of those who have chosen Buddhism in the past half century have done so under the tutelage of teachers from Asia, American Buddhism is, for the most part, not an immigrant or an ethnic religion.

In these terms, American Islam sits midway between Hinduism and Buddhism. About two-thirds of the Muslims in America are immigrants and their offspring, with origins primarily in the Middle East and South Asia. But one-third are African Americans, many of whom are heirs of the black Muslim movement who followed Warith Deen Mohammed, son of Elijah Muhammad, into orthodox Sunni Islam after Elijah's death. Islam in the United States is thus a substantially but not entirely immigrant religion that brings several very different minority ethnic groups into a universalistic community, or *ummah*, as Muslims refer to it. In its multiethnic, heavily immigrant constituency, although not its organizational structure, American Islam is comparable to early-twentieth century American Catholicism.

According to the Pew U.S. Religious Landscape Survey, approximately 4.7 percent of the U.S. population in 2007 adhered to a religion other than Christianity. (The ARIS figure for 2008 was 4.4percent.) Because Jews alone constituted about 4 percent of the (much smaller) U.S. population in the 1950s, we cannot say with a great deal of confidence that the non-Christian share of the U.S. religious population of the United States has grown to unprecedented levels. But it is certainly the case that the United States is more religiously diverse than ever before, with substantial representation of nearly every religion in the world. Yet because of the far greater number of individuals who claim no religious identity than was the case in the 1950s, it is also true that the U.S. population is overall significantly less religious than in Herberg's time.

Immigrant origins: This is where the question of the national origin of immigrants comes decisively into play. Europe became massively secularized after the previous peak of immigration at the turn of the twentieth century. Thus, among post-1965 immigrants, with the exception of those from China, the 15 percent minority of immigrants to the United States who hail from Europe have the lowest level of home country religious observance. Mexico is by far the top "sending country," and the Philippines and India are perennially in the top five. Precisely those countries are among the most religiously active in the world. Thus, far from being a limitation on the applicability of Herberg's paradigm, the shift of sending countries away from Europe and toward Latin America, Asia, and Africa has provided new Christian, Muslim, and Hindu populations who—it is reasonable to expect—would find attractive the implicit promise that it is "in and through religion" that they will find "an identifiable place in American life."

Post-1965 Immigration in the Light of the American Religious and Racial Order

Although the United States was not founded as a "Christian nation," religion was deeply implicated in the founding of the American republic, not only in the deistic language of the Declaration of Independence but also in the Constitution. The same process of compromise that counted an enslaved African as three-fifths of a person also precluded Congress from either establishing a national religion or abolishing the existing state establishments of religion (e.g., in Connecticut and Massachusetts). Slaveholders and proto-abolitionists had to compromise. So also did deists, Unitarians, Congregationalists, Presbyterians, Anglicans, and Baptists—all of whom were at least vaguely Protestant but many of whom did not honor the religious credentials of the others. There could be no "Christian" religious criterion for citizenship, not even one that would exclude the then widely despised Catholics. The "establishment" and "free exercise" clauses of the First Amendment thus not only enshrined individuals' rights to believe as they wish and join the churches of their choice but also entailed their right to organize their own churches. These religious guarantees, along with the "states' rights" guarantees demanded by slaveholders, promoted the flourishing of private associations, including churches, in the newly united states. From the outset, the new nation was, although not Christian, distinctly friendly to religion.[21]

The resulting nineteenth-century "churching of America" enlisted common people on the frontier into religious associations that had been previously the preserve of east coast elites. Long before the Civil War, the plebeian Methodists and Baptists had overtaken the "big three" religions—colonial Congregationalist, Episcopalian, and Presbyterian—in membership, and, for the first time, organized religion became a popular institution in America. At the end of the twentieth century, religious association was still the most equitably available vehicle of civic participation.[22]

But if there was no religious test for citizenship in the new nation, there could be a racial one for immigrants, and the First Congress supplied it in the United States Naturalization Law of March 26, 1790. Under this law, which was not definitively repealed until 1952, in order to become a naturalized U.S. citizen, one had to be a "free white person." White Catholic and Jewish immigrants could gain citizenship. Nonwhites could not. In this sense, as repulsive as the idea sounds today, the United States was founded not as a Christian nation but a white nation. Race was a category applied to determine the invidious distribution of rights. Religion was a protected sphere through which rights could be claimed.

Before the Civil War, blacks were enlisted into Methodist and Baptist churches in the slaveholding south and the Free Soil north, and the first separate African American denominations were organized in the north. But it was especially after the war that "the newly emancipated Negroes carried out the work of separation and independent organization with astounding energy and success." The quoted observation is that of none other than Will Herberg,[23] who recognized the same typically American religious dynamic in the founding of what is now called the "Black Church" tradition as in the churching of those crossing the frontier and those crossing the Atlantic. For Herberg, the Black Church was "an anomaly" only with respect to the "triple melting pot" scheme. (Interracial marriage was not only rarer in his day than in ours; in some states, it was also a felony.) Thus, the path that would later be followed by the 1880–1920 immigrants and their heirs was pioneered by African Americans, for whom it was eventually also "largely in and through religion that they found an identifiable place in American life."[24]

The Civil War ended chattel slavery, but the systematic subjugation of African Americans soon took on a new life in Jim Crow laws, which persisted until they were overturned by the civil rights movement in which the Black Church played an essential role. One of the achievements of that movement was to deprive explicit racism of any moral high ground. Another was to open political and economic opportunities for many blacks. But America had not become post-racial, and racial stereotyping became ever more exquisitely coded.

Although the civil rights movement itself owed much of its effectiveness to the Black Church, some observers expected that the movement's opening of opportunities for African Americans in politics and the economy might undermine the Black Church itself, depriving it of its near-monopoly on African American civic life. Fifty years later, that expected demise had not come about, in part because churches both attacked the remaining obstacles and equipped constituents to take advantage of the opportunities that did exist. The Black Church remains an indispensable vehicle for the articulation of African American experience.[25]

Thus, it remains true in the twenty-first century that "African Americans exceed national rates for church membership, church attendance, self-identification as being 'born again,' and beliefs that religion is very important in their own life and that religion can answer many of today's problems. . . . [B]lack adolescents . . . as well as adults . . . and elderly persons . . . all demonstrate higher levels of religious involvement that do their respective white age counterparts."[26] Of all the racial/ethnic groups in the United States, blacks are the least likely to be religiously unaffiliated and, among the small minority who are unaffiliated, the least likely to be truly secular. The reason is that African Americans have their own church. That is what might be called the bright side of America's notorious religious racial segregation.

Another highly churched group, second only to African Americans in their regular Christian participation, are Korean Americans. By the year 2010, 1.5 million Korean Americans had set up over 4,000 congregations. Among other things, leadership roles in the Korean immigrant church provided a social space in which men, disappointed with the careers they were able to pursue in the United States, could recapture some of the respect they felt was their due. Korean American women could converse with each other at church in the language they could not use while serving their white American customers in the small businesses so many of them ran. For the first generation, church was, among other things, an ethnic refuge that made it possible to survive in an alien society.[27]

But the second generation were fluent in English from an early age, and they typically went on to university and then pursued professional careers. Respectful of their parents and, for the most part, devoted to their Christian faith, many nonetheless found the style of worship in their parents' churches oppressive and boring. They gravitated to the English language worship services that the more progressive of the immigrant churches offered and, once in college, flocked to the Korean American Christian fellowships that were to be found on elite university campuses from coast to coast. The more reflective of them asked why—given their fluency in English and acculturation to American ways, their promising career prospects, and their devotion to a universalistic faith—they should so segregate themselves from their white co-religionist classmates. They, and the researchers among them, discreetly pondered the extent to which their own ethnically specific congregations were a refuge from the racialization to which they were subject in America.[28] Although intermarriage rates were high, enthusiastic Korean American Protestants were not becoming part of the Protestant "melting pot." Like African Americans, they continued to attend their own churches.

Muslims are another marginalized group who have availed themselves of the advantages of religious organization, but in their case, religion is at least in part a cause of their persecution as an antidote to it. The three largest constituent groups in American Islam embody different additional identities that stigmatize them in the contemporary American context. Arab Muslims are counted "white" in official racial statistics but "Arabs" rate low in public opinion. Indo-Pakistani Muslims are officially classified as racially "Asian," which is to say "nonwhite." African Americans, of course, are classified as racially "black." But qualifying these typically stigmatized attributions with "Muslim" not only does not improve the picture; it also makes it worse. "Muslim" is the least favored religious identity in American public opinion, outranking only "atheist."[29]

An outsider might well ask why a person living in America, free to affirm or deny a religious label, would rationally invite discriminatory behavior by being publicly Islamic, wearing hijab or a beard and taking a midday Friday break to pray at the mosque. Nonetheless, Muslims in the United States became more assertive about just such identifying behavior in the two decades surrounding the turn of the twenty-first century, well before the terrible events of September 11, 2001. Many young American-raised Muslims became more public about their religion than were their parents. After 9/11, they and their co-religionists were subject to a backlash of increasingly suspicious scrutiny, intrusive screening at airports, and downright hate crimes.

Two major studies of American Muslims' post-9/11 experience documented not only that backlash but also a response to it that was unanticipated by researchers. They found that Muslim groups "stepped up to take more public and visible roles as defenders and interpreters of Muslims in America. . . . [B]oth despite and because of the backlash and difficulties of recent events, Islam is becoming more civically engaged and more 'American' as a result."[30] For this reason, historians of American Islam years hence will likely look back on 9/11 not as a turning point but as a chapter in the story of their incorporation into American society. Between 2000 and 2011, the number of mosques in America grew by 74 percent. Their leaders' already overwhelming agreement that Muslims should be involved in American society became even more unanimous, and the proportion of those leaders who regard American society as hostile to Islam dropped from over a half to only a quarter. Publicly embracing Islam is far from a guarantee of just treatment, but it is also not a sign of alienation. Islam is turning out to be a platform for ultimate incorporation in American society.

In this respect, Muslims were in part following the path cleared by American Jews, who, by the first decade of the twenty-first century, were the most highly esteemed religious community in America but one still subject to anti-Semitic attacks. In effect, Muslims are daring the United States to live up to its promise of religious freedom.

Buddhists may serve as a test case of religious over-racial exclusion. As we have noted, of the people in the United States who practice or identify with Buddhism, about one-third, many of whom are socially prominent and socioeconomically privileged, are white, and were not raised as Buddhist. As whites in a society that has historically been more determined to police racial than religious boundaries, we can expect that white Buddhists will be able to take their inclusion more or less for granted. In a 2010 survey, Buddhists ranked just below Jews and (not surprisingly) well above Muslims in the proportion of Americans who view them favorably. In the same poll, Buddhists effectively tie with Jews in having the fewest Americans who are prejudiced against them, fewer than the "Christians" (often a code word for conservative Protestants) whose reputation has been tarnished in the eyes of a substantial fraction of their countrymen.[31]

What about Mexicans? They are by far the largest post-1965 immigrant group as well as the source of the greatest replenishment of America's Christian, specifically Catholic, ranks. Yet, in the polarized political climate of the early twenty-first century, their religious profession did not seem to immunize them from a resurgent strain of nativism (albeit one masked by a concern about "illegal" immigrants). Although Muslims are far from esteemed in American public opinion, they do not seem to occasion as much anger as do Mexicans, who in too many U.S. contexts are expected to prove that they have a right to be here, no matter how many generations that may have been. Their presence in the United States has become an issue, but the issue is not their religion. Many experience it as their race. Others argue that it's their native language.[32] What is the role of religion?

An assessment of the situation of Mexican immigrants is complicated by the fact that, regardless of their intention, Mexicans are assigned to the preexisting "Hispanic" or "Latino" ethno-racial group, and it is that category to which most of the available quantitative data pertain. But that broad panethnic category is highly heterogeneous in terms of national origin, racial phenotype, and length of time in the United States (from one year to more than a century), as well as religion.

Although the majority (at least 60 percent) of Hispanics are Catholic, Hispanic Protestants became increasingly visible by the end of the twentieth century. According to the Pew and ARIS surveys, 22 to 23 percent of Hispanics were Protestant in 2007–2008. Conservatively estimated, that means there are more Latino Protestants in the United States than Jews, or than Muslims, Hindus, and Buddhists put together. Sizable percentages of new arrivals from Puerto Rico and Guatemala bring Protestantism with them, and their typically small congregations often keep them in touch with the homeland. On the other hand, many native-born cradle-Catholic Hispanics convert to Protestantism, some because of intermarriage and others because of disaffection with the Catholic church. Their congregations can serve as vehicles of assimilation to working-class or middle-class white American culture.

Nonetheless, Mexico is one of the most thoroughly Catholic nations in the world, and, at 70–75 percent, Americans of Mexican ancestry are the most staunchly Catholic of all Hispanics. Meanwhile, European Americans have been deserting the church in droves. Mexicans and their offspring are the future of the U.S. Catholic Church, and the church has awakened to that fact.

But the church has not always made it easy for its Mexican constituents. In 1851, soon after the U.S. conquest of northern Mexico, Fr. Jean-Baptiste Lamy became bishop of the new American territory of New Mexico, replacing the indigenous clergy and devotional style with his own austere, hierarchical brand of Catholicism. Through *Death Comes for the Archbishop*, the fictionalized biography by Willa Cather, Anglo Americans were invited to admire Lamy's genuine fortitude and commitment, but they were blinded to the damage he, and the church regime he represented, did to the relationship between the church and the formerly Mexican nationals he was put in charge of. "Hispanics who were incorporated into the United States underwent the disestablishment of their religion along with widespread loss of their lands, economic well-being, political clout and cultural hegemony."[33]

The descendants of those of whom it is said "the border crossed" are now greatly outnumbered by the descendants of those who began crossing the border in the 1870s, immigrants properly speaking, and the record of the Catholic church in the southwest is mixed and is by no means uniformly hostile to Mexicans. Yet the widespread pattern by which the church patronized and marginalized its Mexican-origin constituents, as if they were not real Americans, persisted for more than a century. In the 1970s, the U.S. Catholic Church began fitfully to redress these insults, responding initially to bottom-up pressures originating in San Antonio. Eventually as a body—but not necessarily in all its members—the church became more friendly to Hispanics just as immigration from Mexico swelled to unprecedented numbers.

Perhaps the most dramatic organizational turnaround was in the previously inhospitable archdiocese of Los Angeles, where Cardinal Mahony forcefully condemned such anti-immigrant measures as Proposition 187 in 1994 and HR 4437 (the "Sensenbrenner Bill") in 2006. In Chicago, Catholic parishes were at the heart of the huge mass mobilization against HR 4437 in the spring of 2006.[34] Immigrants, especially those from Mexico, had found their most prominent institutional advocate.

To earn the loyalty of its soon-to-be Hispanic majority, an increasing number of leaders and parishes across the expanse of the church have argued that the church has to de-center European-origin norms. Masses delivered in Spanish are a first step. Livelier singing is another. Yet another is incorporation of popular rites such as *quinceañeras* and presentations of babies. The church is implicated more publicly when popular or canonical rites are performed on the street, as are the house-to-house Christmas pilgrimages called *las posadas navideñas* and the Good Friday passion play called *Via Crucis*. Theological issues are raised when the message of Good Friday is shifted from Christ Died for Your Sins to Jesus Suffers with Us.[35] Catholic and other U.S. religious institutions are being changed by post-1965 immigration, just as the Protestant, Catholic, and Jewish institutions of the 1950s bore the imprint of nineteenth-century immigration.

The challenges posed to the Catholic Church by Mexican immigration are enormous. For example, the church's capacity to provide the religious education it gave to the children of previous waves of Irish, Polish, and Italian immigrants is severely hampered by the disappearance of the inexpensive teachers once supplied by women's religious orders. Yet for a population with a lengthy history in the United States and great numbers of both highly assimilated and marginalized members, the complex expanse of the church offers many niches for Mexican Americans of different cultural proclivities. English-dominant members of second and later generations can be instructed by homilies in English masses in the same parish where, on a different Sunday, they can join their parents and grandparents to enjoy the music and rituals of a Mexican-inflected Spanish mass. As in the past, the Catholic Church both helps immigrants adapt and adapts to them.

RELIGION AS A CONTEXT OF RECEPTION

I have argued that post-1965 immigrants to the United States still look to religion to secure a place in American society. In so doing, they take advantage of the long-standing American pattern by which religion is a preferred vehicle for immigrant incorporation. The 2009 Social Science Research Council report called that idea a "truism." The American Mosaic Project, a 2003 survey based at the University of Minnesota, set out to determine whether, in the wake of the gains for racial and ethnic equality since the 1960s, religion still enjoyed such a place in U.S. public opinion. Expecting to find that the positive evaluation of religion as a mark of distinction relative to race has been overstated in the conventional wisdom, the researchers found that religion still has the edge. In response to questions about the suitability of religious and racial/ethnic organization as "a good way to become established in a local community," far more respondents chose religious organizations. White respondents, perhaps less attuned to the need for any communal organization, were least likely to choose either but chose religion over race/ethnicity by more than a two-to-one margin. Blacks and Hispanics were more likely to regard both forms of organization as advantageous but still were more likely to choose religious organizations. On the question of whether the respondent had been discriminated against because of race or religion, only Jews, overwhelmingly white, reported higher incidents of religious discrimination. Not surprisingly, three to five times as many black and Hispanic respondents reported being discriminated against on racial rather than religious grounds. "In general, race is more likely than religion to be associated with social conflict and less likely than religion to be seen as chosen or as deeply connected with personal identity or a common moral culture."[36]

As we have seen, the New Immigrant Survey shows that immigrants' religious participation increases over time in the United States. But immigrant religion does not have the same standing in other societies. Ongoing research by Phillip Connor shows both that the religious participation of immigrants' offspring is less conducive to occupational success in Europe than in the United States and that it tends to decrease over time. Connor's findings give new evidence for the conclusions of a review essay by Nancy Foner and Richard Alba contrasting religion's "positive role in immigration adjustment and assimilation in the United States" to its more problematic role in Western Europe.[37]

In an ingenious three-country research design, sociologist Margarita Mooney explored religion as a context of immigrant reception in three strategically different societies, the United States, Quebec, and France. Mooney's immigrant group were Haitian Catholics, and they were living in Miami, Montreal, and Paris. The Haitians were uniformly pious across all three contexts ("Faith makes us live," they said), but those in Miami were more confident about their and their children's futures. One reason was that their overt religiosity was more welcome in the United States than in Quebec and France, where religion is, of course, tolerated but supposed to be kept to oneself. But the more important reason, which Mooney stresses, is that the Catholic Church served more effectively as an institutional mediator in Miami than it did in Montreal or Paris. Because of the pro-religious public culture of the United States, Catholic leaders could intercede with the state to help provide needed services to Haitians.[38]

Variation across countries in religion's role in immigrant incorporation is a research frontier. But the generalization that religion, in general, contributes to immigrant incorporation specifically in the United States is as true for post-1965 immigrants as it was for those of the previous century. America is exceptionally religious among modern societies not because it was founded as a Christian nation but because the founders established rules for religion that both encouraged religious organization and allowed religion to articulate intergroup difference. The boundaries of allowable difference are far broader now than the founders could possibly have imagined. But as Herberg showed, Jews, as well as Christians, were already firmly inside them a half century ago.

Notes

1. Will Herberg, *Protestant–Catholic–Jew: An Essay in American Religious Sociology*, rev. ed. (Garden City, NY: Doubleday Anchor, 1960), 40.
2. Martin Marty, "Introduction *to Protestant—Catholic—Jew*, by Will Herberg (reissue; Chicago: University of Chicago Press, 1983), ix.
3. Herberg, *Protestant–Catholic–Jew*, 40.
4. Ibid., 27–28.
5. Raymond Brady Williams, *Religions of Immigrants from India and Pakistan: New Threads in the American Tapestry* (Cambridge: Cambridge University Press, 1988), 1; R. Stephen Warner, "Work in Progress Toward a New Paradigm for the Sociological Study of Religion in the United States," *American Journal of Sociology* 98 (Mar. 1993): 1060; R. Stephen Warner and Judith G. Wittner, eds., *Gatherings in Diaspora: Religious Communities and the New Immigration* (Philadelphia: Temple University Press, 1998), 15–16; R. Stephen Warner, *A Church of Our Own: Disestablishment and Diversity in American Religion* (New Brunswick.: Rutgers University Press, 2005), 236; Helen Rose Ebaugh and Janet Saltzman Chafetz, *Religion and the New Immigrants: Continuities and Adaptations in Immigrant Congregations* (Walnut Creek, CA: Alta Mira Press, 2000), 17–18; Diana

Eck, *A New Religious America: How a "Christian Country" Has Become the World's Most Religiously Diverse Nation* (San Francisco: Harper, 2001), 61–64; Charles Hirschman, "The Role of Religion in the Origins and Adaptation of Immigrant Groups in the United States," *International Migration Review* 38 (Fall 2004): 1209; Alejandro Portes and Rubén G. Rumbaut, *Immigrant America: A Portrait*, 3rd ed. (Berkeley: University of California Press, 2006), 393–395; Nancy Foner and Richard Alba, "Immigrant Religion in the U.S. and Western Europe: Bridge or Barrier to Inclusion?" *International Migration Review* 42 (Summer 2008): 363; Richard Alba, Albert J. Raboteau, and Josh DeWind, eds., *Immigration and Religion in America: Comparative and Historical Perspectives* (New York: New York University Press, 2009), 1–2; Pyong Gap Min, *Preserving Ethnicity Through Religion: Korean Protestants and Indian Hindus across Generations* (New York: New York University Press, 2010), 27; Ilana Redstone Akresh, "Immigrants' Religious Participation in the United States," *Ethnic and Racial Studies* 34 (Apr. 2011): 647.

6. Alba et al., *Immigration and Religion*, 1–2.
7. Williams, *Religions of Immigrants*, 11.
8. Ibid.
9. Herberg, *Protestant–Catholic–Jew*, 172.
10. Prema A. Kurien, *A Place at the Multicultural Table: The Development of an American Hinduism* (New Brunswick: Rutgers University Press, 2007), 150.
11. Herberg, *Protestant–Catholic–Jew*, 27–28.
12. Ibid., 30.
13. R. Stephen Warner, Elise Martel, and Rhonda E. Dugan, "Islam Is to Catholicism as Teflon Is to Velcro: Religion and Culture Among Muslimas and Latinas," in *Sustaining Faith Traditions in America: Race, Ethnicity, and Religion among the Latino and Asian American Second Generation*, eds. Carolyn Chen and Russell Jeung (New York: NYU Press, 2012), 46–68.
14. Min, *Preserving Ethnicity*; Kurien, *A Place at the Multicultural Table*.
15. Karen J Chai, "Competing for the Second Generation: English-Language Ministry at a Korean-American Church," in Warner and Wittner, *Gatherings in Diaspora*, 295–331; Rebecca Y. Kim, *God's New Whiz Kids? Korean American Evangelicals on Campus* (New York: NYU Press, 2006).
16. Warner et al., "Islam Is to Catholicism"; Robert Courtney Smith, *Mexican New York: Transnational Lives of New Immigrants* (Berkeley: University of California Press, 2005); Tomás R. Jiménez, *Replenished Ethnicity: Mexican Americans, Immigration, and Identity* (Berkeley: University of California Press, 2010); Virgil Elizondo, *Galilean Journey: The Mexican-American Promise* (Marynoll, NY: Orbis Books, 1983).
17. Fenggang Yang, *Chinese Christians in America: Conversion, Assimilation, and Adhesive Identities* (University Park: Penn State University Press, 1999); Chai, "Competing for the Second Generation;" Kim, *God's New Whiz Kids?*; Jeffrey M. Burns, "¿Que Es Esto? The Transformation of St. Peter's Parish, San Francisco, 1913–1990," in *Portraits of Twelve Religious Communities*, vol. I of *American Congregations*, eds. James P. Wind and James W. Lewis (Chicago: University of Chicago Press, 1994), 396–463; Charles W. Dahm, *Parish Ministry in A Hispanic Community* (Mahwah, NJ: Paulist Press, 2004); John Y. Fenton, *Transplanting Religious Traditions: Asian Indians in America* (New York: Praeger, 1988); Kurien, *A Place at the Multicultural Table*; Yvonne Yazbeck Haddad and Adair T. Lummis, *Islamic Values in the United States: A Comparative Study* (New York: Oxford University Press, 1987); Karen Isaksen Leonard, *Muslims in the United States: The State*

of Research (New York: Russell Sage Foundation, 2003); Paul D. Numrich, *Old Wisdom in the New World: Americanization in Two Immigrant Theravada Buddhist Temples* (Knoxville: University of Tennessee Press, 1996); Wendy Cadge, *Heartwood: The First Generation of Theravada Buddhism in America* (Chicago: University of Chicago Press, 2005); Carolyn Chen, *Getting Saved in America: Taiwanese Immigration and Religious Experience* (Princeton: Princeton University Press, 2008). See also Min Zhou and Carl L. Bankston III, *Growing Up American: How Vietnamese Youth Adapt to Life in the United States* (New York: Russell Sage, 1998).

18. For the New Immigrant Survey, see Akresh, "Immigrants' Religious Participation"; Kosmin, Barry A., and Ariela Keysar. 2009. American Religious Identification Survey (ARIS 2008) Summary Report. Hartford, CT: Institute for the Study of Secularism in Society and Culture. http://commons.trincoll.edu/aris/publications/2008-2/aris-2008-summary-report/Accessed May 16, 2014; Pew Research Center, Pew Forum on Religion & Public Life, "U.S. Religious Landscape Survey: Religious Affiliation: Diverse and Dynamic" (Feb. 2008), http://religions.pewforum.org/pdf/report-religious-landscape-study-full.pdf, accessed Jan. 4, 2012; Pew Research Center, Pew Forum on Religion & Public Life, "Faith on the Move: The Religious Affiliation of International Migrants" (Mar. 2012), http://features.pewforum.org/religious-migration/Faithonthemove.pdf, accessed Mar. 9, 2012. On the National Survey of American Life, see Linda M. Chatters, Robert Joseph Taylor, Kai McKeever Bullard, and James S. Jackson, "Race and Ethnic Differences in Religious Involvement: African Americans, Caribbean Blacks, and Non-Hispanic Whites," *Ethnic and Racial Studies* 32 (Sept. 2009): 1143–1163. ("Asian Americans: A Mosaic of Faiths," a report released by the Pew Research Center: Pew Forum on Religion & Public Life in 2012 (http://www.pewforum.org/Asian-Americans-A-Mosaic-of-Faiths.aspx,) presents new information relevant to Pew's February 2008 "U.S. Religious Landscape Survey" by substantially increasing the estimated proportion of Asian Americans among American Buddhists from one-third to three-fifths. Unlike earlier studies, the Mosaic of Faiths survey was administered in a half dozen or more Asian languages, in addition to English, which appears to have been especially significant in increasing responses of Vietnamese Americans, more than 40 percent of whom claimed a Buddhist identity on the survey.

19. Akresh, "Immigrants' Religious Participation."

20. Compare Eck, *A New Religious America*, and R. Stephen Warner, "The De-Europeanization of American Christianity," in *A Nation of Religions: Pluralism in the American Public Square*, ed. Stephen Prothero (Chapel Hill: University of North Carolina Press, 2006), 233–255.

21. William J. Novak, "The American Law of Association: The Legal-Political Construction of Civil Society," *Studies in American Political Development* 15 (2001): 163–188; Steven Waldman, *Founding Faith: Providence, Politics, and the Birth of Religious Freedom in America* (New York: Random House, 2008); R. Stephen Warner, "Parameters of Paradigms: Toward a Specification of the U.S. Religious Market System," *Nordic Journal of Religion and Society* 21 (2008): 129–146.

22. Roger Finke and Rodney Stark, *The Churching of America, 1776–2005: Winners and Losers in Our Religious Economy*, rev. ed. (New Brunswick: Rutgers University Press, 2005); Sidney Verba, Kay Lehman Schlozman, and Henry E. Brady, *Voice and Equality: Civic Voluntarism in American Politics* (Cambridge: Harvard University Press, 1995).

23. Herberg, *Protestant–Catholic–Jew*, 113

24. Ibid., 27–28.

25. C. Eric Lincoln and Lawrence H. Mamiya, *The Black Church in the African American Experience* (Durham: Duke University Press, 1990).

26. Chatters et al., "Race and Ethnic Differences," 1144.

27. Won Moo Hurh and Kwang Chung Kim, "Religious Participation of Korean Immigrants in the United States," *Journal for the Scientific Study of Religion* 29 (Mar. 1990): 19–34.

28. Chai, "Competing for the Second Generation"; Kim, *God's New Whiz Kids?*

29. Penny Edgell, Joseph Gerteis, and Douglas Hartmann, "Atheist as 'Other': Moral Boundaries and Cultural Membership in American Society," *American Sociological Review* 71 (Apr. 2006): 211–234.

30. Rhys H. Williams, "Creating an American Islam: Thoughts on Religion, Identity, and Place," *Sociology of Religion* 72 (Summer 2011): 127–153, citing Anny Bakalian and Mehdi Bozorgmehr, *Backlash 9/11: Middle Eastern and Muslim Americans Respond* (Berkeley: University of California Press, 2009), and Louise Cainkar, *Homeland Insecurity: The Arab American and Muslim American Experience After 9/11* (New York: Russell Sage Foundation, 2009). See also Ihsan Bagby, *The American Mosque 2011* (Hartford, CT: Hartford Institute for Religion Research, 2012), http://faithcommunitiestoday.org/sites/faithcommunitiestoday.org/files/The American Mosque 2011 web.pdf, accessed Mar. 22, 2012; Pew Research Center, "Muslim Americans: No Signs of Growth in Alienation or Support for Extremism," (Aug. 2011), http://www.people-press.org/files/legacy-pdf/Muslim-American-Report.pdf, accessed Apr. 17, 2012; and Katie Day, Faith on the Avenue: Religion on a City Street (New York: Oxford University Press, 2014), chapter 6.

31. Gallup Center for Muslim Studies, "In U.S., Religious Prejudice Stronger Against Muslims" (Jan. 21, 2010), http://www.gallup.com/poll/125312/religious-prejudice-stronger-against-muslims.aspx, accessed Feb. 7, 2012; Robert Wuthnow and Wendy Cadge, "Buddhists and Buddhism in the United States: The Scope of Influence," *Journal for the Scientific Study of Religion* 43 (Sept. 2004): 363–380.

32. Aristide R. Zolberg and Long Litt Woon, "Why Islam is Like Spanish: Cultural Incorporation in Europe and the United States," *Politics & Society* 27 (Mar. 1999): 5–38; Edward E. Telles and Vilma Ortiz, *Generations of Exclusion: Mexican Americans, Assimilation, and Race* (New York: Russell Sage, 2008).

33. Timothy Matovina, *Latino Catholicism: Transformation in America's Largest Church* (Princeton: Princeton University Press 2012), 16.

34. Stephen P. Davis, Juan R. Martinez, and R. Stephen Warner, "The Role of the Catholic Church in the Chicago Immigrant Mobilization," in *¡Marcha! Latino Chicago and the Immigrant Rights Movement*, eds. Amalia Pallares and Nilda Flores-González (Urbana and Chicago: University of Illinois Press 2010), 79–96.

35. Elizondo, *Galilean Journey*; Dahm, *Parish Ministry in A Hispanic Community*; Matovina, *Latino Catholicism*.

36. Douglas Hartmann, Daniel Winchester, Penny Edgell, and Joseph Gerteis, "How Americans Understand Racial and Religious Differences: A Test of Parallel Items from a National Survey," *Sociological Quarterly* 52 (2011): 336. Although the authors' title and abstract specify a contrast between "racial" and "religious" differences, their interview invited respondents to answer in terms of their "ethnicity," a less contentious category than "race" in popular opinion. Nonetheless, their data show that religion retains its advantage.

37. Phillip Connor and Matthias Koenig, "Bridges and barriers: religion and immigrant occupational attainment across integration contexts." International Migration Review 47 (spring 2013): 3–38; Foner and Alba, "Immigrant Religion in the U.S. and Western Europe."

38. Margarita Mooney, *Faith Makes Us Live: Surviving and Thriving in the Haitian Diaspora* (Berkeley: University of California Press, 2009).

Bibliography

Alba, Richard, Albert J. Raboteau, and Josh DeWind, eds. *Immigration and Religion in America: Comparative and Historical Perspectives.* New York: New York University Press, 2009.

Bagby, Ihsan. *The American Mosque 2011.* Hartford, CT: Hartford Institute for Religion Research, 2012.

Burns, Jeffrey M. "¿Que Es Esto? The Transformation of St. Peter's Parish, San Francisco, 1913–1990." In *Portraits of Twelve Religious Communities.* Vol. I of *American Congregations,* edited by James P. Wind and James W. Lewis, 396–463. Chicago: University of Chicago Press, 1994.

Cadge, Wendy. *Heartwood: The First Generation of Theravada Buddhism in America.* Chicago: University of Chicago Press, 2005.

Chai, Karen J. "Competing for the Second Generation: English-Language Ministry at a Korean-American Church." In *Gatherings in Diaspora: Religious Communities and the New Immigration,* edited by R. Stephen Warner and Judith G. Wittner, 295–331. Philadelphia: Temple University Press, 1998.

Chen, Carolyn. *Getting Saved in America: Taiwanese Immigration and Religious Experience.* Princeton: Princeton University Press, 2008.

Connor, Phillip, and Matthias Koenig, "Bridges and Barriers: Religion and Immigrant Occupational Attainment Across Integration Contexts." *International Migration Review* 47 (spring 2013.): 3–38.

Dahm, Charles W. *Parish Ministry in A Hispanic Community.* Mahwah, NJ: Paulist Press, 2004.

Davis, Stephen P., Juan R. Martinez, and R. Stephen Warner. "The Role of the Catholic Church in the Chicago Immigrant Mobilization." In *¡Marcha! Latino Chicago and the Immigrant Rights Movement,* edited by Amalia Pallares and Nilda Flores-González, 79–96. Urbana and Chicago: University of Illinois Press 2010.

Day, Katie. *Faith on the Avenue: Religion on a City Street.* New York: Oxford University Press, 2014.

Ebaugh, Helen Rose, and Janet Saltzman Chafetz. *Religion and the New Immigrants: Continuities and Adaptations in Immigrant Congregations.* Walnut Creek, CA: Alta Mira Press, 2000.

Eck, Diana. *A New Religious America: How a "Christian Country" Has Become the World's Most Religiously Diverse Nation.* San Francisco: Harper, 2001.

Elizondo, Virgil. *Galilean Journey: The Mexican-American Promise.* Marynoll, NY: Orbis Books, 1983.

Fenton, John Y. *Transplanting Religious Traditions: Asian Indians in America.* New York: Praeger, 1988.

Finke, Roger, and Rodney Stark. *The Churching of America, 1776–2005: Winners and Losers in Our Religious Economy.* Rev. ed. New Brunswick: Rutgers University Press, 2005.

Foley, Michael W., and Dean R. Hoge. *Religion and the New Immigrants: How Faith Communities Form Our Newest Citizens.* New York: Oxford University Press, 2007.

Haddad, Yvonne Yazbeck, and Adair T. Lummis. *Islamic Values in the United States: A Comparative Study*. New York: Oxford University Press, 1987.

Herberg, Will. *Protestant-Catholic-Jew: An Essay in American Religious Sociology*. Rev. ed. Garden City, NY: Doubleday Anchor, 1960.

Jiménez, Tomás R. *Replenished Ethnicity: Mexican Americans, Immigration, and Identity*. Berkeley: University of California Press, 2010.

Kim, Rebecca Y. *God's New Whiz Kids? Korean American Evangelicals on Campus*. New York: NYU Press, 2006.

Kniss, Fred, and Paul D. Numrich. *Sacred Assemblies and Civil Engagement: How Religion Matters for America's Newest Immigrants*. New Brunswick: Rutgers University Press, 2007.

Kurien, Prema A. *A Place at the Multicultural Table: The Development of an American Hinduism*. New Brunswick: Rutgers University Press, 2007.

Leonard, Karen Isaksen. *Muslims in the United States: The State of Research*. New York: Russell Sage Foundation, 2003.

Lincoln, C. Eric, and Lawrence H. Mamiya. *The Black Church in the African American Experience*. Durham: Duke University Press, 1990.

Matovina, Timothy. *Latino Catholicism: Transformation in America's Largest Church*. Princeton: Princeton University Press, 2012.

Min, Pyong Gap. *Preserving Ethnicity Through Religion: Korean Protestants and Indian Hindus Across Generations*. New York: New York University Press, 2010.

Mooney, Margarita. *Faith Makes Us Live: Surviving and Thriving in the Haitian Diaspora*. Berkeley: University of California Press, 2009.

Numrich, Paul D. *Old Wisdom in the New World: Americanization in Two Immigrant Theravada Buddhist Temples*. Knoxville: University of Tennessee Press, 1996.

Portes, Alejandro, and Rubén G. Rumbaut. *Immigrant America: A Portrait*. 3rd ed. Berkeley: University of California Press, 2006.

Smith, Robert Courtney. *Mexican New York: Transnational Lives of New Immigrants*. Berkeley: University of California Press, 2005.

Telles, Edward E., and Vilma Ortiz. *Generations of Exclusion: Mexican Americans, Assimilation, and Race*. New York: Russell Sage, 2008.

Verba, Sidney, Kay Lehman Schlozman, and Henry E. Brady. *Voice and Equality: Civic Voluntarism in American Politics*. Cambridge: Harvard University Press, 1995.

Waldman, Steven. *Founding Faith: Providence, Politics, and the Birth of Religious Freedom in America*. New York: Random House, 2008.

Warner, R. Stephen. *A Church of Our Own: Disestablishment and Diversity in American Religion*. New Brunswick.: Rutgers University Press, 2005.

Warner, R. Stephen. "The De-Europeanization of American Christianity." In *A Nation of Religions: Pluralism in the American Public Square*, edited by Stephen Prothero, 233–255. Chapel Hill: University of North Carolina Press, 2006.

Warner, R. Stephen, Elise Martel, and Rhonda E. Dugan. "Islam Is to Catholicism as Teflon Is to Velcro: Religion and Culture Among Muslimas and Latinas." In *Sustaining Faith Traditions in America: Race, Ethnicity, and Religion among the Latino and Asian American Second Generation*, edited by Carolyn Chen and Russell Jeung, 46–48. New York: NYU Press, 2012.

Warner, R. Stephen, and Judith G. Wittner, eds. *Gatherings in Diaspora: Religious Communities and the New Immigration*. Philadelphia: Temple University Press, 1998.

Williams, Raymond Brady. *Religions of Immigrants from India and Pakistan: New Threads in the American Tapestry*. Cambridge: Cambridge University Press, 1988.

Yang, Fenggang. *Chinese Christians in America: Conversion, Assimilation, and Adhesive Identities*. University Park: Penn State University Press, 1999.

Zhou, Min, and Carl L. Bankston III. *Growing Up American: How Vietnamese Youth Adapt to Life in the United States*. New York: Russell Sage, 1998.

CHAPTER 25

....

IMMIGRATION, RACE, AND ETHNICITY IN AMERICAN FILM

....

STEVEN ALAN CARR

ON January 24, 1916, and after weeks of advance publicity and adulatory reviews of showings in other cities, the highly acclaimed motion picture *The Birth of a Nation* (Epoch, 1915) opened for an exclusive engagement at the Majestic Theatre in Fort Wayne, Indiana. Based on Thomas F. Dixon's 1905 novel *The Clansman* and a subsequent stage adaptation, America's first motion picture blockbuster almost immediately catapulted into popular consciousness with its visual innovations and epic narrative spanning slavery, the Civil War, and Reconstruction. Despite its reprehensible glorification of the Ku Klux Klan, the film, in Janet Staiger's words, became "encrusted with a history of responses and debates which make it a symbol of more than racist propaganda."[1] That encrustation had already begun well before the film's release in Fort Wayne, but once the film actually opened for local audiences, its immediacy created a new dimension for local audiences to make sense of the film. The *Fort Wayne Sentinel* reported that at the city premiere, "audiences burst into applause as the three thousand riders of the Klan dash down the hillside . . . to the rescue of their rights." Of course, the film narrative only could depict such vigilantism after it showed the Klan trying "to quell the uprising of the vicious and evil whites and the ignorant blacks." The *Sentinel* referred to the freed slave Gus in lascivious pursuit of the white Elsie Stoneman, not by name but as "a four legged beast." Yet curiously, the newspaper hailed the film adaptation as "a plea for peace" and "a particularly moving appeal" for greater understanding. It found that like Dixon's book, the film afforded "Northerners . . . a new viewpoint even if their fathers fought and bled in those awful years."[2] Whatever the film's "plea for peace" and understanding might have been, it engaged its audiences not through its ideological purity but through a racism mottled with pleas for tolerance and understanding. Clearly, *The Birth of a Nation* was "more than racist propaganda" for *The Fort Wayne Sentinel* as well as for those audiences deeply moved by their first encounter with the sweep and spectacle of the film.

Nearly 100 years later, the local reception of *The Birth of a Nation* beyond cities like New York still has something to tell us about immigration, race, and ethnicity in film. Films from the past can generate historical mirages for the present, not because they can do but because of what we desire them to do. Today, the public wants these films to offer some essential expression of the past that other forms of historical evidence do not provide. For all of their seeming promise to distill some prior cultural essence, though, films of the past do not tidy up as historical evidence for the present. As a historical document, *The Birth of a Nation* alone cannot fully explain an effusive review of the local premiere of the film in both relaying that an audience cheered the KKK and in lauding the film's perceived message of tolerance. The same challenge emerges for the study of immigration, race, and ethnicity in American film. The studies of immigration, race, and ethnicity themselves are messy and full of contradictions; films from the past do not eliminate these contradictions. Any study of immigration, race, and ethnicity in film undoubtedly will contribute to this confusion, not clarify it.

Perhaps this confusion derives from the desire to use films as a way to streamline this history. Though not exclusively so, the basic premise for studying race, ethnicity, and immigration since the 1960s has presumed that film is merely a vessel, and matters of immigration, race, and ethnicity are what pour out as the contents. In other words, studying immigration, race, and ethnicity in relation to film is simply a matter of studying these identities and representations as they exist in film. Can immigration, race, and ethnicity in American film extend beyond cinematic representation to encompass, for example, studying flesh and blood audiences attending a film or even a theatrical performance?

If we return to Fort Wayne a decade before the release of *The Birth of a Nation*, there are two tantalizing press accounts of the African American audiences who clearly were not the target audience for *The Birth of a Nation*. In 1904, the *Fort Wayne Daily News* reported that a judge had thrown out a court case brought by Charles Williams against Frank E. Stouder, manager of the Masonic Temple theater, "for refusal to admit him . . . because he was a colored man." Almost a year later, the *Fort Wayne Journal-Gazette* reported on page 5 that a melée had occurred at the same theater:

> A party of negroes which attended the Temple theater last night came nearly spending a night at police headquarters and as a result some affidavits may be filed this morning. It seems that one swain took a strange damsel to the show and his old sweetheart was a member of the party. After the play, the old sweetheart ran up to the beau and requested a word with him. It is said he thereupon threatened to throw her down the stairs. He alleges she tore his coat. The entire company then repaired to the police station to tell of the trouble, but when the officers threatened to lock them up they dispersed.

Neither story had anything to do with images in film nor even with movie-going; in both cases, the incidents presumably took place at stage performances. Yet such accounts raise some useful and relevant questions. Were African Americans regularly refused admission to movie theaters? Did they often attend the theater in Fort Wayne, and, if so, did they also attend the films frequently screened as early as 1897 at these venues? How did both white and black audiences attend the theater? Did these audiences sit together or separately, and did they choose where they sat, or did the theater determine seating? Did the theater regularly refuse admission to African Americans or only occasionally? Were these newspaper accounts part of an attempt to diminish and marginalize African American spectatorship, perhaps a way to reinforce the kinds of images of African Americans depicted in films like *The Birth of a Nation*? Were these stories just anomalies? Was the latter story perhaps an ingenious ruse fabricated by the theater to help provide additional publicity for its current dramatic offering?

With their sketchy accounts of an African American audience, these early newspaper reports highlight how little we know of race as well as ethnicity and immigration as they relate to film. Here, we might reflect on these identities not just as images but also as a complex cultural network inclusive of the multiple dimensions of popular entertainment. Also, we might consider how this network included not just films themselves but also audiences who attended these films. What did movie-going as a cultural practice mean in the first half of the twentieth century? How did intertextual networks of literature, stage, journalism, and other films both open and limit potential ways to make sense of these films? How might racial, ethnic, and immigrant identities have mattered to the actual process of movie-making?

Furthermore, approaching immigration, race, and ethnicity as these topics relate to film must address how these relationships have changed over time and in spaces devoted to popular entertainment. As both Vivian Sobchak and Robert Stam have observed, Mikhail Bakhtin's notion of the chronotope—a configuration of textual motifs along a time-space continuum—remains uniquely suited to film analysis. Bakhtin describes the chronotope where "time . . . thickens, takes on flesh, becomes artistically visible; likewise, space becomes charged and responsive to the movements of time, plot and history."[3] Immigration, race, and ethnicity likewise do not remain static and immutable constructs and likewise become "charged and responsive to the movements of time, plot and history."[4] Their presence in film, as well as their relation to the entirety of the social context for movie-going, constitutes its own chronotope playing out across the changing dimensions of movie-going that occurred in both time and in identifiable spaces dedicated to leisure and entertainment. The chronotope need not exist only in the text. It also can map out the thickening and increasingly visible set of relationships between texts and specific audiences charged with and responsive to movements taking place in both space and time.

The chronotope of immigration, race, and ethnicity in relation to film can reveal a great deal about the multidimensional and hybridized nature of this cultural complex. The concept of race meant one thing at the beginning of the twentieth century, perhaps a vague concept that conflated biology with national origin. By the 1920s and 1930s, and with the advent of eugenics and race science, it meant something quite different: race was a scientific but nonetheless arbitrary construction organizing allegedly biological traits, especially as a way to legally and socially subordinate specific groups. Along with the treatment of immigrant and ethnic groups, race could powerfully reinforce existing attitudes—or create new ones—justifying socioeconomic disparities and orders. In more limited and contentious ways, it could help ameliorate the consequences of socio-economic subordination.

As social constructs, immigration, race, and ethnicity have considerable overlap with one another. Each is itself hybridized and thus inflects what movie-going might mean to diverse audiences. As its own construct, the concept of ethnicity today is probably closer to how people used to discuss race: simply as a way to conceive of commonalities between various groups on the basis of religion, culture, and national origin. Immigration became a way to conceive of these groupings in terms of people displaced and dispersed from their homeland. African American theatergoers thus shared a common bond as an ethnic group, but social constructs simultaneously racialized their image both in films as well as in their belonging to an audience. Just as the connotations of immigration, race, and ethnicity have changed continuously over time, so too have the cultural practices of attending a show. The press accounts of African American theater-going and the city premiere of *The Birth of a Nation* some ten years after those reports already mark shifts taking place locally, both in cinematic depictions of race as well as in the cultural practice of being part of an audience. Occurring at various rates of change and scale, the dynamic relationship between film and immigration-race-ethnicity happens not just at the macro level of social and cultural trends but also at a local level that has its own distinct textures and inflections as well.

Is a Holocaust Film a Jewish Film?

The shifting parameters of what race, ethnicity, and immigration might mean to movies and movie-going help delineate the multidimensional and multitemporal nature of this relationship. Newspapers helped construct a reading position for audiences that could at once invoke the mode of melodrama as audiences cheered the Klan chasing down "a four legged beast," yet also identify a message in the film of tolerance and understanding. A decade earlier, press accounts described, however incompletely, the practice of African American theater-going. To understand a shifting set of parameters for what immigration, race, and ethnicity in relation to film might mean, one must look beyond only cinematic images. As a chronotope, the relationships, spaces, and contexts between and within which audiences consumed these images continually shifted and changed. These relationships and contexts included who saw these films, where they saw them, how people understood movie-going as a cultural practice, the connections audiences made between films and other kinds of popular entertainment, and, finally, how audiences understood cultural identity as a part of the movie-making process itself.

If the texture and inflection of the local community emerges as one site among many to examine the chronotope of how film exists in a relationship to immigration, race, and ethnicity, another potential site involves the popular practice of cataloging and inventorying images depicting immigration, race, and ethnicity. To illustrate the need to reflect upon the culturally constructed nature of this practice, let us jump ahead some thirty years to consider this deceptively simple question regarding ethnicity and film: is a Holocaust film necessarily a Jewish film? The answer is not so simple. Does this body of films include only features depicting recognizably Jewish characters or overtly addressing the Holocaust and Nazi anti-Semitism? Anti-Nazi films of the 1930s and 1940s had few identifiably Jewish characters but were rich with contextual meanings readily identifiable to Jewish audiences. In many cases, non-theatrical titles screened only in churches, schools, and the military went further than feature films in addressing the Holocaust and Nazi anti-Semitism. Limiting study to only overt depictions excludes films not necessarily Jewish but specifically marketed to Jewish audiences, or films that were popular with these audiences. In other cases, audiences widely understood films such as *The Life of Emile Zola* (Warner Bros., 1937) to be about Nazi anti-Semitism, even though the biopic ostensibly is about the nineteenth-century French novelist and his involvement in the Dreyfus Affair, a well-known incident of French anti-Semitism. Like *Zola*, films made by Jewish creative personnel during this period frequently lacked overt depictions of Jewish characters or themes but certainly made evocative and implicit references to them.

Because the basic question, "what is a Jewish film?" engenders such varied and protean responses, this chapter moves beyond only cataloging these films and considers a multifaceted approach to the topic. This approach must account for movie-going in all of its dimensions. More than viewing images of Jews or the Holocaust, it involves overlapping methods of textual analysis, production history, and audience reception. Not only do we need a normative framework that seeks to expand the canon of "usual suspects" but one that also seeks to expand our definitions of what studying movie-going in relation to ethnicity—as well as immigration and race—might involve. For each mediated text, these norms include evaluating each film on the basis of the following criteria:

- Significance of artistic achievement
- Facticity and authenticity of representation
- Influence upon subsequent films and genres
- Notable conditions of production, such as on-location shooting or use of survivor reenactments
- Critical reception at the time of release
- Influence upon audiences and subsequent audience expectations regarding how to represent Judaism, anti-Semitism, and the Holocaust

Establishing a transparent set of conventions for discussing the impact and qualities of Holocaust as well as other films involving ethnicity, race, and immigration potentially opens new possibilities for which films and what aspects of them merit discussion. Rather than rely upon a relatively limited canon established mostly through popular reviews or auteurist scholarship, these discussions might focus more on the material

forces establishing that canon. If we can discuss artistic achievement on a par with facticity and authenticity, for example, we can appreciate a relatively low-budget film such
as *The Last Stop* (Times, 1948), shot on location at Auschwitz by a team of female survivors. Neither ignoring nor dwelling upon a specifically Jewish dimension of Nazi anti-
Semitism, this foreign film was, for many American audiences, the first encounter, after
documentary newsreels, with a Holocaust film.

If some discussions regarding Holocaust-themed films involve more than considering what makes these titles "great masterpieces," others alternatively focus upon decidedly mimetic and ethical questions regarding how well these mediated representations
performed. Are they "realistic?" Do they engage in stereotypes? Do they, in Lawrence
Langer's words, "universalize" the Holocaust into a series of digestible yet banal lessons for us to learn?[5] Or worse, do they trivialize the Holocaust as a form of mere entertainment? Just as questions of aesthetic value and canon inclusion have no permanent
resolution, questions of mimesis and representational ethics are impermanent because
our norms and conventions for what constitutes a "realistic" or "ethical" treatment also
remain in flux. Upon release, anti-Nazi and Holocaust "comedies" routinely generated
controversy over tastelessness, but films such as *To Be or Not to Be* (United Artists, 1940),
The Producers (AVCO, 1967), and, more recently, *Life Is Beautiful* (1997; Miramax, 1998),
all eventually merited places, albeit ones subject to continued contestation, in the canon
of anti-Nazi and Holocaust-themed films and, in some cases, even Jewish-themed ones.

Although both aesthetic and mimetic approaches to these films will and should continue to discuss and debate the merits of individual films, these discussions should not
operate to the exclusion of a more systematic approach to considering how these films
represent Holocaust and Jewishness, or how actual audiences might have perceived
these representations. Tastes change; standards of realism shift according to conventions of the time; and methods of evaluating a film, whether by director, genre, or individual film, all come into and out of style. If the study of Holocaust and Jewish films is to
maintain credibility, it must be able to historicize and account for these shifts rather than
simply perpetuate or naturalize them.

In addition to moving beyond the established practice of attempting to inventory
these films, we also must move beyond what I call the "reflection paradigm." Annette
Insdorf's groundbreaking *Indelible Shadows* offers a telling example of just how difficult it is to define a Holocaust film. The films included in her survey are not Holocaust
films but are films that stand in relation to the Holocaust. Defining the Holocaust film as
that which "illuminates, distorts, confronts, or reduces the Holocaust," Insdorf explores
this relationship thematically, in terms of "cinematic language," "narrative strategies,"
depictions of Nazi atrocities, and, finally, those films that shape "documentary material through a personal voice."[6] Maintaining this distinction between the totality of an
event that can never submit fully to representation and the representation itself has a
long and respected tradition which we should continue to observe. But how does this
tradition help us to make sense of a science fiction action adventure film like *X-Men*
(Twentieth Century-Fox, 2000), with its opening explicitly set in a Nazi death camp? As
Lawrence Baron has noted, some critical responses concluded that this was yet another

trivialization of the Holocaust. Baron's essay argued, however, that the film functions on multiple levels, appealing to a teenage male audience while simultaneously reflecting allegorical connections between the Jewish-American experience and dialectical anxieties over state-sanctioned discrimination in both the United States as well as in Nazi Germany. Baron noted that the comic books on which the film is based are even more explicit in making these connections.[7] Clearly, no one looks to *X-Men* for an accurate depiction of a concentration camp. But can we so easily dispense with its allegory or its complex networks of historical meaning simply because it comes from a comic book and appears to trivialize the Holocaust in ways that higher-brow documentary and fiction does not?

The identity politics of what constitutes a Jewish film move us even further from a clear answer to this deceptively simple question. Lester Friedman's *Hollywood's Image of the Jew*, a 1982 pioneering study of representations of Jews in American film, made a similar argument as did Insdorf: film exists in relation to the American Jewish experience rather than embodying some part of that experience. To understand Jewish film, one has to understand "how Jews had been portrayed in American films." These portrayals, in turn, "could say something about Jews as well as about Americans."[8] Two years after the publication of Friedman's book, Patricia Erens proposed a more systematic, genre-oriented framework to examine representations of Jews in American cinema. Like Friedman, she conceived of film narratives as "incorporating Jewish elements" that "relate to American society in general and to the American-Jewish community in particular." And, like Friedman, she argued that these films reflect something of "actual experiences and latent attitudes" both toward and among the Jewish community.[9]

Insdorf, Friedman, and Erens all staked out an important and necessary distinction at a time when film studies still had to achieve respect as an academic discipline: the cinematic representation is not interchangeable with the thing represented. Furthermore, being able to distinguish between cinematic depictions and what those depictions represent can yield greater insight into protean subjects like the Holocaust or Jewish identity. And while these pioneering works have their limitations, as any scholarship has, they helped establish a paradigm for analyzing film as reflection. This chapter thus is not so much a critique of that paradigm as it is an attempt to rethink a different set of possibilities outside the reflection paradigm.

The Life of Emile Zola (Warner Bros., 1937) illustrates the limitations of this paradigm. Does it constitute a Jewish film? Is it an anti-Nazi film? Does the film provide an example of how Hollywood treated anti-Semitism? Except for a single fleeting close-up of the word "Jew" appearing in a shot, the film makes no explicit reference to Zola's involvement in combating anti-Semitism during the infamous Dreyfus Affair. Yet in depicting an event that audiences absolutely would have recognized as being about the infamous Dreyfus affair, Warner Bros. actively marketed the film to Jewish audiences and encouraged them to draw the topical and relevant parallels to contemporary Europe. The problem is not that there is a "reflection" paradigm. The problem is that this dominant paradigm cannot fully account for what *The Life of Emile Zola* actually did with audiences in 1937. And yet for Holocaust- and Jewish-themed films, the reflection paradigm operates largely to the exclusion of other production- or audience-oriented paradigms that might better explain what audiences did with films like *The Life of Emile Zola*.

IMMIGRATION AND THE HOLLYWOOD QUESTION

The Life of Emile Zola demonstrates how the reflection paradigm as a dominant mode of studying immigration, race, and ethnicity in film can only account for explicit representations. Within the chronotope of immigration, race, and ethnicity in relation to film, the paradigm cannot account for the range of meanings that immigrant and ethnic audiences could have assigned to them, or the ways in which motion picture studios attempted to market these films to specific audiences. In addition, as Fort Wayne African American spectatorship and the exhibition of *The Birth of a Nation* in the city demonstrated, issues of race—and, by extension, immigration, and ethnicity—extended well beyond cinematic representation to suffuse a divergent set of practices and meanings characterizing spectatorship.

Because immigrant identity is the most hybridized among race and ethnicity, as a part of the chronotope of film in relation to these identities, its discussion poses some distinct challenges. Immigrants never are just immigrants alone; they are immigrants plus something else. In relation to film, immigration almost always involves discussions of race and/or ethnicity as well. It is possible, nevertheless, to discuss race and racism or ethnicity and ethnic groups without discussing immigration. Any discussion of immigration in film, therefore, must account for how perceptions of immigration frequently express overlapping attitudes regarding race and ethnicity.

My book, *Hollywood and Anti-Semitism*, demonstrates that fears of immigration stoked what I called the "Hollywood Question." A stock set of ethnic and even racialized Jewish stereotypes, the Hollywood Question was more than just representations in films, though it certainly included those images. The Hollywood Question encompassed a whole set of social and cultural issues articulated beyond film, expressing its fears and desires through popular literature, debates over censorship, political cartoons, legislative testimony, and other discursive modes. The Hollywood Question only explicitly conveyed anti-Semitic attitudes on occasion. More often, it politely questioned whether Jews working within the film industry suffered too greatly from their immigrant parvenu backgrounds and ethnic motivations to handle the great responsibility of arriving at the helm of the most powerful media industries of public influence.

The film industry, of course, responded to this widespread perception of ethnic motivation in a variety of allusive ways, for to confront it directly would have given these perceptions additional credibility. One way to gauge the industry response to the Hollywood Question is to examine its depictions of the immigrant and the ghetto. In "Wretched Refuse: Watching New York Ethnic Slum Films in the Aftermath of 9/11," I argued that along with Richard Slotkin's frontier myth, "the myth of the city as a cramped, stifling breeding ground for antisocial and even pathological behavior has blinded us to the additional consequences of suburban revolutions, the rise of transnationalism, and the forces of globalization."[10] The essay argued that two United Artists films, *Street Scene* (1931) and *Dead End* (1937), represented paradigmatic shifts popularizing the view of the immigrant ghetto as a harsh, filthy, and animalistic environment of human beings inhumanely crowded into tenements. Despite the potential for sordid narrative details, both films possessed extraordinary cultural pedigree. Adapted from a Pulitzer Prize-winning play by Elmer Rice, *Street Scene* featured the familiar trope of an Irish-Jewish romance, set amid the harsh, violent, and even murderous conditions of the ghetto. Thematically and stylistically similar to *Street Scene*, *Dead End* self-consciously engaged social issues through its recombination of these elements with the gangster film. Also adapted from a popular Sidney Kingsley play by fellow playwright Lillian Hellman, *Dead End* was justly celebrated for its elaborate recreation of the Lower East Side on a studio soundstage.

In addition to drawing upon the prestige of their origins as well-respected plays, both *Street Scene* and *Dead End* operated squarely within the conventions of the social-problem film genre. Rather than indict the immigrants themselves, both films asserted that the harsh living conditions depicted were what bred such undesirable behaviors. The notion that one could take the immigrant out of the ghetto, but never the ghetto out of the immigrant, easily transplanted itself into popular literature *about* Hollywood. In Budd Schulberg's classic Hollywood novel, *What Makes Sammy Run?*, the book's narrator, Al Mannheim, answered the eponymous question by returning to the Lower East Side, the "breeding ground for the predatory germ that thrived in Sammy's blood, leaving him one of the most severe cases of the epidemic."

Novels like *What Makes Sammy Run* offer a kind of codex to decipher how films like *Street Scene* and *Dead End* depict immigrants. The immigrant ghetto represented the antithesis of assimilation for which many American Jews strove. When Mannheim visited Sammy's birthplace, he only could imagine

> Sammy Glick rocking in his cradle of hate, malnutrition, prejudice, suspicions, amorality, the anarchy of the poor; I thought of him as a mangy little puppy in a dog-eat-dog world. I was modulating my hate for Sammy Glick from the personal to the societal. I no longer even hated Rivington Street but the idea of Rivington Street, all Rivington Streets of all nationalities allowed to pile up in cities like gigantic dung heaps smelling up the world, ambitions growing out of filth and crawling away like worms.

As I argued in "Wretched Refuse," the logical consequence of such attitudes was the physical erasure of human "dung heaps" and, in their place, urban renewal projects like the World Trade Center, which, in this case, obliterated Little Syria, a once-thriving Arab neighborhood that was the oldest Middle Eastern Muslim-Christian community in the United States. Built atop a haphazard patchwork of ethnic immigrant urban neighborhoods and markets, such revitalization projects destroyed the so-called ghetto and, in its place, erected modern, sleek, and streamlined architectural monuments to a burgeoning internationalism, modernity, technocracy, and global capital.

The topic of immigration, race, and ethnicity in film obviously encompasses much more than a single chapter can cover. What is offered here is a different way of thinking about these topics, considering the texture and flavor of what movie-going might have been for diverse audiences and how this experience was mediated through other activities, like attending a play or reading literature. I have also suggested some strategies to move beyond the limits of canonical films that are often discussed because of their explicit representations. Instead, we might do well to consider the multiple meanings and interpretations diverse audiences could have derived from a wider range of films that may or may not have explicitly depicted immigration, race, or ethnicity. And finally, I have suggested that the depiction of immigrants in film may have operated as part of a larger discourse that negotiated perceptions of Hollywood as being essentially ethnic and immigrant.

Other scholarship would do well to explore further the chronotope of immigration, race, and ethnicity in relation to film. Although this chapter does not address depictions of other groups, such as Asians or Native Americans, studying film in relation to these groups also can move beyond the reflection paradigm and consider how such images operated within the political economy of the film industry according to production, distribution, and exhibition. We also might consider how criticism of stereotypes in film at the time helped mediate audience interpretations. Additional scholarship might further explore the relationships between a film like *The Birth of a Nation* and other live performances, such as minstrel shows or the use of blackface. How did immigration, race, and ethnicity operate within the Hollywood industrial mode of production? How did representations of immigrants, race, and ethnicity draw from intertextual sources, such as theater and literature? How did the industry work to exclude stereotypes and regulate ethnic representations? How did attitudes toward other ethnic groups, such as Germans immediately after World War I, influence popular perceptions of the film industry? How did practices such as segregation or publicity for specific films regulate audiences and how audiences assigned meaning? How did specific genres inflect common themes of immigration, race, and ethnicity? And finally, how did films other than the Hollywood feature depict immigration, race, and ethnicity? In addition to the work of independent African American filmmakers such as Oscar Micheaux, a variety of short subjects and non-theatrical films also existed. Much scholarship already has begun to address a number of these issues and continues to question established paradigms of where to look and what to see when studying immigration, race, and ethnicity in film.

NOTES

A portion of this essay was revised and expanded for New World, Old Hate: Antisemitism in North America, Steven K. Baum et al., eds. (Leiden, NL: Brill, in press).

1. Janet Staiger, *Interpreting Films: Studies in the Historical Reception of American Cinema* (Princeton, NJ: Princeton University Press, 1992), 139.
2. "A Wonderful Picture, The Birth of a Nation," *The Fort Wayne Sentinel*, Jan. 25, 1916, 6.
3. Mikhail Mikhailovich Bakhtin, "Forms of Time and of the Chronotope in the Novel: Notes Toward a Historical Poetics," *The Dialogic Imagination: Four Essays*, ed. Michael Holquist,

trans. Caryl Emerson and Michael Holquist (Austin, TX: University of Texas Press, 1981), 86.

4. Ibid., 86.

5. Lawrence J. Langer, *Preempting the Holocaust* (New Haven, CT: Yale University Press, 1998), 8–10.

6. Annette Insdorf, *Indelible Shadows: Film and the Holocaust*, 3rd ed. (1983; Cambridge, UK: Cambridge University Press, 2003), xvi.

7. Lawrence Baron, "X-Men as J Men: The Jewish Subtext of a Comic Book Movie," *Shofar* 22 (1) (2003): 45–46.

8. Lester D. Friedman, *Hollywood's Image of the Jew* (New York: Ungar, 1982), xviii.

9. Patricia Erens, *The Jew in American Cinema* (Bloomington: Indiana University Press, 1984), xi.

10. Steven Alan Carr, "Wretched Refuse: Watching New York Ethnic Slum Films in the Aftermath of 9/11," in *The City That Never Sleeps: New York and the Filmic Imagination*, ed. Murray Pomerance (New Brunswick, NJ: Rutgers University Press, 2007), 231.

BIBLIOGRAPHY

Carr, Steven Alan. *Hollywood and Anti-Semitism: A Cultural History Up to World War II.* Cambridge Studies in the History of Mass Communication. Cambridge, UK: Cambridge University Press, 2001.

Schulberg, Budd. *What Makes Sammy Run?* 1941. New York: Random House, 1952.

Slotkin, Richard. *Regeneration Through Violence: The Mythology of the American Frontier, 1600–1860.* Norman, OK: University of Oklahoma Press, 1973.

Sobchak, Vivian. "Lounge Time: Postwar Crises and the Chronotope of Film Noir." In *Refiguring American Film Genres: Theory and History*, edited by Nick Browne, 129–170. Berkeley, CA: University of California Press, 1998.

Stam, Robert. "Palimpsestic Aesthetics: A Meditation on Hybridity and Garbage." In *Performing Hybridity*, edited by May Joseph and Jennifer Natalya Fink, 59–78. Minneapolis, MN: University of Minnesota Press, 1999.

....

CHAPTER 26

LANGUAGE RETENTION/ LANGUAGE SHIFT, "ENGLISH ONLY," AND MULTILINGUALISM IN THE UNITED STATES

....

JOSHUA A. FISHMAN

QUESTION: How long does the immigrant stock around the world hang on to the languages that they bring with them from elsewhere?

ANSWER: IF they move to a highly interactive and modernizing Western setting, not long (two to three generations). This situation is almost always true, but the United States has an exceptional story to tell in this connection, if it is looked at in greater detail and in longer depth. It is a story with real ups and downs and zigs and zags, rather than a simple monotonic descending curve story. Here's how it goes.

LANGUAGE RETENTION

....

This subtopic is actually bidirectional, including "Language Shift" as its polar opposite, and came into use in American English in 1966 with the designation "Language Maintenance and Language Shift" in Joshua Fishman's then unprecedented review of some two dozen non-English languages on which the American decennial census had been reporting since before the turn of the twentieth century.[1] Spanish was then (1960) the first most numerous and widespread among them, with 3.3 million claimants, second place being held by German (3.1 million claimants).

However, even then in (1960), Spanish was already by far the most frequent non-English mother tongue claimed by the fourth generation (i.e., by individuals both of whose grandparents were American-born). The dynamics in the fourth generation behind the greater prospects of Spanish vis-à-vis German after the turn of the century are still very much with us today. Einar Haugen had taught us that this continent's non-English languages were subdivisible into three historical time sequences: native, imperial, and immigrant.[2] However, what the latter subgroupings hide is the fact that by the time of the fourth generation, Spanish had become ever so much more nativized in the United States than had German and, therefore, no longer essentially depended upon replenishment from the Old World for its prowess in the New World.

Initially, between 1880 and 1950, German had ruled the foreign language roost in the United States. There were German-speaking (praying and sermonizing) churches galore, both for Protestants and Catholics, dozens of German-English public schools and ethnic community schools (both church-related and secular), German periodical publications, German books (including encyclopedias and works specializing in technology, science, and agriculture), German theological schools, German colleges, German radio programs, and German summer camps for children and sports and swim clubs for adults of all ages. Indeed, Germans had established in America a cross-section of the sociocultural environment they had left (or not quite left) behind in Europe. They constituted at times as many as a quarter of the total American white population and even more than that of all Germans living outside of the fatherland, in Canada, South America, South Africa, Australia, the Balkans, and the Baltic states (which were virtually German colonies). Germans supported an "organization for the study of Germans living abroad" with their own schools and other institutions aplenty, "just like at home!"[3] Indeed, German, Germans, and Germany were welcome everywhere in the United States as upstanding members of the "better half" of their new countries of residence, very much as Germany itself was within the world's family of nations. German was the favorite foreign language of American high school students, German colleges in Europe were the favorites of American graduate students studying abroad, and, all in all, all things German projected a kind, nonviolent, and largely bourgeois image of themselves for many years.[4]

Brief Detour

It would be an injustice to leave this topic without at least mentioning two others related to it. Among the more than 80.5 million white Americans at that time (the latter part of the nineteenth century), around 18.4 million claimed mother tongues other than English, and more than 15.3 million of the latter claimed languages other than German and Spanish. Among all of those claiming non-English mother tongues, there were then over a million each of claimants who specified French (1.4 million), Italian (3.7 million), Yiddish (1.7 million), or Polish (2.4 million) and millions whose claims were dispersed across nearly twenty other languages from all over the world. These language groups collectively sponsored tens of thousands of schools (from Sunday school only to all day during every weekday), thousands of periodic publications, hundreds of radio programs, and houses of worship in which some language other than English was used for sermons and services.[5] In all, this was an amazingly large, diverse, widespread, and largely unappreciated, although culturally creative, group of languages, stemming from every corner of the world (although primarily from Europe and from southern and eastern Europe).

Of course, except for the misnamed Pennsylvania "Dutch," the presence of all the languages and the German prominence was substantially dependent on the foreign relations between the United States and their original countries of origin. In the case of German, these relations suddenly went from bad to worse after 1914. And after several subsequent generations of depicting all that was German as cruel, ugly, reprehensible, and anti-democratic, the possibility of any large further German immigration into the United States for the foreseeable future ceased.

In the meantime, Spanish in the United States always benefited from the proximity of Latin America, the seemingly unlimited number of its willing wage laborers—who arrived from the relatively porous American southern borders—and the favorable differences in living standards and interpersonal agreeableness. Both its numbers and stability make Spanish a towering exception today among the non-English languages of the United States in terms of the generational structure of its mother tongue claimants, because for almost all other non-English languages in America, there are virtually no claimants beyond the third generation. Spanish is still very much alive into the fourth generation and probably even well beyond into the fifth; after the third, no further generational counts are tabulated, because the majority are quite obviously native of native background by then. The constant influx of Spanish speakers throughout the United States and the ease and inexpensive nature of travel between this country and the Spanish-speaking countries of origin provide the Spanish language with continuity. The fact that Puerto Rico has made Spanish a co-official language and, therefore, "untouchable" in the eyes of federal law or of the mainland states where Puerto Ricans have resettled has allowed Spanish to have an unassailable and irreversible foothold in the United States. The constant stream of newcomers regularly refreshes and renews the fluency of fourth- (and beyond) generation Hispanics who might otherwise stray into Anglo lifestyles.[6]

Spanish has captured the foreign language market in America, but Hispanic universities have not yet captured the market for Americans studying abroad (as did German universities earlier). The chief problem that the roughly 8 to 10 million Spanish speakers now on this side of the Rio Grande pose for the Anglo-majority is, at base, a demographic one. Left to their own resources, there are Anglos who have feared a slow but inevitable transfer of power to a growing Latino transethnification and translingualization of the country. In connection with such issues, basic biases and emotions have been called into play, unreasonable as they may be, revealing deeply entrenched and protected political and economic concerns that were formerly and are still largely believed to be at stake as to "who is really in charge of this country: 'them' or 'us;?" Three other language groups also have somewhat delayed language-shift patterns: the Old Order Pennsylvania Amish/Mennonites, a few Amerindian peoples, and the Ultra-Orthodox Yiddish-speaking Hasidim, but they are all both numerically insignificant and geographically isolated in comparison with the "Spanish colossus." Instead of English being feared in Latin America as the "colossus of the North," Spanish now apparently elicits just such a fear among some Anglos or anglicized Americans north of the border.

"English Only," "English Official," and, of Course, "English Plus"

The "home of the free and the land of the brave" has never lacked for exclusionist movements vis-à-vis "outsiders," particularly if they were of the non-white and the non-north-western-European kind. Accordingly, it should be no surprise that Spanish, too, has faced such opposition. By the mid-1940s, Spanish and Hispanics as a whole were added to the list of earlier linguistic and ethnolinguistic "suspects" because of their not being "really" in the white, Anglo-Saxon, Protestant mold. The addition of Hispanics to the list of targets of anti-foreignism (previously restricted to individuals of Amerindian, Irish Catholic, Francophone Catholic, Italian Catholic, Jewish, Chinese, and other Asian and Pacific affiliations) was almost a predictable rite of passage for Hispanics. This hostility could and should have been expected by the time it arrived as a nationwide, rather than simply a Southwestern, phenomenon. It appeared in the mid-1950s under the leadership of two conservative spokespersons, John Tanton and S.I. Hayakawa. Because of their inadvertently revealing remarks expressing their blatant ethno-racial biases, the organization they founded ("English Only") soon lost the support of most of its early prominent members, but it did manage to place in some thirty state constitutions provisions that prohibited education and/or some other state functions or services in languages other than English. No federal legislation along these lines has been passed since the Supreme Court's famous 1923 decision in *Meyer v. Nebraska*, in which that state's prohibition of the use of vernaculars other than English in the instruction of minors was declared unconstitutional.[7] In the light of the Court's proceedings at that time, all states passing "English Only" or "English Official" (see below) legislation have exercised considerable care not to infringe upon rights to use other languages for purposes of health education, public safety, or earning a living. More recent civil rights legislation has also led most "English-Only" or "English-Official" legislation to carefully exempt from their intended coverage any states' provision of essential services in all areas of medical, legal, health, job-training or retraining, and other emergency/essential care and services.

The "English-Official" movement was also initiated by, among others, some of the early advocates of "English Only" who sought to avoid the "witch hunt" and "free speech" protests elicited by the rhetoric of "English Only" Newt Gingrich, a prominent conservative Republican tactician, a former speaker of the U.S. House of Representatives, and an early champion of "English-Official" considered "English Only" as "undemocratic." He believed that advocating "English Only" was not only incorrect but also unhelpful, claiming that "other languages" may not only be an asset but also sometimes even a necessity for Americans. He and his movement actually encouraged their adherents to learn other languages, particularly individuals concerned with fostering some other language related to their own family's history and traditions recently referred to as "heritage languages."[8] Therefore, what "English Official" advocates is support of English in the United States as the language that is most symbolic and definitive of government intentions and that is "the default language of government operations"[9]

This newer emphasis appears to some observers to be merely an attempt to "complete the consolidation of the USA," rather than opposition to languages other than English. The country's current "foreign language islands" are now believed to be likened to the multinational empires of old, for example, ancient Persia and Rome, with their ethnic provinces. More modern examples of this type of polity-organization are the Austro-Hungarian Empire and the Czarist Empire, both of which met early demises in some part due to the avoidable internal pressures stemming from their unassimilated and disputatious minority ethnic groups. Had these polities lasted long enough and had their revised policies been appropriate and timely enough for this purpose, they too could have become nation-states (i.e., states that become tightly integrated nations) like Spain, France, and England. The conversion of England into multiethnic Great Britain is an example of the reversibility of developmental processes, a possibility that may yet be germane to the United States.

Beliefs and Attitudes

Members of all speech communities also hold various beliefs and attitudes about the varieties in their speech repertoires. One such frequently encountered set of beliefs and attitudes (here referred to as "attributes") are those shown in Table 26.1, below, to which the definitions indicated further below, under bilingualism, apply.[10]

Spain, France, and England too had once been exceedingly multiethnic but finally succeeded in "digesting," that is, assimilating their ethnic minorities sufficiently to enable them to become consolidated nation-states in their own right. Otherwise, they too would, no doubt, have broken up into separate nation-states, as ultimately did Yugoslavia and Czechoslovakia. It is, presumably, toward the avoidance of any such eventuality, and without any malevolent intent whatsoever, that both "English Only" and its toned-down successor "English Official" now claim to be dedicated. It is because of the much-reduced vitriol or sharpness of the alarms and serious criticisms that once issued forth from these two camps with respect to their earlier "worst scene scenarios" that some have begun to think that a former point of crisis has been seen as having at least temporarily passed. Indeed, relative to the turmoil of their earlier years, both have become merely quiescent "areas of interest." Perhaps the third area to which we now turn will provide some contrast in this connection.

Table 26.1 *Varieties of "Varieties" (types of languages)*

Literary: The variety used in print or in educated writing, e.g., Standard English.

Vernacular: The variety used in ordinary (informal) educated speech: informal speech between good friends.

Dialect: Hierarchically a dialect is a variety of the vernacular that has become associated with a given region or social class, e.g., Brooklynese or "upper-class airs." A dialect is always a "dialect of . . .", i.e., it is not a freestanding entity, and, when used correctly, the designation is not meant as a "put-down." Dialects in many countries are objects of general respect and considerable academic study (e.g., in Germany or Scandinavia).

Creole: A variety created naturally, i.e., out of necessity, among a population having no mother tongue in common, out of the vocabulary and grammar of different previously existing varieties, and a variety that has then continued in use subsequently, to then become the mother tongue of a new generation of speakers, e.g., Jamaican Creole.

Pidgin: A former Creole that has not yet become the mother tongue of a new generation, e.g., speech between recent immigrants and local natives, whether or not they influence one another, but in which neither group passes the resulting fused variety along to its own children because of their differing lifestyles and experiences.

Classical: A variety that has lost its vernacular (spoken) functions but that has been retained in writing and reading functions and/or in formal speech or prayer, e.g., Latin or Biblical Hebrew.

International Auxiliary: An "artificial language" that has been purposely created to foster intergroup communication between communities that do not have or do not want to employ any vernacular in common, so as not to give either party an unfair advantage, e.g., Esperanto.

Code: A disguised variety formed by the systematic inversion of syllables or substitution of letters and, therefore, understandable only to those who have a key to these changes, e.g., "Pig Latin."

N.B.: The fortunes of history and the acts of individuals may cause "promotions" and "demotions" up and down the list of the above varieties, e.g., former creoles may still be known by the name "Creole" (in fact, this may even remain their official name), even after they have attained several generations of mother-tongue speakers and, therefore, have changed structurally accordingly and become recognized dialects or vernaculars themselves.

BILINGUALISM

Unlike "English Only" and "English Official," bilingualism has considerable academic depth and breadth. At the very outset, it must be noted that in the United States, under the U.S. Constitution, the federal government is not directly responsible for providing public education. Public education is an activity left essentially to the individual states to implement, and although all states require roughly the same number of years of compulsory school attendance (eight to ten), the result is one of the least centralized and most disorganized educational systems in the modern world. This condition immediately renders difficult any discussion or focused ameliorative attention to the problems of education in the United States.

For the purposes of parsimony, the discussion below will follow several of the conventions adopted by specialists in sociolinguistics.[11] Accordingly, we will take bilingualism to reflect any culturally appropriate mastery of two or more "languages" of any kind. Languages can be of several different varieties, namely literary [L], vernacular [V], dialect [D], creole [K], pidgin [P], classical [Cl], international auxiliary [I], and code [Co]. These terms will be explained in the next paragraph. Control of at least two distinct realizations of any of these varieties of language constitutes bilingualism, whether in written, read, or purely oral functions. Furthermore, various degrees of fidelity to a certain community or group standard are encountered among the communities' members, using these varieties, such that differences in their use between individual speech, although present, are far from random (thereby facilitating interpersonal communicability). According to this approach, a "country bumpkin" who moves to the big city in order to earn more income will probably (or his or her children will probably) become bilingual if the "city speech" is acquired (vernacular) before the "country speech" variety (dialect) is lost. This example also applies to immigrants who move from one country to another. Examples of both kinds of bilingualism are common in the United States and throughout the world. And, both kinds of bilingualism imply that as societal complexity increases and human mobility increases, almost everyone becomes "bilingual" (which includes trilingual, quadralingual, etc.) in the usual modern course of events. Eight varieties of language will be recognized, and although more can easily be suggested, these particular eight have been chosen partially because they "scale," that is, they stand in a very particular ordered relationship to one another.

Members of speech communities also hold various beliefs and attitudes about their respective speech repertoires. One such frequently encountered set of beliefs and attitudes (referred to as "attributes" in Table 26.2, below), to which the subsequently following definitions apply.

The varieties shown in Table 26.2 can also stand in one of four sociolinguistic relationships vis-à-vis each other: Ausbau, Abstand, Imbau, and none

In connection with bilingual education in the United States, an authoritative decision must be reached as to whether any two languages shown in Table 26.3 are Ausbau varieties that are so similar that they require separate recognition by the educational authorities. Because two different states may be involved in any decision, they could conceivably reach different conclusions, for example, in connection with whether children speaking Black English do or do not require bilingual education because they do not speak regionally standard school English, or whether Portuguese and Cape Verdean are sufficiently different.

As seen in Table 26.2, many bilinguals utilize varieties that differ in their attributes. Spanish-English bilinguals in the American Southwest may believe that their variety of spoken Spanish has greater historicity than does their variety of Texas English. Of course, all of the attributes set forth in Table 26.2 are highly "perspectival," that is, they are accepted as having been attained only by the bulk of the members of any given variety's own speech community and, not necessarily, by the members of any other. The fact that Americans take American English to be an autonomous variety

Table 26.2 *Distribution of varieties across attributes*

ATTRIBUTES

Varieties	V	H	A	S
LITERARY	X	X	X	X
VERNACULAR	X	X	X	-
DIALECT	X	X	-	-
CREOLE	X	-	-	-
CLASSICAL	-	X	X	X
INTERNATIONAL	-	-	X	X
CODE	-	-	-	X

V=Vitality: the attribute of being judged to have many mother-tongue speakers.

H=Historicity: the attribute of being at least three generations older than anyone now alive.

A=Autonomy: the attribute of a variety that can establish its own internally recognized rules.

S=Standardization: the attribute of establishing its own internally and externally recognized rules.

Table 26.3 *Sociolinguistic relationships between varieties*

(1) *Ausbau languages*[1] are those originally closely related varieties that have purposively been developed away from one another, so that the weaker one will not be viewed as "merely a dialect" of the stronger one (e.g., American and British English during the lifetime of Noah Webster);

(2) *Abstand languages* are two frequently interacting languages that are considered to be sufficiently dissimilar from each other for neither of them to be considered as merely a dialect of the other, even though "purification" efforts may still be felt to be necessary (e.g., English and French) at various points in their histories;

(3) *Imbau languages*[2] are those whose "excessive" similarity has not been overcome, and, therefore, the weaker is abandoned or absorbed by the stronger (i.e., Samnorsk vis-á-vis Riksmal or Landsmal in Norway;

(4) *None* (i.e., no relationship): languages that are not in sufficient interaction for their relative statuses with respect to each other to be a matter of societal concern, (e.g., English and Czech).

[1] Heinz Kloss, "German-American Language," in *Language Loyalty*, 206–252.

[2] Fishman, "Rethinking the Ausbau-Abstand Dichotomy into a Continuous and Multivariate system," *International Journal of the Sociology of Language* 191 (May 2008):17–26.

does not oblige the English to think so too. On the other hand, when the residents of Mombay decided that "M-o-m-b-a-y" was the preferred spelling of their city's name, it, instead of Bombay, became the standardized spelling all over the modern world as well, at least wherever Hindi is recognized as possessing its own standardization relative to Urdu.

Bilingualism in the United States is most commonly of the "compound" type rather than the "coordinate" type and increasingly becomes coordinate the longer a respective speech community live surrounded by the Anglo-majority and remain dependent upon them for their income, education, and many leisure time activities, particularly those involving the electronic media. In compound bilingualism, the two languages are customarily not rigorously separated from each other, neither in function nor in structure. Interference becomes more noticeable between them, that is, bilingual individuals use languages almost randomly with other similarly bilingual individuals. Sentences, phrases, and even words revealing aspects of both languages are formed, for example, "I start a sentence in one language *y lo termino en la otra*."

In coordinate bilingualism, most utterances are much more commonly in accord with the rules of only one language at a time, with no jumps from one to another within the same utterance.[12] Indeed, such communities may even be diglossic (i.e., each variety has clearly separate functions that are used in mostly different settings (e.g., the language acquired at home is not acquired at school).[13] Another way of expressing the same phenomenon is to say that the languages are used in ways that reveal them to be much more compartmentalized when they function in coordinate rather than compound bilingualism. Keeping the two languages studiously apart, even though all interlocutors are bilingual, ultimately leads to better maintenance of the weaker language in the broader community, whereas compound bilingualism more quickly leads to language shift toward the dominance of the stronger language in the broader community. Accordingly, it should come as no surprise that most bilingualism in the United States is now of the compound type, where most bilinguals lack the institutions (schools, writers) to guard their mother tongues from English interference. Over time, this leads to the attenuation of bilingualism both among individuals as well as in the bilingual community as a whole. Then bilingual radio and television programs more quickly transfer over to being only in English, bilingual schools are no longer needed, and bilingual families no longer exercise care that their young maintain the family's bilingual traditions vis-à-vis style of discourse in speech.

On the other hand, much affection and interest toward the weaker language may continue, even after its active use has become much attenuated. Such continuation of affect is often put to use by educators and parents who seek to restart bilingual schools (particularly at the early childhood or kindergarten levels), and it is, more generally, the foundation for "language return" or "reversing language shift" movements that may experience limited success, as, for example, in New Zealand among Maoris and in Hawaii in places where Hawaiian was generally no longer being put to use. Such "revitalization" movements have generally not succeeded even in connection with ethnic revival movements, the case of Hebrew being a major (and, thus far, not duplicated) partial exception in this regard. The loss of community bilingualism may well be more irremediable on a wider scale than is the loss of other aspects of culture, notwithstanding the continued presence of exceptional personalities who continue to master both varieties well.[14]

THE CREATION OF A LANGUAGE-CONSCIOUS
AND LANGUAGE-VALUING AMERICA

To a considerable degree, the attenuations of language retention, of "English-Only" sentiments, and of maximal bilingualism may all be understandable as outgrowths of America's growing globalization. As the world becomes smaller and culturally more homogeneous, more and more Americans are (or may become) convinced that they can do without the existence of non-English languages in their very midst and the continued (and largely unsuccessful) efforts to stabilize them and to reverse their attrition. Unfortunately, such views would be mistaken on all grounds. The world is still fairly full of linguistic diversity, as its 8,000 to 10,000 languages reveal and as testified to by the dedication of the European Union to its multilingual operation, and as is evident from the increasing success of a new organization, Terralingua, in the pursuit of its prize-winning work of enumerating and cultivating the indigenous languages, knowledge systems, folklores, plants, vegetation, animals, and food types of the planet. The more that Terralingua searches for such evidence, the more instances of each it finds and the more highly they are found to be intercorrelated with language diversity. Earlier researchers seemed to adopt overly broad typologies, and the more these are replaced by more appropriate narrower ones, the more varieties there are to keep track of. Languages and language and culture systems are not decreasing but, counter to currently popular wisdom, are actually growing in number. This amazing fact has also now been independently confirmed several times by experienced researchers of the Summer Institute of Linguistics in Arlington, Texas.

Thus, there seem to be at least two large and complementary sociolinguistic processes that are generally ongoing in the United States and in the world at large. The first leads to the amalgamation of existing varieties and the second to their further continuation. During its first two centuries, America has devoted most of its attention to the first tendency. Perhaps it will devote the next two centuries to the second. Several problems stand in the way of any such reversal, not the least of which is the paucity of major career and income incentives (of a magnitude to compare with those now available in engineering, medicine, or law) pertaining to maintaining and increasing one's humanistic and communication skills. Perhaps for this goal to be obtained, America has to learn to speak and listen in mini-scales (vis-à-vis mere varieties, rather than just with respect to standardized mini-scales). Thus far, there has not been any binding decision as to whether a language-conscious America—that is, a United States in which all languages spoken by speech communities (rather than only those attained on an individual elective basis)—should be openly acknowledged as being in accord with the "American dream" and, therefore, eligible for whatever support, defense, and assistance may be required for the continued ability to serve the health, and self-assurance necessary for the pursuit of happiness of the members of each speech community. The United States is still very young and accordingly very much "a work in progress" in many ways, and it may well learn to reject the self-defeat implicit in many of its language and culture predictions in the recent past. The path of future scholarship could very profitably be oriented in the direction with which we propose to complete the present discussion.

On the Multidirectionality of Social Processes: Some Tentative Conclusions as Suggestions

The outcomes recorded above are not inevitable, universal, or even necessarily irreversible. They are, in many respects, similar to minority-language efforts in many parts of the world that can best be defined as reflecting the processes of urbanization, modernization, and globalization. These several processes taken together tend overall to move interacting populations in the sociolinguistic direction of the dominant or hegemonic language that can now most often be seen or interpreted as benefiting those populations most in material and social mobility terms. When most minority-language speakers are immigrants, many of whom have left behind their older and more conservative relatives, such change is likely to be rapid as well as marked. Elsewhere in the world, more stable and less uprooted populations speaking a multitude of different languages have lived side by side for generations, in circumstances of slower and more controlled social change, often without any major dislocations in their normal and previously established speech (and writing) patterns.

However, social change is neither uncontested nor, as some have assumed, unidirectional. The alienation and anomie commonly elicited by rapid and far-reaching social change often elicit oppositional or corrective reactions that actually lead to language maintenance, revival, or renewal movements in conjunction with language and also with religion, traditional values, clothing patterns, politics, and outlooks more generally. There have certainly been such counterreactions in the United States too, and although they have been minor compared to the change forces discussed earlier, all social groups contain a variety of different opinions, and just as many may welcome social change as others will oppose it and organize accordingly. Revival movements seeking a full or partial return to former life patterns, including language revitalization movements, have occurred and have left their sociolinguistic marks as well among Protestants, Catholics, and Jews in both urban and especially rural settings in the United States. A major reversal in America's economic prospects might very well foster such developments on the national sociolinguistic scene as well. Amerindian and other more peripheral groups in relation to the American mainstream are particularly prone to such revivalist movements and join them earlier than do most others. In times of trouble, the old ways, the old religion, and the old language all function as magnets that evince renewed attraction and bring renewed hope to many who never expected that it "would happen to them."

Another related area of change over time in this topic area is the ever greater relationship to mainstream language problems and issues. In this way, languages evince an ability to be reinterpreted not only as a return to the old but also as new ways to cope with broader and thoroughly American (rather than only as distinctly minority) issues. Language maintenance and bilingualism are now more commonly presented as contributions to the general American good and welfare as a whole. Thus "English plus" and bilingual education have come to be presented not as narrowly minority-intended or minority-focused issues but as issues that are actually for the benefit of all Americans. Would not all Americans benefit from a country that is linguistically better attuned to world markets and to interaction and competition on the world scene with apparently more multilanguage understanding and competency than many Europeans and East Asians? Such a mainstream-oriented focus on what were heretofore presented and considered only from the point of view of minority-focused interests is actually a genuine Americanization (rather than a feigned) legitimization of purported foreign languages, by means, arguments, and efforts that were not previously available to those who now utilize them creatively, rather than merely as a tactic for circumventing opposition or attracting support for old views. As immigrants and other linguistic, religious, and social minorities increasingly become different, are seen as different, and also see themselves differently than before, they not only change their former language interests and behaviors, but they also accommodate them to the new and constantly growing role of American realities and opportunities in their lives.

America is a land of endless autonomies.[15] Autonomies in culture and in politics involve constant and repeated attempts to find compromises between independence, on the one hand, and incorporation on the other. Note the *"libre y asociado"* status of Puerto Rico, allowing it to be both "free" and Spanish-speaking as well as "associated" and English-speaking. It turns out that language areas such as those we have been discussing here are among the most renegotiable elements of cultural autonomy, pertaining as they do not only to the lives of individuals but also to the operation of the press, the mass media, religion, politics, government participation, and commerce and industry. The Americanization of language maintenance, language advocacy, and multilingualism represents small-scale but ingenious triumph over the earlier travails of language shift and the tragedy of "English Only."

Is English in the United States thriving, or is it crumbling and breaking up into not only new American Englishes but also an increasing number of Black Englishes and an ever greater variety of Hispanic Englishes as second dialects? Strange as it may seem,

English is actually dong both things simultaneously. Upper-class Black and Puerto Rican Englishes, recognizably different though they are, are both examples of the best kinds of spoken and written English to be encountered in the United States today (as anyone who has carefully examined the English of President Obama and his family and the English of the English Department at the University of Puerto Rico at Rio Piedras can easily ascertain). The users of these many varieties of English easily switch from their basolect (the most dialectal of their dialect varieties) to their acrolect (the most standard of their standard varieties). They do so without hesitation when situationally required, but they do so perfectly and effortlessly as well, indicating that they are all used expertly and with native proficiency. Who would have thought 100 years ago, when massive Americanization and anti-hyphenation campaigns were being urgently launched, that this kind of internal diversification would be as marked as it still is today in native American English? More than anything else, this reveals the "wheels within wheels" that constitute the American language scene today. A little bit of everything is going on somewhere all of the time, and, as a result, sociolinguistics has become a multitasking paradise and a multi-splendored area for studying the true complexities of American reality in the living fields of American language, history, and ethnicity. American sociolinguistics, like American history, does not repeat itself, but it circles in ever larger and more inclusive spheres that capture the total and often unpredictable history and culture of a continent (not just a country) with which the entire world is trying to catch up. Clearly, language in America has entered a new stage, namely, one in which a person can end a sentence with a preposition, a prescriptively unacceptable grammar practice merely a few decades ago.

Notes

1. Joshua A. Fishman, ed., *Language Loyalty in the United States: The Maintenance and Perpetuation of Non-English Mother Tongues by American Ethnic and Religious Groups* (London: Mouton, 1966).
2. Einar Haugen, *Bilingualism in the Americas* (Tuscaloosa: University of Alabama Press, 1956).
3. Otto Lohr, *Deutschland und Übersee* (Herrenalb: Erdmann, 1962).
4. Heinz Kloss, "German-American Language Maintenance Efforts," in *Language Loyalty in the United States*, 206–252.
5. Fishman, *Language Loyalty*.
6. Jane M. Christian and Chester C. Christian Jr., "Spanish Language and Culture in the Southwest," in *Language Loyalty*, 280–317; Guadalupe Valdez, Joshua Fishman, Rebecca Chávez, and William Pérez, *Developing Minority Language Resources: The Case of Spanish in California* (Clevedon, England: Multilingual Matters, 2006).
7. Meyer v. Nebraska, 262 U.S. 390, 393 (1923).
8. Donna Brinton, Olga Kagan, and Susan Baukus, *Heritage Language Education* (New York: Routledge, 2007).
9. ProEnglish, "Why ProEnglish Opposes H.R. 2499," https://www.proenglish.org/data/backgrounders.html?id=218:why-proenglish-opposes-hr-2499-&catid=48.

10. Joshua A. Fishman, *European Vernacular Literacy: A Sociolinguistic and Historical Introduction* (Clevedon, England: Multilingual Matters, 2010).
11. Ibid.
12. Veroboj Vildomec, *Multilingualism* (Leyden, Netherlands: A.W. Sijthoff, 1963).
13. Alan Hudson, "Diglossia: A Bibliographic Review," *Language in Society* 21 (Dec. 1992): 611–674; Alan Hudson, "Outline of a Theory of Diglossia," *International Journal of the Sociology of Language* 157 (Sept. 2002): entire issue.
14. Joshua A. Fishman, ed., *Can Threatened Languages Be Saved? Reversing Language Shift Revisited: A 21st Century Perspective* (Clevedon, England: Multilingual Matters, 2001).
15. Hurst Hannum, *Autonomy, Sovereignty, and Self-Determination: The Accommodation of Conflicting Rights*, rev. ed. (Philadelphia: University of Pennsylvania Press, 1996).

BIBLIOGRAPHY

Brinton, Donna, Olga Kagan, and Susan Baukus. *Heritage Language Education.* New York: Routledge, 2007.

Christian, Jane M., and Chester C. Christian Jr. "Spanish Language and Culture in the Southwest" In *Language Loyalty in the United States: The Maintenance and Perpetuation of Non-English Mother Tongues by American Ethnic and Religious Groups*, edited by Joshua A. Fishman et al, 280–317. London: Mouton, 1966.

Fishman, Joshua A., ed. *Can Threatened Languages be Saved? Reversing Language Shift Revisited: A 21st Centery Perspective.* Clevedon, England: Multilingual Matters, 2001.

Fishman, Joshua A., ed. *European Vernacular Literacy: A Sociolinguistic and Historical Introduction.* Clevedon, England: Multilingual Matters, 2010.

Hannum, Hurst. *Autonomy, Sovereignty and Self-Determination: The Accommodation of Conflicting Rights.* Rev. ed. Philadelphia: University of Pennsylvania Press, 1996.

Haugen, Einar. *Bilingualism in the Americas.* Tuscaloosa: University of Alabama Press, 1956.

Kloss, Heinz. "German-American Language Maintenance Efforts." In *Language Loyalty in the United States: The Maintenance and Perpetuation of Non-English Mother Tongues by American Ethnic and Religious Groups*, edited by Joshua A. Fishman, 206–252. Berlin: Mouton, 1966.

Lohr, Otto. *Deutschland und Übersee.* Herrenalb: Erdmann, 1962.

Valdes, Guadalupe, Joshua A. Fishman, Rebecca Chávez, and William Pérez. *Developing Minority Language Resources: The Case of Spanish in California.* Clevedon, England: Multilingual Matters, 2006.

Vildomec, Veroboj. *Multilingualism.* Leyden, Netherlands: A.W. Sijthoff, 1963.

CHAPTER 27

....

MELTING POTS, SALAD
BOWLS, ETHNIC MUSEUMS,
AND AMERICAN IDENTITY

....

STEVEN CONN

In July 2011, Virginia Congressman James Moran introduced legislation to create the National Museum of the American People. The new museum, he announced, would focus on the history of immigration and immigrants. The proposal "may be idealistic," Representative Moran told the press, "but I do think there's merit in the idea of showing all the American people how all the various threads of ethnicities and races and religions came together."[1] Right away, people started calling it the Melting-Pot Museum.

Congress will be asked to authorize the museum and designate a space for it on the National Mall. The funding will be raised privately. All of which means that, as I write this, the museum is still a long way off.

Still, there was a certain foot-in-mouth urgency to Moran's announcement of the project. He worried out loud (and in front of the press) about the proliferation of ethnically specific museums and about the money Congress appropriated to fund them. More than that, he worried that this proliferation also meant a balkanization of audience. As he put it: "The Museum of American History is where all the white folks are going to go, and the American Indian Museum is where Indians are going to feel at home. And African Americans are going to go to their own museum. And Latinos are going to go their own museum. And that's not what America is all about. . . . It's a matter of how we depict the American story and where do we stop?" said Moran, and he went on: "The next one will probably be Asian Americans. The next, God help us, will probably be Irish Americans."[2]

The remarks were impolitic—and Moran was roundly and predictably attacked for them—but they were not altogether wrong either. The tourist traffic in and out of the nation's capital will probably ensure that the ethnically specific museums on the Mall get a healthy attendance. But nationally, the survey evidence we have suggests that Moran is right: Polish Americans tend to go to the Polish American museum, and while the curators there would love to show Ukrainian Americans the exhibits, Ukrainian Americans go to the Ukrainian American museum.[3]

At a higher level of abstraction, Moran also put his finger on what we might call the problem of narrative in American history museums. Given how much Americans venerate our past, or claim to, it comes as something of a surprise to realize that there are only a handful of history museums which attempt to tell the Big Story of American history, whatever that story might be.

Instead, the vast majority of history museums tell a small and usually local tale. And most focus on a particular moment in time—whether the 1770s in Williamsburg or the mid nineteenth century at Connor Prairie in Indiana. Even on the Mall, the National Museum of American History is largely a hodge-podge of collections that reflect its origins as a museum of technology, rather than being a comprehensive narrative of the country's history.

The nation does have two prominent museums dedicated to immigration, one on either coast. Ellis Island, in New York harbor, served as the primary entry point for Atlantic immigrants between 1892 and 1954 by which time it had processed roughly 12 million new arrivals. After it had fallen into disuse and disrepair, Ellis Island reopened as a museum of the immigrant experience in 1990, run by the National Park Service.

Across the country, in San Francisco Bay, the Immigration Station on Angel Island functioned as "the Ellis Island of the West" from 1910 until 1940, though by comparison the number of immigrants who came through the station was tiny. Likewise, the treatment of those arrivals, mostly Chinese, was often harsh and degrading. Angel Island functioned more as a detention center than as a way-station. After World War II, Angel Island became part of the California State Park system, and the Station is now open as a museum, having been renovated in 2009.

Both these museums are rooted in their sites. The stories they tell are connected to a specific place at a specific moment in time, and in no small measure this contributes to the power of those stories. But it also makes them much like other site-specific history museums. Neither, in other words, tries to capture a grand historical narrative.

Moran has offered his melting pot museum to fill that void. A museum created to insist that the story of America is the story of *e pluribus unum*.

"Ethnic" but Not Immigrant: African American and Native American Museums

It is worth starting with a distinction. The best survey we have documents well over 1000 ethnically oriented sites—museums, galleries, gardens, historic homes, and more. But roughly 25 percent of those are sites related to Native America and nearly 200 are devoted to African American history and life. Given the histories of those two groups of people, it hardly seems right to lump them in with museums devoted to the more conventional immigrant narrative, like Swedish museums or Ukrainian museums. After all, as Malcolm X put it: "We didn't land on Plymouth Rock; the rock was landed on us."

In fact, though it is hard to know with exact precision which constitutes the first group-specific museum, pride of place probably goes to the African American museum at Hampton University, founded just after the Civil War in 1868. Since then, African American historical and cultural sites have been established all over the country, in major cities and in small towns. There is even an African American history museum in Boise, Idaho.

The sheer number of these places is matched by their variety. They range from major research facilities, like the Schomburg Center for Research in Black Culture in New York, which holds 5 million items, to small house museums, like the Peter Mott House in Lawnside, New Jersey, open as of this writing just one afternoon each week.

Given that variety, it is hard to generalize about these institutions, but it is fair to say that many, and especially the older ones, focused on telling the story of African American uplift. They celebrate the lives of particularly successful and prominent individuals—like the W. C. Handy Museum and Library in Florence, Alabama—and testify to the achievement of a people who moved from slavery to freedom. It is also fair to say that many were founded to preserve the objects and archives of African America precisely because these things were being systematically ignored in larger mainstream institutions.

More recently, a number of older museums and a handful of new ones have wrestled with the thorny task of presenting slavery, segregation, and racism more broadly to a museum public. Under pressure from political activists and scholars alike, Williamsburg has included slavery as part of its interpretive program, after having resolutely ignored the question for years. Several museums devoted to the Civil Rights movement have opened, and while they tell the heroic and triumphal story of that movement, they cannot ignore the ugly fact that this nation condoned and supported segregation for nearly a century. The brutal realities of slavery have been confronted at the Underground Railroad Museum in Cincinnati. The experience of slavery is also at the center of the Old Slave Mart Museum in Charleston. In 2010, a new exhibit in Philadelphia brought the fact of slavery to Independence National Historical Park. After excavations revealed where the original Executive Mansion had been located, the new exhibit highlights the slaves George Washington brought with him to Philadelphia while he served as the nation's first president. Located just yards from the Liberty Bell, the "President's House" juxtaposes the two central facts of the nation's founding: freedom and slavery.

Even more numerous and various, Native American sites are, in some ways, also even more problematic. Among the roughly 300 such places are archaeological sites, ethnographic museums, ethnographic collections housed in art museums and natural history museums, historic sites, and dozens of tribal museums.

It is an inventory so big and broad as scarcely to make sense as a single category. Tying them together, perhaps, has been a vexing debate over perspective and point of view. Put bluntly: who gets to tell the story of Native America, and how?

Initially, of course, that question had a simple answer. European Americans did the excavating, and the collecting, and they put the material they found, stole, bought or otherwise appropriated in museums of their own design. They relied on the intellectual frameworks of anthropology to construct those exhibits and thus told the story from that point of view.

By the 1960s, that dynamic came under attack, and it has been challenged by a number of exhibits and museums put together by Native Americans from a Native American perspective. Older institutions have invited members of Native groups into the museum to curate exhibits or to create new interpretations of objects. And some Native groups have built a new generation of museums that tell the story of their tribe. Perhaps the most spectacular of these is the Mashantucket Pequot Museum and Research Center in Connecticut.

This drive for Native Americans to tell their own stories in their own ways reached both its climax and its anticlimax with the opening of the National Museum of the American Indian (NMAI) on the National Mall in 2004. Part of the Smithsonian complex, the NMAI instantly became the most prominent Native American museum in the country. Early in the process of planning, the museum decided to invite "community curators" to help design the exhibits. This was a response to the fact that Indians have always been "portrayed from the outside," and the promise at NMAI was something different, "our way of looking at Native American history."

The result was disappointing and widely criticized.[4] Rather than telling a different story, or even a familiar one from a different angle, the NMAI opened as an extravagant jumble. It underscored that simply allowing insiders to tell insider history does not guarantee a compelling or even coherent story.

SEPARATE AND CENTRAL?

After subtracting the African American and Native American museums, we are still left with over 700 museums devoted to and run by particular ethnic groups, mostly those originating in Europe. (The largest collection is the roughly 115 museums devoted to Jewish Americans and to the Holocaust.) In fact, these museums feature 55 different ethnic groups, according to Chicago's Museum of Science and Industry President Emeritus Victor Danilov—from the Acadian Museum in Erath, Louisiana, to the Welsh-American Heritage Museum in Oak Hill, Ohio.[5]

Some are quite elaborate, like the Balzekas Museum of Lithuanian Culture in Chicago, which has its own large facility, charges admission, and keeps regular hours. Others are almost poignantly modest, like the Romanian Museum in the same city, whose folk-costume collection had been kept in the house of the Romanian woman who had brought the traditional clothing to America. It has now abandoned plans to build its own bricks-and-mortar museum and makes its collection available online instead.

On June 2, 1926, Sweden's Crown Prince Gustav Adolph came to Philadelphia and laid the cornerstone for what would become the American Swedish Historical Museum. The event was deliberately heavy with symbolism. The Crown Prince picked up his shovel at the very southern end of the city, on the grounds of the Sesquicentennial Exposition, which celebrated the 150th anniversary of the Declaration of Independence. And, as it happened, the grounds of the fair—in 1926 a largely unoccupied piece of marsh and swamp—turned out to be part of the land-grant Sweden's Queen Christina had given settler Sven Skute in 1653. It was a perfect way for Swedish Americans to connect their own history to the larger history of the United States.

The museum was dedicated 12 years later in 1938, this time to mark the tercentenary of the arrival of Swedes in North America. When it opened formally to the public, it was not necessarily the first museum to focus on (and celebrate) a particular ethnic group in the United States—the Vesterheim Norwegian-American Museum in Decorah, Iowa, had been founded in 1877—but it did constitute the grandest encapsulation of the central tension found in most ethnically specific museums: an insistence, on one hand, on the separateness and distinctiveness of a particular ethnic group, while, on the other hand, an assertion of the central contributions that group has made to the larger American whole. When it opened, the American Swedish Historical Museum aimed "to become not only a depository for objects and exhibits of various kinds which throw light on Swedish contributions to American progress, but [also to] endeavor to be an information bureau on all phases of Swedish life, Swedish activities and Swedish accomplishments in science, art, literature, inventions and other fields."[6]

Their purpose sounds a lot like the mission statement of the Arab American National Museum, which opened almost three quarters of a century later in Dearborn, Michigan: "The Arab American National Museum's mission is to document, preserve, celebrate, and educate the public on the history, life, culture and contributions of Arab Americans. We serve as a resource to enhance knowledge and understanding about Arab Americans and their presence in the United States."[7]

The challenge for ethnic museums is to present the unique and specific character of different cultures while not portraying that culture as so distinct as to be outside the mainstream of American life.

THE RISE OF ETHNIC MUSEUMS AND THE DECLINE OF ETHNICITY

In 1972, Michael Novak published his bombshell of a book *The Rise of the Unmeltable Ethnics*. The book was as controversial as it was, in some ways, prescient. The very title challenged the central mythology about American immigration and ethnicity. Ethnics—and Novak largely meant the descendants of Southern and Eastern European immigrants who formed the backbone of what was already the waning industrial working-class—had not been melted down.

In fact, they had been alienated thoroughly by the WASP elite (read: the Left) which viewed them as so many Archie Bunkers. They were tired of being cast as racists (never mind that plenty of them may have been), and they were tired of being condescended to by liberal egg-heads about their education, their occupations and their Catholicism.

Novak's book was many things. Part political program (it helped usher in the term "white ethnic" as part of our political vocabulary), part pop-sociology, part auto-therapeutic exercise—he spent much of the book ranting at a vague and ill-defined WASP conspiracy—a milestone on Novak's own journey from the political left to the political right.

As much as anything, it captured a mood that had been percolating since the end of the Second World War. For many Americans of that "greatest generation," World War II functioned in an almost Turnerian way. In order to defeat the forces of fascism, disparate groups of hyphenated Americans were forged into a unified fighting force. This was often portrayed wonderfully in the war movies of the day. The "wop" and the "Pollack" and the "Jew," drafted into the army or navy, were at each other's throats at the beginning of the movie, but by the end they have found camaraderie fighting the Germans or the Japanese. Fighting together, they became Americans, unhyphenated.

Reassuring as this myth of America united across ethnic divisions might have been, after the war growing numbers of Americans began to question the idea. For example, Salo Baron, a professor of history at Columbia, complained to a conference in 1954 that the writing of American history "has evinced little interest in the ethnic and religious minorities, despite the fact that this nation consists of an agglomeration of these minorities."[8] While older generations of immigrants had changed their names and learned English to become more American, some of their children and grandchildren embraced ethnicity as a badge of pride.

While it might go too far to say that ethnic museums were the institutions built by those defiant and unmeltable ethnics, they certainly grew out of this renewed interest in ethnic identity, and often out of a grassroots frustration that the American mainstream did not appreciate ethnic cultural heritage. Of those 700-plus ethnic institutions mentioned earlier, a majority were founded after 1945 and most of those, it is safe to say, were founded even more recently. By the 1990s, the cities of New York and Chicago each had roughly two dozen ethnic museums, springing from, as the New York Times put it, "the surge of ethnic self-consciousness of recent decades."[9]

In that sense, these museums tracked a much larger cultural phenomenon. The aftermath of World War II witnessed the high-water mark of what we might call a spirit of universalism: the creation of a United Nations; a vogue for pan-Africanism; even Edward Steichen's 1955 photographic project Family of Man all spoke to a hopeful sense that human differences were trivial compared to the fate we all shared.[10] The mid-century optimism about unity began to dissolve by the late 1960s and 1970s into a focus on particularity, sometimes embittered and angry. As historian John Higham observed, "The tendency of cultural pluralists to emphasize the separateness of ethnic cultures in this country [took] on a darker, anti-American meaning. Now any claim for centered-ness, any affirmation of a unifying national culture, became *ipso facto* oppressive."[11] *Pluribus* supplanted *unum*; "we" was replaced with "us," and worse, with "me."

After all, if black Americans could assert that black was beautiful, and if Native Americans could celebrate their difference from mainstream America, why not dis-solve that big, baggy category of "white Americans" into its constituent parts too? Say it strong, say it loud, I'm Polish and I'm proud.

There are two obvious ironies that play out in many of these ethnic museums.

The first is that while they are predicated on the notion of ethnic difference and par-ticularity, taken together, there is a remarkable sameness to them all. I have already dis-cussed the line many of them walk between setting themselves apart from the rest of the nation, and situating themselves in the middle of it. What that translates into inside the museum is a narrative that is similar from place to place.

Broadly speaking—and I hope not to exaggerate too much—it is a story of first arriv-als, the struggles of settling into a new world (perhaps in a big industrial city; perhaps out on the agricultural frontier), hardships that lead to triumph and success, often illus-trated by particular individuals.

So, to take one example, the Danish Immigrant Museum in Elkhorn, Iowa, was founded in 1983 and now owns over 35,000 objects. The central exhibit at the museum is titled (and trademarked) "Across Oceans, Across Time" and offers visitors the chance to "learn about the impact that Danish immigrants and their descendants had and con-tinue to have in American society, and about the strong relationship that exists between the two countries."[12]

It is, generally, a happy, uncomplicated tale. In this way, many of these museums pres-ent "heritage" more than history. Notice how often the word appears in the names of these places: the German Heritage Museum (Cincinnati), the Germans from Russia Heritage Society (Bismarck, ND), the Texas Czech Heritage and Cultural Center (La Grange). And on and on it goes from the Cambodian American Heritage Museum in Chicago to the Polish Heritage Association of the Southeast in Aiken, South Carolina.

The distinction between heritage and history may be fine, but it is significant, and it has been best parsed by David Lowenthal. "History," Lowenthal writes, "tells all who will listen to what has happened and how things came to be as they are. Heritage passes on exclusive myths of origin and continuance endowing a select group with prestige and common purpose." A reporter for the *New York Times* certainly noticed that desire for prestige when he toured many of the city's ethnic museums: "All of the Manhattan museums I visited seem to have ardent staffs who realize that if not for them certain cul-tures would not earn the respect they deserve in the city's mosaic."[13]

There's nothing wrong, necessarily, with celebrating heritage (and heritage, as opposed to history, is always warm and fuzzy), except when it is conflated with history. At the very least, "heritage" tends to downplay what we might call the intraethnic dirty laundry—the darker side of these immigrant communities. Joseph Scelsa, who founded New York's Italian American Museum, assured visitors that "the museum's mission is to present the whole story, the true story, whatever the story is." But he went on: "There's so little of [the negative] that it shouldn't overshadow everything else." As Lowenthal puts it, "History is for all, heritage for ourselves alone. . . . We exalt our own heritage not because it is demonstrably true but because it *ought* to be."[14]

And these museums trade on nostalgia for the "old country" that many of the original immigrants might find puzzling. As I write, plans are under way in East Durham, New York, for the creation of an ersatz nineteenth-century Irish village. One wonders what the refugees from the potato famine would make of that.

The second irony, of course, is that these museums have appeared exactly as real ethnic distinctions have largely vanished. Individuals and groups have embraced ethnicity in an attempt to hold on to an identity which is already slipping away precisely because those unmeltable ethnics have joined the mainstream of American life—especially its consumer culture—successfully and often with enthusiasm. Michael Novak raged at a WASP conspiracy against his Southern and Eastern European people, but his blame was misplaced. The real "attack" on ethnic culture has come from McDonalds and Disney, not the Yale Club or the *New York Review of Books*.

Ethnic museums, then, have arisen precisely as the other institutions of ethnic life have declined. They take the place of the fraternal organizations and mutual aid societies and labor unions and religious congregations and athletic clubs in an attempt to preserve a world that has been lost. The Italian American Museum in Manhattan's Little Italy section opened in 2008. According to the 2010 census, the percentage of Italian Americans in the 24-square-block neighborhood had shrunk to 5 percent (down from 50 percent in 1950). The census could not find a single Italian-born resident among the 8600 souls who call the area home.[15]

If it is true that the appearance of ethnic museums tracks the decline of ethnic specificity and insularity, then we might well expect to see museums devoted to the ethnicity of more recent immigrants opening in the future as those groups move more and more into the mainstream of American life—say, a museum of Dominican American life in Washington Heights, New York, or a museum of Guatemalan American culture in Adams-Morgan, Washington, D.C.

Further, ethnic museums suppose an easy notion of ethnic purity that belies the reality of American life. What, after all, does it mean to be "Polish," say, if one's mother, or husband, or nephew is Irish, or Italian, or Mexican? That, of course, is the reality for a great many Americans. I heard a joke circulating as a kid growing up in Philadelphia in the 1970s: Q: Given the assimilation of Jews these days, how could you tell which parents were Jewish? A: They send their kids to Quaker schools. To speak only of my own family, I have a grandfather originally from Lithuania, a grandmother from Quebec, a sister from Korea, a daughter from China, a brother-in-law from Colombia, and an uncle from France. Which ethnically specific association should we join?

Or which museum should we visit? In 1937, a year before the American Swedish Museum opened, the *Washington Post* noted approvingly that "the goal and purpose of the museum have attracted interest and sympathy among many Americans who are not of Swedish descent."[16] But, as mentioned earlier, the more recent evidence we have, such as it is, suggests that this proliferation of ethnically specific institutions has created a proliferation of (ever smaller) ethnically specific audiences. Without a genealogical rooting interest, will many people care about these institutions?

THE RISE OF ETHNIC MUSEUMS AND THE DECLINE OF PLACE

Let's make another distinction, this one geographical.

Many of these ethnic museums are urban institutions. They serve to mark the presence of particular groups as part of that great urban mosaic. Chicago, New York, Los Angeles, Philadelphia, Cleveland are all home to a number of these museums.

At least as many, probably, are located in much smaller places. Of the two Finnish American museums, for example, one is found in Portland, Oregon, the other in Hancock, Michigan. Likewise, Chicago is home to one of the nation's two Slovenian museums; the other is located in Enon Valley, Pennsylvania.

They present a record of different experiences: urban vs. rural; industrial vs. agricultural; provincial vs. cosmopolitan. And they participate in the economy of tourism in different ways.

Over the last decade or two, "heritage" tourism has become an increasingly big business in the even larger industry of tourism. (There is even now an academic conference devoted to the phenomenon of tourism.) The National Trust for Historic Preservation defines heritage tourism as "travelling to experience the places and activities that authentically represent the stories and people of the past." Ethnic museums would seem to offer that.

If "heritage tourism" is another way of saying "marketing niche," then the bulk of it takes place in areas where the tourist market is already large. That is to say, in the big cities. Washington, D.C. attracts the largest number of African American heritage tourists each year, followed by Philadelphia. Miami has marketed itself increasingly as a place for Hispanic tourists. In this sense the ethnic museums and festivals of Chicago and Boston are promoted as yet more things for tourists to see in places already rich in such destinations.[17]

The challenge is obviously much greater in America's rural and remote places, despite the fact that it is easier to feel nostalgic over homespun and horse-drawn wagons than it is for cold-water walk-ups.

By every measure, except perhaps a certain flavor of political rhetoric, rural and small-town America is suffering, especially in the middle of the country. The industrial economy has vanished, while the agricultural economy has industrialized. In places that relied on the former—places like East Palestine, Ohio, once home to a large ceramics industry—the loss of jobs has left an unfillable economic hole. In the farm belt, concentration and corporatization have all but killed off family farming and the towns that grew up to support it.

Ethnic museums have been embraced, therefore, by local boosters and politicians as a way of attracting tourists and their money to those places that have otherwise been left behind. Elkhorn, Iowa, has a population of under 1000 people. But the Danish Immigrant Museum located there claims a membership of 3000 and roughly 130,000 visitors annually. Clearly it provides a boost to the local economy. Wilbur, Nebraska, has about twice as many people, but the Wilbur Czech Museum has not become a destination on the same scale, despite the fact that none other than President Ronald Reagan proclaimed Wilbur the "Czech Capital of the United States."

Whether or not ethnic museums and heritage tourism can revive the economies of small towns and rural areas, these museums serve another important function. While a small handful of them make claims to national significance, the vast bulk of them connect a specific ethnic group to a specific place. The Lithuanian Museum and Cultural Center in Frackville, Pennsylvania, focuses on the immigrants who came to work in the coal fields that surround that town.

That is no small service. If ethnic differences have largely disappeared in America as a result of mass media, mass culture, intermarriage, and the rest, then it is also true that the American landscape has been homogenized to a remarkable extent in the last half century as well. Places as well as people have lost much of their distinctiveness under an ever rising tide of strip malls and subdevelopments.

Many of these small ethnic museums function, therefore, not only to give dignity and voice to particular ethnic groups, but to give dignity to the places those people came to and refashioned in specific ways when they arrived. They help give meaning to place in a nation where that sort of meaning is becoming harder and harder to find.

Ethnic History as American History

Representative James Moran has offered his National Museum of the American People as an antidote to the proliferation of hyphenated museums that has occurred. In so doing, he has also asserted that if there is a single through-line in American history—a meta-narrative if you will—it is the story of immigrants and immigration. Not specific immigrants in isolation, mind you, but immigrants moving from their specificity into something we call American-ness. That idea is not new, of course. As long ago as 1916, Randolph Bourne extolled the virtues of a "Trans-National America."[18] But given the fractured nature of American historical writing, given the suspicion in many quarters of grand narratives and whiggish national myths, Moran's idea is provocative.

While his museum is still in its incipient stages, as I write this the National Museum of African American History and Culture is scheduled to open on the National Mall in 2016. Created by an act of Congress in 2003, this museum on the face of it would seem to be another example of the kind of museum that has made Moran (and others) so weary.

It is certainly true that African American museums in other cities cater largely to African American visitors, and in this, as I mentioned earlier, they are no different from the other ethnic museums. However, while it is too early yet to know what the results will be in this new national museum, its director Lonnie Bunch has hinted that things might be considerably more interesting.

In an interview he gave to the *New York Times*, Bunch made it clear that he was crafting his exhibits mindful of the ethnic balkanization that has resulted in so many other museums, and, more immediately, of the disappointing response that the National Museum of the American Indian has received. "This museum is not being built as a museum by African Americans for African Americans," Bunch said to the reporter. "The notion that is so important here is that African American culture is used as a lens to understand what it means to be an American."[19]

Bunch's remark suggests that the museum will do more than simply instill pride among African Americans in their history, or somehow attempt to explain black America to white America, but will rather demonstrate the central truth that there would be no America as we know it without African Americans and vice versa. If the National Museum of African American History and Culture can accomplish that, then it will have achieved something remarkable and rare.

Notes

1. Quoted in "Congressman Backs Melting-Pot Museum," *New York Times* July 7, 2011.
2. Quoted in "Washington Whispers," *US News and World Report*, May 12, 2011.
3. I thank Peter Linett, principle Slover Linnet Strategies consulting firm, for this information.
4. See, among others, my review of NMAI: "Heritage vs. History at the National Museum of the American Indian," *Public Historian* 28 (2006), pp. 69–74.
5. See Victor Danilov, *Ethnic Museums and Heritage Sites in the United States* (Jefferson, NC: McFarland & Company, Inc., 2009).
6. Museum official quoted in "Swedish Museum Contains Art of Early Settlers," *Washington Post*, April 18, 1937.
7. From the museum website, [www.arabamericanmuseum.org], accessed August, 2011.
8. Irving Spiegel, "Histories of the U.S. Held Incomplete," *New York Times*, September 14, 1954.
9. See Joseph Berger, "Ethnic Museums Abounding," *New York Times*, July 4, 2003 and Andrew Bagnato, "Ethnic Museums Bursting at the Seams," *Chicago Tribune*, February 2, 1986.
10. For the best discussion of this see David Hollinger's essay " 'How Wide the Circle of We?': American Intellectuals and the Problem of the Ethnos since World War II," *American Historical Review 98* (1993), pp. 317–337.
11. John Higham, "Multiculturalism and Universalism: A History and Critique," *American Quarterly 45* (1993), p. 206.
12. Museum website [www.danishmuseum.org], accessed August, 2011.
13. Joseph Berger, "Ethnic Museums Abounding," *New York Times*, July 4, 2003.
14. Scelsa quoted in Carlin Romano, "Italian American Museum Opens in New York's Little Italy," *Philadelphia Inquirer*, October 13, 2008; David Lowenthal, *Possessed by the Past* (New York: Free Press, 1996), p. 128.

15. Sam Roberts, "New York's Little Italy, Littler by the Year," *New York Times* February 21, 2011.
16. "Swedish Museum Contains Art of Early Settlers," *Washington Post*, April 18, 1937.
17. See, for example, Jan Rath, ed., *Tourism, Ethnic Diversity and the City* (New York: Routledge, 2007).
18. Bourne's essay appeared originally in *The Atlantic* in July, 1916.
19. See Kate Taylor, "The Thorny Path to a National Black Museum," *New York Times*, January 22, 2011.

BIBLIOGRAPHY

Brasley, Eric and Stephanie. "African American Museums and Historical Societies," in *Handbook of Black Librarianship*, edited by E.J. Josey and Marva L. DeLoach, 349–368 (Lanham, MD: Scarecrow Press, 2000).
Buttlar, Lois, ed. *Guide to Information Resources in Ethnic Museum, Library and Archival Collections in the United States* (Westport, CT: Greenwood Press, 1996).
Conn, Steven. "Heritage vs. History at the National Museum of the American Indian," *Public Historian 28* (2006), 69–74.
Conn, Steven. *Do Museums Still Need Objects?* (Philadelphia: U of Penn Press, 2010).
Danilov, Victor. *Ethnic Museums and Heritage Sites in the United States* (Jefferson, NC: McFarland & Company, Inc., 2009).
Davilos, Karen Mary. *Exhibiting Mestizaje: Mexican (American) Museums in the Diaspora* (Albuquerque: NM: University of New Mexico Press, 2001).
Frazier, Nancy. *Jewish Museums in North America: A Guide to Collections, Artifacts and Memoribilia* (New York: Wiley, 1992).
Higham, John. "Multiculturalism and Universalism: A History and Critique," *American Quarterly 45* (1993), 195–215.
Hollinger, David. "'How Wide the Circle of We?': American Intellectuals and the Problem of the Ethnos since World War II," *American Historical Review 98* (1993), 317–337.
Lowenthal, David. *Possessed by the Past* (New York: Free Press, 1996).
Rath, Jan, ed., *Tourism, Ethnic Diversity and the City* (New York: Routledge, 2007).
Stone, Peter, ed. *The Presented Past: Heritage, Museums and Education* (New York: Routledge in association with English Heritage, 1994).

CHAPTER 28

NEW APPROACHES IN TEACHING IMMIGRATION AND ETHNIC HISTORY

JOHN J. BUKOWCZYK

THE advent of new technologies, innovative methods of instruction, and greater availability of source materials online has changed teaching in the field of American immigration and ethnic history considerably during the past few decades, but ultimately, the value of teaching in the field rests upon the same fundamentals as the value of scholarship in it, namely, what questions the researcher and teacher ask and the intellectual framework within which those questions are located. As changes in the larger society have changed scholarship in the field, so too have they changed teaching. It is often claimed that a great gulf separates the work of scholar and teacher, but indeed scholarship and teaching are—or should be—co-constitutive and mutually reinforcing practices. In this sense, all of the preceding essays in this volume can be read not only as primers on the state of research in the field but also as introductions to the problems and debates shaping new approaches in the classroom.

As research paradigms have shifted, so too have the ways in which scholar-teachers have guided inquiry and organized knowledge in their classes. A generation (or two) ago, American immigration and ethnic history was centered largely on the movement of persons from Europe across the Atlantic. It often began with an idealized image of "the peasant," as drawn by Oscar Handlin in his widely influential Pulitzer Prize-winning book, *The Uprooted* (1951).[1] It rested, in the main, on the mechanistic metaphor of so-called push- and pull-factors to explain the causes of immigration and, for the most part, focused upon immigration to the United States—the land of the free and the home of the brave. The story of immigrants in the United States recounted the progressive process of adaptation, acculturation, and assimilation, with courses treating, in serial fashion, select immigrant groups. Course texts meanwhile often followed the categories of immigrant life in a framework associated with structural-functionalist sociology—family, religion, crime (dysfunction), community, and so forth—and instruction was, in character, largely didactic.

While the older schema no doubt persists, today the most sophisticated teaching in the field differs dramatically from these older byways. Contemporary approaches are theoretically informed, interdisciplinary in content, and frequently comparative. Classes now incorporate not only European/Atlantic migration but also internal, regional, hemispheric, and trans-Pacific flows, often concentrating on recent movements of the latter. The mechanical push-pull model, meanwhile, has given way to the study of transnational and diasporic migration streams and systems of migration, the interactions between and among donor and receiver societies and economies (with the lines often blurred between the two), the social and cultural—and subjective—causes of migration that produce complex translocal and transnational movements and connections, and the dynamic influence of policies and of the state. All of these often are filtered through and shaped by postcolonial discourse.

In consequence, while scholars may debate how new is "transnationalism" or how appropriate the term "diaspora,"[2] virtually no population movements or ethnic group interactions fall outside of contemporary pedagogy in the immigration and ethnic history field, including movements in the pre-Columbian and colonial eras.[3] The field now encompasses not only traditional international movements of persons and stock ethnic and assimilation themes but also an array of other subjects and concepts, including the social construction of race, race and ethnic relations (and, of course, racism), immigrant incorporation and integration,[4] ethnohistory,[5] and internal migration to, from, and within regions the older historiography often overlooked.[6] With its newly expanded field of vision and mission, what was once narrowly defined as American immigration and ethnic history has become perhaps the most comprehensive and integrative subject area within the U.S. history curriculum and subdiscipline.[7]

FROM IMMIGRATION TO
MIGRATION HISTORY

Probably the single most important influence on reorienting teaching in the field away from its focus on immigration to America and toward the study of migration was the publication in 1964 of Frank Thistlethwaite's essay, "Migration from Europe Overseas in the Nineteenth and Twentieth Centuries."[8] In place of the Mayflower and Statue of Liberty mythos that fashioned America as the cradle of liberty and the allure of freedom as the central "pull-factor" drawing the oppressed to these shores, Thistlethwaite introduced a more complicated analysis of population displacements and migration streams that ebbed and flowed with the dynamic and interacting changes taking place within, between, and among donor and receiver societies in an integrated Atlantic world. Scholars, particularly in historical sociology, thereafter widened the field of vision to encompass the Pacific Rim and linked population movements more explicitly to the systematic operation of global capitalist, colonial, and imperialist (and neocolonial and neo-imperialist) relations between economic core and economic periphery and, as variously described, dominant and subordinate/subaltern peoples and societies.[9] This train of analysis removed the history of immigration from its previous location in the liberal political narrative—the apotheosis of which may have been President John F. Kennedy's *A Nation of Immigrants*[10]—and linked it to political economy, demography, and labor markets. This line of inquiry has led to fully integrating U.S. immigration and ethnic history into a global history of migration.[11]

The widening out of scholarship and teaching on the subject of migration occurred, of course, within a context of profound changes taking place at home and abroad. Anti-racialism in reaction to the Holocaust and within the pull-and-tug of a Cold War politics that vied for the hearts and minds of peoples of color in the so-called Third World, the anti-colonial movement abroad and civil rights movement at home, and the political and economic coming of age of the sons and daughters of America's so-called "new immigrants" from southern, central, and eastern Europe all influenced academic discourse on immigration and made possible the Immigration Reform Act of 1965. Although that legislation may have been intended by its supporters as a redress of past inequities in the law, and although its sponsors might have imagined that immigration itself was all but over, that is to say, an accomplished fact,[12] the 1965 act ultimately led to the racial and ethnic remaking of America at a time when international capitalist development abroad was destabilizing the most remote corners of the planet and setting in motion population movements that arguably have overshadowed in importance if not proportional volume those of the previous three centuries.[13] These developments, combined with the political mobilization of America's visible minorities and growing world sympathies for refugee peoples, not only reoriented academic treatments of the subject of immigration but also remade attitudes about and academic approaches to immigration control and immigration restriction. Thus historian John Higham's classic rendition of nineteenth-century nativism as a symptom of crises of confidence in the American body politic, *Strangers in the Land*,[14] has given way to a dark narrative of immigration restriction as systematically racist in practice and of immigration policy as racialist in intent.[15]

The reorientation of teaching and research on the subject of migration and immigration control not surprisingly has pushed immigration and ethnic history courses toward a broad consideration of ethics, morality, and public policy. On balance, has immigration been "good" or "bad"? And, one should add: "good for whom?" or "bad for whom?" Which immigrants have been considered "desirable" and which not? How is "desirability" defined, and who sets the criteria? With these questions has come the logical corollary, a question that ties all the others together: What is America? In confronting such questions, students meanwhile have needed to engage the larger subject of nations and nationalism, which takes them into the proverbial heart of darkness of the modern (and postmodern) world.[16] Are nation and race inextricably connected? Is America, in particular, simply a liberal democracy or a racial-nation, and its government a racial state?[17]

Other developments, domestic and foreign, continue to challenge the immigration and ethnic history curriculum. Attitudes toward race and nation have changed, and sympathies have grown for refugee peoples fleeing natural disasters, war, "ethnic cleansing," genocide, crime, and ethnic dislocations. Continuing international migration has altered America's racial and ethnic composition profoundly; at home, Americans have witnessed the post-9/11 "thickening" of the U.S. border, a surge in nativism (particularly with regard to Arabs and Muslims in the United States),[18] and the rise of the so-called security state, epitomized by passage of the 2008 Patriot Act. Increased migration flows across America's southern border meanwhile have intensified antagonism among many native-born Americans toward Mexican and Central American immigrants. Together these changes have pressed courses in our subdiscipline to question when, by what means, and even whether a nation has a right to control its borders. Migration and immigration—in particular, the act of changing one's residence and loyalties—historically have been fundamentally subversive of the idea of the nation-state. Current trends involving globalization and transnationalism have impelled students to ask not only what is the nation but also *whether* the nation; that is to say, in a globalizing world, are nations obsolete?

From Cultural Pluralism
to Multiculturalism

The same forces that have impinged upon inquiry involving migration and immigration control also have remade the study of ethnic difference in American society. It was nearly a century ago that President Woodrow Wilson remarked, "America does not consist of groups."[19] During the first half of the twentieth century, as fear of "hyphenism" waned, public policy and private practice at all levels shifted from Americanization and assimilation along the lines of Anglo-conformity or of the so-called "melting pot"[20] to a general tolerance of ethnic difference (at least as it involved white European ethnic groups) within a broad civic framework of American citizenship, loyalty, and patriotism that accepted the proposition that "hyphens could connect as well as divide."[21] Among intellectuals, cultural pluralism found venerable expression in the work of Horace Kallen and Randolph Bourne;[22] and through the 1930s the idea was promoted by the popular writer Louis Adamic[23] and by students of historian Frederick Jackson Turner and others of their ilk, whom historian Jon Gjerde has referred to as the "ethnic Turnerians."[24] Despite the assimilationism of the 1950s, by the following decade cultural pluralism had become the reigning paradigm in the academy, with the publication of influential works by social scientists such as Nathan Glazer and Daniel Patrick Moynihan and landmark works by several historians.[25] Rudolph Vecoli refuted Oscar Handlin's *The Uprooted* point-for-point, arguing for the dogged persistence of transplanted ethnic cultures; Herbert Gutman examined the serial remaking of the American working class as a result of successive waves of immigration; Timothy Smith argued that in America, ethnic groups coalesced around religion.[26] These scholarly interventions (as contemporary scholarly jargon might now call them) were embedded in and helped create the so-called New Social History whose signature aim was to study "history from the bottom up."[27]

Revisionist scholarship and teaching after the 1960s, despite tendencies to romanticize its subjects, was not unaware of the historical limitations of American pluralism and of the groups—typically America's visible minorities—it had left out. But it awaited a new wave of scholarship—often conducted in area studies and ethnic studies programs or departments and by members of the various visible (or "racial") minorities themselves—to mount a fundamental challenge to the pluralist formula. While the term "multiculturalism" has often been used as a simple synonym for "diversity," as a critical theoretical and political concept, it recognized that American society contained oppressed racial minorities that never had been integrated into a pluralistic American whole. These racialized minorities differed from white ethnic groups insofar as they were subjected to a more durable system of class and racial inequality and institutional racism and have remained structurally separate and subordinate. As mass migration and changing attitudes about immigration control have subverted the idea of "the nation," multiculturalist attitudes on groupness thus also suggested a new American motto: not *E pluribus unum*, but *E pluribus plural*.[28]

With the recognition of structural inequalities that were arranged according to a racial hierarchy within the larger society came, for example, various redistributive, compensatory, and reparatory social programs and initiatives aimed at legally defined racial minorities, most notably, affirmative action.[29] Within the academy, courses in immigration and ethnic history have had to engage a new set of questions concerning systematic and racially and economically determined limits on the structure of opportunity in America; language issues (viz., bilingual education, Black English); intergroup relations; group and majority rights; prejudice and discrimination; institutional racism; birthright citizenship and the problem of statelessness;[30] and, most basically, social justice. Within this schema, students have had to consider how and why all "minority" groups have not been treated equally in either their experience or within the operation of the law[31] and whether and in what ways the loss of "unity" poses a problem to the United States as a polity, society, and nation-state.[32] Are contemporary immigrants—and their children—following familiar paths of adaptation, assimilation, incorporation, and integration, or are they not?[33] How should historians address and incorporate postcolonial concepts like biculturalism, border-crossing, alterity, and hybridity and older intellectual constructs like syncretism, ethnicization, or ethnogenesis? The concept of hybridity, in particular, offers especially interesting, if not unproblematical, models of cultures in contact.[34] The concept of intersectionality has highlighted the unique results when different types of inequality and discrimination overlap.

The rise of groupness and the challenges to a unitary American nation-state logically lead to more elemental and personal questions. Evocative of liberal critiques of Horace Kallen and in defense of individualism, one feminist theorist has asked: "Is multiculturalism," with its support for the autonomy of often hierarchical and gendered ethnic groups, "bad for women?"[35] Likewise, when one asks, "What is America?", meanwhile, one only logically must need also to ask, "What is an American?" In the meantime, if the most emblematic postmodern question has been "Who am I?," and if America does in fact consist of irreducible groups, what logically also follows is the corollary question: "Who are *we*?"—the "we" now being ethnic or racial groups.

Ethnic and Racial (and Other) Identities

In the face of profound changes in American society and sweeping curriculum revisions in the field of immigration and ethnic history, gone are the days when a central project of a university education was the construction of a unitary American civic identity. But despite the rise of the so-called New Ethnicity in the 1970s,[36] progressive assimilation—effected through the instrumentalities of upward mobility, social integration, and especially intermarriage among white ethnics—had erased ethnic markers, dissolved ethnic institutions and affiliations, and weakened ethnic attachments.[37] By the 1980s, scholarly discussion of tangible topics like "institutional completeness," "ethnocultural" voting, and social mobility had fallen away as scholars now touted the elective nature of white ethnicities as "ethnic options," ethnic identity by consent rather than descent, the homogenization of white ethnic groups into the generic category of European American, ethnicity as "symbolic," and the advent of a post-ethnic America.[38]

But a new and more visible ethnic reality in America belied these descriptions and pressed new topics and themes onto course syllabi in the field, despite recent assertions (I think unfounded) that America had entered a post-racial phase. Membership in various white ethnic groups could be decided—and the groups themselves defined—by examining who was left out, with aspirants to inclusion fighting over the porousness of group boundaries.[39] But for America's visible ethnic minorities—those groups whose members, to paraphrase John Quincy Adams, could not shed their foreign skins[40]—the problem of identity was, in a sense, overdetermined by complexion and also by American concepts of race (like the "one-drop" rule).[41] In recognition of the fact that "race" has been a social construct, some social scientists have replaced the term with "racism" and "racialization" as social descriptors and analytical categories.[42] Alternately, one might argue that the concept of race has been reified or has taken on a discursive life of its own.[43] In either case, in contemporary immigration and ethnic history classes, as in the larger society, the problem of race—and racial Otherness[44]—has emerged as perhaps the central political and intellectual issue of our time, even as the field has moved beyond the binary categories of black and white to consider other racial groups—and groupings—and their various interactions.[45]

A host of scholars of various disciplines and ethnocultural backgrounds has produced literally hundreds of works that have examined the experiences of African American,

Latinx/Latino/Latina, Native American, Middle Eastern American, and Asian American peoples and identities, and these studies have revolutionized content in immigration and ethnic history courses.[46] As cultural pluralism may have tended to romanticize white ethnic pasts, the emergent multiculturalism—a variety of approaches that recognized the racial character of American society and its implications for groupness—not only raised questions about social justice but also asked whether or to what extent identity could or should be understood as essential and hence the walls of difference permanent and the chasms separating races and ethnic groups unbridgeable. Essentializing identity and difference in this way (and through various forms of "identity politics") has posed a significant problem for *historical* approaches to these topics, themes, and issues in the classroom, as in society. Historicizing ethnic identity has prompted scholars to consider it in relationship to performativity.

These challenges can be addressed by alternative strategies of analysis and teaching derived from comparative and diachronic structural analysis of class and power and the ways in which these both have constructed identities and difference and arranged them in hierarchies of subordination and domination over time. With the establishment of race as an independent category of analysis,[47] critical race studies in various forms[48] thus have influenced the history curriculum in ways that, for example, essentialized Afrocentric approaches have not.[49] Meanwhile, scholars and teachers have examined a subject that historically had been taken for granted in the United States, the normative nature of whiteness. As ethnicity implies a set of practices and relationships—of mutualism, reciprocity, inequality, etc.[50]—so too has race. Indeed, as logically there can be no "up" without "down," no "in" without "out," in the American racial context, it can be argued that "black" and "white" (and Otherness and white) also are co-constitutive social categories. What followed from this line of thinking has been the need to interrogate the social construction of whiteness (see the essay on whiteness in this volume).[51]

Insights concerning racial identity formation and the similarities and difference in migration and ethnic experience(s) invite more nuanced comparison of, metaphorically speaking, the black, the brown, the red, the yellow, and the white (and maybe soon the olive)—and the metaphorical gray areas lying between these fixed racial categories.[52] Such insights encourage instructors and their students to interrogate stereotypes, like Jews or Asians as so-called "model minorities";[53] to parse the separate histories of racialized ethnic groups within broad racial categories;[54] to consider how all "white" people (viz., Italian Americans, Greek Americans, Polish Americans) are not the same;[55] and to explore how, in a putatively "color-blind" society, racism can persist in the absence of racists.[56]

Perhaps the newest questions involving racial identity have focused on multiraciality,[57] an area of study rendered especially topical by the election of President Barack Obama. Also, fresh research and teaching have begun a critical examination of colorism and those distinctions based not upon "race" per se, but rather upon color.[58] But race and color have not been the only points of identity complicating inquiry in the immigration and ethnic history field. Scholar-teachers have discovered other aspects of identity and social existence that have informed all topics and issues in the field and thus also need to be engaged in the classroom. Literatures in, for example, women and gender studies (including the study of masculinities), LGBTQ studies (lesbian, gay, bisexual, transgender, and queer studies), disability studies, and labor and working-class history gradually are remaking—or have remade—both scholarly and pedagogical practice in the field and require full integration into the curriculum.[59] One should expect that new work in material culture and cultural studies, postmodern geography, visual studies, and childhood studies may have a similar impact.

New Teaching Resources and Methods

As the problematics of identity formation have come to occupy an important place in immigration and ethnic history classes, scholar-teachers have sought new teaching resources and new methods of instruction in order to take greater advantage of student interest in an area which directly touches their own lives. In former times, instructors may have taken small classes on excursions to museums or on field trips to local historical sites, but now, such adventures are interwoven with critical discussion of commemoration and historical memory—its preservation and presentation.[60] The digital age, meanwhile, has provided instructors and students with access to a virtual world resplendent with possibilities.[61] Online research in census, passenger record, and genealogical databases—accessible at, for example, http://libertyellisfoundation.org (sponsored by the Statue of Liberty-Ellis Island Foundation), www.ancestry.com, and other various and changing URLs—have created new research possibilities for students, even at institutions in the most remote locales, and have inspired interest in social history (although not necessarily by that name, as the subdiscipline of social history has been overshadowed by newer approaches since the 1980s). Family history projects, often popular with instructors and their students, have found in these electronic sources new research tools that build on students' technical skills and bridge across disciplines. Family and community history projects naturally also tap oral history sources, although, as with public history, students need a sharp awareness of methodological and theoretical dimensions of this research technique that is a far cry now from what they (or their instructors) once might have imagined as "just talking to people."[62] The same can be said of contemporary use of sources like immigrant letters, which, like oral history testimony, also cannot necessarily be taken at face value.[63]

The digital revolution also has affected the *process* of learning, perhaps more so in disciplines like history that stress inquiry and investigation over memorization of a body of information. Students can become more active learners using online resources that encourage them to develop their intellectual curiosity through use of, for example, search engines and hypertext links (links to related websites that typically appear as colored or underlined words within a text). Participatory websites like Wikipedia (www.wikipedia.com), online journals, and blogs enable students to become amateur historians, afford opportunities for online discussion of historical questions or historically informed public policy issues or current events, and make it possible for students to publish online. These websites also provide new sources of historical information (albeit of varying and frequently unknown reliability and uncertain authorship).

Electronic communication has revolutionized the day-to-day conduct of courses—from planning through grading, making them more student-centered, interactive, and collaborative. Students venture to query instructors at distant institutions for assistance with research projects or bibliographies. Instructors share syllabi in online forums, blogs, and databases. And links to teaching resource sites in the immigration and ethnic subfield can be accessed online through the websites of, for example, the Immigration and Ethnic History Society (https://iehs.org); the Roy Rosenzweig Center for History and New Media (https://rrchnm.org); History Matters: The U.S. Survey Course on the Web, http://historymatters.gmu.edu/); the Library of Congress: American Memory (https://memory.loc.gov); the Harvard University Library's Open Collection "Immigration to the United States, 1789–1930 (https://library.harvard.edu/collections/immigration-united-states-1789-1930); the Gilder Lehrman Institute (www.gilderlehrman.org/history-now); and an ever varying and changing list of personal and institutional web pages.[64] Students also have greater access to print materials via, for example, Google Books, Google's massive book-scanning project (http://books.google.com/), conducted in collaboration with a number of major research libraries; open-source initiatives like Project Gutenberg (www.gutenberg.org); and various commercial sites.

The quest to personalize history teaching in the immigration and ethnic history field and render it more immediate and relevant to students also has allowed instructors to employ these and other new resources, many now vastly more accessible through online purchase or access, including online course reserves, electronic journals (available through, for example, JSTOR or Project Muse), course homepages, and so forth. In content, they also have shifted in focus, as the field has migrated away from its former European/Atlantic orientation. Courses employ immigrant novels and memoirs, but tried-and-true standards like Upton Sinclair's *The Jungle*, Jane Addams's *Twenty Years at Hull House*, and Anzia Yezierska's *Bread Givers* have been augmented by a wide variety of titles, often by writers of color like Maxine Hong Kingston's *The Woman Warrior* or W.E.B. Du Bois' *Dark Princess*.[65] The information age, meanwhile, also has rendered untold new audio and visual resources available for classroom use via outlets like Hula (www.hulu.com) and YouTube (https://www.youtube.com/, for clips of historical speeches, newsreels, musical performances, and the like) and through more conventional means, like DVDs, but these sources nowadays also require more nuanced treatment, methodologically and theoretically informed by literature in visual sociology and kindred disciplines.

The introduction of new digital media into the history classroom has not been without its complications and challenges, which have affected all historical subfields. The availability of digital sources, while allowing more extensive and robust research, has created problems because of their sheer volume, not least of which may be the impression that now, more than ever before, one can never truly "complete" research on a topic, or that with as much information on a subject as is now available online, there truly is "no new thing under the sun." Users also should ponder the implications of the fact that prominence of search results depends upon the search algorithms employed by search engines to prioritize them and the sites' internal policies regarding provision of web content (as well as any library policies in force restricting or censoring the latter). The democratization of digital knowledge encouraged by the web thus is delimited and potentially imperiled by policies governing web access and use; by corporate—or in some places governmental—control; and the general commodification of information. Related to this is the problem of bias in websites, clues to which might be parsed from knowing their creators and sponsors and why they were created, information often difficult to glean. From a different quarter, indiscriminate reliance on web sources of questionable quality and classroom use by students of electronic devices like cell phones have facilitated various forms of academic dishonesty (most notably, plagiarism), creating huge problems for testing and grading in courses and also damaging students' educational experience. While encouraging student inquiry and democratizing knowledge, the web also may undercut the *idea* of expertise and thereby undermine history as a *discipline* that rests on rules of evidence, argumentation, attribution, and documentation. Documentation of web sources and verification of web-based information is made more difficult by their frequently ephemeral nature.

As students (and sometimes their instructors) abandon print for electronic sources, new challenges emerge for library administrators who have to allocate scarce funds between print and electronic acquisitions. Infrastructure (staff, software, and hardware) to bring new digital media into libraries and classrooms (including remote access and distance learning) involves financial costs unknown to universities and colleges of yesteryear. Historians, technical support staff, and librarians (or, rather, specialists in the "information sciences") have scarcely begun to resolve all of the issues involved with the digital revolution and are unlikely to do so for many years to come.

Finally, another stark new dimension, inseparable from the use of digitized resources and new media, are thorny legal issues involving, for example, liability, privacy, and intellectual property. In our litigious age, students cannot be conveyed offsite without administrative permission and liability waivers signed by the students themselves. Assigning students family history projects systematically disadvantages students from alienated, distant, or broken families—perhaps disproportionately so for the minority and the poor—and thereby reproduces the endemic bias in favor of upper-middle-class, native-born whites that plagues higher education in the United States. Oral histories, even for simple college papers, should not be undertaken without the informed consent of the interview subjects, waiving interviewer liability and transferring property rights to the interview content to the interviewer. Institutions often require that research of this nature pass through institutional review channels, typically a human subjects or human investigation committee, as perhaps mandated by federal regulations. The reproduction of print, audio, or visual materials, beyond "fair use" (whose legal definition, available online, is itself subject to some debate), requires formal permission from copyright holders and may entail the payment of permission fees. Failure to comply with any of the above legal requirements may place both instructor and institution in some legal peril of civil damage claims and even criminal liability. Resistance to these legal impediments and hurdles and resentment of the monetization or commercialization of intellectual property have given rise to an open-source movement, and the full legal, ethical, and practical issues pertaining to or arising from the new digital age as it relates to teaching and learning have yet to be resolved.[66]

RETROSPECT AND PROSPECT

While the full impact of the digital revolution in the academy has yet to be felt or fully understood, the social revolution in American society, as described above, not only transformed immigration and ethnic history teaching but also gave rise to alternative academic practices that represented minority perspectives[67] and promoted new questions about how groups would relate to American society and to each other. Like the old America, the new America, as one scholar has described it, is a "forgetful nation," and becoming an American may be simply a process of selective forgetting.[68] Anglo Americans may have forgotten their own unwashed pasts; and white ethnics may have remembered and honored their own but perhaps not others' histories. As white Euro-Americans now perhaps forget, visible minorities and their children may now also only selectively remember, with both prone to denying similar recognition to persons and groups in some ways profoundly different, but in other way profoundly similar to themselves. Although incorporating postcolonial questions and themes would enhance the field of immigration and ethnic history, extending history and expanding memory remain, perhaps, its central scholarly and pedagogical contribution. As scholar-teachers now pursue the field of immigration and ethnic history, they thus can infuse new meaning into Oscar Handlin's noble observation:

> Once I thought to write a history of the immigrants in America. Then I discovered that the immigrants *were* American history.[69]

In doing so, they need to grapple with a final, though perennial, and most important question: What should America be?

NOTES

Portions of this essay are drawn from J. Bukowczyk, "Immigrants and Others" and "Immigration, Race, and Ethnicity in American Life," and are used here by permission of the author. Thanks are extended to Ronald Bayor for his comments on the manuscript.

1. Oscar Handlin, *The Uprooted: The Epic Story of the Great Migrations that Made the American People* (Boston: Little, Brown, 1951).
2. Rogers Brubaker, "The 'Diaspora' of Diaspora," *Ethnic and Racial Studies* 28 (1) (Jan. 2005): 1–19.

3. Bernard Bailyn, *The Peopling of British North America: An Introduction* (New York: Alfred A Knopf, 1986); Bernard Bailyn, *Voyagers to the West: A Passage in the Peopling of America on the Eve of the Revolution* (New York: Alfred A Knopf, 1986); David Hackett Fischer, *Albion's Seed: Four British Folkways in America* (New York and Oxford: Oxford University Press, 1989); Ramón Gutiérrez, *When Jesus Came, the Corn Mothers Went Away: Marriage, Sexuality, and Power in New Mexico* (Stanford, CA: Stanford University Press, 1991), 1500–1846; Alan Taylor, *American Colonies: The Settling of North America* (New York: Viking, 2001).

4. Gary R. Mormino and George E. Pozzetta, *The Immigrant World of Ybor City: Italians and Their Latin Neighbors in Tampa, 1885–1985* (Gainesville: University Press of Florida, 1998).

5. Richard White, *The Middle Ground: Indians, Empires, and Republics in the Great Lakes Region* (Cambridge, UK, and New York: Cambridge University Press, 1991), 1650–1815; R. David Edmunds, "Native Americans, New Voices: American Indian History, 1895–1995," *American Historical Review* 100 (3) (June 1995): 717–740.

6. Jon Gjerde, *The Minds of the West: Ethnocultural Evolution in the Rural Middle West, 1830–1917* (Chapel Hill: University of North Carolina Press, 1997); Elliott Robert Barkan, *From All Points: America's Immigrant West, 1870s–1952* (Bloomington: Indiana University Press, 2007); Ira Berlin, *The Making of African America: The Four Great Migrations* (New York: Viking, 2010); James N. Gregory, *The Southern Diaspora: How the Great Migrations of Black and White Southerners Transformed America* (Chapel Hill: University of North Carolina Press, 2005).

7. Reviews of developments—and future directions—in the field have appeared in several forums and special issues of the *Journal of American Ethnic History*, specialized books and essays, and encyclopedias. See, for example, Stephan A. Thernstrom, ed., *The Harvard Encyclopedia of American Ethnic Groups* (Cambridge: Belknap Press, 1982); Ronald H. Bayor, ed., *Multicultural America: An Encyclopedia of the Newest Americans*, 4 vols. (Santa Barbara: Greenwood, 2011); Virginia Yans-McLaughlin, *Immigration Reconsidered: History, Sociology, and Politics* (New York: Oxford University Press, 1990); John J. Bukowczyk and Nora Faires, "Immigration History in the United States, 1965–1990: A Selective Critical Appraisal," *Canadian Ethnic Studies\Études Ethniques au Canada* 33 (2) (1991): 1–23; "Forum: Immigration History—Assessing the Field," *Journal of American Ethnic History* 18 (4) (Summer 1999): 40–166; Donna R. Gabaccia, "Migration and the Making of North America," special issue, *Journal of American Ethnic History* 20 (3) (Spring 2001); "Forum on Future Directions in American Immigration and Ethnic History," *Journal of American Ethnic History* 25 (4) (Summer 2006): 68–167; "Forum on New Directions in Irish Immigration and Ethnic History," *Journal of American Ethnic History* 28 (4) (Summer 2009): 66–135. While there is no "perfect" survey of the field, see Roger Daniels, *Coming to America: A History of Immigration and Ethnicity in American Life*, 2nd ed. (New York: Harper Collins, 2002).

8. Frank Thistlethwaite, "Migration from Europe Overseas in the Nineteenth and Twentieth Centuries," Rapports, Comité International des Sciences Historiques, V, 32–60 (Stockholm, 1960), 32–60, reprinted in *Population Movements in Modern European History*, ed. Herbert Moller (New York: MacMillan, 1964), 73–91.

9. See Lucie Cheng and Edna Bonacich, eds., *Labor Immigration Under Capitalism: Asian Workers in the United States Before World War II* (Berkeley: University of California Press, 1984); Ronald T. Takaki, *A Different Mirror: A History of Multicultural America*

(Boston: Little, Brown, 1993); Paul Spickard, *Almost All Aliens: Immigration, Race, and Colonialism in American History and Identity* (New York: Routledge, 2007).

10. John F. Kennedy, *A Nation of Immigrants* (New York: Anti-Defamation League of B'nai B'rith, 1959).

11. See Linda Basch, Nina Glick Schiller, and Cristina Szanton Blanc, *Nations Unbound: Transnational Projects, Postcolonial Predicaments and Deterritorialized Nation-States* (New York: Routledge, 1993); Robin Cohen, *Global Diasporas: An Introduction* (London: UCL Press, 1997); Robin Cohen, *Migration, Diasporas, and Transnationalism* (Cheltenham, UK, and Northampton, MA: E. Elgar Publishers, 1999); Saskia Sassen, *Globalization and Its Discontents: Essays on the New Mobility of People and Money* (New York: New Press, 1998); Dirk Hoerder, *Cultures in Contact: World Migrations in the Second Millennium* (Durham: Duke University Press, 2002); Timothy J. Hatton and Jeffrey G. Williamson, *Global Migration and the World Economy: Two Centuries of Policy and Performance* (Cambridge and London: MIT Press, 2005); Patrick Manning, *Migration in World History* (London and New York: Routledge, 2005); Donna R. Gabaccia and Vicki L. Ruiz, *American Dreaming, Global Realities: Rethinking U.S. Immigration History* (Urbana: University of Illinois Press, 2006). Transnational approaches in U.S. immigration and ethnic history reflect a similar movement within the broader U.S. history field. See Thomas Bender, *A Nation Among Nations: America's Place in World History* (New York: Hill and Wang, 2006); Thomas Bender, *The La Pietra Report: A Report to the Profession* (Organization of American Historians, Sept. 2000).

12. David M. Reimers, "An Unintended Reform: The 1965 Immigration Act and Third World Immigration to the United States," *Journal of American Ethnic History* 3 (1) (Fall 1983): 9–28.

13. See David M. Reimers, *Still the Golden Door: The Third World Comes to America* (New York: Columbia University Press, 1985); Reed Ueda, *Postwar Immigrant America: A Social History* (Boston and New York: Bedford/St. Martin's, 1994); Daniels, *Guarding the Golden Door*; Rogers Brubaker, *Ethnicity Without Groups* (Cambridge: Harvard University Press, 2006).

14. John Higham, *Strangers in the Land: Patterns of American Nativism, 1860–1925* (1963; New York: Antheneum, 1974).

15. Kitty Calavita, *Inside the State: The Bracero Program, Immigration, and the I.N.S.* (New York and London: Routledge, 1992); Matthew Frye Jacobson, *Barbarian Virtues: The United States Encounters Foreign Peoples at Home and Abroad, 1876–1917* (New York: Hill and Wang, 2000); Erika Lee, *At America's Gates: Chinese Immigration during the Exclusion Era, 1882–1943* (Chapel Hill: University of North Carolina Press, 2003); Mae Ngai, *Impossible Subjects: Illegal Aliens and the Making of Modern America* (Princeton: Princeton University Press, 2004).

16. See Benedict Anderson, *Imagined Communities: Reflections on the Origin and Spread of Nationalism*, rev. ed. (1983; London and New York: Verso, 2006); Bhabha, *Nation and Narration*; Eric J. Hobsbawm, *Nations and Nationalism Since 1780: Programme, Myth, Reality*, 2nd ed. (Cambridge and New York: Cambridge University Press, 1992, 1993); Anthony D. Smith, *The Ethnic Origins of Nations* (Oxford, UK: Blackwell, 1986).

17. Bob Blauner, *Still the Big News: Racial Oppression in America* (1972; Philadelphia: Temple University Press, 2001); Etienne Balibar and Immanuel Wallerstein, *Race, Nation, and Class: Ambiguous Identities* (London and New York: Verso, 1991); David Theo Goldberg, *The Racial State* (Malden, MA, and Oxford, UK: Blackwell, 2002).

18. Amaney Jamal and Nadine Naber, eds., *Race and Arab Americans Before and After 9/11* (Syracuse: Syracuse University Press, 2008).

19. Frederick C. Luebke, *Bonds of Loyalty: German-Americans and World War I* (DeKalb: Northern Illinois University Press, 1974), 142.

20. J. Hector St. Jean de Crèvecoeur, "What Is an American?" in *Letters from an American Farmer and Sketches of Eighteenth-Century America* (1782; New York: Penguin Books, 1986), 66–105; Israel Zangwill, *The Melting-Pot: Drama in Four Acts* (1909, 1911; Whitefish, MT: Kessinger Publishing, 2010).

21. John J. Bukowczyk, *A History of the Polish Americans* (1987; New Brunswick and London: Routledge, 2008), 70. On the fate of the assimilation model, see Russell A. Kazal, "Revisiting Assimilation: The Rise, Fall, and Reappraisal of a Concept in American Ethnic History," *American Historical Review* 100 (2) (Apr. 1995): 437–471; Gary Gerstle, "Liberty, Coercion, and the Making of Americans," *Journal of American History* 84 (2) (Sept. 1997): 524–558.

22. Horace M. Kallen, "Democracy Versus the Melting Pot," in *Culture and Democracy in the United States* (1915; New Brunswick and London: Transaction Publishers, 1998), 15–117; Randolph Bourne, "Trans-National America," in *War and the Intellectuals*, ed. Carl Resek (1917; New York: Harper and Row, 1964), 107–123.

23. John P. Enyeart, "Revolutionizing Cultural Pluralism: The Political Odyssey of Louis Adamic, 1932–1951," *Journal of American Ethnic History* 34(3) (Spring 2015): 58–90.

24. Jon Gjerde, "New Growth on Old Vines—The State of the Field: The Social History of Immigration and Ethnicity in the United States," *Journal of American Ethnic History* 18 (4) (Summer 1999): 39–65.

25. See Nathan Glazer and Daniel Patrick Moynihan, *Beyond the Melting Pot: The Negroes, Puerto Ricans, Jews, Italians, and Irish of New York City* (Cambridge: M.I.T. Press, 1963).

26. Rudolph J. Vecoli, "'Contadini' in Chicago: A Critique of *The Uprooted*," *Journal of American History* 51 (3) (Dec. 1964): 404–417; Herbert Gutman, "Work, Culture and Society in Industrializing America, 1815–1919," *American Historical Review* 78 (3) (June 1973): 531–588; Timothy L. Smith, "Religion and Ethnicity in America," *American Historical Review* 83 (5) (Dec. 1978): 1155–1185.

27. While coinage of the phrase, "New Social History," has been attributed to historian Jesse Lemisch, it may be traced back to historian Theodore Blegen and, before him, Frederick Jackson Turner. See Staughton Lynd, "Reflections on Radical History," *Radical History Review* 79 (Winter 2001); 104, accessed June 19, 2011, http://muse.jhu.edu/journals/rhr/summary/v079/79.1lynd.html; Gjerde, "New Growth on Old Vines," 61, n17.

28. David Theo Goldberg, *Multiculturalism: A Critical Reader* (Cambridge, MA, and Oxford: Blackwell, 1994); Charles Taylor et al., *Multiculturalism: Examining the Politics of Recognition* (Princeton: Princeton University Press, 1994).

29. John David Skrenty, *The Ironies of Affirmative Action: Politics, Culture, and Justice in America* (Chicago: University of Chicago Press, 1996).

30. Linda K. Kerber, "Presidential Address: The Stateless as the Citizen's Other: A View from the United States," *American Historical Review* 112 (1) (Feb. 2007): 1–34.

31. Ethno-religious groups probably have enjoyed the greatest, constitutionally guaranteed rights and protections. For complicated reasons—both political and historical—legally defined and protected ethno-racial minorities have benefited more than the various working-class white ethnic groups. See John David Skrentny, *The Minority Rights Revolution* (Cambridge: Harvard University Press, 2002).

32. Arthur M. Schlesinger Jr., *The Disuniting of America: Reflections on a Multicultural Society* (1991; New York: Norton, 1992); Samuel Huntington, *Who Are We? The Challenge to America's National Identity* (New York: Simon and Schuster, 2004).

33. Alejandro Portes and Rubén G. Rumbaut, *Immigrant America: A Portrait* (Berkeley: University of California Press, 1990); Alejandro Portes and Rubén G. Rumbaut, *Legacies: The Story of the Immigrant Second Generation* (Berkeley: University of California Press and New York: Russell Sage Foundation, 2001); Roger Waldinger and Mehdi Bozorgmehr, eds., *Ethnic Los Angeles* (New York: Russell Sage Foundation, 1996); Nancy Foner, *From Ellis Island to JFK: New York's Two Great Waves of Immigration* (New Haven: Yale University Press and New York: Russell Sage Foundation, 2000).

34. Pnina Werbner and Tariq Modood, *Debating Cultural Hybridity: Multi-Cultural Identities and the Politics of Anti-Racism* (Atlantic Highlands, NJ, and London: Zed Books, 1997); John Hutnyk, "Hybridity," *Ethnic and Racial Studies* 28 (1) (Jan. 2005): 79–102.

35. Susan Moller Okin, *Is Multiculturalism Bad for Women?*, ed. Joshua Cohen, Matthew Howard, and Martha Nussbaum (Princeton: Princeton University Press, 1999).

36. See Michael Novak, *Unmeltable Ethnics: Politics and Culture in American Life*, rev. ed. (1972; New Brunswick: Transaction Publishers, 1996); Matthew Frye Jacobson, *Roots Too: White Ethnic Revival in Post-Civil Rights America* (Cambridge: Harvard University Press, 2006). The white ethnic revival seemed to fulfill the prediction of historian Marcus Lee Hansen: "what the son wishes to forget, the grandson wishes to remember." See Marcus Lee Hansen, *The Problem of the Third Generation Immigrant* (Rock Island, IL: Augustana Historical Society, 1938), reprinted in Peter Kivisto and Dag Blanck, eds., *American Immigrants and Their Generations: Studies and Commentaries on the Hansen Thesis after Fifty Years* (Urbana and Chicago: University of Illinois Press, 1990).

37. Ruby Jo Reeves Kennedy, "Single or Triple Melting Pot? Intermarriage Trends in New Haven, 1870–1940," *American Journal of Sociology* 49 (Jan. 1944): 331–339; Will Herberg, *Protestant-Catholic-Jew: An Essay in American Religious Sociology* (Garden City, NY: Anchor Books, 1960); Milton Gordon, *Assimilation in American Life: The Role of Race, Religion, and National Origins* (New York: Oxford University Press, 1964).

38. Raymond Breton, "Institutional Completeness of Ethnic Communities and the Personal Relations of Immigrants," *American Journal of Sociology* 70 (1964): 193–205; Ronald P. Formisano, "The Invention of the Ethnocultural Interpretation," *American Historical Review* 99 (2) (Apr. 1996): 453–477; Mary C. Waters, *Ethnic Options: Choosing Identities in America* (Berkeley: University of California Press, 1990); Stephan Thernstrom, *The Other Bostonians: Poverty and Progress in the American Metropolis, 1880–1970* (Cambridge: Harvard University Press, 1973); Josef F. Barton, *Peasants and Strangers: Italians, Rumanians and Slovaks in an American City, 1890–1950* (Cambridge: Harvard University Press, 1975); John Bodnar, Michael Weber, and Roger Simon, *Lives of Their Own: Blacks, Italians, and Poles in Pittsburgh, 1900–1960* (Urbana: University of Illinois Press, 1982); Werner Sollors, *Beyond Ethnicity: Consent and Descent in American Culture* (1986; New York: Oxford University Press, 1990); Richard D. Alba, *Ethnic Identity: The Transformation of White America* (New Haven: Yale University Press, 1990); Herbert Gans, "Symbolic Ethnicity: The Future of Ethnic Groups and Culture in America," *Ethnic and Racial Studies* 2 (Jan. 1979): 1–20; David A. Hollinger, *Postethnic America: Beyond Multiculturalism*, rev. ed. (1995; New York: Basic Books, 2006).

39. See Fredrik Barth, introduction to *Ethnic Groups and Boundaries: The Social Organization of Culture Difference* (1969; Long Grove, IL: Waveland Press, 1998), 9–38.

40. Werner Sollors, *Beyond Ethnicity: Consent and Descent in American Culture* (New York: Oxford University Press, 1986), 2.

41. The one-drop rule, also termed hypodescent, refers to the pseudo-scientific racialist belief that the slightest percentage of African ancestry made a person "black."

42. See Michael Banton, *The Idea of Race* (Boulder, CO: Westview Press, 1977); Michael Banton, *Racial Theories*, 2nd ed. (Cambridge: Cambridge University Press, 1998).

43. Rohit Barot and John Bird, "Racialization: The Genealogy and Critique of a Concept," *Ethnic and Racial Studies* 24 (4) (July 2001): 601–618.

44. Influential in the development of this theme was Edward W. Said, *Orientalism* (New York: Pantheon, 1978).

45. Nancy Foner and George M. Fredrickson, eds., *Not Just Black and White: Historical and Contemporary Perspectives on Immigration, Race, and Ethnicity in the United States* (New York: Russell Sage Foundation, 2004); Eduardo Bonilla-Silva, "From Bi-racial to Tri-racial: Towards a New System of Racial Stratification in the USA," *Ethnic and Racial Studies* 27 (6) (Nov. 2004): 931–950.

46. See, for example, Gary Y. Okihiro, ed., *Margins and Mainstreams: Asians in American History and Culture* (Seattle: University of Washington Press, 1994); Mary C. Waters, *Black Identities: West Indian Immigrant Dreams and American Realities* (New York: Russell Sage Foundation and Cambridge and London: Harvard University Press, 2001); Karen Leonard, *Muslims in the United States: The State of Research* (New York: Russell Sage Foundation, 2003); John A. Arthur, *African Women Immigrants in the United States: Crossing Transnational Borders* (New York: Palgrave Macmillan, 2009); Laird W. Bergad and Herbert S. Klein, *Hispanics in the United States: A Demographic, Social, and Economic History, 1980–2005* (Leiden: Cambridge University Press, 2010).

47. Michael Omi and Howard Winant, *Racial Formation in the United States: From the 1960s to the 1980s* (New York: Routledge, 1994); Paul Gilroy, *"There Ain't No Black in the Union Jack": The Cultural Politics of Race and Nation* (1987; Chicago: University of Chicago Press, 1991).

48. Richard Delgado and Jean Stefancic, *Critical Race Theory: An Introduction* (New York: New York University Press 2001).

49. Molefi Kete Asante, *The Afrocentric Idea*, rev. ed. (Philadelphia: Temple University Press, 1998); Stephen Howe, *Afrocentrism: Mythical Pasts and Examined Homes* (London and New York: Verso, 1998); Clarence E. Walker, *We Can't Go Home Again: An Argument About Afrocentrism* (Oxford and New York: Oxford University Press, 2001); Tunde Adeleke, *The Case Against Afrocentrism* (Jackson: University of Mississippi Press, 2009).

50. See Brubaker, *Ethnicity Without Groups*. Brubaker's explication of ethnicity takes inspiration from E.P. Thompson's treatment of class. See E.P. Thompson, preface to *The Making of the English Working Class* (New York: Pantheon, 1963), 9–14.

51. See also Reginald Horsman, *Race and Manifest Destiny: The Origins of American Racial Anglo-Saxonism* (Cambridge: Harvard University Press, 1981); Alexander Saxton, *The Rise and Fall of the White Republic: Class Politics and Mass Culture in Nineteenth-Century America* (London and New York: Verso, 1990); David Roediger, *Towards the Abolition of Whiteness: Essays on Race, Politics, and Working-Class History* (London and New York: Verso: 1994); David Roediger, *The Wages of Whiteness: Race and the Making of the American Working Class* (New York: Verso, 1999); David Roediger, *Working Toward Whiteness: How America's Immigrants Became White: The Strange Journey from Ellis Island* (New York: Basic Books, 2005); Robert A. Orsi, "The Religious Boundaries of an

Inbetween People: Street Feste and the Problem of the Dark-Skinned Other in Italian Harlem, 1920–1990," *American Quarterly* 44 (3) (Sept. 1992): 313–347; Noel Ignatiev, *How the Irish Became White* (New York: Routledge, 1995); James R. Barrett and David Roediger, "Inbetween Peoples: Nationality and the 'New Immigrant' Working Class," *Journal of American Ethnic History* 16 (3) (Spring 1997): 3–44; Matthew Frye Jacobson, *Whiteness of a Different Color: European Immigrants and the Alchemy of Race* (Cambridge: Harvard University Press, 1998).

52. See, for example, Scott Kurashige, *The Shifting Grounds of Race: Black and Japanese Americans in the Making of Multiethnic Los Angeles* (Princeton: Princeton University Press, 2007); Wendy D. Roth, *Race Migrations: Latinos and the Cultural Transformation of Race* (Stanford; Stanford University Press, 2012).

53. Frank H. Wu, *Yellow: Race in America Beyond Black and White* (New York: Basic Books, 2002).

54. See Eiichiro Azuma, *Between Two Empires: Race, History, and Transnationalism in Japanese America* (New York: Oxford University Press, 2005); Deborah Dash Moore, ed., *American Jewish Identity Politics* (Ann Arbor: University of Michigan Press, 2008); Hasia Diner, *We Remember with Reverence and Love: American Jews and the Myth of Silence After the Holocaust, 1945–1962* (New York and London: New York University Press, 2009).

55. Ronald H. Bayor, "Another Look at 'Whiteness': The Persistence of Ethnicity in American Life," *Journal of American Ethnic History* 29 (1) (Fall 2009): 13–30.

56. Eduardo Bonilla-Silva, *Racism Without Racists: Color-Blind Racism and the Persistence of Racial Inequality in the United States* (Lanham, MD: Rowman and Littlefield, 2003).

57. See Jared Sexton, *Amalgamation Schemes: Antiblackness and the Critique of Multiracialism* (Minneapolis: University of Minnesota Press, 2008).

58. See Glenn Crothers and Tracy E. K'Meyer, "'I Was Black When It Suited Me, I Was White When It Suited Me': Racial Identity in the Biracial Life of Marguerite Davis Stewart," special issue (*Women's Voices: Ethnic Lives through Oral History*), *Journal of American Ethnic History* 26 (4) (Summer 2007): 24–49.

59. Donna R. Gabaccia, *From the Other Side: Women, Gender, and Immigrant Life in the U.S., 1820–1990* (Bloomington and Indianapolis: Indiana University Press, 1995); Donna R. Gabaccia and Vicki L. Ruiz, "Migrations and Destinations: Reflections on the Histories of U.S. Immigrant Women," *Journal of American Ethnic History* 26 (1) (Fall 2006): 3–19; Eithne Luibhéid, *Entry Denied: Controlling Sexuality at the Border* (Minneapolis: University of Minnesota Press, 2002); Horacio N. Roque Ramírez, "Introduction: Homoerotic, Lesbian, and Gay Ethnic and Immigrant Histories," special issue, *Journal of American Ethnic History* 29 (4) (Summer 2010): 5–21; Douglas C. Baynton, "Defectives in the Land: Disability and American Immigration Policy, 1882–1924," *Journal of American Ethnic History* 24 (3) (Spring 2005): 31–44; Neil Foley, *The White Scourge: Mexicans, Blacks, and Poor Whites in Texas Cotton Culture* (Berkeley: University of California Press, 1997).

60. John Bodnar, *Remaking America: Public Memory, Commemoration, and Patriotism in the Twentieth Century* (Princeton: Princeton University Press, 1992); Warren Leon and Roy Rosenzweig, eds., *History Museums in the United States: A Critical Assessment* (Urbana: University of Illinois Press, 1989).

61. On the impact of the digital age on history teaching, see Roy Rosenzweig, *Clio Wired: The Future of the Past in the Digital Age* (New York: Columbia University Press, 2011). Also see "Forum on Using Online Resources in Teaching U.S. Immigration and Ethnic History," *Journal of American Ethnic History* 33 (4) (Summer 2014): 31–93.

62. Mary Patrice Erdmans, "The Personal Is Political, but Is It Academic?," special issue (*Women's Voices, Ethnic Lives through Oral History*), *Journal of American Ethnic History* 26 (4) (Summer 2007): 7–23.
63. See Bruce S. Elliott, David A. Gerber, and Suzanne M. Sinke, eds., *Letters Across the Borders: The Epistolary Practices of International Migrants* (New York and Basingstoke, UK: Palgrave Macmillan, 2006).
64. For a select list of U.S. history websites (including sites related to race, ethnicity, migration, immigration, eugenics, etc.), see Kelly Schrum, Alan Gevinson, and Roy Rosenzweig, *U.S. History Matters: A Student Guide to U.S. History Online*, 2nd ed. (Boston and New York: Bedford/St. Martin's, 2009).
65. Upton Sinclair, *The Jungle*, ed. Christopher Phelps (Boston: Bedford St. Martin's, 1906; 2005); Jane Addams, *Twenty Years at Hull House* (Urbana: University of Illinois Press, 1910; 1990); Anzia Yezierska, *Bread Givers: A Struggle Between a Father of the Old World and a Daughter of the New* (1925; New York, Persea, 1975); Maxine Hong Kingston, *The Woman Warrior: Memoirs of a Girlhood Among Ghosts* (New York: Random House, 1976); W.E.B. Du Bois, *Dark Princess: A Romance* (1928; Jackson: University Press of Mississippi, 1995).
66. These issues are explored in Rosenzweig, *Clio Wired*.
67. These included ethnic studies and its related subfields—Asian studies, Chicano/Boricua or Latino/Latina studies, African American or black studies, and so forth. See Johnnella Butler, ed., *Color-Line to Borderlands: The Matrix of American Ethnic Studies* (Seattle and London: University of Washington Press, 2001); Michael Soldatenko, *Chicano Studies: The Genesis of a Discipline* (Tucson: University of Arizona Press, 2009).
68. Ali Behdad, *A Forgetful Nation: On Immigration and Cultural Identity in the United States* (Durham and London: Duke University Press, 2005).
69. Handlin, *The Uprooted*, 3.

Bibliography

Bayor, Ronald H., ed. *Multicultural America: An Encyclopedia of the Newest Americans*. 4 vols. Santa Barbara: Greenwood/ABC-CLIO, 2011.

Conzen, Kathleen Neils, et al. "The Invention of Ethnicity: A Perspective from the U.S.A." *Journal of American Ethnic History* 12 (Fall 1992): 3–41.

Daniels, Roger. *Guarding the Golden Door: American Immigration Policy and Immigrants Since 1882*. New York: Hill and Wang, 2004.

Harzig, Christiane, and Dirk Hoerder, with Donna Gabaccia. *What Is Migration History?* Cambridge, UK: Polity Press, 2009.

Journal of American Ethnic History 25, no.4 (Summer 2006): 68–167. "Forum: Future Directions in American Immigration and Ethnic History."

Øverland, Orm. *Immigrant Minds, American Identities: Making the United States Home, 1870–1930*. Urbana: University of Illinois Press, 2000.

Skrenty, John David. *The Minority Rights Revolution*. Cambridge: Harvard University Press, 2002.

INDEX

Gagliano, Luigi 267
Gallagher, Charles 368
Galton, Francis 250, 257
Gambino, Richard 342
gambling 331–32
Gamio, Manuel 50
Gamm, Gerald 296
gangs 290, 292, 333
Gans, Herbert 404
García, Macario 74
García, María Cristina 385
garment manufacturing 268
Garvey, Marcus 386
Gay New York (Chauncey) 293
Gee Hop case 16
gender issues
    and Atlantic Migration System 39
    and citizenship issues 166
    and colonial North America 109
    and current research agendas 11
    and ethnocultural structure of the
        U.S. 42–45
    gender balance in migrant
        populations 110, 115–16
    and immigration legislation 15, 16
    and immigration scholarship 2–3
    and religious composition of the U.S. 431
    women and the proletarian mass 112–15
general strikes 276
generational change 192–93, 224, 339,
    434, 444–45
genetics 254, 255, 257
genocide 36, 167, 492
"Gentlemen's Agreement," 15, 54, 149
gentrification 297–98
Georgia 7, 82, 138, 359, 361, 369
Gerber, David 426
German Heritage Museum 483
Germans
    and correspondence of
        immigrants 418, 426
    and economic niches 8
    and eighteenth century immigration 36
    and ethnocultural structure of the
        U.S. 42, 44
    and film depictions of race and
        ethnicity 461

Germans from Russia Heritage Society 483
German speakers 463–65
    and immigration reforms 19
    and labor unions 274–75
    and machine politics 313–14
    POWs 47
    and racialization 45
    and religious composition of the U.S. 434
    and rural settlement 111–13
    and U.S. foreign policy 378–80
    and working class 263–64
Germany 40, 47, 382
gerrymandering 311
Gerson, Louis L. 377
Gerstle, Gary 5, 270
ghettos 44
GI Bill 74, 214, 238
Gilder Lehrman Institute 497
Gilman, Charlotte Perkins 251
Gilroy, Paul 405
Gingrich, Newt 345, 466–67
Giuliani, Rudy 312, 329
Gjerde, Jon 402, 492
glass-ceiling limits 62
Glazer, Nathan 185, 202, 204, 341, 343, 375, 492
Glick Schiller, Nina 400–404, 406–8
global capitalism 124–25, 127, 218, 491
globalization
    and border enforcement 137
    and correspondence of immigrants 421
    and film depictions of race and
        ethnicity 460
    and immigrant unions 273–76
    and immigration in American South 356
    and language consciousness 472–73
    and migration history scholarship 492
Goddard, Henry 251–56, 259n 31
Godfather films 325
Gold, Mike 198
Golden Venture 60
Goldfield, David 367
Goldman, Emma 267
gold rush 14, 128, 420
Goldscheider, Calvin 339, 350n 3
Goldstein, Eric 203, 205
González, Rodolfo "Corky," 76
Google Books 497

Johnson-Reed Act (1924) 17, 24, 53, 55, 128, 150, 238
Jones Act 72
Jones and Laughlin Steel Company 92
Jones Brothers 332
Journal of American Ethnic History (JAEH) 2–3, 11, 200
Journal of Delinquency 256
Judeo-Christian identity 153–55, 188
The Jukes (Dugdale) 255
juvenile delinquency 322

Kallen, Horace 151, 492, 493–94
The Kallikak Family (Goddard) 255
Karelia 398–99, 408, 411
Kazal, Russell 5, 202, 205
Kazan, Elia 197–98
Keiser, Richard A. 309–10
Kelley, Florence 49
Kelley Brothers 332
Kellor, Frances 329
Kelly, "Honest John," 304
Kennedy, John F. 54, 79, 148, 491
Kentucky 95
Keohane, Robert 400
Khmers 59
Kibria, Nazli 223
Killers street gang 321
Kim, Claire Jean 346
King, Martin Luther, Jr. 155, 239, 310
King, Rodney 297
King Coal (Sinclair) 199
Kingsley, Sidney 460
Kingston, Maxine Hong 58
kinship ties 332, 405
Kivisto, Peter 201, 389, 402
Klein, Christina 240
Knights of Labor 264, 274
Know Nothings 6, 147
Knox, Howard 255
Koch, Ed 10, 312
Koch, Robert 250
Korean American Christian Fellowship 440–41
Koreans
    and economic niches 8
    and ethnic employment networks 270

and family-based immigration 16
and historical legacy of migration 61, 63
and immigration in American South 358, 363–66
and intermarriage 239
and military wives 55, 240
and panethnicity 220, 223
and religious composition of the U.S. 27, 435, 440–41
and urban ethnic neighborhoods 297
and U.S. foreign policy 388
and women in mass migrations 112, 113
Korean War 55, 431
Korematsu v. United States 176
Korshak, Sidney 326
Kossuth, Lajos 379
Kraut, Alan 247
Ku Klux Klan 6, 172, 184, 361, 452–53, 455
Kurien, Prema 432–33

labor and labor activism
    and Americanization 272
    and civic nationalism 145
    and economy-motivated migration 40–41
    and ethnocultural structure of the U.S. 43
    and immigrant medical exams 250
    and immigration in American South 356–57, 359–63, 361
    labor shortages 73
    and Latino immigration 70
    and migration history scholarship 491
    organization of labor 272
    and organized crime 334
    and racialization 45
    skilled labor 19, 23, 28, 56
    and transnationalism 411
    unionization of immigrant labor 273–76
    and U.S. foreign policy 381
    and working-class communities 262, 263
    and World War I 92–93
    and World War II 48
    See also unions
Laborer's International Union of North America (LIUNA) 362
Labor Republic 398
La Cosa Nostra 326, 330, 334
LaFeber, Walter 375

CPSIA information can be obtained
at www.ICGtesting.com
Printed in the USA
BVHW011322060522
636339BV00010B/35

9 780197 529911